Knowledge and Space

Volume 11

Series editor
Peter Meusburger, Department of Geography, Heidelberg University, Heidelberg, Germany

Knowledge and Space

This book series entitled "Knowledge and Space" is dedicated to topics dealing with the production, dissemination, spatial distribution, and application of knowledge. Recent work on the spatial dimension of knowledge, education, and science; learning organizations; and creative milieus has underlined the importance of spatial disparities and local contexts in the creation, legitimation, diffusion, and application of new knowledge. These studies have shown that spatial disparities in knowledge and creativity are not short-term transitional events but rather a fundamental structural element of society and the economy.

The volumes in the series on Knowledge and Space cover a broad range of topics relevant to all disciplines in the humanities and social sciences focusing on knowledge, intellectual capital, and human capital: clashes of knowledge; milieus of creativity; geographies of science; cultural memories; knowledge and the economy; learning organizations; knowledge and power; ethnic and cultural dimensions of knowledge; knowledge and action; and mobilities of knowledge. These topics are analyzed and discussed by scholars from a range of disciplines, schools of thought, and academic cultures.

Knowledge and Space is the outcome of an agreement concluded by the Klaus Tschira Foundation and Springer in 2006.

More information about this series at http://www.springer.com/series/7568

Johannes Glückler • Emmanuel Lazega
Ingmar Hammer
Editors

Knowledge and Networks

Klaus Tschira Stiftung
Gemeinnützige GmbH

Editors
Johannes Glückler
Department of Geography
Heidelberg University
Heidelberg, Germany

Ingmar Hammer
Department of Geography
Heidelberg University
Heidelberg, Germany

Emmanuel Lazega
Department of Sociology
Institut d'Etudes Politiques de Paris (SPC)
and Centre for the Sociology of
Organizations (CNRS)
Paris, France

ISSN 1877-9220
Knowledge and Space
ISBN 978-3-319-45022-3   ISBN 978-3-319-45023-0 (eBook)
DOI 10.1007/978-3-319-45023-0

Library of Congress Control Number: 2016957854

© The Editor(s) (if applicable) and The Author(s) 2017. This book is published open access.
Open Access This book is distributed under the terms of the Creative Commons Attribution 4.0 International License (http://creativecommons.org/licenses/by/4.0/), which permits use, duplication, adaptation, distribution and reproduction in any medium or format, as long as you give appropriate credit to the original author(s) and the source, provide a link to the Creative Commons license and indicate if changes were made.
The images or other third party material in this book are included in the work's Creative Commons license, unless indicated otherwise in the credit line; if such material is not included in the work's Creative Commons license and the respective action is not permitted by statutory regulation, users will need to obtain permission from the license holder to duplicate, adapt or reproduce the material.
The use of general descriptive names, registered names, trademarks, service marks, etc. in this publication does not imply, even in the absence of a specific statement, that such names are exempt from the relevant protective laws and regulations and therefore free for general use.
The publisher, the authors and the editors are safe to assume that the advice and information in this book are believed to be true and accurate at the date of publication. Neither the publisher nor the authors or the editors give a warranty, express or implied, with respect to the material contained herein or for any errors or omissions that may have been made.

Printed on acid-free paper

This Springer imprint is published by Springer Nature
The registered company is Springer International Publishing AG
The registered company address is: Gewerbestrasse 11, 6330 Cham, Switzerland

Acknowledgments

The editors thank the Klaus Tschira Stiftung for funding the symposia and book series on Knowledge and Space. The teams of the Klaus Tschira Stiftung and the Studio Villa Bosch have always been contributing greatly to the success of the symposia. Together with all the authors in this volume, we are especially grateful to David Antal, James Bell, and Patricia Callow for their tireless dedication to quality as technical editors of all the chapters and as translators for some of them. Volker Schniepp at the Department of Geography at Heidelberg University has generously helped get figures and maps into shape for publication. We also thank all student assistants and colleagues from the Department of Geography who have helped accomplish the symposium as well as this 11th volume in the Klaus Tschira Symposia book series. We are especially grateful to Andreas Kalström, Laura Krauß, Florence Wieder, Pia Liepe, Leslie Ludwig, Katrin Janzen, Christian Wuttke, Anna Mateja Schmidt, Laura Suarsana, Helen Dorn, and Lisa Bührer.

Contents

1 **Exploring the Interaction of Space and Networks in the Creation of Knowledge: An Introduction**................................... 1
Johannes Glückler, Emmanuel Lazega, and Ingmar Hammer

Part I Knowledge About Networks

2 **Reversing the Instrumentality of the Social for the Economic: A Critical Agenda for Twenty-first Century Knowledge Networks**.............................. 25
Nancy Ettlinger

3 **Interpersonal Networks in Foreign Assignments and Intercultural Learning Processes**................................. 53
Erika Spieß

4 **Family Networks for Learning and Knowledge Creation in Developing Regions**............................ 67
Pengfei Li

5 **Studying Networks Geographically: World Political Regionalization in the United Nations General Assembly (1985–2010)**........................... 85
Laurent Beauguitte

6 **(Post)graduate Education Markets and the Formation of Mobile Transnational Economic Elites**............................ 103
Sarah Hall

Part II Network Evolution and Social Outcomes

7 **Organized Mobility and Relational Turnover as Context for Social Mechanisms: A Dynamic Invariant at the Heart of Stability from Movement**......... 119
Emmanuel Lazega

8 **Trajectory Types Across Network Positions: Jazz Evolution from 1930 to 1969**......... 143
Charles Kirschbaum

9 **Topology and Evolution of Collaboration Networks: The Case of a Policy-Anchored District**......... 169
Laura Prota, Maria Prosperina Vitale, and Maria Rosaria D'Esposito

10 **Platforming for Path-Breaking? The Case of Regional Electromobility Initiatives in Germany**......... 191
Jörg Sydow and Friedemann Koll

11 **Brokering Trust to Enhance Leadership: A Self-Monitoring Approach to Leadership Emergence**......... 221
Martin Kilduff, Ajay Mehra, Dennis A. (Denny) Gioia, and Stephen Borgatti

Part III Network Geographies of Learning

12 **How Atypical Combinations of Scientific Ideas Are Related to Impact: The General Case and the Case of the Field of Geography**......... 243
Satyam Mukherjee, Brian Uzzi, Benjamin F. Jones, and Michael Stringer

13 **Connectivity in Contiguity: Conventions and Taboos of Imitation in Colocated Networks**......... 269
Johannes Glückler and Ingmar Hammer

14 **Are Gatekeepers Important for the Renewal of the Local Knowledge Base? Evidence from U. S. Cities**......... 291
Stefano Breschi and Camilla Lenzi

15 **Learning Networks Among Swedish Municipalities: Is Sweden a Small World?**......... 315
Christopher Ansell, Martin Lundin, and Per Ola Öberg

16	The Coevolution of Innovative Ties, Proximity, and Competencies: Toward a Dynamic Approach to Innovation Cooperation .... Uwe Cantner, Susanne Hinzmann, and Tina Wolf	337

The Klaus Tschira Stiftung... 373

Index.. 377

Contributors

Christopher Ansell Department of Political Science, University of California, Berkeley, CA, USA

Laurent Beauguitte UMR IDEES, CNRS, Mont Saint-Aignan, France

Stephen Borgatti Department of Management, University of Kentucky, Lexington, KY, USA

Stefano Breschi Department of Management and Technology, Università L. Bocconi, Milan, Italy

Uwe Cantner Department of Economics, Friedrich Schiller University Jena, Jena, Germany

Maria Rosaria D'Esposito Department of Economics and Statistics, University of Salerno, Fisciano, SA, Italy

Nancy Ettlinger Department of Geography, Ohio State University, Columbus, OH, USA

Dennis A. (Denny) Gioia Department of Management and Organization, The Pennsylvania State University, University Park, PA, USA

Johannes Glückler Department of Geography, Heidelberg University, Heidelberg, Germany

Sarah Hall School of Geography, University of Nottingham, Nottingham, UK

Ingmar Hammer Department of Geography, Heidelberg University, Heidelberg, Germany

Susanne Hinzmann Department of Economics, Friedrich Schiller University Jena, Jena, Germany

Benjamin F. Jones Department of Management and Strategy, Kellogg School of Management, Northwestern University, Evanston/Chicago, IL, USA

Martin Kilduff UCL School of Management, University College London, London, UK

Charles Kirschbaum Insper Instituto de Ensino e Pesquisa, São Paulo, Brazil

Friedemann Koll School of Business & Economics, Path Dependene Research Center, Freie Universität Berlin, Berlin, Germany

Emmanuel Lazega Department of Sociology, Institut d'Etudes Politiques de Paris (SPC) and Centre for the Sociology of Organizations (CNRS), Paris, France

Camilla Lenzi Building Environment Science & Technology, Politecnico di Milano, Milano, Italy

Pengfei Li Department of International Business, HEC Montréal, Montréal, Canada

Martin Lundin Department of Government, Uppsala University, Uppsala, Sweden

Ajay Mehra Gatton College of Business and Economics, School of Management, University of Kentucky, Lexington, KY, USA

Satyam Mukherjee Indian Institute of Management, Udaipur, Rajasthan, India

Per Ola Öberg Department of Government, Uppsala University, Uppsala, Sweden

Laura Prota Department of Economics and Statistical, University of Salerno, Fisciano, SA, Italy

Erika Spieß Department Psychologie, Ludwig-Maximilians-Universität (LMU), Munich, Germany

Michael Stringer Northwestern Institute on Complex Systems, Northwestern University, Evanston, IL, USA

Jörg Sydow School of Business & Economics, Freie Universität Berlin, Berlin, Germany

Brian Uzzi Kellogg School of Management, Northwestern University, Evanston, IL, USA

Maria Prosperina Vitale Department of Economics and Statistics, University of Salerno, Fisciano, SA, Italy

Tina Wolf Department of Economics, Friedrich Schiller University Jena, Jena, Germany

Chapter 1
Exploring the Interaction of Space and Networks in the Creation of Knowledge: An Introduction

Johannes Glückler, Emmanuel Lazega, and Ingmar Hammer

A Conversation Between Spatial and Network Perspectives of Knowledge

The book series on Knowledge and Space explores the nature of human knowledge from a geographical perspective. How to create, share, and adopt new knowledge is a core question in the social sciences. Processes of learning and knowledge creation are the result of social practice and always take place in space and in specific geographical contexts. The eleventh volume is the outcome of the symposium entitled "Topographies and Topologies of Knowledge" in the series of Klaus Tschira Symposia on Knowledge and Space held at the Villa Bosch Studio in Heidelberg. This book focuses on the conceptual and empirical intersections of the geographical and network dimensions of social practice in accounting for the creation and reproduction of knowledge. By taking up this dialogue between the fields of geography and social network studies, the book is conceived to bridge a research gap between two analytic perspectives that until recently have developed more in parallel to each other than in mutual exchange between scholars. The intention of its chapters is to broaden and deepen understanding of the specific characteristics not only of space and connectivity but also of their mutual and interactive effect on knowledge creation.

J. Glückler (✉) • I. Hammer
Department of Geography, Heidelberg University,
Berliner Straße 48, D-69120 Heidelberg, Germany
e-mail: glueckler@uni-heidelberg.de; hammer@uni-heidelberg.de

E. Lazega
Department of Sociology, Institut d'Etudes Politiques de Paris (SPC) and,
Centre for the Sociology of Organizations (CNRS), 19, rue Amélie, 75011 Paris, France
e-mail: emmanuel.lazega@sciencespo.fr

© The Author(s) 2017
J. Glückler et al. (eds.), *Knowledge and Networks*, Knowledge and Space 11,
DOI 10.1007/978-3-319-45023-0_1

Geography and Networks

The network perspective has been influential in geography since the 1960s, when formal network analysis was used in what was called network geometry. By adopting the concept of topology from mathematics (Matthes, 1912), geographers integrated topographic and topological perspectives into the analysis of spatial networks. With this new method, geographers sought to solve puzzles such as the traveling salesman[1] to determine optimal routes involving the shortest paths in transport and utility networks (Greenberg, Carey, Zobler, & Hordon, 1971; Sagers & Green, 1982). Haggett and Chorley (1969) developed a comprehensive approach for the optimization of network geometry, which they considered to be the most interesting research topic of location theory at the time. This research has become an important topic especially in engineering disciplines such as operations research, computation science, mathematics, and economics. Journals such as *Networks and Spatial Economics* and *Operations Research* focus on models, techniques, algorithms, and research questions and on ways that production networks, supply chain management networks, infrastructure, and communication networks can be organized and optimized.

Since the 1980s, the research interest in geography has increasingly shifted from material to social connections and from a quantitative to a rather qualitative approach to capturing the multidimensional processes developing in local and global environments. Unlike physical infrastructure, social relationships do not necessarily follow a linear logic by which costs rise or connectivity weakens as distance increases. Geometric distance cannot be accepted as a sufficient condition for determining social interactions. Instead, the availability and use of communication and transport technologies mediate the relationship between physical proximity and social interaction. The relation between space and social interaction depends on the actor's choice of technology and mobility (Glückler, 2007). Today, geography is interested in the quality rather than the physical metrics of social and organizational relations.

Knowledge is a key resource in economic development, prosperity, and wealth (e.g., Jacobs, 1969; Romer, 1990; Schumpeter, 1911). Knowledge is also socially constructed and diffused in the relational network among people (Brown & Duguid, 1991; Knorr-Cetina, 1981; Wenger, 1998). Geographers have therefore focused on the question to what extent geography influences learning, knowledge creation, and innovation by rejecting the traditional models that calculate the probability of a tie as a function of metric distance (Bathelt & Glückler, 2011; Maskell, 2001; Maskell & Malmberg, 1999). A fundamental observation in the geography of knowledge is that knowledge is often sticky with regard to place and difficult to transfer to or reproduce in other places (Bathelt & Glückler, 2011; Gertler, 1995; Storper, 1997; von Hippel, 1994). This stickiness sometimes leads to idiosyncratic

---

[1] The problem of the traveling salesman consists in finding the minimal route for a journey that starts and ends at the same location and has to pass through a determinate number of intermediary destinations.

knowledge specific to certain places and poses challenges to learning and imitation over distance (Malmberg & Maskell, 2002). From an economic perspective, such epistemic idiosyncrasies may be sources of competitive advantage in some regions where they foster innovative practice, learning, and economic development, while other regions lag behind and face the challenge of catching up.

Researchers interested in geography's particular role in knowledge creation have studied innovative regions with technological and knowledge clusters such as Silicon Valley (Klepper, 2010; Saxenian, 1994), Boston (Bathelt, 2001; Glaeser, 2005; Tödtling, 1994), Bangalore (Lorenzen & Mudambi, 2013), and London (Cook, Pandit, Beaverstock, Taylor, & Pain, 2007; Keeble & Nachum, 2002) to find out how physical proximity and face-to-face contact help create and circulate new ideas and knowledge. Geographical proximity allows for planned as well as serendipitous encounter and interaction, and it allows for learning even in the absence of immediate social relations simply by virtue of one's "being there" (Gertler, 1995, p. 1) and observing others in proximity (Malmberg & Maskell, 2002). In this context, Abbott (2001) cited French sociologist Émile Durkheim (1897/1951, p. 123):

> A cough, a dance-motion, a homicidal impulse may be transferred from one person to another even though there is only chance and temporary contact between them. They need have no intellectual or moral community between them nor exchange services, nor even speak the same language, nor are they more related after the transfer than before (p. 141).

In summary, the discipline of geography has developed a deep and diversified understanding of learning, knowledge creation, and innovation in and between places and spaces. Geographical places may become specific milieus (Camagni, 1991; Meusburger, 2009) where people enjoy access to localized knowledge and where they learn from others to come up with new ideas and innovations themselves. But the social and more formal understanding of relational processes has been neglected until recently.

Social Processes, Social Networks, and Distance

In the social sciences the shoe is on the other foot. Whereas thinking of places and spaces has been a matter of physical distance, formal network theory has deepened human understanding of learning and knowledge creation as a social process. In general, social network researchers are interested in the nature, antecedents, and outcomes of social connectivity. Formal network analysis and the conceptual emergence of relational thinking in the social sciences (see Marsden & Lin, 1982, and Wellman & Berkowitz, 1988, for instance) have led to new research designs and have yielded ground-breaking empirical discoveries that challenge established categorical reasoning. New theoretical perspectives, methodologies, and concepts have been developing within the framework of relational thought (Doreian, Batagelj, & Ferligoj, 2005; Kilduff & Tsai, 2003; Snijders & Steglich, in press-a; Wasserman & Faust, 1994). Some scholars push this relational thinking as far as arguing that the basic assumption of a relational social science is the "anticategorical imperative"

(Emirbayer & Goodwin, 1994, p. 1414). It stipulates understanding social phenomena such as identity, power, conflict, social capital, and knowledge as expressions and consequences of the positions and associations that actors enjoy or endure within systems of social interdependencies and relations rather than as substantialist, monadic entities with predetermined characteristics (Bathelt & Glückler, 2005). In a relational perspective the focus is on individual and collective opportunities for action, and these opportunities are thought of as being facilitated by the specific context and structure of social relations.

Beyond early radical relational sociologies, current theories move on, prodded by the founding fathers of contemporary structuralism (e.g., White, 2008) to combine relational and categorical approaches as well as relational and cultural perspectives that bring classical social science theory and network analyses into a neostructural framework (e.g., Brandes, 2016; Breiger, 1974, 1990, 2010; Snijders, 2005; Snijders & Steglich, in press-b). From these perspectives a relational topology is also a social space in which specific social processes driven by these relationships take place in a meaningful way for the actors themselves (Lazega & Pattison, 2001). Generic social processes examined by the social sciences since their emergence (e.g., solidarity and discrimination, collective learning and socialization, social control and conflict resolution, and regulation and institutionalization) are partly the product of the regularities constructed in the management of interdependencies between actors in conflict and/or in cooperation. These processes facilitate the management of collective action's dilemmas at each level of agency. The role of network analysis evolves toward modeling these processes and helping with theorizing them.

Building knowledge in individual and collective learning is precisely one such generic process. Such a theoretical perspective necessarily implies an analytical focus on connectivity in social and economic action. Those new theories and concepts have been the key ground-breaking insights into models and concepts of knowledge creation and knowledge diffusion. How does knowledge about this generic process benefit from this approach? Network analyses from several angles are useful for answering this question. Learning, knowledge creation, and innovation are all fruit of the circulation and interpretation of information, the co-creation of new ideas, cumulative experience, and cognition. People relate to other people inside and outside organizations in order to exchange information, knowledge, goods, services, and capital. The myriad individual and collective actors and the relations they sustain are the building blocks of social networks. Relationships are important for the acquisition of information (Borgatti & Cross, 2003), and the creation of knowledge has been recognized as a social, interactive process (Lawson & Lorenz, 1999). Networks are not merely a representational form of social relations but also a social context. A network is "a specific set of linkages among a defined set of persons, with the additional property that the characteristics of these linkages as a whole may be used to interpret the social behavior of the persons involved" (Mitchell, 1969, p. 2). This definition implies that the specific structure of relations may be used to draw inferences and expectations pertaining to individual and collective action (Gulati, 1995; Mizruchi, 1994). Networks affect opportunities for action (Burt, 1992).

Therefore, the capacity to learn collectively depends on specific relational infrastructures (Lazega, 2016; Lazega, Bar-Hen, Barbillon, & Donnet, 2016) that are available for such a social process. One exemplary source of knowledge and learning is advice-seeking. Advice does more than transmit information that will be used to build knowledge. What is being pragmatically transmitted in an advice relationship is also a framework for the evaluation and interpretation of this information, the elements necessary for the evaluation of its appropriateness as a basis for knowledge-building. This point is where relational infrastructures such as social status and social niches come in. For example, recognition of status gratifies the advisers by providing them with an incentive to share their knowledge and their experience (Blau, 1964).

Advice networks are highly interdependent with collaboration, friendship, and other types of social networks that help mitigate the status rule (Lazega & Pattison, 1999): Both collaboration and friendship can lead to advice and vice-versa. This multiplexity indicates the presence of reference groups or epistemic communities. A longitudinal analysis of advice networks adds to the picture by showing that, in many organizations examined by researchers, advice-seeking converges toward senior members recognized for having the "authority to know". They provide social approval for specific decisions and contribute to the integration of the organization because they link the individual, group, and organizational levels. This alignment is a key ingredient of intraorganizational collective learning. In addition, the dynamics of advice networks are cyclical: A pattern of centralization—decentralization—recentralization is generated by epistemic leaders seeking a balance between overload and conflict (Lazega et al., 2016). The described mechanism suggests that epistemic leaders who drive collective knowledge-building through alignments are precisely those who can remain at the top of the epistemic pecking order throughout the cyclical process.

Social network studies also point to a number of structural conditions that are conducive to innovation, such as the number of relationships (e.g., Powell, Koput, & Smith-Doerr, 1996; Zaheer, Gözübüyük, & Milanov, 2010), the quality of those relationships (Granovetter, 1985; Uzzi & Lancaster, 2003), and the location of an actor in the overall structure of a network (Whittington, Owen-Smith, & Powell, 2009). Researchers have found various structural concepts to be positively related with innovation, such as actor centrality (Owen-Smith & Powell, 2004; Whittington et al., 2009), boundary-spanning locations between one's own group and other groups (Krackhardt & Stern, 1988), and intermediate positions between a core and a periphery (Cattani & Ferriani, 2008). Theories of structural holes (Burt, 1992, 2004; Obstfeld, 2005) and of structural folds (Vedres & Stark, 2010) have developed rich explanations of how network location affects the access to information and the co-creation of knowledge. The existence and the quality of relations as well as specific structural characteristics of locations have been theorized as helping or hindering social outcomes such as economic performance or innovativeness. The geography of learning, knowledge, and innovation as a social process between people of different places and spaces has become an important research issue in social network analysis. But despite the growing literature in that field, one of the main criticisms concerning relational thinking is the reductionist, geometric focus on distance. Geography is often treated only as a cost function of linear distance rather than as a matter of multifaceted and rich social context (Daraganova et al., 2012; Doreian & Conti, 2012).

Beyond Disciplinary Silos: The Uncharted Interrelation of Learning, Knowledge, Relations, and Space

Despite the potential of combining the relational and the geographical perspectives, there has long been unintended silence between the two fields in knowledge studies. Geography has endorsed the term *network* as a rich metaphor of social cohesion and cooperation rather than of formal structure (Grabher, 2006); network research has often ignored the spatial dimension of social networks and used regions merely as a convenient shell for the empirical analysis of interpersonal and interorganizational relations. Recently, however, scholars from various fields in the social sciences have realized that both dimensions—geography and relational thinking—are important for knowledge creation and learning (e.g., Doreian & Conti, 2012; Glückler, 2013). Gatherings such as the Capturing Context Conference (Columbia University, June 2009) and the International Workshop on Social Space and Geographic Space (University of Melbourne, September 2007) and a special issue of *Social Networks* in 2012 have brought together researchers interested in discussing new research questions and solutions at the intersection of the two fields (Adams, Faust, & Lovasi, 2012). Overall, the interdisciplinary study of knowledge creation and innovation at the junction of space and social networks has only emerged in recent years. A closer look at the recent literature that has included both spatial and network dimensions in the study of innovation suggests that networks, geography, and knowledge are conditionally related to each other. At least four linkages within this conceptual triangle have been studied empirically: (a) geography as a condition of network formation, (b) geography as a moderator of the effects of network on knowledge, (c) networks as a moderator and (d) networks as a mediator[2] of the effects that geography has on knowledge. With the "agentic turn" (Kilduff & Brass, 2010, p. 336) and an expanding perspective on multilevel networks, a fifth linkage emerges, (e) agency as a moderator of "places" in multilevel relationships on collective learning. We briefly summarize some of the insights of these studies in order to identify the uncharted interrelation of knowledge, networks, and space.[3]

---

[2] A moderator variable governs (e.g., increases or decreases) the strength of a relationship between two other variables, whereas a mediator variable explains the relationship between two other variables (Baron & Kenny, 1986).

[3] The following discussion on the interrelation of geography and network studies is based on Glückler (2013).

Space as a Condition for Network Formation

One dominant line of research has focused on the geographical constraints on the very process of network formation[4] and its evolution. This approach is based on findings that geographical proximity tends to facilitate network formation; it increases the likelihood for social encounter, the exchange of information, and the creation of social relations (Allen, 1977; Zipf, 1949). Empirical research on network evolution confirms the plausible expectation that new relations are more likely to emerge in geographical proximity than over large distance (Broekel & Boschma, 2012; Glückler, 2010; Powell, White, Koput, & Owen-Smith, 2005). Recent research in evolutionary economic geography has underscored the association between geographical proximity and tie formation in networks by empirically controlling for other forms of proximity (Balland, 2012). These and other accounts of geographical constraints of network formation and evolution form part of what Borgatti and Halgin (2011) would classify as geographical theories of networks. Consequently, networks are located in space, and the creation of new linkages seems to be somewhat affected by this geography. Conversely, the creation of new ties in a network is an important strategy for bridging physical separation and enable communication and exchange over large distance (Glückler, 2005). The mutual conditionality between space and networks is thus a fascinating and still unexplored area of research. More complicated, however, is the question of how space and networks interact in their combined effect on the creation and reproduction of knowledge.

Space as a Moderator of Network Effects on Knowledge

The first interactive linkage between space and networks points to the moderating effect of space on the impact of network on innovation. In an interesting research design, Owen-Smith and Powell (2004) analyzed Boston-based biotech firms and their global alliance network. They found that although actor centrality was an important factor of innovativeness in the global network, it was insignificant within the regional network. Defying the intuition of network theorists, firms were equally likely to innovate independent of their position's centrality in the network as long as they were connected to the local alliance network. Geographical proximity thus moderated the effect of network centrality on innovation. One explanation of this finding is that proximity allows for knowledge spillovers within the entire network of alliances and beyond the dyadic alliances. In a subsequent analysis of U.S. biotechnology, Whittington et al. (2009) demonstrated that the innovativeness of biotech firms benefits from geographical proximity and network centrality in ways that

---

[4] See Adams et al. (2012), in particular Butts, Acton, Hipp, and Nagle (2012); Daraganova et al. (2012); Doreian and Conti (2012); Lomi and Pallotti (2012); Viry (2012); Preciado, Snijders, Burk, Stattin, and Kerr (2012); Sailer and McCulloh (2012); Takhteyev, Gruzd, and Wellman (2012); Verdery, Entwisle, Faust, and Rindfuss (2012).

depend on a variety of factors. The effect of the centrality of firms in the interorganizational network was very much a function of proximity: Highly central firms were more likely to be innovative if sited close to other firms than if sited far away from them. This finding corresponds with those reported in more recent studies in the context of trade fairs (e.g., Brailly, Favre, Chatellet, & Lazega, 2016a; Favre, Brailly, Chatellet, & Lazega, 2016; Piña-Stranger & Lazega, 2010).

Connectivity as a Moderator of Spatial Effects on Knowledge

The same kind of effect seems to be at work in the opposite case. It is usually accepted that information transfer and knowledge spillovers dwindle with geographical distance. In the context of international technology transfer between units of multinational corporations, Hansen and Løvås (2004) explicitly focused on interaction effects between the major factors of technology transfer. Their analysis conveyed that the relations between distributed organizational units clearly moderate the association between technology transfer and geography. Units were found more likely to transfer technology successfully over large distances if they were connected through interpersonal ties or through formal organizational linkages than if there were no such links. Bell and Zaheer (2007) suggested that the kind of relationship, whether at the individual, organizational, or institutional level, varies in its dependence on geographical proximity. Empirically, they reported rather counterintuitive evidence for what they call geographic holes, that is, situations where information flow is facilitated between friends when they are geographically distant. In a similar vein, research on contractual alliances (Rosenkopf & Almeida, 2003) and informal business relationships alike (Glückler, 2006) illustrates how relationships substitute for local search and how they help bridge distance. Lastly, learning-by-hiring can be useful for extending the hiring firm's geographic reach and access to remote knowledge (Song, Almeida, & Wu, 2003). In all these research designs, the existence and characteristics of networks affect the strength of the association between geography and knowledge.

Connectivity as a Mediator of Geographical Effects on Knowledge

A fourth stream of innovation research suggests that networks mediate the entire effect of geography on innovation. Empirically, patents are cited more frequently within the region in which they were invented than in others (Jaffe, Trajtenberg, & Henderson, 1993; Thompson & Fox-Kean, 2005). This finding supported the argument that trajectories of technological knowledge are spatially sticky. However, new research designs were needed to examine how these local spillovers happened. Almeida and Kogut (1999) found that local spillovers did not occur equally across regions and that those regions with the strongest spillovers in technological development were the ones where job mobility was restricted mostly to intraregional job moves. Using network analysis, even more sophisticated research designs have illustrated that patent citations tend to be local because inventors tend to change jobs locally and stay within their labor-market region (Breschi & Lissoni, 2009). This evidence suggests that the most fundamental reason why geography matters for localized knowledge creation is the relative immobility of researchers. The job mobility of inventors increases the transfer of technological knowledge (measured as patent citations) between firms independently of geography (Rosenkopf & Almeida, 2003). In support of this conclusion, Breschi, Lenzi, Lissoni, and Vezzulli (2010) offered evidence that proximate and remote job moves occur in equal proportions, and Song et al. (2003) demonstrated that both proximate and distant hiring of inventors lead to effective transfer in technological knowledge as measured by patent citations. A second example of how networks mediate the relation between space and knowledge is provided in the context of information search. Borgatti and Cross (2003) found that when one knows an informant and can access that source, physical proximity is no longer associated with information transfer.[5] In summary, this line of research suggests that the association between geography and knowledge is not a direct effect, that it is mediated through inventor mobility, the accessibility of other partners, and prior knowing.

Agency as a Moderator of Relational "Places" in Multilevel Relationships on Collective Learning

Social scientists, especially sociologists and geographers, have arguably been building a strong alliance in the social sciences to measure, model, and understand the multilevel dynamics of places, positions, and the effects of such dynamics on all the generic social processes we are interested in, notably knowledge-building and collective learning. In particular, when complex position in an organized system of places allows actors to try and change that formal structure (albeit with varying success), scholars interested in spatial and organizational movement can help combine institutional locations, position in relational infrastructures (e.g., status and niches), and geographical place (e.g., Bathelt & Glückler, 2011; Glückler & Hammer, 2012).

Social processes such as collective learning and knowledge creation are also contingent on multilevel interdependencies and require unprecedented amounts of coordination among actors at and across given levels. Actors think in multilevel terms ("this person is a big fish in a big pond") and are required to manage these

---

[5] Mediation implies that the mediated variable (proximity) predicts the mediating variables as well as the dependent variable (e.g., innovation, information exchange) and that the coefficient for the mediated variable becomes insignificant when the mediators are included in the model (Baron & Kenny, 1986).

exceptionally complex interdependencies (e.g., functional, epistemic, normative, emotional) in sophisticated ways at different levels simultaneously. Actors thus face multiple dilemmas of collective action. Without this multilevel coordination between individuals, between organizations, and between individuals and organizations, neither individuals nor organizations can access or mobilize on their own all the resources that are needed to produce, compete, and survive.

Collective learning and knowledge-building are heavily dependent on the existence of such superimposed levels of agency, each of them characterized by horizontal interdependencies that sociologists can examine as sets of local social systems. Interpersonal interdependencies consist of individuals tied together within or across organizations through cowork, advice, friendship, and the rules that organize their social exchanges. The content of these relationships varies. This level of agency is different from that of the organizations to which these same individuals are affiliated. Interorganizational interdependencies are created most often by contractual agreements between organizations specifying the contributions, rights, and responsibilities of each organization in the pursuit of a particular objective, but they also depend on the existence of institutions that guarantee the credibility of those contractual agreements. Economic, contracting activity has been shown, for instance, to depend heavily on collective learning and knowledge-building at the interpersonal level (Brailly et al., 2016a, 2016b). Cross-level interactions between individuals and organizations as well as reliance on collective learning built into such cross-level interactions are vital in the organizational society. In a multilevel context where each level has its own temporality, synchronization costs are efforts—made by individuals and by organizations in very asymmetrical ways—to keep pace with each other by reshaping a structure of opportunity and constraints. Given this complexity, geography's focus on the spatiality of knowledge creation is crucial to social sciences that need the dynamics of multilevel structures to understand current organizational societies.

Enhancing the Conversation

This book intends to open the floor for engaged conversation between topographies and topologies of knowledge. As the brief appraisal of these different lines of research suggests, the empirical evidence of the association between geography, networks, and knowledge is still inconclusive. To some scholars, geography appears to be a force; to others, a moderator. To still others it is only an indirect factor mediated by more important factors such as connectivity. These empirical contingencies may be consequences of the variety and incomparability of methodologies and measures as well as of the kinds of knowledge and networks observed. Whereas geography is often observed either as a binary (inside/outside a region) or as a measure of geometric distance, network relations and the types of knowledge and relations vary widely. Relations in networks range from informal to contractual relationships and from individual to organizational levels. New knowledge is usually measured as successful patent applications, although innovation occurs in many other forms, too. These different semantics and metrics are likely to produce different effects and may cause much of the observed contingencies. What this nascent research indicates is that both networks and geography play elementary roles in understanding the creation, use, and reproduction of knowledge. Yet researchers are only at the beginning of a more comprehensive understanding of the way in which the two modes of being there and being connected are interrelated in the social creation of new ideas and innovations.

We contend that the complex interrelations between networks, space, and knowledge can be solved only if approaches from different disciplines are combined in a multidisciplinary way. Their individual contributions help integrate both network arguments of connectivity and geographical arguments of contiguity and contextuality into a more comprehensive understanding of the ways in which people and organizations are constrained by and make use of space and networks for learning and innovation. Examples are the cases that call for recognition that social and collective learning is moderated by economic networks, intercultural relations, or relational turnover. Another example is when the contributors to this book extend the current research frontier by solving the puzzle of how learning in the past shapes knowledge creation in the future, or how positions of institutions and people shape the geography of learning and knowledge creation. Coming from the fields of geography, sociology, economics, political science, psychology, management, and organizational studies, the authors of the chapters in this volume develop conceptual models and propose empirical research that illustrate the ways in which networks and geography play together in processes of innovation, learning, leadership, and power.

Structure of the Book

The research questions raised in the following fifteen chapters stem from three main perspectives. The first addresses the significance of knowledge about networks and the insight that relational thinking serves as a principle bridging between economic, social, and geographic issues. Networks are moderator, mediator, and input factors for learning, knowledge, and innovation in and between places and space. The contributors to this part of the volume consider relations between the social and the economic dimensions and trace social networks of knowledge through the spheres of business, education, polity, and family, expanding knowledge about the meaning and role that relational aspects have in both the social and economic dimensions.

Networks are embedded systems of multiple social or economic relationships developed through the agency of different actors. These systems encompass different relational places, so social relations and their effect on learning and innovation are constantly in flux. The second perspective picks up on that stream of research by presenting an evolutionary viewpoint on networks and space. The authors add to the discussion about models of relational systems by conceptualizing and exploring them; explaining and investigating mechanisms, structures, and the development of tie formation and agency; and identifying the benefit of relational systems for regions. This section shows knowledge about the evolution of relational structure to be a key determinant of social and regional development.

The third perspective presented in this volume integrates geography, connectivity and knowledge creation. The authors adopting it take space, networks, and actors to be origins of new knowledge and innovation. Those rather economic models not only help improve individual, regional, and organizational innovation but also show how the desired outcome is achievable. In short, the contributors to this volume bring together new research questions, concepts, and empirical work from economics, geography, sociology, and management science to offer new insights by combining the relational view of networks with the geographical view of locations and space with respect to knowledge and learning.

Knowledge About Networks

Part I, consisting of five contributions, points to the importance of knowledge about networks. This section of the volume highlights from a theoretical point of view the relational dimension as a multilevel problem mutually influenced by social, economic, individual, and geographical issues. The authors, with their research agendas, carve out how new perspectives on those manifold relationships broaden human knowledge about relational issues surrounding the intersection of knowledge, space, and agency. In the opening chapter, "Reversing the Instrumentality of the Social for the Economic: A Critical Agenda for twenty-first-century Knowledge Networks," Nancy Ettlinger reverses the direction of causality between the economic and the social dimensions of knowledge networks and questions the classical argument that social aspects serve economic outcomes. She develops a critical agenda for two purposes. First, she uses theories about knowledge generation, the generation of economic knowledge, and networks to develop social knowledge by dissolving frictions caused by difference and constructing an inclusive system of collaborative work. Second, she uses the market itself to adapt new corporate strategies to social ends in the course of sustaining, if not augmenting, productivity.

The chapter thereafter elaborates on the growing importance of intercultural competence and learning in a world of rapid internationalization and globalization. The text outlines a possible solution to the following problem: When employees of small- and medium-sized enterprises and large corporations are sent on foreign assignments, the ensuing clash of cultures could lead to emotional or psychological withdrawal although the business opportunity calls for social closure. Setting out from the individual's point of view, the author, Erika Spieß, elaborates a model that takes various influential factors into account, such as the social network of expats, cultural processes, and the current economic and political environment. In a broader interpretation, this chapter can be seen as an initial empirical perspective on and solution to the agenda that Ettlinger discusses. By developing models that offer an insight into how intercultural learning processes take place, researchers learn how economic factors influence the social dimension when the learning process is triggered by economic requirements, namely, the pursuit of international business.

The fourth chapter, by Pengfei Li, takes a more conventional perspective by investigating how social aspects influence the economic dimension. He examines the role of family and friendship networks as bridges for technology diffusion in developing countries. When regional economies take off, the role of family networks in localized learning weakens. By contrast, another kind of social network, friendship ties, are more open and dynamic in fostering regional innovation in the knowledge economy. The transformation from family- to friend-based learning is not easy. Many developing economies become stuck in a transition stage that arises after the collapse of traditional social connections and before the establishment of generalized trust and formal institutions has created spontaneous associations of individuals. Concentrating on the interdependencies between different forms of social relationships, Pengfei Li conceptualizes how this transition could take place.

In the fifth chapter Laurent Beauguitte considers the "national–local" aspect as a moderator of global networks. He unravels the increasing interaction of local, global, economic, and social issues by investigating processes of political regionalization on a world scale. Starting from the assumption that political actors are called upon to work more and more often on a supranational basis, he proposes that this arrangement is not only a response to global economic processes but also a reaction to the rise of global issues demanding a change in governance. He analyzes the United Nations General Assembly (UNGA) from 1985 to 2010. With nearly all states being represented in this organization, it allows him to observe patterns of cooperation on a world scale from both dynamic and thematic points of view. A variation of the search for equivalence allows him to map the geographical clusters revealed by voting positions. In a second analysis he examines patterns of speeches and reveals the rising importance of regional groups at the UNGA. Lastly, Beauguitte proposes a theoretical model of cooperation among actors at the UNGA.

In the final chapter of Part I, Sarah Hall discusses networks as a moderator of individual learning by examining new strategies in undergraduate and graduate education markets. Her treatment builds on the investigation that this section's other authors conduct into the interrelationship between social and economic issues. She finds that policy-makers and employers in advanced economies have increasingly framed both kinds of market as an important way to improve graduate employability and enhance economic growth within "knowledge-based economies." However, graduates seeking to enter those elite labor markets have faced increased competition in recent years, driven, for instance, by the financial crises after 2007. Sarah Hall analyzes an emerging strategy that has received less attention than others: the growing use of postgraduate educational services and training. She argues that attaining additional credentials is an important strategy among graduates seeking entry into elite global labor markets and, consequently, for the production, reproduction, and circulation of geographically variegated economic elite knowledge practices.

Network Evolution and Social Outcomes

Part II of the book addresses the matter of network evolution and its impact on individuals and regions. Emmanuel Lazega offers a neostructural perspective on how organized mobility and relational turnover (OMRT) constitute important dimensions of the social context in which social mechanisms are deployed. He investigates how rotation across a carrousel of organizational places and subsequent relational turnover create a relational infrastructure that shapes the social process of collective learning. An advice network among lay judges serves as an empirical context in which to develop a "spinning-top model" of collective learning. It accounts for the dynamics of these networks, in particular their cyclical centralization and decentralization over time, with OMRT in the organization providing the energy that drives this evolution. Emmanuel Lazega identifies stability from movement at the heart of collective learning and from its multilevel character and consequences.

Charles Kirschbaum investigates how the relational environment mediates individual possibilities. He studies a 40-year evolution in jazz to analyze how that relational field affects the trajectories of individual musicians. By using relational data on the credits of 5571 albums to extract social-network statistics, he builds ideal-typical trajectories of musicians' paths. Additionally, Kirschbaum uses methods of block-modeling to map the field's development in light of the positioning of trajectory types and the evolution of styles. He demonstrates how the field of jazz moved from a normative to a more competitive structure as older generations were co-opted by new ones.

The ninth chapter advances knowledge about the topology and evolution of collaboration networks in a policy-anchored, high-tech district in Italy. Laura Prota, Maria Prosperina Vitale, and Maria Rosaria D'Esposito use prespecified block-modeling to identify the structural configuration of collaboration over time, tracing the evolutionary path of collaboration within the district. Providing an assessment of the district management strategy, their empirical results show that initial collaboration assumed a core–periphery configuration characterized by a single, small bridging core of research organizations. Gradually, this configuration changed, developing a large cohesive nucleus connected to global partners through generalized bridging ties.

Jörg Sydow and Friedemann Koll investigate the possibility of designing regional technological capabilities by injecting related variety into regional development processes not only in terms of knowledge resources but also of agents, activities, and relations—a problem they conceptualize as "platforming." Using a case-study approach to the electromobility initiative in Germany, the authors investigate the potential of platforming for unlocking such path dependencies. The empirical results lead them to conclude that platforming may contribute to path-forming, but not necessarily to path-*breaking*, at a regional level.

The final chapter in this section takes up the question of tie formation and governance from the perspective of agency. Studying a high-tech firm employing 116 professionals, authors Martin Kilduff, Ajay Mehra, Dennis Gioia, and Stephen

Borgatti develop a fine-grained picture of the emergence of informal leadership. They find that high self-monitoring emergent leaders notice problems and ameliorate them by providing advice and brokering relationships across social divides. Occupying a structurally advantageous position may well be more advantageous for some individuals (i.e., high self-monitors) than for others (i.e., low self-monitors). This study adds to the understanding of the contingency related to the social outcomes of a particular structural position.

Network Geographies of Learning

Part III of this book focuses on the different forms of network outcomes, especially learning, knowledge, and innovation. The researchers in this section deepen the knowledge about how networks moderate, mediate, and contribute to individual and collective learning and about how history as well as social and geographical factors influence those outcomes. Satyam Mukherjee, Brian Uzzi, Ben Jones, and Michael Stringer investigate in chapter twelve how novelty builds on conventional and atypical knowledge alike. Their analysis of 17.9 million papers spanning all scientific fields suggests that science follows a nearly universal pattern, with the highest-impact science being grounded primarily in exceptionally conventional combinations of prior work yet simultaneously featuring an intrusion of unusual combinations. Novel combinations of prior work are rare, yet teams are more likely than solo authors to insert novel combinations into familiar knowledge domains.

In the chapter thereafter, Johannes Glückler and Ingmar Hammer theorize the interactive effect of connectivity and spatial proximity on mechanisms of learning. They argue that connectivity among firms facilitates purposive collaboration and forms of friendly imitation, whereas spatial proximity also enhances the mutual visibility among even disconnected firms, raising the incentives for unfriendly forms of rival learning and unilateral imitation. Drawing on the case of an organized business network of independent IT firms in eastern Germany, the analysis demonstrates that the co-occurrence of connectivity and colocation facilitates both friendly and unfriendly practices of imitation. The social tensions that emerge from unfriendly imitation are mitigated by social conventions and sanctions and thus promote realization of individual and long-term collective opportunities.

Since the path-breaking work by social scientists and statistical methodologists, the sense of the importance that agency, roles and positions have for knowledge creation has sharpened. "Are gatekeepers important for the renewal of the local knowledge base? Evidence from U.S. cities" broaden knowledge about roles, positions, and knowledge creation within a geographical framework. In chapter fourteen, Stefano Breschi and Camilla Lenzi offer an exploratory perspective on the importance of gatekeepers for the expansion and renewal of the knowledge base of U.S. cities. The authors propose and test a number of indicators accounting for what the gatekeeper does to mediate knowledge flows across cities. Their findings indicate that external direct relations are the key mechanism injecting fresh knowledge into a city and amplifying opportunities for technological recombination. Conversely, the greater the reliance on external relations governed by gatekeepers, the less the impact on the expansion and renewal of a city's knowledge base. Distributed, networked learning processes are widely touted as a basis for superior performance.

Recognizing a lack of knowledge about how learning networks operate in the aggregate, Christopher Ansell, Martin Lundin, and Per Ola Öberg seek to widen the view on networks and learning. They take an explicitly geographical perspective into account by utilizing a unique dataset on learning among Swedish municipalities. The authors find that municipalities learn from their near neighbors, especially those in the same county. This research also provides evidence that Swedish municipalities are a "small world" linked together at the national level. Two mechanisms knit the Swedish municipalities together. First, county seats serve as "hubs" that bind local clusters. Second, local clusters aggregate into regional clusters. Despite a high degree of local clustering, hubs and regions provide a structural basis for the national diffusion of policy ideas and practices among Swedish municipalities.

In the final chapter of the book, Uwe Cantner, Susanne Hinzmann, and Tina Wolf take a dynamic approach to investigating the coevolution of cooperation ties and various dimensions of proximity between potential collaboration partners. Specifically, they highlight the predominant role of cognitive proximity for the continuity of innovation-oriented alliances and take into account that this proximity changes over time. They find partner-switching more often than the repetition of collaboration. Neither knowledge transfer nor mutual experience with cooperation shows significant effects on repeated cooperation. Instead, the authors find cooperation to be favored by similarity (overlap) between the firms' knowledge bases, an imbalance in the reciprocal potential for knowledge exchange, the general experience the partners have with collaboration, and similarity in the degree of popularity of collaboration partners.

Conclusion

With this book we continue the interdisciplinary discussion on relational, geographical, and knowledge perspectives. Researchers from different disciplines have long developed important insights from their very different perspectives, and every perspective has its own strengths and weaknesses. In drawing on the strengths of each discipline and its specific point of view, the understanding of the interdependencies between networks, learning, and space becomes increasingly comprehensive. Collectively, the chapters in this volume are but a small step in this endeavor, yet we believe that all the contributions herein offer new research questions, alternative research designs, and discerning solutions to the issues to which they call attention. May it serve as a prospect and source of discoveries that will further expand interdisciplinary inquiry into the nexus of geography, networks, and knowledge.

References

Abbott, A. D. (2001). *Time matters: On theory and method*. Chicago: University of Chicago Press.
Adams, J., Faust, K., & Lovasi, G. S. (2012). Capturing context: Integrating spatial and social network analyses. *Social Networks, 34,* 1–5. doi:10.1016/j.socnet.2011.10.007
Allen, T. J. (1977). *Managing the flow of technology: Technology transfer and the dissemination of technological information within the R&D organization*. Cambridge, MA: MIT Press.
Almeida, P., & Kogut, B. (1999). Localization of knowledge and the mobility of engineers in regional networks. *Management Science, 45,* 905–917. doi:10.1287/mnsc.45.7.905
Balland, P.-A. (2012). Proximity and the evolution of collaboration networks: Evidence from research and development projects within the Global Navigation Satellite System (GNSS) industry. *Regional Studies, 46,* 741–756. doi:10.1080/00343404.2010.529121
Baron, R. M., & Kenny, D. A. (1986). The moderator–mediator variable distinction in social psychological research: Conceptual, strategic, and statistical considerations. *Journal of Personality and Social Psychology, 51,* 1173–1182. doi:10.1037/0022-3514.51.6.1173
Bathelt, H. (2001). Regional competence and economic recovery: Divergent growth paths in Boston's high technology economy. *Entrepreneurship & Regional Development, 13,* 287–314. doi:10.1080/08985620110067502
Bathelt, H., & Glückler, J. (2005). Resources in economic geography: From substantive concepts towards a relational perspective. *Environment and Planning A, 37,* 1545–1563. doi:10.1068/a37109
Bathelt, H., & Glückler, J. (2011). *The relational economy: Geographies of knowing and learning*. Oxford: University Press. doi:10.1111/jors.12024_4
Bell, G. G., & Zaheer, A. (2007). Geography, networks, and knowledge flow. *Organization Science, 18,* 955–972. doi:10.1287/orsc.1070.0308
Blau, P. M. (1964). *Exchange and power in social life*. New York: John Wiley & Sons.
Borgatti, S. P., & Cross, R. (2003). A relational view of information seeking and learning in social networks. *Management Science, 49,* 432–445. doi:10.1287/mnsc.49.4.432.14428
Borgatti, S. P., & Halgin, D. S. (2011). On network theory. *Organization Science, 22,* 1168–1181. doi:10.1287/orsc.1100.0641
Brailly, J., Favre, G., Chatellet, J., & Lazega, E. (2016a). Embeddedness as a multilevel problem: A case study in economic sociology. *Social Networks, 44,* 319–333. doi:10.1016/j.socnet.2015.03.005
Brailly, J., Favre, G., Chatellet, J., & Lazega, E. (2016b). Market as a multilevel system. In E. Lazega & T. A. B. Snijders (Eds.), *Multilevel network analysis for the social sciences: Theory, methods and applications* (pp. 245–271). Methodos Series: Vol. 12. London: Springer.
Brandes, U. (2016). Network positions. *Methodological Innovations, 9,* 1–19. doi:10.1177/2059799116630650
Breiger, R. L. (1974). The duality of persons and groups. *Social Forces, 53,* 181–190. doi:10.1093/sf/53.2.181
Breiger, R. L. (Ed.). (1990). *Social mobility and social structure*. Cambridge, UK: University Press.
Breiger, R. L. (2010). Dualities of culture and structure: Seeing through cultural holes. In J. Fuhse & S. Mützel (Eds.), *Relationale Soziologie: Zur kulturellen Wende der Netzwerkforschung* (pp. 37–47). Wiesbaden: Verlag für Sozialwissenschaften.
Breschi, S., Lenzi, C., Lissoni, F., & Vezzulli, A. (2010). The geography of knowledge spillovers: The role of inventors' mobility across firms and in space. In R. A. Boschma & R. Martin (Eds.), *The handbook of evolutionary economic geography* (pp. 353–369). Cheltenham: Edward Elgar. doi:10.4337/9781849806497.00025
Breschi, S., & Lissoni, F. (2009). Mobility of skilled workers and co-invention networks: An anatomy of localized knowledge flows. *Journal of Economic Geography, 9,* 439–468. doi:10.1093/jeg/lbp008
Broekel, T., & Boschma, R. (2012). Knowledge networks in the Dutch aviation industry: The proximity paradox. *Journal of Economic Geography, 12,* 409–433. doi:10.1093/jeg/lbr010

Brown, J. S., & Duguid, P. (1991). Organizational learning and communities-of-practice: Toward a unified view of working, learning, and innovating. *Organization Science, 2,* 40–57. doi:10.1287/orsc.2.1.40

Burt, R. S. (1992). *Structural holes: The social structure of competition.* Cambridge, MA: Harvard University Press.

Burt, R. S. (2004). Structural holes and good ideas. *American Journal of Sociology, 110,* 349–399. doi:10.1086/421787

Butts, C. T., Acton, R. M., Hipp, J. R., & Nagle, N. N. (2012). Geographical variability and network structure. *Social Networks, 34,* 82–100. doi:10.1016/j.socnet.2011.08.003

Camagni, R. (1991). Local 'milieu', uncertainty and innovation networks: Towards a new dynamic theory of economic space. In R. Camagni (Ed.), *Innovation networks: Spatial perspectives* (pp. 121–144). London: Belhaven Press.

Cattani, G., & Ferriani, S. (2008). A core/periphery perspective on individual creative performance: Social networks and cinematic achievements in the Hollywood film industry. *Organization Science, 19,* 824–844. doi:10.1287/orsc.1070.0350

Cook, G. A. S., Pandit, N. R., Beaverstock, J. V., Taylor, P. J., & Pain, K. (2007). The role of location in knowledge creation and diffusion: Evidence of centripetal and centrifugal forces in the City of London financial services agglomeration. *Environment and Planning A, 39,* 1325–1345. doi:10.1068/a37380

Daraganova, G., Pattison, P., Koskinen, J., Mitchell, B., Bill, A., Watts, M., & Baum, S. (2012). Networks and geography: Modelling community network structures as the outcome of both spatial and network processes. *Social Networks, 34,* 6–17. doi:10.1016/j.socnet.2010.12.001

Doreian, P., Batagelj, V., & Ferligoj, A. (2005). *Generalized blockmodeling.* Cambridge, UK: University Press.

Doreian, P., & Conti, N. (2012). Social context, spatial structure and social network structure. *Social Networks, 34,* 32–46. doi:10.1016/j.socnet.2010.09.002

Durkheim, E. (1951). *Suicide: A study in sociology.* New York: Free Press. (Original work published 1897)

Emirbayer, M., & Goodwin, J. (1994). Network analysis, culture, and the problem of agency. *American Journal of Sociology, 99,* 1411–1454. Retrieved from http://www.jstor.org/stable/2782580

Favre, G., Brailly, J., Chatellet, J., & Lazega, E. (2016). Inter-organizational network influence on long-term and short-term inter-individual relationships: The case of a trade fair for TV programs distribution in sub-Saharan Africa. In E. Lazega & T. A. B. Snijders (Eds.), *Multilevel network analysis for the social sciences: Theory, methods and applications* (pp. 295–314). Methodos Series: Vol. 12. London: Springer.

Gertler, M. S. (1995). "Being there": Proximity, organization, and culture in the development and adoption of advanced manufacturing technologies. *Economic Geography, 71,* 1–26. doi:10.2307/144433

Glaeser, E. L. (2005). Reinventing Boston: 1630–2003. *Journal of Economic Geography, 5,* 119–153. doi:10.1093/jnlecg/lbh058

Glückler, J. (2005). Making embeddedness work: Social practice institutions in foreign consulting markets. *Environment and Planning A, 37,* 1727–1750. doi:10.1068/a3727

Glückler, J. (2006). A relational assessment of international market entry in management consulting. *Journal of Economic Geography, 6,* 369–393. doi:10.1093/jeg/lbi016

Glückler, J. (2007). Economic geography and the evolution of networks. *Journal of Economic Geography, 7,* 619–634. doi:10.1093/jeg/lbm023

Glückler, J. (2010). The evolution of a strategic alliance network: Exploring the case of stock photography. In R. Boschma & R. Martin (Eds.), *The handbook of evolutionary economic geography* (pp. 298–315). Cheltenham: Edward Elgar. doi:10.4337/9781849806497.00023

Glückler, J. (2013). Knowledge, networks and space: Connectivity and the problem of non-interactive learning. *Regional Studies, 47,* 880–894. doi:10.1080/00343404.2013.779659

Glückler, J., & Hammer, I. (2012). Multilaterale Kooperation und Netzwerkgüter [Multilateral cooperation and network goods]. In J. Glückler, W. Dehning, M. Janneck, & T. Armbrüster

(Eds.), *Unternehmensnetzwerke: Architekturen, Strukturen und Strategien* (pp. 139–162). Heidelberg: Springer Gabler. doi:10.1007/978-3-642-29531-7_8

Grabher, G. (2006). Trading routes, bypasses, and risky intersections: Mapping the travels of 'networks' between economic sociology and economic geography. *Progress in Human Geography, 30,* 163–189. doi:10.1191/0309132506ph600oa

Granovetter, M. (1985). Economic action and economic structure: The problem of embeddedness. *American Journal of Sociology, 91,* 481–510. doi:10.1086/228311

Greenberg, M. R., Carey, G. W., Zobler, L., & Hordon, R. M. (1971). A geographical systems analysis of the water supply networks of the New York metropolitan region. *The Geographical Review, 61,* 339–354. doi:10.2307/213432

Gulati, R. (1995). Does familiarity breed trust? The implications of repeated ties for contractual choice in alliances. *Academy of Management Journal, 38,* 85–112. doi:10.2307/256729

Haggett, P., & Chorley, R. J. (1969). *Network analysis in geography.* London: Edward Arnold.

Hansen, M. T., & Løvås, B. (2004). How do multinational companies leverage technological competencies? Moving from single to interdependent explanations. *Strategic Management Journal, 25,* 801–821. doi:10.1002/smj.413

Jacobs, J. (1969). *The economy of cities.* New York: Random House.

Jaffe, A. B., Trajtenberg, M., & Henderson, R. (1993). Geographic localization of knowledge spillovers as evidenced by patent citations. *Quarterly Journal of Economics, 108,* 577–598. doi:10.2307/2118401

Keeble, D., & Nachum, L. (2002). Why do business service firms cluster? Small consultancies, clustering and decentralization in London and southern England. *Transactions of the Institute of British Geographers, New Series, 27,* 67–90. doi:10.1111/1475-5661.00042

Kilduff, M, & Brass, D. J. (2010). Organizational social network research: Core ideas and key debates. *The Academy of Management Annals, 4,* 317–357. doi:10.1080/19416520.2010.494827

Kilduff, M., & Tsai, W. (2003). *Social networks and organizations.* London: Sage.

Klepper, S. (2010). The origin and growth of industry clusters: The making of Silicon Valley and Detroit. *Journal of Urban Economics, 67,* 15–32. doi:10.1016/j.jue.2009.09.004

Knorr-Cetina, K. (1981). *The manufacture of knowledge: An essay on the constructivist and contextual nature of science.* Oxford: Pergamon Press.

Krackhardt, D., & Stern, R. N. (1988). Informal networks and organizational crises: An experimental simulation. *Social Psychology Quarterly, 51,* 123–140. Retrieved from http://www.jstor.org/stable/2786835

Lawson, C., & Lorenz, E. (1999). Collective learning, tacit knowledge and regional innovative capacity. *Regional Studies, 33,* 305–317. doi:10.1080/713693555

Lazega, E. (2016). Synchronization costs in the organizational society: Intermediary relational infrastructures in the dynamics of multilevel networks. In E. Lazega & T. A. B. Snijders (Eds.), *Multilevel network analysis for the social sciences: Theory, methods and applications* (pp. 47–77). Methodos Series: Vol. 12. London: Springer.

Lazega, E., Bar-Hen, A., Barbillon, P., Donnet, S. (2016). Effects of competition on collective learning in advice networks. *Social Networks, 47,* 1–14. doi:10.1016/j.socnet.2016.04.001

Lazega, E., & Pattison, P. E. (1999). Multiplexity, generalized exchange and cooperation in organizations: A case study. *Social Networks, 21,* 67–90. doi:10.1016/S0378-8733(99)00002-7

Lazega, E., & Pattison, P. E. (2001). Social capital as social mechanisms and collective assets: The example of status auctions among colleagues. In N. Lin, K. Cook, & R. S. Burt (Eds.), *Social capital: Theory and research* (pp. 185–208). New York: Aldine de Gruyter.

Lomi, A., & Pallotti, F. (2012). Relational collaboration among spatial multipoint competitors. *Social Networks, 34,* 101–111. doi:10.1016/j.socnet.2010.10.005

Lorenzen, M., & Mudambi, R. (2013). Clusters, connectivity and catch-up: Bollywood and Bangalore in the global economy. *Journal of Economic Geography, 13,* 501–534. doi:10.1093/jeg/lbs017

Malmberg, A., & Maskell, P. (2002). The elusive concept of localization economies: Towards a knowledge-based theory of spatial clustering. *Environment and Planning A, 34,* 429–449. doi:10.1068/a3457

Marsden, P. V., & Lin, N. (Eds.). (1982). *Social structure and network analysis.* Beverley Hills: Sage.

Maskell, P. (2001). Towards a knowledge-based theory of the geographical cluster. *Industrial and Corporate Change, 10*, 921–943. doi:10.1093/icc/10.4.921

Maskell, P., & Malmberg, A. (1999). Localised learning and industrial competitiveness. *Cambridge Journal of Economics, 23*, 167–185. doi:10.1093/cje/23.2.167

Matthes, F. E. (1912). Topology, topography and topometry. *Bulletin of the American Geographical Society, 44*, 334–339. Retrieved from http://www.jstor.org/stable/199822

Meusburger, P. (2009). Milieus of creativity: The role of places, environments, and spatial contexts. In P. Meusburger, J. Funke, & E. Wunder (Eds.), *Milieus of creativity: An interdisciplinary approach to spatiality of creativity* (pp. 97–153). Knowledge and Space: Vol. 2. Dordrecht: Springer. doi:10.1007/978-1-4020-9877-2_7

Mitchell, J. C. (1969). The concept and use of social networks. In J. C. Mitchell (Ed.), *Social networks in urban situations: Analyses of personal relationships in central African towns* (pp. 1–50). Manchester: Manchester University Press.

Mizruchi, M. S. (1994). Social network analysis: Recent achievements and current controversies. *Acta Sociologica, 37*, 329–343. doi:10.1177/000169939403700403

Obstfeld, D. (2005). Social networks, the tertius iungens orientation, and involvement in innovation. *Administrative Science Quarterly, 50*, 100–130. doi:10.2189/asqu.2005.50.1.100

Owen-Smith, J., & Powell, W. W. (2004). Knowledge networks as channels and conduits: The effects of spillovers in the Boston biotechnology community. *Organization Science, 15*, 5–21. doi:10.1287/orsc.1030.0054

Piña-Stranger, A., & Lazega, E. (2010). Inter-organisational collective learning: The case of biotechnology in France. *European Journal of International Management, 4*, 602–620. doi:10.1504/EJIM.2010.035591

Powell, W. W., Koput, K. W., & Smith-Doerr, L. (1996). Interorganizational collaboration and the locus of innovation: Networks of learning in biotechnology. *Administrative Science Quarterly, 41*, 116–145. doi:10.2307/2393988

Powell, W. W., White, D. R., Koput, K. W., & Owen-Smith, J. (2005). Network dynamics and field evolution: The growth of interorganizational collaboration in the life sciences. *American Journal of Sociology, 110*, 1132–1205. doi:10.1086/421508

Preciado, P., Snijders, T. A. B., Burk, W. J., Stattin, H., & Kerr, M. (2012). Does proximity matter? Distance dependence of adolescent friendships. *Social Networks, 34*, 18–31. doi:10.1016/j.socnet.2011.01.002

Romer, P. M. (1990). Endogenous technological change. *Journal of Political Economy, 98*, 71–102. Retrieved from http://www.jstor.org/stable/2937632

Rosenkopf, L., & Almeida, P. (2003). Overcoming local search through alliances and mobility. *Management Science, 49*, 751–766. doi:10.1287/mnsc.49.6.751.16026

Sagers, M. J., & Green, M. B. (1982). Spatial efficiency in Soviet electrical transmission. *Geographical Review, 72*, 291–303. doi:10.2307/214528

Sailer, K., & McCulloh, I. (2012). Social networks and spatial configuration—How office layouts drive social interaction. *Social Networks, 34*, 47–58. doi:10.1016/j.socnet.2011.05.005

Saxenian, A. L. (1994). *Regional advantage: Culture and competition in Silicon Valley and Route 128*. Cambridge, MA: Harvard University Press.

Schumpeter, J. A. (1911). *Theorie der wirtschaftlichen Entwicklung* [A theory of economic development]. Berlin: Duncker und Humblot.

Snijders, T. A. B. (2005). Models for longitudinal network data. In P. J. Carrington, J. Scott, & S. Wasserman (Eds.), *Models and methods in social network analysis* (pp. 215–247). Structural Analysis in the Social Sciences: Vol. 28. Cambridge, UK: Cambridge University Press.

Snijders, T. A. B., & Steglich, C. E. G. (in press-a). *Actor-based models for analyzing network dynamics*. Structural Analysis in the Social Sciences series. Cambridge, UK: Cambridge University Press.

Snijders, T. A. B., & Steglich, C. E. G. (Eds.). (in press-b). *Social network dynamics by examples*. Structural Analysis in the Social Sciences series. Cambridge, UK: Cambridge University Press.

Song, J., Almeida, P., & Wu, G. (2003). Learning-by-hiring: When is mobility more likely to facilitate interfirm knowledge transfer? *Management Science, 49*, 351–365. doi:10.1287/mnsc.49.4.351.14429

Storper, M. (1997). *The regional world: Territorial development in a global economy*. New York: Guilford Press.
Takhteyev, Y., Gruzd, A., & Wellman, B. (2012). Geography of Twitter networks. *Social Networks, 34*, 73–81. doi:10.1016/j.socnet.2011.05.006
Thompson, P., & Fox-Kean, M. (2005). Patent citations and the geography of knowledge spillovers: A reassessment? *American Economic Review, 95*(1), 450–460. doi:10.1257/0002828053828509
Tödtling, F. (1994). Regional networks of high-technology firms: The case of the Greater Boston Region. *Technovation, 14*, 323–343. doi:10.1016/0166-4972(94)90075-2
Uzzi, B., & Lancaster, R. (2003). Relational embeddedness and learning: The case of bank loan managers and their clients. *Management Science, 49*, 383–399. doi:10.1287/mnsc.49.4.383.14427
Vedres, B., & Stark, D. (2010). Structural folds: Generative disruption in overlapping groups. *American Journal of Sociology, 115*, 1150–1190. doi:10.1086/649497
Verdery, A. M., Entwisle, B., Faust, K., & Rindfuss, R. R. (2012). Social and spatial networks: Kinship distance and dwelling unit proximity in rural Thailand. *Social Networks, 34*, 112–127. doi:10.1016/j.socnet.2011.04.003
Viry, G. (2012). Residential mobility and the spatial dispersion of personal networks: Effects on social support. *Social Networks, 34*, 59–72. doi:10.1016/j.socnet.2011.07.003
von Hippel, E. (1994). "Sticky information" and the locus of problem solving: Implications for innovation. *Management Science, 40*, 429–439. doi:10.1287/mnsc.40.4.429
Wasserman, S., & Faust, K. (1994). *Social network analysis: Methods and applications*. Cambridge, UK: Cambridge University Press.
Wellman, B., & Berkowitz, S. D. (1988). *Social structures: A network approach*. Structural Analysis in the Social Sciences: Vol. 2. Cambridge, UK: Cambridge University Press.
Wenger, E. C. (1998). *Communities of practice: Learning, meaning, and identity*. Cambridge, UK: Cambridge University Press.
White, H. C. (2008). *Identity and control: How social formations emerge*. Princeton: Princeton University Press.
Whittington, K. B., Owen-Smith, J., & Powell, W. W. (2009). Networks, propinquity, and innovation in knowledge-intensive industries. *Administrative Science Quarterly, 54*, 90–122. doi:10.2189/asqu.2009.54.1.90
Zaheer, A., Gözübüyük, R., & Milanov, H. (2010). It's the connections: The network perspective in interorganizational research. *Academy of Management Perspectives, 24*(1), 62–77. doi:10.5465/AMP.2010.50304417
Zipf, G. K. (1949). *Human behavior and the principle of least effort*. Cambridge, MA: Addison-Wesley Press.

Open Access This chapter is distributed under the terms of the Creative Commons Attribution 4.0 International License (http://creativecommons.org/licenses/by/4.0/), which permits use, duplication, adaptation, distribution and reproduction in any medium or format, as long as you give appropriate credit to the original author(s) and the source, provide a link to the Creative Commons license and indicate if changes were made.

The images or other third party material in this chapter are included in the work's Creative Commons license, unless indicated otherwise in the credit line; if such material is not included in the work's Creative Commons license and the respective action is not permitted by statutory regulation, users will need to obtain permission from the license holder to duplicate, adapt or reproduce the material.

Part I
Knowledge About Networks

Chapter 2
Reversing the Instrumentality of the Social for the Economic: A Critical Agenda for Twenty-first Century Knowledge Networks

Nancy Ettlinger

Divergent Trends in the New Millennium: Setting an Agenda

Taking stock of changing realities, in this chapter I take note of an emergent production system around the turn of the twenty-first century that pivots on new approaches to innovation and, relatedly, on open networks to access dispersed knowledges. At the same time, it is sensible to recognize pressing social problems associated with dramatically increasing socioeconomic polarization and precarious livelihoods worldwide, as well as persistent problems of segregation that inform the nature of exclusions. Although the new system of production is lucrative for firms, its contribution to social problems has been negative at best because new networking strategies remain exclusive, while being highly exploitative in new ways. At this critical juncture in the global economy, my aim in this chapter is to bring a sociopolitical agenda to new economic realities that would service economic agents and goals while developing a means to extend living-wage and stable work in knowledge networks to diverse people, and in the process dissolve frictions of difference through collaborative work relations. Based on a critical synthesis of information drawn from case studies across wide-ranging literatures (economic geography and sociology; social theory; and business, management, and information science), I conceptualize a strategy for making use of new networking strategies that is inclusive and shaped by social goals.

The ensuing argument begins with conceptualizing a reversal of the usual instrumentality of the social for the economic. I contextualize the agenda in terms of the above-stated critical juncture in the global economy, namely new types of economic knowledge networks that reap enormous rewards for corporations without, however, attention to dire and worsening social needs and problems. I conclude this

---

N. Ettlinger (✉)
Department of Geography, Ohio State University,
1036 Derby Hall, 154 North Oval Mall, Columbus, OH 43210-1361, USA
e-mail: ettlinger.1@osu.edu

section with a call for imbricating *social* knowledges with an understanding of economic knowledge networks. In the next section I discuss a particular social problem, segregation, which spatially expresses exclusions in everyday life. Crucially, segregation is driven by ignorance; therefore, constructively engaging segregation requires targeting ignorance by developing social knowledges—per the frame of this edited collection, specifically in the context of knowledge networks. I turn then to the literature on knowledge generation and exchange in economic-oriented literatures to cull insights regarding requirements for the development of socially oriented issues of trust and mutual respect that underpin collaborative project work. One limitation of this literature is that it presents a faceless landscape of actors, and thereby elides issues of difference. In light of my goal to conceptualize the proactive construction of diverse and inclusive knowledge networks, I then draw insights from the business, management, and information science literatures on potential problems of the frictions of difference in on-the-ground as well as virtual workplaces. While useful, this literature nonetheless lacks attention to social goals—back to the problem of the usual instrumentality of the social for the economic—and thus requires attention to the multidimensionality of problems. As I will elaborate, I envision the construction of a web of inclusive knowledge networks in what I call "mediated crowdsourced project work," supported by government and other organizations to ensure continual, living-wage employment in ephemeral networks that form, dissolve, and form anew with different membership to meet the requirements for particular constellations of expertise across projects. At the outset I envision such a project at the metropolitan scale where field research can identify the domain of skills in local populations, allowing for such projects to extend beyond localities over time. My aim is to develop a critical agenda—as opposed to a blueprint or policy brief—to clarify the issues, the logics, and, moreover, the need to chart a new course, while avoiding the replication of existing ills. The vision here derives analytically from a critique of the existing system and a problematization of those new features of the production apparatus that require reconfiguration to achieve social as well as economic goals.

Despite this admittedly ambitious agenda, precedents for discrete components nonetheless exist in various contexts. Open network strategies such as crowdsourcing connect firms seeking expertise or intellectual property with individuals who may be disassociated from firms (although not in association with stable, living-wage jobs). The U.S. government has supported the formation of open networks constituted by firms (although not open networks that draw from a skilled population of workers who may be disassociated from firms). Governments outside the United States support enterprises that privilege social objectives and community well-being over economic goals (although not in connection with new types of knowledge networks). Field research has identified skill sets among marginalized, populations (although not in association with new approaches to production and not necessarily remunerative). The novelty of the agenda I develop, then, lies in the imbrication of components among discrete projects in a holistic approach to achieve both social and economic change.

The Nature of Economic Networks in Relation to Social Issues

Analyses of economic networks for goods and services commonly cast people as instrumental to the effective functioning of networks. The social capital that accrues to such networks is seen to result in productivity, innovativeness, resilience, and the like.[1] This relation between people and networks, with the former serving the latter, is sensible in the context of neoliberal society, which encompasses researchers as much as their subjects and objects of study. As critical philosopher and historian Michel Foucault (2004/2008) argued, neoliberal practices transform the social into economic opportunity, reflected in the academic conceptualization of social relations as instrumental to economic goals.

I aim to conceptualize a reversal of the usual relation between the social and the economic to engage specifically how economic knowledge networks can enhance social relations. How, then, might economic networks contribute to social change? The question appears to counter neoliberal logic. However, as research on economic networks has pointed out, constructive social relations in the arena of production and innovation depend on effective collaboration, trust, and mutual respect (Bourdieu, 1986; Glückler, 2005). Thus, the process of achieving social goals embeds economic goals (Cantener, in this volume). Such nesting is not, however, necessarily implicated when the goal is conceived economically because economic goals often are achieved at the expense of the social, notably labor.[2] The overall strategy I offer aims at subverting the usual logic of instrumentality by rendering economic effectiveness useful for social relations without, however, negating the importance of social relations for economic performance. I advocate a *counter-conduct*[3] that works from within the dynamics of the system, consistent with Foucault's (1996, p. 387) provocative point that effective critique and resistance "relies upon the situation against which it struggles" and is immanent to the system of governance. Per Foucault (1996, p. 386) resistance "is not simply a negation, but a creative process," which can take shape in an agenda for positive social change.

---

[1] Alternatively, Bourdieu's (1986) discussion of social capital casts individuals' membership in a network as benefitting individuals, notably regarding their social positioning. This view does not negate the instrumental view of people relative to economic networks, but it offers more in terms of potential benefits of social capital. This said, the concern of this chapter is less with the benefits of network relations to an individual and more with a specifically relational view of social interaction, that is, the development of constructive relations among individuals based on the development of trust, mutual respect, and the like.

[2] Achieving economic goals at the expense of social goals can be a matter of exploiting vulnerable workers for the sake of personal or shareholder gain. Other processes include myopic strategic planning (Ettlinger, 2008) as well as implicit biases against, and thus exclusion of, talented people who may be outside entrenched power networks (Ettlinger, 2003; Faulconbridge, 2007; Faulconbridge and Hall, 2009).

[3] Foucault conceptualized systems of governance in terms of the *conduct of conduct* (e.g., Foucault, 2004/2007), with reference to the strategies, tactics, and programs that guide actors to make choices (often unconsciously) in accordance with societal norms. Counter-conduct, then, is the governance of practices that counter those norms (e.g., Foucault, 2004/2007, p. 201).

A Critical Juncture in the Global Economy: Open Innovation and Networks

The impetus for a normative agenda is recognition of a critical juncture in the global economy in which an emergent mode of production associated with new networking strategies reaps considerable rewards for firms and shareholders, but exacerbates already precarious ways of earning a living and, more generally, inequality in the context of deepening socioeconomic polarization worldwide (Beck, 1999/2000; Standing, 2011). The aim is not to dismantle existing corporate strategies, an unfeasible strategy, but rather to conceptualize ways to make use of them by reconfiguring goals to privilege the sociopolitical without jettisoning the economic—admittedly difficult, but plausible.

The emergent system of production is characterized overall by *openness* (Ettlinger, 2014) regarding two overlapping systems: innovation, and networks to access labor. Networks connect with innovation as a means by which firms access expertise and intellectual property. However, networks also enable firms to access labor for non-innovative yet menial activity, and the processes for connecting with this labor market differ.[4] In keeping with the theme of this volume, my focus in this chapter is on networks in relation to innovative activity, specifically knowledge networks.

Novel forms of knowledge networks have evolved in the context of what has been termed *open innovation* in the business literature. The term was coined in 2003 by former corporate manager and Berkeley scholar Henry Chesbrough (Chesbrough, 2006a, 2006b; Chesbrough , Vanhaverbeke, & West, 2006). The first survey of open innovation was conducted in 2013, encompassing large firms in the United States and Europe with sales of more than 250 million dollars; results showed that over three quarters of the firms actively pursued open innovation strategies and, moreover, support for open innovation among top managers is increasing (Chesbrough & Brunswicker, 2013).

Open Innovation and Networks

Open innovation refers to the eclipsing of a longstanding tradition of in-house innovation by new practices whereby firms develop innovations on the terrain of interorganizational relations. Although firms externalized production under the regime of flexible accumulation beginning around 1980 in the United States and Britain and

---

[4] Amazon.com's Mechanical Turk subsidiary (Mechanicalturk.com) exemplifies non-routine but menial work. Skilled labor is required, but for relatively low-skilled tasks that nonetheless are non-routine and therefore unamenable to operation by artificial intelligence. Amazon.com lists jobs or human intelligence tasks (HITs) for other companies that pay Amazon.com 10% of the fee for completed tasks. People are paid extremely low wages by the task, not the unit of time—a situation that has been likened to "piece work" in a digital sweatshop.

more recently in continental Europe, innovation nonetheless largely remained an in-house activity. Around the turn of the twenty-first century, firms began externalizing innovation, in part as deepening vertical disintegration (associated with flexible accumulation) gradually produced unanticipated benefits for large firms, namely the possibility of learning from suppliers and making use of innovations they developed—a trajectory facilitated by the increasing ubiquity of personal computer hardware and software (Gawer & Cusumano, 2002, p. 5). Further, as availability of venture capital from venture capital firms declined over the last decade, many large firms internalized venture capital programs (corporate venture capital, CVC) to invest in small to medium-sized firms (SMEs) to develop innovations pertinent to their (the large firms') competencies(Van de Vrande, Vanhaverbeke, & Duysters, 2011).[5]

Push factors for open innovation included the increasing costs of technology development, which have prompted firms across the size spectrum to develop strategies to spread expenses to reach beyond their boundaries for problem solving and intellectual property. Further, many large firms lack sufficient internal expertise, in part as a vestige of lean management in the 1980s, when firms laid off many personnel, including researchers; accordingly, firms increasingly access expertise externally (Chesbrough, 2006a, p. 190). The goal set by Proctor and Gamble's newly appointed chief economic officer in 2000 is telling: to acquire 50 % of the company's innovations from external sources (Huston & Sakkab, 2006).

Beyond the development of innovative capabilities among suppliers in the context of relations between large and small firms, open innovation also entails interfirm relations among large firms that interlink business models based on new innovations, notably in industries that produce multi-component products (Chesbrough, 2006a, 2006b; Cooke, De Laurentis, MacNeill, & Collinge, 2010; Gawer, 2009; Gawer & Cusumano, 2002). The main imperative in open innovation is to continually move to new innovative activity in concert with other firms producing related products and services.[6]

The management of innovation across the spectrum of firms practicing open innovation has occurred in the context of the development of a relatively new demand environment: *customized* demand, which requires combinations of expertise that cannot be anticipated (Goldman, Nagel, & Preiss, 1995). Although, in principle, firms under such circumstances can continually add to their repertoire of skill through mergers, acquisitions, and continual hiring of experts, the high costs of

---

[5] For a survey in 2013 of the top 50 *Forbes Global* 2000 firms with CVC programs, see Battistini, Hacklin, and Baschera (2013).

[6] Intel's activity in the 1990s serves as an instructive example of interlinked activity among firms and novel strategies to coordinate innovativeness (see discussion in Gawer & Cusumano, 2002). By the late 1980s the pace of Intel's innovation in its core product, computer microprocessors, exceeded the pace of innovation in IBM's personal computer (PC) architecture. In response, Intel staffed a new lab with *software* engineers to find new uses for its hardware (microprocessors), in turn to stimulate demand for a new generation of personal computers that require Intel's core product. Its strategy in the next decade and into the twenty-first century has been "to establish the technologies, standards and products necessary to grow demand for the extended PC through the creation of new computing experiences" (cited in Gawer & Cusumano, 2002, p. 25).

such a strategy often prompt firms to look instead for expertise among external sources (Grant, 1998). From the vantage point of structural hole theory, linkages to an increasingly broad range of organizations increase social capital, provide a means by which individual firms can overcome structural gaps (Burt, 1992; Burt, Hogarth, & Michaud, 2000; Garrigos-Simon, Alcami, & Ribera, 2012), and enhance innovative capacity based on increasingly diverse knowledges (Frey, Lüthje, & Haag, 2011; Poetz & Schreier, 2012). *Agility,* defined in this context as the capacity of firms to tap external resources efficiently and rapidly, is a key asset of organizations (Goldman et al., 1995; Greis & Kasarda, 1997).[7] Outsourcing in the context of open innovation, even if exploitative, is prompted at the outset not by lowest cost of labor and products in externalized production, as in a Coase (1937)-inspired model of economic activity, but rather by the need to incorporate expertise external to a firm in projects that crosscut firms, as in a Hayek (1945)-inspired conceptualization. Per Hayek (1945), the world constantly changes, requiring an effective means of culling dispersed knowledges. Assuming all individuals possess unique knowledge, a central problem for Hayek was how dispersed knowledges might be accessed. The contemporary answer to Hayek's problem regarding innovation is open networks, in contrast to the tradition of relatively closed organizational forms (Lazega, in this volume). Whereas just-in-time manufacturing networks associated with flexible production tended to evolve as relatively closed with "strategic bridges" (Burt, 1992, 2005) forged between networks to facilitate flows of new information, Web 2.0 information and communications technologies (ICTs) have facilitated the development of open networks that draw from dispersed knowledges across firms (Garrigos-Simon et al., 2012).

Crucially, firms have opened their boundaries in the realm of innovation not only to other firms, both small and large, but also to freelancers "on the street," who may not necessarily be associated with firms and conceivably may even be unemployed. The governing apparatus of this labor market is crowdsourcing, which is one of several short-run avenues by which firms ensure fast profitability to complement long-term investment strategies and meet the demands of shareholders. Other short-run avenues include licensing in ready-to-go innovations to avoid their expense as well as time to invention and innovation; licensing out warehoused inventions that

---

[7] The concept of agility was first developed in U.S. defense-related production and eventually became wedded with the concept of the virtual enterprise in the early 1990s (Goldman et al., 1995; Goranson, 1999). The Advanced Research Projects Agency (ARPA) and the Pentagon created a program managed by several military services (especially the Air Force) and the National Science Foundation (NSF) to develop an organizational strategy to respond to unexpected problems in a post-Cold War environment; the research firm Sirius-Beta developed a key role in the program, connecting the idea of effectively and rapidly tapping external resources (agility) with the idea of ephemeral networks (the virtual enterprise). The NSF supported research centers at universities, pilot production programs, and information networks regarding the new paradigm. In 1991 the NSF supported a workshop at Lehigh University in Pennsylvania. Political support and thus defense dollars eventually diminished, although the NSF continued its support for programs, conferences, workshops, and publications to disseminate the new paradigm to the private sector.

have not been commercialized[8]; and partnering with universities, think tanks, and non-governmental organizations (Chesbrough, 2006a; Fabrizio, 2006).

Companies crowdsource by sending out open, electronic calls for inventions or expertise when problems emerge and require solution. For example, in 2002 Proctor and Gamble wanted to find a way to print edible pictures on each potato chip in a Pringles can; their electronic call was answered by the owner of a small bakery in Bologna, Italy, who had invented a way to print edible pictures on cakes and cookies; more generally, Proctor and Gamble has developed a strategy it calls "Connect+Develop" to replace the more traditional mentality of in-house research and development (Huston & Sakkab, 2006). Other companies orchestrate high-stakes online competitions as a growth strategy to access inventions that would enhance core competencies. Cisco Systems, for example, arranged an online competition for an invention related to its core competency in internet technology in 2007, offering a prize of 250,000 dollars to the winner; 2500 inventors across 104 countries competed, with rules stipulating that the winner would sign over the commercial rights of the invention to Cisco (Jouret, 2009). This one-time cost was offset considerably by the long-term billion-dollar business that Cisco launched using the winning invention as a platform.

Many firms now outsource crowdsourcing, giving rise to a new breed of firms that connect *seekers* (firms looking for new technology or expertise) with *solvers* (firms or individual actors with intellectual property or expertise who may be disassociated from firms)—the contemporary answer to Hayek's concern for how to access dispersed knowledges. Useful classifications of these mediators[9] exist (e.g., Feller, Finnegan, Hayes, & O'Reilly, 2009),[10] but the rapid evolution and internal diversification among these firms render the classifications insightful mainly in clarifying an initial division of labor. For example, some of these firms specialized in connecting seeker firms with experts selling existing intellectual property, while others connected seekers with experts selling their expertise to solve problems; some specialized at the outset in demand-driven activity such as classifying and cataloguing problems that solvers search, while others focused on supply-side activity such as finding solutions sought by firms. Most of these firms gradually have diversified internally, developing an array of activities and services to complement

---

[8] Around 90 % of Proctor and Gamble's patents in 2002 were never commercialized as innovations—a situation that is emblematic of tendencies to warehouse inventions (Chesbrough, 2006a, p. 9). In the context of open innovation, dormant inventions take on new value as a means to earn revenue quickly as other firms look to license in new technologies to avoid the costs of technology development.

[9] These third-party organizers conventionally are termed "intermediaries." Taking a cue from Bruno Latour's (2005) compelling argument that "intermediary" implies neutrality, I use the term "mediator."

[10] Feller et al.'s (2009) classification of mediators includes the following exemplars: Innocentive, founded in 2001; NineSigma, founded in 2000; Yet2, founded in 1999; YourEncore, founded in 2003; and InnoCrowding, founded in 2006. Companies specializing in connecting freelancers in software development, website design, customer service, and translation in low-wage countries with businesses (including SMEs) in high-wage countries include: oDesk, launched in 2005; Freelancer, launched in 2009; and Guru, launched as eMoonlighter in 1998 (Korkki, 2014).

the kind of activities that characterized their niche as they emerged at the outset as a secondary market for innovation.

Whereas all the above-mentioned mediators broker networks characterized by a hub-and-spoke structure in which the mediating firm is the connector but the network of individual solvers (people) lacks connectivity, another model of open networks entails networks of solver firms (not people) that collaborate relative to customized demand. In this latter system one firm receives customized orders from seeker firms and subsequently coordinates expertise amongst solver firms in ephemeral networks. Firms coalesce temporarily in projects to combine expertise to solve a problem; networks dissolve following completion of projects, and form anew with new memberships relative to the required expertise. This type of solver network is exemplified by the Agile Web, a virtual corporation established in 1995 and constituted by 20 small-to-medium-sized manufacturing firms that were selected from a population of over 700 prescreened firms in northeastern Pennsylvania; by 1999 it obtained over 50 million dollars in orders (Sheridan, 1993, 1996). In 2000, G5 Technologies, a company in New Jersey, acquired the Agile Web to enhance its array of collaborative business services and internet-based software technologies; as a subsidiary, the Agile Web remained intact, providing collaborative product design and manufacturing solutions (PR Newswire Association LLC, 2000). Similarly, KICMS is an association established in South Korea in 2004 that coordinates collaboration on research among large numbers of SMEs (around 4000), while also providing consulting services and assistance to the SMEs in developing markets (Lee, Park, Yoon, & Park, 2010).

To date, then, there are firms that access innovative expertise among individual people (not firms) in a hub-and-spoke approach in which there is no collaboration among solvers, and there are firms that access expertise among firms (not people) that engage in collaborative problem solving and temporarily coalesce in networks. The former case represents a lucrative model for firms that contracts with people, not firms, but is hardly a source of remunerative, living-wage jobs; each contest has one or a few winners and often thousands of losers who self-fund, and moreover, sign away their intellectual property rights when submitting their contributions. The latter case represents an effective organizational model to meet economic (not social) goals, and the customized orders reach firms, not individual people. Consider, then, the possibility of combining elements of each of these types of knowledge networks to constitute a hybrid system that serves social as well as economic goals.

Making Use of New Knowledge Networks to Develop Social Knowledges

I am interested in the proactive construction of one type of activity: mediators, which may be non-profit and at least partially government funded, that could connect firms as well as other organizations (e.g., government-funded and non-profit organizations, academic institutions) with appropriate networks of solvers who are people, not firms, to collaborate in remunerative, problem-solving activity. Based on information drawn from numerous cases studies, I develop a normative argument about the social as well as economic potential of this organizational approach to innovation that I term *mediated crowdsourced project work*. At this critical juncture in the global economy I am interested in how new approaches to accessing expertise in open networks, notably crowdsourcing, might be constructed so as to erode precarious conditions of work while serving to dissolve frictions of difference among people who might otherwise not interact in an increasingly segregated world.

Mediated crowdsourced project work is germane for two main reasons. First, the effort and ability of firms to reach innovative freelancers disassociated from firms and even unemployed conceivably can avoid institutionalized discrimination at the outset because actors in crowdsourced activity are recruited on the basis of their expertise relative to specified problems, not their work associations, previous history, or formal education. If we accept that many people earning below a living wage have well-developed skills, even if informally developed, then this system in principle has the potential to be inclusive, although to date, inclusivity has not been a goal and indeed has not been served. Second, the immateriality of collaboration in knowledge networks associated with project work (as opposed to selling intellectual property) brings people into contact with one another on the basis of their expertise. If innovative *communities of practice*[11] that are tapped for expertise were to open to diverse actors, then people who might otherwise not interact beyond superficial exchanges could gain trust and mutual respect through working together in meaningful interaction aimed at effective problem solving.

The idea of people developing mutual respect and trust in the process of using complementary expertise to solve problems for firms suggests that people learn about each other and develop social knowledges in the process of work with economic, material objectives. This is key, although the content of social knowledges typically is absent from analysis of economic networks in light of the conventional instrumentality of the social for the economic.

I suggest extending types of knowledges in economic-oriented literatures to include social knowledges, which I define as the generation of knowledges about actors' lives and circumstances, talents, idiosyncrasies, tragedies, and humor. Existing typologies of economic knowledges are rooted in Karl Polanyi's (1958, 1966) distinction between tacit and coded knowledges. Frank Blackler's (1995) elaborated typology includes embrained knowledge (rooted in an individual's cognitive abilities); embodied knowledge (practical knowledge developed in specific physical contexts, as in project work); encultured knowledge (rooted in shared

---

[11] The term "communities of practice," CoPs (Amin & Cohendet, 2004; Amin & Roberts, 2008; Lave & Wenger, 1991; Wenger, 1998; Wenger, McDermott, & Snyder, 2002), refers to context-specific practices that foster innovativeness among entrepreneurs through collaboration. An independent but parallel concept is "ba," which translates from Japanese as "place," in reference to public arenas in which innovative knowledges are generated and exchanged (Nonaka, 1994; Nonaka & Konno, 1998). Both concepts emerged with a localized context in mind, but evolved to consider collaborative practices across space.

understanding developed through socialization); embedded knowledge (subjective knowledge embedded in a context), and encoded knowledge (knowledge that can be presented in manuals, books, websites, and the like). The addition of social knowledges to existing typologies rests on the recognition of *problems* of social interaction. In an inclusive framework, exclusions wrought of segregation require attention.

Problematizing the Social: Conceptualizing Exclusion in Relation to Social Knowledges

Constructing networks among people who might otherwise not interact due to membership in different affinity groups (by class, race, ethnicity, gender, and the like) is fraught with problems in light of people's life experience in a hyper-segregated world. Although segregation commonly is viewed in the context of residential areas and school districts, occupational segregation also is well documented. Further, the management literature has documented frictions of difference within occupations in both material and virtual workplaces, as well as tendencies for people to want to work with people similar to themselves (e.g., Brown, Jenkins, & Thatcher, 2012; Joshi, 2006). Electronic workplaces in association with e-collaboration have been shown to embed implicit sociolinguistic biases regarding gender (Gefen, Geri, & Paravastu, 2007); moreover, different modes of e-communication have been shown to foster or inhibit constructive social relations in the context of diverse participants (Brown et al., 2012). Difference matters, consistent with geographer Mark Graham's (2011a) more general point that virtual space embeds biases relative to the range of axes of difference that exist in material space, while also creating new axes of difference. Recognizing persistent problems of difference departs from various sanguine views, such as the notion that activity in virtual space portends a more democratic future (e.g., see critical reviews by Graham, 2011b; Etling, Faris, & Palfrey, 2010), or that convivial interaction among diverse groups signifies the dissolution of frictions of difference, despite the superficiality of interaction (Gilroy, 2004, 2005).

Segregation along any of many or a combination of axes of difference contributes to the increasingly polarized nature of our world because it blocks access to information and opportunity to groups that lack resources, and moreover, it renders those without access out-of-sight and out-of mind (Young, 2000). Drawing from the theory of communicative action (Habermas, 1984), we can understand segregation in terms of the absence of communication among different groups via the construction of invisible and sometimes visible walls among groups, which then generate misinformation and the production of homogenizing and typically derogatory stereotypes. Misinformation in turn produces fear and discriminatory practices, which reinforce segregationist tendencies.

If segregation is understood as the socio-spatial production of ignorance, whether on the ground or virtually, then the task is to dissolve ignorance by developing new social knowledges through meaningful interaction (Ettlinger, 2009). I pursue new types of knowledge networks as a possible context for social change in association with the emergence of open innovation. The recognition of social knowledges in typologies of knowledge suggests important implications for adapting theory of knowledge generation regarding competitiveness to the domain of social relations while recognizing the benefits for economic performance. In light of the relative absence of attention to problems of knowledge generation in the realm in social theory, I turn now to literature on economic networks for clues regarding knowledge generation and sharing, with the aim of using these insights toward social knowledges in the context of economic dynamics.

Adapting Theories of (Economic) Knowledge Networks to Social Relations: Generating and Sharing Knowledges, and the Nagging Problem of Trust and Familiarity

Research in economic geography and sociology and allied fields in business and management has grappled with the "soft" issue of trust as a linchpin in the generation of knowledges for innovative activity among firms. Despite an absence of interest in the content of social knowledges and their usefulness for social issues, this literature nonetheless is germane because it clarifies the complexity of establishing trust and mutual respect, irrespective of the agenda.

Economic geographers in particular have engaged the spatiality of trust. The idea emanating from economic sociology that economic action is socially embedded (Granovetter, 1985) became axiomatic in economic geography, which initially meshed social with *local* embeddedness (Hess, 2004). However, the idea that feelings of trust associated with knowledge generation and exchange necessarily require the familiarity of physical, face-to-face interaction (e.g., Gertler, 2003; Morgan, 2004; Scott & Storper, 2003) eventually became upended in topological renditions of networks conceptualized in non-Euclidean space (e.g., Adams, 1998; Allen, 2009; Amin & Cohendet, 2004).[12] Unbounding learning regions opened analysis to networks and collaboration spread across space (Amin, 2004; Goodwin, 2013) and

---

[12] The sense of space from a Euclidean and topographic perspective represents the relation between two points in space as a straight line; space is understood as a container, constituted by locations that can be mapped as Cartesian coordinates. A non-Euclidean and topological sense of space recognizes that in practice the relation between two points in space may be non-linear due to physical, social, cultural, political, and economic barriers; space is folded. The non-Euclidean, topological perspective recognizes that relations between people across space may be stronger than relations between people at the same location, countering longstanding assumptions about the positive correlation between physical and social distance. Doreen Massey's (1993, 2005) "progressive sense of place" understands places as points of articulation between processes in local contexts and the wide-ranging experiences of people in places who have traversed many contexts; accordingly, places are characterized by diverse and not necessarily harmonious realities and identities. See also John Allen's (2003, 2009) scholarship on topologies of power.

the recognition of multiple types of proximities—physical, organizational, cultural, social, institutional, virtual—each with their own configurations of constraints and opportunities (Amin & Roberts, 2008; Bathelt, Feldman, & Kogler, 2011; Boschma, 2005; Jones & Search, 2009). Critiques of earlier notions of cozy, localized networks recognized that such networks may not result in innovativeness, as previously thought (Gordon & McCann, 2005), or they often are ineffective (Ettlinger, 2008; Hadjimichalis & Hudson, 2006). Moreover, localized networks became problematized in terms of negative tendencies toward "spatial myopia" (Maskell & Malmberg, 2007) or "lock-in" and innovative stagnation (Boschma, 2005). In contrast, global relations based on strategic bridging of knowledges across different networks suggested productive and creative possibilities (e.g., Bathelt, Malmberg, & Maskell, 2004).

However, the implications for knowledge generation have become complex and contingent. Far from a "flat world" of knowledge generation as a result of a wider range of opportunities across space (Friedman, 2005), there are concerns about what kinds of knowledge transfers are possible across space, in part due to the problem of trust among actors who lack familiarity with one another. Whether using Karl Polanyi's (1958, 1966) simple dichotomy of coded and tacit knowledge or more elaborated versions, there seems to be a consensus that a certain type of knowledge, *relational* knowledge, labeled "tacit" knowledge in Polanyi's conceptualization or *encultured* and *embedded* knowledges in Blackler's (1995) scheme, is *less* open to activity spread across space (e.g., Bathelt et al., 2004; Faulconbridge, 2006; Jones, 2007). People are reluctant to share their knowledges without having established familiarity (Han & Hovav, 2013). This may seem like a déjà vu—that research on networks and knowledge exchange is back to the original problem of necessitating face-to-face interaction, thereby limiting opportunities across space. Yet the situation is more complex, for several reasons.

First, from an epistemological vantage point, the process by which researchers of different camps have interpreted trust and familiarity relative to space differs. *Topographically* oriented research that assumes the dependence of trust formation on face-to-face contact emanates from analysis that begins with a particular spatial configuration of economic activity. In contrast, *topologically* oriented research, which has focused on communities of practice across space, directs attention not to what knowledge is generated by a particular spatial configuration of activity, but rather, what *practices* in the everyday economy do or do not require face-to-face interaction (Amin & Roberts, 2008; Faulconbridge, & Hall, 2009; Jones, 2008); analytically researchers start with, rather than infer, processes, and thereby can avoid spurious conclusions about processes of interaction based on patterns of activity. Moreover, this latter approach permits sensitivity to variation in conditions for sharing and exchanging knowledges relative to different industry contexts (Brenner, Cantner, & Graf, 2013; Tether, Li, & Mina, 2012).

Second, substantively, the spatiality of networks changes over time (Glückler, 2007). Spatially proximate ties made at one point in the evolution of a network can anchor relations as members of a network change location over time, and new ties can be developed while older ties dissolve. Moreover, the dynamics of any one network change as ties develop and evolve among actors in different networks.

Third, and relatedly, interdisciplinary research has suggested that with all the sophistication of ICTs, face-to-face communication remains the richest, especially for complex situations (e.g., Glückler & Schrott, 2007; Kock & Nosek, 2005). Interestingly, the competitive practice of bridging relations between actors in different networks has been shown to depend on bonding relations *within* networks (Kraut, Steinfeield, Chan, Butler, & Hoag, 1999; Han & Hovav, 2013). Accordingly, management techniques such as brainstorming and focus groups have been recommended at the outset of a project to cultivate bonding and anchor effective social relations that can evolve outside conditions of initial spatial proximity (Han & Hovav, 2013). Actually, the nature of the "location" of actors itself is fluid, if we consider cases of temporary spatial proximity owing to the mobility of many professionals (Almeida & Kogut, 1999; Torre & Rallet, 2005; Williams, 2006), and possibilities for the construction of temporary spatial clusters of innovation (e.g., Maskell, Bathelt, & Malmberg, 2006).

Finally, certain types of ICTs such as teleconferencing permit face-to-face relations across space, thereby creating virtual localization, overcoming the constraint of physical distance. However, research has shown that increased e-networking depends on effective and constructive personal relations within networks (Kraut et al., 1999), or at least in particular culture-specific contexts (Burt et al., 2000). These findings corroborate more general findings that effective bridging between networks of any kind (material or virtual) is contingent upon internal relations. Knowledge is subjective, and thus personal experience and *relational* capital (Kale, Singh, & Perlmutter, 2000) are pivotal resources at the outset of any project (Nonaka, 1994; Nonaka & Konno, 1998). Unsurprisingly, then, research on suites of ICTs for e-collaboration has suggested that asynchronous communication (e.g., discussion boards, e-mail, blogs, audio or video streaming, databases, or document libraries) are more appropriate at a *later* stage in a project, *after* actors' relations become anchored in early synchronous communication (e.g., through video, and audio conferencing, electronic chatting, or instant messaging) (Han & Hovav, 2013). This technosocial framework is consistent with research that advocates beginning project work with focus groups and brainstorming sessions, focusing on other types of communication later in the evolution of a project (Kraut et al., 1999).

It seems, then, that relational knowledge does not necessarily require face-to-face interaction, and further, localization can be achieved virtually across space with appropriate ICTs, as well as physically in short-run clustering of people from different places (Bathelt & Turi, 2011).

But here is the rub: Just as in problems of de-segregation in housing and school districts, co-location of project participants, whether virtual, physical, or temporary, does not necessarily produce trust.[13] A simple, basic, practical point complicates

---

[13] Approaching segregation relative to predefined, bounded residential areas, school districts, or workplaces is problematic because the problem is identified in terms of location, without regard for processes of inclusion and exclusion. The locational conceptualization of segregation underscores the conventional de-segregation strategy that locates diverse people in the same physical or virtual place. This locational strategy ironically is repeated over time and across space, despite documentation of persistent segregation with*in* apparently integrated areal units such as school districts

matters, namely, what people think of each other a priori, and the nature of power relations, affect prospects for knowledge sharing (Brown, Jenkins, & Thatcher, 2012). Moreover, research has shown that knowledges are communicated in verbal and nonverbal ways, including body language and other contextual cues (e.g., Harvey, Novicevic, & Grarrison, 2004), potentially inhibiting productive interaction in physical or virtual face-to-face settings (Brown et al., 2012; Shachaf, 2007). Bias is embodied, reinforcing the importance of incorporating faces as well as bodies in research on networks. Critical human geographers writing about issues in field strategies have highlighted some of the problems of, for example, focus groups, wherein power relations can surface and thereby produce silences among some members (Hyams, 2004). Similarly, in the business world, brainstorming sessions can inhibit creativity as different participants take on more and less responsibility in a group-think culture (Cain, 2012). Sometimes network analyses incorporate power relations (e.g., Faulconbridge & Hall, 2009) regarding, for example, selective recruitment by gatekeepers and executive search firms (Faulconbridge, Beaverstock, Hall, & Hewitson, 2009), agents' relational positioning (Weller, 2009), different kinds of proximities (Jones & Search, 2009), and uneven access to circuits of knowledge (Faulconbridge, 2007; Grabher, 2002).[14] And sometimes research in economic geography on networks connects with gender issues (Blake & Hanson, 2005; Hanson & Blake, 2009; McDowell, 2000). However, there is relative silence on issues of race and ethnicity and, more generally, issues of difference broadly construed.[15] The "soft" field of feelings and interpersonal relations remain central yet relatively unexplored.[16]

(Riley & Ettlinger, 2011) and neighborhoods (Joseph, Chaskin, & Webber, 2007). Given that the usual goal is defined not in terms of the nature of interaction, but rather in terms of the pattern of co-location, success is relatively easily achieved, perhaps in part explaining views that segregation is not really a problem. In contrast, a topological and non-Euclidean (as opposed to topographic and Euclidean) approach to segregation recognizes that segregation ripples through everyday life at fine scales, *within* so-called mixed residential communities such as schools, as well as in workplaces, including virtual workplaces.

[14] See Christopherson and Clark (2007) for a discussion of power relations in firm networks in which the actors are represented at the scale of firms.

[15] For example, Ash Amin, who has written extensively on issues in economic geography on knowledge generation (Amin, 2004; Amin & Cohendet, 2004; Amin & Roberts, 2008), has published on issues of race (e.g., Amin, 2010) and more general social theory (Amin & Thrift, 2013), but this part of his scholarship tends to be discrete from his publications on issues in economic geography. Similarly, Doreen Massey, whose early scholarship (Massey, 1984) paved the way for analysis of spatial divisions of labor, eventually departed from issues of firms and the economy (e.g., Massey, 1991, 2005).

[16] The allusion to emotions here differs from ideas about "emotional intelligence" in the business and management literature, which engages emotions in the context of fixed hierarchical structures and focuses on particular actors who are leaders to manage the emotions of their staffs—a top-down approach that implicitly is about policing emotions to fit with a prescribed configuration of emotion and reason to accommodate firm goals of productivity. The perspective here differs insofar as first, the usual instrumentality of the social for the economic is reversed, and second, emotions are not to be managed or possibly suppressed, but rather understood so as to enable constructive relations (Ettlinger, 2004).

The Difference that Difference Makes

Injecting problems of difference (along any of many axes) into the problematic arena of knowledge generation and sharing deepens already existing challenges. Thinking about difference entails more than adding Others to existing groups of workers; rather, it requires altering strategies that might otherwise be developed. For example, whereas there seems to be a consensus from e-collaboration and general management and organization studies that techniques for social bonding and building social awareness should be developed at the start of a project, whether in virtual or physical face-to-face settings (Han & Hovav, 2013; Kraut et al., 1999), difference might be served best differently. Research on heterogeneous groups recognizes that although diversity is seen instrumentally as productive due to a multiplicity of knowledges and perspectives (Shachaf, 2007), people nonetheless prefer to work and interact with those most similar to themselves, and moreover, are reluctant to share their knowledges with Others (Brown et al., 2012) in the context of prevailing preconceived views and derogatory stereotypes (Brown et al., 2012; Giambatista & Bhappu, 2010). Admittedly, economic performance can be served while social identities and relations are not, but, beyond ethics, economic productivity at the expense of the social arguably is sub-optimal because constructive social relations are strategic for economic performance.

Interestingly, research specifically on collaboration when difference is considered suggests a trajectory of communication strategies in which the outset of a project might benefit from *a*synchronous modes of communication or possibly avatars (Kock & Nosek, 2005, p. 3), and subsequently move to face-to-face interaction, virtually or physically, followed by diverse modes of communication depending on project needs (Brown et al., 2012). Asynchronous modes of communication, which lack physical cues, conceal at least some elements of difference,[17] permitting more focus at the outset on the objective content of interaction (Brown et al., 2012; Giambatista & Bhappu, 2010; Shachaf, 2007),[18] and possibly facilitate a formulation of identities at least partially unencumbered from visual cues among diverse actors at the start of new project (Amiri, Gholipour, & Sohrabi, 2011). A trajectory of asynchronous and synchronous communication is best conceptualized as dialectical rather than unilinear to permit adaptation to unanticipated dynamics (Brown et al., 2012). The difference that difference makes in the strategic design of project communications would seem to occur notably at the outset, entailing a reversal of the conventional logic for the appropriate communication platform at this stage.

But if the ultimate aim targets social relations in the course of project work, there remains more to consider. If a principal task is to develop social knowledges, beyond sharing economic knowledges in collaborative project work, then at least a portion

---

[17] Emoticoms, grammar, and the like are not, however, hidden in asynchronous communication (Brown et al., 2012).

[18] See also Harvey, Novicevic and Grarrison (2004) and Kock and Nosek (2005) on the strengths and limitations of different modes of communication in general.

of overall collaboration should entail some physical face-to-face interaction through work as well as social time. Personal relations matter in the sharing of knowledges, or more generally, private resources (Hambley, Kline, & O'Neil, 2007; Kraut et al., 1999; Uzzi, 1999). Further, the creation of a space and time for people to learn about each other in the course of collaborating on a project is complex because social learning is far from automatic. Rather, it requires careful planning of the mundane—seating arrangements, for example—to avoid the self-segregation during social time that has been documented in apparently "mixed" residential complexes and lunchrooms in schools.[19]

The idea here is to take what we know about the value of routinized rhythms of interaction from communities of economic practice in innovative activity (Brown & Duguid, 1991), and introduce such routinization in new social relations formed around collaborative project work.[20] Drawing from what we know about path dependence and the value of respect for another's work for future interaction, the sharing of knowledges about people as well as project work positions future social relations constructively. Pragmatically, the agenda produces logistical problems as well as the expense of ensuring participants' travel to a central place for the portion of project work requiring physical face-to-face interaction (see Feller, Finnegan, Hayes, & O'Reilly, 2012, regarding the critical role of stability for open innovation). In this regard, public-private partnerships may be crucial to provide continual support.

Envisioning Socially Responsive, Collaborative Knowledge Networks in the New Economy

The short-term nature of collaboration and the continual reconfiguration of proactively constructed networks ensure a continual meeting ground of diverse actors. The main drawback of network ephemerality from the vantage point of solvers is the potential instability of work.[21] Especially in light of one of the objectives to

---

[19] Lee's (2007) provocative account of a neighborhood's effort to deter Vancouver planners, engineers, politicians, and developers from moving ahead with plans for demolition and gentrification is instructive. Organizers of the movement against demolition and gentrification recognized that the actors behind these plans regarded the neighborhood as blight, and did not have any idea or even image of the people living in the neighborhood. Rather than protest, community leaders invited city officials and representatives of the new planning movement to their neighborhood for festivals, dinner, and walking tours, paying close attention to mundane details such as seating arrangements at dinner and the like. The face-to-face interaction and development of personal relations culminated in the termination of city plans for demolition and gentrification following what might be described as a concert of orchestrated "situated practices" that emplaced actual faces and livelihoods in the image of the neighborhood.

[20] The rhythms of working together and getting to know one another might otherwise be stated in terms of the socialization stage in Nonaka's conceptualization of knowledge generation (Nonaka, 1994; Nonaka & Konno, 1998).

[21] There also is a drawback of ephemeral networks from the vantage point of economic activity and goals, namely that the complex problem of establishing trust must be continually engaged—a

serve diverse labor markets in the context of increasing socioeconomic polarization, the type of system I advocate is one that should have the support of local and federal governments and other public and private organizations to sustain continual employment through a web of solver networks.

There is an existing model for such support, although the solvers in this model are firms (not individual people) and the goal is economic, not social. The previously mentioned Agile Web was formed and operated under the auspices of the state-funded Ben Franklin Technology Partners at Lehigh University in Pennsylvania. The center works with federal, state, and regional agencies, universities, and the private sector in a mission to achieve technology-based economic development. Prior to the formation of the Agile Web, the National Science Foundation funded an "Agility Forum" at Lehigh University, which laid a foundation for the development of the Web. The funded conceptualization and planning of the Agile Web occurred over a period of 2 years.

Consider the possibilities if federal, state, and regional agencies, universities, and the private sector were to reconfigure goals so as to value the social in the course of achieving economic ends. There are precedents for such reconfiguration, although not specifically in the context of open innovation and related network strategies (Gibson-Graham & Cameron, 2010; Gibson-Graham, Cameron, & Healy, 2013). One is the Mondragón Cooperative Corporation (MCC), which was founded in 1956 in Spain's Basque region with funding by business owners, institutions, workers, and municipal government. The MCC persists through the present as a business group based on democratic governance and a privileging of social and community objectives. Although it developed as a regional industrial complex spanning manufacturing, finance, distribution, housing, services, research, education, and training, it now has operations worldwide. Another model was Tony's Blair's "Third Way" programs in the United Kingdom in which the U.K. government provided financial and bureaucratic support for the development of "social enterprises" defined with reference to social and community objectives. In Australia, the Victoria government allocated 9.2 million dollars to a community enterprise strategy, and with the Brotherhood of St. Laurence supports 42 localities in the development of community enterprises. This selection of exemplars in different contexts demonstrates the plausibility of government and various local institutions and actors taking a proactive and supportive role in the systematic development of enterprises oriented to social and community goals. J. K. Gibson-Graham and Jenny Cameron (2010) have indicated that some social enterprises are remunerative and some are not; some "fail" yet serve an important role in providing a platform for the participants to move on to other enterprises, and in that sense, can reasonably be understood more as successes than failures.

My concern here is for remunerative and continual employment in mediated crowdsourced project work in the context of open innovation and related knowledge

---

problem that closed networks need not engage. As previously indicated, however, closed networks have other problems, and further, changing conditions have required increasing openness. The task then, is how to engage the new realities constructively, creatively, and effectively.

networks. The imperative for the provision of continuous, living-wage work across ephemeral networks derives from a fundamental concern for problems of underconsumption among increasingly large numbers of people worldwide, as well as the ills of the credit economy, in turn related to insufficient or no wages (Lazzarato, 2011/2012). The agenda to construct collaborative networks of people, not firms, connects with an innovation of open networks associated with open innovation: crowdsourcing. Although crowdsourcing often is exploitative (Howe, 2008; Korkki, 2014), I suggest treating it as a tool to achieve social objectives by creating a time and space for diverse people to realize their talents while being paid a living wage, and in the process develop meaningful knowledges about each other using multiple modes of communication in the course of sharing economic knowledges in temporary, collaborative networks that respond to customized demand for expertise in the context of open innovation.

Municipal governments might well consider it desirable to develop localized networks that are inclusive to avoid local socioeconomic and political tensions wrought of exclusionary processes. The multidimensionality of the agenda developed in this chapter suggests that it may be prudent to spatially fix it initially at the local scale to permit localized field research for the identification and establishment of knowledge networks in connection with the intricate dynamics of classifying problems relative to requisite sets of expertise. This sort of project need not, however, remain spatially bounded. Considering the long-run possibility of such projects worldwide, local mediators (supported by government at different scales) could work to ensure continual employment via local projects while connecting with other projects in other places; the local versus extra-local issue can, but need not, be a zero-sum game with appropriate goals, planning, and local participation. The evolution of the Mondragon Cooperative Corporation from localized to globally extensive is a case in point, although as J. K. Gibson-Graham (2006, p. 123) has pointed out, it is unclear whether democratic practices and the privileging of social objectives extend to offshore operations. Indeed, a transfer of social relations across space is anything but perfunctory and hardly a seamless operation; for this reason, beginning mediated crowdsourced project work at the metropolitan scale is pragmatic.

One central problem is recruitment. Recall Cisco's open electronic call for expertise and the considerable response across the world—2500 inventors across 104 countries. While many of those responding may well be without stable employment despite their skills, they nonetheless are "plugged in" to a global network, even if exploitative. In addition to all those who did not win Cisco's one-time prize, consider also the large numbers of people who remain unplugged from opportunities—as previously explained, a defining feature of segregation. People in untapped labor markets live in resource-poor areas that lack access to lucrative information, in part due to the absence of material and immaterial resources as well as institutionalized discrimination.

Extending knowledge networks to untapped labor markets, including people who are talented but lack formal work and educational experience, requires field research as a crucial complement to electronic communication to engage the complex terrain of sedimented exclusions.[22] Placing appropriate computer hardware and software in such communities at central-access locations would be ineffective without also seeking out and connecting with local gatekeepers as well as would-be gatekeepers across multiple community groups engaged in a wide range of activities.[23] While incorporating new members into a community of practice requires significant effort (de Vreede et al., 2007), the challenges are multiplied when new members come from previously excluded communities. The role of mediators entails coordinating, connecting, facilitating, and indeed empowering (Obstfeld, 2005).[24]

To avoid the pitfalls of top-down programs, it would be especially helpful if leaders of field research were recruited from within excluded neighborhoods (Kindon, Pain, & Kesby, 2007). An important part of the field research in these contexts entails assisting people who have been undervalued and might otherwise self-select out of opportunities to recognize and draw upon their strengths. Jenny Cameron and Katherine Gibson (2004) carried out precisely this type of field work in Australia, where they sought out people in communities devastated by industrial restructuring; crucially, these researchers recognized that the devastation was as much subjective as a matter of objectified conditions. Using field strategies such as focus groups, they helped people develop new subjectivities, based on recognition of their skills and talents despite exclusion from the market. In mediated crowdsourced project work, field research also must entail a constructive way to screen and evaluate expertise that would have to depart from existing techniques such as competitions (Howe, 2008; Lampel, Jha, & Bhalla, 2012; Villarroel, Taylor, & Tucci, 2013), which are win-lose propositions and incompatible with the objectives I have laid out. Face-to-face focus groups may be at least one viable alternative (Schweitzer, Buchinger, Gassmann, & Obrist, 2012). Admittedly, the task is huge, encompassing field research, continual classification of seeker problems in connection with appro-

---

[22] Although formal education often is used as a proxy measure for skill, this measure misses the variety of avenues by which people develop skills and knowledges. This much has been recognized by the business world, which has recognized that many educational systems around the world lack appropriate training for many workplaces. In response, training increasingly is linked to continuous learning in ongoing on-the-job training (Marković, 2008). Accordingly, many firms develop rigorous recruitment and selection criteria based on apparent intelligence, sense of responsibility, ambition, and the like and subsequently train workers themselves rather than rely on educational institutions.

[23] I include legal as well as illegal activity here. Regarding the latter, the view here is that illegal activity is most fruitfully engaged by providing new opportunities and practices, not by imprisoning and more generally constraining people who have been subjected to institutionalize discrimination—a system that has been shown to multiply existing problems. The view overall is consistent with Foucault's point that arriving at new truths requires the development of new practices, as opposed to proselytizing (1980, p. 133) or repression, which produces rather than eliminates actions on a targeted population (Foucault, 1976/1990).

[24] Obstfeld (2005) countered Burt's (1992) *tertius gaudens* (the third party that profits and plays one party off another) with *tertius iungens* (the third party that joins, unites, facilitates, connects, creates).

priate solvers (Feller et al., 2012), and effective communication among all actors orchestrating the different components of the project.

The dynamics of the mediated crowdsourced project work I envision entail something akin to the Agile Web, except that the solvers are talented people, not firms, who are identified at the outset and continually across a metropolitan region. In an era of increasingly customized demand, wide-ranging problems (from mechanical to electronic) that emerge are crowdsourced. In the scenario laid out in this chapter, crowdsourcing targets networks of diverse solvers (people) who would earn a living wage by collaborating in problem solving and the development of innovations demanded by seekers (private as well as public, organizations). Networks, coordinated by mediators between seekers and solvers, form around particular problems, dissolve, and form again with different membership relative to the expertise required for new problems. As networks form and reconfigure relative to the constitution of membership, each solver interacts with an increasingly wide array of people while developing social knowledges in the course of each collaboration. The point is to construct social knowledges to erode ignorance in the course of fluid, living-wage, collaborative work, supported by public and private institutions that serves both the economy and its people. The process renders economic space social and vice versa.

Conclusion: A Matter of Values

The agenda of this chapter is to conceptualize how to work towards social ends by recognizing and acting on the role of meaningful social knowledges in the pursuit of knowledges for economic gain. The context is the emergence of new production dynamics and labor recruitment strategies amid dramatically increasing socioeconomic polarization and exclusion. To date, crowdsourcing associated with open innovation has proven to be lucrative for firms but also highly exploitative and exclusive. Recognizing insidious dimensions of the market, the underlying suggestion here is to make use of the market, not to work against it, with public and private support for social as well as economic objectives. If the social and the economic as well as the cultural and political are mutually constituted, then it is sensible to refuse the conventional privileging of one dimension, the economic, at the expense of another, commonly the social. I have privileged social over economic goals to encompass strategies that might otherwise be jettisoned, but economic goals remain nested in the broader project. At this critical juncture in the global economy, the agenda I have in mind entails nothing less than reconfiguring the values that govern our lives.

Acknowledgments I thank Johannes Glückler and his team at the University of Heidelberg for organizing and graciously hosting the symposium on "Topographies and Topologies of Knowledge," and their invitation to me to participate. I also thank Johannes as well as Alistair Fraser and Kath Gibson for their thoughtful and constructive comments on an earlier draft of this chapter.

References

Adams, P. (1998). Network topologies and virtual place. *Annals of the Association of American Geographers, 88*, 88–106. doi:10.1111/1467-8306.00086

Allen, J. (2003). *Lost geographies of power*. Malden: Blackwell.

Allen, J. (2009). Powerful geographies: Spatial shifts in the architecture of globalization. In S. R. Clegg, & M. Haugaard (Eds.), *The SAGE handbook of power* (pp. 157–174). London: Sage.

Almeida, P., & Kogut, B. (1999). Localization of knowledge and the mobility of engineers in regional networks. *Management Science, 45*, 905–917. doi:10.1287/mnsc.45.7.905

Amin, A. (2004). Regions unbound: Towards a new politics of place. *Geografiska Annaler, 86*, 33–44. doi:10.1111/j.0435-3684.2004.00152.x

Amin, A. (2010). The remainders of race. *Theory, Culture & Society, 27*(1), 1–23. doi:10.1177/0263276409350361

Amin, A., & Cohendet, P. (2004). *Architectures of knowledge: Firms, capabilities, and communities*. New York: Oxford University Press.

Amin, A., & Roberts, J. (2008). Knowing in action: Beyond communities of practice. *Research Policy, 37*, 353–369. doi:10.1016/j.respol.2007.11.003

Amin, A., & Thrift, N. (2013). *Arts of the political: New openings for the left*. Durham: Duke University Press.

Amiri, B., Gholipour, A., & Sohrabi, B. (2011). The influence of information technology on organization behavior: Study of identity challenges in virtual teams. *International Journal of e-Collaboration, 7*(2), 19–34. doi:10.4018/jec.2011040102

Bathelt, H., Feldman, M. P., & Kogler, D. F. (Eds.). (2011). *Beyond territory: Dynamic geographies of knowledge creation, diffusion and innovation*. New York: Routledge.

Bathelt, H., Malmberg, A., & Maskell, P. (2004). Clusters and knowledge: Local buzz, global pipelines and the process of knowledge creation. *Progress in Human Geography, 28*, 31–56. doi:10.1191/0309132504ph469oa

Bathelt, H., & Turi, P. (2011). Local, global and virtual buzz: The importance of face-to-face contact in economic interaction and possibilities to go beyond. *Geoforum, 42*, 520–529. doi:10.1016/j.geoforum.2011.04.007

Battistini, B., Hacklin, F., & Baschera, P. (2013). The state of corporate venturing: Inside of a global study. *Research-Technology Management, 56*(1), 31–39. doi:10.5437/08956308X5601077

Beck, U. (2000). *The brave new world of work* (P. Camiller, Trans.). Malden: Polity Press. (Original work published 1999)

Blackler, F. (1995). Knowledge, knowledge work and organizations: An overview and interpretation. *Organization Studies, 16*, 1021–1046. doi:10.1177/017084069501600605

Blake, M. K., & Hanson, S. (2005). Rethinking innovation: Context and gender. *Environment and Planning A, 37*, 681–701. doi:10.1068/a3710

Boschma, R. (2005). Proximity and innovation: A critical assessment. *Regional Studies, 39*, 61–74. doi:10.1080/0034340052000320887

Bourdieu, P. (1986). The forms of capital. In J. Richardson (Ed.), *Handbook of theory and research for the sociology of education* (pp. 241–258). New York: Greenwood.

Brenner, T., Cantner, U., & Graf, H. (Eds.). (2013). Introduction: Structure and dynamics of innovation networks. *Regional Studies, 47*, 647–650. doi:10.1080/00343404.2013.770302

Brown, J. S., & Duguid, P. (1991). Organizational learning and communities-of-practice: Toward a unified view of working, learning, and innovation. *Organizational Science, 2*, 40–57. doi:10.1287/orsc.2.1.40

Brown, S., Jenkins, J. L., & Thatcher, S. M. B. (2012). E-Collaboration media use and diversity perceptions: An evolutionary perspective of virtual organizations. *International Journal of e-Collaboration, 8*(2), 28–46.

Burt, R. (1992). *Structural holes: The social structure of competition*. Cambridge, MA: Harvard University Press.

Burt, R. (2005). *Brokerage and closure: An introduction to social capital*. New York: Oxford University Press.
Burt, R., Hogarth, E., & Michaud, C. (2000). The social capital of French and American managers. *Organization Science, 11*, 123–147. doi:10.1287/orsc.11.2.123.12506
Cain, S. (2012, January 13). The rise of the new groupthink. *New York Times*, Retrieved from http://nyti.ms/1wUaLCc
Cameron, J., & Gibson, K. (2004). Participatory action research in a poststructuralist vein. *Geoforum, 36*, 315–331. doi:10.1016/j.geoforum.2004.06.006
Chesbrough, H. (2006a). *Open business models: How to thrive in the new innovation landscape*. Boston: Harvard Business School Press.
Chesbrough, H. (2006b). *Open innovation: The new imperative for creating and profiting from technology*. Boston: Harvard Business School Press.
Chesbrough, H., & Brunswicker, S. (2013). *Managing open innovation in large firms: Survey report, executive survey on open innovation*. Berkeley: Fraunhofer.
Chesbrough, H., Vanhaverbeke, W., & West, J. (Eds.). (2006). *Open innovation: Researching a new paradigm*. New York: Oxford University Press.
Christopherson, S., & Clark, J. (2007). Power in firm networks: What it means for regional innovation systems. *Regional Studies, 41*, 1223–1236. doi:10.1080/00343400701543330
Coase, R. (1937). The nature of the firm. *Economica, 4*, 386–405. doi:10.1111/j.1468-0335.1937.tb00002.x
Cooke, P., De Laurentis, C., MacNeill, S., & Collinge, C. (Eds.). (2010). *Platforms of innovation: Dynamics of new industrial knowledge flows*. Northampton: Edward Elgar.
de Vreede, G.-V., Tarmizi, H., & Zigurs, I. (2007). Leadership challenges in communities of practice: Supporting facilitators via design and technology. *International Journal of e-Collaboration, 3*(1), 1–18. doi:10.4018/jec.2007010102
Etling, B., Faris, R., & Palfrey, J. (2010). Political change in the digital age: The fragility and promise of online organizing. *SAIS Review, 30*(2), 37–49. Retrieved from http://nrs.harvard.edu/urn-3:HUL.InstRepos:4609956
Ettlinger, N. (2003). Cultural economic geography and a relational and microspace approach to trusts, rationalities, networks, and change in collaborative workplaces. *Journal of Economic Geography, 3*, 145–171. doi:10.1093/jeg/3.2.145
Ettlinger, N. (2004). Towards a critical theory of untidy geographies: The spatiality of emotions in consumption and production. *Feminist Economics, 10*(3), 21–54. doi:10.1080/1354570042000267617
Ettlinger, N. (2008). The predicament of firms in the new and old economies: A critical inquiry into traditional binaries in the study of the space-economy. *Progress in Human Geography, 32*, 45–69. doi:10.1177/0309132507083506
Ettlinger, N. (2009). Surmounting city silences: Knowledge creation and the design of urban democracy. *International Journal of Urban and Regional Research, 33*, 217–230. doi:10.1111/j.1468-2427.2009.00840.x
Ettlinger, N. (2014) The openness paradigm. *New Left Review, 89*, 89–100.
Fabrizio, K. R. (2006). The use of university research in firm innovation. In H. Chesbrough, W. Vanhaverbeke, & J. West (Eds.), *Open innovation: Researching a new paradigm* (pp. 134–160). New York: Oxford University Press.
Faulconbridge, J. R. (2006). Stretching tacit knowledge beyond a local fix? Global spaces of learning in advertising professional service firms. *Journal of Economic Geography, 6*, 517–540. doi:10.1093/jeg/lbi023
Faulconbridge, J. R. (2007). Relational networks of knowledge production in transnational law firms. *Geoforum, 38*, 925–940. doi:10.1016/j.geoforum.2006.12.006
Faulconbridge, J. R., Beaverstock, J. V., Hall, S., & Hewitson, A. (2009). The "war for talent": The gatekeeper role of executive search firms in elite labour markets. *Geoforum, 40*, 800–808. doi:10.1016/j.geoforum.2009.02.001

Faulconbridge, J. R., & Hall, S. (Eds.). (2009). Organizational geographies of power [Special issue]. *Geoforum, 40*, 785–789. doi:10.1016/j.geoforum.2009.09.003

Feller, J., Finnegan, P., Hayes, J., & O'Reilly, P. (2009). Institutionalizing information asymmetry: Governance structures for open innovation. *Information Technology and People, 22*, 297–316. doi:10.1108/09593840911002423

Feller, J., Finnegan, P., Hayes, J., & O'Reilly, P. (2012). "Orchestrating" sustainable crowdsourcing: A characterization of solver brokerages. *Journal of Strategic Information Systems, 21*, 216–232. doi:10.1016/j.jsis.2012.03.002

Foucault, M. (1980). Truth and power (C. Gordon, L. Marshall, J. Mepham, & K. Soper, Trans.). In C. Gordon (Ed.), *Power/knowledge: Selected interviews and other writings 1972–1977* (pp. 109–133). New York: Pantheon.

Foucault, M. (1990). *The history of sexuality: Volume 1. An introduction* (R. Hurley, Trans.). New York: Vintage Books. (Original work published 1976)

Foucault, M. (1996). Sex, power and the politics of identity (L. Hochroth, & J. Johnston, Trans.). In S. Lotringer (Ed.), *Foucault live: Interviews, 1961–1984* (pp. 382–390). New York: Semiotext(e) (Interview conducted by B. Gallagher, & A. Wilson, Toronto, 1982).

Foucault, M. (2007). *Security, territory, population: Lectures at the Collège de France, 1977–1978* (G. Burchell, Trans.). In M. Senellart (Ed.), New York: Palgrave. (Original work published 2004)

Foucault, M. (2008). *The birth of biopolitics: Lectures at the Collège de France, 1978–1979* (G. Burchell, Trans.). In M. Senellart (Ed.), New York: Palgrave Macmillan. (Original work published 2004.)

Frey, K., Lüthje, & Haag, S. (2011). Whom should firms attract to open innovation platforms? The role of diversity and motivation. *Long Range Planning, 44*, 397–420. doi:10.1016/j.lrp.2011.09.006

Friedman, T. L. (2005). *The world is flat: A brief history of the twenty-first century*. New York: Farrar, Straus and Giroux.

Garrigos-Simon, F. J., Alcami, R. L., & Ribera, T. B. (2012). Social networks and web 3.0: Their impact on management and marketing of organizations. *Management Decision, 50*, 1880–1890. doi:10.1108/00251741211279657

Gawer, A. (Ed.). (2009). *Platforms, markets and innovation*. Northampton: Edward Elgar.

Gawer, A., & Cusumano, M. A. (2002). *Platform leadership: How Intel, Microsoft, and Cisco drive industry innovation*. Boston: Harvard Business School Press.

Gefen, D., Geri, N., & Paravastu, N. (2007). Vive la difference: The cross-culture differences within us. *International Journal of e-Collaboration, 3*(3), 1–16. doi:10.4018/978-1-87828-991-9.ch174

Gertler, M. (2003). Tacit knowledge and the economic geography of context, or the undefinable tacitness of being (there). *Journal of Economic Geography, 3*, 75–99. doi:10.1093/jeg/3.1.75

Giambatista, R. C., & Bhappu, A. D. (2010). Diversity's harvest: Interactions of diversity sources and communication technology on creative group performance. *Organizational Behavior and Human Decision Processes, 111*, 116–126. doi:10.1016/j.obhdp.2009.11.003

Gibson-Graham, J. K. (2006). *A postcapitalist politics*. Minneapolis: University of Minnesota Press.

Gibson-Graham, J. K., & Cameron, J. (2010). Community enterprises: Imagining and enacting alternatives to capitalism. In P. Healey, & J. Hillier (Eds.), *The Ashgate research companion to planning theory: Conceptual challenges for spatial planning* (pp. 291–298). Burlington: Ashgate.

Gibson-Graham, J. K., Cameron, J., & Healy, S. (2013). *Take back the economy: An ethical guide for transforming our communities*. Minneapolis: University of Minnesota Press.

Gilroy, P. (2004). *After empire: Melancholia or convivial culture?* London: Routledge.

Gilroy, P. (2005). Melancholia or conviviality: The politics of belonging in Britain. *Soundings, 29*(1), 35–46.

Glückler, J. (2005). Making embeddedness work: Social practice institutions in foreign consulting markets. *Environment and Planning A, 37,* 1727–1750. doi:10.1068/a3727

Gückler, J. (2007). Economic geography and the evolution of networks. *Journal of Economic Geography, 7,* 619–634. doi:10.1093/jeg/lbm023

Glückler, J., & Schrott, G. (2007). Leadership and performance in virtual teams: Exploring brokerage in electronic communication. *International Journal of e-Collaboration, 3*(3), 1–13. doi:10.4018/978-1-59904-955-7.ch076

Goldman, S. L., Nagel, R. N., & Preiss, K. (1995). *Agile competitors and virtual organizations: Strategies for enriching the customer*. New York: Van Nostrand Reinhold.

Goodwin, M. (2013). Regions, territories and relationality: Exploring the regional dimensions of political practice. *Regional Studies, 47,* 1181–1190. doi:10.1080/00343404.2012.697138

Goranson, H. T. (1999). *The agile virtual enterprise: Cases, metrics, tools*. Westport: Quorum Books.

Gordon, I. R., & McCann, P. (2005). Innovation, agglomeration, and regional development. *Journal of Economic Geography, 5,* 523–543. doi:10.1093/jeg/lbh072

Grabher, G. (2002). Cool projects, boring institutions: Temporary collaboration in social context. *Regional Studies, 36,* 205–214. doi:10.1080/00343400220122025

Graham, M. (2011a). Time machines and virtual portals: The spatialities of the digital divide. *Progress in Development Studies, 11,* 211–227. doi:10.1177/146499341001100303

Graham, M. (2011b). Cloud collaboration: Peer-production and the engineering of the Internet. In S. Brunn (Ed.), *Engineering earth* (pp. 67–83). New York: Springer.

Granovetter, M. (1985). Economic action and social structure: The problem of embeddedness. *American Journal of Sociology, 91,* 481–510.

Grant, R. M. (1998). Prospering in dynamically competitive environments: Organizational capability as knowledge integration. In A. Y. Illinitch, A. Y. Lewin, & R. D'Aveni. (Eds.), *Managing in times of disorder: Hypercompetitive organizational responses* (pp. 297–318). Thousand Oaks: Sage.

Greis, N. P., & Kasarda, J. D. (1997). Enterprise logistics in the information era. *California Management Review, 39*(4), 55–78. 10.2307/41165910

Habermas, J. (1984). *The theory of communicative action*. Boston: Beacon Press.

Hadjimichalis, C., & Hudson, R. (2006). Networks, regional development and democratic control. *International Journal of Urban and Regional Research, 30,* 858–872. doi:10.1111/j.1468-2427.2006.00687.x

Hambley, L. A., Kline, T. J. B., & O'Neil, T. A. (2007). Virtual team leadership: Perspectives from the field. *Organizational Behavior and Human Decision Processes, 103,* 1–20. doi:1016/j.obhdp.2006.09.004

Han, J. Y., & Hovav, A. (2013). To bridge or to bond? Diverse social connections in an IS project team. *International Journal of Project Management, 31,* 378–390. doi:10.1016/j.ijproman.2012.09.001

Hanson, S., & Blake, M. (2009). Gender and entrepreneurial networks. *Regional Studies, 43,* 135–149. doi:10.1080/00343400802251452

Harvey, M., Novicevic, M. M., & Grarrison, G. (2004). Challenges to staffing global virtual teams. *Human Resource Management Review, 14,* 275–294. doi:10.1016/j.hrmr.2004.06.005

Hayek, F. A. (1945). The use of knowledge in society. *The American Economic Review, 35,* 519–530.

Hess, M. (2004). 'Spatial' relationships? Towards a reconceptualization of embeddedness. *Progress in Human Geography, 28,* 165–186. doi:10.1191/0309132504ph479oa

Howe, J. (2008). *Crowdsourcing: Why the power of the crowd is driving the future of business*. New York: Crown Business.

Huston, L., & Sakkab, N. (2006). Connect and develop: Inside Proctor and Gambles's new model for innovation. *Harvard Business Review, 84*(3), 58–66. Retrieved from https://hbr.org/2006/03/connect-and-develop-inside-procter-gambles-new-model-for-innovation

Hyams, M. (2004). Hearing girls' silences: Thoughts on the politics and practices of a feminist method of group discussion. *Gender, Place and Culture, 11,* 105–119. doi:10.1080/0966369042000188576

Jones, A. (2007). More than 'managing across borders?' The complex role of face-to-face interaction in globalizing law firms. *Journal of Economic Geography, 7,* 223–246. doi:10.1093/jeg/lbm003

Jones, A. (2008). Beyond embeddedness: Economic practices and the invisible dimensions of transnational business activity. *Progress in Human Geography, 32,* 71–88. doi:10.1177/0309132507084817

Jones, A., & Search, P. (2009). Proximity and power within investment relationships: The case of the UK private equity industry. *Geoforum, 40,* 809–819. doi:10.1016/j.geoforum.2009.09.002

Joseph, M. L., Chaskin, R. J., & Webber, H. S. (2007). The theoretical basis for addressing poverty through mixed-income development. *Urban Affairs Review, 42,* 369–409. doi:10.1177/1078087406294043

Joshi, A. (2006). The influence of organizational demography on the external networking behavior of teams. *Academy of Management Review, 31,* 583–595 doi:10.5465/AMR.2006.21318919

Jouret, G. (2009). Inside Cisco's search for the next big idea. *Harvard Business Review, 87*(9), 43–45. Retrieved from https://hbr.org/2009/09/inside-ciscos-search-for-the-next-big-idea

Kale, P., Singh, H., & Perlmutter, H. (2000). Learning and protection of proprietary assets in strategic alliances: Building relational capital. *Strategic Management Journal, 21,* 217–237. doi:10.1002/(SICI)1097-0266(200003)

Kindon, S., Pain, R., & Kesby, M. (Eds.). (2007). *Participatory action research approaches and methods: Connecting people, participation and place.* New York: Routledge.

Kock, N., & Nosek, H. (2005). Expanding the boundaries of e-collaboration. *IEEE Transactions on Professional Communication, 48,* 1–9. doi:10.1109/TPC.2004.843272

Korkki, P. (2014, February 15). Small business, joining a parade of outsourcing. *The New York Times.* Retrieved from http://nyti.ms/1dwGYcr

Kraut, R., Steinfeild, C., Chan, A. P., Butler, B., & Hoag, A. (1999). Coordination and virtualization: The role of electronic networks and personal relationships. *Organization Science, 10,* 722–740. doi:10.1287/orsc.10.6.722

Lampel, J., Jha, P. P., & Bhalla, A. (2012). Test-driving the future: How design competitions are changing innovation. *Academy of Management Perspectives, 26*(2), 71–85. doi:10.5465/amp.2010.0068

Latour, B. (2005). *Reassembling the social: An introduction to actor-network-theory.* New York: Oxford University Press.

Lave, J., & Wenger, E. (1991). *Situated learning: Legitimate peripheral participation.* New York: Cambridge University Press.

Lazzarato, M. (2012). *The making of the indebted man: An essay on the neoliberal condition,* (J. D. Jordan, Trans.). Los Angeles: Semiotext(e). (Original work published 2011)

Lee, J.-A. (2007). Gender, ethnicity, and hybrid forms of community-based activism in Vancouver, 1957–1978: The Strathcona story revisited. *Gender, Place and Culture, 14,* 381–407. doi:10.1080/09663690701439702

Lee, S., Park, G., Yoon, B., & Park, J. (2010). Open innovation in SMEs—An intermediated network model. *Research Policy, 39,* 290–300. doi:10.1016/j.respol.2009.12.009

Marković, M. R. (2008). Managing the organizational change and culture in the age of globalization. *Journal of Business Economics and Management, 9,* 3–11. doi:10.3846/1611-1699.2008.9.3-11

Maskell, P., Bathelt, H., & Malmberg, A. (2006). Building global knowledge pipelines: The role of temporary clusters. *European Planning Studies, 14,* 997–1013. doi:10.1080/09654310600852332

Maskell, P., & Malmberg, A. (2007). Myopia, knowledge development and cluster evolution. *Journal of Economic Geography, 7,* 603–618. doi:10.1093/jeg/lbm020

Massey, D. (1984). *Spatial divisions of labor: Social relations and the geography of production.* New York: Routledge.

Massey, D. (1991). Flexible sexism. *Environment and Planning D: Society and Space, 9,* 31–57. doi:10.1068/d090031
Massey, D. (1993). Power-geometry and a progressive sense of place. In J. Bird, B. Curits, T. Putnam, G. Robertson, & L. Tickner (Eds.), *Mapping the futures: Local cultures, global change* (pp. 60–69). New York: Routledge.
Massey, D. (2005). *For space.* London: Sage.
McDowell, L. (2000). Feminists rethink the economic: The economics of gender/the gender of economics. In L. Clark, M. P. Feldman, & M. S. Gertler (Eds.), *The Oxford handbook of economic geography* (pp. 497–517). New York: Oxford University Press.
Morgan, K. (2004). The exaggerated death of geography: Learning, proximity and territorial innovation systems. *Journal of Economic Geography, 4,* 3–21. doi:10.1093/jeg/4.1.3
Nonaka, I. (1994). A dynamic theory of organizational knowledge creation. *Organization Science, 5,* 14–37. doi:10.1287/orsc.5.1.14
Nonaka, I., & Konno, N. (1998). The concept of "Ba": Building a foundation for knowledge creation. *California Management Review, 40,* 40–54.
Obstfeld, D. (2005). Social networks, the *tertius iungens* orientation, and involvement in innovation. *Administrative Science Quarterly, 50,* 100–130. doi:10.2189/asqu.2005.50.1.100
Poetz, M. K., & Schreier, M. (2012). The value of crowdsourcing: can users really compete with professionals in generating new product ideas? *Journal of Product Innovation Management, 29,* 245–256. doi:10.1111/j.1540-5885.2011.00893.x
Polanyi, M. (1958). *Personal knowledge.* Chicago: University of Chicago Press.
Polanyi, M. (1966). *The tacit dimension.* Garden City: Anchor Books.
PR Newswire Association LLC (2000). G5 Technologies Completes Acquisition of Agile Web, Inc. Retrieved from http://www.thefreelibrary.com/G5+Technologies+Completes+Acquisition+of+Agile+Web,+Inc-a065158785
Riley, C., & Ettlinger, N. (2011). Interpreting racial formation and multiculturalism in a high school: Towards a constructive deployment of two approaches to critical race theory. *Antipode, 43,* 1250–1280. doi:10.1111/j.1467-8330.2010.00825.x
Schweitzer, M., Buchinger, W., Gassmann, O., & Obrist, M. (2012). Crowdsourcing: Leveraging innovation through online idea competitions. *Research-Technology Management, 55*(3), 32–38. doi:10.5437/08956308X5503055
Scott, A. J., & Storper, M. (2003). Regions, globalization, development. *Regional Studies, 37,* 579–593. doi:10.1080/0034340032000108697
Shachaf, P. (2007). Cultural diversity and information and communication technology impacts on global virtual teams: An exploratory study. *Information and Management, 45,* 131–142. doi:10.1016/j.im.2007.12.003
Sheridan, J. H. (1993). Agile manufacturing: Stepping beyond lean production. *Industry Week, 242*(8), 30–46.
Sheridan, J. H. (1996). The Agile Web: a model for the future? *Industry Week, 245*(5), 31–35.
Standing, G. (2011). *The precariat: The new dangerous class.* New York: Bloomsbury.
Tether, B. S., Li, Q. C., & Mina, A. (2012). Knowledge-bases, places, spatial configurations and the performance of knowledge-intensive professional service firms. *Journal of Economic Geography, 12,* 969–1001. doi:10.1093/jeg/lbs015
Torre, A., & Rallet, A. (2005). Proximity and localization. *Regional Studies, 39,* 47–59. doi:10.1080/0034340052000320842
Uzzi, B. (1999) Embeddedness in the making of financial capital: How social relations and networks benefit firms seeking financing. *American Sociological Review, 64,* 481–505. Retrieved from http://www.jstor.org/stable/2657252
Van de Vrande, V., Vanhaverbeke, W., & Duysters, G. (2011). Additivity and complementarity in external technology sourcing: The added value of corporate venture capital investments. *IEEE Transactions on Engineering Management, 58,* 483–496. doi:10.1109/TEM.2010.2091134
Villarroel, J. A., Taylor, J. E., & Tucci, C. L. (2013). Innovation and learning performance implications of free revealing and knowledge brokering in competing communities: Insights from the

Netflix Prize challenge. *Computational and Mathematical Organization Theory, 19,* 42–77. doi:10.1007/s10588-012-9137-7

Weller, S. A. (2009). Shifting spatialities of power: The case of Australasian aviation. *Geoforum, 40,* 790–799. doi:10.1016/j.geoforum.2009.04.003

Wenger, E. (1998). *Communities of practice: Learning, meaning, and identity.* Cambridge, UK: Cambridge University Press.

Wenger, E., McDermott, R., & Snyder, W. M. (2002). *Cultivating communities of practice.* Boston: Harvard Business School Press.

Williams, A. M. (2006). Lost in translation? International migration, learning and knowledge. *Progress in Human Geography, 30,* 588–607. doi:10.1177/0309132506070169

Young, I. M. (2000). *Inclusion and democracy.* New York: Oxford University Press.

Open Access This chapter is distributed under the terms of the Creative Commons Attribution 4.0 International License (http://creativecommons.org/licenses/by/4.0/), which permits use, duplication, adaptation, distribution and reproduction in any medium or format, as long as you give appropriate credit to the original author(s) and the source, provide a link to the Creative Commons license and indicate if changes were made.

The images or other third party material in this chapter are included in the work's Creative Commons license, unless indicated otherwise in the credit line; if such material is not included in the work's Creative Commons license and the respective action is not permitted by statutory regulation, users will need to obtain permission from the license holder to duplicate, adapt or reproduce the material.

Chapter 3
Interpersonal Networks in Foreign Assignments and Intercultural Learning Processes

Erika Spieß

Globalization and Foreign Assignment

Due to the pressures of competition resulting from the globalization of markets, international experience has gained importance, and in fact become a vital asset (Carpenter, Sanders, & Gregerson, 2001; Landy & Conte, 2008). Multinational companies, in particular, regard foreign assignment experience as a market advantage (Spreitzer, McCall, & Mahoney, 1997). For employees, international professional experience in this context has become a prime prerequisite for becoming an executive (Daily, Certo, & Dalton, 2000).

This growing trend to send staff on foreign assignment is accompanied by a need to know what has to be done for expatriates to adjust successfully. Employees working in a foreign country are confronted with major changes in various areas, changes requiring their preparation prior to the foreign sojourn and support during it. If this does not occur, there is a risk that employees may feel stressed, be unable to work effectively, and, if worst comes to worst, have to end their sojourn prematurely.

The different phases of a foreign assignment (Kühlmann & Stahl, 2001/2006)—preparation, sojourn, and return—harbor certain risks. Due to time constraints, preparation is often inadequate or does not occur at all. The risks associated with the assignment are country-specific as well as of a private nature. Western expatriates in China experienced a "classic" culture shock (Selmer, 1999) and transferees uninterested in the country of assignment had difficulty adapting and, consequently, being effective for the company (Selmer, 2001). The larger the cultural distance to the country of origin the more difficult a foreign assignment may turn out to be (Wang, 2002). There is the danger of culture shock limiting an expatriate's ability to do

---

E. Spieß (✉)
Department Psychologie, Ludwig-Maximilians-Universität (LMU),
Leopoldstraße 13, 80802 Munich, Germany
e-mail: erika.spiess@psy.lmu.de

© The Author(s) 2017
J. Glückler et al. (eds.), *Knowledge and Networks*, Knowledge and Space 11,
DOI 10.1007/978-3-319-45023-0_3

his or her job. A lack of appreciation for returnees by company and home colleagues has been observed as a problem during the return phase (Kupka, Everett, & Cathro, 2008; Szkudlarek, 2010).

To facilitate adjustment during the sojourn, some large corporations institute comprehensive mentoring programs embedded in personnel development measures and processes (Noe, Greenberger, & Wang, 2002). Hechanova, Beehr, and Christiansen's (2003) meta-analysis described the antecedents and consequences of the adjustment of transferees on foreign assignment. Self-efficacy—the belief in one's ability to act, the frequency of interaction with people from the host country, interpersonal skills, and family support proved to be the main predictors for successful adjustment to the entire environment.

For instance, Wang and Kanungo (2004) demonstrated that the role of interpersonal networks is often neglected, although it has a direct and significant positive influence on the transferee's well-being. Caligiuri and Lazarova (2002) developed a model showing the relationship between social network, social support, and adjustment. They assumed that social interaction and social support (e.g., family members, coworkers in the country of sojourn, transferees from home and other countries) could help activate psychological resources with the capacity to intensify recognition and confirmation, attributes that in turn can substantially improve intercultural adjustment. Social support can act as a buffer against stress that usually occurs as the transferee tries to adjust to the new environment. Successful intercultural adjustment is closely related to network partners and social support.

In the following I present Kurt Lewin's field theory as a theoretical framework for my discussion of networks, social support in different fields of application, and personal initiative and for my examination of the relationship between social support and work adjustment. In conclusion results are considered regarding their specific meaning for the intercultural learning process and within the framework of field theory.

Theoretical Framework

Lewin's field theory is an important model for explaining economic action in significant fields of application. The central idea of Lewin's theory is that people are drawn to some things in their environment and repelled by others. In the Lewinian sense, all actors are situated in a field: They act, bring things into motion, influence others, launch campaigns, and are, for their part, exposed to various, even antagonistic behavioral forces. The advantage of the concept of *field* is its understanding that a person exists in a field of tensions, with the tensile and pressure forces within the field enabling a description of human behavior. In contrast to behaviorism's mechanistic image, field theory assumes that a person is active, perceiving and assessing his or her surroundings (Lewin, 1943, 1951/1963). Lewin (1939) regards the psychological environment functionally as "a part of one interdependent field, the life-space, the other part of which is the person" (p. 878). He expresses this in his famous formula: "Behavior = Function of person and environment = Function of life-space" (p. 878).

"Lewin's field theory states that it is possible to understand the basis for changing the behavior of individuals and groups by constructing a 'life space' comprising the psychological forces influencing their behavior at a given point in time" (Burnes & Cooke, 2012a, p. 409). According to Burnes and Cooke (2012a), field theory played a central part in all of Lewin's work by allowing him to understand the forces that would need to be either strengthened or weakened in order to bring out desired behavior. Burnes and Cooke (2012a) reviewed and reevaluated field theory, arguing that the main reason for the decline of field theory was Lewin's pursuit of mathematical rigor over practical relevance. In psychology, field theory is closely associated with Gestalt psychology.

Six fundamental characteristics underpin Lewin's field theory (Burnes & Cooke, 2012a, p. 411; Lewin, 1943):

1. Constructive method: The meaning of any concept is derived from its relationship to other concepts.
2. Dynamic approach: Lewin saw equilibrium in social life as a dynamic process where change occurs, but a recognizable form is maintained.
3. Psychological approach: The elements of an individual's or group's life space must be based on their perception of their reality at the time rather than seeking to construct it from the objective viewpoint of an observer.
4. Analysis beginning with the situation as a whole: All psychological events are conceived to be a function of the life space. One needs to consider the situation as a whole.
5. Behavior as a function of the field at the time it occurs: The focus is on the behavior of an individual in the "here and now." Behavior is not caused by something in the past or the future, but is grounded in the totality of the present situation.
6. Mathematical representations of the psychological situation: Lewin maintained that psychology had to represent behavior in mathematical terms.

Lewin saw field theory as a way of combining scientific rigor and practical relevance by offering a rigorous, theory-based method for analyzing behavior and as a practical approach to changing behavior by allowing individuals to understand their actions better. He saw behavior as the product of the environment and of the way in which individuals interpret external stimuli (Burnes & Cooke, 2012a, p. 412). Five of the fundamental principles were derived from Gestalt psychology; the sixth principle was inspired by Cassirer's philosophy of science.

After Lewin's death in 1947, his work on group dynamics, action research, and his three-step model of change was taken up by other scholars and became the basis of organizational development (OD). His work on field theory went into decline until the 1990s, when it once again began to attract the attention of scholars and practitioners to behavioral and organizational change (Burnes & Cooke, 2012a, p. 416). There is "a growing recognition of the relevance of Lewin's work to contemporary organizational concerns, especially change, ethics and values" (p. 418).

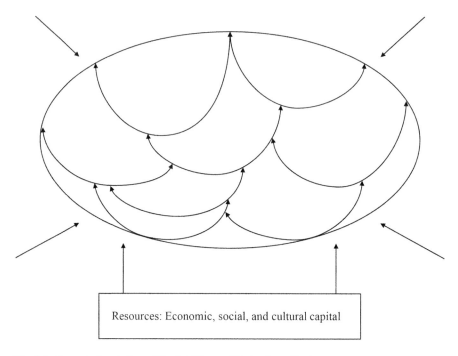

Fig. 3.1 Expanded metaphor of the field theory (Design by author)

Burnes and Cooke (2012b) asserted that the core components of OD have strong connections with the work of Kurt Lewin, summarizing that "Lewin's field theory was a significant break with the contemporary view of human behavior. It offered a holistic view of human behavior that focused on the entirety of a person or groups perceptual or psychological environment" (p. 420).

Bourdieu's (1983) sociocultural approach points out the different assumptions of active actors in an economic field. He differentiates between economic, cultural, and social capital. Economic capital comprises material resources such as income and money; social capital comprises relations and social networks; and cultural capital comprises resources such as cultivation, education, and lifestyle. Bourdieu stresses the specialness of cultural capital, whose transmission occurs within the family. Incorporating this cultural capital takes a lot of time (e.g., education). An economic field is distinguished by especially high dynamics, with the situation and individuals characterized by rapid change, competition, and quick action. Additional features are limited rationality and acting under great uncertainty. Typical in the Lewinian sense is the analysis of the interaction between the actors and the situation at hand. In Bourdieu's (1983) extension of field theory, the actors' social, cultural, and economic resources must also be considered. Figure 3.1 is simply an abstract metaphor for the forces interacting in an economic context (Spieß, 2006).

Lewin's field theory provides a suitable framework, representing a metaphor and a model for the process-like course of psychoeconomic fields of topics. The inclusion of actors' assumptions—their economic, social, and cultural capital—in Lewin's field theory offers a more precise and differentiated view. Among the various applications of field theory, Elsass and Veiga (1994), for example, used field theory as a way to explain acculturation within organizations.

The Role of Networks

The concept of flexible, open organizations, which are willing to learn, continues to replace rationalistic and rule-oriented notions of appropriate behavior in organizations. In this regard, networks can be seen as structures that are more suitable than bureaucratic organizations.

A network is defined by the cooperative work of its participants, as well as by stability, voluntariness of participation, trust, individual objectives, and the objectives of the network partners, including autonomy and interdependency (Borgatti & Foster, 2003). The *ego-centered network* is a distinct type of network, focused on an actor (ego), who then identifies the network partners (alteri). This is the conceptual basis for the coauthored studies by Stroppa and Spieß (2010, 2011) discussed in this chapter.

The participants in a network are influenced by group processes, which leads to network partners interacting primarily with people similar to themselves (regarding race, gender, and status). This produces fewer conflicts, but also results in less diversity (e.g., creativity in terms of product development). Networks have unique structural forms that offer certain advantages over those of hierarchies and markets (Powell, 1990). They are flexible and fast-working, offer favorable terms for learning processes and knowledge exchange, and reduce the level of uncertainty, which is particularly high for market-related transactions.

The development and sustainability of networks relies heavily on trust. Networks facilitate access to specific resources and information (Borgatti & Foster, 2003). According to Sydow (1992), networks establish a link between organizational and interorganizational flexibility, with openness forming one of their core characteristics.

Making organizations more efficient by decentralizing and restructuring them reduces the existing division of labor, so an objective is to form networks of equal, self-regulating organizational entities. However, these networks can only work if decision-making processes and employee cooperation are successful (Cross, Kaše, Kilduff, & King, 2013).

One functional characteristic of networks is social support, which offers network participants reliability and gives them backing. Social control, however, is also a functional network characteristic linked to social support—for example, in terms of norm orientation and the transmission of values. Networks can play an important role regarding foreign assignments.

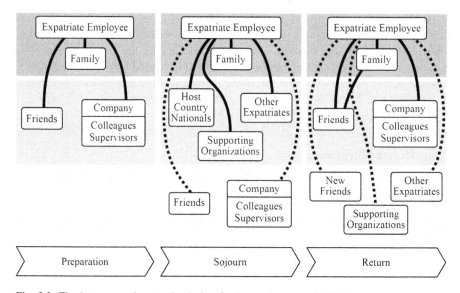

Fig. 3.2 The interpersonal networks during foreign assignment. Solid lines represent stronger relationships and dotted lines weaker ones. From Spieß (2009, p. 172) (Copyright 2009 by Oldenbourg. Reprinted by permission)

In a coauthored qualitative study focusing on interpersonal networks of expatriates (Spieß, Schaaf, & Stroppa, 2009) I considered the network partners present during the different phases of the foreign assignment who form the social net and grant social support. The procedure and instruments of the qualitative study were guided interviews with expatriates of small and medium-sized companies from April to July 2006. Guidelines were developed for each of the phases of preparation, sojourn, and return. The participants were 16 respondents: male, between 27 and 47 years old, working in medium-sized companies in Munich and surroundings in the fields of electronics, conveyor systems, paper manufacturing, engineering, and mechanical engineering. Their destinations were China, Japan, Thailand, and Indonesia.

In the preparation phase of an assignment the network partners are different than those during the sojourn or return, including, for example, family, friends, colleagues, superiors, and the organization itself. During the sojourn the network expands to include contacts with host-country nationals, other expatriates, and the organizations that provide support to the expatriates—contacts that can then continue to exist as part of the network after the return. The interpersonal networks are further divided into sub-networks, with the respondents in the study viewing the professional network as separate from the private network. Family and friends form part of the private network, whereas colleagues, superiors, and the organization itself are part of the professional network.

Figure 3.2 illustrates interpersonal networks during foreign assignment. Results of the 2009 study showed that all respondents attached great value to their families. In the phase of sojourn a change could be noted. The expatriate employees lost contact with their old friends and colleagues, but formed contacts with other expatriates and host-country nationals, as well as receiving help from support organizations. When they returned, this constellation changed again and they lost contact with their new friends and other expatriates.

Respondents regarded family as highly important in every phase of the assignment, which is why the concept of *family* is located adjacent to the expatriate employee in Fig. 3.2. This does not imply that the family always stands by the expatriate's side. Rather, the figure refers to the ideational value of family as such, a perspective that is even more compelling when one is separated from the family. During the preparation phase family is followed in precedence by friends, colleagues, superiors, and the organization itself. Respondents also pointed out that keeping in contact with family members demanded additional effort during the sojourn. Contacts with friends, in particular, suffered due to the lack of time. This was reflected in statements such as "One can only work, eat, and sleep," or, if the expatriate was accompanied by a spouse, "Only a busy wife is a good wife, a bored wife is torture."

During the sojourn, this list expands to include new colleagues, other expatriates, and host-country nationals, as well as the supporting organizations. The relationship with friends from home becomes less important (indicated by the dotted lines in Fig. 3.2). In the phase of returning, the expatriates try to reestablish contact with the network partners from the preparation phase and to maintain relationships newly formed during the sojourn, but these, too, lose importance. It is, therefore, crucial to point out that there is hardly any networking activity between the network partners themselves. The connecting lines in Fig. 3.2 show relationships between the expatriate employee and various network partners, but only a single link among the network partners. In their review of organizational social network research, Kilduff and Brass (2010) emphasized its focus on relations between actors.

The Role of Social Support

In recent years, a number of research projects have focused on social support in various contexts, including family, friends, and work (e.g., Glazer, 2006; Stroebe & Stroebe, 1998). The concept of social support is founded in various research traditions that also deal with the interrelationship of social support and mental health.

From the standpoint of a resource concept (Udris, 1997), social support is not only an external resource that a person receives but also an internal resource that an individual can develop (Udris & Frese, 1999). Dücker (1995) describes various forms of support experienced by members of a network: material support (e.g., financial), support in the form of helping behavior (e.g., care in the case of illness), emotional support (e.g., affection, trust, or sympathy), feedback (e.g., social confirmation), informative support, orientation assistance (e.g., advice), and positive social activities (e.g., fun and recreation).

Many studies (overview in Cohen & Wills, 1985) have shown a positive influence of social support at work on the well-being of those receiving it. Frese and Semmer (1991) named further social support mechanisms. First, social support is a primary need expressing humans' phylogenetic urge to work in a social group. The lack of social support automatically leads to a diminution of well-being. And second, the positive feedback connected with social support directly affects self-confidence and, thus, other components of mental well-being. Social support and the formation of networks are, therefore, closely related. The network concept is considered broad and multidimensional (Inkpen & Tsang, 2005) and consequently suited as an umbrella concept for social support.

In the case of foreign assignment, various relationships within the interpersonal network of an expatriate are of interest, including those with the spouse, friends, and coworkers, mattering in both the home country and the country of sojourn. These networks may be considered an objective reality within which there are dyadic relationships of different strengths.

Social support is an essential component of our daily lives and takes on a special significance in the context of assignment to a foreign country. Adelman (1988) expressed it as follows: "Our ability to cope with daily stressors, critical life transitions and environmental or cultural change is inextricably tied to the social ecology in which we are embedded" (p. 183). The entire social network and the accompanying social support of family, friends, and coworkers are of eminent importance in eliminating the risk of failure of the foreign assignment.

The mentioned risks and the antecedents for successful adjustment have been primarily studied in large corporations (e.g., Mendenhall & Oddou, 1985; Ward & Rana-Deuba, 1999). The situation in small and medium-sized companies remains unclear, but it may be assumed that it is especially difficult, because small companies do not have the corresponding resources at their disposal. In this context, interpersonal networks for small and medium-sized company transferees on foreign assignment are gaining significance, although the involved company often underestimates their effect.

Social Support and Firm Size

A study published in "Expatriates' Social Networks: The Role of Company Size" by Stroppa and Spieß (2010) extended and tested Caligiuri and Lazarova's (2002) model for the influence of support provided by different network partners (supervisors, coworkers, friends, spouses) on received socioemotional and instrumental support. This model was extended by examining the impact of company size on effectiveness of support. Ninety expatriates were questioned during their foreign assignment: 45 from small and medium-sized enterprises (SMEs) and 45 from large companies. As expected expatriates who received support from their network partner coworkers during their foreign sojourn also received more instrumental support. In addition, the study confirmed that the type of company moderated the relationship between the network partner (friends) and socioemotional and instrumental support. The type of company had more influence on that support when there were no network partners (friends) available for the expatriates, and less when those contacts did exist. SMEs and their expatriate employees had less experience with environmental factors in different countries, less power to withstand the demands of host governments, and less reputation and financial resources, as well as fewer resources for managing international operations. In the future, therefore, it is very important that firms, especially SMEs, develop concepts for the effective support of staff on foreign assignment.

Social Support and Host-Country Nationals

Social support can be regarded as especially significant in the context of sojourners. Sources of support are wide ranging and can include many different social groups, such as family, friends, peers, coworkers, and supervisors.

A study published in "Social Support on International Assignments: The Relevance of Socioemotional Support From Locals" (Podsiadlowski, Vauclair, Spieß, & Stroppa, 2013) identified the importance of support from host-country nationals. Using the matching or specificity hypothesis, which suggests that the right match between type and source of support is needed to increase well-being (Viswesvaran, Sanchez, & Fisher, 1999, p. 318), the authors postulated that sojourners' satisfaction would increase if there were an optimal match between the type and source of social support (Madjar, 2008). One hundred thirty-one English-speaking participants living in New Zealand were sampled via a snowballing technique (Podsiadlowski et al., 2013). The results showed that both types of social support—instrumental and socioemotional—were positively related to satisfaction with the sojourn, with socioemotional support being more important in predicting satisfaction with a sojourn than instrumental support, and support from host-country nationals being the most important source of social support. Furthermore, there was partial support for the matching specificity hypothesis. Only the amount of support from host-country nationals was a significant moderator and only the relationship between socioemotional support and satisfaction with a sojourn was moderated. The authors found only partial support for the matching or specificity hypothesis. The study's findings showed that it did not apply to instrumental support. Additionally, results showed that the right match between socioemotional support and source of support was more specific than expected. Only socioemotional support provided by host-country nationals increased satisfaction with the sojourn. Support from home did not moderate the relationship between socioemotional support and satisfaction. This indicates that only host-country nationals are able to provide relevant socioemotional support if individuals are faced with uncontrollable stressors.

To summarize, the most important predictors for satisfaction with a sojourn were support from host-country nationals and perceived socioemotional support. Not only did socioemotional support from host-country nationals have a positive effect, support received from other foreigners living in the respective country was not sufficient to assure a sojourner's well-being. Support from home was actually counterproductive for satisfaction with the sojourn. Findings (Podsiadlowski et al., 2013) emphasized the importance of receiving considerable socioemotional support from host-country nationals for a successful international assignment.

The Role of Personal Initiative

Personal Initiative is defined as a behavioral syndrome relating to individuals with an active, self-initiated approach to work that exceeds normal work behavior. Personal initiative is characterized by the following aspects (Frese, Kring, Soose, & Zempel, 1996): it is consistent with the organization's mission, has long-term focus, is goal-directed and action-oriented, is persistent in the face of barriers and setbacks, and is self-starting and proactive. Social support and personal initiative have a strong relationship with successful work adjustment.

A study carried out by Stroppa and Spieß in 2011 adapted components of Fay and Frese's (2001) nomological network of personal initiative and Caligiuri and Lazarova's (2002) model for the influence of social support on adjustment. On this basis the authors developed and tested a model for the relationship between personal initiative, social support, and work adjustment. One hundred twenty-seven respondents answered an online questionnaire during and after their foreign sojourn. The study demonstrated that personal initiative moderates the relationship between social support from coworkers and job performance. Results showed that personal initiative of the expatriates and social support received from supervisors—but not from their coworkers—predicted job satisfaction, job stress, and job performance of the expatriates. The fact that personal initiative had a main effect on all three indicators of successful work adjustment indicates that it is a very important predictor for successful adjustment.

Consequences for the Intercultural Learning Process

Increasing internationalization demands intercultural action. From a psychological point of view, this interaction is special because it involves an overlapping situation. When meeting people of another culture one is in one's own culture as well as in another culture. The paradox is to adapt in a situation in which one becomes particularly aware of belonging to another culture (Lewin, 1963). This requires special preparation and training workshops.

The intercultural learning process can be described by the construct of intercultural sensitivity. Bennett's (1998) Developmental Model of Intercultural Sensitivity (DMIS) consists of three ethnocentric stages (denial, defense, minimization) and three ethnorelative stages (acceptance, adaptation, integration) constituting a continuum ranging from denial of difference to integration of difference. Denial of cultural difference is the state in which one's own culture is experienced as the only real one. Other cultures are either not perceived at all, or they are construed in rather vague ways. Defense against cultural difference is the state in which one's own culture is experienced as the only viable one. Minimization of cultural difference is the state in which elements of one's own cultural worldview are experienced as universal. Acceptance of cultural difference is the state in which one's own culture is experienced as just one of a number of equally complex worldviews. Adaptation to cultural difference is the state in which the experience of another culture yields perception and behavior appropriate to that culture. Integration of cultural difference is the state in which one's experience of self is expanded to include the movement in and out of different cultural worldviews (Hammer, Bennett, & Wiseman, 2003, p. 424–425).

Hammer et al. (2003) summarized that, in general, the more ethnocentric orientations can be seen as ways of avoiding cultural difference, either by denying its existence, by raising defenses against it, or by minimizing its importance (p. 426). The more ethnorelative worldviews are ways of seeking cultural difference, either by accepting its importance, by adapting perspective to take it into account, or by integrating the whole concept into a definition of identity.

This theoretical framework provided conceptual guidance for Hammer et al. (2003) as they undertook the construction of the Intercultural Development Inventory (IDI) to measure the orientations toward cultural differences described in the DMIS. The result of this work is a 50-item, paper-and-pencil instrument (with 10 additional demographic items).

Referring to Lewin's field theory it is important to consider individual points of view and competencies as well as the social network, social support, cultural processes, and the current economic and political environment. The intercultural learning process, as well as intercultural sensitivity, is also important for foreign assignments and can help establish and connect networks more successfully. For this purpose, psychologists offer a measuring instrument, for example, the intercultural development inventory (Hammer et al., 2003). In addition to further intercultural learning and sensitivity, suitable trainings are also interesting and helpful.

The process of a foreign assignment can be viewed within the framework of Lewin's field theory, with the interaction between people and their environment clearly recognizable. According to the cited research (Stroppa & Spieß, 2010, 2011; Podsiadlowski et al., 2013), a personal characteristic such as personal initiative is important, with it moderating the relationship between social support from coworkers and job performance. Environmental factors such as the size of the company also play a role.

Social support importantly involves a social interaction between the provider of support and the recipient, who can not only ask for support or aid, but also reject it. In the context of foreign assignments the support of superiors and colleagues and especially of host-country nationals (Podsiadlowski et al., 2013) has proven to be very important. Social support can also be seen as an aspect of networks, which can form connections within the field, possibly bringing together different strengths. I would therefore recommend a stronger coordination between the existing networks.

My viewpoint also corresponds with Kilduff and Brass's (2010) observation that organizational social network research assumes dyadic relationships do not occur in isolation. However, the field of foreign assignments, which is marked by attracting and repelling forces, includes far more. Global development and climatic, economic, and cultural influences also have to be taken into consideration as highly relevant factors.

References

Adelman, M. B. (1988). Cross-cultural adjustment: A theoretical perspective on social support. *International Journal of Intercultural Relations, 12,* 183–204. doi:10.1016/0147-1767(88)90015-6

Bennett, M. J. (1998). Intercultural communication: A current perspective. In M. J. Bennett (Ed.), *Basic concepts of intercultural communication: Selected readings* (pp. 1–34). Yarmouth: Intercultural Press.

Borgatti, S. P., & Foster, P. C. (2003). The network paradigm in organizational research: A review and typology. *Journal of Management, 29,* 991–1013. doi:10.1016/S0149-2063(03)00087-4

Bourdieu, P. (1983). The field of cultural production, or: The economic world reversed. *Poetics, 12,* 311–356. doi:10.1016/0304-422X(83)90012-8

Burnes, B., & Cooke, B. (2012a). Kurt Lewin's field theory: A review and re-evaluation. *International Journal of Management Reviews, 15,* 408–425. doi:10.1111/j.1468-2370.2012.00348.x

Burnes, B., & Cooke, B. (2012b). The past, present and future of organization development: Taking the long view. *Human relations, 65,* 1395–1429. doi:10.1177/0018726712450058

Caligiuri, P., & Lazarova, M. (2002). A model for the influence of social interaction and social support on female expatriates' cross-cultural adjustment. *International Journal of Human Resource Management, 13,* 761–772. doi:10.1080/09585190210125903

Carpenter, M. A., Sanders, G., & Gregerson, H. B. (2001). Bundling human capital with organizational context: The impact of international experience on multinational firm performance and CEO pay. *Academy of Management Journal, 44,* 493–511. doi:10.2307/3069366

Cohen, S., & Wills, T. A. (1985). Stress, social support, and the buffering hypothesis. *Psychological Bulletin, 98,* 310–357. doi:10.1037//0033-2909.98.2.310

Cross, R., Kaše, R., Kilduff, M., & King, Z. (2013). Bridging the gap between research and practice in organizational network analysis: A conversation between Rob Cross and Martin Kilduff [Special issue]. *Human Resource Management, 52,* 627–644. doi:10.1002/hrm.21545

Daily, C. M., Certo, S. T., & Dalton, D. R. (2000). International experience in the executive suite: The path to prosperity? *Strategic Management Journal, 21,* 515–523. doi:10.1002/(SICI)1097-0266(200004)21:4<515::AID-SMJ92>3.0.CO;2-1

Dücker, B. (1995). *Stress, Kontrolle und soziale Unterstützung im industriellen Bereich* [Stress, control and social support in the industrial sector]. Bonn: Holos.

Elsass, P. M., & Veiga, J. F. (1994). Acculturation in acquired organizations: A force-field perspective. *Human Relations, 47,* 431–453. doi:10.1177/001872679404700404

Fay, D., & Frese, M. (2001). The concept of personal initiative: An overview of validity studies. *Human Performance, 14,* 97–124. doi:10.1207/S15327043HUP1401_06

Frese, M., Kring, W., Soose, A., & Zempel, J. (1996). Personal initiative at work: Differences between East and West Germany. *Academy of Management Journal, 39,* 37–63. doi:10.2307/256630

Frese, M., & Semmer, N. (1991). Stressfolgen in Abhängigkeit von Moderatorvariablen: Der Einfluß von Kontrolle und sozialer Unterstützung [Consequences of stress in dependence to moderator variables: The influence of control and social support]. In S. Greif, E. Bamberg, & N. Semmer (Eds.), *Psychischer Stress am Arbeitsplatz* (pp. 135–153). Göttingen: Hogrefe.

Glazer, S. (2006). Social support across cultures. *International Journal of Intercultural Relations, 30*, 605–622. doi:10.1016/j.ijintrel.2005.01.013

Hammer, M. R., Bennett, M. J., & Wiseman, R. (2003). Measuring intercultural sensitivity: The intercultural development inventory. *International Journal of Intercultural Relations, 27*, 421–443. doi:10.1016/S0147-1767(03)00032-4

Hechanova, R., Beehr, T. A., & Christiansen, N. D. (2003). Antecedents and consequences of employees' adjustment to overseas assignment: A meta-analytic review. *Applied Psychology, 52*, 213–236. doi:10.1111/1464-0597.00132

Inkpen, A. C., & Tsang, E. W. K. (2005). Social capital, networks, and knowledge transfer. *Academy of Management Review, 30*, 146–165. doi:10.5465/AMR.2005.15281445

Kilduff, M., & Brass, D. J. (2010). Organizational social network research: Core ideas and key debates. *Academy of Management Annals, 4*, 317–357. doi:10.1080/19416520.2010.494827

Kühlmann, T. M., & Stahl G. K. (2006). Problemfelder des internationalen Personaleinsatzes [Problem areas of international personnel placement]. In H. Schuler (Ed.), *Lehrbuch der Personalpsychologie* [Textbook of personnel psychology] (revised and expanded 2nd ed., pp. 533–558). Göttingen: Hogrefe. (Original work published 2001)

Kupka, B., Everett, A. M., & Cathro, V. (2008). Home alone and often unprepared: Intercultural communication training for expatriated partners in German MNCs. *International Journal of Human Resource Management, 19*, 1765–1791. doi:10.1080/09585190802323819

Landy, F. J., & Conte, J. M. (2008). Work in the 21th century: An introduction to industrial and organizational psychology. *Personnel Psychology, 61*, 447–450. doi:10.1111/j.1744-6570.2008.00119_2.x

Lewin, K. (1939). Field theory and experiment in social psychology: Concepts and methods. *American Journal of Sociology, 44*, 868–896. doi:10.1086/218177

Lewin, K. (1943). Defining the "field at a given time". *Psychological Review, 50*, 292–310. doi:10.1037/h0062738

Lewin, K. (1963). *Feldtheorie in den Sozialwissenschaften: Ausgewählte theoretische Schriften* [Field theory in social science: Selected theoretical papers] (A. Lang & W. Lohr, Trans.). Bern: Hans Huber. (Original work published 1951)

Madjar, N. (2008). Emotional and informational support from different sources and employee creativity. *Journal of Occupational and Organizational Psychology, 81*, 83–100. doi:10.1348/096317907X202464

Mendenhall, M., & Oddou, G. (1985). The dimensions of expatriate acculturation: A review. *Academy of Management Review, 10*, 39–47. doi:10.2307/258210

Noe, R. A., Greenberger, D. B., & Wang, S. (2002). Mentoring: What we know and where we might go. *Research in Personnel and Human Resources Management, 21*, 129–174. doi:10.1016/S0742-7301(02)21003-8

Podsiadlowski, A., Vauclair, C.–M., Spieß, E., & Stroppa, C. (2013). Social support on international assignments: The relevance of socioemotional support from locals. *International Journal of Psychology, 48*, 563–573. doi:10.1080/00207594.2012.669042.

Powell, W. W. (1990). Neither market nor hierarchy: Network forms of organizations. *Research in Organizational Behavior, 12*, 295–336. Retrieved from http://woodypowell.com/wp-content/uploads/2012/03/10_powell_neither.pdf

Selmer, J. (1999). Culture shock in China? Adjustment pattern of western expatriate business managers. *International Business Review, 8*, 515–534. doi:10.1016/S0969-5931(99)00018-9

Selmer, J. (2001). Psychological barriers to adjustment and how they affect coping strategies: Western business expatriates in china. *International Journal of Human Resource Management, 12*, 151–165. doi:10.1080/09585190010014106

Spieß, E. (2006). Lewin's contribution to economic psychology. In J. Trempala, A. Pepitone & B. H. Raven (Eds.), *Lewinian Psychology—Proceedings of the international conference: Kurt Lewin: Contribution to contemporary psychology* (pp. 208–218). Bydgoszcz: Wielki University Press.

Spieß, E., Schaaf, E., & Stroppa, C. (2009). Netzwerke sozialer Unterstützung bei Auslandsentsendungen nach Asien [Networks of social support during foreign assignments in

Asia]. In T. Kühlmann & H. D. Haas (Eds.), *Internationales Risikomanagement— Auslandserfolg durch grenzüberschreitende Netzwerke*. [International risk management—success in foreign assignments through crossbordering networks] (pp. 155–183). Munich: Oldenbourg. doi:10.1524/9783486592719

Spreitzer, G. M., McCall, M. W., & Mahoney, J. D. (1997). Early identification of international executive potential. *Journal of Applied Psychology, 82,* 6–29. doi:10.1037/0021-9010.82.1.6

Stroebe, W., & Stroebe, M. (1998). *Lehrbuch der Gesundheitspsychologie: Ein sozialpsychologischer Ansatz* [Textbook of health psychology: A social psychological approach]. Frankfurt: Dietmar Klotz.

Stroppa, C., & Spieß, E. (2010). Expatriates social networks: The role of company size. *The International Journal of Human Resource Management, 21,* 2306–2322. doi:10.1080/09585192.2010.516586

Stroppa, C., & Spieß, E. (2011). International assignments: The role of social support and personal initiative. *International Journal of Intercultural Relations, 34,* 234–245. doi:10.1016/j.ijintrel.2010.09.008

Szkudlarek, B. (2010). Reentry—A review of the literature. *International Journal of Intercultural Relations, 34,* 1–21. doi:10.1016/j.ijintrel.2009.06.006

Sydow, J. (1992). *Strategische Netzwerke: Evolution und Organisation* [Strategic networks: Evolution and organisation]. Wiesbaden: Gabler. doi:10.1007/978-3-322-86619-6

Udris, I. (1997). Soziale Unterstützung [Social support]. In S. Greif, H. Holling, & N. Nicholson (Eds.), *Arbeits- und Organisationspsychologie. Internationales Handbuch in Schlüsselbegriffen* (pp. 421–425) [Work and organizational psychology. The international handbook of key terms]. (3rd ed.). Weinheim: Psychologie Verlags Union.

Udris, I., & Frese, M. (1999). Belastung und Beanspruchung [Stress and strain]. In C. Graf Hoyos & D. Frey (Eds.), *Arbeits- und Organisationspsychologie. Ein Lehrbuch* (pp. 429–445) [Work and organizational psychology. A textbook]. Weinheim: Beltz-PVU.

Viswesvaran, C., Sanchez, J. I., & Fisher, J. (1999). The role of social support in the process of work stress: A meta-analysis. *Journal of Vocational Behavior, 54,* 314–334. doi:10.1006/jvbe.1998.1661

Wang, X. (2002). Expatriate adjustment from a social network perspective: Theoretical examination and a conceptual model. *International Journal of Cross-Cultural Management, 2,* 321–337. doi:10.1177/147059580223003

Wang, X., & Kanungo, R. N. (2004). Nationality, social network and psychological well-being: Expatriates in China. *The International Journal of Human Resource Management, 15,* 775–793. doi:10.1080/0958519042000192942

Ward, C., & Rana-Deuba, A. (1999). Acculturation and adaptation revisited. *Journal of Cross-Cultural Psychology, 30,* 422–442. doi:10.1177/0022022199030004003

Open Access This chapter is distributed under the terms of the Creative Commons Attribution 4.0 International License (http://creativecommons.org/licenses/by/4.0/), which permits use, duplication, adaptation, distribution and reproduction in any medium or format, as long as you give appropriate credit to the original author(s) and the source, provide a link to the Creative Commons license and indicate if changes were made.

The images or other third party material in this chapter are included in the work's Creative Commons license, unless indicated otherwise in the credit line; if such material is not included in the work's Creative Commons license and the respective action is not permitted by statutory regulation, users will need to obtain permission from the license holder to duplicate, adapt or reproduce the material.

Chapter 4
Family Networks for Learning and Knowledge Creation in Developing Regions

Pengfei Li

Social Learning Processes in Developing and Developed Contexts

With the rise of the knowledge economy, learning and knowledge creation rather than material resources and assets are becoming competitive advantages of regions and countries. Unlike concrete inputs, which are produced mechanically, intangible knowledge is created through agents' interaction and communication, which are structured by social relations and norms within organizations, communities, and societies. Accordingly, knowledge-creating regions both in traditional sectors (e.g., the Third Italy) and high-tech industries (e.g., Silicon Valley) are characterized by intensive interaction of professionals and accommodating business culture in local communities. It has thus become widely accepted that the long-term success of regional economies increasingly depends on social learning processes—localized and globalized—of individuals and organizations. Daily practices of agents develop specialized language, frameworks, and conventions as codes of communication and rules of interaction by which individually, organizationally, and regionally embedded knowledge can be mobilized and cross-fertilized in continuous codification and internalization processes (Amin & Cohendet, 2004; Bathelt & Glückler, 2011; Malmberg & Maskell, 2006; Saxenian, 2007).

As significant as these knowledge-based theories of regional economies are, developing regions have received scant attention in the theoretical discussion of social learning processes. In those contexts formal institutions such as the legal

---

I am grateful to the East China Normal University, Department of Urban and Regional Economics as well as the University of Toronto, Department of Political Science for supporting my work on this chapter.

P. Li (✉)
Department of International Business, HEC Montréal,
3000 Chemin de la Côte-Sainte-Catherine, Montréal H3T 2A7, Canada
e-mail: li.pengfei@hec.ca

system usually do not function well. It is the *in*formal norms and social structures (e.g., family networks) that tend to be more important for communication and collaboration. However, some researchers have long argued that these informal networks contribute to the backwardness of developing regions (Banfield, 1958; Putnam, Leonardi, & Nanetti, 1993). These divergent arguments about the part that social networks play in developing and developed economies raise the question of why local informal relations in developing economies cannot generate the social learning process that occurs in a developed context.

Focusing on family ties, I aim to provide a provocative answer to this question by arguing that family networks can facilitate technology diffusion but not knowledge creation. My purpose is not to investigate family and friendship ties in social and political arenas. Family and friendship networks are discussed in this chapter only in terms of social learning mechanisms. I argue that ties between family members, though strong, can—unlike ties between friends—act as bridges in local and global knowledge networks. Compared to open networks of friends, family ties tend to be exclusive and hierarchical. Structured differently, friendship and family networks generate heterogeneous and homogeneous knowledge pools within themselves, respectively. This observation implies that friendship networks supplant family ties as local economies upgrade.

Exploration of family networks in developing regions may advance the discussion of knowledge in space in three ways. First, it offers a knowledge-based explanation for the advent of many industrial clusters and agglomerations in developing countries. Drawn from common features of innovative regions, traditional cluster theories do not have much power to account for localized industries in developing contexts. Many clusters in those contexts develop endogenously from intensive learning through kinship networks (Henn, 2012; Li, Bathelt, & Wang, 2012; Meagher, 2007; Nadvi, 1999). Second, this chapter's inquiry into different structures of family and friendship networks in a dynamic perspective adds to an evolutionary understanding of networks and knowledge in economic geography (Glückler, 2007). Rather than viewing regions in developing and developed contexts as two different worlds, I look at how developing regions with family-based learning networks can transform into innovative economies with open and dynamic social structures. I suggest that many developing and developed areas are facing similar challenges when it comes to socially restructuring themselves to improve their ability to mobilize local and global knowledge. Third, I shed light on the role that family structure plays in developing regions and argue that family ties as strong bridges can accelerate technology diffusion in local communities rather than hamper economic development.

I begin by summarizing the contradictory evaluation of family organization over the course of economic development. In the section thereafter I revisit Granovetter's (1973) argument of the strength of weak ties and examine the basic structure of family networks, asserting that strong family ties can be bridges for intensive interaction and technology learning in local settings. My study of family networks then continues by turning attention to the weakness of kinship connections as compared to another kind of social network, friendship ties. I illustrate why the two kinds of network differ structurally in terms of knowledge creation and why localized learning in developing communities can be expected to evolve from closed to open networks.

Family Ties and Economic Development

The family is a basic social organization in both traditional and modern societies. Family and kinship groups, connected biologically, constitute a natural association of individuals and influence economic behaviors to different degrees from one society to the next. In traditional communities, where family structures predominate, individuals are both economically and socially affiliated to their families. These family networks become an institution through which seniors are empowered with authority over resource allocation and the resolution of disputes among family members. Societies of this kind are by nature composed of families rather than individuals because individuals in these contexts cannot freely make choices and take actions. Family control reduces labor participation, geographical mobility, and civil engagement and results in low economic development (Alesina & Giuliano, 2013; Bertrand & Schoar, 2006). Strong family structure has therefore long been generally regarded as an obstacle to the development of capitalism. The point is illustrated by the underdevelopment of capitalism in some family-dominated societies such as traditional China and southern Italy (Banfield, 1958; Weber, 1951) and by the fact that family and kinship networks declined with the ascendance of modern corporations and economic development in Europe (Greif, 2006). Strong family structures are still found to be related to the low development of some European regions (Duranton, Rodríguez-Pose, & Sandall, 2009). These arguments on the incompatibility of family ties in capitalism depend on the idea that activities of individuals cannot be organized beyond the family level in a society with excessively strong family structures and, hence, that civic spirit and public institutions cannot take root therein.

Unlike western individualistic societies, Asian societies tend to emphasize family values strongly. The successes of several Asian economies in the past decades therefore defy the understanding that family ties inhibit the development of capitalism. In these economies a keen sense of family obligation motivates individuals to work hard and reduce consumption in order to support family members, especially the next generation, and to increase their education. Strong family ties, as an important kind of social capital, help develop human capital (Coleman, 1988). Besides improving the labor market, strong commitment to the family also accelerates capital accumulation because family workers tend to consume less and save more than singles do. Family structure thereby contributes to the growth of Asian economies (Whyte, 1996). Since the Asian financial crisis in the 1990s, however, it has been recognized that family involvement in Asian economies is, to a large extent, responsible for the weakness of those economies (Perkins, 2000). At the national level, cronyism—family networks among political authorities such as Suharto's family in

Indonesia—brings about severe corruption and thwarts efficient investment (Kang, 2003). At the firm level, family ties discourage the participation of nonfamily professionals in family firms and restrict the growth of those enterprises (Cai, Li, Park, & Zhou, 2013; Weidenbaum & Hughes, 1996).

Although contradictory, the preceding arguments generally focus on the relationship between family structure and market development in that family ties affect resource allocation and labor participation. The presumption in those negative understandings of family ties is that individuals would make right and rational choices without family bonds and that market economies would therefore develop efficiently. In the positive evaluation of family values, family considerations force labor into the production process of capitalism and contribute to capital accumulation. In general, these arguments contextualize family ties in the neoclassical framework of economic development and have not directed much attention to the role of family structure in knowledge-sharing and learning. From a historical perspective, these arguments make sense because family economies often emerge in the early stages of capitalism and are regarded as irrelevant to the knowledge economy. However, this view of family ties can be questioned. Because acquisition of technical and business know-how is always crucial in economic development processes even in their early periods (Mokyr, 2004), it becomes important to discuss whether family networks can promote knowledge-sharing and creation.

Empirical investigation of this question in the context of regional economies has led to contradictory findings. In an exploration of high-tech industries in the Research Triangle region of North Carolina (near Durham, Raleigh, and Chapel Hill), Renzulli, Aldrich, and Moody (2000) suggested that family ties can aid the diffusion of homogeneous information but are of little help to technological entrepreneurship. By contrast, research on start-ups in traditional industries in developing economies shows that entrepreneurs' family networks convey industrial information and professional advice, which are crucial for the establishment of small businesses (Anderson, Jack, & Drakopoulou-Dodd, 2005; Jack, 2005). Indeed, some research on industrial clusters in developing contexts shows that family and kinship networks can act as important learning channels for local entrepreneurs and firms. In a cluster producing surgical instruments in Pakistan, extended family ties were found to stimulate technical knowledge-sharing between firms and encourage interfirm cooperation in local business communities (Nadvi, 1999). Li et al. (2012) also documented how family-based learning has transformed some rural villages in South China into a large cluster of aluminum-processing activities over the past 20 years. Munshi (2011) and Henn (2012) further showed that kinship and ethnic networks in an Indian diamond cluster not only functioned as a localized channel of learning but also acted as a transnational knowledge bridge connecting local communities with global diamond centers in Europe and America.

As noteworthy as these empirical studies on family ties in regional contexts can be, they do not yield a coherent framework for explaining why family ties can channel learning in some settings but not in others. There is also little theoretical knowledge about the structure of family networks and how knowledge can diffuse within them.

Strong Family Ties as Knowledge Bridges in Local Communities

The manner in which knowledge can be shared among individuals and firms depends largely on the structure of the social networks within which they are embedded (Granovetter, 1973). Characterized by intensive interaction and high intimacy between two agents, strong ties involve much, sometimes perhaps too much, communication. The result is that understandings, ideas, and judgments on issues of mutual interest become homogenized in strong ties. Groups connected by strong ties tend to be closed. This characteristic—the closeness tendency—makes reputation reliable and punishment enforceable (Coleman, 1988). It is easy to illustrate: Given that agents B and C are both strongly connected with A, it is most unlikely that B and C will not be connected with each other. With this reasoning Granovetter (1973) deduced his famous argument: For a bridge that is the only path between two agents, "except under unlikely conditions, no strong tie is a bridge" (p. 1364). As the only form of bridges, weak ties turn out to be highly significant in the knowledge economy because they can provide varieties of information and connect different groups and communities. Applying this idea to community development, Granovetter (1973) argued that communities would be fragmented into cliques if only strong ties existed within them.

Granovetter's argument on the significance of weak ties rests on the closeness tendency of strong ties. In defending this concept, he generally interpreted social ties as friendships,[1] which can be measured by the amount time that individuals spend together. He admitted that "implicit here is Homans's idea that 'the more frequently persons interact with one another, the stronger their sentiments of friendship for one another are apt to be'" (Homans, 1950, p. 133, as cited in Granovetter, 1973, p. 1362). Granovetter's argument of the strength of weak ties is thereby cast within the framework of friendship networks, relations that people create and sustain through intended actions.

However, there is another, unique kind of social network, the family tie, which develops in a different way. If one measures the strength of social ties by trust and the emotional commitment of individuals, ties within the family can be strong even without its members being together for a long time. For instance, the bond between long-separated family members is usually very strong when they unite. As a biological and social association of individuals, family ties entail many meanings. For example, family members can be those whom an individual can trust, from whom that person receives emotional support, for whom she or he is responsible, and with whom he or she consults before making decisions. In many ways family can be interpreted as a social structure of economic actions. Because this chapter focuses on learning and knowledge generation, the following discussion centers on family ties as a mode of social interaction for sharing *economic* knowledge. Although husband and wife usually do not work in the same field and individuals may prefer not

---

[1] Granovetter's (1973) understanding of social networks does not include family ties.

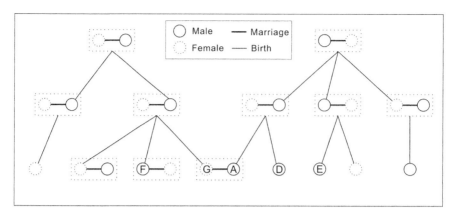

Fig. 4.1 Structure of family networks (Design by author)

to talk about work with family members, the high level of trust commonly present in family networks makes the exchange of economic knowledge virtually inevitable. How does this family-based knowledge-sharing come about?

Figure 4.1 depicts the structure of a typical family network.[2] Unlike friendship ties, family networks are hierarchical like trees, stratified in generations. Within family trees a husband and a wife, linked horizontally, constitute a pair of nodes in the network. Family ties develop vertically by birth and horizontally by marriage. Created primarily through birth and marriage, all family ties are strong in terms of trust, intimacy, and emotional commitment. As in friendship networks, the strength of a relationship between two individuals in family networks depends on the length of the path between them. In Fig. 4.1, for example, brothers A and D are closer (only two steps between them) than cousins A and E (four steps). Given the different strengths of the relations between brothers and cousins, why are A, D, and E not connected directly in Fig. 4.1? The reason is that brothers, cousins, and other kinship connections are *derived* ties; their relationships are derived from the basic structure of the family networks shown in Fig. 4.1. A and D are brothers because they have common parents, and A and E are cousins because they have common grandparents. Family connections among A, D, and E are created by virtue of their ties with common parents or grandparents. Direct links between A and D or E will be redundant because their connections through parents and grandparents already show their relations. The same consideration also applies to other kinship relations in Fig. 4.1. In fact, distant relatives, especially those between extended families, such as E and F, have few chances of being together and knowing each other.

---

[2] Specifically, Figure 4.1 shows a biological structure of family networks (a map of the biological relationships between family members) and their social structure (a pattern of interaction and communication). Social practices in family networks vary in different cultural contexts and time periods. The arguments formulated in this chapter rest on my own observations, which apply to developing economies (especially China) and should not be overgeneralized. I thank Johannes Glückler for this point.

Although they can be contacted through some family members, they are more likely to be as distant as strangers. The fact that they are mutually accessible suggests the role that some family members and ties have as bridges.

In Fig. 4.1 the marriage of A and G creates a bridge between two extended families. Before the marriage, the two extended families were unconnected. After the marriage, although most family members in the two groups still do not know each other,[3] they are connected through the sole tie between A and G. In this sense every marriage acts as a bridge in family networks. This bridging function of marriage can partly explain why marriage is so important in traditional societies: It may be the only bridge to leverage resources and knowledge beyond families in such a low-trust context (see Padgett & Ansell, 1993, for an analysis of the Medici family network in the Renaissance, for example). Through marriage, hierarchical family ties, too, can be bridges. For instance, if D marries, then the path between A and D, together with their marriage ties, becomes the bridge between their wives' families.

Knowledge and information can be quickly and reliably shared across family groups through bridges. Suppose that D has some information or opportunity that can be of interest to F. In daily conversation between A and G, A may accidentally divulge this information to G, who, realizing the potential of the information for her brother F, would facilitate information flows between F and D. If further communication and interaction between F and D is required, A and G will endorse these actions. The advantage of family bridges is that, as strong ties, they can be particularly effective for repeated interaction and learning, not just one-time information- or opportunity-sharing. Such intensive learning is extremely important for technology diffusion because manufacturing know-how and technical skills are learned in a systematic way by trial and error.

Having described the structure of family networks, I now turn to probe the role that family bridges can play for knowledge-sharing in industrial communities. If strong family ties can be bridges—in contradiction to Granovetter's (1973) conclusion that no strong tie is a bridge—then local communities, even those with only strong ties, can be closely connected rather than fragmented into cliques. At this point a difference in focus has to be clarified. Not everyone in local communities is highly relevant to economic development, which is primarily related to agents with a spirit of entrepreneurship and an interest in technological and business learning. As an economic geographer, I thus focus this chapter on social networks of a specific local group—entrepreneurs and professionals—rather than on the general social structure of local communities. This perspective narrows the argument derived from the concept of family bridges. I assert that local *business* communities can be closely connected through family bridges. Tentative evidence tends to suggest that at least this connection is possible in developing regions in which family relations of entrepreneurs are a notable feature. For example, 35 % of the entrepreneurs in a diamond cluster in India and 57 % of their children married within the local industrial community (Munshi, 2011). In the early development stages of an industrial cluster for aluminum extrusion in China in the 1990s, many entrepreneurs

---

[3] They may meet once at A and G's wedding.

were from a local clan whose members shared a rare family name (Li et al., 2012). Both cases suggest that cluster development in developing economies can be promoted by family ties of entrepreneurs. Indeed, industrial communities in developing countries rely more heavily on family ties than clusters in developed contexts, which are embedded in networks of friends, alumni, and ethnic groups. A key question, then, is why family networks matter in industrial communities in developing regions? Particularly, what is the structure of family networks that can give rise to knowledge diffusion to sustain local industrial development?

Before theoretical and empirical exploration of these questions, it should be recognized that communities with a single kind of tie are imaginary. Local business communities actually consist of different kinds of relations encompassing both families *and* friends, both strong and weak ties. Figure 4.2 shows a theoretical social network in an industrial community of entrepreneurs, for whose interconnections family bridges are pivotal. This social network has four components. Entrepreneur H, who has three family bridges and one friendship bridge, occupies a central position linking the four components of the local business community. Now suppose H learns new technology or business know-how from the outside of the community. Through family and friendship bridges, this knowledge can quickly spread across the whole local community (through eight steps in Fig. 4.2), suggesting that entrepreneurs in closely connected communities can rapidly learn new knowledge through family networks. This family-based learning may explain why many industrial clusters in Asia have been able to develop swiftly over the past decades, even in areas with poor industrial bases. For example, most of the entrepreneurs in the aluminum extrusion cluster in China did not initially know how to extrude the metal, but technical know-how was soon shared with them by an engineer who, just like H in Fig. 4.2, established family bridges in the local business community (Li et al., 2012).

Family-based localized learning can be paramount in the development of industrial clusters in developing economies. Given the increasing global brain drain, it is, with few exceptions, hard for most developing regions to attract highly skilled people worldwide. A dynamic learning community of educated immigrants and professionals tends to be beyond the capacity of many developing areas, at least for the time being. People thus often believe it is almost impossible for traditional communities to generate and support a learning economy. Family-based learning suggests that this conviction may not be true. In developing regions, family networks are usually social structures that exist before local industrial development. Channeled by family bridges, business and technical knowledge can be quickly shared in well-connected traditional communities. That dissemination is conducive to entrepreneurship and endogenous economic growth. From a knowledge perspective, theoretical and empirical investigation affords evidence that family ties can encourage economic development and suggests that the chances of successful industrialization will substantially increase if it is compatible with local social structures such as family networks (Woolcock & Narayan, 2000).

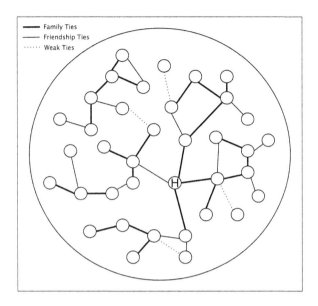

Fig. 4.2 A community well connected by bridges between family members and friends (Design by author)

From Families to Friends: Building Knowledge-Creating Economies in Developing Contexts

The role of family ties as bridges for localized learning should not be overemphasized, because family bridges have important weaknesses. First, stability of family ties is at odds with what dynamic learning requires in some fields. Family ties created through marriage and birth tend to be a lifetime commitment, meaning that family networks develop very slowly and selectively. The fact that they emerge only gradually implies that the number of bridges each individual or family can have through the strong ties of kinship is restricted by the size of the family. At the individual or community level, effective family bridges as knowledge pipelines therefore cannot increase substantially in a short period. In sectors such as high-tech industries, where short life cycles of products and technologies require a consistent combination of new ideas from various sources, family networks are incapable of channeling the needed knowledge flows. Stable family ties work best for learning from certain sources in a mature technological field (e.g., traditional industries) or in trading activities that require a high level of trust rather than technological innovation (e.g., the diamond sector).

Second, localization of family networks reduces the variety of knowledge that family bridges can provide, since geographical proximity of family members restricts their function as pipelines for external learning. In developing contexts traditional family networks generally do not go beyond local communities. The chances that family bridges will become global pipelines are quite low in such

Table 4.1 Comparison of family and friendship networks

Dimensions	Family ties	Friendship networks
Formation	Marriage and birth	Common experience, personality
Structure	Hierarchical, exclusive	Open, inclusive
Duration	Lifelong	Flexible
Strength	Strong	Strong or weak
Knowledge	Homogenous	Heterogeneous
Power	Patriarchal, imbalanced	Equal, reciprocal
Action	Involuntary	Voluntary

settings. Even in cases where family connections extend internationally through emigrant entrepreneurs, external knowledge tends to confine itself to some groups in the family rather than to diffuse throughout the locale (Henn, 2012).

Third, family networks as hierarchical structures foster knowledge diffusion rather than knowledge creation. Unlike other social connections, family ties entail an imbalanced distribution of power between individuals, usually in favor of seniors and males in traditional communities. Economic knowledge within families thus usually flows either horizontally (across families) by means of marriage bridges or vertically from the old to the young (Sussman, 1959). In that kind of learning process, the roles of agents as knowledge transmitters or receivers are assigned ex ante by their positions in family structures. Knowledge thereby tends to diffuse in a unidirectional manner in family networks. Because family ties are strong, such knowledge diffusion processes can be quick; because family networks are stable, the variety of knowledge in local communities can shrink rapidly.

In contrast to this process of knowledge diffusion, knowledge *creation* comes from collision of different ideas and from reflection on traditional thinking. Knowledge creation requires dynamic interaction of individuals, which is inconsistent with the structured flows of knowledge in family networks. Although useful for technology diffusion at the individual or community level, family networks may therefore be unhelpful to knowledge creation.

If family ties do little to build an innovative regional ecosystem, how can developing regions that industrialize through family-based learning transform into a knowledge economy? Another basic kind of social network, friendship ties, will gain increasing significance in the transformation process because friendship networks constitute a more open and dynamic structure for learning than family ties do (see Table 4.1). Unlike family ties created by marriage and birth, friendship is built from a sharing of common experience, an agreement on common rules, and an attraction between personalities. Friends are chosen independently, made through mutual acceptance, and endorsed by personal trust. Friendships are thus an autonomous association of individuals, open in structure and flexible in duration and strength. The easiest way to make friends is to be introduced by common friends. Granovetter (1973) argues this point by demonstrating the closeness tendency of strong friendship ties. In friendship networks only weak ties with acquaintances can become bridges, which elicit new information and opportunities. Therefore, heterogeneous knowledge can be cross-fertilized for innovation in societies through weak friendship bridges. Furthermore, the mutual obligation inherent in friendship enables friends to organize, disband, and reorganize in technical communities. These dynamic combinations of relations offer possibilities for knowledge creation and disruptive innovation. As Fukuyama (1995) put it, friends represent a spontaneous sociability of individuals and constitute an important kind of social capital in a modern society:

> The most useful kind of social capital is often not the ability to work under the authority of a traditional community or group, but the capacity to form new associations and to cooperate within the terms of reference they establish. (p. 27)

If the preceding theoretical constructs of family and friendship networks are correct, then the significance of family ties for business and technology learning is likely to wane as regional or national economies upgrade, while friendship networks will gain momentum. This transformation is consistent with Giddens's (1990) view of the modernization process, in which individuals experience intimacy less from families than from friends. The evolutionary framework of family and friendship networks is supported by provocative evidence as well. Using world social survey data, Bertrand and Schoar (2006) and Alesina and Giuliano (2013) found strong family connections to be related to a lack of generalized trust and weak formal institutions in societies. More directly, an international comparison of entrepreneurs' social networks (Drakopoulou-Dodd & Patra, 2002) suggested that, in a fairly developed economy, entrepreneurs' social connections consist more of friends than of families and relatives.

Although the rationale of the evolution from families to friends is clear in theory, this transition is not easy in reality because the breakdown of family networks and the construction of generalized trust for friends are two different processes (Fukuyama, 1995). Family ties stable over one generation can decline quickly across generations. Increasing geographical mobility of new generations decreases connections among family members in traditional communities whether this effect is desired or not. Talented young individuals may even intend to disconnect from their families in order to avoid commitment to less able relatives (Munshi & Rosenzweig, 2005). Members of new generations who are more mobile than those of previous ones may also be unable to connect closely with each other or the rest of their families because of a lack of time spent together (Li et al., 2012). The transition from family ties to ties of friendship is complicated further by the challenge of developing generalized trust and creating autonomous associations in societies (Portes & Landolt, 2000). Based on mutual agreement, friendship must develop naturally. Legal systems may back up individuals' interaction and collaboration, but compulsory regulations cannot guarantee the creation of voluntary associations. It takes time for individuals to reach consensus on their identities and build accepted codes of interaction. Only after that point can spontaneous associations of friends prosper as the main infrastructure for social learning in societies.

Developing regions usually become stuck in a transitional stage, in which local family structure was destroyed while generalized trust in societies has not been cre-

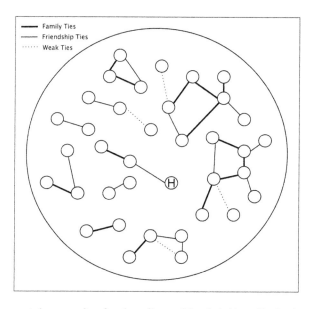

Fig. 4.3 A fragmented community after the collapse of family bridges (Design by author)

ated (Fukuyama, 1995). This situation, which is neither mechanically nor organically solidified in Durkheim's (1893/1997) sense,[4] corresponds to the worst conceivable combination of community- and society-based governance for economic development argued by Rodríguez-Pose & Storper (2006). Falling into this transitional stage can be an unanticipated consequence of public policies, such as an unsuccessful plan for urban renewal (Jacobs, 1961) or a blind liberalization strategy (Meagher, 2007), which destroy the social structure of traditional communities but cannot build an interactive environment for new social and economic orders. It can also be an unavoidable outcome of rapid industrialization that quickly undermines traditional family solidarity while formal institutions and a spirit of civic engagement are still developing, as in modern China. Figure 4.3 illustrates a fragmented community in transition after the erosion of family bridges and before the development of friendship bridges. In contrast to Granovetter's (1973) argument that strong ties create separate cliques, it is the *decline* of strong family ties, especially family bridges, that pulls the community apart. New external knowledge, even if accessible to some local entrepreneurs, is difficult to share in a fragmented community of this kind. As a result, the community's ability to absorb technological and business know-how becomes weak. Local firms with no social networks for learning and with weak capacity for innovation have no choice but to enter a race to

---

[4] Developing societies in this transitional stage are not socially integrated with individuals who have common beliefs (mechanical solidarity) or who depend on each other in the division of labor (organic solidarity) in Durkheim's (1893/1997) sense.

the bottom by competing on low costs. This situation describes many industrial clusters in developing contexts.

Just as the transition from families to friends sheds light on the challenges that developing regions face, it can be relevant for developed economies as well. In the global knowledge economy successful regions increasingly need to acquire and mobilize distant resources, ideas, and innovations, a task that requires generalized trust in talented people regardless of their races, religions, and national origins. Dynamic regional economies, such as Silicon Valley, have been creating an open, friendly social structure to attract immigrant technocrats from all over the world. These mobile professionals act as global knowledge brokers to facilitate cross-border learning and innovation (Saxenian, 2007). In both developing and developed countries, regions without this social infrastructure for global learning are becoming either isolated or passively integrated into global networks of leading clusters through transnational brain drains. A new core-and-periphery pattern in the global knowledge economy may develop along with the great transition of social learning from closed to open networks. In this sense developed and developing regions are up against the same challenge of the transformation process.

Conclusion

Social networks for interactive learning are essential for regional knowledge economies. Exploration of socialized knowledge networks in industrial communities is conducted mainly in successful regions in western individualistic societies. Developing regions are widely seen to be grappling with challenges that are no longer concerns in developed economies, such as the development of civic spirit and the enforcement of formal regulations. A fundamental difference between developing and developed economies is perhaps that individuals in developing contexts are more committed to families in traditional communities and, hence, act less independently than individuals in developed countries. These distinctions make developing regions appear to be a different world. In economic geography, a field in which knowledge-based theories of clusters are derived from practices of regional economies in developed contexts, the conditions of developing regions have received scant attention in theoretical discussion of knowledge in space. Focusing on developing regions, I pursue an alternative frame of reference: the evolution of social learning processes in traditional communities. Specifically, I have posed two theoretical questions. First, can knowledge be shared in a structured way within family networks, and if so, how? Second, if family ties can channel knowledge flows, why is family-based learning so inconspicuous in innovative regions?

The first question invites an investigation into the anatomy of family networks. Unlike friendship connections, family ties are created primarily by birth and marriage, and marriage-based linkages can work as bridges for information-sharing between extended family groups. The connecting role of marriage implies that strong family ties can be bridges, which differ from weak friendship bridges as argued by Granovetter (1973). As bridges, family ties can channel knowledge fertilization between two groups; as strong ties, family bridges can be extremely helpful for technological learning that requires repeated communication and interaction. In traditional communities family bridges can enable entrepreneurs to learn business and technical know-how quickly. Traditional family structure is thus not a handicap of being less developed but rather an advantage for catching up.

The second question requires interpreting the role of family networks for learning from a dynamic perspective. After industrialization, regional economic growth relies more on technological innovation and knowledge creation than on resource utilization and business imitation. Being stable and hierarchical in structure, family networks are most likely to channel and bridge knowledge flows in one direction from fixed sources. Being localized, family ties are numerically restricted as translocal knowledge pipelines. The variety of knowledge pools in family networks therefore tends to decline after rapid diffusion of technology. In that stage the significance of ties with friends tends to surpass that of family ties in encouraging knowledge creation, because friendship networks are more dynamic and open for new information than family ties are. It is beyond the scope of this chapter to document the transformation process from family- to friend-based learning. The challenge for many developing economies is that family networks in local business communities can quickly collapse in new generations of entrepreneurs while generalized trust and formal institutions as foundations for spontaneous associations of individuals take a long way to develop in societies.

The great transition from family-based industrial communities to friend-based learning regions confronts developing economies and many developed areas alike. The turbulent global knowledge economy requires regions to develop global connections of transnational professionals and entrepreneurs regardless of their backgrounds, yet only a few leading clusters have successfully constructed a friendly social infrastructure to attract talented immigrants and mobilize innovation on a global scale. Divergence among clusters and regions may increase in the global knowledge economy along with the transition from closed to open social learning processes.

In examining the dynamics of family networks from the perspective of learning in industrial communities, I do not tend to argue that there is a trend toward substituting friends for families as the only, or even the main, social structure in societies. This dualistic interpretation of families and friends clearly does not hold from a sociological perspective. The family remains a basic part of social organization in modern societies and is not going to disappear.

Acknowledgments I thank Johannes Glückler for the invitation to the conference on "*Topographies and Topologies of Knowledge*" and I am grateful to participants of the conference for their suggestions on this chapter as well as to the Department of Political Science, University of Toronto, Canada and the East China Normal University, Department of Urban and Regional Economics for supporting my work on the manuscript. The chapter has also been presented at the University of Toronto, National University of Singapore, and the annual meeting of Association of

American Geographers in Chicago. I appreciate the comments by the audience at these meetings as well, particularly from Harald Bathelt, Melanie Fasche, Daniel Gabaldon, Sebastian Henn, Yutian Liang, and Xiaojun You. Comments from anonymous reviewers and Johannes Glückler have also been very helpful. Lastly, I owe my thanks to David Antal, this volume's technical editor, for his excellent editorial job. All errors are mine.

References

Alesina, A., & Giuliano, P. (2013). Family ties. *National Bureau of Economic Research* (Working Paper No. 18966). Retrieved from http://www.nber.org/papers/w18966.pdf

Amin, A., & Cohendet, P. (2004). *Architectures of knowledge: Firms, capabilities, and communities*. Oxford: University Press.

Anderson, A. R., Jack, S. L., & Drakopoulou-Dodd, S. (2005). The role of family members in entrepreneurial networks: Beyond the boundaries of the family firm. *Family Business Review, 18*, 135–154. doi:10.1111/j.1741-6248.2005.00037.x

Banfield, E. C. (1958). *The moral basis of a backward society*. Glencoe: Free Press.

Bathelt, H., & Glückler, J. (2011). *The relational economy: Geographies of knowing and learning*. Oxford: University Press. doi:10.1111/jors.12024_4

Bertrand, M., & Schoar, A. (2006). The role of family in family firms. *Journal of Economic Perspectives, 20*(2), 73–96. doi:10.1257/jep.20.2.73

Cai, H., Li, H., Park, A., & Zhou, L.-A. (2013). Family ties and organizational design: Evidence from Chinese private firms. *Review of Economics and Statistics, 95*, 850–867. doi:10.1162/REST_a_00268

Coleman, J. S. (1988). Social capital in the creation of human capital. *American Journal of Sociology, 94*, 95–120. Retrieved from http://www.jstor.org/stable/2780243

Drakopoulou-Dodd, S., & Patra, E. (2002). National differences in entrepreneurial networking. *Entrepreneurship & Regional Development, 14*, 117–134. doi:10.1080/08985620110111304

Duranton, G., Rodríguez-Pose, A., & Sandall, R. (2009). Family types and the persistence of regional disparities in Europe. *Economic Geography, 85*, 23–47. doi:10.1111/j.1944-8287.2008.01002.x

Durkheim, E. (1997). *The division of labor in society* (7th ed.) (G. Simpson, Trans.). New York: Free Press. (Original work published 1893)

Fukuyama, F. (1995). *Trust: The social virtues and the creation of prosperity*. New York: Free Press.

Giddens, A. (1990). *The consequence of modernity*. Stanford: University Press.

Glückler, J. (2007). Economic geography and the evolution of networks. *Journal of Economic Geography, 7*, 619–634. doi:10.1093/jeg/lbm023

Granovetter, M. S. (1973). The strength of weak ties. *American Journal of Sociology, 78*, 1360–1380. Retrieved from http://www.jstor.org/stable/2776392

Greif, A. (2006). Family structure, institutions, and growth: The origins and implications of Western corporations. *The American Economic Review, 96*, 308–312. doi:10.1257/000282806777212602

Jack, S. L. (2005). The role, use and activation of strong and weak network ties: A qualitative analysis. *Journal of Management Studies, 42*, 1233–1259. doi:10.1111/j.1467-6486.2005.00540.x

Jacobs, J. (1961). *The death and life of great American cities*. New York: Vintage books.

Henn, S. (2012). Transnational entrepreneurs, global pipelines and shifting production patterns: The example of the Palanpuris in the diamond sector. *Geoforum, 43,* 497–506. doi:10.1016/j.geoforum.2011.10.009

Homans, G. C. (1950). *The human group.* New York: Harcourt, Brace & Company.

Kang, D. C. (2003). Transaction costs and crony capitalism in East Asia. *Comparative Politics, 35,* 439–458. Retrieved from http://www.jstor.org/stable/4150189

Li, P.-F., Bathelt, H., & Wang, J. (2012). Network dynamics and cluster evolution: Changing trajectories of the aluminium extrusion industry in Dali, China. *Journal of Economic Geography, 12,* 127–155. doi:10.1093/jeg/lbr024

Malmberg, A., & Maskell, P. (2006). Localized learning revisited. *Growth and Change, 37,* 1–18. doi:10.1111/j.1468-2257.2006.00302.x

Meagher, K. (2007). Manufacturing disorder: Liberalization, informal enterprise and economic 'ungovernance' in African small firm clusters. *Development and Change, 38,* 473–503. doi:10.1111/j.1467-7660.2007.00420.x

Mokyr, J. (2004). *The gifts of Athena: Historical origins of the knowledge economy.* Princeton: University Press.

Munshi, K. (2011). Strength in numbers: Networks as a solution to occupational traps. *The Review of Economic Studies, 78,* 1069–1101. doi:10.1093/restud/rdq029

Munshi, K., & Rosenzweig, M. (2005). Economic development and the decline of rural and urban community-based networks. *The Economics of Transition, 13,* 427–443. doi:10.1111/j.1468-0351.2005.00231.x

Nadvi, K. (1999). Shifting ties: Social networks in the surgical instrument cluster of Sialkot, Pakistan. *Development and Change, 30,* 141–175. doi:10.1111/1467-7660.00110

Padgett, J. F., & Ansell, C. K. (1993). Robust action and the rise of the Medici, 1400–1434. *American Journal of Sociology, 98,* 1259–1319. Retrieved from http://www.jstor.org/stable/2781822

Perkins, D. H. (2000). Law, family ties and the East Asian way of business. In L. E. Harrison & S. P. Huntington (Eds.), *Culture Matters: How Values Shape Human Progress* (pp. 232–243). New York: Basic Books.

Portes, A., & Landolt, P. (2000). Social capital: Promise and pitfalls of its role in development. *Journal of Latin American Studies, 32,* 529–547. Retrieved from http://journals.cambridge.org/article_S0022216X00005836

Putnam, R. D., Leonardi, R., & Nanetti, R. Y. (1993). *Making democracy work: Civic traditions in modern Italy.* Princeton: University Press.

Rodríguez-Pose, A., & Storper, M. (2006). Better rules or stronger communities? On the social foundations of institutional change and its economic effects. *Economic Geography, 82,* 1–25. doi:10.1111/j.1944-8287.2006.tb00286.x

Renzulli, L. A., Aldrich, H., & Moody, J. (2000). Family matters: Gender, networks, and entrepreneurial outcomes. *Social Forces, 79,* 523–546. doi:10.1093/sf/79.2.523

Saxenian, A. (2007). *The new argonauts: Regional advantage in a global economy.* Cambridge, MA: Harvard University Press.

Sussman, M. B. (1959). The isolated nuclear family: Fact or fiction. *Social Problems, 6,* 333–340. doi:10.2307/799367

Weber, M. (1951). *The religion of China: Confucianism and Taoism* (H. H. Gerth, Trans.). Glencoe: Free Press.

Weidenbaum, M. L., & Hughes, S. (1996). *The bamboo network: How expatriate Chinese entrepreneurs are creating a new economic superpower in Asia.* New York: Free Press.

Whyte, M. K. (1996). The Chinese family and economic development: Obstacle or engine? *Economic Development and Cultural Change, 45,* 1–30. Retrieved from http://www.jstor.org/stable/1154365

Woolcock, M., & Narayan, D. (2000). Social capital: Implications for development theory, research and policy. *The World Bank Research Observer, 15,* 225–249. doi:10.1093/wbro/15.2.225

Open Access This chapter is distributed under the terms of the Creative Commons Attribution 4.0 International License (http://creativecommons.org/licenses/by/4.0/), which permits use, duplication, adaptation, distribution and reproduction in any medium or format, as long as you give appropriate credit to the original author(s) and the source, provide a link to the Creative Commons license and indicate if changes were made.

The images or other third party material in this chapter are included in the work's Creative Commons license, unless indicated otherwise in the credit line; if such material is not included in the work's Creative Commons license and the respective action is not permitted by statutory regulation, users will need to obtain permission from the license holder to duplicate, adapt or reproduce the material.

Chapter 5
Studying Networks Geographically: World Political Regionalization in the United Nations General Assembly (1985–2010)

Laurent Beauguitte

The study of networks from the viewpoint of a geographer does not mean studying geographical networks as technical infrastructures, especially when one is interested in geopolitical phenomena. It means that the relational nature of a given spatial phenomenon seems to demand a specific approach, that is, a network one, and that formalization via a graph (a set of nodes, a set of links between these nodes, and some attributes) allows discovering unrevealed aspects of a sociospatial fact. The study of networks often means adopting an interdisciplinary posture, applying tools and methods developed in other academic fields, and conducting solid conceptual analysis. For instance, whereas distance and centrality are useful concepts in both geography and social network analysis, their definition and implications for research remain quite different and need to be adapted from one academic field to another to remain efficient and relevant.

This chapter presents results on the political regionalization process on a world scale, a process understood as the reinforcement of supranational structures based on geographical proximity. I presume that political actors, and especially state representatives in intergovernmental organizations, are constrained to work more and more often supranationally because of the globalization process, a process that can be understood neither solely nor primarily as an economic or financial phenomenon but rather as an increase in global issues demanding global responses and a governance shift (e.g., global warming, migrations, and energy). Although much has been published on economic regionalization since the 1990s (e.g., Mansfield & Milner, 1999), the political aspects have been quite neglected, and when they are studied, especially in international relations, the approach is mainly qualitative and purely conceptual (Barnett & Duvall, 2005; Diehl, 2005). The approach investigated in this chapter is taken from the behavioral school of international relations: If political regionalization is occurring, it should be possible to measure it, produce indicators,

---

L. Beauguitte (✉)
UMR IDEES, CNRS, 7 rue Thomas Becket, 76821 Mont Saint-Aignan, France
e-mail: laurent.beauguitte@cnrs.fr

and validate the hypothesis by using quantitative and reproducible methods. Because a political process by nature involves relations among actors, network analysis appears to be a relevant tool to investigate this regionalization.

I begin with a short overview of network analysis in geographical studies because the similarity in vocabulary between the sciences can hide a large gap in methods, procedures of validation, and questions of research. Opportunities for political geography will be highlighted. Because techniques of network analysis are rarely used in geopolitical studies nowadays, the strengths and relevance of political geography will be underscored. The next section presents the main hypothesis, the field of observation (the United Nations General Assembly from 1985 until 2010), and the methodological choices made to study world political regionalization. The final section presents the main results obtained and underlines the relevance of network analysis for investigating questions of political regionalization. If tools of network analysis prove valuable in highlighting processes of innovation, they can also produce innovative results when brought to bear on many research questions. Geographical logics of coalition and policy-making, which in this chapter are investigated on a world scale but can be studied from a multiscalar perspective, can greatly benefit from such input (Hafner-Burton, Kahler, & Montgomery, 2009).

Network Studies in (Political) Geography: A Quick Refresher

Because I am a geographer, my academic training involved a specific relationship with the network approach, and I feel it necessary to describe geographical network analysis briefly before highlighting the opportunities that network analysis offers in geopolitical investigations. There is no pretense that this description is exhaustive, and it is based largely on a French perspective. Network literature has grown so voluminous and diverse since the mid-1990s that it has become nearly impossible for one individual to follow all the developments—although an overview of relations between complex network studies and geography was recently proposed (Ducruet & Beauguitte, 2013). This chapter therefore offers not a definitive state-of-the-art treatment of geographical networks but rather some observations on the disciplinary biases inherent in network approaches as well an appeal for dialogue between disciplines. Since the inception of political geography, its practitioners, like those of international relations, have intensely investigated the question of power. Although many definitions of this central concept have been proposed, the canonical one by Dahl (1957) remains one of the most elegant: "A has power over B to the extent that he can get B to do something that B would not otherwise do" (pp. 202–203). This definition underlines the strong relational nature of power. It cannot be considered an attribute of an individual actor; it implies relations between actors and at least dyadic examinations.

Network as a Fashionable Metaphor

Not surprisingly, the term *network* is polysemous. Its three most widely accepted definitions can be found in current geographical literature: network as a metaphor; network as a technical infrastructure; and—similar to, but distinct from, network studies in the strict sense—network as relational flows between places. The predominant definition of the word is its metaphorical one: A network is a social process (migratory network) or a system of relations (network of cities) that crosses borders. It is fluid, moving, and dynamic. In this sense the network is always the opposite of an enclosed and stable territory. The study of networks from this perspective does not involve any methodological choice, and the term *network* could simply be replaced by another (Glückler, 2013; Grabher, 2006). In political geography this metaphorical usage is especially strong given the presumed weakening of the level of the state, which is being overwhelmed by transboundary movements and the supranational nature of financial and economic actors. P. Taylor's publications of the Globalization and World Cities Research Network[1] are quite representative of this trend, which moves away from the state level to consider mainly relations among the so-called world cities. Although many of these papers are quite interesting from a thematic perspective, *network* remains an emblematic word that implies neither conceptual nor methodological change. More interesting for my topic is the coexistence of two intersecting research traditions, one dedicated to technical networks and the other dedicated to flow studies.

Two Geographic Traditions: Infrastructure Networks and Flow Studies

As for the nonmetaphorical network, two main approaches exist in current geographical research: technical networks and flow studies. Studies of infrastructure networks (transport, energy, communication) were predominant starting with the seminal doctoral dissertation by Kansky (1963) until the middle of the 1990s and remain at the core of network studies in geography today. Although a minority of geographers tried to mix methods and propose new ways to study transportation networks (Ducruet, Ietri, & Rozenblat, 2011; Gleyze, 2007), the canonical tradition using the series of indices by Kansky (different ratios between the number of edges, the number of vertices, and the number of cycles derived from graph theory) prevails. It should be noted that in the vast majority of cases, networks are planar— often valued and nondirected—a characteristic that may help explain the lack of methodological dialogue with social network analysis, in which a network is more often Boolean, directed, and nonplanar. Even though some methodological

---

[1] http://www.lboro.ac.uk/gawc/

innovation has taken place, especially with respect to place accessibility and multilevel analysis (Mathis, 2003), dialogue with other social sciences remains the exception rather than the rule. However, these studies can provide valuable input for political geography because the structure and characteristics of technical networks can reveal social, economic, and spatial patterns. In what became for decades the reference handbook of network analysis in geography (Haggett & Chorley, 1969), one small example puts into perspective the physical aspects, socioeconomic variables (e.g., urbanization, hierarchy of cities), and indices of road and rail networks (pp. 88–89). The density and connectivity of technical networks are factors that reveal the level of regional or national wealth that can explain given patterns of relations among these actors.

Another trend in geographical research is relational by nature because it involves the study of flows between places. The use of a model inspired by laws of gravitation became a convenient tool in the 1960s and has been common since then to study and model patterns of interaction (Nystuen & Dacey, 1961; Tobler, 1970). Based on valued flows (goods, communication, migration), the techniques developed did not involve any dialogue with social network analysis. Note also that this literature barely makes explicit reference to the term *network*. However, several recent works by physicists draw on these interaction models mixed with complex network approaches and generally demonstrate that the two methods produce complementary results (Gorman et al., 2007). Interest in such approaches for political geography cannot be underestimated; they are able to reveal, for instance, preferential relations as well as barriers between pairs of actors. Mixing tools from flow studies and network analysis clearly appears promising for investigating globalization processes at multiscalar levels (Van Hamme & Grasland, 2011).

Some Recent and Welcome Changes

The soaring number of physicists and computer scientists in the network field since the 1990s has changed the landscape on two fronts. First, some geographers were quick to adopt new measurements from related works (clustering coefficient, power law degree distribution). Rozenblat's papers on economic and transport relations between world cities are good examples of this imitation process (Rozenblat & Melançon, 2007). This early acceptance can be explained by the not-so-new character of the scale-free network as a power law distribution, which is a common and well-known process in several social sciences (e.g., rank distribution of cities in urban geography, Zipf's word distribution in textual analysis). It must also be mentioned that the conclusions offered in the works on world cities remain classic yet are somehow deceptive: Using so-called innovative methods to show that Paris, London, New York, and Tokyo are the main world cities appears to contribute little to geographical knowledge (Rozenblat & Melançon, 2007). More noteworthy is the interest some physicists are taking in spatial networks and models and the methods proposed to analyze them (Barthelemy, 2011; Gastner & Newman, 2006). Methods from social network analysis were less widely adopted by geographers, but several recent papers have indicated the use of the block model and equivalence (Drevelle, 2013), density and nodes centrality measures (Comin, 2009; Maisonobe, 2013), and k-cores to reveal a world center–periphery structure (Van Hamme & Pion, 2012). Once again, the emerging hybridization of disciplinary traditions appears quite interesting for geopolitical studies. It does not mean that network analysis is the only way to study conflicts or patterns of relations between actors, whatever the level of analysis. However, it is worth considering that, for some specific questions, network analysis can reveal unexpected facts and trends.

In summary, network analysis appears to be of major interest for geopolitical studies, especially when one is investigating power and hierarchy among actors. In the following sections I describe the investigation of patterns of relations among actors in the United Nations General Assembly (UNGA), using network analysis to test whether political regionalization is taking place on a world scale.

A Relational Approach to the United Nations General Assembly

Since the 1950s, and especially at the zenith of the behaviorist school of international relations (1960s and 1970s), a long tradition of United Nations (UN) studies has explored relations between actors, consequences of decolonization, the rise of ideological groups advocating a more equitable economic system than the existing one, the socializing effect of UN sessions, and the specific position of states in the UN system (although this list is far from exhaustive). The existence of blocs, regional or ideological, in the UN system, particularly in the UN General Assembly, triggered a profusion of books, reports, and papers, mainly in the Anglophonic academic sphere. Proposing even a short overview of this literature would hardly be feasible, even if the scope were limited to quantitative approaches (for a good starting point, see Beauguitte, 2011).

The UNGA is of significant interest for researching political geography. During a session, nearly all the world's political actors exchange ideas, discuss problems, confront each other, and attempt to assemble the pieces for more efficient world governance. Network analysis appears relevant mainly because decisions in the UNGA involve discussions, negotiations, and relations between actors, and there are documents available from which to draw the relational pattern between these actors. Of course, data collected reflect only the final step of dialogue, and the ways to achieve agreement among actors are generally unknown. At least three mechanisms have been identified in the literature: free agreement (two actors are like-minded on a specific topic), bargaining (A votes yes on this topic if B votes yes on another topic), and pressure (A must vote this way to get financial support from B). A well-known example of bargaining is the relationship between the Arab League and the African Union. Since the 1970s, the African Union has supported Arab

League positions on Palestine, whereas the Arab League has supported the African Union's position on economic development. Examples of pressure are less well-documented but are occasionally mentioned in the minutes of the meetings, albeit without precise targets. Before examination of the voting behavior and speech patterns in the UNGA, a short review of the UN system seems appropriate to justify some methodological choices.

Studying the UN System from a Geographical Point of View

The UN organization can be considered a relational system and a bureaucratic organization at the same time. First, positions of actors in the UN system depend on the relative positions of other actors. Moreover, an actor's behavior in one specific organ can in certain cases be explained by the position of this actor in another organ of the UN system. One familiar example is the voting behavior of the United Kingdom and France in the UNGA—they often vote differently from other member states of the European Union (EU)—behavior that can be explained only by their permanent member status in the Security Council. Another relational aspect relates to the possibility of action in the UN system in general and in the UNGA specifically: Any decision involves a dense network of relations with other actors, with all decisions being adopted by consensus or majority.

But the UN system is also a bureaucratic organization where the behaviors of actors are highly predictable (needed to strengthen cooperation), where stability outweighs evolution, and where reform is always a long and costly process. One of the most famous examples of this bureaucratic aspect is the reform of the Security Council, which generated hundreds of speeches, reports, and recommendations but not one single concrete decision.

Since its creation, the UN system has been extensively studied by academics, especially by North American academics in the fields of political science and international relations—the U.S. government has always paid a great deal of attention to UN activities and has financed numerous research projects. Geographers have paid scant attention to the UN's decision-making processes. However, at least two aspects are of particular interest: the geography of cooperation and conflict, and scale issues related to daily operations. Because nearly all states are represented in the UNGA, this institution allows one to observe patterns of cooperation on a worldwide scale, from both dynamic and thematic points of view, and studying voting behavior provides some valuable geopolitical input.

A brief explanation of the purpose and function of the UNGA seems warranted at this point. The aim of the UNGA, according to the UN Charter signed in 1945, is to "consider the general principles of cooperation in the maintenance of international peace and security, including the principles governing disarmament and the regulation of armaments" (Charter of the United Nations, Article 11) and to initiate studies and make recommendations for the purpose of (a) promoting international cooperation in the political field and encouraging the progressive development of international law and its codification; (b) promoting international cooperation in the economic, social, cultural, educational, and health fields; and (c) assisting in the realization of human rights and fundamental freedoms for all without distinction as to race, sex, language, or religion (Charter of the United Nations, Article 13).

When a member state, a regional group, or an ad hoc group of states submits a resolution proposal to the General Assembly, there can be one of two outcomes. The first and most frequent one is the resolution's adoption by consensus without any vote. Depending on the session, between two thirds and three quarters of all resolutions are adopted by consensus. A vote indicates a controversial issue, and member states have four options (only member states are able to vote): vote yes, abstain, vote no, or abstain. The last option often indicates a small and/or failed state that cannot obtain a permanent delegation in the UNGA. It should also be noted that nearly all states are UNGA members: The Holy See and the State of Palestine have observer status (they can sponsor a resolution but cannot vote), and Taiwan is the only independent state not recognized by the UN system, a situation due to the strong and persistent opposition of China.

Geographical Voting Patterns in the UNGA

Studying votes in the UNGA has had a long academic tradition since the seminal paper by Ball (1951). The main hypothesis is that states that vote the same way on a vast range of topics are supposedly politically close and like-minded. Kissack (2007) noted that studying votes has advantages as well as drawbacks, and among the latter is the inability to infer any cooperative behavior from results obtained. In other words, in an arena where many resolutions are ritually adopted year after year over several decades, two states can exhibit the same voting behavior without having any actual relation. However, in an arena where two thirds of the resolutions are adopted by consensus, putting an issue up for vote already indicates a lack of consensus. Whereas a similar vote does not necessarily imply a close relation, a dissimilar vote conversely indicates opposition between two actors. When dozens of votes are considered, similar voting patterns can infer a relation between a pair of actors. Moreover, the autonomy of actors is not equally distributed: Some delegations have dozens of members (e.g., diplomats, lawyers, and counselors), whereas delegations from the poorest countries have only two to five members. It is obviously difficult for the small delegations to study all proposed resolutions, to consider their legal implications, and so on, and voting behavior will depend on group directives rather than on national orientation.

For the two sessions considered here (the 42nd and 63rd), voting results were selected according to (a) resolutions and (b) member states. First, tables recording all voting results per session were made from the UNBISnet website, which provides all details of states' behavior per resolution.[2] Then, near-unanimous resolutions

---

[2] http://unbisnet.un.org/

were deleted (less than 5 % of no votes or abstentions). The resolution-based selection was motivated by the presence of very specific resolutions on Israel for which only Israel and the United States voted against or abstained. These two states are clearly peripheral in the UNGA, and including these votes would not provide any supplementary information. The second selection, based on member states, comprised those states that were often absent and not able to vote. Keeping the threshold used in previous studies, I chose to delete states that did not participate in at least 30 % of the votes. Failing to omit these states would produce a group lacking political consistency. The final tables included 158 states and 145 resolutions for the 42nd session (1987–1988) and 178 states and 68 resolutions for the 63rd session (2009–2010). These basic measurements are congruent with the general trend in the UNGA in this period: a rising number of member states (with the addition of former Eastern-bloc countries in the 1990s and many small states in the 2000s) and a diminishing number of resolutions put to a vote.

Several network approaches can be used to study voting behavior in the UNGA. The most common method is to create a multibipartite state-resolution graph and to transform it into a state-state similarity matrix with range values from 0 (two states always vote in a different way) to 100 (two states always vote the same way). One issue concerns the threshold process because finding a value suitable for different sessions seems challenging. The solution proposed by Beauguitte (2011) was to choose the same statistical threshold for all similarity tables in order to allow comparison. However, transformation from continuous to discrete values remains quite unsatisfactory. Although some authors proposed this approach in the 1960s (Lijphart, 1963), multivariate analysis (mainly principal component analysis) soon became the canonical method of handling this data.

An alternative option that allows keeping link weights is to adopt a variation of the CONCOR method adapted for valuable matrices; the classification procedure groups together states that have the same relational profile. Figure 5.1 shows the regional structure based on voting behavior before the end of the Cold War (42nd session, 1987–1988), and Fig. 5.2 reflects the situation in 2010 (63rd session, 2009–2010). The considerable cluster inertia is quite surprising but confirms results obtained in previous research (Voeten, 2000). Even today, there is one Northern bloc in opposition to one Southern and Eastern bloc. In 2009 the East appeared smaller because eastern European countries began to behave like western ones—adhesion or application to the EU—but the main fracture between developed and less developed countries continued to be the dominant pattern. The voting pattern of Turkey, one of the few countries showing a marked change, was becoming more and more like that of western countries. The cluster inertia is also related to the structure of resolutions voted upon in the UNGA. The Israeli–Palestinian conflict is the subject of more than one third of all resolutions voted upon in each session. Regarding this issue, the West strives for a balanced stance, whereas other members share a pro-Palestinian approach, which partly explains their cohesiveness. In 2009 there appeared a tiny group of small developing island states that tended to vote like Southern-bloc states, except when resolutions concern global warming.

5 Studying Networks Geographically: World Political Regionalization in the United... 93

Fig. 5.1 Political regions in the UNGA in 1987 (42nd session). From UNBISnet (Performed by Philcarto. Design by author)

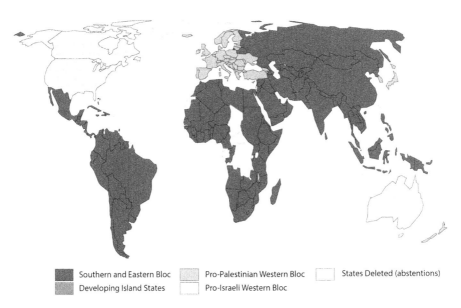

Fig. 5.2 Political regions in the UNGA in 2009 (63rd session). From UNBISnet (Performed by Philcarto. Design by author)

This clustering approach is of particular interest because it is able to sum up thousands of statements, speeches, and resolutions in order to produce an artificial map of political regions. The map does not necessarily signify that two member states in the same group always behave in the same way or share common views on the vast range of topics examined in the UNGA. However, it does provide an initial delineation that should be kept in mind for in-depth study.

Other approaches appear valuable and can provide relevant results, such as investigating resolutions' sponsors by topic or similarities among resolutions to see whether or not the same type of resolution (on human rights or economic development) tends to produce highly interconnected graphs. However, studying voting behavior provides only a partial picture of relational patterns in the UNGA because only one third of resolutions are included.

Whereas studying voting behavior is a traditional way to view relations in the UNGA, the study of speeches remains less developed even though the General Assembly can be considered an arena of words rather than decision-making. Each year, representatives from nearly all countries (Taiwan excepted) issue statements on a broad range of issues, and these speeches can be considered the official position of those states' governments. But states are not the only speakers, and the study of speeches supports multiscalar analysis.

Speech Dynamics in the UNGA: A Network Approach

Various individuals make statements in the UNGA: representatives of states (nearly 80 % of all statements during a session for the period under consideration), representatives of groups, of institutions from the UN system, and, less often, representatives from NGOs (e.g., the Red Cross) or institutions external to the UN system (e.g., the European Commission). In the last two decades, a change in speech dynamics has occurred. Groups issued more and more statements on a growing range of topics, and states' representatives have supported their statements more and more often, two patterns that could be a relevant indicator confirming the political world regionalization hypothesis. Minutes of meetings from 1990 to 2010 were reviewed to collect all speeches that affirmed "state A supports group a," and these data were studied as bipartite graphs. Occurrences of such speeches were transformed into a state-group matrix in which each case indicates the number of times a state A supported a statement made by a group a. The poor quality of documents from older sessions prevents automatic word-searching, and data-gathering was therefore manual and time consuming.

Table 5.1 Main properties of bipartite state–group network

Session	No. of states	No. of groups	Density	Diameter	Components
45 (1990–1991)	10	3	.367	3	2
51 (1996–1997)	52	6	.196	6	2
57 (2002–2003)	54	14	.098	7	5
63 (2009–2010)	100	14	.129	6	3

Source: UNGA verbatim records

Statements by Regional Groups and States

Table 5.1 provides a general picture of this phenomenon. The increase in the number of states that support a group's statements is quite impressive (from 10 to 100 in 20 years), whereas the progression of groups is less marked (from 3 to 14).

Before the graphs from Fig. 5.3 are interpreted, one distinction is necessary regarding the type of groups investigated. Some groups can be called ideological because they defend specific points of view on topics examined in the UNGA, whereas others can be labeled regional because their main ambition is integration at a supranational level—although some regional formations may indeed be based on ideological considerations. (The EU, for instance, is based mainly on the liberal free-market ideology.) Among the initial groups, the Nonaligned Movement (NAM) and the Group of 77 (now called the Group of 77 plus China) are emblematic of the 1970s at the UNGA, with NAM supporting an alternative political path between capitalism and socialism and the G77 promoting a new and less disparate world economic order. These two groups remain active, giving voice to the weakest states and advancing their claims.

In 1990 (Fig. 5.3, Session 45) the situation was quite simple: The European Commission was the only group whose statements were regularly supported by its member states. Although the EC was not the only group to make statements, individual states did not support statements made by other groups. The other two supported groups (G77 and the least developed countries) can be considered ideological because they do not promote a regional integration process but defend a more general point of view based on uneven economic development.

Six years later (Fig. 5.3, Session 51) the situation was not so different, although there were more member states that supported groups' statements. Although EU member states often supported EU statements, most of the links in the component illustrated on the left reflected ideological considerations (degree equal to 6 for NAM, degree equal to 9 for the G77 plus China). Nevertheless, the increase in the number of regional groups in the strict sense (Latin America and the Caribbean, the Rio Group, and the Organization of African Unity) was notable, and some member states chose to support one group or another, depending on the topic under consideration.

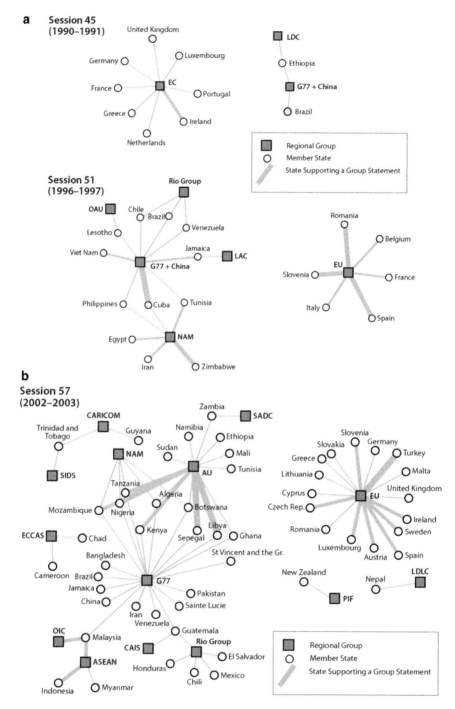

Fig. 5.3 Bipartite UNGA state-group graphs. *ASEAN* Association of Southeast Asian Nations, *AU* African Union, *CAIS* Central American Integration System, *CARICOM* Caribbean Community, *EC* European Commission, *ECCAS* Economic Community of Central African States, *EU* European Union,

The 57th session (2002–2003) shows the growing importance of regional groups for all member states, European or otherwise. The G77 plus China maintained its central position, and NAM moved to a more peripheral position. All other groups that appear affirmed regional integration as one of their main objectives. Once again, the EU was a component isolated from other countries and included only member states (and candidates). This picture confirms previous results according to which the EU is simultaneously one of the most cohesive groups in the UNGA and one of the most isolated because it is unable to attract support from other actors (Gowan & Brantner, 2008). The situation in 2009—not reproduced here because the density of the graph renders it unreadable—confirms this evolution: the rising importance of regional groups, the rising number of states supporting several groups depending on the topic examined, and the cohesiveness and isolation of the EU. Further studies are needed, especially to investigate concrete mechanisms of cooperation that groups set up to achieve these results. One can assume that this trend reflects an increasingly pressing need for member states to see that taking action through a supranational framework is more efficient than taking action as individual member states. However, major powers—the best example being the United States, which never appears on these graphs—do not necessarily need regional groups. When political regionalization occurs, it is primarily for actors unable to influence world decisions by themselves. Another question concerns how the UNGA itself functions. As regional groups become more active (sponsoring resolutions, making statements, and collaborating with one another), will the organization be able to change its procedures to take this dynamic into account or will it remain a strictly international organ? The fact that the EU recently gained a higher participation status—EU representatives (rather than representatives of the state leading the EU) can now make statements and propose resolutions—indicates that organizational change is possible to reinforce the role of regional groups.[3]

From Empirical Observations to Models of Cooperation and Regionalization

A complementary approach to this discursive regionalization dynamic is to build ideal types based on the expected behavior of actors instead of measuring the expansion of phenomena from one session to the next. This exercise is interesting principally because it identifies the relation between actors and their motivations and

Fig. 5.3 (continued) *G77* Group of 77, *LAC* Latin America and the Caribbean, *LDC* Least Developed Countries, *LDLC* Least Developed and Landlocked Countries, *NAM* Nonaligned Movement, *OIC* Organization of Islamic Cooperation, *OAU* Organization of African Unity, *PIF* Pacific Islands Forum, *SADC* Southern African Development Community, *SIDS* Small Island Developing States (Source: UNGA verbatim records. Design by author)

---

[3] http://www.unbrussels.org/general-assembly-grants-eu-higher-participation-status.html (retrieved June 16, 2014)

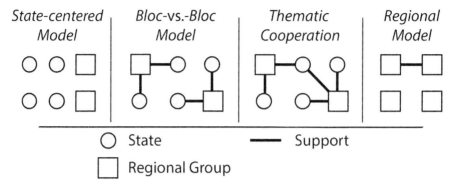

Fig. 5.4 Theoretical models of regional cooperation (Design by author)

connects this trend to conceptual inquiries in political geography and international relations. Of course, as always, models are not claimed to represent reality in all its dimensions. They are propositions of a simplified structure that depicts main relations between prominent actors. A model can also serve as a guideline to relate actual evolution to conceptual inquiries regarding relations between actors on a world scale.

This regionalization trend poses two main questions, one about cooperation and the other about the scalar level of decision-making. From a thematic and geopolitical point of view, the rise in regional groups can be regarded as the expression of political regionalization based on cooperation between actors—primarily, but not exclusively, national ones. This concept is clearly related to globalization as regionalization emerges as a process in which nation states within geographic proximity take collective measures to cope with problems of global governance…the more regionalized the world, the more necessary, enabled and willing for regions to construct connections with each other [sic]. (Song, 2007, p. 67)

This process does not mean the end of bilateral relations or the end of the state level, but it does involve a new paradigm for comprehending world structures (Chen, 2005). One main challenge in the near future will be to improve coordination of national interests and group dynamics and to engage the main powers (United States, Russia, or China) in this process. The multilevel scale of governance inside international organizations also offers a new angle of research. Although member states continue to get their own agendas into the international forum, their actions are increasingly constrained by supranational structures. Figure 5.4, which is based on both theoretical considerations and the data analysis presented in Table 5.1, attempts to model this process of regionalization, in which four different types of cooperation emerge.

The four hypothetical graphs in Fig. 5.4 show the evolution from a pure state-centered situation to an ideal regional configuration. These graphs sum up three key hypotheses on world political regionalization: (a) the presence of regional groups is increasing, (b) states are using regional groups more and more often to achieve their aims, and (c) cooperation between regional groups is rising. Of course, the hypotheses apply only if the globalization process continues, change that should not be taken for granted. One can certainly envision a process of shrinking globalization in which ever more barriers are erected at the state level. The rising anti-European feeling serves as a reminder that history does not stand still and that social processes are far from being linear or predictable.

In the first graph on the far left, several groups make statements and member states make statements, but there are no links between these two categories of actors. The second graph depicts conflict between two groups that have the support of their respective members: The EU-versus-the-rest-of-the-world configuration observed in recent years closely resembles this pattern. It is also the model that best lends itself to partitioning the political world. The third graph reflects a situation in which member states, depending on the topic, choose to support one group or another, which happens with increasing frequency in the UNGA in the case of the South American and Pacific island states. The final graph models a situation in which a process of cooperation emerges between regional groups and in which all statements by the states assume a supranational scale. This ideal is still a long way off because national interests are predominant among the most powerful states.

Although these models can be helpful for highlighting processes in a specific arena and for providing points of comparison, they portray only one of many possible progressions. From a thematic point of view, political regionalization is mostly a weapon of the weak. Since the 1970s, groups have been used by small, recently decolonized, and peripheral member states in the UNGA, and it is not by chance that the United States and Russia are not represented in the graphs in Fig. 5.3. Three major kinds of group relations can be found in the UNGA. Some states do not need them (United States, Russia), some powerful states use groups only to reinforce their interests (France, United Kingdom, and China), and some states need groups to be heard (the least developed states). It seems that two kinds of political regionalization are distinguishable: voluntary and constrained. The first includes wealthy states aiming to reinforce their position and internal cohesiveness (the EU); the second subsumes states too weak to influence decisions by themselves. Qualitative methods are needed to confirm this hypothesis because network analysis does not allow differentiating these two types of groups.

Concluding Remarks

Is network analysis necessary? Did the results obtained in this study need these techniques and methods or can they be obtained by other means? The clustering method used to produce the maps in Figs. 5.1 and 5.2 is not completely satisfactory, and other statistical multivariate techniques could easily be applied to data on voting behavior. The results arrived at are congruent with those produced by other means, but the interpretation of classes remains more difficult than with a principal component analysis, for example. Where scales of speeches are concerned, network analysis appears much more relevant than votes and reveals patterns of interaction not easily identifiable by other means. So the answer is partly yes: Network analysis, like any other technique, is not a one-size-fits-all solution. It is able to produce unexpected discoveries in geopolitical research.

From a geopolitical perspective network analysis seems a useful tool with which to investigate regionalization processes, for these processes reinforce links—either cooperative or conflicting—between several types of actors. If the UNGA comprises mainly states and groups, then several other forums, notably the major UN-organized conferences, involve very different actors (e.g., firms, NGOs, experts), and a network approach would be helpful to improve the understanding of contemporary dynamics in world governance. If geography matters, it is primarily because spatial proximity appears to favor cooperation. Furthermore, patterns of relations create political regions of like-minded actors, and discontinuities are likely to appear between these regions. For instance, a recent study on human rights issues have revealed the gap between Europe, Africa, and the Middle East (Beauguitte, 2012).

Network analysis is ultimately a powerful way to communicate results, although the readability of graphs needs improving (Bahoken, Beauguitte, & Lhomme, 2013; Henry, Fekete, & McGuffin, 2007). Last but not least, network analysis also represents an excellent way to cross disciplinary boundaries and encourage discussion among researchers.

References

Bahoken, F., Beauguitte, L., & Lhomme, S. (2013). La visualisation des réseaux. Principes, enjeux et perspectives [The visualization of networks: Principles, stakes and perspectives]. *Groupe f.m.r. working paper*. Retrieved from http://halshs.archives-ouvertes.fr/docs/00/83/99/05/PDF/fmr18_visualisation.pdf

Ball, M. (1951). Bloc Voting in the General Assembly. *International Organization, 5*, 3–31. doi:10.1017/S0020818300029805

Barnett, M., & Duvall, R. (Eds.). (2005). *Power in global governance*. Cambridge, UK: University Press.

Barthelemy, M. (2011). Spatial networks. *Physics Report, 499*, 1–101. doi:10.1016/j.physrep.2010.11.002

Beauguitte, L. (2011). *L'Assemblée générale de l'ONU de 1985 à nos jours. Essai de géographie politique quantitative* [United Nations General Assembly of 1985 in our days: Essay on quantitative political geography] (Doctoral dissertation, University of Paris 7). Retrieved from http://hal.archives-ouvertes.fr/docs/00/63/44/03/PDF/These_Beauguitte_2011_ONU_et_Systeme_Monde.pdf

Beauguitte, L. (2012). L'ONU contre la peine de mort. La puissance normative de l'UE en question [The UN against the death penalty. The question of the normative power of the EU]. *L'Espace politique* [online], *18*. doi:10.4000/espacepolitique.2432

Charter of the United Nations. (1945). http://www.un.org/en/sections/un-charter/un-charter-full-text/index.html

Chen, Z. (2005). NATO, APEC, and ASEM: Triadic interregionalism and global order. *Asia Europe Journal, 3*, 361–378. doi:10.1007/s10308-005-0005-7

Comin, M. N. (2009). *Réseaux de villes et réseaux d'innovation en Europe: structuration du système des villes européennes par les réseaux de recherche sur les technologies convergentes* [Networks of cities and networks of innovation in Europe: The structuring of the European system of cities through research networks dedicated to converging technologies]. (Doctoral dissertation, University Paris I, Panthéon-Sorbonne).

Dahl, R. A. (1957). The concept of power. *Behavorial Science, 2*, 201–215. doi:10.1002/bs.3830020303

Diehl, P. F. (2005). *The politics of global governance: International organizations in an interdependent world.* Boulder: Lynne Rienner.

Drevelle, M. (2013). Structure des navettes domicile-travail et polarités secondaires autour de Montpellier [Structures of commuting traffic and secondary polarity around Montpellier]. *M@ppemonde, 107.* Retrieved from http://mappemonde.mgm.fr/num35/articles/art12304.html

Ducruet, C., & Beauguitte, L. (2013). Spatial science and network science. Review and outcomes of a complex relationship. *Networks & Spatial Economics, 14*, 297–316. doi:10.1007/s11067-013-9222-6

Ducruet, C., Ietri, D., & Rozenblat, C. (2011). Cities in worldwide air and sea flows: A multiple networks analysis. *Cybergeo, 528.* Retrieved from http://cybergeo.revues.org/23603 doi:10.4000/cybergeo.23603

Gastner, M. T., & Newman M. E. (2006). The spatial structure of networks. *The European Physical Journal B, 49*, 247–252. doi:10.1140/epjb/e2006-00046-8

Gleyze, J. F. (2007). Effets spatiaux et effets réseau dans l'évaluation d'indicateurs sur les nœuds d'un réseau d'infrastructure [Making allowances for spatial and network effects when assessing indicators of infrastructure network nodes]. *Cybergeo, 370,* Retrieved from http://cybergeo.revues.org/5532 doi:10.4000/cybergeo.5532

Glückler, J. (2013). Knowledge, networks and space: Connectivity and the problem of non-interactive learning. *Regional Studies, 47*, 880–894. doi:10.1080/00343404.2013.779659

Gorman, S. P., Patuelli, R., Reggiani, A., Nijkam, P., Kulkarni, R., & Haag, G. (2007). An application of complex network theory to German commuting patterns. In T. L. Friesz (Ed.), *Network science, nonlinear science and infrastructure systems* (pp. 167–185). International Series in Operations Research & Management Science: Vol. 102. New York: Springer. doi:10.1007/0-387-71134-1_8

Gowan, R. & Brantner, F. (2008). *A global force for human rights? An audit of european power at the UN.* European Council on Foreign Relations, Policy paper 2. http://ecfr.eu/content/entry/the_european_union_at_the_united_nations

Grabher, G. (2006). Trading routes, bypasses, and risky intersections: Mapping the travels of 'networks' between economic sociology and economic geography. *Progress in Human Geography, 30*, 163–189. doi:10.1191/0309132506ph600oa

Hafner-Burton, E. M., Kahler, M., & Montgomery, A. H. (2009). Network analysis for international relations. *International Organization, 63*, 559–592. doi:10.1017/S0020818309090195

Haggett, P., & Chorley, R. J. (1969). *Network analysis in geography.* London: Edward Arnold.

Henry, N., Fekete, J. D., & McGuffin, M. J. (2007). NodeTrix: A hybrid visualization of social networks. *IEEE Transactions on Visualization and Computer Graphics, 13*, 1302–1309. doi:10.1109/TVCG.2007.70582

Kansky, K. J. (1963). *Structure of transportation networks: Relationships between network and regional characteristics* (Doctoral dissertation). Research papers: Vol. 84. Chicago: University of Chicago.

Kissack, R. (2007). European Union member state coordination in the United Nations system: How to measure cohesion. *CFSP Forum, 5*(2), 3–5.

Lijphart, A. (1963). The analysis of bloc voting in the General Assembly: A critique and a proposal. *The American Political Science Review, 57*, 902–917. doi:10.2307/1952608

Maisonobe, M. (2013). Diffusion et structuration spatiale d'une question de recherche en biologie moléculaire [Diffusion and spatial structuring of a research question in molecular biology]. *M@ppemonde, 110.* Retrieved from http://mappemonde.mgm.fr/num38/articles/art13202.html

Mansfield, E. D., & Milner, H. V. (1999). The new wave of regionalism. *International Organization, 53*, 589–627. doi:10.1162/002081899551002

Mathis, P. (Ed.). (2003). *Graphes et réseaux, modélisation multi-niveau [Graphs and networks, multilevel modeling]*. Paris: Hermes Lavoisier.

Nystuen, J. D., & Dacey, M. F. (1961). A graph theory interpretation of nodal regions. *Papers of the Regional Science Association, 7,* 29–42. doi:10.1007/BF01969070

Rozenblat, C., & Mélançon, G. (2007). A small world perspective on urban systems. In F. Bavaud & C. Mager (Eds.), *Handbook of theoretical and quantitative geography* (pp. 431–467). Lausanne: University of Lausanne. Retrieved from http://wp.unil.ch/citadyne-news/files/2012/05/ROZENBLAT_MELANCON_CITADYNE_2009.pdf

Song, W. (2007). Regionalisation, inter-regional cooperation and global governance. *Asia Europe Journal, 5,* 67–82. doi:10.1007/s10308-006-0094-y

Tobler, W. (1970). A computer movie simulating urban growth in the Detroit region. *Economic Geography, 46,* 234–240. doi:10.2307/143141

Van Hamme, G., & Grasland, C. (Ed.). (2011). Statistical toolbox for flow and network analysis. *EuroBroadMap working paper*. Retrieved from http://halshs.archives-ouvertes.fr/docs/00/65/45/32/PDF/EWP_flows_networks_toolbox.pdf

Van Hamme, G., & Pion, G. (2012). The relevance of the world-system approach in the area of globalization of economic flows and networks. *Geografiska Annaler: Series B, Human Geography, 94,* 65–82. doi:10.1111/j.1468-0467.2012.00396.x

Voeten, E. (2000). Clashes in the Assembly. *International Organization, 54*(2), 185–215. Retrieved from http://journals.cambridge.org/action/displayAbstract?fromPage=online&aid=164773&fileId=S0020818300440981

Open Access This chapter is distributed under the terms of the Creative Commons Attribution 4.0 International License (http://creativecommons.org/licenses/by/4.0/), which permits use, duplication, adaptation, distribution and reproduction in any medium or format, as long as you give appropriate credit to the original author(s) and the source, provide a link to the Creative Commons license and indicate if changes were made.

The images or other third party material in this chapter are included in the work's Creative Commons license, unless indicated otherwise in the credit line; if such material is not included in the work's Creative Commons license and the respective action is not permitted by statutory regulation, users will need to obtain permission from the license holder to duplicate, adapt or reproduce the material.

Chapter 6
(Post)graduate Education Markets and the Formation of Mobile Transnational Economic Elites

Sarah Hall

This chapter is set within the resurgence of interest in economic elites across the social sciences (see, for example, Daloz, 2010; Savage & Williams, 2008). Clearly understanding the activity of economic elites, including those who work in the financial services focused on in this chapter, is not an entirely new endeavor within economic geography and the broader social sciences (see, for example, McDowell, 1997; Thrift, 1994). Building on this work, however, the recent and growing interest in elites marks the development of a more sustained academic engagement aimed at understanding not only the background of elites but also the nature of their work and its significant implications for the global economy. Beyond the academy, this developing interest in elites has received considerable impetus from the 2007 to 2008 financial crisis and the ensuing recession because of how the elites' working practices, particularly those undertaken by investment bankers in financial services in the area of securitization (the process of transforming an illiquid asset into a security), which are argued to have been central to both causing the crisis and contributing to its geographically disparate consequences (Tett, 2009).

Inspired by this growing interest in elites and their working practices, I focus in this chapter on the role of postgraduate education in facilitating entry into—and upward career progression within—early-career labor markets in investment banking in London's international financial district. I take as my starting point the considerable attention that has been paid to the role of educational background in elite formation, led by the work of Bourdieu (1989/1996). The development of this work, particularly in the sociology of education, has documented how individuals strategically accumulate credentials in order to secure positional advantage vis-à-vis other job seekers in their chosen labor market (see, in particular, Brown & Hesketh, 2004). I develop this literature by examining how education beyond the first degree

---

S. Hall (✉)
School of Geography, University of Nottingham,
Sir Clive Granger Building, Nottingham NG7 2RD, UK
e-mail: sarah.hall@nottingham.ac.uk

level (i.e., beyond bachelor's degree) represents an important means by which early-career financial elites are inculcated into the meanings and competencies associated with normalized, legitimated business practices in London and into the corporate culture of their employing firm.

I suggest that these forms of education, alongside the more widely studied forms of educational background, have important implications for both the spatial and social mobility of financial elites. My approach advances understandings of the spatial mobility (or otherwise) of financial elites. In this respect work on elites has more generally often labeled them as, for example, a transnational capitalist class (Sklair, 2001) or global elites (Castells, 1996). These labels, and the discourses that surround them, suggest a highly mobile group of topologically linked individuals who are only loosely embedded in topographical space while being situated within particular geographical locations, cities, or regions. However, by focusing on the role of education in elite formation, I suggest that elites combine elements of both topological mobility and connectedness with topographical specificity because their working practices and careers are shaped in part by the still largely national educational systems in which they are produced and the distinctive working cultures associated with different, place-based economies—the international financial centers in the case of the financial elites I study here. Meanwhile, I suggest that socially the case of finance demonstrates how many of the networks created through postgraduate education continued to be structured along social lines. In particular, mobility into and within elite financial labor markets remains comparatively limited to an educational and occupational elite, in spite of the widely held view that the growing importance of postgraduate education signaled the rise of a more meritocratic global economy—and City of London in particular—where individuals can succeed if they invest appropriately in their human capital (Becker, 1994). Taken together, I therefore argue that postgraduate education is an important but hitherto comparatively overlooked element in creating financial elites who combine elements of topological financial networks inseparable from the topographical dimensions of socioeconomic practice in financial services.

I develop these arguments over four further sections. In the next section, I examine how work on the role of educational background, particularly in the sociology of education, can be developed to provide a fuller understanding of the role of ongoing education in shaping socioeconomic practice within elite labor markets. I then introduce the different elements of the postgraduate landscape as they pertain to financial elites working in investment banking in the City of London. In the final substantive section of the chapter, I consider the spatial implications of this ongoing education for a group of early-career financial elites employed by investment banks often assumed to be unproblematically transnational and highly geographically mobile. I conclude by reflecting on the implications of this argument for work on the geographies of elites more generally and on their spatial and social (im) mobility.

Financial Elites, Education, and Socioeconomic Practice in the City

As noted in the introduction, the relationship between educational background and entry into elite networks has been extensively studied, led by the work of Pierre Bourdieu (1980/1990, 1989/1996). A central component of this research is Bourdieu's identification of three interrelated forms of capital (economic, social, and cultural) that form an individual's habitus (Bourdieu, 1980/1990). Work in the sociology of education has focused particularly on institutional capital, arguing that it is gained through the acquisition of education credentials, as well as through membership in other formal groups (see, for example, Waters, 2007). However, although Bourdieu only discusses education explicitly in relation to institutional capital, research, particularly in the sociology of education, has revealed how education also plays an important role in the acquisition of the other forms of cultural and embodied capital as individuals learn accepted ways of being and doing through their educational experiences (Brown, 2000; Brown & Hesketh, 2004; Waters, 2009).

This emphasis on the ways in which institutional, cultural, and embodied capital is acquired through education has been particularly evident regarding the relationship between education and the financial elites focused on in this chapter. Most notably, in the case of the City of London educational credentials from a small number of fee-paying public schools and elite universities, the University of Oxford and Cambridge in particular, have been identified as key determinants of successful entry into London's financial labor markets prior to the deregulatory changes of Big Bang in 1986, (Kynaston, 2002; McDowell, 1997). Educational credentials obtained from these institutions acted as a form of institutionalized cultural capital by indicating the possession of the objectified and embodied forms of cultural capital associated with "gentlemanly" capitalism (Augar, 2001). Indeed, as Thrift (1994, p. 342) has argued, gentlemanly capitalism was based "on values of honor, integrity, courtesy and so on, and manifested in ideas of how to act, ways to talk [and] suitable clothing" (see also Tickell, 1996). These embodied forms of working in the City have been argued to have had important implications for how the City was regulated by dense social networks based on shared educational backgrounds, through which trust based relationships could be formed (Pryke, 1991). More recent work has revealed how newer forms of educational credentials continue to reproduce the importance of the relationship between the educational background-based entry into financial elite labor markets and the embodied, institutional, and cultural capital needed to work successfully in these environments. For example, Masters of Business Administration (MBA) alumni networks from leading business schools have been shown to be an important way of securing upward career progression within investment banks, especially those headquartered in the United States where the MBA is more fully integrated into investment banking career pathways (Hall, 2008).

However, despite the acknowledged importance of educational background in securing entry into these elite labor markets, it is important not to paint a naively simple picture in which obtaining credentials from elite educational institutions was the only way of entering financial services work in the City of London. Such caution is particularly important given the marked changes in the nature of elite financial labor markets and work in the City of London that have occurred since much of the literature on "gentlemanly capitalism" was written in the 1980s and 1990s. Of particular importance for my focus on investment banking labor markets in this chapter are the changes associated with financial services work during the period of rapid-finance-led growth and innovation in the 2000s (Engelen, Konings, & Fernandez, 2010; Froud, Johal, Leaver, & Williams, 2006). Alongside the growth of new financial products, particularly securitization requiring greater technical competency and quantitative skills, this period saw elite financial labor markets in London expand beyond employment in merchant and investment banks to include new forms of financial intermediation offered by actors including private equity firms, hedge funds, and sovereign wealth funds (Folkman, Froud, Johal, & Williams, 2007; Wójcik, 2011). The related diversification and growth in elite financial labor meant that the old-school-network forms of recruitment based on educational background could no longer provide the number of elites demanded by financial labor markets (Leyshon & Thrift, 1997), suggesting changes in the relationship between education and elite financial work. In particular, these developments indicate that research needs to focus not only on the relationship between educational background and financial elites, but also on the ways in which education, including that undertaken after a first undergraduate degree, was important in securing entry into elite financial labor markets and inculcating individuals into the required skills, competencies, and new forms of embodied and cultural capital demanded by the changing nature of the City of London. These concerns form the basis of the rest of this chapter, in which I draw on the case of early-career investment bankers in examining the intersection between postgraduate education and everyday socioeconomic practice in the City in order to better understand the role of education in inculcating elites into particular working environments and its geographical implications for those persons often assumed to be globally mobile financial elites.

Postgraduate Education and Legitimate Elite Financial Practice

To address these concerns, I turn to a set of arguments made by Bourdieu (1980/1990, 1989/1996) concerning everyday socioeconomic practice, to his work on doxa—an idea still not widely developed in relation to education (although, see also Faulconbridge & Hall, 2014). In so doing, my analysis draws on the wider interest in normalized practice within socioeconomic life as it relates to processes of learning and the reproduction of practices in geographically specific ways (Amin & Cohendet, 2004; Wenger, 1998). For Bourdieu, assumptions and understandings about appropriate everyday practice in any given context, or doxa, strongly influence an individual's actions and thoughts. This insight is important for the arguments in this chapter for two main reasons. First, the concept of doxa suggests that the everyday socioeconomic practices of financial elites need to be understood in relation to the geographically specific understandings of what constitutes legitimate behavior in any given spatially situated economy. This raises significant questions about the role of education in reproducing these understandings because its part in inculcating early-career elites into the accepted and legitimated forms of action within—as regards this chapter—the City of London. Second, and following on, Bourdieu highlights through his work on doxa the situated nature of elite action. By considering the situated and co-constitutive characteristics of education and doxa in a particular field, it becomes possible to highlight the causes of geographically variegated elite practice.

The research I present in the rest of this chapter develops these insights by examining the role of post-first-degree (undergraduate) education in shaping the beliefs, attitudes, and working practices of earlier-career financial elites in the City of London. In other words, I seek to address in this chapter how education is used to inculcate these elites into the situated nature of legitimate socioeconomic activity in London's financial district. In so doing, I challenge assumptions that education facilitates the reproduction of a globally homogeneous elite class, entry into which has become more meritocratic because of the declining importance of educational background. Rather, I use these theoretical insights to reveal the ways in which elite financial work combines both topological and topographical components at different stages in the career life course to enhance social and spatial mobility for some while restricting it for others.

Researching Early-Career Financial Elites in London's Financial District

The analysis below is based on original empirical research conducted with early-career investment bankers and others professionals in London's international financial district. The research centered around 105 interviews conducted with that can be broken down into: investment bankers working in London at an early stage in their careers to discuss their postgraduate education and training experiences (53 interviews including U.K. and non-U.K. nationals); human resource managers in investment banks in London (6 interviews); educators and managers of for-profit financial business education firms in London (10 interviews); and lecturers and managers in international business schools (36 interviews). Interviews were transcribed in full and analyzed iteratively, with theoretical frameworks used to guide the initial coding. All respondents have been made anonymous and unidentifiable in the analysis below. These interview datasets were triangulated with desk-based reviews of: investment bank and education providers' websites to gather information about the wider educational landscapes available for early-career investment bankers; business and specialist new providers to document recent developments in postgraduate education and training in elite financial labor markets; policy documents from U.K. government departments, particularly the Department for Innovation, Universities, and Skills (DIUS), the Department for Business, Innovation and Skills, and Her Majesty's (HM) Treasury; and organizations working to support graduate employability in the United Kingdom, particularly the Higher Education Funding Council for England (HEFCE).

Education and the Process of Learning the Legitimate Socioeconomic Practice of a City Financial Elite

As I have documented elsewhere (Hall & Appleyard, 2009, 2011), ongoing postgraduate education for early-career financial elites can be divided into three broad types, each of which is aimed at inculcating financiers into a particular set of legitimated knowledge's that are deemed important in order to work within investment banking in the City of London. First, education plays an important role in circulating and legitimating the technical know-how or "calculative devices" (Callon & Muniesa, 2005) important within the increasingly technical nature of contemporary investment banking in the City. A second form of education focuses on the "psy-knowledges" (Rose, 1998) deemed important within such labor markets and include topics such as leadership, while the third form of education concentrates on ensuring that early-career investment bankers meet the regulatory clearances required to offer investment advice in the United Kingdom. At one level, these types of postgraduate educational experience for early-career investment bankers support unquestioned assumptions about education's role in inculcating individuals into the dominant global discourses that surround financial services (on which see Clark, 2011), particularly into its technical and quantitative nature, which has intensified since the rise of securitization in the 2000s. As one interviewee noted in talking about a graduate training scheme undertaken with the other graduate recruits at the employing investment bank:

> At the beginning stage, it's the technical experience, the grounding that we do…it is very broad; it's quite theoretical as well. You don't get the experience of actually applying it. (Analyst, investment bank, London, June 2008)

This reflects changes to the investment banking business model associated with the rise of securitization and structured finance. The new approach shifted the emphasis away from the areas of mergers and acquisitions and consulting that until then had dominated investment banking in the City (see Augar, 2009), with the increasingly valued technical know-how and modeling skills supplanting the client services and client interactions previously so important in an era of "gentlemanly capitalism." However, within this education into the language of global finance (Clark, 2011) here was widespread recognition that education was much more important than simply facilitating the learning of the key tenets of quantitative finance. Rather—building here on my earlier discussion on education's role in reproducing legitimate forms of socioeconomic practice—it was widely acknowledged to be an important set of activities inculcating new-graduate hires into the meanings, cultures, and beliefs that legitimate certain forms of technical know-how. Indeed, one interviewee put it very strongly, arguing that the technical know-how of quantitative finance in isolation was "irrelevant to your career" (Investment bank analyst, City of London, London, June 2008). This suggests that postgraduate education plays an important role in allowing new early-career elites to learn the cultural meanings surrounding the implementation of technical know-how in ways deemed legitimate and appropriate by colleagues, clients, and rival banks within the City of London. As the following interview summarized:

> You obviously need the theoretical background but something I've always experienced is that you have a theoretical background in something so principled, you then have the technical professional [knowledge] in a particular issue but it is almost impossible to remember that without the practical application as well. So I think they need to be very closely aligned and you can't really have one without the other—things that are really important in the workplace like presentation skills, soft skills, knowing how to approach a client and how to address them. (Investment bank president, London, September 2006)

Two elements of the way in which postgraduate education inculcates elites into the legitimated form of socioeconomic practice in the City are particularly important in this respect. First, education is essential in reproducing the discourse of client service that is a longstanding component of City-specific legitimate socioeconomic activity. This form of embodied know-how resonates in some ways with the emphasis on client service important in discourses of "gentlemanly capitalism" (see Anderson-Gough, Grey, & Robson, 2000; Clark & O'Connor, 1997; Thrift, 1994). Evidence of this was frequently commented on, with the following example being indicative:

> I think in general, one of the biggest skill sets that's required is client facing skills. Just the ability to communicate clearly and concisely (Investment bank vice president, London, October 2006).

While socialization into client service is partially achieved through observing more senior colleagues, postgraduate education also plays an important part, with education providers devising innovative teaching techniques to facilitate this form of learning, often also including elements of observation. Of particular importance in this respect is the use of simulations, in which client-facing situations are enacted in the classroom using actors and finance firm senior employees. Education providers seek to offer participants opportunities to learn about the meanings and competencies associated with commercially sensitive client advice through a combination of observation (of both actors and more senior colleagues) and feedback provided after the simulation by the educators themselves and senior colleagues.

Postgraduate education is also important because it informs new recruits about legitimated meanings and competencies associated with City practice by inculcating them into specific organizational and corporate cultures referred to by Erica Schoenberger (1997) as the "social conventions" within firms. These include informal know-how about acceptable workplace behavior and shared interpretations of the regulatory norms of London's financial district The importance of this aspect of education illustrates that despite the firms' broadly similar knowledge bases they seek as competitors to differentiate themselves by emphasizing how their ability to deliver what would be considered appropriate advice is influenced by strengths associated with particular, firm-specific cultures of practice. In financial firms, compulsory courses for all new recruits are run in-house on a regular basis, sometimes by senior staff and sometimes by for-profit education firms. This type of education is concerned with socializing individuals into the organizationally acceptable ways of using the standard technologies or "calculative devices" (Callon & Muniesa, 2005) underpinning most investment bank transactions. Here competency relates to knowledge about firm-specific parameters for the particular risk valuation techniques to be used (see Hall, 2008).

Such technology-specific education is supported by the wider socialization objectives of investment banks' induction programs targeting new-graduate recruits with the goal of informing individuals about how to fulfill the expectations of both the City field and the firm's senior professionals in terms of everyday practice. The approach is described by the following interviewee:

> There is also quite a lot of time dedicated to them instilling and communicating the values of the company and what is going to be expected of people and giving guidance on the key values, what it means to be professional, what the standards are, and what you are expected to project on a day to day basis, so yes, quite a lot of time is spent on that in the beginning. I think people expect that. (Investment bank vice-president, London, 2010)

Taken together, these elements reveal how postgraduate education is crucial in inculcating new recruits in investment banks into the legitimated and expected forms of socioeconomic practice within these elite labor markets. In so doing, postgraduate education moves considerably beyond simply circulating and facilitating the reproduction of technical know-how within wholesale financial workplaces in London's financial district, to include a range of embodied and sociocultural forms of knowledge.

Societally and Territorially Embedding Early-Career Financial Elites Through Education

The analysis so far has revealed the central role of postgraduate education in providing new recruits with an understanding of the legitimate meanings, competencies, and technologies (and their use) associated with City practice. At first glance, this analysis might be read as a story about the role of education in helping reproduce elites using practices attuned to the globally dominant discourses that shape the financial services sector (on which see Clark, 2011). However, although the kinds of education experienced by early-career elites in the City allows some such attuning to global investment banking labor markets, education also acts in important ways to situate City elites in a London-specific mode of practice. These educational activities suggest that in addition to facilitating entry into the topological networks characteristic of financial elites and elites more generally in a process well documented in the literature, postgraduate education also serves to societally and territorially embed financiers, temporally at least, in particular national and city-specific international financial districts. This involvement demonstrates how the topological and topographical are entwined within financial elite labor markets, as well as the role of education within this. In the following, I draw attention to two ways in which postgraduate education serves to embed early-career financial elites into the U.K. national economy and the City-specific international financial district in London in particular: first, briefly, by examining the role of education in inculcating elites into the regulatory frameworks of London and the United Kingdom; and second, by examining the intersection of what remain predominately national education systems with the more transnational qualities of elite financial labor markets.

Beginning with geographically specific financial services regulatory frameworks, postgraduate education gained importance because it provided individuals the opportunity to study for the credentials needed to practice as a financier and to offer investment advice in the City. At the time this chapter's research was undertaken, this meant being registered with the Financial Services Authority (FSA) in the United Kingdom, as the following interviewee summarized (for a fuller discussion of this element of postgraduate education geographies see Hall & Appleyard, 2009):

> The FSA exams basically mean I can work in the United Kingdom—if I work overseas then I'd have to go through a similar process—it's not necessarily a huge problem but it does mean for the moment I'm really a British banker and there would be some delay in terms of me generating revenue if I move to Dubai. (Investment bank vice president, London, 2010)

Beyond this regulatory element, the second way elite education served to embed financiers into particular forms of practice and associated career pathways was through its relationship to the broader national education landscape in the United Kingdom. In this respect, although financial labor markets are often assumed to be global in scope, a significant proportion of new recruits to the City come from the United Kingdom. These individuals typically hold undergraduate degrees from either Oxbridge or the Russell Group, a collection of 24 of the most research-intensive and selective universities in the United Kingdom. This fact poses important questions about how a predominately national education system intersects with the more global nature of elite financial labor markets and what the implications of this are for early-career financial elites working in investment banking in London's financial district. As Brown and Hesketh (2004, p. 23) argue in regard to graduate labor markets more generally:

> Some occupational elites operate in a global rather than a local context, but they accumulate elite credentials and other cultural assets within national and local contexts. How domestic competitions are organized continue to be important to understanding the fates of the eventual winners and losers.

In the case of finance, one of the most distinctive features of the U.K. university system impacting how early-career elites enter financial labor markets are the numeracy skills required by the increasingly technical nature of investment banking work. While earlier generations of investment bankers in the City held degrees in a diverse range of disciplines, throughout the 2000s the recruitment strategies of investment banks favored the hiring of individuals holding undergraduate—and increasingly master's and Ph.D—degrees in numerate subjects, notably mathematics and physics (Hall & Appleyard, 2009; Wilmott, 2000). This preference was driven by a growing need for numerate graduates to undertake the financial modeling and analysis underpinning the securitized financial products dominating the investment banking business model in the 2000s (see also Ho, 2009 on the case of Wall Street, New York). However, investment banks have become increasingly concerned about the skills of U.K. educated graduates and their ability to meet the operational needs of investment banks, reflecting wider concerns surrounding the skill sets and employability of U.K. graduates, particularly in science, technology, engineering, and medicine (STEM subjects, on which see CBI, 2011; DIUS, 2009). As the following interviewee summarized:

> I guess very generally there has been actually a problem with British students coming into banking. We find that they are just not coming through the interview process or screening process and I think that's probably true across the board of most banks. (Human resources director, investment bank, London, September 2006)

As a result, in an effort to enhance students' positional advantage within increasingly competitive financial labor markets, postgraduate education for U.K. graduates entering finance increasingly concentrates on sharpening those numerical skills that employers feel undergraduate education has left underdeveloped, The nature of postgraduate education for investment bankers has become tailored to reflect both the wider educational landscape of the United Kingdom in which it is situated and the labor market demands made of domestic and international new recruits into investment banking, as this example shows:

> Because we can't always get the technical skills we want domestically, increasingly we hire international graduates on that basis but then recognize that we might need to invest a little more in their soft skills and their expectations about working in the City. That's not to say we only hire internationally, not at all, but we know that the needs of analysts tends to be different depending on where they studied for their first degree, so, we'll work with talented U.K. hires to develop their technical skills, using specialist courses and that kind of thing. (Human resources director, investment bank, London, 2009)

In conjunction with education aimed at meeting the regulatory clearances needed to practice as a financier, postgraduate education thus serves as an important set of activities not only by facilitating the mobility of individuals into elite financial labor markets but also by serving to—temporarily at least—limit their mobility and territorially and to embed them societally in the legitimate forms of socioeconomic practice associated with the international financial center where they work (London's financial district in the case of this chapter). Indeed, interviewees' frequently commented on the ways in which they had to use training and orientation sessions to learn about working in other financial districts in order to overcome some of this geographical stickiness, as the following example demonstrates:

After my initial training in New York, I was then sent on, I think, six rotations where I was working for a short period in different functions globally. It was all about learning through doing, getting a feel for the working culture, the hours, the dress, how you handle clients and of course colleagues. But that wasn't just in London even though that is where I work now. (Investment bank vice president, London, 2009)

Taken together, this suggests that postgraduate education plays an important role in inculcating early-career financial elites into the topological networks and the more topographical requirements of working in London's international financial district. Indeed, these multiple spatitialities have become increasingly marked as elite financial labor markets demand ever more quantitative skills from graduates, something that has not been a historic strength of the U.K. education system producing many of the early-career elites.

Conclusions

This chapter has taken the growing interest in economic elites as its starting point to examine the comparatively neglected role of postgraduate education in facilitating entry into and upward mobility within elite financial labor markets in London's international financial district, particularly in its investment banks. Much of the attention to date has emphasized the role of educational background at a small number of elite, fee-paying public schools and universities in the graduate recruitment process and the importance of the shared educational experience in the development of trust-based relationships between bankers and their historic regulator, the Bank of England, in the City of London (see Pryke, 1991). The research presented in this chapter builds on these insights to sharpen the focus on the significance of ongoing education beyond the first degree and second schooling in shaping the nature of socioeconomic practice in the City. In this regard, I have argued that training early-career elites in the technical know-how required to work in investment banks in London's contemporary international financial district is only part of the function these forms of educational experiences fulfill. Rather, education within investment banks through graduate training schemes and that provided by specialist business education providers plays an important role in inculcating new investment bank employees into the expected and legitimated practices, meanings, competencies, and cultures associated with working in investment banking in the City of London.

The wider significance of this chapter is twofold. First, theoretically, the analysis reveals the value of extending work on the sociology of education beyond the existing focus on the multiple forms of capital reproduced through educational background to include questions raised by Bourdieu's wider concepts of field, habitus, and doxa. By examining what these concepts reveal about practice, this chapter has begun to develop a valuable approach for considering how education within elite occupations not only plays an important role for individuals in securing entry into labor markets, but also serves to (re)produce understandings of legitimated forms of practice. In particular, and in relation to the focus of this book more generally, such an understanding is important because it challenges assumptions that investment bankers are a globally mobile, homogeneous financial class. Rather, education plays an important role in embedding (see Hess, 2004) them societally and territorially in the distinctive cultures of particular financial centers at different points in their careers. This finding reinforces recent arguments in economic geography that the topological nature of financial networks cannot be separated from the topographical dimensions of socioeconomic practice (see Pike & Pollard, 2010).

Second, empirically, by focusing on the educational experiences of early-career elites, the analysis here has revealed the need for work on corporate and industry cultures and practices to study more carefully on the role of postgraduate educational spaces in the (re)production of situated practices. This is important because the cultures of practice within elite work have been the subject of considerable media and popular debate concerning their continued exclusionary tendencies and the implications of this for the possible growth trajectories of the global economy following the financial crisis (Cabinet Office, 2009; Treasury Committee, 2010). In this respect, it would appear that claims of the end of "gentlemanly capitalism" has heralded a more meritocratic City where upward career progression is equally available to all recruits provided they invest appropriately in their human capital through further postgraduate education and training have been exaggerated. Rather, individuals are involved in obtaining training and using it strategically to enhance their employability and positional advantage relative to other early-career elites in what remain highly competitive elite labor markets. This suggests that further postgraduate education might represent an important site of intervention if political aims to alter the culture of the City and render it more meritocratic and sustainable in terms of its financial practices are to be fully realized.

Acknowledgements The research reported in this chapter was funded by the Nuffield Foundation (SGS/3204) and the Economic and Social Research Council (RES–061–25–0071).

References

Amin, A., & Cohendet, P. (2004). *Architectures of knowledge: Firms, capabilities and communities*. Oxford: University Press.
Anderson-Gough, F., Grey, C., & Robson, K. (2000). In the name of the client: The service ethic in two professional services firms. *Human Relations, 53,* 1151–1174. doi:10.1177/0018726700539003
Augar, P. (2001). *The death of gentlemanly capitalism: The rise and fall of London's investment banks* (2nd ed.). London: Penguin.
Augar, P. (2009). *Chasing Alpha: How reckless growth and unchecked ambition ruined the City's golden decade*. London: Bodley Head.
Becker, G. (1994). *Human capital: Theoretical and empirical analysis with special reference to education*. Chicago: University of Chicago Press.
Bourdieu, P. (1990). *The logic of practice* (R. Nice, Trans.). Stanford: University Press. (Original work published 1980)
Bourdieu, P. (1996). *The state nobility: Elite schools in the field of power* (L. C. Clough, Trans.). Stanford: University Press. (Original work published 1989)

Brown, P. (2000). The globalisation of positional competition? *Sociology, 34,* 633–653. doi:10.1177/S0038038500000390
Brown, P., & Hesketh, A. (2004). *The mismanagement of talent: Employability and jobs in the knowledge economy.* Oxford: University Press.
Cabinet Office, (2009). Unleashing aspiration: The final report on fair access to the professions (Ref:296833/07 09). Retrieved from http://webarchive.nationalarchives.gov.uk/+/http:/www.cabinetoffice.gov.uk/media/227102/fair-access.pdf
Callon, M., & Muniesa, F. (2005). Peripheral vision: Economic markets as calculative collective devices, *Organization Studies, 26,* 1229–1250. doi:10.1177/0170840605056393
Castells, M. (1996). *The information age: Economy, society and culture: Vol. 1. The rise of the network society.* Oxford: Blackwell.
CBI (2011). *Building for growth: Business priorities for education and skills.* London, UK: CBI. Retrieved from http://www.cbi.org.uk/media/1051530/cbi__edi_education___skills_survey_2011.pdf
Clark, G. L. (2011). Myopia and the global financial crisis. *Dialogues in Human Geography, 1,* 4–25. doi:10.1177/2043820610386318
Clark, G. L., & O'Connor, K. (1997). The informational content of financial products and the spatial structure of the global finance industry. In K. Cox (Ed.), *Spaces of Globalization: Reasserting the power of the local* (pp. 89–114). New York: Guildford Press.
Daloz, J.-P. (2010). *The sociology of elite distinction. From theoretical to comparative perspectives.* Basingstoke: Palgrave Macmillan.
Department for Education and Skills (DIUS), (2009). *The demand for science, technology, engineering and mathematics skills.* London: Crown Copyright.
Engelen, E., Konings, M., & Fernandez, R. (2010). Geographies of financialization in disarray: The Dutch case in comparative perspective. *Economic Geography, 86,* 53–73. doi:10.1111/j.1944-8287.2009.01054.x
Faulconbridge, J. R., & Hall, S. (2014). Reproducing the city of London's institutional landscape: The role of education and the learning of situated practices by early-career elites. *Environment and Planning A, 46,* 1682–1696. doi:10.1068/a45392
Folkman, P., Froud, J., Johal, S., & Williams, K. (2007). Working for themselves? Capital market intermediaries and present day capitalism. *Business History, 49,* 552–572. doi:10.1080/00076790701296373
Froud, J., Johal, S., Leaver, A., & Williams, K. (2006). *Financialization and strategy. Narrative and numbers.* London: Routledge.
Hall, S. (2008). Geographies of business education: MBA programmes, reflexive business schools and the cultural circuit of capital. *Transactions of the Institute of British Geographers, 33,* 27–41. doi:10.1111/j.1475-5661.2007.00288.x
Hall, S., & Appleyard, L. (2009). City of London, city of learning? Placing business education within the geographies of finance. *Journal of Economic Geography, 9,* 597–617. doi:10.1093/jeg/lbp026
Hall, S., & Appleyard, L. (2011). Trans-local academic credentials and the (re)production of financial elites. *Globalisation, Societies and Education, 9,* 247–564. doi:10.1080/14767724.2011.577177
Hess, M. (2004). Spatial relationships? Towards a reconceptualization of embeddedness. *Progress in Human Geography, 28,* 165–186. doi:10.1191/0309132504ph479oa
Ho, K. (2009). *Liquidated: An ethnography of Wall Street.* Durham: Duke University Press.
Kynaston, D. (2002). *The City of London: Vol. 4. Club no more, 1945–2000.* London: Pimlico.
Leyshon, A., & Thrift, N. (1997). *Money/Space: Geographies of monetary transformations.* London: Routledge.
McDowell, L. (1997). *Capital culture: Gender at work in the City of London.* Oxford: Blackwell.
Pike, A., & Pollard, J. (2010). Economic geographies of financialization. *Economic Geography, 86,* 29–51. doi:10.1111/j.1944-8287.2009.01057.x
Pryke, M. (1991). An international city going global: Spatial change in the City of London. *Environment and Planning D: Society and Space, 9,* 197–222. doi:10.1068/d090197

Rose, N. (1998). *Inventing our selves: Psychology, power and person hood*. Cambridge, UK: University Press.
Savage, M., & Williams, K. (2008). Elites: Remembered in capitalism and forgotten by social sciences. In M. Savage & K. Williams (Eds.), *Remembering elites* (pp. 1–24). Oxford: Blackwell.
Schoenberger, E. (1997). *The cultural crisis of the firm*. Oxford: Blackwell.
Sklair, L. (2001). *The transnational capitalist class*. Oxford: Blackwell.
Tett, G. (2009). *Fool's gold: The inside story of J.P. Morgan and how Wall St. greed corrupted its bold dream and created a financial catastrophe*. New York: Free Press.
Thrift, N. (1994). On the social and cultural determinants of international financial centres: The case of the City of London. In S. Corbridge (Ed.), *Money, power and space* (pp. 327–355). Oxford: Blackwell.
Tickell, A. (1996). Making a melodrama out of a crisis: Reinterpreting the collapse of Barings Bank. *Environment and Planning D: Society and Space, 14*, 5–33. doi:10.1068/d140005
Treasury Committee (2010). Women in the City. Tenth report of session 2009–10. London, UK: House of Commons. Retrieved from http://www.publications.parliament.uk/pa/cm200910/cmselect/cmtreasy/482/482.pdf
Waters, J. L. (2007). Roundabout routes and sanctuary schools: The role of situated educational practices and habitus in the creation of transnational professionals. *Global Networks, 7*, 477–497. doi:10.1111/j.1471-0374.2007.00180.x
Waters, J. L. (2009). In pursuit of scarcity: Transnational students, employability and the MBA. *Environment and Planning A, 41*, 1865–1883. doi:10.1068/a40319
Wenger, E. (1998). *Communities of practice: Learning meaning and identity*. Cambridge, UK: Cambridge University Press.
Wilmott, P. (2000). The use, misuse and abuse of mathematics in finance. *Philosophical Transactions of the Royal Society A, 358*, 63–73. doi:10.1098/rsta.2000.0519
Wójcik, D. (2011). Securitization and its footprint: The rise of the US securities industry centers 1998–2007, *Journal of Economic Geography, 11*, 925–947. doi:10.1093/jeg/lbq045

Open Access This chapter is distributed under the terms of the Creative Commons Attribution 4.0 International License (http://creativecommons.org/licenses/by/4.0/), which permits use, duplication, adaptation, distribution and reproduction in any medium or format, as long as you give appropriate credit to the original author(s) and the source, provide a link to the Creative Commons license and indicate if changes were made.

The images or other third party material in this chapter are included in the work's Creative Commons license, unless indicated otherwise in the credit line; if such material is not included in the work's Creative Commons license and the respective action is not permitted by statutory regulation, users will need to obtain permission from the license holder to duplicate, adapt or reproduce the material.

Part II
Network Evolution and Social Outcomes

Chapter 7
Organized Mobility and Relational Turnover as Context for Social Mechanisms: A Dynamic Invariant at the Heart of Stability from Movement

Emmanuel Lazega

Movements following paths that Harrison White (1970) calls "vacancy chains" (p. 17) can be seen as forms of rotation across systems of places that are often socially organized circuits.[1] White calls such movements "mobility in loops" (p. 380). From his structural perspective, not all loops or systems of places are necessarily visible to the actors involved, or even to managers of organizations who track, measure, and sometimes steer other people's careers. Internal or external labor markets were the first contexts White (1970) identified for such circuits. These loops are also the daily focus of attention of lay citizens and professional observers alike, representing revolving doors for a wide range of actors. That group includes high-status people between the business world and government—from investment banks to the Treasury, for example. It is composed partly of workers subjected to employment "flexibility" and struggling step by step to make the necessary moves a reality while keeping limbos between jobs as short as possible. It also encompasses managers rotating their employees and themselves from one service to the other in the company, as with associates assigned to different partners and clients of the firm in successive and heterogeneous task forces. It consists, too, of directors moving from one corporate board to the other in a closed chain, and of sales representatives participating each year in dozens of recurrent and similar trade fairs of their industry (Brailly, Favre, Chatellet, & Lazega, 2015). Many analogous circuits

---

[1]The term *place* is used here in a general sense to refer to a location that can be occupied by an individual in any formally organized circuit, which can be geographical, organizational, or both. It is to be distinguished from the term *position* (White, Boorman, & Breiger, 1976)—a set of structurally equivalent actors called a "social niche" (Lazega, 2001, p. 25) when the ties between actors in the position are dense. A position makes sense in a system of positions (or niches) that differs from, though always combined and coevolving with, the system of places (Lazega, 2013). Space (contiguity) and network (connectivity), for example, are both different and related.

E. Lazega (✉)
Department of Sociology at the Institut d'Etudes Politiques de Paris,
Centre for the Sociology of Organizations, 19 rue Amélie, 75007 Paris, France
e-mail: emmanuel.lazega@sciencespo.fr

exist around and beyond labor markets as well. Migrants in comparatively wealthy countries attract people from the same place of origin and sometimes return there after having been overused to sweep floors and dig holes. Students can spend semesters pursuing their curriculum in universities of different countries before returning to their alma mater. Geographers and sociologists can ultimately examine broad residential forms of mobility of individuals and entire communities. By doing so, they see, for example, mobility in loops of neighborhoods or as life-cycle-related mobility of young adults moving together into new places, then to bigger places when they have children, then to smaller ones when the children leave home.

Sociologists have also looked independently at turnover in networks of personal relations. In an increasingly rich body of literature, they have described and modeled relational turnover, using statistical tools designed to deepen the understanding of network dynamics (Snijders, 1996; 2005). Relational turnover is defined in this chapter as the set of changes observed in an actor's relationships between two moments in time (e.g., the creation or addition of new relationships, the destruction or disappearance of previous relationships, and the maintenance of relationships). Dynamic models of coevolution of behavior and networks are based on analyses of this relational turnover in members' profiles and in the composition and structure of the collective. When people close their eyes and ignore a situation marked by conflicts of interest, is it because they have become friends with someone who tends to do the same thing and influences them in that direction? Or is it because from the outset they chose friends from among people who, like themselves, close their eyes when confronted by situations of this kind? Often, both answers are true, but each effect has a relative weight that can be measured only by observing and analyzing behavioral changes and relational turnover over time. Without such analyses of coevolution of behavior and relational turnover, intuitions about concerted ignorance as a complex phenomenon, i.e. difficult to observe, remain poor and explanations of this phenomenon as a social process remain untested.[2] The act of changing structural forms and relational infrastructures triggers changes in social processes downstream. All the main social phenomena, such as solidarity, exclusion and discrimination, social control, conflict resolution, learning, socialization, regulation, and institutionalization, have a relational dimension, are a function of relational infrastructures, and reshape structure, at least opportunity structures.[3]

---

[2] In many ways work by Snijders (1996, 2005) strongly reflects the best social science epistemological practice in which researchers measure, formalize, and model the coevolution of behaviour and interdependencies, of interdependencies and conflicts between actors, both individual and collective. This approach compares models against reality and measurements of reality, but also inspires new intuitions about realities too complex and difficult to observe directly. In short, models, measurements, theories, and the object of analysis coevolve.

[3] The list of social processes that facilitate collective action between status competitors and that can be modeled by network analysis is indefinite (i.e., there is no finite list of these processes) because no social processes exist without a relational dimension. Relational processes that characterize collective action undertaken by interdependent entrepreneurs have been the object of neostructural formalizations: integration, assimilation, cooptation, balance of power, evaluation of product quality, exploitation, extraction of economic performance, discrimination, and desolidarization. These

Often overlooked in the literature, however, is the systematic, recursive, and transformative link between the two realities—mobility (rotation) across systems of places and relational turnover—and that link's implications for social life. There is a connection between movement and human relationships, for actors switch places in these circuits and change occurs as a consequence, at least in part, in their respective sets of relationships—and, by extension, in their relational capital. In addition, the latter change affects the evolution of the system of places itself, an evolution that is apparent only if places are regarded not as purely contextual and exogenous but rather as endogenized by members themselves and thus as endogenous to the mechanisms under study. The connection between movement and relational capital is often explored in detail in specific areas of social life. Migration networks, for example, are prototypical. When members of a family migrate across continents, separations between them and the family remaining in the country of origin are often devastating for individuals and social communities. The focus in studies on their situation is therefore justifiably on coping with the costs of leaving families behind, on marginality, loneliness, and the creation and management of new relationships by agents striving for their own or their children's social mobility and assimilation. But the mechanics and social costs of this link also deserve exploration, as do the effects that such movements have on the structure and governance of the system of places. It is about the stability and change of the system and the opportunity structure that it represents for its members.

The structuration, or transformation, of organized mobility and relational turnover (OMRT) may be called the complex dynamics that lead individuals and organizations to change part of their relational and social capital as they switch places in relatively closed, partly overlapping loops, whether formally institutionalized or emergent. These dynamics trigger social processes that may, under specific circumstances, reshape the initial opportunity structure of some members of the setting but not that of others. Each domain of social and economic life and every field of attendant research in the social sciences has its OMRT structuration processes. I define OMRT structuration as the dynamic link—as mediated by "dynamic invariants"—between places and positions. I use the label *organized* to qualify mobility, for both social actors and the social system create paths and rules for movements that are not allowed to be random. Whether physical or social or both, these linked, articulated movements and changes are fundamental to social structure and social order in the

---

processes, which together contribute, for example, to cooperation between competitors, remain separate only for analytical purposes. They are dynamically linked, as by retroactive effects. The redefinition of rules can engender new solidarities. Normative beliefs produced by the regulatory process influence choices of advisors and, hence, learning, among other processes. Controversies in part energize the evolution of structures that facilitate collective learning. They contribute to the endogenous formation of the constraints that actors can then consider legitimate or not legitimate and that they submit to more or less voluntarily. Research is only just beginning on the manner of connection (articulation) between these processes and the forms of social discipline that they create (see Lazega, 2009; 2012).

organizational society (Perrow, 1991).[4] They are created by the social organization of these milieus and end up, under conditions that remain to be spelled out, restructuring these milieus, taking some members somewhere and others nowhere. Dynamics of OMRT are not simply a recursive and alternating movement between two separate poles influencing each other while competing in doing the same thing. OMRT dynamics involve more complex evolution because they have an impact on fundamental social processes. These processes all have a relational dimension, and all depend on relational infrastructure that facilitates their deployment (Lazega, 2001, 2003, 2012).

A neostructural approach to the relationship between behavior and position in the social structure takes these dynamics into account and provides this endogenous understanding of social change and system stability.[5] From this perspective, position in the structure is not a static place in a static order. It results from specific social dynamics. These dynamics can be approached through the notion and measurements of relational infrastructures, i.e. social forms in the sense meant by Simmel (1908/2009). At least two such forms are needed to position actors in the structure, describe their attempts to modify their opportunity structure, and explain the deployment of generic social processes that help them, as members of a collective, deal with the pitfalls of collective action (e.g., freeloading and crowding in the production and consumption of collective goods). The two social forms are niches and status, which represent underlying social differentiations, horizontal and vertical, in the social space. It is not surprising that status as a social form is key to the deployment of social processes. In general, sociological theory, status refers to a member's relative position in the formal hierarchy of the group, as well as in its internal networks of exchanges (Blau, 1964; Hughes, 1945; Lenski, 1954; Merton, 1957). Members' status can be understood as a translation of their present and past contributions to the group's cooperative system into a right to participate actively, and sometimes to lead. Sociological classics have long stressed the salience of many dimensions of social status and social approval. Weber (1924), for example, distinguished between three—economic (based on the control of production apparatus), social (based on honor and prestige derived from birth and from human capital, or education), and political (based on control of the state apparatus)—which can overlap in stable economic conditions.

---

[4] The term *organizational society* has several dimensions. According to Perrow (1991), it means that large-scale public or private organizations "absorb" (p. 726) societal functions that can be performed by communities. It also means that a system of interdependent organizations interlinked at the mesolevel in a multilevel network shapes the opportunity and constraint structure of citizens by coordinating, for example, various forms of opportunity-hoarding (Tilly, 1998). Lastly, the term *organizational society* is a metaphor for the tendency of individuals to act at the individual and organizational levels simultaneously and for the observation that domination (in the sense meant by Weber, 1924) is linked to the control of organizations as "tools with a life of their own" (Selznick, 1949, p. 24).

[5] Contemporary neostructuralism is different from the structuralism of the 1960s in that the former draws on a theory of individual and collective action to articulate structure, culture, and agency (Archer, 1988; Lazega & Favereau, 2002).

This chapter focuses on status to theorize the relationship between OMRT dynamics and social processes, in particular collective learning. In neostructural vocabulary social processes differ from OMRT dynamics. In a collective of interdependent members, social processes are combined and iterated actions and interactions that help these members manage the dilemmas of collective action by constituting a form of social discipline that the same members consider to be legitimate, at least temporarily. OMRT dynamics are the micro- and macrophenomena that shape and reshape these social processes and can be considered as being among the determinants thereof. The process taken as an example in this chapter is collective learning. In this process status is a central relational infrastructure (Blau, 1964; Krackhardt, 1990; Lazega, 1992). Indeed, the quest for status (an individual's importance) in the collective, which presupposes participation in status competition, is another way of seeking to modify one's opportunity structure to one's advantage. Social status is an inevitable basis for strategies intended to modify opportunity structures. In effect, the multiple dimensions of social status can be measured as concentrations of different kinds of resources. Network analysis offers measures (essentially, centrality and prominence), that identify heterogeneous and *endogenous* forms of status (and not simply exogenous forms as in Weber). From a more endogenous perspective, a person can achieve status in many local ways, such as by demonstrating great competence, assuming administrative responsibilities, gaining popularity, concentrating various sorts of specific assets, or even receiving the endorsement of members with status. Status competition paves the way to a mandate to represent the collective, control resources, gain authority, and define the terms of social exchanges, but also to protect one's regulatory interests and partially resist being thrust from "above" into overt competition.

Status will thus help construe and measure these dynamics for an indispensable process of collective action and social life in communities in which it is a notable relational infrastructure: collective learning. This example will illustrate that such infrastructures have a salient role in linking OMRT and social processes. Theorizing these dynamics shows that geographers, historians, and sociologists have a strong interest in collaborating in research on OMRT structuration and on the social costs it entails.

Illustration: A Spinning-Top Model of Collective Learning

It may be useful to start this exploration with an empirical case study that illustrates some of the complexities of OMRT dynamics. The research was used to explore the OMRT model and permits a look at intraorganizational learning networks at the intersection of the sociology of organizations, economic sociology, and the sociology of law. Intraorganizational learning has been considered a significant process in organizations ever since the publication of March and Simon's (1958) perspective. The relevance of studying this process has grown with the number of knowledge-intensive organizations, which thrive on innovation, and with the concomitant search for new competitive advantages. Learning as a relational and interactive process can be captured through the study of advice networks. In organized contexts it is usually possible to consult with someone through social exchange in which members obtain advice in exchange for recognition of the advisor's status and authority (Blau, 1955), which can be called *epistemic status*. Members with epistemic status usually have hierarchical authority, professional authority, or expert authority, if not two or even all three of these forms of authority combined (Lazega, 1992).[6]

The case is based on an organizational and longitudinal network study of advice-seeking among judges at the Commercial Court of Paris. The French Commercial Court is a judicial, local, first-level *consular* jurisdiction dealing with commercial litigation and bankruptcies in the French economy.[7] Its judges are unpaid lay volunteers from the local business community, and they are expected to pool their experience and knowledge of business practices and customs in order to find solutions to conflicts therein. They are elected or coopted for 2- or 4-year terms (but no more than 14 years) by an electoral body composed of other judges already sitting at the same court and by representatives of the trade associations of the Chamber of Commerce of their local jurisdiction. Most consular judges remain for the whole 14-year tenure, allowing social groups to form and be sustained within the organization. Of the 156 consular judges at the Commercial Court of Paris in 2005, 38% were bankers and insurers, for the financial industry is currently the only one that can afford to send large numbers of senior managers to perform as judges in such an institution (see Lazega, Lemercier, & Mounier, 2006; Lazega & Mounier, 2009, 2012; Lazega, Mounier, Snijders, & Tubaro, 2012; Lazega, Sapulete, & Mounier, 2011).

The court is composed of 20 specialized and general chambers dealing with bankruptcies and widely diverse forms of commercial litigation (such as corporate law, European Union law, international law, unfair competition, multimedia, and new technologies). It handles around 12% of all the commercial litigation in France, including large and complex cases for which companies decide not to go to arbitration courts. The consular judges rotate annually from one chamber to another. The policy of rotating judges across the chambers is intended to prevent corruption and

---

[6] Expert authority can be defined as professional authority exercised among nonprofessionals, i.e. by sharing minimal knowledge for action with the latter across the professional/lay boundary.

[7] An explanation of the term *consular* is in order. The *consulat* was a mode of urban government practiced in the Middle Ages in the southern part of the Kingdom of France by cities with a right to self-administration and self-defense. *Consulatus* is a noun formed from *consul*, meaning "council." The word referred to a community's ability to deliberate in an assembly (likewise called the *consulat.*). Urban communities governed by a *consulat* could call themselves cities. All had markets, and many had fairs. In a *régime consulaire* the community governed itself through *consuls*, who varied in number and qualification. Merchants organized as socially distinct guilds occupied a pivotal place in the *régime consulaire*. Drawing on the *lex mercatoria* (commercial law), they managed to negotiate, with the emerging French state, something akin to joint regulation of their business activities within the *consulat* framework: Their local self-regulation was to be founded on the state's sanctioning power. The state, whose own administration was still embryonic, may paradoxically have seen this cooptation by local merchants as a means of further extending its central control over the country. A major component of the *consular regime* is the *tribunal de commerce*, or commercial court, whose purview evolved over time.

conflicts of interests (as could occur if judges were to come from the banking industry and concentrate in bankruptcy chambers).

Tasks are complex, and judges have discretion in many areas of business law. Disagreements over solutions to many legal problems abound. Commercial litigation varies, with conflict resolution often depending on knowledge of the specific business and industry in which the conflict has arisen. To manage these uncertainties intraorganizationally, the judges are keen on seeking each other's advice, drawing on their professionally heterogeneous set of colleagues. When a judge coming from the hotel industry must decide in a case brought by two opposing banks, for example, she has many banking-sector colleagues with whom she can consult about customs and current issues in the financial industry or about banking law.

Data for this chapter was gathered at three points in time (fall 2000, fall 2002, and fall 2005). All the judges were interviewed face to face about their advice-seeking among each other. The following name generator was used:

> Here is the list of all your colleagues at this Tribunal, including the President and Vice-Presidents of the Tribunal, the Presidents of the Chambers, the judges, and "wise men." Using this list, please check the names of colleagues from whom you have asked advice about a complex case in the previous two years or with whom you have had basic discussions outside formal deliberations in order to elicit a different point of view on it.

A high average response rate (87.1 %) over the three stated periods made it possible to reconstitute the entire advice network (outside formal deliberations) among judges at this courthouse at each point in time. The number of judges at the court from 2000 to 2005 varied from 151 to 156.

Longitudinal analyses of the advice network among these lay judges have facilitated a close look at the structural factors that explain relational turnover in the network—that is, the creation of new ties and the discontinuation of previous ones. This work was based on Snijders's (1996, 2005) *Siena* models of dynamic analysis of the evolution of this network (see Lazega et al., 2006; Lazega et al., 2012). They tease out a cyclical process of centralization and decentralization in the network over time. Movement in this organizational system of places, change in the system of places, and the attendant emergence of status are all visible in this cycle of centralization–decentralization. Through these cyclical dynamics individuals eventually attain epistemic status and displace incumbent status-holders at the top of the hierarchy. Such evolution helps reproduce the persistent organizational structure and characterizes the continuous collective learning process in the organization.

OMRT Transformations as Determinants of Collective Learning: Cyclical Dynamics of Advice Networks

An advice network represents a set of paths through which appropriate information circulates among members of an organized setting. The allocation of this resource through informal ties and interactions reduces the costs of its acquisition during the process of making decisions to solve problems. Members of organizations see expertise and experience as accumulated by the organization, and they rely constantly on advice from others. However, intraorganizational learning through advice-seeking does not simply result from the accumulation of individually and informally acquired information. The process is socially organized in a sophisticated way.

In organizations examined by researchers, advice-seeking converges toward senior and recognized members and reflects a process of epistemic alignment with (or orientation to) members who have gained epistemic status and the "authority to know," who give social approval for specific decisions, and who contribute to integrating the organization by linking the individual, group, and organizational levels. This alignment may be thought of as a key ingredient of intraorganizational learning. Providing a social incentive for actors to share their knowledge and experience with others, a status hierarchy helps explain the social organization of the learning process. For example, social exchange and status help solve a learning dilemma in which it is rational for individuals to pursue the maximum organizational share of joint learning by taking more knowledge than they give. At the same time, the relative withholding of knowledge reduces the total amount of joint learning from which persons attempt to appropriate their individual share (Larsson, Bengtsson, Henriksson, & Sparks, 1998).

Because advice networks are usually shaped by such status 'games', they are usually highly centralized. They exhibit a pecking order that often closely follows the hierarchical structure of the organization (Lazega, 2014). Members of formal organizations rarely declare that they seek advice from "people below" in this pecking order. In addition to a core set of central advisors, the periphery of the network can be complex and characterized by homophilous (Lazega & van Duijn, 1997) horizontal ties (i.e., ties among peers). Members use such ties to mitigate the negative effects that this strict rule can have on intraorganizational action and learning (e.g., unwillingness to show that one does not know the answer to a question). Advice networks thus tend to be both hierarchical and cohesive (at least within subsets of peers), with the hierarchical dimension usually being stronger than the cohesive one. In some firms advice ties are crucial in facilitating the flows of other kinds of resources in coworkers' and friendship ties (Lazega & Pattison, 1999).

A "spinning-top model" accounts for the dynamics of advice networks in organizations by furnishing a main metaphor for research on the relationship between formal organization and intraorganizational process. It shows that intraorganizational collective learning depends on the organization's capacity to generate an elite group of authoritative advisors with epistemic status that remains stable. By contrast, advice ties among other organizational members undergo rapid turnover (due, say, to rotation policy, career movement, or the need for new knowledge that old advisors cannot offer; Ortega, 2001; Kane, Argote, & Levine, 2005). More generally, the spinning-top model illustrates a new approach to the relationship between formal organization and informal social behavior and processes.

As a model for a dynamic process, the spinning-top heuristic brings together at least three components: a rotating body, a rotation axis, and a fragile equilibrium that depends partly on characteristics of the first two components. I define these terms metaphorically and loosely. The rotating body represents the learning organization—the population of judges who switch places once a year in a circular system of places, as with a carrousel or "mobility in loops" (White, 1970, p. 380). The rotation axis represents a pecking order: a vertical differentiation between the judges and the emergent hierarchy of members with epistemic status. This axis can be pictured as the spinning top's shaft, which supplies the angular momentum that keeps the spinning top erect. It allows learning to take place in a system that remains stable thanks to its movement. The fragile equilibrium created by the rotation movement represents the structural condition for learning collectively in the organization and depends on the stability of the rotation axis and the shape of the organization. Time is taken into account through rotation and speed. These members have the authority to know in the organization. Formal structure is summarized in rotation rules across intraorganizational boundaries and in status differences. Infrastructural stability, that is necessary for collective learning and social processes in general, comes from movement.

The endogenous evolution of advice networks is characterized by three interrelated moments. First, the centrality of members with high epistemic status varies over time. It initially tends to be reinforced. Pivotal members become ever more central in a Matthew effect (Merton, 1968): The more they attract advice-seekers, the more their reputation grows and, in turn, the more they are sought out. Among other members, there spreads the impression that turning to such a source for advice is safe and legitimating for their own knowledge claims, and that making this choice signals a rise in relative status. Concentration of epistemic authority thereby intensifies with the centralization of advice networks as learning comes to depend on a dwindling number of sources of authoritative knowledge.

Second, in real-life organizations this centralization creates an overload for members with high epistemic status. These members tend to manage this overload by sharing some of their epistemic status, redirecting advice-seekers to other sources through recommendations. When advice from the handful of the supercentral advisors becomes inaccessible, irrelevant, inaccurate, untimely, or rare, members turn to these other advisers, creating new epistemic stars. Sharing epistemic status (a form of delegation) enlarges the number of advisers and lessens the centralization of the network.

Third, the expansion in the number of central members with high epistemic status in the organization creates a problem of epistemic conflicts, consensus, and coordination among epistemic authorities. If it is easy to co-orientate with them, equilibrium is established. If not, conflicts between epistemic authorities trigger recentralization. When collective action eventually becomes endangered by an excessive number of epistemic leaders, some of them withdraw or retire, and others are disqualified in one way or another. As their numbers decrease, it becomes easier at the top to recreate consensus around a common definition of the situation, to give coherent social benchmarks for homogeneous judgments of appropriateness (Lazega, 1992).

These dynamics of centralization and decentralization in advice networks may not be purely endogenous. In other words, it might not be that overload due to centralization leads the supercentral advisors to redirect advice-seekers to surrogates and thereby create new epistemic stars. The pattern of advice relations can be influenced by the content of the advice sought, and external events may make one potential advisor a better source of advice than another. Nonetheless, the existence of this endogenous dimension of the process provides at least one mechanism that explains how particular supercentral elites are able to stabilize their position and surf at the top of the structure thanks to strong competition for epistemic authority and status.

This picture is heuristic for several reasons. First, it suggests that time is important in allowing organizations to select members who possess epistemic status. The epistemic status of a person appreciates with his or her reputation for expertise, with the capacity to provide quality control without raising excessive controversy or conflict over the definition of the situation, and with the trained capacity to speak legitimately on behalf of the collective. Acquiring this status takes effort and time. The authority to know stems from prolonged individual and collective investment that can be ruined if members with epistemic status leave or behave too opportunistically. The equilibrium achieved by the spinning top thus suggests that members with status and epistemic authority in the organization have a strong incentive to keep both over time, even at extra expense, to avoid losing advantages that come with their relative standing (see Frank, 1985).

Second, this heuristic suggests that the equilibrium achieved by the spinning top is fragile. It is not only the centrality but also the number of members with high epistemic status that varies over time. There are several conceivable reasons for this number's fluctuation. One is that members tend to choose advisors whom they perceive to be the most popular (i.e., already chosen by a large number of colleagues). Because such widely sought-out members within the organization are perceived to be safe and legitimate choices as advisors, their reputation grows. Given the micropolitical perspective that all people seek status and that they believe they will improve theirs, access to advisors higher up the ladder becomes in itself a sign of relative status. The implication is that a member highly sought out in time t_1 will be even more intensely sought out in time t_2.

Another reason for the rise and fall in the number of members with high epistemic status is that the first period in this process demands too much of the small circle of highly central advisors. Because these individuals often manage the overload by delegating, by referring the advice-seeker to other advisors, the number of new central advisors inflates to the point that the stability of the pecking order is jeopardized. Even without such delegation, however, the equilibrium remains fragile, and for the same reasons. These elites must thus work together to avoid destructive status competition between them and avert infighting over the definition of the situation. In turn, this strategy either triggers formal attempts at coordination among the elites or reduces the number of central advisors through retirement or delegitimation.

The existence of this oscillation in the centralization of the advice network was detected through dynamic analyses of the network's evolution (see Table 7.1). This

Table 7.1 Collective learning as a cyclical process: increase, then decrease, of centralization in an advice network over time

Independent variables	Parameters for period 1[a] (Wave 1–Wave 2)	Parameters for period 2[b] (Wave 2–Wave 3)
Rate parameter	22.25 (2.03)	30.58 (3.14)
Density	−1.74 (0.09)	−2.23 (0.18)
Reciprocity	0.95 (0.16)	0.71 (0.13)
Transitivity	0.50 (0.04)	0.19 (0.01)
Popularity of alter	3.34 (0.40)	3.84 (0.25)
Activity of alter	−14.44 (1.84)	−1.86 (1.87)
3-cycles-of-generalized-exchange effect	−0.29 (0.09)	−0.07 (0.01)

Note: Adapted from Lazega et al. (2006), p.119
[a] $N=91$. [b] $N=113$. Standard errors are in parentheses

approach entailed a close look at the structural factors that explain the network's relational turnover, that is, the creation of new ties that are added to or supplant hitherto existing ones.

This heuristic spinning-top model helps illustrate an OMRT context for processes such as intraorganizational learning. The dynamics of the advice network examined in this commercial court can indeed be represented intuitively as a spinning top. They are driven by the rotation rule in the formal structure of organization. Because judges seek advice first within their own Chamber, and because they change Chamber every year, the relational turnover in this network is high. Each year, each judge leaves behind several advisors and creates new advice ties within his or her new Chamber. This turnover, however, is compensated for by the creation of a set of advisors with epistemic status to whom judges turn for advice thanks to the Chamber in which they work. The centrality scores of members with epistemic status rise, then tend to decline over time, showing that the stabilization of this elite set of judges adds to the complexity of the dynamics of advice networks. Those dynamics come to include formally induced homophily, relational turnover, emergence of status as an endogenous effect reinforcing exogenously defined status, centralization of the advice network, and strategies of stabilization of this elite under capacity constraints. It is likely that empirical observation will find a perpetual cyclical pattern of centralization and decentralization in the advice network and that relative structural stability is achieved in part through OMRT.

These detailed analyses show that most judges achieve centrality over time, some of them to the point of losing part of it and their corresponding status in the cyclical dynamics precisely because they succeeded at sharing their status by delegating a degree of their advisory function to other colleagues (Lazega et al., 2011). Lack of space in this volume precludes detailed treatment of the substantive reasons for these dynamics of the advice networks in this specific context. The complex story behind this process of collective learning is a matter of alignment with the supercentral judges who maintain themselves by trying to exercise epistemic control and balance excessive requests for advice (when too few colleagues occupy the top of the pecking order) and to build consensus among the epistemic leaders (when too many of them occupy the top of the pecking order).

Further analyses (Lazega & Mounier, 2009) have shown that this relationship between networks, rotation across places, and learning leads to collective learning when judges make decisions requiring their discretion. Such circumstances include the choice of whether or not to award damages (punitive or otherwise), to intervene in boards (by supporting minority shareholders against the management of a company), or to intervene in markets (by preventing a given party from terminating a contract that was meant to support a weaker party). What is learned in the process of collective learning, through a status game leading to upward and outward spirals of temporary epistemic status, is the solution that the court considers to be appropriate for problems for which the law does not always provide clear answers. For example, in controversies pitting bankers against colleagues mainly from the building industry, collective learning leads most judges to align their deliberations and decisions with the solutions proposed by bankers who hold a law degree. Collective learning thereby becomes equated with a form of normative alignment (if not institutional capture; see Lazega, 2011; Lazega & Mounier, 2012) by which most judges are receptive to the solutions outlined by the dominant players in this institution (Lazega et al., 2012).

Dynamic Invariant: Stability from Movement and Emergence of Epistemic Status in OMRT Structuration

These processes are not simple. The spinning-top heuristic suggests that centralization of advice networks can remain stable or eventually expand or contract to find a balance between elite overload and conflicts between interpretations that these heterogeneous elites offer. This metaphor leads to the following claim about the structure and dynamics of advice networks and intraorganizational learning. Intraorganizational learning, as an informal process, depends on at least three factors: (a) the way that members manage their advice ties in the context of this formal organization; (b) the ways that central advisors handle overload and conflicts between definitions of the situation; and (c) the ways that formal structure can help actors deal with the advice network's oscillation between centralization and decentralization. In effect, variations in centralization over time suggest that this oscillation serves as a pump in the spinning top. If OMRT can be represented by a spinning top, it is because this image accounts for one of the main processes taking place in OMRT: the emergence of status in organized social settings.

The extent to which the emergent relational infrastructure in an organization remains the same over time—despite the combined turnover of its members and turnover in their respective relational profile—is one of the most interesting questions raised by structural analyses applied in organized social settings. In this case the emergent structure of this organization remains the same overall. The finding is that the emergent relational structure remains unchanged. This answer is a function of the degree to which observers focus on structure and on the dimensions of the structure they examine. As shown in the following section, the existence of a pecking order and of the core–periphery structure itself remains relatively stable thanks to their intertwining with formal hierarchy and status competition. But social differentiation measured in terms of role relationships and the division of labor shows that the relational structure does *not* remain the same, depending on when and where observers look at the process. Intraorganizational relational processes, such as collective learning, impose varying constraints on different kinds of members over time, and the overall relational structure reflects their changing responses to those limitations. Because the processes vary, so does the relational structure, as does the resulting emergent overall structure. Even when these dynamics are the same, they do not produce identical outcomes. They transform very different initial situations. Radical, orthodox structuralism turns out to be wrong.

OMRT and Catch-up Dynamics at Superimposed Levels of Agency

Where does the energy for rotation in OMRT come from to begin with? Posing this question is like asking what OMRTs take place in which context. Granted, OMRTs are the context of social processes, but they are themselves embedded in a wider, macrosocial context. In the example of the spinning top, the energy comes from an organizational rule that obliges representatives of an institution to switch places, a compelled rotation that is meant to control their behavior given the exogenous suspicion of corruption. But at the interorganizational level such rules do not always exist in such a formalized way. Nevertheless, if organizations are open systems, then they are part of interorganizational systems of interdependencies (observed as "networks") and are thus part of somewhat self-contained systems with a certain level of closure and their own dynamics. Movement makes sense from both below (the perspective of individual actors who orient their actions to multiple levels) and above (the fact that mesosocial order and agency take place in superimposed systems of interdependencies and collective agency) (Lazega, Jourda, & Mounier, 2013; Lazega, Jourda, Mounier, & Stofer, 2008).[8] In such multilevel systems the temporalities of each level differ from each other. Each level must adjust and adapt to the evolution of the other level. Attempts at synchronization, however, are usually more costly for one level than for another. The level that is dominated will be compelled to pay for synchronization. This imposition can take the form of catching up in the competition for status.

The answer to the question about the origin of the energy for OMRT rotation therefore has to do with the functioning of the mesolevel in its macrocontext. The

---

[8] This logic is related to a theory of action that stresses attempts by actors to reshape their opportunity structure (see Lazega & Mounier, 2002; Tilly, 1998).

energy stems from the way power and class struggles function in the organizational society: in collective efforts to hoard opportunities and to saddle others with constraints while still encouraging or obliging everyone to compete for these same opportunities and resources. The clearest way to comprehend the origins of the energy for rotation in OMRT is to understand that it is used to concentrate power in a stratified organizational society, a society made of superimposed levels of agency. Such a society spends a great deal of energy catching up in status-related competition imposed from above, self-imposed from below, or both. That struggle is not so much about catching up with the Joneses next door as it is about adjusting to top-down constraints on maintaining or enhancing one's status. The promise of sharing power and status takes the power differentials generated by the structure of organizational society and turns them into a source of energy. Of course, decentralization is followed by recentralization. But each step in this catch-up cycle is what produces the energy for OMRT.

These OMRT are intrinsically multilevel, and the only way to understand them is to develop models depicting the dynamics of multilevel networks. These developments will be at the heart of future explorations in the social sciences. The mesosocial order and the multilevel dimension of social phenomena show that systems of superimposed interdependencies (one interorganizational, the other interindividual) create dynamics specific to each level. But because levels are partly interlocked, dynamics across levels drive each other. Drawing on Simmel's (1908/2009) ideas about social circles and Breiger's (1974) "dual" approach to the coconstitution of individuals and groups in society, sociologists have begun to look at the dynamics of multilevel structure and their consequences for societies (Lazega & Snijders, 2016).

Articulation of distinct levels of action for that purpose can be partly accounted for, beyond bipartite structures, with a method called *structural linked design*, which brings together networks of different levels by using individuals' affiliation ties, be they single or multiple (see Fig. 7.1). Statistical analyses of linked-design data (Wang, Robins, Pattison, & Lazega, 2013; 2015) show that two levels are not just superimposed but highly intertwined without being necessarily rigidly nested. That relationship implies that changes in ties at one level contribute to changes in ties at the other level even if the capacity to force changes at the other level varies with socioeconomic attributes of the actors.

At each level actors attempt to structure the contexts of their interactions and have to manage the attendant contextually imposed constraints by trying to redesign their opportunity structures. In this approach each complete network is examined separately and then combined with that of the other level by means of information about each individual's membership in the first network (interindividual) and in one of the organizations of the second network (interorganizational). Work undertaken so far within this framework has shown that dual or multiple positioning in superimposed systems of interdependencies makes it possible to formulate and test precise hypotheses about the relation between members' position in the structure and individual achievements, especially when this positional reckoning is based on

Fig. 7.1 Real life multilevel network based on a linked-design approach to studying an interindividual advice network (*bottom*), an interorganizational contract network (*top*), and vertical affiliation ties for the individuals in the organizations (Illustration by J. Brailly)

strategies of actors. Using this multilevel approach and reasoning in terms of the dynamics of these networks will help specify OMRT dynamics.

This form of dual positioning in the structural contextualization of action distinguishes between two levels of agency (one individual, the other organizational) and their coconstitution, but without conflating them. Insofar as each level constitutes a production and exchange system that has its own logic—its own division of labor and system of roles—it is important to examine the various levels separately (as is usually the case in the literature) but also jointly. Studying the levels jointly means identifying, in particular, the actors who profit from comparatively easy access to resources that circulate at each level, and it means measuring their relative achievement. The term *strategy* refers to the fact that actors manage their interdependencies at different levels by appropriating, accumulating, exchanging, and sharing resources, both with peers and with hierarchical superiors or subordinates. One observes these strategies by looking at the choices made by interindividual and interorganizational exchange partners.

In the multilevel context of this organizational society, individual actors can try to reshape their complex opportunity structure by creating new ties and languages that escape the control of the organizations with which they are affiliated. In the multilevel system actors try to take advantage of spatial and temporal gaps between different levels of agency. By doing so, they reap benefits that may prompt them to move and set up new organizations that are meant to protect access to these benefits and to hoard the new opportunities created by breaking off the constraints that had been imposed on them by their former affiliations and bosses. Under specific circumstances, ongoing interactions between interpersonal and interorganizational networks therefore bring about changes, as opposed to mere consolidation, at each level. These changes may be great enough to reconfigure the multilevel system if they drive the creation of new organizational actors (new collectives). Culture plays a substantial part in these dynamics. No collective can be set up without the language needed to formulate the conditions under which "synergy" (Archer, 2013, p. 13) is achieved and without institutionalization of its rules. The major task of culture is thus to produce the language for creating relationships with heterogeneous others and to strengthen the institutional dimension of organizations that emerge from this effort. The multilevel and cultural dimensions of collective action are the two sources of energy that coevolve with OMRT transformations and affect social processes such as collective learning.

Why would individuals willingly incur the costs of adjustments and adaptation? Answers to this question abound. People may be coerced into accepting such behavior if they are the weakest parties in the system. They may want to increase their status. Or it may be culturally and symbolically rewarding to do so. From the perspective of the individual actors, such movements (across places) and associated relational changes are part of the costs or benefits of reshaping opportunity structures, if not opportunity-hoarding, in the organizational and class society. Saying that structure reflects both opportunity and constraint is equivalent to saying that individual actors eventually try to manage the constraints in order to reshape their opportunity structure in this organizational society. The opportunities include, for example, those of landing a job, obtaining funding for a project, arranging credit for an apartment, finding a place in a suitable kindergarten or school for the children, and maintaining a steady flow of business.

Individuals trying to reshape their opportunity structure can be portrayed as strategic, but interdependent, actors who seek contexts in which they can find and exchange these resources at low cost. Once in such contexts they can seek various forms of concentration of these resources—an initial dimension of power—and thereby enable themselves to define the terms of such exchanges, to determine the rules of the game. At the individual level this set of goals is the answer to the question about the source of the energy for rotations and movements across places: It comes from efforts to close the gap between levels of agency. It comes from the competition for status.

This view calls for a contemporary definition of social class that is more complex than existing ones, for relatively invisible dimensions of opportunity structures are growing in significance at the intra- and interorganizational levels. Tilly (1998) offered such an organizational view of mechanisms that generate inequality. They are the organizational structures that allow for exploitation, entrench it, and make it seem natural. From this perspective contemporary social stratification also articulates exploitation (by the elites who hold many of the resources and much of the power in society) and opportunity-hoarding (by intermediary classes) as two complementary means for perpetuating inequality. Opportunity monopolists organize themselves legally and socially in ways far less conspicuous than the distinction between the bourgeois and the proletarians, constructing well-organized communities able to dominate the opportunities created by movement. It is not easy to see whether someone has the opportunities that others may not have. These opportunities are comparable to the very efficient implicit or informal rights, often self-granted in an organized group, that are linked to the positions in the inconspicuous relational structure (White, 1970).

Organizations, for example, help align social cleavages to create a system of inequality in which these cleavages reinforce each other, achieving exclusion and exploitation. In the monopolization of opportunities, Tilly (1998) saw the key mechanism that reproduces social inequality, joining the mesosocial level to the macrosocial level. Organizations and stratifications reinforce each other, even though the knowledge of their own opportunity structures for the individual actors is not obvious or the modality and the yield of monopolizing are not mechanical. They depend on the link-up of a long-term process at the macrolevel and the operations of local organizations with their stabilized and specific social disciplines. The starting point proposed by Tilly is a complex socioeconomic process at the heart of the neostructural approach to relations between the meso- and macrosocial levels. Neostructural sociologists can measure and model this monopolization by using social and organizational network analysis as a method that was developed for updating the various forms of conflicts and interdependencies between actors and between categories of actors.

If synchronization is necessary for the organization to benefit from the individual action of its members, especially from individual action that takes place outside the organization, creating asynchronies is sometimes what helps individuals break free. Collective action at two vertically interdependent levels of agency can thus also be a story of one level's emancipation from the influence of the other and of either catching up with that other level or creating a new emergent structure (or, more modestly, a new substructure). The lag between the two vertically interdependent levels of collective agency can be considered the main source of morphogenesis, and the generalization of lags can be seen as the cause of morphogenesis unbound: Structuration at one level drives structuration at the other in mostly conflicting, chaotic, and unequal ways. There is not always time to adjust and adapt; enormous waste and disorganization may characterize the multilevel structuration process.[9] When agents emancipate and create their own organizations, structure and culture

---

[9] Because this morphogenesis creates dynamics of multilevel networks marked by different levels of agency, a new family of models is needed to account for such dynamics. This family of models could be a multilevel extension of Snijders's (1996) model of network dynamics and could use characteristics of a level 2 network as a set of exogenous factors in the evolution of a level 1 network and vice versa. The coevolution of both level networks is added to the coevolution of behavior and relational choices. In terms of model specification, new independent variables from interorganizational networks operate at the interindividual level and vice versa. A multilevel version of Snijders's model of network dynamics could, for example, introduce dual alters or induced potentials (extended opportunity structures as defined by Lazega et al., 2013) into Snijders's formalism in order to propose concepts such as multilevel closure and to measure the effects that one level of agency has on the other.

can be brought together as status and rules by which opposing parties collaborate nevertheless. Catching up "depends upon the swift succession of positive feedback cycles…, all of which lead to new variety fostering further variety" (Archer, 2013, p. 14).

It also matters who manages to stabilize their powerful position in multilevel, OMRT systems. Analyses in the courthouse case study above show that organizational members who have enough staying capacity, status, and epistemic authority also represent specific forces in the joint regulation of markets: bankers with a law degree. The study shows that advice-seeking does converge toward central and supercentral members and reflects a process of epistemic alignment with members who have gained the authority to know, who provide social approval for specific decisions. Actors and their groups do not learn mechanically. This capacity to learn collectively depends particularly on their stability and reframing capacities in changing networks, that is, on their switching capacities across social boundaries (Breiger, 2010; White, 2008). Members with specific forms of status frame collective action by providing the judgments of appropriateness that are shared in collective learning (Lazega, 1992).

OMRT is thus based on limited transformation of the structure (examined in this chapter through the status system), which could nevertheless either be controlled homeostatically or change more profoundly. This juncture is where such transformation can, in turn, change the social processes that help members manage the problems of collective action.

Endogenizing Systems of Places: OMRT Research Agenda for Sociology and Geography

Reasoning in terms of OMRT dynamics is important because it helps one understand how stability in the system can be precisely created by the enormous quantity of movement that it organizes, directly or indirectly. New attention to OMRT dynamics is also needed because they assume new forms in contemporary society (Archer, 2013, 2014). Speed matters more than ever in everything, members are exposed to increasingly open competition as they descend through the social hierarchy, and social control has become ever more intrusive. When various sorts of mobility slow down or accelerate, new people are left behind and disenfranchised in many respects, exclusion that reproduces or creates new social inequalities and hierarchies. Actors who know how to instrumentalize organizations do better than others because they can navigate or even reshape the prior system of places. Relational capital of individuals and social capital of organizations have always been leading determinants of inequalities (Breiger, 1990, 2011). Some people's movements and mobility create and recreate the stability and wealth of other people, including the capacity of those others to acquire and capitalize resources (e.g., status) and positions (e.g., niches) in advantageous relational infrastructures. In the organizational society individuals are part of organizational systems, and organizations are part of interorganizational systems. The coevolution of the levels is not necessarily peaceful and harmonious. Synchronization entails costs of adaptation to the other level, and the costs of adjustments in dual and asynchronized opportunity structures are dumped onto the weakest parts of the system (Lazega, 2013, 2014, 2015). These costs can be measured only if one understands how OMRT dynamics shape the coevolutionary, recursive nature of the transformations they create—that is, structural emergence.

Much remains to be done to carry out this program. Changes in social mechanisms that help members of collective actors manage the problems of collective action are occurring in contexts defined more and more by OMRT dynamics and structuration derivable from residential, educational, and professional forms of mobility. Collective learning is only one of the processes that help members of society deal with these dilemmas (Glückler & Hammer, 2012, 2014; Lazega, 2012). The capacity of societies to adapt to changes and environments that they themselves have brought about depends on their OMRT dynamics.

In addition, this chapter's exclusive emphasis on status as a relational infrastructure of vertical differentiation is due only to lack of space. Other such social forms, such as horizontally discrete social niches and systems of niches, can be regarded as linchpins between OMRT and collective action. They represent forms of the social division of labor in all socially organized contexts, with their multilevel and superimposed role systems. Social niches in their system of niches are among the relational infrastructures that precondition social processes such as solidarity and social control. They are part of the definition of the initial system of places across which mobility takes place to begin with. Niches and status alike are forms by which socially rational actors seek to structure the contexts of their interactions and their social and economic exchanges. If the changes in the system of places itself are interpreted as OMRT driven and as the ultimate expression of domination, then places will no longer be regarded as exclusively exogenous entities in the social sciences but rather as coevolutionary detrminants and outcome of social processes.

It is fundamental to understand that the links between interdependent processes also have an effect on the relational infrastructures reconstituted by the observer and endogenized by the actors. These effects lie at the origin of the dynamics of relational structures: New rules can reconfigure a system of niches; exercise of social control can encourage the emergence of new forms of social status and modify principles of status consistency. In turn, the new processes that result from these changes facilitate new modes of coordination. To improve the understanding of what agency means in this interpersonal, interorganizational, and dynamic context, neostructural sociologists must still develop methods that combine the systematic study of longitudinal and multilevel data on identities, trajectories (in the long term), exchange networks, and representations (or controversies). The fact that new rules can reconfigure a system of places is not obvious. Orthodox structuralists have challenged such statements (Pizarro, 1999, 2007). It is on this point that sociologists, geographers, and historians need to collaborate when pursuing the joint research agenda of tracking OMRT and their effects on collective action.

Indeed, it may be that the social sciences are able to treat these systems of places, these forms of the division of labor, as endogenous only with the assistance of geographers or other specialists on spatial and organizational movement (Bathelt & Glückler, 2011; Glückler, 2012, 2013). Geographers become crucial in the description and modeling of OMRT dynamics of all kinds because the social reality that such researchers observe is spatial, organizational, relational, multilevel, and dynamic. Contemporary public statistical datasets are ill suited for this purpose and for the measurement of OMRT dynamics in interaction with social stratification in the organizational society. Geographers and sociologists can design joint research projects on residents switching neighborhoods (e.g., Lévy, 1998), people migrating from countryside to the city and back (Lemercier & Rosental, 2008), entire populations making an exodus from one continent to the other, and the changes occurring at the meso- and macrolevels because of such movements. Much of what happens in social life at meso and macro levels combined is OMRT-related phenomena characterized by the dynamics of multilevel structures where relational infrastructures necessarily function as gears driving evolution. They can be reconstituted in all areas of social life provided that a longitudinal perspective articulates coevolutionary changes across places (mobility) and in relationships (networks). Neostructural sociologists argue that social change at the mesolevel must be examined process by process at each level of agency (interindividual or interorganizational). To describe and analyze these systems adequately, the challenge is in observing and reconstructing these combined dynamics in interdisciplinary collaboration conceived to make sense of vast amounts of heterogeneous data gathered on various scales. That work will provide the framework for building a general theoretical approach to such OMRT phenomena with up- and down-stream effects.

Mapping and modeling OMRT is how geographers and sociologists can account for the link between the meso- and macrolevels, indeed for the way in which mesolevel actors build the macrolevel. Therefore, their function in documenting and explaining social change is to explore these OMRT dynamics at multiple levels simultaneously. These modalities are the ways in which actors manage the multilevel dimension of their society, moving (or not) from one level to the other and organizing these adjustments and their costs. As shown in analyses of regulation and governance, such exploration can yield a theory of action to guide dynamic, multilevel modeling and, eventually, to afford a fresh look at politics. In this respect much remains to accomplish.

Acknowledgment I thank David Antal, Julien Brailly, Johannes Glückler, and Andreas Kalström for very helpful suggestions. Support for writing this chapter was provided by Sorbonne Paris-Cité as part of the program *Dynamique des réseaux multiniveaux* (DYREM).

References

Archer, M. S. (1988). *Culture and agency*. Cambridge, UK: Cambridge University Press.
Archer, M. S. (Ed.). (2013). *Social morphogenesis*. Studies in Social Morphogenesis: Vol. 1. Dordrecht: Springer.
Archer, M. S. (Ed.). (2014). *Late modernity: Trajectories towards morphogenic society*. Studies in Social Morphogenesis: Vol. 2. Dordrecht: Springer.
Bathelt, H., & Glückler, J. (2011). *The relational economy: Geographies of knowing and learning*. Oxford: University Press.
Blau, P. M. (1955). *The dynamics of bureaucracy*. Chicago: University of Chicago Press.
Blau, P. M. (1964). *Exchange and power in social life*. New York: John Wiley & Sons.
Brailly, J., Favre, G., Chatellet, J., & Lazega, E. (2015). Embeddedness as a multilevel problem: A case study in economic sociology, *Social Networks*. Advance online publication. http://dx.doi.org/10.1016/j.socnet.2015.03.005
Breiger, R. L. (1974). The duality of persons and groups. *Social Forces, 53*, 181–190. doi:10.2307/2576011
Breiger, R. L. (1990). *Social mobility and social structure*. Cambridge, UK: University Press.
Breiger, R. L. (2010). Dualities of culture and structure: Seeing through cultural holes. In J. Fuhse & S. Mützel (Eds.), *Relationale Soziologie. Zur kulturellen Wende der Netzwerkforschung* (pp. 37–47). Dordrecht: Springer.
Breiger, R. L. (2011). Some challenges in multilevel social network research. Keynote address at the Conference on Research on the Organizational Society: Advances in Multilevel and Dynamic Network Analysis, Observatoire des Réseaux Intra- et Inter-Orgaisationnels (ORIO), Dauphine, France.
Frank, R. H. (1985). *Choosing the right pond: Human behavior and the quest for status*. Oxford: University Press.
Glückler, J. (2012). Organisierte Unternehmensnetzwerke: Eine Einführung [Introduction to organized corporate networks]. In J. Glückler, W. Dehning, M. Janneck, & T. Armbrüster (Eds.), *Unternehmensnetzwerke. Architekturen, Strukturen und Strategien* (pp. 1–18). Heidelberg: Springer Gabler.
Glückler, J. (2013). The problem of mobilizing expertise at a distance. In P. Meusburger, J. Glückler, & M. el Meskioui (Eds.), *Knowledge and the economy* (pp. 95–109). Knowledge and Space: Vol. 5. Dordrecht: Springer.
Glückler, J., & Hammer, I. (2012). Multilaterale Kooperation und Netzwerkgüter [Multilateral cooperation and network goods]. In J. Glückler, W. Dehning, M. Janneck, & T. Armbrüster (Eds.), *Unternehmensnetzwerke. Architekturen, Strukturen und Strategien* (pp. 139–162). Heidelberg: Springer Gabler.
Glückler, J., & Hammer, I. (2014). Organized networks and the creation of network goods. Unpublished manuscript, Department of Geography, University of Heidelberg, Germany.
Hughes, E. C. (1945). Dilemmas and contradictions of status. *American Journal of Sociology, 50*, 353–359. Retrieved from http://www.jstor.org/stable/2771188
Kane, A. A., Argote, L., & Levine, J. M. (2005). Knowledge transfer between groups via personnel rotation: Effects of social identity and knowledge quality. *Organizational Behavior and Human Decision Processes, 96*, 56–71. doi:10.1016/j.obhdp.2004.09.002
Krackhardt, D. (1990). Assessing the political landscape: Structure, cognition, and power in organizations. *Administrative Science Quarterly, 35*, 342–369. doi:10.2307/2393394
Larsson, R., Bengtsson, L., Henriksson, K., & Sparks, J. (1998). The interorganizational learning dilemma: Collective knowledge development in strategic alliances. *Organization Science, 9*, 285–305. http://dx.doi.org/10.1287/orsc.9.3.285
Lazega, E. (1992). *Micropolitics of knowledge: Communication and indirect control in workgroups*. New York: Aldine–de Gruyter.

Lazega, E. (2001). *The collegial phenomenon: The social mechanisms of cooperation among peers in a corporate law partnership.* Oxford: University Press.

Lazega, E. (2003). Rationalité, discipline sociale et structure [Rationality, social discipline, and structure]. *Revue Française de Sociologie, 44,* 305–329. doi:10.3917/rfs.442.0305

Lazega, E. (2009). Cooperation among competitors: Its social networks through network analyses. *SocioLogica [Italian Journal of Sociology Online, 1].* doi:10.2383/29560. With comments by L. Burroni, S. Mützel, & H. C. White: http://www.sociologica.mulino.it/journal/issue/index/Issue/Journal:ISSUE:7

Lazega, E. (2011). Four and half centuries of new (new) law and economics: Legal pragmatism, discreet joint regulation and institutional capture at the Commercial Court of Paris. In U. de Vries & L. Francot-Timmermans (Eds.), *Law's environment: Critical legal perspectives* (pp. 179–204). The Hague: Eleven International Publishing.

Lazega, E. (2012). Sociologie néo-structurale [Neostructural sociology]. In R. Keucheyan & G. Bronner (Eds.), *Introduction à la théorie sociale contemporaine* (pp. 113–130). Paris: Presses Universitaires de France.

Lazega, E. (2013). Network analysis and morphogenesis: A neo-structural exploration and illustration. In M. S. Archer (Ed.), *Social morphogenesis* (pp. 167–186). Studies in Social Morphogenesis: Vol. 1. Dordrecht: Springer.

Lazega, E. (2014). Morphogenesis unbound from the dynamics of multilevel networks: A neo-structural perspective. In M. S. Archer (Ed.), *Late modernity: Trajectories towards morphogenic society* (pp. 173–191). Studies in Social Morphogenesis: Vol. 2. Dordrecht: Springer.

Lazega, E. (2015). Body captors and network profiles: A neo-structural note on digitalized social control and morphogenesis. In M. S. Archer (Ed.), *Generative mechanisms transforming the social order* (pp. 113–133). Studies in Social Morphogenesis: Vol. 3. Dordrecht: Springer.

Lazega, E., & Favereau, O. (2002). Introduction. In O. Favereau & E. Lazega (Eds.), *Conventions and structures in economic organization: Markets, networks, and hierarchies* (pp. 1–28). Cheltenham: Edward Elgar.

Lazega, E., Jourda, M.-T., & Mounier, L. (2013). Network lift from dual alters: Extended opportunity structures from a multilevel and structural perspective. *European Sociological Review, 29,* 1226–1238. doi:10.1093/esr/jct002

Lazega, E., & Snijders, T. A. B. (Eds.). (2016). *Multilevel network analysis for the social sciences: Theory, methods and applications* (Methodos series). Dordrecht: Springer.

Lazega, E., Jourda, M.-T., Mounier, L., & Stofer, R. (2008). Catching up with big fish in the big pond? Multi-level network analysis through linked design. *Social Networks, 30,* 159–176. http://dx.doi.org/10.1016/j.socnet.2008.02.001

Lazega, E., Lemercier, C., & Mounier, L. (2006). A spinning top model of formal structure and informal behavior: Dynamics of advice networks among judges in a commercial court. *European Management Review, 3,* 113–122. doi:10.1057/palgrave.emr.1500058

Lazega, E., & Mounier, L. (2002). Interdependent entrepreneurs and the social discipline of their cooperation: The research program of structural economic sociology for a society of organizations. In O. Favereau & E. Lazega (Eds.), *Conventions and structures in economic organization: Markets, networks, and Hierarchies* (pp. 147–199). Cheltenham, Edward Elgar.

Lazega, E., & Mounier, L. (2009). Polynormativité et contrôle social du monde des affaires: le exemple de l'interventionnisme et de la punitivité des juges du Tribunal de Commerce de Paris [Polynormativity and social control in the business world: Judges' interventionism and punitivity at the Paris Commercial Court]. *Droit et Société, 71,* 103–132. Retrieved from http://basepub.dauphine.fr/xmlui/bitstream/handle/123456789/4594/Polynormativite.PDF?sequence=2

Lazega, E., & Mounier, L. (2012). Networks of institutional capture. In B. Vedres & M. Scotti (Eds.), *Networks in social policy problems* (pp. 124–137). Cambridge, UK: University Press.

Lazega, E., Mounier, L., Snijders, T. A. B., & Tubaro, P. (2012). Norms, status and the dynamics of advice networks. *Social Networks, 34,* 323–332. doi:10.1016/j.socnet.2009.12.001

Lazega, E., & Pattison, P. E. (1999). Multiplexity, generalized exchange and cooperation in organizations: A case study. *Social Networks, 21,* 67–90. doi:10.1016/S0378-8733(99)00002-7

Lazega, E., Sapulete, S., & Mounier, L. (2011). Structural stability regardless of membership turnover? The added value of blockmodelling in the analysis of network evolution. *Quality & Quantity, 45,* 129–144. doi:10.1007/s11135-009-9295-y

Lazega, E., & van Duijn, M. (1997). Position in formal structure, personal characteristics and choices of advisors in a law firm: A logistic regression model for dyadic network data. *Social Networks, 19,* 375–397. http://dx.doi.org/10.1016/S0378-8733(97)00006-3

Lemercier, C., & Rosental, P.-A. (2008, September). Les migrations dans le Nord de la France au XIXe siècle. Nouvelles approches, nouvelles techniques en analyse des réseaux sociaux [Migrations in northern France in the nineteenth century: New approaches, new techniques in analysis of social networks]. Lille, France. Retrieved from https://halshs.archives-ouvertes.fr/halshs-00319448

Lenski, G. E. (1954). Status crystallization: A non-vertical dimension of social status. *American Sociological Review, 19,* 405–413. Retrieved from http://www.jstor.org/stable/2087459

Lévy, J.-P. (1998). Dynamiques du peuplement résidentiel [Dynamics of residential settlement]. *Sociétés Contemporaines, 29,* 43–72.

March, J. G., & Simon, H. A. (1958). *Organizations.* New York: John Wiley & Sons.

Merton, R. K. (1957). *Social theory and social structure* (2nd ed.). New York: Free Press.

Merton, R. K. (1968). The Matthew effect in science. *Science, 159,* 56–63. doi:10.1126/science.159.3810.56

Ortega, J. (2001). Job rotation as a learning mechanism. *Management Science, 47,* 1361–1370. doi:10.12.87/mnsc.47.10.1361.10257

Perrow, C. (1991). A society of organizations. *Theory and Society, 20,* 725–762. doi:10.1007/BF00678095

Pizarro, N. (1999). Appartenances, places et réseaux de places. La reproduction des processus sociaux et la génération d'un espace homogène pour la définition des structures sociales [Appearance, places, and network places: The reproduction of social processes and the generation of a homogeneous space for the definition of social structures]. *Sociologie et Societies, 31,* 143–161. doi:10.7202/001568ar

Pizarro, N. (2007). Structural identity and equivalence of individuals in social networks, beyond duality. *International Sociology, 22,* 767–792. doi:10.1177/0268580907082260

Selznick, P. (1949). *TVA and the grassroots: A study in the sociology of formal organization.* Berkeley: University of California Press.

Simmel, G. (2009). *Inquiries into the construction of social forms* (A. J. Blasi, A. K. Jacobs, & M. Kanjirathinkal, Eds. & Trans., with an introduction by H. J. Helle). 2 Vols. Leiden: Brill. (Original work published 1908)

Snijders, T. A. B. (1996). Stochastic actor-oriented models for network change. *Journal of Mathematical Sociology, 21,* 149–172. doi:10.1080/0022250X.1996.9990178

Snijders, T. A. B. (2005). Models for longitudinal network data. In P. J. Carrington, J. Scott, & S. Wasserman (Eds.), *Models and methods in social network analysis* (pp. 215–247). Cambridge, UK: University Press.

Tilly, C. (1998). *Durable inequality.* Berkeley: University of California Press.

Wang, P., Robins, G., Pattison, P., & Lazega, E. (2013). Exponential random graph models for multilevel networks. *Social Networks, 35,* 96–115. doi:10.1016/j.socnet.2013.01.004

Wang, P., Robins, G., Pattison, P., & Lazega, E. (2015). Social selection models for multilevel networks. *Social Networks.* Advance online publication. http://dx.doi.org/10.1016/j.socnet.2014.12.00

Weber, M. (1924). *Gesammelte Aufsätze zur Soziologie und Sozialpolitik* [Collected essays on sociology and social policy]. Tübingen: J. C. B. Mohr.

White, H. C. (1970). *Chains of opportunity: System models of mobility in organizations.* Cambridge, MA: Harvard University Press.

White, H. C. (2008). *Identity and control: How social formations emerge* (2nd ed.). Princeton: University Press.

White, H. C., Boorman, S. A., & Breiger, R. L. (1976). Social structure from multiple networks, In: Blockmodels of roles and positions. *American Journal of Sociology, 81,* 730–780.

Open Access This chapter is distributed under the terms of the Creative Commons Attribution 4.0 International License (http://creativecommons.org/licenses/by/4.0/), which permits use, duplication, adaptation, distribution and reproduction in any medium or format, as long as you give appropriate credit to the original author(s) and the source, provide a link to the Creative Commons license and indicate if changes were made.

The images or other third party material in this chapter are included in the work's Creative Commons license, unless indicated otherwise in the credit line; if such material is not included in the work's Creative Commons license and the respective action is not permitted by statutory regulation, users will need to obtain permission from the license holder to duplicate, adapt or reproduce the material.

Chapter 8
Trajectory Types Across Network Positions: Jazz Evolution from 1930 to 1969

Charles Kirschbaum

The study of organizational fields has been prevalent throughout organizational studies, strategic management, economic sociology and economic geography. The *field construct* has emerged as a powerful analytical concept that affords a holistic view of a social system. In this chapter, I espouse the idea that a field is a social space that encloses the main aspects of certain actors' institutional lives, and where the field's actors interact with each other in a more intensive way compared to their interactions with outside actors (DiMaggio & Powell, 1983). Specifically, the jazz field includes musicians, critics, schools, magazines, and so on. Its formal and informal institutions include, inter alia, how music is constructed and interpreted, as well as the main practices in recruiting musicians for recording sessions. Its interactions include, inter alia, relational events such as playing together in jam sessions or in studios.

Throughout this chapter, my concern is to contribute to the literature of field dynamics. In particular, I explore the transition from a normative to a competitive configuration (Anand & Peterson, 2000). In a normative field, social action is usually driven by rule-following, with these norms being enacted by central and dominant players. In competitive fields, by contrast, central actors dominate other actors, too, but norm-following does not rely on rule enforcement. Softer power, such as influence, becomes much more prevalent in competitive fields.

To be sure, both these field ideal types evoke the core-and-periphery framework, as though such a structure could be taken for granted. However, a closer inspection of the concrete historical process that leads from one ideal type to another can shed light on whether such a structure remains the same and indicate the extent to which topological changes during the process constitute main events and turning points. This examination may reveal that a core-periphery structure looks very similar in

---

C. Kirschbaum (✉)
Insper Instituto de Ensino e Pesquisa,
Rua Quatá 300, Vila Olímpia 04546042, São Paulo, Brazil
e-mail: charlesk1@insper.edu.br

© The Author(s) 2017
J. Glückler et al. (eds.), *Knowledge and Networks*, Knowledge and Space 11,
DOI 10.1007/978-3-319-45023-0_8

both ideal types, although the core is fragmented and rearranged in the course of the process.

Although this macro-topological investigation is itself important to understanding field dynamics, I claim in this chapter that it is necessary to add the actor's trajectory into the analysis. If a field migrates from a normative logic toward a competitive one, what happens to the members of the incumbent elite? Assuming that they are able to sustain their dominant position through coercion or by hoarding key resources in the field, what is their fate as the field migrates to a competitive logic? Are they displaced and expelled? Or are they able to reconnect?

The goal of this paper is to address these lines of inquiry by using of the coevolutionary and network perspectives, taking as an example the evolution of jazz musicians' trajectories from 1930 to 1969. I begin by exploring the structural changes in the jazz field during those almost four decades. I have also obtained a blockmodeling image of musicians' networks throughout this period in order to understand how musicians associated with different trajectories were positioned vis-à-vis each other. The jazz case provides a rich context for understanding the shift between types of field configurations given the transformations it experienced during these decades and the correspondent impact on musicians' trajectories (Kirschbaum, 2007). Furthermore, the geographic location of recording sessions became less centralized in New York (specifically) and the United States (in general). Results shown later in the chapter suggest that competitive fields present a lower distinction between core and periphery than do normative fields. Increasing centrifugal forces causes a paradigm crisis. As a result, although a new elite emerges and become central, members of the former elite eventually play the role of brokers when younger musicians become distant from each other.

Normative and Competitive Field Structures

Anand and Peterson (2000) and Peterson and Anand (2002) identify two kinds of organizational fields: normative and competitive.[1] Within normative fields, individuals are driven mainly by norms established by dominant authoritative actors. Central players dominate peripheral actors by controlling the field's main resources and *schemata*.[2] It is unsurprising, therefore, that innovations are usually introduced top-down, relatively buffered from competitive pressures. Along these lines, a classical example of a normative field is described by DiMaggio's (1991) research on U.S. art museums that shows central players sanctioning the field's norms.

---

[1] Fields are defined as "a community of organizations that partakes a common meaning system and whose participants interact more frequently and fatefully with one another than with actors outside the field" (Scott, 1995, p. 56).

[2] A schema is defined as "the set of shared assumptions, values, and frames of reference that give meaning to everyday activities and guide how organization members think and act" (Rerup & Feldman, 2011, p. 578).

In contrast, individuals in competitive fields are less constrained by normative rules and driven more by competitive forces. In contrast to action driven by normative rules established by authority, action impelled by competitive forces registers a balance between innovation and imitation (Anand & Peterson, 2000). Leblebici, Salancik, Copay, & King (1991) provide the example of the transformation of the radio broadcasting industry in the United States, showing that most innovations were introduced by peripheral actors.

Both these ideal-type depictions of a field evoke a core-periphery network topology. But while innovations within normative fields are first adopted at their core, in competitive fields they are initially created and adopted on the periphery. Nevertheless, in both depictions it is assumed that the overall core-periphery structure remains the same, or that changes are too subtle to be accounted for. Undoubtedly it is possible to envisage distinct mechanisms in play that help generate equivalent core-periphery structures. Within normative fields, dominant actors are assumed to use their power to remain at the core of the field. Conversely, new musicians entering the field are attracted to established players, a process that creates an asymmetric structure (Barabási, 2003). Because individuals prefer to connect to prominent actors who control key resources, peripheral actors will connect more frequently to core actors than with each other. As a result, a core-periphery structure emerges in which the field is dominated by a cohesive core that is surrounded by a fragmented periphery.

Alternative mechanisms may also work to generate an equivalent core-periphery structure in competitive fields. Although core actors cannot simply coerce peripheral actors to follow standards and rules, they may be able to exert influence. This occurs because central actors have better access to information (Lena & Pachucki, 2013). Furthermore, peripheral actors may still attempt to connect to core actors in order to associate with high-status musicians (Podolny, 2001).

In spite of this apparently similar outcome in competitive and normative fields, it can be asked whether the asymmetry between core and periphery is actually the same. While most resources in normative fields are controlled by core actors, in competitive fields resources are more freely allocated among musicians. To illustrate this distinction, it is useful to look at a recording session in these different settings. In the normative phase of the jazz field, bandleaders are usually hired by recording companies under long-term contracts. This situation gives bandleaders considerable powers of discretion to employ sidemen of their choosing for the planned recording sessions. In the competitive phase of the jazz field, by contrast, musicians do not have long-term contracts with recording companies (Perrow, 1986). Although the latter approach represents an instability factor, it also encourages a musician to constitute a band by inviting sidemen to play together, with lower production costs making it possible for them to record samples to send to recording companies. The combination of the centripetal tendency (new musicians continuing to look to play with core actors) with the centrifugal force (cheap production and distribution costs enabling higher levels of entrepreneurship activity) can result in a core-periphery structure in which peripheral actors may present higher cohesion among themselves than is seen in a normative configuration's structure. This discussion leads me to investigate the following aspects underlying normative and competitive fields: Is there a core-periphery structure within both normative and competitive fields? Are these structures distinct from each other? What can be learned from the process of transition from one configuration to another?

So far I have explored the macro-topological structure of competitive and normative fields. In the next section, I explore the musicians' trajectories as an analytical dimension additional to the topological.

Networked Trajectories

Most analyses of field structure rely on topological descriptions. In each cross-sectional analysis (or temporal *slice*), individuals are aggregated into positions. Rarely is an individual's history in the field preserved. The best way to illustrate this problem is by evoking a *Markovian* world. In a Markov chain approach, social systems are modeled as if trajectory were meaningless. Hence, if individuals are allocated to a position (whether core or periphery) at a given point in time, it does not matter where they were before that point. While this kind of approach simplifies the analysis, it generates several problems. First, it assumes that those individuals have no memory, and that their past experience is entirely subsumed in their present location. Second, from a relational point-of-view, it assumes that other individuals will be indifferent to one's trajectory, without any consideration of reputation, pedigree, and other biographical factors.[3]

In contrast, the existing literature has shown that trajectory is an important construct because it reveals how similar outcomes are attained through different processes among, for instance, firms (Stark & Vedres, 2006), poets (Dubois & François, 2013), or painters (Accominotti, 2009). Moreover, I argue that individual trajectories do indeed matter and that these are best understood as embedded in the field's historical evolution (Bourdieu, 1993; Giuffre, 1999).

In order to illustrate this idea, I take the example of a normative field, which is typically characterized by stable stylistic rules enacted by dominant players. One possible career track is the *elite* trajectory, represented by individuals who attain centrality in the field and who remain in central positions for a long period of time. On the other hand, there may be individuals who stay on the periphery but are able to survive in the field for a long time as well. Finally, some musicians might stay in the field only for a short time, limited to the periphery. One important line of inquiry is studying how dominant players interact with individuals from other trajectories. Do elite trajectory individuals relate only among themselves? If *wanna-be* trajectory musicians (short-lived and peripheral) attempt to break into the field, in what circumstances are they able to play with elite musicians? In normative fields, one

---

[3] A third point could be added to this list: The sequence of events does not matter (Abbott, 2001). I do not explore this third point in this chapter because it would require an approach similar to sequence analysis.

can envisage a social system in which tiers of players relate to each other. Dominant musicians (with a high centrality and a long period in the field) recruit musicians from a surrounding tier (mid-periphery players, with long periods in the field). The latter, in turn, recruit players, but having fewer opportunities than dominant players, they are only able to secure shorter-duration performance gigs for their recruits. As a result, some of these more peripheral sidemen will have to leave the field to earn an adequate income from other sources.

By contrast, when a field migrates from a normative to a competitive configuration, new elites challenge previous ones in order to establish new paradigms. From this perspective, artists who start their trajectory as avant-garde challengers to the established artistic idiom strive for recognition among peers and critics. If this recognition is granted, these individuals are likely to attain a dominant position in the field (Bourdieu, 1993, 1996). What effect does this type of disruption have on the fate of individual trajectories? Taking trajectory as a key analytical concept again, how do individuals with different trajectories relate to each other?

If all that is being observed is a turning point, whereby one paradigm is displaced by another (i.e., the field remains normative and only a change of stylistic paradigm occurs), then it could be suggested that an established elite is replaced by a new one. Concretely speaking, the new elite would have strong presence at the field's core and also demonstrate a long period in the field, like the previous elite. Nonetheless, distinct apex moments may be found from one generation to the next.

However, when a field migrates from a normative to a competitive configuration, dominant actors are less able to maintain hegemony, and new elites displace existing ones over shorter temporal cycles. As a consequence, musicians with a history of presence at the field's core may also present shorter permanence in the dominant position. But what happens to the "fallen" elite? Do they become obsolete, as though musicians were similar to technologically outdated pieces of machinery? Are they able to reconnect with other musicians outside of the new elite? Displaced musicians might be compelled to play with peripheral musicians. If so, it should be possible to observe a higher level of social intercourse between musicians from different trajectories in competitive fields. This discussion leads me to ask how competitive fields impact the length of musicians' occupation of dominant positions.

The main goal of this preliminary discussion is to identify the initial challenges to understanding the evolution of a field vis-à-vis its embedded trajectories, while evoking a set of basic building blocks in order to construct its narrative.

Data Collection

Source of Relational Data

Musicians establish various types of relationships, from friendships to romantic affairs, in contexts ranging from joint session recordings to non-recorded jam sessions. Innovations can, of course, emerge as a result of all of these interactions. Nonetheless,

I focus on one specific kind of relationship: joint session recordings. In joint session recordings, musicians are in their closest contact with the commercial side of the jazz art world, and their final product success has a direct impact on their trajectories. To gather the album data, I consulted the Crazy Jazz website. Crazy Jazz is a compact disk (CD) seller specializing in jazz titles. The universe of music albums at Crazy Jazz comprises 5572 LPs (long play albums records) produced between 1930 and 1969.[4]

The ideal would be to consider only those titles that reflect original recording sessions as relational data. However, many of the titles available are collections and compilations that could interfere with an accurate interpretation. Collection titles could establish relationships that did not exist (e.g., the compilation *All Star Swing Players* could wrongly link Benny Goodman to Duke Ellington). On the other hand, compilations may cover a lengthy period of the artist's production and include changes of style, making it difficult to identify when relationships with other players were established, and when the artist in question developed a certain style (e.g., Dizzy Gillespie's biography could mistakenly relate swing to Afro-Cuban jazz).

In order to minimize these effects, I eliminated collection albums from the database. Nonetheless, I could not simply eliminate compilation albums, because several titles were originally released individually as singles and later reissued on compilation CDs. As a solution, I limited compilations to a maximum 5-year range, taking the release year as the initial year of the period covered.[5]

Preparation of the Network

From the information taken from the LPs and their featured artists, I built three preliminary databases: a list of musicians, a list of LPs, and a list of relationships between LPs and musicians.

The LP database was divided into 85-year periods: 1930–1934, 1935–1939, 1940–1944, 1945–1949, 1950–1954, 1955–1959, 1960–1964, and 1965–1969. For each period, I counted the number of titles recorded by all pairs of musicians. In order to build the database of ties, I considered only those pairs that had at least two titles recorded in common. Next, I dichotomized all relationships without considering the strength of the tie. Table 8.1 shows descriptive statistics for each period's network.

---

[4] It is worth highlighting the consequences of building this database using currently available commercial data as its main source. The first consequence is that I have had to rely on Crazy Jazz's criteria when it comes to defining what is relevant. In terms of revenues, low-selling albums might not be included, although they may well have reflected important relationships at their time. Additionally, Crazy Jazz's commercial classification of what jazz is may differ substantially from the viewpoints of other members of the jazz community. These sampling constraints underline the exploratory status of this paper. See DiMaggio (1987) on classification problems in art, as well as proposed solutions using network analysis.

[5] In future investigations I intend to turn to a direct analysis of recording sessions in order to eliminate the distortions I experienced with the LP titles.

8 Trajectory Types Across Network Positions: Jazz Evolution from 1930 to 1969

Table 8.1 Descriptive Statistics for the Jazz Field from 1930 to 1969

Statistic	Periods							
	1930–1934	1935–1939	1940–1944	1945–1949	1950–1954	1955–1959	1960–1964	1965–1969
Group size	449	959	939	1338	1217	1822	1739	1543
Density	0.0239	0.0143	0.0144	0.0103	0.0102	0.0076	0.0069	0.0066
Normalized average degree	2.392	1.426	1.438	1.031	1.018	0.758	0.758	0.656
Normalized degree variance	3.906	2.175	2.055	1.089	0.941	0.755	0.755	0.375
Normalized average betweenness	0.536	0.211	0.213	0.173	0.218	0.129	0.129	0.195

Analytical Strategy

Classifying Trajectories

My first concern was to gain an understanding of different trajectory types by examining relevant factors. I selected three aspects: lifespan, average betweenness centrality, and the number of periods of membership in the network's core. In this section I explore each of these dimensions in turn.

Probably the most critical indication of an artist's success is the ability to earn an adequate income in the chosen artistic field. Zuckerman, Kim, Ukanwa, and Rittman (2003) show how novice film actors frequently submit themselves to typecasting in order to establish a foothold in the industry. Even if an artist is able to enter the industry, survival is never entirely guaranteed, because fads and shifts in fashion can impact an artist's fate (Hirsch, 1972/2011). Hence, one's lifespan is a measure of success in a networked industry.

Better connections with other players increase the likelihood of an artist being able to exploit resources. On the other hand, higher coupling to the industry structure can constrain the artist's action and creativity. Nonetheless, more resources and information generally increase the odds of an artist being employed in the most attractive opportunities (Granovetter, 1973/2011). The method I chose to measure the resources available to an individual was to calculate the average *betweenness centrality* across his or her lifespan in the field because it indicates the extent to which an actor functions as a broker for a network's paths (Hanneman, 2001).

Kadushin (2004) observes that the stability of a field can be grasped by the composition of a network's core. A polarized core can trigger social changes. Core membership empowers its holders to influence a field's rules. Core members are able to establish a consensus among different actors. Conversely, membership in the core provides the opportunity to disrupt the current consensus and to fight to establish new rules. It can be asked whether membership in a network's core does not automatically entail a high betweenness centrality, making dimensions such as betweenness and core membership redundant. This correlation would be high for *star* networks in which the center is occupied by a single member and all peripheral actors are connected only to the center. In more decentralized networks, peripheral actors might control critical resources despite their positions. Conversely, novice actors might have a very early opportunity to develop a project with a core actor. In doing so, they would become central actors as well. However, if their only connection is to their "godfather" at the core, they have relatively less freedom of action than better connected peripheral actors.

I performed a K-means cluster analysis using the variables *average betweenness centrality, lifespan (periods),* and *number of periods at the core* to obtain six clusters of musicians (see Table 8.2). The limitation of the period of analysis to the years 1930–1969 resulted in left and right censoring effects, given that it therefore did not encompass the entire history of jazz. For instance, the trajectory of a musician that began in 1925 would have a longer lifespan than the trajectory captured in my analysis. In order to mitigate left and right censoring effects, I excluded from the trajec-

Table 8.2 K-means cluster analysis of trajectories

Key trajectory variables	Cluster					
	1	2	3	4	5	6
Average betweenness centrality	0.29	0.03	0.98	0.52	2.80	0.13
Lifespan (periods)	6.55	1.16	6.63	3.88	6.40	3.69
Number of periods at the core	0.70	0.02	3.89	2.26	1.80	0.21
Number of individuals	180	3614	71	128	5	725

tory analysis those musicians who consistently had decreasingly betweenness centrality as of period one, and those who had consistently increasing betweenness centrality up to period eight. I included these in the Clusters 7 and 8, respectively (see Table 8.2 for the number of musicians in each cluster). Looking at Table 8.2, one can distinguish different types of trajectories and propose some tentative classifications:

Cluster 1: *Ivory Tower*. Cluster 1 presents the second longest lifespan (6.55 periods); however, it has a low presence in the core (0.7) and average betweenness is only 0.29. This suggests a group of musicians who are able to sustain themselves in the network, but have limited involvement with both the core and with other musicians. Examples of musicians in this cluster are Duke Ellington and Ella Fitzgerald.

Cluster 2: *Wanna-be*. Musicians in Cluster 2 present the lowest betweenness average (0.03), lowest lifespan (1.16), and lowest membership in the core (0.02). Unsurprisingly, it is also the largest cluster, with 3614 musicians. This is the typical fate of novice musicians: After a few appearances and slammed doors, they choose to leave the industry.

Cluster 3: *Elite*. This cluster has the longest average lifespan (6.63 periods) and the highest presence at the core (3.89 periods). It also has the second highest average betweenness centrality. I labeled the musicians "elite" because of their low number (only 73 musicians), their long presence in the network, and high core presence. Examples of musicians in this cluster are Dizzy Gillespie, Louis Armstrong, Miles Davis, and Stan Getz. Cluster 4: *Shooting Stars*. Members of this cluster have half the *Elite*'s average betweenness (0.52) and medium lifespan (3.88). However, they have the second highest core membership (2.26), higher than those in the *Ivory Tower* cluster, who presented a longer time in the network. This suggests that members of *Shooting Stars*, though able to remain at the core for a significant portion of their lifespan (almost 60% of their lives), are unable to maintain their positions for as long as *Elite* musicians. Remarkable examples of *Shooting Stars* are Charlie Parker and Artie Shaw, both of whose trajectories ended prematurely.

Cluster 5: *Ivy League*. There are only a handful of members (five) in this cluster. However, they share some interesting characteristics with other trajectory types. Like their *Ivory Tower* and *Elite* colleagues, they have a long lifespan (6.4) and a medium level of membership in the core (1.8), but the highest average betweenness centrality. It is worth mentioning them by name: Benny Goodman, Henry "Red" Allen, Sidney Bechet, Don Byas, and Woody Herman. These are founders of swing music who were able to survive in the network. In contrast to Louis Armstrong, who knew how to reposition himself at the core, these players remained on the outskirts of the core. Although not always in the core spotlight, recording with these players was just as coveted as playing with *Elite* musicians.

Cluster 6: *Up-Starters*. This is the second largest group (725 musicians), with an average lifespan similar to *Shooting Stars*. However, their average betweenness and membership in the core are low (0.13 and 0.21, respectively), higher only than the *Wanna-be* cluster. I identified important musicians in this cluster, including the likes of Dave Brubeck and Quincy Jones. Nonetheless, this may indicate that musicians who were commercially successful were not necessarily active at the core of the jazz community during their heyday.

I would like to point out some potential issues with the *Elite* and *Shooting Stars* clusters. Both groups spent an average 60% of their lifespans in the core, a statistic that suggests the existence of different generations. Failure to distinguish between generations might lead to poorer comprehension of the trajectory of different musicians. For this reason, I split these two clusters into two generations using a 2-mode faction search. The *Elite* first generation spans from 1930 to 1944 (Cluster 31), while the second generation spans from 1945 to 1969 (Cluster 32). The *Shooting Star* first generation runs from 1930 to 1949 (Cluster 41), while the second generation runs from 1950 to 1969 (Cluster 42). See Table 8.3 for descriptive statistics on these new clusters. Table 8.4 summarizes the evolution of musicians by each trajectory type.

Blockmodeling the Jazz Field

In order to obtain a topology of the jazz field structure over time, I applied a blockmodeling approach from the social networks analysis tradition. The use of blockmodeling has become widespread in organizational research. DiMaggio (1986) was

Table 8.3 Clusters Obtained by Splitting *Elite* and *Shooting Star* Groups

Key trajectory variables	Clusters			
	31	32	41	42
Average betweenness centrality	1.29	0.84	0.51	0.52
Lifespan (periods)	7.14	6.41	3.74	3.94
Periods at the core	4.00	3.84	2.15	2.30
Number of individuals	22	49	39	89

Note. Cluster 3 (*Elite*) split into first generation (1930–1944) Cluster 31 (*Elite-1*) and second generation (1945–1969) Cluster 32 (*Elite-2*). Cluster 4 (*Shooting Star*) split into first generation (1930–1949) Cluster 41 (*Shooting Star-1*) and second generation (1950–1969) Cluster 42 (*Shooting Star-2*). (Design by the author)

Table 8.4 Evolution of trajectory types in the Jazz field

Type of trajectory	1930–1934	1935–1939	1940–1944	1945–1949	1950–1954	1955–1959	1960–1964	1965–1969
	Trajectory type musicians per period							
1	70	118	144	132	119	142	106	105
2	188	519	418	622	497	930	881	142
5	5	4	4	4	4	3	3	1
6	64	181	237	394	382	442	350	207
7	74	41	16	10	7	7	7	5
8	9	38	26	40	53	124	232	957
31	17	19	20	21	18	20	19	15
32	13	23	42	47	47	49	44	40
41	6	10	12	17	23	28	27	21
42	3	6	20	51	67	76	70	50
Total	449	959	939	1338	1217	1821	1739	1543
	Percentage of trajectory type per period							
1	16%	12%	15%	10%	10%	8%	6%	7%
2	42%	54%	45%	46%	41%	51%	51%	9%
5	1%	0%	0%	0%	0%	0%	0%	0%
6	14%	19%	25%	29%	31%	24%	20%	13%
7	16%	4%	2%	1%	1%	0%	0%	0%
8	2%	4%	3%	3%	4%	7%	13%	62%
31	4%	2%	2%	2%	1%	1%	1%	1%
32	3%	2%	4%	4%	4%	3%	3%	3%
41	1%	1%	1%	1%	2%	2%	2%	1%
42	1%	1%	2%	4%	6%	4%	4%	3%
Total	100%	100%	100%	100%	100%	100%	100%	100%

Note. Cluster 1: *Ivory Tower*; Cluster 2: *Wanna-be*; Cluster 5: *Ivy League*; Cluster 6: *Up-Starters*; Cluster 31: *Elite*, first generation (1930–1944), Cluster 32: *Elite*, second generation (1945–1969); Cluster 41: *Shooting Star*, first generation (1930–1949); Cluster 42: *Shooting Star*, second generation (1950–1969). (Design by the author)

one of its first proponents and used the approach to study the relation among theater managers in the United States. Other seminal works using blockmodeling are Mohr's study (1994) of non-profit organizations at the beginning of the twentieth century, and Padget and Ansell's (1993) investigation of relationships among Florentine families in order to understand the rise of the Medici. The idea behind blockmodeling is to group together those individuals who share similar patterns of relationships with other individuals in the network (see Breiger, 2004, for a review of the methodology). As a result, musicians placed in the same block will be structurally similar, meaning that they will be likely to display the same pattern of ties to other actors in the network. Nevertheless, structurally similar actors are not necessarily connected.

There are several methodologies for obtaining block models from a given network (for a review, see Ferligoj, Doreian, & Batagelj, 2011). CONCOR

(CONvergence of iterated CORrelations) is the oldest and works as follows: First the algorithm calculates the correlation between each pair of actors in a series of iterations. The aim is to identify those actors with the highest likeliness of ties. Then, based on the matrix of correlations, it splits the network into two partitions. I chose to split the network three times, thereby obtaining eight blocks. As Hanneman (2001) indicates, there is no good or bad number of blocks. I chose eight blocks because this number would yield a less complex output.

I used UCINET 6.64, a network analysis software, to obtain a permutated matrix and its respective image matrix. The image matrix is obtained from the permuted matrix by calculating the density of ties in each block. Next, I dichotomized the density matrix of each period using the following procedure: If the density of a given block was above the average density of the image matrix, I considered a tie to exist between a pair of blocks (represented as a solid line in Fig. 8.1a–h). If the density of a block was between the average density and half of this value, I considered this a weaker tie (represented by a dashed line in Fig. 8.1a–h). In the case of diagonal blocks (reflexive relationships), the higher the density, the higher the likeliness of including a cohesive group of musicians.

Figure 8.1a–h show the results of this blockmodeling of the jazz musician networks. I also identified the most important blocks for each trajectory type as follows: Whenever the percentage of a particular trajectory type was above 12.5 % (the expected percentage average per block, given the eight blocks generated by CONCOR), I identified the number of musicians from that category who are members of that block. Furthermore, in order to increase the clarity of the schemes, I left blank isolated blocks with no relevant trajectory type.

Relationships Between Trajectory Types

In order to understand the relations between the trajectory types over time, I built density matrices for each period, associating pairs of trajectory types. In an approach similar to the blockmodeling exercise, I obtained an image matrix (see Fig. 8.2a–h). This image matrix is dichotomized: Above average density is marked "1," while below average density is marked "0."

Several phenomena can become evident through this analysis. First, it is possible to ascertain to whom each trajectory type was related during each period. Some of the questions I address with this approach, therefore, are how *Elite* Cluster members interact and whom an emerging *Elite* member dealt with before attaining a dominant position. Second, in a strictly regulated society where social roles are highly differentiated, role types cannot freely interact with one another. The less differentiated a society (i.e., interactions between individuals are mainly driven by the social norms embedded in social roles), the more outbound are the ties observable between groups. From this perspective, the greater the number of ties, the less differentiated one trajectory type is from another. Third, by analyzing the sociograms generated by the dichotomized matrixes it is possible to identify which trajectory types are

8 Trajectory Types Across Network Positions: Jazz Evolution from 1930 to 1969

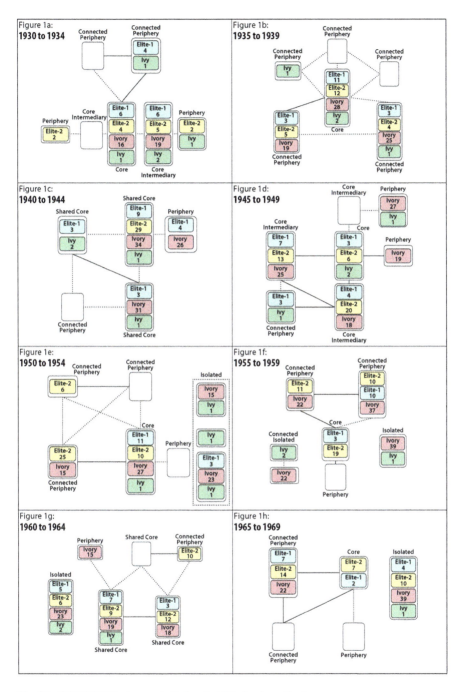

Fig. 8.1 CONCOR blocks per studied period (Design by author)

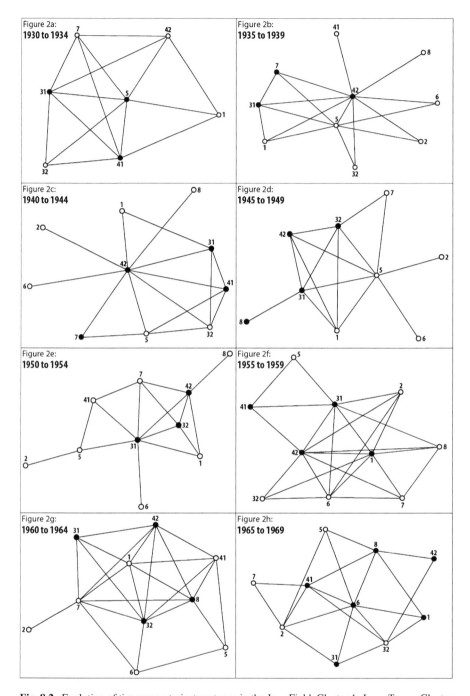

Fig. 8.2 Evolution of ties among trajectory types in the Jazz Field. Cluster 1: *Ivory Tower*; Cluster 2: *Wanna-be*; Cluster 5: *Ivy League*; Cluster 6: *Up-Starters*; Cluster 31: *Elite-1*, first generation (1930–1944), Cluster 32: *Elite-2*, second generation (1945–1969); Cluster 41:*Shooting Star-1*, first generation (1930–1949); Cluster 42 *Shooting Star-2*, second generation (1950–1969). Black nodes = cohesive groups; white nodes = non-cohesive groups. (Design by author)

Table 8.5 QAP matrix Pearson Correlation between periods

Period	Period							
	1930–1934	1935–1939	1940–1944	1945–1949	1950–1954	1955–1959	1960–1964	1965–1969
1930–1934	1							
1935–1939	0.186	1						
1940–1944	0.295	0.434*	1					
1945–1949	0.405*	0.691***	0.386*	1				
1950–1954	0.473**	0.46**	0.371	0.754***	1			
1955–1959	−0.027	0.354**	0.306*	0.092	0.406**	1		
1960–1964	0.036	−0.163	0.364***	0.117	0.405***	0.189	1	
1965–1969	−0.289**	−0.132	−0.163	−0.058	0.004	−0.089	0.333**	1
1930–1934	1							

Note $*p<.05$; $**p<.01$; $***p<.001$
Two-tailed tests.

central, which roles are peripheral, and which trajectory types play a brokerage role. The results of this analysis are shown in Fig. 8.2a–h. I have left the original cluster numbering visible on the sociograms. White nodes denote below-average-density cells, which can be interpreted as groups with low cohesiveness.

I also verified how similar each period was to any other period of time. Webster, Freeman, and Aufdemberg (2001) argue that actors in similar social contexts will establish similar network patterns. Following this analytical approach, I used Ucinet's QAP Matrix tool to obtain a matrix of Pearson correlations among all periods (Table 8.5). The diagonal under the main diagonal (with 1 s) represents the correlations between subsequent periods. Given the high incidence of right and left censored trajectories in the periods 1930–1934 and 1965–1969, I warn against possible misinterpretations of the very low Pearson correlation at both extremes of this diagonal. Hence, I excluded Clusters 7 and 8 (left and right-censored trajectories) from this analysis in order to mitigate their phasing out and phasing in effects.

Results: The History of Jazz from a Structural Perspective

The Pre-swing Era: 1930 to 1934

In the early thirties, jazz was considered a dead style, alive only in the memories of connoisseurs nostalgic for a pre-Depression America (Lopes, 2002). "Sweet" bands, headed by classical-music-educated maestros such as Paul Whiteman, controlled the emerging phonographic industry of the period. Nonetheless, some sidemen musicians such as Benny Goodman, who played for big bands and had contact with early jazz musicians, started to introduce "hot" elements. The musical style they were developing would be eventually called *swing*. It is worth noting that more than 90% of the recording sessions were concentrated in three cities: New York, Chicago, and London (Fig. 8.3). This geographic concentration was reinforced by the recording industry structure.

It is evident that during this period *Ivory Tower* and *Ivy League* musicians dominated the network's core (Fig. 8.1a in the *Core* and *Core Intermediary* blocks). Both generations of the *Elite* Cluster were already present, but they played a minor role, which can be observed by the limited number of musicians in these categories (Table 8.4). In Fig. 8.4 it is apparent that betweenness centrality was higher than degree centrality, indicating that few musicians were instrumental in playing the role of brokers.

Figure 8.2a shows the relationship between trajectory types. It is interesting to observe that despite the large number of ties between trajectory types, only three

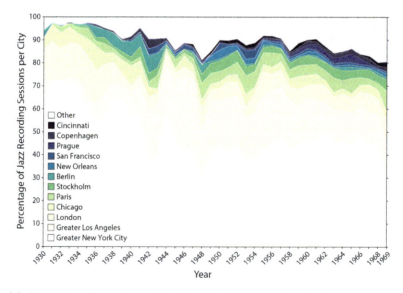

Fig. 8.3 Distribution of recording sessions by major city (Design by author)

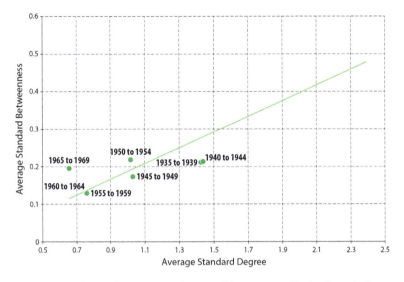

Fig. 8.4 Evolution of centrality measures: degree and betweenness (Design by author)

groups are cohesive: *Elite-1*, *Ivy League*, and *Shooting Star-1*. *Elite-1* and *Ivy League* clearly occupy a central role vis-à-vis other trajectory types, suggesting that those two groups played a coordinating role in this field.

The Swing Era: 1935–1945

The consolidation of swing as a popular style came in the late 1930s. The popularity of its musicians enabled them to bridge racial chasms, as exemplified by Goodman's partnership with Teddy Wilson. A close connection with a monopolistic recording industry also helped structure a centralized organizational field. As Peterson and Anand (2002) observe, in the mid-1940s the phonographic field in the United States migrated from a normative to a competitive model. Several explanations exist for this shift. The first relates to the domain of law and regulation. The founding of Broadcast Music, Inc (BMI) in 1942 broke the American Society of Composers and Publishers' (ASCAP) monopoly on music royalty distribution agreements and permitted the shift from the New York Tin Pan Alley formula to the introduction of new styles (Hobsbawm, 1989; Peterson & Anand, 2002). The number of recording sessions fell dramatically in 1942 (see Fig. 8.5), which had the effect of loosening the leadership of established swing musicians.

An inspection of the geographic distribution of the sessions reveals that New York and Los Angeles still accounted for the majority in the mid-1940s. However, there was a clear shift from New York to Los Angeles due to the usage of jazz in movies (Fig. 8.3). In Europe, jazz declined in London, but expanded in pre-World-War-II

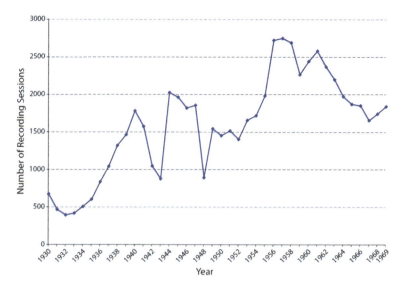

Fig. 8.5 Evolution of recorded jazz sessions included in the sample (Design by author)

Germany. After the 1942–1944 musicians' strike against the recording industry in the United States ended the number of recording sessions soared (see 1944 in Fig. 8.3). Due to World War II, though, this recovery mainly occurred in the United States, while the European share dwindled (see Fig. 8.5).

The shift from a normative to a competitive field is observed in the field articulation. Figure 8.4 indicates that the periods 1935–1939 and 1940–1944 both have low betweenness and high degree centrality (a combination typical of more cohesive networks). In this type of configuration, brokerage is less important. The loose articulation of the field, along with the presence of experienced sidemen, was a crucial ingredient in the subsequent revolution of the jazz field. Nonetheless, older generations still controlled the field. A low QAP (Quadratic Assignment Procedure) correlation is observable between period 1 (1930–1934) and period 2 (1935–1939) (Table 8.5). This may be explained by a structural change in the network. As cohesion increased, so concentric paths became established. In contrast, the patterns of relationships did not change dramatically from period 2 (1935–1939) to period 3 (1940–1944) (Table 8.5 shows a 0.43 Pearson correlation, similar to Webster et al.'s (2001) level). This suggests that with the articulation in the 1935–1940 period relationships changed at a slower pace.

In Fig. 8.1b a *Core* block articulating the field's record production is quite clear. *Ivory Tower* musicians predominated over other trajectory types (Fig. 8.1b). Nonetheless, a connected periphery started to emerge, which balanced the dominance of the core. In Fig. 8.1c the emergence of shared *Core* blocks can be seen. *Ivory Tower*, *Ivy League*, and *Elite-1* musicians were still controlling the field. There was, however, no clear-cut core articulating the entire structure. It is worth noting that 29 musicians from *Elite-2* (or 75 % of this generation) were already present in the field, all concentrated in a single block.

Figure 8.2b, c reveal details of interactions between trajectory types. *Shooting Star-2* musicians (Cluster 42) came to dominate the interactions in both periods. In view of the fact that *Shooting Star* musicians experienced short periods at the core, my findings suggest that in parallel to the institutionalization of swing most interactions were articulated by players with lower permanence in the network. It is also worth noting that despite the concentration of all *Elite-2* musicians in the same block (as pointed out for Fig. 8.1c) they were not cohesive as a trajectory type (Fig. 8.2c). As a possible interim interpretation, I suggest that their relationships during this period were not best captured within the phonographic industry, but in more informal, less commercial, uncoupled locations such as jam sessions and night clubs (Becker, 2004).

The Bop/Cool Era: 1945 to 1960

Peterson and Anand (2002) note that by the mid-1940s a new Federal Communication Commission (FCC) regulation had broken the monopoly held by the major radio stations. Furthermore, in 1948 there was a second musicians' strike in the U.S. recording industry, leading to a general decline in recording sessions (see Fig. 8.5). The emergence of television networks also impacted the radio industry. Companies shifted their advertising budgets toward television, causing the radio networks to view smaller and local radio stations as unattractive. Both factors—the end of the radio stations' monopoly and the emergence of television networks—led to the sale of licenses to local entrepreneurs. As a result, a flood of new licenses were issued to local radio stations, which had few resources to invest in live shows. Instead, they played albums published by small recording companies, increasing the diversity of styles reaching the public (Peterson & Anand, 2002, p. 268). With this change, promoters of new styles were able to challenge the dominance of established musicians. It is worth noting that when the number of recording sessions did once again increase again the strike (see 1950 in Fig. 8.5), New York and Los Angles were unable to retain the geographic concentration they had held during World War II.

In the mid-1950s this picture changed as young America embraced *rock*. Jazz as an embracing paradigm lost touch with a large share of the American audience, resulting in its loss of dominance to rock music in the sales charts published in *Billboard* magazine. In spite of these changes, demand for jazz recording sessions was still rising at the end of the 1950s (see Fig. 8.5). Although the New York scene did remain stable, most of the growth came from Los Angeles and European-based recording sessions (see Fig. 8.3). These changes in the industry and the demographics of jazz musicians accelerated the shift from the normative to the competitive configuration.

To be sure, relationships across periods were reasonably stable (see Table 8.5, correlations were around 0.4). Furthermore, an examination of the field's blockmodel structure (Fig. 8.1d–f) shows the stability of a core and connected periphery configuration, reinforcing the idea of a fairly cohesive field. Yet in Fig. 8.4 a slight shift from the superiority of degree centrality towards betweenness centrality is detectable. When the field reaches the 1955–1959 period, there is a relative equilibrium between the average betweenness centrality and the average degree centrality, indicating that the field was swinging back towards a more centralized configuration.

Elite-2 musicians, mostly associated with the emerging *bop* style, were important players from 1945 to 1960. In Fig. 8.1d it is evident that *Elite-2* musicians dominated the core, partially displacing *Ivory Tower* and *Elite-1* musicians to the periphery or to the outskirts of the core. Nonetheless, in an increasingly open system as the phonographic field was becoming (Perrow, 1986, pp.178–218), uncontested dominance was not guaranteed. During the following period, from 1950 to 1954, *Elite-2*'s dominance of the core was shared with *Elite-1* and *Ivory Tower* (Fig. 8.1e).

It was first during the 1945–1949 period that *Elite-1* and *Elite-2* trajectory musicians became more prominent than other trajectory types (Fig. 8.2d). This prominence was maintained throughout the ensuing period (Fig. 8.2e). Although *Shooting Star* trajectory musicians had been prominent during the previous period (see Fig. 8.1c), they were now pushed into a more peripheral role.

However, the leadership of *Elite-2* members was not sustained for long: It soon became a dispersed and low cohesion group (Fig. 8.2f). Although *Elite-2* musicians were still central (Fig. 8.1f), they showed low levels of collaboration among themselves, spending more effort in exploring outbound relationships. In contrast, those in the *Elite-1* and *Ivory Tower* clusters, along with both generations of *Shooting Stars*, were the only cohesive groups in this period. These findings have several implications. In the previous period, *Shooting Star* musicians were central in the interactions (Fig. 8.2b, c), but *Elite* and *Ivory Tower* musicians dominated the most prominent blocks (Fig. 8.1b, c). Now, however, *Elite* musicians were both central in the interactions (Fig. 8.2d–f) and dominant in the *Core* blocks (Fig. 8.2d–f).

The Jazz Renaissance: 1960–1969

During the 1960s, jazz became increasingly associated with the "older generation," and its decline quickened (see Fig. 8.5). In response to this downturn several musicians looked for outside the traditional canon for ways to reinvigorate that field of music. For instance, Miles Davis introduced *fusion*, while Stan Getz helped bring Bossa Nova to American jazz. All these efforts to mitigate jazz's decline led to an increasingly loosely coupled field. To be sure, there was abundant reaction to disqualify some of these new idioms. Miles Davis's fusion was thought to be more a style of rock than of jazz, while Coleman's *free jazz* was unacceptable to some traditional jazz musicians. Geographically, this period also represents a sharp decline in the U.S.-centrism of jazz. The large American cities cited in Fig. 8.3 represented

71% of recording sessions in 1960, falling to 54% by 1969. By contrast, the large European cities cited in Fig. 8.3 had 19% of recording sessions in 1960, but rising to 27% towards 1969.

Jazz scholars identify this period as strongly fragmented because of the adoption of distinct styles. Figure 8.4 shows that the average betweenness centrality during this period is higher than the average degree centrality, indicating higher reliance on brokers. With greater stylistic differentiation emerging, musicians can be expected to play increasingly among peers sharing the same style. The shift from the more cohesive configuration seen in the 1945–1960 period to the less cohesive configuration of the 1945–1960 period is also accompanied by a stark change in the pattern of relationships (see Table 8.5 for the statistically non-significant correlation between the 1955–1959 and 1960–1964 periods).

Figure 8.1g shows the division of the field's core into two, nonetheless interconnected, shared cores. In other words, although musicians were going in different directions, the process cannot be termed fragmentation, because the field's blocks remain connected. *Elite* musicians (from both generations) are represented occupying the shared *Core* blocks together with *Ivy League* musicians. Figure 8.2g reveals a rearticulation of *Elite-2* from 1960 to 1964, with the cluster occupying a more central role, articulated with *Shooting Star-2* and *Elite-1*.

In the period from 1965 to 1969, the network was relatively stable in comparison to other periods (see Table 8.5, 0.333 correlation across periods), while the tendency for further prominence of brokerage over cohesion was still operating. Table 8.1 indicates that the average betweenness centrality is higher than the average degree centrality. In comparison to the previous period, a clearer core-periphery configuration (Fig. 8.1h) is seen.

During this period, several *Elite-2* musicians were present at the core (Fig. 8.1h). As a group, though, *Elite-2* became less cohesive (Fig. 8.2h). New groups emerged as central and cohesive, like Cluster 6, the *Up-Starters* (Fig. 8.2h). It is worth noting that *Elite-2* was neither able to entirely displace older groups nor become a perennial cohesive group. In addition, Fig. 8.2h shows a return of *Elite-1*, although the expectation would be for the core to be held by the newly established generation. This evidence suggests that, given a stylistic crisis in the field, previous *Elite* generations were able to fill the void left by the competing new generation.

Discussion

The above analysis reveals a rearrangement in the field structure. While the field was relatively centralized (both geographically and socially) during the 1930–1934 period, it became more cohesive in the following periods, regaining a higher centralization toward the 1965–1969 period (Fig. 8.4). In broad strokes, this is observable throughout the different blockmodeling configurations (Fig. 8.1a–h). A clear core-periphery structure is discernible during the 1930–1934 period, with the peripheral blocks becoming more connected throughout the coming periods, and shared core positions emerging. Peripheral blocks remain connected, despite the higher centralization of the 1964–1969 period and the reemergence of a distinct core position.

Hence, it can be inferred that in normative fields there is high centralization and a core-periphery distinction. With a shift to a competitive field, more spontaneous interactions take place, leading to better distribution of interactions throughout the field. The field again attains a higher centralization, possibly due to stylistic differentiation and geographic localism. Yet there is lower core-periphery distinction compared with the 1930–1934 period.[6]

It is evident that *Shooting-Star* musicians were prominent in the network (Fig. 8.2b, c) at the dawn of the transition of the jazz field from normative to competitive, In the 1945–1949 period, *Elite* musicians attained this centrality. However, this achievement of centrality was fairy unstable: *Elite* musicians across generations displaced each other. Looking at *Elite* musicians vis-à-vis the blocks in which they are located (Fig. 8.1a–h), it seems, though, that *Elite* prominence consolidated up to the 1945–1949 period. The distinction between these two sets of analyses sheds light on the value of blockmodeling: While cohesion-based prominence is important (Fig. 8.2a–h), structural equivalence (Fig. 8.1a–h) allows identification of those musicians who dominate blocks analytically constructed to capture asymmetries across relationships. In substantial terms, if individuals who dominate core blocks are not the same as those whose centrality is cohesion-based, it can be inferred that a loosening has occurred between global and local key players. While the global key players might enjoy higher brokerage gains, local key players may be able to command specific styles, fads, and fashions, as suggested by the prominence of musicians with short-timespan trajectories.

In most periods, *Elite* Cluster musicians dominate the *Core* blocks in both the normative and competitive field configurations—unsurprising given that this grouping was obtained by clustering together musicians with high betweenness centrality and long lifespan. However, during the reconfiguration years (from 1945 to 1964), the *Elite* musicians were also prominent in its cohesion-based centrality. Hence, during the transition from one configuration to another, the *Elite* musicians played both the high-cohesiveness and high-status roles. But when the field became relatively centralized again, and musicians dispersed into distinct styles, younger generations yielded the central position to older musicians.

Conclusions

Aldrich (1999) suggests that communities evolve in a nested way. He suggests a coevolutionary approach concerned with how sets of populations coevolve over time. From this perspective, trajectories are constrained and supported by a

---

[6] Of course, here I am assuming that the field reached in equilibrium in 1969. Further analyses of right-censored data could show a decline in interperipheral connections.

macro-structure. Conversely, the macro-structure is shaped by the nested micro-trajectories. The idea of coevolution can be extrapolated to different levels of analysis: regions, countries, organizations, and individuals. A field's evolution in terms of its structural and normative elements is better explained by describing the coevolution among its members.

This research contributes to the literature in question by showing that changes in the jazz field structure from normative to competitive in the mid-1940s occurred in tandem with significant changes in the positioning of jazz musicians within the network.

This research presents an empirical puzzle: More competitive structures are beneficial for emerging artists because they grant them better access to resources previously concentrated in established musicians' hands. Consequently, the shift from a normative to a competitive field is likely to enhance individual creativity and allow for the emergence of a new elite. However, if the new elite is unable to establish a new normative era and to curtail the competitive forces, its new styles may be quickly put to the test and its central position disputed by even more recently recognized musicians. As a result, the drive for innovation and better positions leads to the weakening of a field's paradigm. Once faced with a crisis and the additional challenge of reestablishing normative controls, newly ensconced musicians are likely to look to previously predominant musicians who still retain social capital and status. A radical shift toward a competitive field is therefore likely to reestablish formerly prevailing musicians in core positions, contrary to a common sense intuition that those musicians would be left to occupy peripheral areas of the network.

Acknowledgments I would like to thank the CAPES (Coordination for the Improvement of Higher Education Personnel) Foundation for the support received.

References

Abbott, A. (2001). Temporality and process in social life. In A. Abbott (Ed.), *Time matters: On theory and method* (pp. 209–239). Chicago: The University of Chicago Press.
Accominotti, F. (2009). Creativity from interaction: Artistic movements and the creativity careers of modern painters. *Poetics, 37,* 267–294. doi:10.1016/j.poetic.2009.03.005
Aldrich, H. E. (1999). *Organizations evolving.* London: Sage.
Anand, N., & Peterson, R. A. (2000). When market information constitutes fields: Sensemaking of markets in the commercial music industry [Special issue]. *Organization Science, 11,* 270–284. Retrieved from http://www.jstor.org/stable/2640261
Barabási, A. L. (2003). *Linked: How everything is connected to everything else and what it means for business, science, and everyday life.* New York: Plume.
Becker, H. S. (2004). Jazz places. In A. Bennett & R. A. Peterson (Eds.*), Music scenes: Local, translocal, and virtual* (pp. 17–27). Nashville: Vanderbilt University Press.
Bourdieu, P. (1993). *The field of cultural production. Essays on art and literature.* New York: Columbia University Press.
Bourdieu, P. (1996). *The rules of art: Genesis and structure of the literary field.* Cambridge, UK: Polity Press.

Breiger, R. L. (2004). The analysis of social networks. In M. Hardy & A. Bryman (Eds.), *Handbook of data analysis* (pp. 505–526). London: Sage.
DiMaggio, P. J. (1986). Structural analysis of organizational fields: A blockmodel approach. In B. Staw & L. Cummings. (Eds.), *Research in organizational behavior* (Vol. 8, pp. 335–370). Greenwich, CT: JAI Press.
DiMaggio, P. J.(1987). Classification in art. *American Sociological Review, 52,* 440–455. Retrieved from http://www.jstor.org/stable/2095290
DiMaggio, P. J. (1991). Constructing an organizational field as a professional project: U.S. art museums, 1920–1940. In W. W. Powell & P. J. DiMaggio (Eds.), *The new institutionalism in organizational analysis* (pp. 267–292). Chicago: The University of Chicago Press.
DiMaggio, P. J., & Powell, W. W. (1983). The iron cage revisited: Institutional isomorphism and collective rationality in organizational fields. *American Sociological Review, 48,* 147–160. Retrieved from http://www.jstor.org/stable/2095101
Dubois, S., & François, P. (2013). Career paths and hierarchies in the pure pole of the literary field: The case of contemporary poetry. *Poetics, 41,* 501–523. http://doi.org/10.1016/j.poetic.2013.07.004
Ferligoj, A., Doreian, P., & Batagelj, V. (2011). Positions and roles. In J. Scott & P. J. Carrington (Eds.), *The SAGE handbook of social network analysis* (pp. 434–446). Los Angeles: Sage.
Giuffre, K. (1999). Sandpiles of opportunity: Success in the art world. *Social Forces, 77,* 815–832. Retrieved from http://www.jstor.org/stable/3005962
Granovetter, M. S. (1973). The strength of weak ties. *American Journal of Sociology, 78,* 1360–1380.
Hanneman, R. A. (2001). *Introduction to social network methods.* Retrieved from http://www.researchmethods.org/NETTEXT.pdf
Hirsch, P. M. (2011). Processing fads and fashions: An organization-set analysis of cultural industry systems. In M. Granovetter & R. Swedberg (Eds.), *The sociology of economic life* (3rd ed., pp. 340–356). Boulder: Westview Press. (Original work published 1972)
Hobsbawm, E. J. (1989). *The jazz scene.* London: Weidenfeld & Nicolson.
Kadushin, C. (2004). *Introduction to social network theory.* Unpublished manuscript. Retrieved from http://melander335.wdfiles.com/local--files/reading-history/kadushin.pdf
Kirschbaum, C. (2007). Careers in the right beat: US jazz musicians' typical and non-typical trajectories. *Career Development International, 12,* 187–201. doi:10.1108/13620430710733659
Leblebici, H., Salancik, G. R., Copay, A., & King, T. (1991). Institutional change and the transformation of interorganizational fields: An organizational history of the U.S. radio broadcasting industry. *Administrative Science Quarterly, 36,* 333–363. doi:10.2307/2393200
Lena, J. C., & Pachucki, M. C. (2013). The sincerest form of flattery: Innovation, repetition, and status in an art movement. *Poetics, 41,* 236–264. doi:10.1016/j.poetic.2013.02.002
Lopes, P. D. (2002). *The rise of a jazz art world.* Cambridge, UK: University Press.
Mohr, J. W. (1994). Soldiers, mothers, tramps and others: Discourse roles in the 1907 New York City charity directory. *Poetics, 22,* 327–357. doi:10.1016/0304-422X(94)90013-2
Padget, J. F., Ansell, C. K. (1993). Robust action and the rise of the Medici, 1400–1434. *American Journal of Sociology, 89,* 1259–1319
Perrow, C. (1986). *Complex organizations. A critical essay.* New York: Random House.
Peterson, R. A., & Anand, N. (2002). How Chaotic Careers Create Orderly Fields. In M. A. Peiperl, M. B. Arthur, & N. Anand (Eds.), *Career creativity: Explorations in the remaking of work* (pp. 257–279). Oxford: University Press.
Podolny, J. M. (2001). Networks as the pipes and prisms of the market. *American Journal of Sociology, 107,* 33–60. doi:10.1086/323038
Rerup, C., & Feldman, M. S. (2011). Routines as a source of change in organizational schemata: The role of trial-and-error learning. *The Academy of Management Journal, 54,* 577–610. doi:10.5465/AMJ.2011.61968107
Scott, W. R. (1995). *Institutions and organizations.* Thousand Oaks: Sage.
Stark, D., & Vedres, B. (2006). Social times of network spaces: Network sequences and foreign investment in Hungary. *American Journal of Sociology, 111,* 1367–1411. doi:10.1086/499507

Webster, C. M., Freeman, L. C., & Aufdemberg, C. G. (2001). The impact of social context on interaction patterns. *Journal of Social Structure, 2*. Retrieved from http://www.cmu.edu/joss/content/articles/volume2/Webster.html

Zuckerman, E. W., Kim, T.-Y., Ukanwa, K., & von Rittmann, J. (2003). Robust identities or nonentities? Typecasting in the feature-film labor market. *American Journal of Sociology, 108*, 1018–1074. doi:10.1086/377518

Open Access This chapter is distributed under the terms of the Creative Commons Attribution 4.0 International License (http://creativecommons.org/licenses/by/4.0/), which permits use, duplication, adaptation, distribution and reproduction in any medium or format, as long as you give appropriate credit to the original author(s) and the source, provide a link to the Creative Commons license and indicate if changes were made.

The images or other third party material in this chapter are included in the work's Creative Commons license, unless indicated otherwise in the credit line; if such material is not included in the work's Creative Commons license and the respective action is not permitted by statutory regulation, users will need to obtain permission from the license holder to duplicate, adapt or reproduce the material.

Chapter 9
Topology and Evolution of Collaboration Networks: The Case of a Policy-Anchored District

Laura Prota, Maria Prosperina Vitale, and Maria Rosaria D'Esposito

Despite all the increased mobility of capital, goods, and labor, modern globalization has failed to produce a placeless market economy. Contrary to expectations, local differences have radically emerged, creating uneven economic landscapes (Amin & Thrift, 1995). Regions and localities increasingly compete to attract and retain resources through innovation (Cooke, 2005; Cooke, Uranga, & Etxebarria, 1997; Morgan, 2007). Innovation, from this perspective, is intended as a collaborative process linking science, technology, industries, and institutions within a coherent system able to produce positive spillovers and favor systemic learning (Asheim, Smith, & Oughton, 2011; Morgan, 2007).

From a theoretical point of view, these interactions are likely to produce vital regional innovation systems with enhanced potential for growth (Doloreux & Parto, 2004). The industrial-cluster model proposed by Porter represented a first concrete example of this process of systemic learning. Since Porter's conceptualization (Porter, 1998), clusters have become a flagship model for innovation all over the world, inspiring policies in Europe and other OECD countries at all levels as well as in emerging economies. As clusters were replicated and sustained by public policies, there emerged an array of diverse empirical applications reflecting different aims, governance, institutions, and composition. According to Martin and Sunley (2003), however, this organizational variety made the very meaning of the cluster concept vague and pointless, calling for a detailed classification of experiences and practices.

L. Prota (✉) • M.P. Vitale • M.R. D'Esposito
Department of Economics and Statistics, University of Salerno,
Via Giovanni Paolo II 132, I-84084 Fisciano, SA, Italy
e-mail: laura_p@fastmail.fm; mvitale@unisa.it; mdesposito@unisa.it

© The Author(s) 2017
J. Glückler et al. (eds.), *Knowledge and Networks*, Knowledge and Space 11, DOI 10.1007/978-3-319-45023-0_9

The initial enthusiasm for clusters gradually thus dampened, and thought turned to the question of what type of connections were really to be encouraged, given that "being connected" is just not enough. Moreover, the promised gains of regional competitiveness were difficult to assess, given that the institutional complexity involved in regional innovation systems could not be easily translated into *competitiveness* as though clusters were firms (Martin & Sunley, 2003). The evaluation of regional innovation systems is even more problematic when clusters' members have key public targets, as in the case of policy-anchored districts, whose major drivers can be government tenants such as capital cities, military or defense facilities, public universities, or national research centers (Markusen, 1996). The specific issues inherent in these policy-anchored districts still need to be properly addressed.

Researchers contributing to a growing body of studies are investigating social network analysis as an effective means with which to examine the structure and dynamics of regional innovation systems. Collaboration networks represent the backbone of systemic learning. According to Powell et al., (1996), the wider the industrial knowledge base is, the more collaboration networks become essential for exploiting and exploring a firm's capabilities. Such networks are not one-time dyadic interactions aimed at filling in a firm's gaps in knowledge. On the contrary, networks are the loci of innovation representing the means through which collective learning unfolds. Studying clusters as networks has therefore become increasingly popular in the literature. Network analysis has been used to explain how the innovative capacity and performance of firms vary with network attributes such as centrality or density (Boschma & Ter Wal, 2007; Giuliani, 2007; Tsai, 2001). Alternatively, network properties and configurations were explained as resulting from firms' characteristics, such as knowledge bases (Baum, Shipilov, & Rowley, 2003). However, to the best of our knowledge, there are no studies formally analyzing networks as coordination mechanisms administered by a formal local institution devoted to orchestrating the network's developmental trajectory (Provan, Fish, & Sydow, 2007).

Our study contributes to this literature on regional innovation systems through a formal network analysis of a network-administered, policy-anchored district, Ingegneria dei Materiali polimerici e compositi e Strutture (IMAST), located in the region of Campania in southwestern Italy. Policy-anchored districts are often criticized as suffering from technological and political lock-in, where member organizations are well-established, large corporations primarily interested in consolidating and reproducing a given structure through multiple embedding mechanisms (Tödtling & Trippl, 2005). We want to determine the extent to which a process of consolidation of existing structures applies to IMAST or whether behavioral changes are emerging.

IMAST is a high-tech district focusing on polymeric and composite materials, engineering, and structures. This modern corporate research center was built in 2004 on the initiative of a public university, a national research center, and a set of public and private firms in strategic industries such as aeronautics, transport, and defense. A dedicated administration was established with the explicit mission of orchestrating members' relations and facilitating the integration of the different knowledge bases for the common goal of fostering exploratory research on complex polymers.

An ideal core–periphery configuration is taken as a benchmark against which to compare the evolution of the observed patterns of collaborations within the IMAST project network. We conduct a prespecified blockmodel analysis of IMAST's collaboration network for research and development (R&D) in each of the 7 years from 2006 to 2013 to determine how far its observed topology was from a core–periphery model configuration at each time point (Doreian, Batagelj, & Ferligoj, 2005). The core–periphery model used as a benchmark was defined as a multiple-core model with a bridging core connecting all the others (Kronegger, Ferligoj, & Dorein, 2011).

Blockmodeling can provide a synthetic and effective visualization of the evolutionary trajectory of the cluster. It is thus possible to use prespecified blockmodeling to assess the extent to which the observed trajectory was path dependent. From an evolutionary perspective, we operationalize the concept of structural variations introduced by Glückler (2007) to explain how a developmental trajectory can be shifted away from its path. Lastly, we examine what type of actors occupied key structural positions and what degree of positional mobility there was in the period examined.

The available theories on cluster configuration and evolution are reviewed in the first section, with particular attention to the core–periphery model. The second section introduces the case study characteristics and the data used for the analysis. In the third section we illustrate the method of prespecified blockmodeling and operationalize key indicators of path reproduction and variation. The fourth and fifth sections contain the results of our prespecified blockmodeling analysis, which shows the evolutionary trajectory of IMAST. This part of the chapter also has a detailed discussion of the organizations' attributes. The final section presents our conclusions and recommendations.

Cluster Topologies in the Literature: Generative Processes and Configurations

Innovation in a knowledge economy is conceptualized as an interactive process of learning that involves different actors in a system (Cooke & Morgan, 1999). This learning process is shaped by a variety of institutional routines and practices, defined as organizational patterns of behavior. The delicate role of managing collaborations and harmonizing practices and routines is particularly sensitive when technology- and science-based organizations are called on to coexist within the same cluster (Autio, 1998). In these cases a dedicated administration can be instituted as a knowledge integrator in the network-administered organizations (NAO) (Provan & Kenis, 2008). The literature on innovative clusters does not directly examine top-down management strategies of collaborations, probably because top-down management is not an ideal model that fits all cases. However, several economic processes have been identified as generative of cluster topologies from a bottom-up perspective. These processes suggest that a core–periphery structure is the most likely one to emerge in innovation networks.

Owen-Smith and Powell (2004) identified geographical proximity and ownership as the main explanation for cluster configurations. In their view, geographical proximity facilitates informal knowledge transfers by providing trust-based channels of communication. In the absence of face-to-face interactions that are perceived as secure, information needs to be formally protected. Distant knowledge transfers, therefore, are more likely to occur through codified conduits of knowledge regulated by property rights.

These underlying processes have been shown to affect the resulting structure of the network providing different positional advantages to actors. Owen-Smith and Powell (2004), for example, estimated a model using data on the Boston biotechnology industry and showed how geographical proximity and ownership have an impact on centrality. Geographical proximity favored a process of embedding by which groups became cohesive over time. Cohesiveness benefited all members, regardless of their centrality. Conversely, in geographically sparse communities, being central is essential to success. The study by Owner-Smith and Powell showed that ownership also mattered in terms of configuration. When clusters were driven by private commercial firms, networks ties likely spread across the globe to reach key partners. Policy-anchored districts, by contrast, tended to take root in the community to which they belonged, thus creating dense local networks.

The dyad of *local–tacit* versus *global–formal* knowledge transfers was discussed by Bathelt, Malmberg, and Maskell (2004), who argued that both these types of interactions need to coexist. Cognitive proximity is considered in their study as the baseline mechanism of cluster topology. Based on the consideration that collaboration requires a certain degree of cognitive distance, local buzz is seen as a way to reduce distance and acquire familiarity with different knowledge bases. In order to maintain creative diversity within the cluster, it is simultaneously essential to have intakes of fresh information via pipelines connecting the buzz to the rest of the world. Should the buzz prevail, the cluster risks technological lock-in. Should pipelines overmultiply, the cluster risks disintegration. Finding the balance between inward- and outward-looking ties is, therefore, key to sustainable cluster development.

Zooming out from individual ties, we note that the configuration resulting from the process of cognitive recombination is a core–periphery model in which the buzz represents the cohesive nucleus of the topology and the pipelines its periphery. In a study on the wine districts in Italy, Giuliani (2007) also underlined the importance of knowledge bases in producing a core–periphery network configuration. She considered two distinct relations: a knowledge network built on survey data tracing technical advice, and a business network recording any type of business relations among cluster firms. A model was then estimated to understand the effect of knowledge bases and firms' characteristics on degree centrality. Estimation results were reinforced by calculating a core index to locate core actors within the networks. Results showed that the two networks had very different configurations. Although the business network was complete, representing a collective and pervasive community, the knowledge network was highly centralized, producing a selective and uneven environment. At the core of the knowledge network sat the firms with the strongest knowledge bases.

Furthermore, Balland, Suire, and Vicente (2010) distinguished the effect of geographical proximity and knowledge bases by project phases such as in a knowledge value chain approach. In this very thought-provoking study, two-mode data on the Global Navigation Satellite System in Europe (GNASS) were used to define two network projections. The first network projection, describing project-to-project relations, was used to divide projects into three phases of the knowledge value chain: exploration, integration, exploitation. The second network, showing an organization-to-organization network, was used to distinguish firms by their knowledge bases: synthetic, analytic, and symbolic. Finally, a blockmodel was used to find cohesive local clusters and pipelines linking these clusters to global partners. Results from social network analysis showed that the project network indeed took a core–periphery configuration, the core consisting of exploitative projects close to the marketing phase and with a high concentration of pipelines. By contrast, local embeddedness dominated the periphery where exploratory projects required trust to exchange sensitive information and reach closure.

The relation between the core and the periphery of an innovation network was further discussed by Glückler (2014) with an analysis of BASF's cross-departmental knowledge flow linking the center to a peripheral unit in Argentina. The study demonstrates that the periphery can become a particularly suitable location to develop controversial innovations due to its organizational features. The unit examined was able not only to capitalize on its local market connections to develop a new business model but also to exploit the global organizational viscosity of BASF by establishing contacts with distant units.

From this literature it emerges that geographical and cognitive proximities as well as ownership can set in motion underlying processes that ultimately produce core–periphery structures. The extent to which an observed network approximates a core–periphery model can be captured through blockmodeling. This method is well established in social network analysis and has been used since the 1970s to reduce a network to its key topological features (Doreian et al., 2005). In this chapter, we use a variant of blockmodeling that permits prespecifying a theoretical core–periphery model and then using it as a benchmark against which to measure the configuration of the observed project networks over time.

The temporal dimension is particularly important in this study because it allows one to understand the extent to which the district development trajectory was path dependent (Martin & Sunley, 2006). The presence of a core–periphery structure in a specific moment of a cluster life does not necessarily mean that the structure will persist in the future. In this study we consider the emergence of a core–periphery structure as an indication that an underlying process of preferential attachment is taking place. This process implies that new ties are more likely to form around already central actors, reinforcing the cohesiveness of the core against the periphery (Glückler, 2007). However, this correspondence between topologies and processes persists only if the processes are protracted.

From an evolutionary perspective variations can occur such that the entire system shifts toward a new configuration. Variations are defined as ties (or behaviors) capable of modifying the whole structure because their formation countervails the prevailing reproductive rule of the system. Glückler (2007) identifies three types of variations with potential structural impact: (a) ties that establish global bridges between the local cluster and distant alters (e.g., the pipelines theorized by Bathelt et al., 2004); (b) ties that establish local bridges by connecting groups that are proximate but disconnected (due to gaps in the knowledge bases, for instance); and (c) actors who are part of different groups and act as brokers. All these types of variations are operationalized by making explicit hypotheses on the expected location of block-model inconsistencies. Before we move on to the method, the next section introduces the case study and the data used for the analyses.

The Case Study: The Experience of Italian Technological Districts

Influenced by the theory of regional innovation systems, European policies have encouraged the creation of several R&D infrastructures (Landabaso, Oughton, & Morgan, 1999). In this section we focus on the specific case of policy-anchored technological districts (TDs). As reported in Lazzeroni (2010): "A technological district is defined as a territorial system specialised in hi-tech activities and endowed with factors that determine system innovativeness" (p. 48). In Italy this policy orientation led the Ministry of Education, Universities, and Research to set up 29 TDs between 2002 and 2004. The creation of TDs was the implementation of a region-oriented policy aimed at fostering innovation and competitiveness through "local aggregations of high-tech activities, made up by public research centers, firms and local governments, geographically concentrated" (Bertamino, Bronzini, De Maggio, & Revelli, 2014, p. 6). Thus, TDs are characterized by three elements: territoriality, specialization in high technology, and system innovativeness. TDs represent a key region-oriented policy instrument aimed at stimulating interorganizational collaborations through subsidization (Fornahl, Broekel, & Boschma, 2011).

Even though TDs stem from the same policy, they have different specializations, governance systems, and geographical contexts. Given the high level of heterogeneity characterizing these clusters, cross-cutting comparisons remain problematic (Lazzeroni, 2010; Miceli, 2010). We undertake an in-depth analysis of a specific case study by adopting an evolutionary perspective aimed at capturing changes with respect to a theoretical model (for a related approach, see Prota, D'Esposito, De Stefano, Giordano, & Vitale, 2013; Prota & Vitale, 2014; or Ardovino & Pennacchio, 2012; Capuano, De Stefano, Del Monte, D'Esposito, & Vitale, 2013).

The case study investigated, IMAST, conducts exploratory research on composite materials and polymers engineering. It was conceived as a corporate research center bringing together in horizontal collaborations the largest Italian firms in strategic industries such as defense, aerospace, aeronautics, maritime shipping, and transport.[1] Beyond this highly technological core, the district was also given a science base through involvement of public universities and the national research institute. The governance was a holding of industrial and public laboratories and institutes. This holding was managed by a dedicated administration whose role was to orchestrate collaborations to promote horizontal partnerships and encourage the recombination of knowledge bases. The explicit mission of the district, as knowledge integrator, was to intensify public-private collaborations and to put in place private-to-private interactions connecting firms from different industries within and outside the district.[2]

This cross-sectoral approach to baseline research was orchestrated by the administration through active management of the network. Not only were projects were selected, but district members and external partners were called upon to participate in order to encourage the convergence between science and technology. IMAST management was able to attract an increasing number of firm leaders (the number doubled during the 10 years examined), and the science base was expanded to involve an increasing number of departments, universities, and institutes. In the following section the R&D collaboration network among members is first defined and then analyzed by means of social network analysis.

The data in this chapter refer to all IMAST R&D projects subsidized by both national and international grants. These projects can be used to study the structure of collaboration networks linking members among themselves and with the rest of the world.[3] They also express IMAST's policy on collaboration insofar as they were the direct result of the administration's innovation strategy.

The data encompass 24 R&D research projects undertaken by the district between 2006 and 2013. These project data constitute a two-mode network of organizations participating in projects. More formally, let N be the set of n TD's members (associated members and external partners) and P be the set of the p R&D projects observed for the n members over time. An affiliation matrix $A(n \times p)$ can be defined. The matrix entry a_{ik} is equal to 1 if the organisation $i \in N$ participates in the project $k \in P$, and is equal to 0 otherwise.

We use the conversion approach (Everett & Borgatti, 2013) to obtain an actor-by-actor adjacency matrix G from the two-mode network. In matrix G the entries are equal to the number of research projects shared by two organizations and 0 if two organisations have never collaborated in a research project. In order to highlight the structural changes that occurred over time, separate adjacency matrices were derived for each year (Prota & Vitale, 2014). Each of these temporal slides can be described as a graph $G_T(N,L,T)$, with T being the set of ordered time points $t \in T$. The set of actors $n \in N$ and the links $l \in L$ change over time according to individual participation in the projects.

---
[1] http://www.imast.biz/index.php?option=com_content&view=article&id=1&Itemid=2&lang=en
[2] The governance structure, the rules, and the composition of the district were highlighted by the manager during an in-depth interview held in February 2014. In particular, the active role of management was clarified by the manager and further discussed with members.
[3] We thank the TD's administrative staff who helped us update the data to March 2013.

In Table 9.1 some whole network measures are provided for each yearly collaboration network examined.[4] The table shows two main waves of funded projects: an initial wave in 2006–2007 when six and seven projects were funded, respectively; and a second wave in 2013 when seven projects started. The number of organizations involved in the collaboration network notably increased over time, going from 19 organizations in 2006 to 82 in 2013. The proportion of associated members to external partners also changed dramatically. From 2006 to 2011, most of the organizations were local research institutions and firms formally engaged with the TD. In 2012 and 2013, the number of external partners exceeded that of associated members. However, the number of the external partners involved in the European R&D project since 2008 is much larger (50 organizations) and has been shrunk to only one representative node in order to simplify the analysis.[5]

Figure 9.1 shows the evolution of the collaboration network. Structural hole measures were used to highlight group clustering.[6] These measures provide information on (i) dyadic constraint, which indicates the extent to which a single organization bridges two cohesive groups; and (ii) associated constraint, which measures the degree of organizational embeddedness within a cohesive group. In the graphs, TD members with high aggregate constraint are drawn closely together, whereas low dyadic constraint is shown as longer links to highlight structural holes.

We note that the one-mode projection of the data has generated perfect cliques in correspondence with joint participation in projects. However, clustering cannot be entirely attributed to this data distortion. Since the very beginning of the TD, a subset of organizations have collaborated on more than one project, suggesting the emergence of a substantially cohesive core. Furthermore, key brokers have characterized the network in each time period. In the start-up phase, only two actors within the TD bridged otherwise disconnected groups. From 2009 onward, however, the number of brokers notably increased.

---

[4] We calculated the reported measures by disregarding isolates (the TD's members not involved in projects in each year).

[5] Given that only six members were involved in the EU project, we decided to subsume all the international partners in one representative node. In this way the pattern of collaborations internal to the TD remained stable, and at the same time the analyses and visualizations were simplified. If we were to count all the partners involved in the European project, the number of external partners collaborating with the TD since 2008 would increase by 50 units.

[6] Pajek software for social network analysis (de Nooy, Mrvar, & Batagelj, 2011) was used for all analyses and visualizations in the study.

Table 9.1 The IMAST[a] collaboration network, 2006–2013

Characteristics	2006 Time 2	2007 Time 3	2008 Time 4	2009 Time 5	2010 Time 6	2011 Time 7	2012 Time 8	2013 Time 9
No. of members	19	24	28	40	39	37	50	82
No. of associated members	18	21	24	29	28	26	24	38
No. of partners	1	3	4	11	11	11	26	44
No. of edges	65	96	116	215	214	218	382	728
New projects	6	5	1	1	0	2	1	7
Active projects	7	12	13	13	11	10	8	12
Density	.38	.348	.307	.276	.289	.327	.312	.219
Average degree	6.84	8	8.29	10.75	10.97	11.78	15.28	17.76

[a]Ingegneria dei Materiali polimerici e compositi e Strutture (technological district). *Source.* Authors' elaborations based on R&D collaboration data within the technological district

Capturing Cluster's Topology with Prespecified Block-Modeling

We used prespecified blockmodeling to gain a synthetic view of the structural evolution of IMAST collaboration network (Fig. 9.1). Blockmodeling is a type of clustering for relational data intended to reduce complex networks into simpler graphs, with nodes representing groups of equivalent actors (positions) and ties representing the relation between positions (roles) (see Ferligoj, Doreian, & Batagelj, 2011; Wasserman & Faust, 1994). These reduced graphs (also called images) are used in this study to facilitate synthetic visualization of the overall topology of the IMAST collaboration network and its evolution.

To reduce a complex network into its image, a single node subsumes similar actors if they are equivalent. This study uses the definition of structural equivalence to reduce IMAST collaboration networks. Actors are considered equivalent if their pattern of ties to and from alters is identical (Lorrain & White, 1971). In practice, when structural equivalence is used, the network matrix is permuted to form either null or

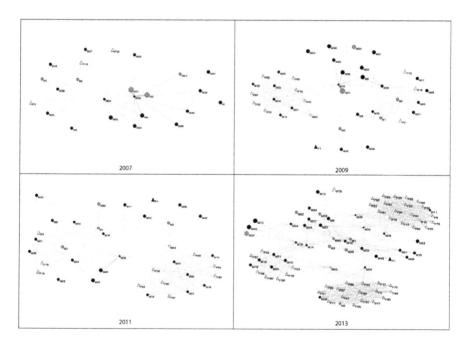

Fig. 9.1 Energized graphs by structural-hole measures of collaboration networks in selected years (2006, 2009, 2011, 2013). *Nodes* represent the IMAST's associated members and external partners; line lengths = dyadic constraint; node size = aggregate constraint; node shape = IMAST's associated member (*circle*), partner (*triangle*); node color: firm (*gray*), research institution (*black*), other organizations (*white*), and external partner (*yellow*) (Source: Authors' elaborations based on R&D collaboration within the technological district)

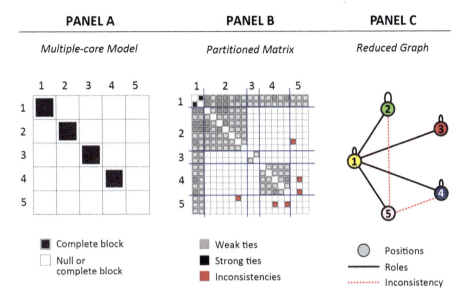

Fig. 9.2 An example of network reduction through prespecified blockmodeling. *Panel A*: A theoretical multiple-core model. *Panel B*: The multiple-core model fit to data. Inconsistencies between observed and expected ties are marked in red. *Panel C*: An example of reduction where the partitioned matrix in *Panel B* is presented as a reduced graph (Source: Authors' elaborations based on R&D collaboration within the technological district)

complete blocks (Batagelj, Ferligoj, & Doreian, 1992; Doreian et al., 2005). The term *block* refers to the ties linking equivalent actors to alters in this permuted matrix.

In prespecified blockmodeling, a hypothesis on the overall configuration of the network is formulated a priori on theoretical grounds. Subsequently, this model configuration is fit to the data by means of a local optimization algorithm. The algorithm partitions the network to minimize the overall number of inconsistencies between the expected and observed ties. Lastly, the permuted matrix can be reduced to a simpler graph (the image), which represents an instance of all the possible configurations compatible with that prespecified block model.

Figure 9.2 presents the prespecified block model used to reduce IMAST networks (Panel A) and exemplifies the process of reduction (Panels B and C). Panel A reports, in a matrix format, the multiple-core blockmodel specified to fit the data. This particular blockmodel was introduced by Kronegger et al. (2011) to study collaboration among Slovenian academics. The rows and the columns of the matrix in Panel A represent groups of organizations, whereas the cells of the matrix indicate how these groups are related to each other (i.e., the role they play in the system). As mentioned, we specified the groups to be formed according to the definition of structural equivalence.

The topological hypothesis advanced by this blockmodel is that multiple cores of completely connected actors exist in the observed network. We express this hypothesis formally by specifying that diagonal blocks are complete. In our specific case, these diagonal cores can be interpreted as research units or project partnerships. In keeping with Kronegger et al. (2011), these cores are hereafter referred to as *simple cores*.

Furthermore, the blockmodel allows simple cores either to be connected to each other through bridging blocks or to stay disjointed. In our specification, off-diagonal blocks can be either null or complete. The former condition is the case when no overlapping exists between two research groups, whereas the latter condition signals brokerage.

The final block (5,5) of the blockmodel representing the periphery of this multiple-core blockmodel is left unspecified so that it can be either complete or null. The network will have a periphery if the last block is null, implying that the actors in the respective cluster 5 will have no relations among themselves. Pajek software for social network analysis was used to fit IMAST project networks to this block model at each time point.

Panel B of Fig. 9.2 reports how the blockmodel fits the IMAST collaboration network in the year 2006. As mentioned, the observed network was permuted using structural equivalence so that organizations (rows and columns of the network matrix) formed either complete or null clusters (identified by blue lines in Panel B). The cells of the network report the number of times actors collaborated with each other. The higher the number of collaorations, the more intense the color.

Inconsistencies between the observed network and the blockmodel hypothesis are reported in red. The location and pattern of inconsistencies can be examined to arrive at a substantive interpretation of blockmodeling solutions (Prota & Doreian, 2016). More specifically, in this study inconsistencies are used to operationalize the key concepts of *cohesive cores* and *structural variations* as discussed in the first section as follows:

1. Complete diagonal blocks with no inconsistencies refer to clusters whose members collaborated on exactly the same research projects or on a single research project. All the organizations participating in the same R&D project are, by definition, collaborating with one another and form a complete clique or a 1-covered block.
2. Complete diagonal blocks with inconsistencies indicate effective cohesive cores. Through the use of structural equivalence, inconsistencies in a complete diagonal block imply nonidentical patterns of ties between a cluster's organizations. In other words, organizations recursively collaborate in slightly different partnerships.
3. A diagonal core is a bridging core when all the off-diagonal blocks associated with it are complete. This operationalization applies to block (1;1) in Panel B of Fig. 9.2, whose associated columns and rows are all complete. In our example the two research institutions in cluster 1 collaborated on all the projects undertaken by the district. By identifying a specific group of organizations participating in all research projects, bridging cores can be taken as a measure of local brokerage as discussed by Glückler (2007).

4. Inconsistencies in null off-diagonal blocks identify brokerage. An example of this pattern of collaboration is shown by the red ties in block (2;5) and (4;5). These inconsistencies show that individual organizations in clusters 2 and 4 are also taking part in the projects undertaken by the organizations in cluster 5. These organizations cross a structural hole.

Note that all the inconsistencies reported in Panel B involve the peripheral block (5;5), which happens to be null for that year. In other words, the network in 2006 indeed took a classic core–periphery structure with a bridging core (block (1;1)) and a disconnected periphery (block (5;5)). An increased number of inconsistencies involving actors in cluster 5 will ultimately have an impact on the core-periphery structure of the network by eliminating the periphery. In that eventuality, this local bridging would represent a structural variation (Glückler, 2007).

Finally, Panel C of Fig. 9.2 illustrates an example of network reduction by which the rows and columns of the partitioned network matrix in Panel B are shrunk to single nodes if they are equivalent. The reduced graph represents the observed configuration consistent with the prespecified blockmodel. In the reduced graph, nodes with loops represent simple cores (complete diagonal blocks in Panel A), whereas ties indicate cross-cluster bridging. Dotted red lines indicate a discrepancy between the network observed and the ideal core-periphery model tested.

Blockmodeling Results

The blockmodel specified in the previous section is used to reduce the observed networks (as illustrated in Fig. 9.3) in each year from 2006 to 2013.[7] The reduced graphs obtained are presented in Fig. 9.3.

Empirical results confirm that a process of structural transition characterized the evolutionary trajectory of the IMAST collaboration network. Between 2006 and 2009, the network configured as a core–periphery model with few inconsistencies. In each year of that period, it was possible to identify a clear bridging core linking all the other clusters in a star configuration. Moreover, during those years, there were only a few cross-cutting ties connecting clusters beyond the bridging core, and they were all defined as inconsistencies (reported as red ties in Fig. 9.3). Lastly, from 2006 to 2008, a clear periphery was identified. Members of cluster 5 did not have collaborations among themselves (there was no loop on the cluster), but they did have systemic ties with the bridging core and sporadic ties with other clusters (inconsistencies).

In 2009 there occurred a variation capable of shifting the network evolutionary path toward a new configuration. The shift is signaled, among the other things, by

---

[7] An increasing number of clusters (from 4 to 10) were used for reduction. Only the best solutions are reported. The chosen solutions are those that minimize the number of clusters and inconsistencies and still provide stable results. One thousand repetitions were done for each fit.

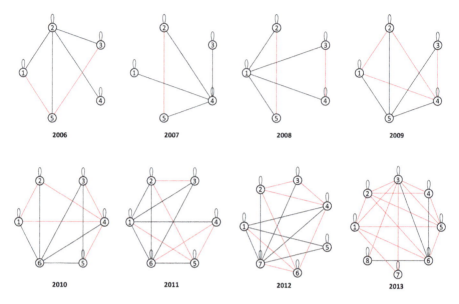

Fig. 9.3 Reduced graphs of IMAST collaboration networks over time. *Nodes* represent clusters of structurally equivalent actors; *links* represent intergroup relations; loops signal within-group connections. *Red ties* signal positive ties in blocks specified as null (bridging ties) (Source: Authors' elaborations based on R&D collaboration within the technological district)

the fact that the periphery (cluster 5) suddenly became the bridging core. Figure 9.3 shows that in 2009 cluster 5 was connected to all the other clusters but it had no loop. That is, its members were disconnected from each other, but they have become key structural brokers within the network. This result alone calls into question the very concept of network periphery. In addition, in 2009 a new bridging core emerged from the inconsistencies in cluster 4. The new bridging core indicates that inconsistencies were becoming structured and that a new collaboration pattern was being established from below.

From 2010 onward, the development trajectory of IMAST remarkably phased away from a core–periphery model, and the pattern identified in 2009 gradually evolved into a new trajectory. In 2010 cluster 6 represented the main bridging core; like cluster 5 in 2009, it also had no loop. This evidence further confirms that structural transformations were taking place at the periphery of the network. Moreover, in 2010 cluster 4 remained a bridging core connected through inconsistencies, just as it was in 2009.

This process of transition from a classic core–periphery model culminated in 2011, when the periphery suddenly disappeared. From 2011 to 2013, all clusters had loops, indicating that intercluster collaborations were occurring. The hypothesis that a core–periphery structure persisted from 2006 to 2013 can therefore be rejected. Instead, the collaboration network evolved toward a new model characterized by multiple bridging cores and an increasing number of sporadic ties linking clusters to one another. In 2012 a third bridging cluster emerged (cluster 3), whereas in 2013 the institutional bridging function seemed to have lost out to increasingly diffused bridging ties captured by the model as inconsistencies.

In the next section the pattern and location of inconsistencies are examined to aid in understanding what types of variations occurred and what types of actors were involved in this process of recombination.

Inconsistency Analysis and Structural Variations

This section includes an in-depth analysis of inconsistencies to aid in understanding (a) what types of variations shifted the IMAST development trajectory from a core–periphery to a multiple cores topology as discussed in the immediately preceding section (Results) and (b) what types of actors were involved in terms of knowledge bases and geographical location.

Inconsistencies in blockmodeling do not have a straightforward interpretation. A blockmodel solution cannot be accepted or discarded based on the number of inconsistencies it produces (Doreian et al., 2005). The number of inconsistencies depends mostly upon the shape of the block (Prota & Doreian, 2016). Rather, inconsistencies need to be interpreted in the light of the equivalence chosen for the reduction. From this perspective, inconsistencies indicate where and how the observed network deviates from the specified block model. With this consideration in mind, we have used blockmodel inconsistencies in this study to operationalize structural variations such as local and global bridging.

To explore the location of the inconsistencies the data produced, we examine the inconsistencies matrices as reported in Fig. 9.4. The matrices offer an alternative visualization of the reduced graph presented in Fig. 9.3 and highlight different aspects of the solutions. Although graphs provide an immediate idea of the evolutionary trajectory of the network, matrices allow a more detailed analysis of inconsistencies' locations. In each reduced matrix of Fig. 9.4, rows and columns represent clusters of similar organizations (nodes in the graphs of Fig. 9.3), and cells represent relations between clusters representing ties in the graphs of Fig. 9.3. Matirx's cells are hereafter referred to as blocks (row #; column #). Black cells indicate complete blocks, and white cells represent null blocks. Numbers indicate inconsistencies.

As expected, complete diagonal blocks without inconsistencies identify organizations collaborating on a single project. We refer to these project groups as simple cores. Simple cores are, for instance, all diagonal blocks in year 2006; block (1;1) in 2009; and all diagonal blocks but blocks 3;3 and 5;5 in 2013.

We defined cohesive cores as complete blocks on the main diagonal with inconsistencies. Examples include block (3;3) in 2007, blocks (2;2), (3;3), and (5;5) in 2011, and blocks (3;3) and (5;5) in 2013, as in Fig. 9.4.

Beyond simple and cohesive cores, the blockmodel also identified bridging cores. Particularly central to the system of collaboration are block (4;4) in 2007, block (5;5) in 2009, and block (6;6) in 2010. These clusters are peculiar insofar as

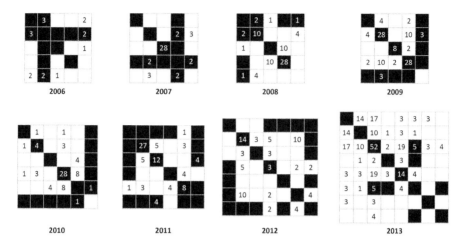

Fig. 9.4 Image matrices of IMAST collaboration networks over time. *Black* cells represent complete blocks; *white* cells represent null blocks; *numbers* indicate inconsistencies between observed and expected ties (Source: Authors' elaborations based on patterns of R&D collaboration within the technological district)

they included only a few organizations linked by strong collaborative ties involving all other clusters (all the blocks on the associated rows and columns are complete). These key bridging cores had ties spanning all the other research units and played the role of pivots for the whole collaboration network.

Finally, the number of positive ties in null blocks signals that individual brokerage was occurring. Figure 9.4 shows that there was a systemic and generalized increase in this type of inconsistency over time. In 2013, inconsistencies spread across full rows and columns in correspondence with cores. This pattern suggests that a single organization acted as a broker linking more cores, as if it were a bridging core embedded within another type of core. Examples are provided by blocks (1;1), (2;2) and (3;3) in 2013 whose associated rows and columns present a significant number of inconsistencies.

To verify this substantive interpretation of the results further, blockmodeling partitions are fitted onto the original network data. In Fig. 9.5, the observed collaboration networks in selected years (2007, 2009, 2011, 2013) are shown by means of blockmodeling partitions.

The changes that occurred within the main cohesive core can be appreciated in Fig. 9.5. Whereas in 2007 all cores were exclusively connected to the bridging core (block (4;4)), in 2013 a large group of local organizations was right in the middle of the graph (red nodes in Figure 9.5, diagonal block 3;3 in Figure 9.4) and was linked to a number of other cores. This group fully represented the heterogeneity of knowledge bases in IMAST: firms from the defense, aeronautics, maritime, transport, aerospace, and automotive industries, and public universities were all embedded within this cluster along with private research centers and universities.

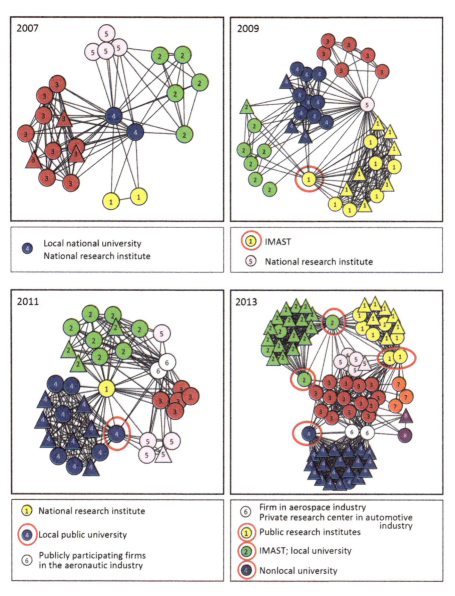

Fig. 9.5 Energized graphs of four collaboration networks (2007, 2009, 2011, 2013). *Circular nodes* represent the technological district's associated members; *triangles* are partners from a different geographical region or nation. *Numbers* indicate clustering partitions. *Red circles* around nodes indicate bridging through inconsistencies (Source: Authors' elaborations based on patterns of R&D collaboration within the technological district)

The graphs in Fig. 9.5 clearly illustrate the transformations related to the role played by the bridging core within IMAST. In 2006 and 2007, the bridging core was the very center of the network. Cluster 4 included the local public university (under whose initiative the district was first instituted) and the national public research institute. In 2009 and 2010 the local public university entered the cohesive block (4;4) (blue nodes in Figure 9.5, block 4;4 in Figure 9.4). The bridging core (pink node in Figure 9.5, block 5;5 in Figure 9.4) was composed, instead, of the national public research institute alone. The district itself, took part in a large European project together with some of the district members, acting as an institutional global broker between the European partners and the district (yellow node circled in red in Figure 9.5, block 4;4 in Figure 9.4). In 2011 a further bridging core emerged within the system, encompassing two firms (white nodes in Figure 9.5, block 6;6 in figure 9.4).

Lastly, in 2013, the only bridging core remeined was this block (6;6) that included a firm and a private research center from two different industries (aerospace and transport). Collaboration, however, assumed a completely new pattern because many actors individually connected cores one another, as was the case with two public research institutes (circled in red) from cluster 1. Similarly, in cluster 2 both IMAST itself and the local public university had explicit brokerage functions. In cluster 4, a university from another region linked the cohesive cluster with the rest of the project members, acting as a global broker.

These ties linking individual organizations from a core with all the members of other cores account for the generalized increase in the inconsistencies reported in the matrix of Fig. 9.4. We have circled these broker organizations in red to indicate that their behavior is inconsistent with the model. It is worth noting that, in 2013, broker organizations connected the local cohesive core (circles) with actors external to the district (triangles). This global brokerage very much recalls the buzz-and-pipeline configuration described by Bathelt et al. (2004).

These results support the conclusion that IMAST is characterized by a clear structural transition from a core–periphery topology toward a new buzz-and-pipeline configuration.

Conclusions

We have tackled the problem of analyzing the topology and evolution of collaborations within a policy-anchored district by using prespecified block modeling. Through analysis of the patterns of collaboration established during the period from 2006 to 2013, our study has traced the evolutionary trajectory of IMAST's R&D collaborations. Given that collaborations were actively managed by the administration, the study has also provided an assessment of the district's governance and inherent innovation policy.

We used prespecified blockmodeling to define a benchmark topology against which to measure structural changes. Empirical results clearly show that the IMAST collaboration network evolved from a neat core–periphery structure toward a new structural topology characterized by an increasing number of local and global brokers' ties. This new topology closely resembles the buzz-and-pipeline model described by Bathelt et al. (2004).

In analyzing this structural change, we have taken an evolutionary approach that takes both retention mechanisms and variations into account (Glückler, 2007). Among the retention mechanisms, the analysis identified the formation of a large cohesive core represennting key knowledge bases of IMAST. Examining the changing composition of this cohesive core over time, we found an increasing integration of the science and technology bases. The core included not only private and public firms but also a growing number of university departments and research institutions. The convergence of knowledge bases through joint research activities undertaken at the core of the district remained a constant characteristic of the district's development.

In addition to this cohesive core, a bridging core also characterized the system at its initial phase. This bridging core can be thought of as IMAST's institutional base constituted by the main local university and the national research institute. Over time, however, not only did the composition of the bridging core change to include firms, but new broker organizations also emerged. By 2013 the bridging function spread across clusters and became a characteristic behavior of broker organizations crossing structural holes rather than an institutional function. We note also that, although the original bridging core linked local cores to one another, new bridging ties linked the local cohesive core to external partners as in a buzz-and-pipeline model (Bathelt et al., 2004).

From a policy perspective, the structural analysis undertaken in this study is important because it allows an assessment of how the network was governed over a 10-year period. The structural changes were the result of an active administration pursuing a coherent development strategy.

A similar analysis can be replicated in other contexts to compare developmental trajectories across other policy-anchored districts in Italy and beyond. If undertaken, such study would probably open new questions about the variety of topologies of innovation networks and the role local institutions play in managing the structural transitions from one topology to another.

References

Amin, A., & Thrift, N. (Eds.). (1995). *Globalization, institutions, and regional development in Europe*. Oxford: University Press.

Ardovino, O., & Pennacchio, L. (2012). *Le determinanti della cooperazione nei distretti tecnologici italiani finanziati dal governo* [The determinants of cooperation in government-sponsored innovation networks: Empirical evidence from Italian technological districts]. *Studi Economici, 108*, 121–149. doi:10.3280/STE2012-108004

Asheim, B. T., Smith, H. L., & Oughton, C. (2011). Regional innovation systems: Theory, empirics and policy. *Regional Studies, 45*, 875–891. doi:10.1080/00343404.2011.596701

Autio, E. (1998). Evaluation of RTD in regional systems of innovation. *European Planning Studies, 6,* 131–140. doi:10.1080/09654319808720451

Balland, P., Suire, R., & Vicente, J. (2010). *How do clusters/pipelines and core/periphery structures work together in knowledge processes?* Papers in Evolutionary Economic Geography (PEEG), #10.08. Retrieved from http://econ.geo.uu.nl/peeg/peeg1008.pdf

Batagelj, V., Ferligoj, A., & Doreian, P. (1992). Direct and indirect methods for structural equivalence. *Social Networks, 14,* 63–90. doi:10.1016/0378-8733(92)90014-X

Bathelt, H., Malmberg, A., & Maskell, P. (2004). Clusters and knowledge: Local buzz, global pipelines and the process of knowledge creation. *Progress in Human Geography, 28,* 31–56. doi:10.1191/0309132504ph469oa

Baum, J., Shipilov, A., & Rowley, T. (2003). Where do small worlds come from? *Industrial and Corporate Change, 12,* 697–725. doi:10.1093/icc/12.4.697

Bertamino, F., Bronzini, R., De Maggio, M., & Revelli, D. (2014). *Local policies for innovation: The case of technology districts in Italy.* Bank of Italy. Retrieved from http://www.bancaditalia.it/pubblicazioni/altri-atti-convegni/2014-innovazione-italia/Bertamino-Bronzini-DeMaggio-Revelli.pdf

Boschma, R. A., & Ter Wal, A. L. J. (2007). Knowledge networks and innovative performance in an industrial district: The case of a footwear district in the south of Italy. *Industry and Innovation, 14,* 177–199. doi:10.1080/13662710701253441

Capuano, C., De Stefano, D., Del Monte, A., D'Esposito, M. R., & Vitale, M. P. (2013). The analysis of network additionality in the context of territorial innovation policy: The case of Italian technological districts. In P. Giudici, S. Ingrassia, & M. Vichi (Eds.), *Statistical models for data analysis* (pp. 81–88). Heidelberg: Springer International Publishing.

Cooke, P. (2005). Regionally asymmetric knowledge capabilities and open innovation: Exploring 'Globalization 2'—A new model of industry organisation. *Research Policy, 34,* 1128–1149. doi:10.1016/j.respol.2004.12.005

Cooke, P., & Morgan, K. (1999). *The associational economy: Firms, regions, and innovation.* Oxford: University Press.

Cooke, P., Uranga, M. G., & Etxebarria, G. (1997). Regional innovation systems: Institutional and organizational dimensions. *Research Policy, 26,* 475–491. doi:10.1016/S0048-7333(97)00025-5

De Nooy, W., Mrvar, A., & Batagelj, V. (2011). *Exploratory network analysis with Pajek* (rev. and expanded 2nd ed.). Cambridge, UK: University Press.

Doloreux, D., & Parto, S. (2004). *Regional innovation systems: A critical synthesis* (Discussion paper No. 2004–17). United Nations University Institute for New Technologies, INTECH. Retrieved from http://www.intech.unu.edu/publications/discussion-papers/2004-17.pdf

Doreian, P., Batagelj, V., & Ferligoj, A. (2005). *Generalized blockmodeling.* Cambridge, UK: University Press.

Everett, M. G., & Borgatti, S. P. (2013). The dual-projection approach for two-mode networks. *Social Networks, 35,* 204–210. doi:10.1016/j.socnet.2012.05.004

Ferligoj, A., Doreian, P., & Batagelj, V. (2011). Positions and roles. In J. Scott & P. J. Carrington (Eds.), *The SAGE handbook of social network analysis* (pp. 434–446). Thousand Oaks: Sage.

Fornahl, D., Broekel, T., & Boschma, R. (2011). What drives patent performance of German biotech firms? The impact of R&D subsidies, knowledge networks and their location. *Papers in Regional Science, 90,* 395–418. doi:10.1111/j.1435-5957.2011.00361.x

Giuliani, E. (2007). The selective nature of knowledge networks in clusters: Evidence from the wine industry. *Journal of Economic Geography, 7(2),* 139–168. doi:10.1093/jeg/lbw020.

Glückler, J. (2007). Economic geography and the evolution of networks. *Journal of Economic Geography, 7,* 619–634. doi:10.1093/jeg/lbm023

Glückler, J. (2014). How controversial innovation succeeds in the periphery? A network perspective of BASF Argentina. *Journal of Economic Geography, 14,* 903–927. doi:10.1093/jeg/lbu016

Kronegger, L., Ferligoj, A., & Dorein, P. (2011). On the dynamics of national scientific systems. *Quality & Quantity, 45,* 989–1015. doi:10.1007/s11135-011-9484-3

Landabaso, M., Oughton, C., & Morgan, K. (1999). Learning regions in Europe: Theory, policy and practice through the RIS experience. *Systems and policies for the global learning economy,* Westport, Connecticut and London, Praeger, 79–110.

Lazzeroni, M. (2010). High-tech activities, system innovativeness and geographical concentration: Insights into technological districts in Italy. *European Urban and Regional Studies, 17,* 45–63. doi:10.1177/0969776409350795

Lorrain, F, & White, H. (1971). Structural equivalence of individuals in social networks. *Journal of Mathematical Sociology, 1,* 49–80. doi:10.1080/0022250X.1971.9989788

Markusen, A. (1996). Sticky places in slippery space: A typology of industrial districts. *Economic Geography, 72,* 293–313. doi:10.2307/144402

Martin, R., & Sunley, P. (2003). Deconstructing clusters: Chaotic concept or policy panacea? *Journal of Economic Geography, 3,* 5–35. doi:10.1093/jeg/3.1.5

Martin, R., & Sunley, P. (2006). Path dependence and regional economic evolution. *Journal of Economic Geography, 6,* 395–437. doi:10.1093/jeg/lbl012

Miceli, V. (2010). *Distretti tecnologici e sistemi regionali di innovazione. Il caso italiano* [Technological districts and regional systems of innovation: The case of Italy]. Bologna: Il Mulino.

Morgan, K. (2007). The learning region: Institutions, innovation and regional renewal. *Regional Studies, 41,* 147–159. doi:10.1080/00343400701232322

Owen-Smith, J., & Powell, W. W. (2004). Knowledge networks as channels and conduits: The effects of spillovers in the Boston biotechnology community. *Organization Science, 15,* 5–21. doi:10.1287/orsc.1030.0054

Porter, M. E. (1998). Clusters and the new economics of competition. *Harvard Business Review, 76*(6), 77–90. Retrieved from EBSCO*host* database.

Powell, W. W., Koput, K. W., & Smith-Doerr, L. (1996). Interorganizational collaboration and the locus of innovation: Networks of learning in biotechnology. *Administrative Science Quarterly, 41,* 116–145. doi:10.2307/2393988

Prota, L., D'Esposito, M., De Stefano, D., Giordano, G., & Vitale, M. (2013). Modeling cooperative behaviors in innovation networks: An empirical analysis. In J. C. Spohrer, L. E. Freund (Eds.), *Advances in the human side of service engineering* (pp. 369–378). Boca Raton: Taylor & Francis.

Prota, L., & Doreian, P. (2016). Finding roles in sparse economic network: Going beyond regular equivalence. *Social Networks, 45,* 1–17. doi:10.1016/j.socnet.2015.10.005

Prota, L., & Vitale, M. P. (2014). A pre-specified blockmodeling to analyze structural dynamics in innovation networks. In D. Vicari, A. Okada, G. Ragozini, & C. Weihs (Eds.), *Analysis and modeling of complex data in behavioural and social sciences* (pp. 221–230). Heidelberg: Springer.

Provan, G. K., Fish, A., & Sydow, J. (2007). Interorganizational networks at the network level: A review of the empirical literature on whole networks. *Journal of Management, 33,* 479–516. doi:10.1177/0149206307302554

Provan, K. G., & Kenis, P. (2008). Modes of network governance: Structure, management, and effectiveness. *Journal of Public Administration Research and Theory, 18,* 229–252. doi:10.1093/jopart/mum015

Tödtling, F., & Trippl, M. (2005). One size fits all? Towards a differentiated regional innovation policy approach. *Research Policy, 34,* 1203–1219. doi:10.1016/j.respol.2005.01.018

Tsai, W. (2001). Knowledge transfer in intraorganizational networks: Effects of network position and absorptive capacity on business unit innovation and performance. *Academy of Management Journal, 44,* 996–1004. doi:10.2307/3069443

Wasserman, S., & Faust, K. (1994). *Social network analysis: Methods and applications.* Cambridge, UK: University Press.

Open Access This chapter is distributed under the terms of the Creative Commons Attribution 4.0 International License (http://creativecommons.org/licenses/by/4.0/), which permits use, duplication, adaptation, distribution and reproduction in any medium or format, as long as you give appropriate credit to the original author(s) and the source, provide a link to the Creative Commons license and indicate if changes were made.

The images or other third party material in this chapter are included in the work's Creative Commons license, unless indicated otherwise in the credit line; if such material is not included in the work's Creative Commons license and the respective action is not permitted by statutory regulation, users will need to obtain permission from the license holder to duplicate, adapt or reproduce the material.

Chapter 10
Platforming for Path-Breaking? The Case of Regional Electromobility Initiatives in Germany

Jörg Sydow and Friedemann Koll

Electromobility Ante Portas?

Formulating platform policies, or "platforming" for short, is becoming increasingly popular in both innovation research and practice, where they are used for either inducing regional knowledge-creating processes or overcoming the closed nature of regional clusters that have, or have been, developed (Asheim, Boschma, & Cooke, 2011; Cooke, 2011). Platforming is the process of arriving at "regional resource configurations based on the past development trajectories but presenting the future potential to produce competitive advantage existing in the defined resource configurations" (Harmaakorpi, 2006, p. 1089). It focuses on injecting diversity or, more precisely, what is commonly called "related variety" (Boschma & Frenken, 2011b; Frenken, van Oort, & Verburg, 2007), into regional developmental processes in terms of knowledge resources, agents, activities, and relations. To this end, platforming sets out from the already existing knowledge base of a particular region but is commonly understood as a strategy that is more combinative than cumulative, as one designed to foster cross-sectorial coordination and learning aimed at cross-fertilization. But can such platforming be used to break away from an established regional knowledge path? That is, can it be used to reconstitute choice for the actors who follow the current path but succeed in deviating from it in some significant way? This definition of path-breaking builds on the increasing convergence in theorizing path dependence, at least in organization science and regional studies.

J. Sydow (✉)
School of Business & Economics, Freie Universität Berlin,
Boltzmannstr 20, 14195 Berlin, Germany
e-mail: joerg.sydow@fu-berlin.de

F. Koll
School of Business & Economics, Path Dependene Research Center,
Freie Universität Berlin, Garystr 21, 14195 Berlin, Germany
e-mail: friedemann.koll@yahoo.com

The electromobility initiative in Germany, launched in response to global warming caused by high carbon emissions, and boosted in the aftermath of the global financial crisis that erupted in 2008, provides a suitable case for investigating the potential of platforming to unlock path dependencies that are likely to be more than technological in nature. Battery electric vehicles (BEVs) might be on the way to becoming the most serious challenger to the traditional fossil-fuel powertrain technology driven by internal combustion engines. Even though significant technological progress is a crucial factor, it is not enough in the development of the electric car (Kirsch, 2000). Battery-charging infrastructure has to be built, new organizations created and existing ones adapted, intelligent traffic concepts developed, and new business models designed to pave the way for this technological alternative. All these technological and socioeconomic challenges are addressed in the corresponding policy initiative, the National Platform for Electromobility (NPE) set up by the federal German government in 2010. Involving all the relevant national actors, yet adopting a clear regional focus, it offers a framework for discerning the extent to which platforming can change an entrenched technological path at a regional level, that is, tightly intertwined with institutional and organizational path dependencies. At the very least, platform policies such as the NPE may be capable of opening new opportunities.

We ask under what conditions platforming may be a suitable, if only a complementary, strategy for regional path-breaking change. To answer this question, we first review the present state of theorizing on path dependence and path-breaking and locate the role of platform policies systematically within this effort, paying particular heed to regional knowledge-creation processes. We then summarize the emergence and development of the electromobility initiative in Germany, which has a strong regional focus, during the four and a half years from summer 2007 through early 2012. After describing our research setting, we explain our research design and methods. That section is followed by a presentation of our empirical insights from two metropolitan regions that differ significantly in their current knowledge resources and their dependence on the automotive industry: the region of Germany's capital city, Berlin, which has little industrial production; and of Stuttgart, a core hub of Germany's automobile production. We begin with the idea that platform policies may, under certain circumstances, contribute to breaking a technological, institutional, and/or organizational knowledge path, or may at least open new opportunities. Our empirical insights lead us to the tentative conclusion that platforming may contribute to path-forming but not necessarily to path-breaking at a regional level.

Our study contributes to the rising discourse on the possibilities and limitations of platforming as a potential "post-cluster" (Cooke, 2011, p. 307) regional policy approach with a particular focus on breaking or forming technological, institutional, and/or organizational paths in regions. With regard to the continuing emphasis on regional knowledge creation and exploitation, our inquiry contributes broadly to the knowledge-based theorizing of regional economic development and, thereby, also to popular evolutionary and institutional theorizing about regional development processes.

The Theory of Path Dependence and Path-Breaking and the Role of Platforming

For decades regional clusters (e.g., Bathelt, 2005; Lazzeretti, Sedita, & Caloffi, 2014; Martin & Sunley, 2003; Porter, 2000) have been seen as hot spots of knowledge creation and transfer or, more broadly, learning (e.g., Bathelt, Malmberg, & Maskell, 2004; Cooke, 2001; Ibert, 2007; Malmberg & Maskell, 2002; Maskell, 2001; Morgan, 1997). This view cumulated over the years into the conception of clusters as *the* institution for knowledge-based economic development, although negative path dependencies and even the dangers of lock-ins have also been recorded with respect to clusters for some time (Grabher, 1993; Hassink, 2005, 2010; Henning, Stam, & Wenting, 2013; Lagerholm & Malmberg, 2009; Martin, 2010; Martin & Sunley, 2006). The path dependence of knowledge development has been noted for regions and geographical network trajectories (Glückler, 2007) as well as for firms and other types of organizations and their knowledge management practices (Coombs & Hull, 1998; Nooteboom, 1997). In regional clusters this phenomenon is, hence, likely to have its roots not only in technological but also institutional and organizational path dependencies (Sydow, Lerch, & Staber, 2010).

Path dependence is mostly used with the broad meaning of "history matters," less often in a much more specific, analytical sense alluding to the seminal works of Paul David (1985) and W. Brian Arthur (1994). In this chapter we adopt this latter understanding, which is currently also conquering the analysis of regional development processes and might eventually be used for additional cumulative knowledge production on cluster formation and transformation processes in economic geography (Bathelt & Boggs, 2003; Boschma & Fornahl, 2011; Henning et al., 2013; Li, Bathelt & Wang, 2012; Tödtling & Trippl, 2013; Wolfe & Gertler, 2006). What is more, we try to clarify the relationships between this particular understanding of path dependence and the challenging task of path-breaking—and the role that platforming may have therein. Such clarification is necessary if actors wish to have strategic influence on the development of a regional cluster.

According to David (1985), who developed this understanding based on his research on QWERTY,[1] *path dependence* is understood as a tapering process triggered by a small event and leading, at least potentially, into a lock-in. For three reasons, this understanding is more specific than the general argument that history matters. First, a small event (which in the case of QWERTY is still debated; see Kay, 2013) triggers the tapering process of becoming more dependent on the course of action embarked on after this event. Second, from a certain point in time often retrospectively called a "critical juncture" (Collier & Collier, 1991), positive feedback mechanisms take over and make it increasingly difficult to leave the given course of action, or path. These mechanisms make the once-chosen path increasingly attractive. Economists typically refer to this phenomenon as "increasing

---

[1] QWERTY refers to the most common keyboard layout for Latin script. The name derives from the sequence of the first six keys in the upper left row of letters when read from left to right.

returns" (Arthur, 1994), although they have also become more receptive to explanations other than decreasing unit costs or network effects (David, 2001). Third, this path-dependent process is likely to lead to a lock-in, that is, a situation in which actors are stuck with former choices because an alternative course of action is no longer feasible.

Building on the works of David and Arthur as well as on that in political science (e.g., Mahoney, 2000; Pierson, 2000; Thelen, 1999), the ascendant theory of organizational path dependence (Sydow, Schreyögg, & Koch, 2009) highlights the importance of imprinting processes, the notion that history already matters in the preformation phase of a path. In keeping with earlier contributions and with much thinking in economic geography (see Henning et al., 2013), this theory also underlines the importance of self-reinforcing processes triggered by one or more events or actions that narrow down alternatives in the formation phase, including coordination, complementarity, and particular kinds of learning effects. Finally, like the original conception by David and Arthur, the theory of organizational path dependence stresses the lack of any realistic alternatives in the lock-in phase. Nevertheless, it asserts the importance of considering agency also in this last phase because agents do not simply have to take the path; they are capable of making on-path changes and, under specific circumstances, of shaping, leaving, or even breaking the existing path.

Although this theory is fairly new, it has already been applied explicitly to the analysis of a nascent cluster (optics), for which the relevance of technological, institutional, and organizational factors for regional path dependence was pointed out by Sydow et al. (2010). More significant, however, the theory of organizational path dependence is consistent with recent developments in the theory of regional path dependence (in the fields of economic geography and regional studies, see especially Henning et al., 2013; Martin & Sunley, 2006). Table 10.1 gives an overview of the most important features of this theorizing in four important streams of literature.

Path-breaking activities, which do not necessarily imply the creation of a new path, can be different in nature and degree, but there is a minimum requirement:

> Since the process of becoming path dependent has been framed as progressively eliminating the scope of decision making, this minimum condition is the effective restoration of a choice situation—the insertion of at least one alternative course of action. However, opening the window for an alternative is necessary but not sufficient. The new alternative has to be a superior one (Arthur, 1994), because implanting an inferior one would not constitute a real choice. (Sydow et al., 2009, p. 702)

Of course, what is perceived as a real choice by the actors or outside observers depends heavily on context. In reality, it is less a question of choice or no choice than of degree. A more realistic understanding of path-breaking would therefore be geared to increasing the scope of choice.

A potential means of path-breaking in this sense is *platforming*, which tries to (re)introduce diversity, related variety in particular, into a developmental process, including a regional knowledge path. In the case of forming a new path, a certain amount and composition of such related variety is required. However, both are hard

Table 10.1 The theory of path dependence in different disciplines and fields of study

Important features	Economics[a]	Political science[a]	Organization science[b]	Regional studies[b]
Primary object of study	Technologies	Institutions	Organizations	Regions, in particular regional clusters comprising all three
Triggering event	Small	Small or big	Event or action	Event or action
Role history	Matters only after the event	Unclear	Historical imprints also matter before the event/action	Historical imprints also matter before the event/action
Self-reinforcing mechanisms	Increasing returns at the center	Learning more generally, complementarity and coordination effects	Coordination and complementarity effects, single-loop learning, adaptive expectations	Coordination and complementarity effects, learning, adaptive expectations
Agency	Agency restricted to reproducing the path	Political interests and power, agency also shaping the path	Interests and power, agency in all phases of the process	Interests and power, agency in all phases of the process
Contributors	David (1985, 2001), Arthur (1994), and many others with mainly an application focus on technological developments; North (1990) famously pointing to economic institutions	Thelen (1999); Pierson (2000); and Mahoney (2000)	Sydow, Schreyögg, & Koch (2009); Sydow, Lerch, & Stabe (2010); Schreyögg, Sydow, & Holtmann (2011); Manning & Sydow (2011)	Grabher (1993); Bathelt & Boggs (2003); Hassink (2005, 2010); Martin & Sunley (2006); Glückler (2007); Lagerholm & Malmberg (2009); Martin (2010); Henning, Stam, & Wenting (2013)

[a]Discipline
[b]Interdisciplinary field of study

to establish ex ante. Breaking an existing path or opening it to additional choices, may call for additional related variety. Admittedly, related variety constitutes an underdetermined and insufficient, but necessary, condition for any concept of path-forming or path-breaking.

Although the idea of platforming has arisen only recently (see also Asheim et al., 2011; Cooke, 2007, 2012; Harmaakorpi, 2006; Harmaakorpi, Tura, & Melkas, 2011), examples are found in a handbook (Cooke & De Laurentis, 2010, pp. 294–309), at the interface of art and food in an Italian region (Lazzeretti, Capone, & Cinti, 2010), in emerging innovation policies of several Finnish regions (Uotila, Harmaakorpi, & Hermans, 2012), and in urban regions of Canada (Wolfe, 2013).

Drawing on the insights these sources provide and anticipating the findings of our own empirical study, we see platforming as building on and steering regional resource configurations and as developing common cognitive-normative frames that foster collaboration, not least between private and public sector organizations, yet also as preventing the collaboration from drifting toward premature rigidity.

The concept of platforming, whether or not appropriately labeled as a postcluster policy approach, is explicitly related by its protagonists not only to cluster policies per se but to regional path dependencies and this type of rigidity in particular (e.g., Cooke, 2011, p. 307). The core concept of platforming, with its powerful idea of related variety borrowed from evolutionary economics, aims directly at counterbalancing the market-driven focus that conventional cluster policies, often with reference to Porter (2000), have on rather closed industries and industry-related settings and their emphasis on the homogeneity of knowledge configurations.

Against this background it comes as no surprise that the spectrum of regional platform actors, activities, resources, and relations is broader than that of clusters and is even less well captured by the industry concept still dominating cluster research and policy. Instead of narrowing the scope of actors and activities, platforming aims at widening it. At least as important, the concept stresses the understanding of regional trajectories and a conscious avoidance of negative path dependence and regional lock-in by promoting the identification and construction of competitive configurations of assets and by providing access to rather diverse knowledge resources through relationship-building and cross-fertilization. Because related variety is a necessary, but not sufficient, condition for path-forming or -breaking, what is needed in addition are events that help focus attention on new circumstances and the urgent need for eventual change in a regional field or cluster. In this respect the concept of *field-configuring events* (FCE), currently on the rise in organization studies (e.g., Schüßler, Rüling, & Wittneben, 2014), is useful and can be related to platforming.

Referring to work by Meyer, Gaba, and Colwell (2005) on the role of conferences for structuring organizational fields, Lampel and Meyer (2008) define FCEs more broadly as

> temporary social organizations such as tradeshows, professional gatherings, technology contests, and business ceremonies that encapsulate and shape the development of professions, technologies, markets, and industries (Meyer et al., 2005). They are settings in which people from diverse organizations and with diverse purposes assemble periodically, or on a one-time basis, to announce new products, develop industry standards, construct social networks, recognize accomplishments, share and interpret information, and transact business. FCEs can enhance, reorient, or even undermine existing technologies, industries, or markets; or alternately, they can become crucibles from which new technologies, industries, and markets emerge. Recognizing this, their organizers often design FCEs with an eye towards influencing field evolution. (p. 1026)

FCEs are thus an important concept for understanding and a means of executing platform policies, no matter whether they are of a rather continuous or disruptive nature. Despite, or because of, the relatedness of the FCE concept to "temporary clusters" (Maskell, Bathelt, & Malmberg, 2006), it has not yet been fully exploited by economic geographers in the context of understanding and influencing regional development.

Regardless of how important FCEs are considered to be for platforming, structures beyond the particular event are needed. These structures allow agents to refer to them as they strive to influence the development of a regional knowledge base, be it at the field, cluster/network, or organizational level (Giddens, 1984). By referring to these rules and resources in practice, agents reproduce or transform these structures, helping others make sense of related variety to establish common ground for their potentially diverse interests. This solid foundation can, in turn, facilitate future collaboration and coordinated action with a comparatively long-term perspective in order to build momentum in and beyond the FCEs.

Studying Electromobility Initiatives in the Metropolitan Regions of Berlin and Stuttgart

Industrial and political actors recently discovered, or rather rediscovered, electromobility as a promising future technology for urban mobility. In a narrow sense, on which we focus in this chapter, this term coined politically by the German federal government refers only to BEVs, range-extended electric vehicles (REEVs), and plug-in hybrids (PHEVs). It is believed that these three constituent technologies will spread at least in urban areas and thereby contribute to the reduction of carbon dioxide once an adequate regional battery-charging infrastructure is provided (German Federal Government, 2009, pp. 5–7).

We begin by explaining our research design and methods and presenting our empirical insights into policy-making at both the federal and state levels in Germany. Focusing for obvious reasons exclusively on the early stages of these processes, we point out the importance of agenda-setting at the federal level before the implementation of the NPE. Then we look into how the creation of the NPE triggered a process of path-formation at both levels. The chapter concludes with an investigation mainly of the NPE's regional effects. Although the German NPE is primarily the outcome of federal policies, it has had a strong regional focus from the outset. This aspect is important in face of the regional battery-charging infrastructure necessary for electromobility. Even more important, as we show, is the fact that the NPE provided significant economic incentives for industries and regional politicians to join the platforming initiative. Whereas the involved industries mainly sought to decrease their technological uncertainty before engaging in serious research and development (R&D), the politicians welcomed the central government's offer of subsidies for platforming initiatives, including regional ones, to promote regional economic development in the emerging field of electromobility.

Research Design and Methods

To capture the developments at the federal and state levels of analysis, we adopted an embedded case study design (Yin, 2009) centered on two regions—Stuttgart and Berlin—that were (and still are) embedded in the broader, very dynamic national context of electromobility in Germany. Taking Pettigrew's (1990) advice to "go for polar types" (p. 275), we chose the most dissimilar regional cases in order to ensure adequate variance across the existing regional knowledge bases and the present dependence on the automotive industry. The Stuttgart region is Germany's leading automotive cluster, with its extraordinary competence in the traditional engineering of parts and components of the internal combustion engine. Original equipment manufacturers as well as several leading first- and second-tier suppliers have their headquarters there. It is also a region already analyzed for path dependence and possible lock-in (Fuchs, 2010; Fuchs & Wassermann, 2005; Kaiser, 2007; Strambach & Klement, 2013). At the other extreme, we opted for the capital region of Berlin, which is characterized by a substandard number of industrial jobs, particularly in the automotive sector. However, Berlin is widely seen as a hot spot for the creative industries (Lange, Kalandides, Stöber, & Mieg, 2008), including alternative means of transportation and mobility. At the onset of the developments in the field of electromobility, the socioeconomic conditions of these two metropolitan regions differed significantly.[2] The study covered a period of more than 4 years starting in summer 2007, when the political agenda-setting gained momentum, and ending in early 2012, when both regions were selected as electromobility showcases, a federal program that funds large-scale regional demonstration projects to consolidate innovative elements of electromobility and make them visible internationally. These projects may be considered as an advance indication that the contours of the new field were becoming fairly clear.

Unexceptionally for case study research, our inquiry draws on multiple sources of evidence (Eisenhardt, 1989). The main sources of data are 27 semistructured interviews conducted by the second author with representatives of relevant groups of actors at the national level (3 interviews) and regional level (16 in the Berlin region, 8 in the Stuttgart region) in mid-2011. At the national level representatives of participating federal authorities were interviewed. At the regional level the interviewees were experts from regional companies, regional institutions, local administrations, and research organizations. The average interview length was 67 min. Twenty interviews were conducted face to face on-site; seven interviews had to take place by telephone. A semistructured guideline was used throughout all interviews to achieve a degree of uniformity concerning the subject matter discussed. Nonetheless, all interviewees were given ample space to express their own experiences and assessments. To elicit personal accounts and chronological narratives, for

---

[2] For instance, two major players in the German automotive industry, Bosch and Daimler, together employ more than 100,000 people in the Stuttgart region, a number exceeding that of all industrial workplaces in the Berlin region.

example, all interviews began with an open invitation such as, "Just start telling me how you personally initially encountered the issue of electromobility." Subsequently, discussion turned to more specific topics in six thematic blocks: (a) the region's socioeconomic conditions when the field of electromobility was still nascent, (b) the general developments in that field, (c) the way(s) in which the interviewee's organization executed and planned activities, (d) the observable actor constellations and hidden interests in the region, (e) an assessment of the attempts at regional coordination between organizations and sectors, and (f) a short reflection and outlook. For the purpose of this publication, relevant quotations have been translated verbatim by the authors.

A second data source for this study is a collection of more than 150 official and internal documents published between summer 2007 and early 2012. It encompasses about 3000 pages of reports, press releases, presentations, and other material stemming from industry and government. This compilation was used predominantly to construct, or reconstruct, the hard facts of the processual developments. A third source of data is the nonparticipant observations made by the second author while at 28 events such as expert meetings, conferences, and project presentations over a 2-year period until fall 2011, attendance that resulted in more than 250 pages of personal notes. This written record covered information he gathered verbally and visually throughout the official program of each event. It included not only notes from presentations and round-table discussions but also personal impressions. Although we are far from claiming that this source even approximates a coherent ethnography, we used them to guarantee a rather nuanced assessment of the "soft facts" about the processual developments in the regional and national context.

To analyze the data, we had all the interview material (more than 30.5 h) fully transcribed and encoded with a QDA software in a thematic and temporal way. We then added the data derived from the official and internal documents and from the personal notes, attached them to the thematic and temporal codings, and further elaborated on them (more than 2250 codes in all). The combination of these three data sources offered multiple perspectives on certain events, processes, relations, interests, and the like. In this phase of data analysis, we created both a national and a regional timeline of the events and processes. Applying a temporal bracketing strategy (Langley, 1999), we decomposed three distinct periods to sequence the processes and events chronologically for analytic purposes. In accordance with the theory of organizational path dependence (Sydow et al., 2009), we call these periods the *preformation phase*, the *critical juncture*, and the *formation phase*. We used them to structure our process description and to support our conceptual argument with empirical evidence that—at least in the case of regional electromobility initiatives—platforming strategies were being used to open the scope for new regional path-building or path-shaping activities at a fairly early stage. Although we assumed continuity within each period and a certain degree of discontinuity at its boundaries, we omitted later phases in the process, particularly the lock-in phase, because there were no indications that the new technology or knowledge path might already have reached that stage. We focused instead on the early phase of a path by zooming in on these periods before, during, and after the critical juncture. We also focused on

FCEs because they are at least potential "critical turning points" (Lampel & Meyer, 2008, p. 1026), where representatives of all the relevant actor groups meet occasionally to structure, or restructure, resource combinations and to keep coordinating joint action—or, more formally, aim to institutionalize the field of electromobility. In each region we identified three events that we classified as potentially *field-configuring* in nature. Taking these steps in data analysis, we conducted a within-case analysis in each region, focusing on a detailed description of the observable events and activities that occurred between mid-2007 and early 2012. Lastly, we compared the cases across the two regions under study to elaborate commonalities and differences between the identified platforming activities.

Preformation Phase: Political Agenda-Setting

Political actions in the field of electromobility go back to a gathering of Germany's federal cabinet in August 2007. The neologism electromobility originally appeared as one of several ways to address the challenges posed by global climate change, growing energy demand, and rising oil prices as documented in the Integrated Energy and Climate Program (German Federal Government, 2007). The assumption in this report was that battery electric vehicles in particular offer two advantages. One is an enormous potential to reduce transport-related carbon dioxide emissions and the country's dependence on oil imports. The other is an apt opportunity to increase the number of primary energy sources by using the full spectrum of renewable energies to power electric vehicles in the medium and long term. This document was the first official reference to electromobility by the German government, which addressed at the very least three different industries: automotive, energy, and information and communication technology (ICT). As one early result and imprint, German car manufacturers and electric utilities announced field experiments with battery electric cars and new infrastructures in several German regions.[3]

In 2008 the German federal government organized the National Strategy Conference on Electromobility to provide the impetus for further action despite the peak of the financial and economic crisis gripping the world at that time. It was the first official venue at which governmental authorities, scientists, and representatives from all the relevant industries met to discuss the country's next strides in the field of electromobility and jointly underlined the future potential of this technological alternative. The necessity of increasing national R&D efforts to maintain the competitiveness of the automotive industry, the backbone of the German economy, also came

---

[3] Even earlier imprints may have been left by the abortive field tests conducted by the German automotive industry on the island of Rügen from 1992 to 1996. Unlike the current experiments, these early ones of the 1990s were predominantly technological in nature. No coordinating national or regional institutions integrated diverse actor constellations from industry, politics, and science, nor were demonstration projects of applied science and technology set up in multiple German regions.

to the fore. Needless to say, this gathering increased regional discussion about what potential reconfigurations of established value-chain architectures could lead to.

The issue of electromobility became even more important almost as a "historical accident" (David, 1985, p. 332) when the federal government announced its second economic stimulus package to mitigate the economic downturn accompanying the global financial crisis. In early 2009 an additional €500 million for R&D, market preparation, and demonstration were provided. Eight electromobility pilot regions, including the metropolitan regions of Berlin and Stuttgart, were selected in the first half of 2009. More than one fifth of the overall budget was earmarked for these regional initiatives.

When the first period of political agenda-setting ended in August 2009, only a few months before federal elections, the German government adopted the National Electromobility Development Plan. Besides focusing on the intensified R&D of battery systems, this incentivized roadmap also drew considerable attention to the regional scale. Among other things, the necessity of an alternative battery-charging infrastructure had to be tested, and the viability of electric vehicles had to be demonstrated in regional projects. In this respect the document comprised a mélange of climate and economic goals pushed forward by political actors, particularly highlighting the market-oriented objective of putting one million electric vehicles on Germany's roads by 2020 (German Federal Government, 2009).

Having gained momentum at the national level, the issue of electromobility spread to the Stuttgart and Berlin regions at the end of 2008—the first time at that level. However, new regional industries to address it did not arise out of nowhere; they branched out from already existing industries (Boschma & Frenken, 2011a). The preexisting local economic and technological environments may thus properly be regarded as either constraining or enabling the emergence (Martin, 2010, p. 20). In short, the two regions in our embedded comparative case study fundamentally differed in the inherited conditions, knowledge bases, and competencies that informed these early activities.

In the Stuttgart region an enabling precondition was evident in efforts to increase the interorganizational coordination of existing activities within the institutionalized automotive cluster in order to face future challenges in the industry. The main thrust of these early networking activities as of 2007 was to safeguard the existing value chain of powertrain technologies based on the internal combustion engine, so the new issue of electromobility was not explicitly addressed. The first reference to this new technological alternative came 1 year later, in late 2008. Key actors from the automotive industry and the energy and ICT sectors took up the then-new subject of electromobility in their joint application to two competitive national funding programs—the prestigious Leading-Edge Cluster Competition and the Electromobility Pilot Regions—announced as part of the German federal government's second economic stimulus package. Above all, these national programs acted as a means of anchoring the issue of electromobility in the existing structure of industry for the first time. In summer 2009 the Stuttgart region was selected as a pilot region. However, the proposal for the R&D-focused Leading-Edge Cluster Competition failed. This outcome greatly disconcerted the region's industrial actors.

The wide automotive supplier base in particular remained largely excluded from subsequent developments in the field of electromobility, for the original equipment manufacturers with headquarters in the region hedged when disclosing their future R&D strategies. This collective uncertainty was reinforced by several studies highlighting the threat of a regional economic downturn as a result of potential structural changes in the region's dominant industrial sector.

By contrast, the dominance of the industrial sector is much less pronounced in the Berlin region. Electromobility was adopted at the outset as a welcome starting point in the search for future topics for regional development at the interface of the transport and energy sectors to help revitalize Berlin's industrial structure. Already evident in the region's economic policy at that time, the renewed attention to the industrial sector strengthened the initial expectations of electromobility. The matter appeared on the agenda in the Berlin region for the first time when German carmakers and utilities called for proposals for demonstration projects to conduct there in 2008. Nearly all the projects that were submitted were of an applied nature. In 2009 the Berlin region was ultimately selected as a pilot region. However, the complexity of unsolved problems related to transport and urban settings surfaced when it came to installing a public charging infrastructure, a process that lagged far behind the initial schedule. In addition, an attempt to put a regional innovation network in place to pool regional companies and research institutions in the field of electromobility failed. As the first phase of path formation ended, political actors engaged in much wishful thinking, ignoring the fact that the region was serving predominantly as a technological playground for industrial actors close to federal policy but with little potential for regional value-creating activities. As noted by an interviewee from the regional innovation agency, "Although it is nice to have projects, it would be even nicer if Berlin were not only the playing field,…if some things were sustained" (Interview B003; June 2011).

Critical Juncture: Organized Calls for Increased Regional Coordination

The rather hasty and haphazard political actions taken before and after adoption of the National Electromobility Development Plan (German Federal Government, 2009) greatly unsettled the agents involved. In autumn 2009 four federal ministries were still equally responsible for the issue of electromobility. Criticism of this complex constellation and the lack of clear governmental leadership mounted in early 2010. For instance, the Commission of Experts on Research and Innovation, whose annual report includes assessment of technological performance in Germany, criticized the lack of coordinated action between the federal government and the federal states and called for increased national R&D efforts to develop international competiveness (Expert Commission on Research and Innovation, 2010, pp. 65–76). The National Academy of Science and Engineering (2010) challenged the government's incomplete focus on market-oriented goals and endorsed instead its own aspiration to make Germany both a lead market and a lead provider, which the academy believed more suitable for safeguarding the future competitiveness of German industry.

As a result, an interdepartmental Joint Unit for Electric Mobility was founded in spring 2010 to pool competencies and the federal government's activities in the field. Since then, this Joint Unit has been the government's sole contact for key stakeholders from industry and research organizations. It is headed by the Federal Ministry of Economics and Technology and the Federal Ministry of Transport, Building, and Urban Affairs. One of the main tasks of this newly created governmental institution was to organize the NPE's constitutive convention. Meanwhile, industrial actors, mainly under the aegis of the Federation of German Industry (BDI) and the German Association of the Automotive Industry (VDA), agreed on a joint approach to collaboration in the projected multistakeholder platform intended to encompass politicians, industry associations, trade unions, the automotive industry, the energy and ICT sector, research organizations, and other interested parties. Before the NPE's inaugural event, which took place in May 2010 with more than 400 invited guests attending, representatives of industry and government agreed to a joint declaration that underscored their commitment to increasing cross-sector and interorganizational coordination despite the manifestly conflicting interests of the relevant stakeholders (German Federal Government, 2010). The NPE now consists of a steering committee, seven specific technological working groups, and almost 150 members in total. The goal is to lay the foundations of a concerted and consistent R&D strategy among key stakeholders from industry, science, and other relevant spheres of society to provide the basis for future governmental financial support. Hence, the NPE became the central place of intersectorial exchange, where major pillars of the burgeoning national innovation system were developed. This organization's creation marks a fundamental break with the previous political goal of establishing a lead market for electromobility. Instead, the industrial dimension of the initiative—the stated aim to become a lead provider—supplemented the climate-policy goals that had dominated when the developments began in the preceding period.

The two regions responded differently to these developments. Whereas a degree of collective uncertainty pervaded the Stuttgart region, hopes about the industrial policy implications grew in the Berlin region. Despite these opposing reactions, the activities that followed had striking similarities. At FCEs in both regions, a targeted appeal to policy-makers was seen as the critical juncture in the attempt to root the issue of electromobility firmly in regional development strategies. At these gatherings industrial and institutional actors clearly articulated their call to establish an interorganizational platform at the regional level and aimed to mobilize political support for such institutionalization. We now present a relatively detailed account of these critical turning points by looking at three potentially field-configuring or -reconfiguring events in both regions.

In retrospect, a cabinet hearing in fall 2009 was the Stuttgart region's first FCE to move common awareness toward BEVs. During this event it was predominantly representatives of the automotive industry who clearly urged the state government to create an organizational body to intensify regional coordination. To quote a participant in the hearing, "the state ministry has to wield the baton" (Flaig, 2009). Only a few days later the call succeeded, and electromobility was henceforth commonly known, in the words of the state's minister president, as "a vital issue for the automotive region" (State Ministry of Baden-Wuerttemberg, 2009). Momentum stemming from this event led to implementation of a state initiative for electromobility in Baden-Wuerttemberg. The main mission of this initiative was to establish a regional knowledge base to promote the industrialization of electromobility along the entire value chain, including the abundant R&D and manufacturing capabilities and capacities in the region. A representative from one of the region's original equipment manufacturers reflected on the regulatory work involved at that time:

> Basically, you have to create some kind of coordinating institution—of course, without telling policy-makers what it should look like....If you continue talking about it, it will bear fruit at some point in time,....[T]his was not only us; others were just as smart and raised this topic. And let's say that is how the formation of political will developed and played out. (Interview S002; September 2011)

In the Berlin region the first FCE took place a few months later. It stemmed from a meeting of a new industrial policy network, the Steering Committee on Industrial Policy, to discuss and amplify measures of the city's reindustrialization process. In the first session of this forum, held in spring 2010, it was agreed to pursue the recent developments in the field of electromobility as a new key aspect in the region's future economic development strategy. The ensuing political wishful thinking was reinforced by a study conducted by an international consulting firm that forecast what in retrospect were very optimistic, if not unrealistic, prospects for the region as a result of the recent developments in the field of electromobility. In the wake of the appeal by representatives of industrial and institutional stakeholders, the Berlin Senate Chancellery released an initial concept paper to confirm its willingness and its commitment to strengthen the efforts in this new area. The draft of this program was circulated by a letter to federal decision-makers and members of the NPE, which was being formed at that time. The shift toward the regional economic dimension of electromobility was highlighted by a member of the steering committee: "Obviously, a region or a city that is in a process of redefining itself anyway and questioning how it can do more regarding the question of industrial policy should grab this opportunity" (Interview B012; August 2011).

During this phase both regions had a diverse set of actors from regional industry, research organizations, industry associations, innovation agencies, trade unions, and municipal authorities who pushed to create new regional institutions such as a formal coordination agency, harmonized local regulations, and stable interorganizational and intersectorial coordination practices. These institutions seem to have been a precondition for embedding the issue of electromobility permanently in future regional development strategies. As one of the first cornerstones, regional agencies were set up as platform organizers early in the next phase. This measure was arguably the main result of the targeted appeal relating to the FCEs in both regions.

Formation Phase: Implementing Cross-Sectorial Platform-Policies

In November 2010 the NPE published its first interim report, which centered on the activities of the seven installed working groups. The members of the NPE were pressed for time because the financial aid provided by the second economic stimulus package was scheduled to end in 2011. Each of the seven technological working groups (e.g., battery systems, electric drivetrains, infrastructures, and framework conditions) was led by an industry representative and consisted of about twenty members. Within the framework of the NPE's interim report, each working group published its own roadmap "to set out the development paths" (National Platform for Electromobility, 2010, p. 5). The work and outcome of these groups clearly indicate that the NPE had already become more than a policy and funding announcement by the government.

In May 2011, just 1 year after the platform had been created, the NPE released its second report, in which the members pushed two central claims. First, they developed the idea of technological "lighthouse projects" (National Platform for Electromobility, 2011, pp. 16–25, e.g., the battery, drivetrain technology, ICT, and infrastructure lighthouses) to foster interorganizational and intersectoral R&D projects. In these projects R&D activities with a "strategic character" (p. 16) were to be bundled in keeping with the proposed roadmaps drawn up by the NPE's working groups. Second, large-scale regional showcases of applied science and technology were to be established to succeed the electromobility pilot regions (pp. 55–57). Only a few days after the report appeared, the federal government itself went public with its own program, in which it basically adopted the NPE's strategic recommendations (German Federal Government, 2011). Simultaneously, the government assured it would provide €1 billion for R&D activities in the upcoming years until late 2013. By contrast, it temporarily excluded direct market incentives, even though the NPE strongly recommended monetary incentives to achieve the ambitious and controversial goal of selling 1 million electric vehicles in Germany by 2020.

In October 2011 the government announced the funding program called Electromobility Showcases, which addressed primarily the regional level. In early 2012, at the end of the period we studied, the regions of Berlin/Brandenburg, Baden-Wuerttemberg, Lower Saxony, and Bavaria/Saxony were selected as the four showcases for Germany. Within a 3-year period the government was to provide a total of €180 million for the projects involved. Given the results of the NPE process—characterized by field-configuring or field-reconfiguring events—and the subsequent government program, it is presumably appropriate to note that the basic contours of a "national innovation system" (Nelson, 1993) for electromobility were developed in this 1-year period.

An important part of the state initiative in the Stuttgart region, besides the promotion of research infrastructure, was the creation of e-mobilBW, an entirely state-owned agency for electromobility and fuel-cell technology. The inaugural meeting of this entity took place in spring 2010. We think of this event as the second FCE in the region. Reflecting on the remarkable difference between this approach and former, uncoordinated practices, one interviewee claimed:

> In Baden-Wuerttemberg we always have a bit of a problem. First, everyone works meticulously on his or her own, and it is sometimes hard if you say it has to be coordinated. But I think we are beyond that phase,...The awareness is there, we have to structure it, we have to somehow bundle it[.]...Therefore, I think we are well on the way right now. (Interview S002; September 2011)

The agency e-mobilBW is governed by a board of directors (politicians) and an advisory board (about 25 representatives of industry, science, and regional institutions). The main goals are to establish an efficient and effective network and cluster management (cf. Sydow, Schüßler & Müller-Seitz, 2016: 103–159) and to serve as a center for consulting and knowledge transfer, aiming to provide for a useful topology of knowledge in the region. Furthermore, the agency is responsible for coordinating activities and creating synergies by also integrating small and medium-sized companies into the innovation process, and it is expected to support the creation of an adequate framework in the fields of infrastructure, education, and training (e-mobilBW, 2012). In 2011 the issue of electromobility was made a new core area in a state-wide automotive network named TecNet automotive bw, a decision that has reinforced the willingness of regional industry actors to engage in interorganizational coordination and projects. As one project executive stated: "Barriers that definitely existed have been lowered. ... The reservation we encounter among the suppliers is not as high as it was 2 years ago. Since we have been involved in these projects, the atmosphere has improved significantly" (Interview S005; September 2011).

Another FCE took place in spring 2011, when the proposal for the third round of the Leading-Edge Cluster Competition was presented publicly to regional stakeholders. Unlike the two abortive attempts in earlier years, this process was organized by e-mobilBW as a single point of contact. In January 2012 the application entitled Cluster Electromobility Southwest—Road to Global Market was ultimately accepted. Involving industries and federal financial support in equal measure, the program committed about €80 million to future R&D projects in the field of electromobility. At that time Daimler and Bosch, two of the leading automotive companies headquartered in the region, announced a joint venture in electric engines, with R&D capacities located in the Stuttgart region and manufacturing capacities at a Bosch site in northern Germany. From then on it became increasingly evident that the installation of research infrastructure and the integration of small and medium-sized companies along the entire value chain were two of the highest priorities for industrializing the R&D results in the region and not elsewhere (e-mobilBW, 2011).

A representative of the automotive industry summarized the common goals and benefits of the regional platforming activities:

> This means that the barriers…have to be highlighted and overcome by joint projects. At the same time, you have to involve medium-sized businesses, which are extremely strong in Baden–Wuerttemberg along this new path….And that is one of the central tasks of the forthcoming Cluster Electromobility Southwest. (Interview S003; September 2011)

In April 2012 the Stuttgart region became a showroom of applied science and technology, a "LivingLab BWe mobil," which is also being coordinated by e-mobilBW. More than 40 projects, encompassing an aggregate volume of some €150 million, have been set up. The programs are intended to reinforce each other, for R&D results can be tested immediately and practical insights taken into account in R&D activities.

In the Berlin region a second FCE also took place early in the formation phase, subsequent to the critical juncture, beginning in autumn 2010 with a high-level meeting of representatives of regional firms, institutions, and research organizations at the invitation of the city's Governing Mayor. It functioned as the starting point for creating the Berlin Agency for Electromobility (eMO), a regional coordinating institution, whose organizational and financial structure was negotiated and presented to selected regional stakeholders. Only a few days later, the establishment of eMO was publicly announced at a large venue to promote Berlin as a site for industry. The Action Plan for Electromobility, published a few months later, was one of the first results (eMO, 2011). At that time the NPE hinted at its expected recommendations to mount large-scale regional demonstration projects as an apt way to promote the development of electromobility. The action plan thus mainly supported the region's willingness to become a national showcase. The normative work done at that time was stressed by an interviewee: "The hope is eminent that if Berlin positions itself within this thematic field, it will get the chance to secure a slice of the new industrial value creation" (Interview B009; August 2011).

The third FCE occurred in summer 2011. Before the application process for the national showcase program, eMO organized a closed multistakeholder workshop with about 60 selected guests. As stated in the internal letter of invitation, the workshop was "to set the corresponding course" for the application. It did so by having the participants slip into the role of other stakeholders in order to become aware of further relevant perspectives and interests. Overall, this 2-day workshop marked the origin of the region's draft application. In the words of one participant,

> Slowly but surely, core areas are being reinforced: Where do we want to go? What could the added value be in comparison to Bavaria or Baden-Wuerttemberg? What is our unique selling point? Now this process is being moderated by the agency, and the workshop was an important milestone. (Interview B007; August 2011)

The Berlin region was chosen as an international showcase in April 2012. About 35 key projects, accounting for a total volume of approximately €165 million (eMO, 2012) were set up. It is now commonly agreed that the upcoming projects of applied science and technology will serve as catalysts to attract R&D capacities. This first step may be the basis for future value creation in the long run. This new perception may be seen as a major result of the platforming activities coordinated by eMO, for it signifies a fundamental shift away from wishful thinking to concrete and viable regional development activities compatible with the region's initial resources, competencies, and knowledge bases. "Getting from mere application to value creation in Berlin—that is the core strategy" (Interview B011; July 2011).

In summary, coordinating agencies were created in the Stuttgart and Berlin regions in 2010 and were implemented as platform organizers to facilitate a decidedly interorganizational exchange among proliferating, divergent interests and to foster and accelerate learning processes. Followed by other FCEs, these pooled knowledge bases provided by eMO and e-mobilBW thenceforth became the central "locale" (Giddens, 1984, p. xxv) for regional coordinating activities. Within these regional platforms central actor constellations stabilized in the field; interaction increased between the various stakeholders from industry, government, and science; and these actors became generally aware that they were involved in a common project. The field has become structured nationally as well as regionally (DiMaggio & Powell, 1983). The incipient coordinating mechanism that connects the nexus of place-specific practices with the rules and resources in the field was arguably the salient result of this early stage of platforming policies in the two regions. Above all, clarification and stabilization of future priorities and project tasks was the main legacy of these regional platforming strategies by the time this phase ended in early 2012. Bearing in mind the interplay of the national and the regional scale, one interviewee with an academic background from the Stuttgart region concluded: "We are beginning to discern the line of march of the regional actors—who are coordinating themselves, of course. This gives them all a measure of certainty. And with this national framework, now this is reinforced even a bit further" (Interview S008; October 2011). However, these positive effects of platforming were not all that was highlighted. One interviewee with the Berlin region in mind also expounded on the problems of potentially dark sides (e.g., premature rigidity) due to increased coordination in this early phase of path-forming activities:

> At some points you make decisions, but I think you have to be smart enough to reconsider [them] once in a while and ask yourself if this is the right path to take. ... I think there is a bit of a danger in wanting to stop or adjust the course once a train has begun moving. (Interview B007; August 2011)

This quotation indicates how much reflexivity was involved in the platforming process; though not everywhere all the time. The upper part of Fig. 10.1 summarizes the development of the national context; the two bottom parts, the developments in the two regions under study—Stuttgart and Berlin—between 2008 and early 2012.

Discussion: Platforming Toward Path-Forming?

The development of urban mobility based on the automotive system in general and cars with a traditional powertrain technology in particular indisputably illustrates a path-dependent process that has locked-in certain regions, indeed even whole

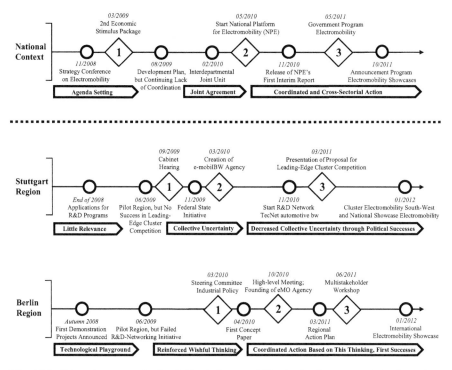

Fig. 10.1 Triggering events in the field of electromobility in the Stuttgart and Berlin regions (Design by authors)

societies, through positive feedback processes, which are fueled across several industries (Cowan & Hultén, 1996; Dennis & Urry, 2009, pp. 54–61; Kirsch, 2000). Given the interlocking technological, economic, and societal complexity of the automotive system, which is deeply ingrained in both the supply and demand side of modern societies with their organizations and institutions, platforming is unlikely to compete seriously with the present path either nationally or regionally. This inability to "unlock regional economies" (Hassink, 2005) particularly characterizes localities such as the Stuttgart region, with its organizations and institutions whose economic future is closely aligned with the automotive system. They depend on the present technology. But, as we have shown, it also distinguishes Berlin and similar regions that depend significantly less on the present powertrain technology.

Nonetheless, platforming is more than just an experimentation with possible future worlds, and as such it is more than only unsettling to actors treading the established and often strategically extended path (Sydow, Windeler, Schubert, & Möllering, 2012). Instead, platforming helps open a window, on the supply side at least, by integrating a related variety of actor groups with divergent interests and complementary resources to foster cross-sectorial coordination and learning aimed at cross-fertilization. It can rather strongly stimulate construction of a complementary institutional infrastructure around which an alternative national or regional knowledge path may finally form. The more reflective, emphatic, and resourceful the platforming initiative is, the more likely this path-forming will be. To achieve these results, platforming requires certain conditions. It must be efficiently and effectively administered. It must be supported by diligently arranged national and regional FCEs and significant resource endowment (e.g., Germany's second economic stimulus package). It must be accompanied by successes (e.g., the creation of new organizations, the launching of R&D projects, and the provision of early infrastructure for electromobility). Platforming also needs a suitable degree of related variety that combines, for instance, a well-prepared top-down approach with a bottom-up approach sensitive to regional competencies and political legacies. However, platforming will contribute to path-forming only if it is somewhat consistent with the expectations of the actors in the region and, in particular, their tolerance for change. Until then, platforming will not gain the momentum necessary even to complement the present knowledge path, let alone break or replace it (Grabher & Stark, 1997).

It has become apparent that platforming activities do not come out of nowhere; they are based on preexisting regional competencies, resources, and knowledgebases (Asheim et al., 2011). Path-forming as a possible result of platforming can thus be fully understood only if one takes into account the preexisting technological, institutional, and organizational structures and paths and the constraining or enabling effects (Martin, 2010) they have on intersectorial and interorganizational coordination and learning activities in a regional setting. More precisely, platforming may be perceived as the locus of "the interaction of differences" (Cooke, 2012, p. 1419) and of purposeful and generative recombinations of existing activities or relations in a region. Besides the region's existing resource bases and other resources injected into the process of platforming, cognitive-normative orientations and context-sensitive framing activities seem to be highly important (Giddens, 1984).

In the two cases presented in this chapter, wishful thinking (the Berlin region) and collective uncertainty (the Stuttgart region) each had lasting impacts on the early formation of a new knowledge path despite quite effective attempts to reframe it. Take, for instance, the opposing motivations to implement the two regional platforms. The creation of the agency eMO in the Berlin region is largely explicable as an effort by regional stakeholders to moderate exaggerated expectations of industrial policy and transform them into a practicable approach. By contrast, the founding of the agency e-mobilBW in the Stuttgart region is interpretable mainly as the result of trying to convert exaggerated perception of threats into a realistic assessment, of seeking to balance protection of the existing industrial structure with encouragement of new technological developments. Whatever the cognitive-normative orientations and intentions behind attempts to promote or prevent the development of a new knowledge path, it seems crucial for the platforming strategy to explicitly address the diversity of stakeholder interests and orientations and allow for serious discourse about them. The two regions we have studied demonstrate that this diversity may, at best, be the source of creativity and novelty. At worst, it can block the collective creation of a proper and superior alternative perhaps needed for "effective restoration of a choice situation" (Sydow et al., 2009, p. 702) across organizational and industrial boundaries alike.

Compared to early experience with platforming in other countries (see Lazzeretti et al., 2010, pp. 31–34 for a review), the German encounter with electromobility seems significantly more burdened with issues of technological, institutional, and organizational path dependence. It also has—at least potentially—much greater socioeconomic scope and relevance. The two metropolitan electromobility regions we have investigated, Stuttgart and Berlin, are economically essential, though for different reasons. At the same time, the technological and institutional breakthrough needed there is more challenging than in others regions, not least because the Stuttgart and Berlin regional platforms established in the shadow of the NPE are, unsurprisingly, more diverse in their actors, activities, resources, and relations. The coordinative challenges facing the regional actors before the desired cross-fertilization is likely to materialize are correspondingly difficult. Despite successful steps toward both the preformation and formation phases in the development of the new knowledge path, it is much too early to say whether a new path really will form and to question the existence of the old.

Conclusions and Directions

Starting necessarily from a focal region's existing knowledge base, platforming is commonly understood as a more combinative than cumulative and more generative than reproductive strategy that uses the related variety of agents, activities, resources, and relations to develop locally adapted solutions designed to avoid premature rigidity. In this regard platforming may complement traditional cluster policies rather than constitute a postcluster policy on its own. As long as cluster approaches do not incorporate additional ideas about related variety, platforming may serve as an effective antivenom to present cluster policies that reflect too little concern with the benefits of having diversity and the impact of rigidity that is too early.

But can a platforming strategy actually be used to break an established knowledge path such as the one related to the traditional powertrain technology driven by the internal combustion engine and embedded in a well-adapted organizational and institutional infrastructure that is itself characterized by path dependencies? To answer this question we examined the recent electromobility initiative in Germany, launched in response to global warming caused by high carbon emissions, and boosted in the aftermath of the global financial crisis in 2008. The case of the National Platform for Electromobility, which was introduced by the German government in 2010 and analyzed at the national level and in terms of two very different metropolitan regions, provided an excellent opportunity to inquire into the potential of platforming to unlock path dependencies.

We focused on the early stages of knowledge-path formation, drawing on theoretical insights into path dependence, path-breaking, platforming, and the role of FCEs in this strategy. We also used detailed data from two embedded and starkly contrasting cases (Yin, 2009) constituted by the Stuttgart and Berlin regions. It is there that the importance of agenda-setting at the federal level featured as prominently as the eventual creation and work of the NPE. Together, these national FCEs triggered—from the top down—a feasible process of regional path-formation flanked by similar regional events. In the years to come such events in the Stuttgart and Berlin metropolitan regions may acquire the critical mass and momentum necessary for new electromobility clusters to emerge. But if this process proves successful at all, it may well have a rather long way to go, and the results in the one region are likely to differ from those in the other, not least because of abundant path dependencies.

The Stuttgart region's inherited conditions, knowledge bases, and competencies on which subsequent complementary activities had to build were as different from those of the Berlin region as were the perceptions of the important regional actors (the collective uncertainty in the former area and the wishful thinking in the latter). Nevertheless, the actors in both regions were quite successful with their reframing activities and pushed to create new regional institutions, such as a formal coordination agency, harmonized local regulations, and stable practices of interorganizational and intersectorial coordination. These institutions seem to have functioned as a precondition for embedding the issue of electromobility rather securely in future regional development strategies. In the formation phase of the new knowledge path, which has only just begun, political successes have helped overcome at least some of the collective uncertainty experienced in Stuttgart and to make initial reality out of at least some of the wishful thinking that characterized the Berlin region. It is still unclear whether economic successes will follow the political achievements, although platform policies were increasingly carefully coordinated between the federal and regional levels. Even less clear is whether new clusters will arise from these activities in the distant future. The observed platforming activities, pushed forward by political initiatives, may be thought of as an important prerequisite of the effort to advance development toward BEVs, but these path-breaking attempts cannot be evaluated yet.

From our analysis we conclude that platforming opens new windows of opportunities but may be less likely to trigger the breaking of a national and regional knowledge path than some of its protagonists may expect (e.g., Cooke, 2007, p. 192; Harmaakorpi, 2006, p. 1090). Instead, platforming for path-breaking may culminate only in path-forming activities with a contingent outcome. This general insight awaits empirical testing in other settings and with research designs and methods more longitudinal than those feasible in the case studies we conducted. It would be useful to compare Germany's institutional specifics, which support collaboration between organizations in general and between firms and the government in particular, with those of other capitalist countries (Hall & Soskice, 2001). Most importantly however, our research on the Stuttgart and Berlin metropolitan regions would have to be extended by several years—until the effects of platforming as path-forming became more visible. The platforming and path-forming processes need analysis even finer-grained than that which was possible in the present study, at least for selected episodes of stability and change. Additional ethnographic techniques would be useful for inquiry into such episodes. That kind of relatively long-term, detailed work would obviously contradict demands to widen the research to other regions and to extend the present study to fields other than electromobility and to nations other than Germany in order to improve the generalizability of our findings.

Despite these clear limitations of our study, we are confident that we have made at least three contributions. First, in terms of research on technological, institutional, and organizational path dependence (David, 1985, 2001; Mahoney, 2000; Manning & Sydow, 2011; North, 1990; Pierson, 2000; Schreyögg, Sydow, & Holtmann, 2011; Sydow et al., 2009, 2010), we have introduced the idea of platforming as a possible instrument for at least shaping, if not breaking, an existing path. Second, in continuing the emphasis that regional knowledge creation and exploitation receives in economic geography (and regional studies generally), we have, in more theoretical terms, also added to the knowledge-based theorizing of regional economic development that reflects the topology as much as the topography of knowledge (Bathelt et al., 2004; Cooke, 2001; Glückler, 2007, 2013; Malmberg & Maskell, 2002). More precisely, our contribution lies in the exploration of platforming and of the concomitant role that field-configuring events have for creating new knowledge that both relates to and diverges from the present knowledge base in a region. Third, our study, particularly its focus on path dependence and possible path-breaking through platforming and attendant field-configuring events, contributes generally to the popular evolutionary and institutional theorizing about regional development processes (see Boschma & Martin, 2010). That thinking seems increasingly sensitive to the importance of individual and organizational agency on the one hand and historical imprints and self-reinforcing, agency-delimiting processes on the other (Henning et al., 2013; Li et al., 2012; Martin & Sunley, 2006; Tödtling & Trippl, 2013). In this sense, we have drawn on the discussion in economic geography about the conceptual relation that platforming and related variety have with the enhancement of regional economic development processes. According to Boschma and Frenken (2011a), neither regional specialization (e.g., cluster policies) nor diversification (e.g., unrelated variety) is constructive in and of itself. Rather, related activities and shared competencies between diverse organizational actors in different industries or areas of expertise (related variety) seem to matter most for achieving knowledge spillovers and creating regional growth processes in a knowledge economy. However, platform policies designed to organize overlapping activities and to coordinate the interrelations of formerly unconnected sectors and interorganizational competencies may ultimately be insufficient on their own to help actors "leave well-trodden paths" (Sydow et al., 2010, p. 176) or to open a window for new path-forming activities. The extent to which they are up to that task remains to be seen. In the case of electromobility, the regional actors—from the demand as well as the supply side—need to stabilize and further institutionalize the preparatory platforming activities constantly. Only then may platforming finally acquire a self-reinforcing dynamic—the main shaper of a regional knowledge path. Despite this promising conceptual perspective, the current development in the field of electromobility still calls for a certain degree of skepticism, even pessimism.

Acknowledgments An early draft of this paper was presented at the symposium entitled "Knowledge & Space—Topographies and Topologies of Knowledge" at the Villa Studio Bosch in Heidelberg, June 12–15, 2013. We thank Johannes Glückler for hosting this stimulating workshop and all the participants for their constructive comments. In addition, we are grateful to Udo Staber, Phil Cooke, and Elke Schüßler for insightful recommendations on how to improve the manuscript.

References

Arthur, W. B. (1994). *Increasing returns and path dependency in the economy*. Ann Arbor: University of Michigan Press.

Asheim, B., Boschma, R. A., & Cooke, P. (2011). Constructing regional advantage: Platform policies based on related variety and differentiated knowledge bases. *Regional Studies, 45*, 893–904. doi:10.1080/00343404.2010.543126

Bathelt, H. (2005). Geographies of production: Growth regimes in spatial perspective (II)—Knowledge creation and growth in clusters. *Progress in Human Geography, 29*, 204–216. doi:10.1191/0309132505ph539pr

Bathelt, H., & Boggs, J. (2003). Toward a reconceptualization of regional development paths: Is Leipzig's media cluster a continuation of or a rupture with the past? *Economic Geography, 79*, 265–293. doi:10.1111/j.1944-8287.2003.tb00212.x

Bathelt, H., Malmberg, A., & Maskell, P. (2004). Clusters and knowledge: Local buzz, global pipelines and the process of knowledge creation. *Progress in Human Geography, 28*, 31–56. doi:10.1191/0309132504ph469oa

Boschma, R. A., & Fornahl, D. (2011). Cluster evolution and a roadmap for future research. *Regional Studies, 45*, 1295–1298. doi:10.1080/00343404.2011.633253

Boschma, R. A., & Frenken, K. (2011a). Technological relatedness and regional branching. In H. Bathelt, M. Feldman, & D. F. Kogler (Eds.), *Beyond territory: Dynamic geographies of knowledge creation, diffusion, and innovation* (pp. 64–81). Regions and Cities, Vol. 47. London, UK: Routledge.

Boschma, R. A., & Frenken, K. (2011b). Technological relatedness, related variety and economic geography. In P. Cooke, B. Asheim, R. A. Boschma, R. Martin, D. Schwartz, & F. Tödtling (Eds.), *Handbook of regional innovation and growth* (pp. 187–197). Cheltenham, UK: Edward Elgar.

Boschma, R. A., & Martin, R. (Eds.). (2010). *The handbook of evolutionary economic geography*. Cheltenham, UK: Edward Elgar.

Collier, R. B., & Collier, D. (1991). *Shaping the political arena: Critical junctures, the labor movement, and regime dynamics in Latin America*. Princeton: University Press.

Cooke, P. (2001). Regional innovation systems, clusters and the knowledge economy. *Industrial and Corporate Change, 10*, 945–974. doi:10.1093/icc/10.4.945

Cooke, P. (2007). To construct regional advantage from innovation systems first build policy platforms. *European Planning Studies, 15*, 179–194. doi:10.1080/09654310601078671

Cooke, P. (2011). Transversality and regional innovation platforms. In P. Cooke, B. Asheim, R. A. Boschma, R. Martin, D. Schwartz, & F. Tödtling (Eds.), *Handbook of regional innovation and growth* (pp. 303–314). Cheltenham, UK: Edward Elgar.

Cooke, P. (2012). From clusters to platform policies in regional development. *European Planning Studies, 20,* 1415–1424. doi:10.1080/09654313.2012.680741

Cooke, P., & De Laurentis, C. (2010). Platforms of innovation: Some examples. In P. Cooke, C. De Laurentis, S. MacNeill, & C. Collinge (Eds.), *Platforms of innovation: Dynamics of new industrial knowledge flows* (pp. 271–310). Cheltenham, UK: Edward Elgar.

Coombs, R., & Hull, R. (1998). 'Knowledge management practices' and path-dependency in innovation. *Research Policy, 27,* 237–253. doi:10.1016/S0048-7333(98)00036-5

Cowan, R., & Hultén, S. (1996). Escaping lock-in: The case of the electric vehicle. *Technological Forecasting and Social Change, 53,* 61–79. doi:10.1016/0040-1625(96)00059-5

David, P. (1985). Clio and the economics of QWERTY. *American Economic Review, 75,* 332–337.

David, P. (2001). Path dependence, its critics and the quest for 'historical economics'. In P. Garrouste & S. Ioannides (Eds.), *Evolution and path dependence in economic ideas: Past and present* (pp. 15–40). Cheltenham, UK: Edward Elgar.

Dennis, K., & Urry, J. (2009). *After the car.* Cambridge, UK: Polity Press.

DiMaggio, P. J., & Powell, W. W. (1983). The iron cage revisited: Institutional isomorphism and collective rationality in organizational fields. *American Sociological Review, 48,* 147–160.

Eisenhardt, K. M. (1989). Building theories from case study research. *Academy of Management Review, 14,* 532–550. doi:10.5465/AMR.1989.4308385

eMO (Ed.). (2011). *Action plan for electromobility Berlin 2020.* Retrieved May 22, 2015, from https://www.berlin-partner.de/fileadmin/user_upload/01_chefredaktion/02_pdf/publikationen/eMO%20Aktionsprogramm%20%28english%29.pdf

eMO (Ed.). (2012). *Berlin–Brandenburg international showcase for electromobility: Application summary.* Retrieved May 22, 2015, from http://www.emo-berlin.de/fileadmin/user_upload/Downloads/English/120904_eMO_Bewerbung_EN.pdf

e-mobilBW (Ed.). (2011). *Structure study BWe Mobile 2011: Baden–Wuerttemberg on the way to electromobility.* Retrieved March 3, 2013, from http://www.e-mobilbw.de/en/publications.html?file=files/e-mobil/content/DE/Publikationen/PDF/e_mobil_structure_study_en.pdf

e-mobilBW (Ed.). (2012). *The e-mobilBW GmbH: Start now in the future of Electric Mobility.* Retrieved March 3, 2013, from http://www.e-mobilbw.de/en/publications.html?file=files/e-mobil/content/DE/Publikationen/PDF/0356_Broschuere_englisch_RZ_5-web_final.pdf

Expert Commission on Research and Innovation (Ed.). (2010). *Report on research, innovation and technological performance in Germany 2010.* Retrieved May 4, 2014 from http://www.e-fi.de/fileadmin/Gutachten/2010_engl.pdf

Flaig, I. (2009, September 30). Land bei Elektroauto im Hintertreffen: Wirtschaft drängt Oettinger [Federal state of Baden–Wuerttemberg falls behind on electric cars: Industry pressures the state's minister president]. *Stuttgarter Nachrichten.* Retrieved from http://www.stuttgarter-nachrichten.de/inhalt.wirtschaft-draengt-oettinger-land-bei-elektroauto-im-hintertreffen.f2289c33-3ac8-40a8-9eec-fd2c713e4b13.html

Frenken, K., van Oort, F., & Verburg, T. (2007). Related variety, unrelated variety and regional economic growth. *Regional Studies, 41,* 685–697. doi:10.1080/00343400601120296

Fuchs, G. (2010). Path dependence in regional development: What future for Baden–Württemberg? In G. Schreyögg & J. Sydow (Eds.), *The hidden dynamics of path dependence: Institutions and organizations* (pp. 178–194). London, UK: Palgrave Macmillan.

Fuchs, G., & Wassermann, S. (2005). Path dependency in Baden–Württemberg: Lock-in or breakthrough? In G. Fuchs & P. Shapira (Eds.), *Rethinking regional innovation and change: Path dependency or regional breakthrough?* (pp. 223–248). New York: Springer.

German Federal Government (Ed.). (2007). *Eckpunkte für ein integriertes Energie- und Klimaprogramm* [Key elements of an integrated energy and climate program]. Retrieved May 4, 2014, from http://www.bmwi.de/BMWi/Redaktion/PDF/E/eckpunkt-fuer-ein-integriertes-energie-und-klimaprogramm.pdf

German Federal Government (Ed.). (2009). *National Electromobility Development Plan*. Retrieved May 4, 2014, from http://www.bmwi.de/English/Redaktion/Pdf/national-electromobility-development-plan.pdf

German Federal Government (Ed.). (2010). *Establishment of the National Platform for Electromobility on May 3, 2010: Joint declaration by the Federal Government and German industry*. Retrieved May 4, 2014, from http://www.bmwi.de/EN/Press/press-releases,did=346562.html

German Federal Government (Ed.). (2011). *Regierungsprogramm Elektromobilität* [Government electromobility program]. Retrieved May 4, 2014, from http://www.bmbf.de/pubRD/programm_elektromobilitaet.pdf

Giddens, A. (1984). *The constitution of society: Outline of the theory of structuration*. Cambridge, UK: Polity Press.

Glückler, J. (2007). Economic geography and the evolution of networks. *Journal of Economic Geography, 7*, 619–634. doi:10.1093/jeg/lbm023

Glückler, J. (2013). Knowledge, networks and space: Connectivity and the problem of non-interactive learning. *Regional Studies, 47*, 880–894. doi:10.1080/00343404.2013.779659

Grabher, G. (1993). The weakness of strong ties: The lock-in of regional development in the Ruhr Area. In G. Grabher (Ed.), *The embedded firm: On the socioeconomics of industrial networks* (pp. 255–277). London, UK: Routledge.

Grabher, G., & Stark, D. (1997). Organizing diversity: Evolutionary theory, network analysis and postsocialism. *Regional Studies, 31*, 533–544. doi:10.1080/00343409750132315

Hall, P. A., & Soskice, D. (Eds.). (2001). *Varieties of capitalism: The institutional foundations of comparative advantage*. Oxford: University Press.

Harmaakorpi, V. (2006). Regional Development Platform Method (RDPM) as a tool for regional innovation policy. *European Planning Studies, 14*, 1085–1104. doi:10.1080/09654310600852399

Harmaakorpi, V., Tura, T., & Melkas, H. (2011). Regional innovation platforms. In P. Cooke, B. Asheim, R. A. Boschma, R. Martin, D. Schwartz, & F. Tödtling (Eds.), *Handbook of regional innovation and growth* (pp. 556–572). Cheltenham, UK: Edward Elgar.

Hassink, R. (2005). How to unlock regional economies from path dependency? From learning region to learning cluster. *European Planning Studies, 13*, 521–535. doi:10.1080/09654310500107134

Hassink, R. (2010). Locked in decline? On the role of regional lock-ins in old industrial areas. In R. A. Boschma & R. Martin (Eds.), *The handbook of evolutionary economic geography* (pp. 450–468). Cheltenham, UK: Edward Elgar.

Henning, M., Stam, E., & Wenting, R. (2013). Path dependence research in regional economic development: Cacophony or knowledge accumulation? *Regional Studies, 47*, 1348–1362. doi:10.1080/00343404.2012.750422

Ibert, O. (2007). Towards a geography of knowledge creation: The ambivalences between 'knowledge as an object' and 'knowing in practice'. *Regional Studies, 41*, 103–114. doi:10.1080/00343400601120346

Kaiser, W. (2007). Regionales Cluster oder globaler Knoten? Automobiltechnik im Raum Stuttgart [Regional cluster or global knot? Automotive engineering in the Stuttgart region]. In H. Berghoff & J. Sydow (Eds.), *Unternehmerische Netzwerke: Eine historische Organisationsform mit Zukunft?* (pp. 175–195). Stuttgart, Germany: Kohlhammer.

Kay, N. M. (2013). Rerun the tape of history and QWERTY always wins. *Research Policy, 42*, 1175–1185. doi:10.1016/j.respol.2013.03.007

Kirsch, D. A. (2000). *The electric vehicle and the burden of history*. New Brunswick: Rutgers University Press.

Lagerholm, M., & Malmberg, A. (2009). Path dependence in economic geography. In L. Magnusson & J. Ottosson (Eds.), *The evolution of path dependence* (pp. 87–107). Cheltenham, UK: Edward Elgar.

Lampel, J., & Meyer, A. D. (2008). Field-configuring events as structuring mechanisms: How conferences, ceremonies, and trade shows constitute new technologies, industries, and markets. *Journal of Management Studies, 45,* 1025–1035. doi:10.1111/j.1467-6486.2008.00787.x

Lange, B., Kalandides, A., Stöber, B., & Mieg, H. A. (2008). Berlin's creative industries: Governing creativity? *Industry & Innovation, 15,* 531–548. doi:10.1080/13662710802373981

Langley, A. (1999). Strategies for theorizing from process data. *Academy of Management Review, 24,* 691–710. doi:10.5465/AMR.1999.2553248

Lazzeretti, L., Capone, F., & Cinti, T. (2010). The regional development platform and 'related variety': Some evidence from art and food in Tuscany. *European Planning Studies, 18,* 27–45. doi:10.1080/09654310903343518

Lazzeretti, L., Sedita, S. R., & Caloffi, A. (2014). Founders and disseminators of cluster research. *Journal of Economic Geography, 14,* 21–43. doi:10.1093/jeg/lbs053

Li, P.-F., Bathelt, H., & Wang, J. (2012). Network dynamics and cluster evolution: Changing trajectories of the aluminium extrusion industry in Dali, China. *Journal of Economic Geography, 12,* 127–155. doi:10.1093/jeg/lbr024

Mahoney, J. (2000). Path dependence in historical sociology. *Theory and Society, 29,* 507–548. doi:10.1023/A:3A1007113830879

Malmberg, A., & Maskell, P. (2002). The elusive concept of localization economies: Towards a knowledge-based theory of spatial clustering. *Environment and Planning A, 34,* 429–449. doi:10.1068/a3457

Manning, S., & Sydow, J. (2011). Projects, paths, and practices: Sustaining and leveraging project-based relationships. *Industrial and Corporate Change, 20,* 1369–1402. doi:10.1093/icc/dtr009

Martin, R. (2010). Roepke lecture in economic geography—Rethinking regional path dependence: Beyond lock-in to evolution. *Economic Geography, 86,* 1–27. doi:10.1111/j.1944-8287.2009.01056.x

Martin, R., & Sunley, P. (2003). Deconstructing clusters: Chaotic concept or policy panacea? *Journal of Economic Geography, 3,* 5–35. doi:10.1093/jeg/3.1.5

Martin, R., & Sunley, P. (2006). Path dependence and regional economic evolution. *Journal of Economic Geography, 6,* 395–437. doi:10.1093/jeg/lbl012

Maskell, P. (2001). Towards a knowledge-based theory of the geographical cluster. *Industrial and Corporate Change, 10,* 921–943. doi:10.1093/icc/10.4.921

Maskell, P., Bathelt, H., & Malmberg, A. (2006). Building global knowledge pipelines: The role of temporary clusters. *European Planning Studies, 14,* 997–1013. doi:10.1080/09654310600852332

Meyer, A. D., Gaba, V., & Colwell, K. (2005). Organizing far from equilibrium: Nonlinear change in organizational fields. *Organization Science, 16,* 456–473. doi:10.1287/orsc.1050.0162

Morgan, K. (1997). The learning region: Institutions, innovation and regional renewal. *Regional Studies, 31,* 491–503. doi:10.1080/00343409750132289

National Academy of Science and Engineering (Ed.). (2010). *Wie Deutschland zum Leitanbieter für Elektromobilität werden kann* [How Germany can become the lead supplier of electromobility]. Berlin: Springer.

National Platform for Electromobility (Ed.). (2010). *Interim report.* Retrieved May 4, 2014, from http://www.bmwi.de/English/Redaktion/Pdf/electro-mobility-report

National Platform for Electromobility (Ed.). (2011). *Second report.* Retrieved May 4, 2014, from http://www.bmwi.de/English/Redaktion/Pdf/second-report-of-the-national-platform-for-electromobility.pdf

Nelson, R. R. (1993). *National innovation systems: A comparative analysis*. Oxford: University Press.
Nooteboom, B. (1997). Path dependence of knowledge: Implications for the theory of the firm. In L. Magnusson & J. Ottosson (Eds.), *Evolutionary economics and path dependence* (pp. 57–78). Cheltenham, UK: Edward Elgar.
North, D. C. (1990). *Institutions, institutional change and economic performance*. Cambridge, UK: Cambridge University Press.
Pettigrew, A. M. (1990). Longitudinal field research on change: Theory and practice. *Organization Science, 1,* 267–292. doi:10.1287/orsc.1.3.267
Pierson, P. (2000). Increasing returns, path dependence, and the study of politics. *American Political Science Review, 94,* 251–267.
Porter, M. E. (2000). Locations, clusters, and company strategy. In G. L. Clark, M. S. Gertler, & M. P. Feldman (Eds.), *The Oxford handbook of economic geography* (pp. 253–274). Oxford: University Press.
Schreyögg, G., Sydow, J., & Holtmann, P. (2011). How history matters in organizations—The case of path dependence. *Management & Organization History, 6,* 81–100. doi:10.1177/17449359 10387030
Schüßler, E., Rüling, C. C., & Wittneben, B. B. F. (2014). On melting summits: The limitations of field-configuring events as catalysts of change in transnational climate policy. *Academy of Management Journal, 57,* 140–171. doi:10.5465/amj.2011.0812
State Ministry of Baden-Wuerttemberg (Ed.). (2009, November 20). *Pressemitteilung 4. Landeskonferenz Automobilwirtschaft Baden–Württemberg* [Press release, 4th conference of the automotive industry in Baden–Wuerttemberg]. Retrieved from http://www.baden-wuerttemberg.de/de/service/presse/pressemitteilung/pid/4-landeskonferenz-automobilwirtschaft-in-baden-wuerttemberg/
Strambach, S., & Klement, B. (2013). Exploring plasticity in the development path of the automotive industry in Baden–Württemberg: The role of combinatorial knowledge dynamics. *Zeitschrift für Wirtschaftsgeographie, 57,* 67–82.
Sydow, J., Lerch, F., & Staber, U. (2010). Planning for path dependence? The case of a network in the Berlin–Brandenburg optics cluster. *Economic Geography, 86,* 173–195. doi:10.1111/j.1944-8287.2010.01067.x
Sydow, J., Schreyögg, G., & Koch, J. (2009). Organizational path dependence: Opening the black box. *Academy of Management Review, 34,* 689–709.
Sydow, J., Windeler, A., Schubert, C., & Möllering, G. (2012). Organizing R&D consortia for path creation and extension: The case of semiconductor manufacturing technologies. *Organization Studies, 33,* 907–936. doi:10.1177/0170840612448029
Sydow, J., Schüßler, E., & Müller-Seitz, G. (2016). *Managing inter-organizational relations*. London: Palgrave Macmillan.
Thelen, K. (1999). Historical institutionalism in comparative politics. *Annual Review of Political Science, 2,* 369–404. doi:10.1146/annurev.polisci.2.1.369
Tödtling, F., & Trippl, M. (2013). Transformation of regional innovation systems: From old legacies to new development paths. In P. Cooke (Ed.), *Re-framing regional development: Evolution, innovation and transition* (pp. 297–317). Regions and Cities: Vol. 62. London, UK: Routledge.
Uotila, T., Harmaakorpi, V., & Hermans, R. (2012). Finnish mosaic of regional innovation system: Assessment of thematic regional innovation platforms based on related variety. *European Planning Studies, 20,* 1583–1602. doi:10.1080/09654313.2012.713331

Wolfe, D. A. (2013). Regional resilience, cross-sectoral knowledge platforms and the prospects for growth in Canadian city regions. In P. Cooke (Ed.), *Re-framing regional development: Evolution, innovation and transition* (pp. 54–72). Regions and Cities: Vol. 62. London, UK: Routledge.

Wolfe, D. A., & Gertler, M. S. (2006). Local antecedents and trigger events: Policy implications of path dependence for cluster formation. In P. Braunerhjelm & M. P. Feldman (Eds.), *Cluster genesis: Technology-based industrial development* (pp. 243–263). Oxford: University Press.

Yin, R. K. (2009). *Case study research: Design and methods* (4th ed.). Applied Social Research Methods Series: Vol. 5. Thousand Oaks: Sage.

Open Access This chapter is distributed under the terms of the Creative Commons Attribution 4.0 International License (http://creativecommons.org/licenses/by/4.0/), which permits use, duplication, adaptation, distribution and reproduction in any medium or format, as long as you give appropriate credit to the original author(s) and the source, provide a link to the Creative Commons license and indicate if changes were made.

The images or other third party material in this chapter are included in the work's Creative Commons license, unless indicated otherwise in the credit line; if such material is not included in the work's Creative Commons license and the respective action is not permitted by statutory regulation, users will need to obtain permission from the license holder to duplicate, adapt or reproduce the material.

Chapter 11
Brokering Trust to Enhance Leadership: A Self-Monitoring Approach to Leadership Emergence

Martin Kilduff, Ajay Mehra, Dennis A. (Denny) Gioia, and Stephen Borgatti

Within work organizations some individuals emerge as leaders in the eyes of others even though these individuals hold no formal authority. For example, wiremen at the Hawthorne Works found in Taylor "a leader of their own, different from the supervisors given them by the company" (Homans, 1951, p. 148). Leaders such as Taylor lack formal power, but may be recognized by peers for their expertise or their access to information. Such emergent leaders build bases of power over time that facilitate managerial goals or, alternatively, threaten the very survival of the organization (Burt & Ronchi, 1990; Krackhardt, 1995).

What kind of person is likely to emerge as an informal leader? Relevant experimental research shows that high self-monitors, the chameleons of the social world, are able to adjust their attitudes and behaviors to the demands of different situations and tend to emerge as informal leaders in temporary groups. By contrast, low self-monitors—who tend to be true to themselves in terms of consistency in attitudes and behaviors across different situations—are less likely to emerge as leaders (e.g., Zaccaro, Foti, & Kenny, 1991; for a review of self-monitoring in the workplace,

---

M. Kilduff (✉)
UCL School of Management, University College London,
1 Canada Square, E14 5AA London, UK
e-mail: m.kilduff@ucl.ac.uk

A. Mehra
Gatton College of Business and Economics, School of Management, University of Kentucky,
Lexington, KY 40506, USA
e-mail: ajay.mehra@uky.edu

D.A.(Denny) Gioia
Department of Management and Organization, The Pennsylvania State University,
452 Business Bldg, University Park, PA 16802, USA
e-mail: dag4@psu.edu

S. Borgatti
Department of Management, University of Kentucky, 338A, Lexington, KY 40506, USA
e-mail: sborgatti@uky.edu

© The Author(s) 2017
J. Glückler et al. (eds.), *Knowledge and Networks*, Knowledge and Space 11,
DOI 10.1007/978-3-319-45023-0_11

see Day & Schleicher, 2006). But these findings have stirred controversy. One skeptic criticized emergent leadership research as lacking external validity, and pointedly predicted that in real-world contexts the attempted leadership behaviors of high self-monitors would be perceived as "both duplicitous and reprehensible" (Bedeian & Day, 2004, pp. 707–708). From this skeptical perspective, the emergence of high self-monitors as leaders represents ephemeral impression management in the context of laboratory experiments.

This skepticism toward high self-monitoring leadership includes a rejection of the possibility that high self-monitors might build trust among their colleagues. The chameleon-like high self-monitors with their changeable attitudes and behaviors are said to lack the "right stuff" to be seen as leaders. The impression management skills characteristic of high self-monitors (involving ingratiation and self-promotion—Turnley & Bolino, 2001) are seen by some leadership experts as likely to undermine the trust of colleagues in real organizations by exemplifying inauthentic leadership (Cooper, Scandura, & Schriesheim, 2005). We address this unresolved controversy concerning high and low self-monitors through an examination of whether and how self-monitoring relates to leadership in organizational contexts.

There are three contributions related to leadership emergence. First is the contribution to leadership research. We show that flexibility (in terms of a high self-monitoring orientation) is associated with brokering trust relations to win attributions of leadership. Second is the contribution to brokerage theory and research. We provide an answer to the puzzle (raised by Burt, 1992) of why some people more than others benefit from the occupation of a brokerage position in the trust network. Third is the contribution to self-monitoring theory and research. We show that the emergence of high self-monitors as leaders is associated with the provision of advice concerning work-related matters to colleagues rather than being merely impression management.

Our research ties in with the long-standing debate concerning the micro-origins of social-structural outcomes. We know that the natural proclivity of individuals is to cluster together in similar groups creating cohesion locally but the possibility of fragmentation at the level of the overall organization (Granovetter, 1973). This paradox of local cohesion within overall fragmentation is a situation that demands informal leadership to connect across clusters (Burt, 1992). The important question arises as to who is likely to exemplify leadership in connecting across social divides. We seek to provide insight into this question in this paper.

Self-Monitoring and Leadership

Self-monitoring theory suggests that high self-monitors, relative to lows, are likely to emerge as leaders in work situations not just in terms of promotions (Kilduff & Day, 1994), but also in terms of informal leadership perceptions. High self-monitors, acutely attentive to social cues, take an active, initiatory posture in social interaction whereas low self-monitors generally adopt a non-directive approach. For example, when two unacquainted people of the same sex find themselves in a waiting room together, those individuals who are higher in self-monitoring tend to speak first and to initiate more frequent conversations (Ickes & Barnes, 1977). The high self-monitors tend to "take the pulse of their social surroundings" (Snyder, 1987, p. 33) in tailoring self-expressions to the role demands appropriate to different well-defined situations. In contrast, low self-monitors tend to "march to the beat of their own inner drummer" (p. 33) in seeking opportunities to be themselves irrespective of the situation. For example, one study showed that those higher in self-monitoring (relative to those lower in self-monitoring) tended to base their estimates of when they should intervene to help a colleague suffering an epileptic fit on information concerning what others had done in a similar situation (Kulik & Taylor, 1981). Further, managers higher in self-monitoring relative to managers lower in self-monitoring tend to be active in the provision of help to those suffering emotional problems in the workplace (Toegel, Anand, & Kilduff, 2007). Overall, high self-monitoring employees (relative to low self-monitoring employees) tend to be actively engaged in more workplace projects (as measured by the number of formal work relationships they develop) (Mehra, Kilduff, & Brass, 2001). Thus, high self-monitors are likely to be perceived as leaders in organizations in part because of their interest in the attitudes and behaviors of others, whereas low self-monitors are less likely to be perceived as leaders because of their consistent focus on themselves. High self-monitors, relative to lows, develop an active repertoire of role enactments related to leadership, including motivating others by setting clear goals, showing that efforts will be rewarded, encouraging others to cooperate, being supportive, and listening to others' suggestions (Snyder, 1987, p. 89). The overall picture, then, suggests that high self-monitors, relative to lows, are more likely to be seen to be involved in informal leadership roles given their focus on engagement with and management of coworkers.

Hypothesis 1: High self-monitors, relative to low self-monitors, are more likely to be perceived as leaders by organizational members.

We want to go beyond this overall prediction to expand our understanding of how self-monitoring relates to informal leadership. A credible argument has been made (Bedeian & Day, 2004) concerning why people in organizations might scorn the leadership of those who appear to flexibly change their opinions. Such inconsistency, it has been argued, is incompatible with being perceived to be a leader. Our understanding of self-monitoring theory leads us to a quite different prediction – that high self-monitors, relative to lows, are likely to be central in terms of providing advice to coworkers.

Giving Advice About Work-Related Matters Within work organizations the provision of advice is a key aspect of the leadership role (Carter, Haythorn, Shriver, & Lanzetta, 1951; Sorrentino & Field, 1986; see the brief review in Neubert & Taggar, 2004, p. 180). People central in advice networks tend to be those who are also recognized as leaders by their colleagues (Bono & Anderson, 2005). And there are several prior studies suggesting the likelihood that self-monitoring orientation relates to involvement in the provision of workplace advice to colleagues.

For example, we know that high self-monitors, relative to lows, are better at scanning the social world for information concerning others, and are also better at remembering such information (Berscheid, Graziano, Monson, & Dermer, 1976). If valuable information is available in the organization relevant to workplace problems, then it is the high self-monitors who are likely to collect and utilize such information. High self-monitors tend to be more successful than low self-monitors at eyewitness identification (e.g., Hosch, Leippe, Marchioni, & Cooper, 1984) and at detecting people's intentions (Jones & Baumeister, 1976). Thus, in work situations, high self-monitors are more likely than the lows to grasp what problems people are trying to solve. Further, high self-monitors strive to establish reputations as generous exchange partners—people who are willing to provide help to others without expecting to be helped in turn (Flynn, Reagans, Amanatullah, & Ames, 2006). Overall, then, high self-monitors are likely to emerge as central in advice giving networks in organizations because they collect important knowledge from the social environment and recognize when such knowledge is likely to be of use in helping others.

Hypothesis 2: High self-monitors, relative to low self-monitors, are more likely to be sought for advice by organizational members.

Finally, we come to the thorny issue of trust. Surely, it must be, as Bedeian has argued (Bedeian & Day, 2004), that the true-to-themselves low self-monitors, consistent in their attitudes across different situations, are more likely to be trusted than the chameleon-like highs? Does not the changeability of the high self-monitoring orientation undermine trust? Self-monitoring theory suggests a more complex picture. Yes, low self-monitors, because of the consistency they demonstrate between their attitudes and behaviors (Zanna, Olson, & Fazio, 1980), can build reputations as principled and autonomous individuals. But, high self-monitors are also likely to exhibit autonomy and independence when normative climates favor such nonconformity (Snyder & Monson, 1975).

Perhaps surprisingly, given the flexibility that high self-monitors exhibit, there is no general association between self-monitoring and conformity to social pressure (Santee & Maslach, 1982; Snyder, 1987, p. 37). Where high self-monitors do exhibit consistency is in presenting a general appearance of friendliness and the absence of anxiety (Lippa, 1978), and this general appearance is likely, one could argue, to engender trust. Thus, on the basis of self-monitoring-theory, it is difficult to formulate any simple relationship between self-monitoring and the extent to which individuals are trusted by others, given that both the principled low self-monitoring orientation and the sociable high self-monitoring orientation offer bases for establishing trust. It is possible, however, to respond to the request from the leading exponent of structural hole theory to "take the next analytical step" (Burt, 1992, p. 275) in understanding why some individuals rather than others benefit from brokerage opportunities in the trust network.

Trust Brokerage From a self-monitoring perspective, there is likely to be a difference in how the low and high self-monitors use their positions in the trust network. All individuals who "broker" between unconnected others occupy positions of autonomy (Merton, 1968; Simmel, 1955) that confer advantages in negotiations (Markovsky, Willer, & Patton, 1988) and in access to diverse knowledge and other resources (Burt, 1992). Such brokers are likely to be seen as leaders (Bavelas, 1950; for a review, see Shaw, 1964). However, the extent to which individuals who broker between disconnected others are able to take advantage of the brokerage position to emerge as leaders in the eyes of others is likely to vary. In the specific case of brokerage in the trust network, the broker connects two other people who do not trust each other, and this situation calls for particular skills in managing relationships. The broker in such a situation is in danger of being regarded by each of the nontrusting parties as partial to the other (Podolny & Baron, 1997, p. 676). High self-monitors, relative to low self-monitors, are more skilled at overcoming such negative impressions (Flynn, Chatman, & Spataro, 2001). Indeed, high self-monitors, relative to low self-monitors, are more skilled at social interactions (Furnham & Capon, 1983) in terms of being active in conversations (Ickes & Barnes, 1977), pacing conversations (Dabbs, Evans Hopper, & Purvis, 1980), using humor (Turner, 1980), and using a range of other techniques to ensure successful interactions (Snyder, 1987, p. 42).

We suggest, therefore, that the relationship between trust brokerage and leadership emergence is likely to be stronger for high self-monitors than for low self-monitors. Relative to low self-monitors, high self-monitors are particularly motivated to construct and project images with the intent of impressing others. Given this "status enhancement motive" (Gangestad & Snyder, 2000) and evidence that high self-monitors are able to act out different, and potentially incompatible, roles with different groups of people (Snyder, 1987, pp. 62–63), we suggest that high self-monitors will be particularly likely to leverage positions of brokerage in the trust network to facilitate the work of others, thus elevating their reputations as emergent leaders.

Hypothesis 3: The relationship between trust brokerage and leadership emergence will be stronger for high self-monitors than for low self-monitors.

Methods

Site We collected data from a high-technology company located in the northeastern United States. The company researched, produced, and marketed high-precision chromatographic equipment that it sold to analytical laboratories and other clients interested in testing the composition of a wide array of products, such as foods, fragrances, environmental pollutants, pharmaceuticals, and petrochemicals. The self-styled "head-coach" founded the company when he quit his job at a rival firm to take advantage of a business incubator program at a nearby university. Twelve years later, when this study was conducted, the company had grown from 1 to 116 employees. The firm used a relatively flat organizational structure (only three formal hierarchical levels) to help it compete in a fast-paced industry dominated by large, well-funded rivals, such as Hewlett-Packard. Of the 116 employees, 95 were in non-supervisory positions. The company was housed in a building purposefully designed to promote informal interactions among all employees. At the heart of the building was a large sunlit atrium, complete with large tropical plants, a waterfall, and a campus-style cafeteria. The firm had won prestigious awards for its entrepreneurial culture, environmentally friendly products, and success in recruiting, training, and promoting women.

Data We collected data on leadership perceptions, self-monitoring, and the trust network using a questionnaire sent to all 116 employees (68 men and 48 women). 102 people responded to the questionnaire, an overall response rate of 88%. Missing data reduced the sample size to 91. Respondents were not significantly different from non-respondents with regard to tenure or sex.

Measures

Trust Network To learn about the network of interpersonal trust relations we used the roster method: we asked respondents to look at a list of employees' names and place a check next to the names of "… those [people] whom you especially trust." We defined trusted individuals as "people with whom you would feel comfortable sharing personal or otherwise confidential information; people who you feel confident would not use the information to take advantage of you." The definition of trust was based on Rousseau, Sitkin, Burt and Camerer (1998), who examined how trust has been conceptualized and measured across a range of social science disciplines. Their review concluded that trust is "a psychological state comprising the intention to accept vulnerability based upon positive expectations of the intentions or behavior of another" (p. 395). This is also the definition used by Dirks and Ferrin (2002, p. 612) in their meta-analytic study of trust in leadership; and it is consistent with the approach to measuring the trust network adopted by Sparrowe and Liden (2005, p. 517). The sociometric data on trust relations were arranged in a 102×102 matrix containing 10,302 observations on all possible pairs of people.

Advice Network We also used the roster method to learn about advice relations. We asked employees to look down a list of names of all employees and place a check next to the names of "… the people from whom you seek advice about work-related matters. These are the people you turn to when you have a work-related problem or when you need advice about a work-related decision you have to make." This definition of advice relations is based on earlier network studies of advice relations in the workplace (e.g., Ibarra, 1992; Sparrowe & Liden, 2005). The sociometric data on advice relations were arranged in a 102×102 matrix containing advice relations among all possible pairs of people.

Independent Variables

Trust Brokerage To assess the extent to which an individual occupied a brokerage position in the trust network, we used the social network software UCINET VI (Borgatti, Everett, & Freeman, 2002) to calculate Burt's measure of "network constraint" (for the mathematical formula and an extended discussion of the measure, see Burt, 1992, pp. 50–81; Borgatti, Jones, & Everett, 1998). Network constraint can range from 0 to 1. A summary index, constraint "measures the lack of brokerage opportunities" (Burt, 2007, p. 125) within a network. The more that a person's contacts are directly tied to one another, the higher is the constraint on the individual. This measure has been widely used to assess structural brokerage in prior studies (e.g., Burt, 1997; Seibert, Kraimer, & Liden, 2001). We reversed the sign of the measure so that the index can be directly interpreted as representing the presence of brokerage opportunities (rather than the absence of brokerage opportunities).

Self-Monitoring We used the revised 18-item, true-false version of the self-monitoring scale to code self-monitoring orientation (Snyder & Gangestad, 1986). Scale items included "I would probably make a good actor," and "I would not change my opinions (or the way I do things) in order to please someone or win their favor" (reverse coded). The 18-item scale has higher internal consistency than the original 25-item measure. Cronbach's alpha for the scale in this study was .80. Research suggests that self-monitoring is a stable aspect of personality through the lifespan (Gangestad & Snyder, 1985; Jenkins, 1993, p. 84). A meta-analytic review of the literature on self-monitoring in the workplace concluded that this scale has sound psychometric properties, as evidenced by high levels of internal consistency, reliability, and predictive validity (Day, Schleicher, Unckless, & Hiller, 2002).

Dependent Variables

Leadership Perceptions The construct of leadership has been conceptualized and measured in a number of different ways in the organizational literature (see R. Hogan, Curphy, & Hogan, 1994). Nonetheless, a longstanding distinction relevant to our investigation is between leadership effectiveness and leadership emergence (Lord, De Vader, & Alliger, 1986). Whereas leadership effectiveness is conceptualized in terms of group and organizational performance, leadership emergence "is based on the extent to which an individual is viewed as a leader by others and is, therefore, inherently tied to others' perceptions" (Day & Schleicher, 2006, p. 693).

We assessed the extent to which respondents perceived others to be leaders by counting the number of times each individual was nominated as a leader. Specifically, we asked each respondent to look down a list of names of employees and place a check next to the name of the individuals whom they perceived to be leaders. We explained on the questionnaire that individuals perceived as leaders "may or may not be officially designated as leaders by...management." We did not specify what we meant by the term "leader" because we were interested in capturing respondents' implicit theories of leadership (Lord & Maher, 1991/1993, p. 11).

Advice Centrality We assessed centrality in the advice network by counting the number of times an individual was identified by others as someone they tended to turn to for advice on work related matters.

Control Variables

Rank This variable was coded as 1 for supervisors and as 0 for non-supervisors. The data for coding this variable came directly from company records. We controlled for rank because high-ranking individuals, due to the resources they control and the prestige they enjoy, are likely to garner informal leadership influence on the basis of their reward power (French & Raven, 1959).

Tenure Taken from company records, this was the number of months the person had been employed by the company.

Job Performance In the research on work organizations, the majority of performance ratings tend to come from supervisors (Bretz, Milkovich, & Read, 1992, p. 331). Meta-analytic evidence suggests that supervisory evaluations represent valid assessments of true performance (Arvey & Murphy, 1998, p. 163). Our three-item measure of job performance was based on confidential ratings provided by each individual's direct supervisor. Performance ratings that are collected for research purposes tend to more reliable and valid than those obtained for administrative purposes (Wherry & Bartlett, 1982). The three items that made up our measure were selected on the basis of multiple discussions with a panel comprising the firm's human resources director, a long tenured member with broad knowledge of the company, and four employees who represented a range of different job types at the firm. The items asked supervisors to rate subordinates in terms of (a) their "overall job performance" (1=poor, 5=excellent); (b) the likelihood that the subordinate would "achieve future career related success (such as promotions, awards, bonuses, and involvement in high profile projects)" at the company; and (c) would be someone the supervisor would pick as a successor for their job (1=highly unlikely; 5=highly likely). The reliability of the scale as measured by Cronbach's alpha was .83.

We considered and then rejected the inclusion of individual sex (male/female) as a control variable. This variable was insignificant in all the analyses reported below, but its inclusion produced poorer fitting models.

Analyses

The dependent variables in our analyses—the number of leadership nominations received by an individual, and the number of times an individual was cited as someone others turned to for work related advice—are count variables. For these kinds of data, Poisson-based regression models are more appropriate than Ordinary Least Squares (OLS) regression. However, our data showed clear evidence of over-dispersion (e.g., after fitting the ordinary Poisson regression model, the Pearson chi-square goodness-of-fit statistic divided by degrees of freedom was much larger than 1). Therefore, we used the negative binomial variant of Poisson regression that explicitly includes a parameter for over-dispersion (see Hilbe, 2008). In negative binomial regression, the log of the expected values (μ) is a linear function of the independent variables plus the dispersion parameter:

$$\log(\mu) = \text{intercept} + b1*X1 + b2*X2 + \ldots + b3*Xm + \varepsilon.$$

We employed the Likelihood Ratio (LR) test to assess the comparative goodness of fit between models (Huelsenbeck & Rannala, 1997). The LR test compares the likelihood scores of two models. The LR statistic, which follows a chi-square distribution, assesses whether the addition of an additional parameter (e.g., self-monitoring) leads to a significantly better fitting model than a baseline model (e.g., a model containing just the control variables). To test the interaction Hypothesis 3, we mean-centered measures of self-monitoring and trust brokerage and multiplied them to create a single interaction term. We then included this interaction term in the regression equation containing control variables, self-monitoring, and trust brokerage.

Results

The descriptive statistics in Table 11.1 show that the typical non-supervisory employee had worked for the firm for four-and-a-half years, was seen as a leader by nine other people, was turned to for advice by 16 other people, and was regarded by the supervisor as a high performer ($M = 10.15$ on a 15-point scale). Compatible with the first two hypotheses, individuals high in self-monitoring, compared with those low in self-monitoring, tended to receive more leadership nominations ($r = .23$, $p < .05$) and more nominations as advice providers ($r = .25$, $p < .05$). Further, self-monitoring was related to the tendency to occupy a role as a broker trusted by those who did not trust each other ($r = 20$, $p < .10$). Tables 11.2 and 11.3 show the results of tests of hypotheses. All of the binomial regression models in these tables demonstrate goodness-of-fit ratios close to one (the chi-square statistic divided by the degrees of freedom) indicating well-fitting models.

Table 11.1 Means, standard deviations, and correlations of the variables

Variable	M	SD	1	2	3	4	5	6
1. Rank	0.22	0.42						
2. Tenure	53.95	39.25	.19					
3. Job performance	10.15	2.75	.25*	.28**				
4. Self-monitoring	0.07	0.08	.18+					
5. Trust brokerage	0.29**	0.14	.08	.20+				
6. Perceived leadership	0.72***	0.29	.23*	.25**	.35***	.23*	.36**	
7. Advice centrality	15.87	11.11	.60***	.28**	.23*	.25*	.52***	.74***

Note $^+p<.10$; $^*p<.05$; $^{**}p<.01$; $^{***}p<.001$

Model 1 in Table 11.2 shows that each of the three control variables (individual's rank, tenure in the organization, and job performance) significantly predicted the extent to which the individual was perceived as a leader. Recall that the first hypothesis suggested that the higher the self-monitoring score, the more the individual would be perceived as a leader. We found support for this prediction in the regression analysis summarized in Model 2, which shows that the addition of self-monitoring significantly improved model fit over the controls-only Model 1 ($\chi=7.86$, $p<.01$).

Thus, high self-monitors tend to be perceived as leaders. But are they also perceived as advice providers as suggested by Hypothesis 2? The answer is yes, as shown by the analyses summarized in Table 11.3. Controlling for the individual's rank, tenure, and job performance, the addition of self-monitoring in Model 2 significantly improved model fit over the base-line Model 1 ($\chi=4.80$, $p<.05$). More co-workers report that high self-monitors, relative to low self-monitors, provide them with advice.

Hypothesis 3 suggested that the self-monitoring scores of those individuals who were trusted by people who distrusted each other would predict emergent leadership. We found support for this trust-leveraging hypothesis. As shown in Table 11.2, Model 5, the interaction between self-monitoring and trust brokerage was significant ($p<.01$). The inclusion of the interaction term improved model fit relative to the main-effects Model 4 ($\chi=5.32$, $p<.05$), suggesting that high self-monitors, relative to low self-monitors, leveraged go-between positions in the trust network to emerge as leaders in the eyes of others.

To more closely examine the form of these interactions, we constructed a split plot following the procedures described in Aiken and West (1991). The form of the plot depicted in Fig. 11.1 shows support for Hypothesis 3: although trust brokerage was positively related to the number of leadership nominations received for both high self-monitors and low self-monitors, this relationship was significantly stronger for highs than for lows.

Table 11.2 Negative binomial regression estimates from analysis predicting perceived leadership

Independent variables	Model 1	Model 2	Model 3	Model 4	Model 5
Rank	1.74 (0.27)***	1.81 (0.26)***	1.35 (0.22)***	1.42 (0.21)***	1.45 (0.20)***
Tenure	0.01 (0.00)***	0.01 (0.00)*	0.01 (0.00)*	0.01 (0.00)+	0.00 (0.00)
Job performance	0.18 (0.05)***	0.15 (0.05)**	0.14 (0.04)**	0.12 (0.04)**	0.11 (0.04)**
Self-monitoring		0.09 (0.03)**		0.07 (0.02)**	0.03 (0.03)
Trust brokerage			17.05 (2.97)***	16.62 (2.92)***	17.71 (2.74)***
Self-monitoring × Trust brokerage					1.58 (0.67)**
Pearson chi square	89.71	91.25	84.70	90.76	89.12
Log likelihood	1411.65	1415.58	1430.72	1434.05	1436.71
Likelihood ratio		7.86**	38.14***	44.80***	5.32*

Note The intercept and dispersion parameters were included in the regression models, but they are not reported here. Numbers in table are parameter estimates (standard errors are in parentheses). The Likelihood Ratio (LR) test is a statistical test of the relative goodness-of-fit across two models. To calculate the LR statistics corresponding to models 2, 3, and 4, we used Model 1 as the baseline model. To compute the LR statistic for Model 5, we used Model 4 as the baseline model

*$p<.05$; **$p<.01$; ***$p<.001$

Table 11.3 Negative binomial regression estimates from analysis predicting advice centrality

Independent variables	Model 1	Model 2
Rank	.68 (0.17)***	0.70 (0.16)***
Tenure	0.01 (0.00)*	0.01 (0.00)*
Job performance	0.04 (0.03)	0.03 (0.03)
Self-monitoring		0.04 (0.02)*
Trust brokerage		
Self-monitoring x trust brokerage		
Pearson chi square	86.75	86.87
Log likelihood	2870.65	2873.25
Likelihood ratio		4.80*

Note The intercept and dispersion parameters were included in the regression models, but they are not reported here. Numbers in table are parameter estimates (standard errors are in parentheses). The Likelihood Ratio (LR) test is a statistical test of the relative goodness-of-fit across two models. To calculate the LR statistic for model 2 we used Model 1 as the baseline model
*$p<.05$; **$p<.01$; ***$p<.001$

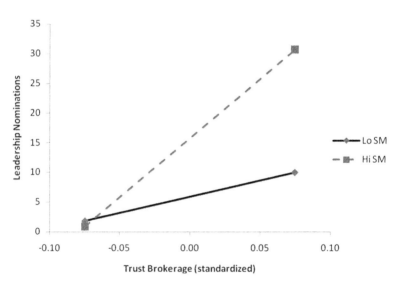

Fig. 11.1 Plot of the relationship between trust brokerage and number of leadership nominations received for high and low self-monitors (Design by authors)

Discussion

Are high self-monitors likely to emerge in actual workplace settings as leaders in the eyes of others? Critics have pointed out that "subjects in laboratory studies... rarely feel accountable to others for the positions they take" (Tetlock, 1992, p. 335) and evidence suggests that laboratory studies may have inflated the relationship between self-monitoring and leadership emergence (Day et al., 2002, p. 394). Our results showed that self-monitoring was significantly related to leadership emergence in the workplace. Further, the leadership emergence of high self-monitors was facilitated by earning the trust of those who did not trust each other. Relative to low self-monitors, the high self-monitors were also active in the provision to colleagues of workplace advice. From these results, we build a picture of the high self-monitoring emergent leader as someone who notices problems and ameliorates them through the provision of advice. The high self-monitoring style of leadership is not, as some have suggested, an epiphenomenon of laboratory experiments, but is recognized by workplace colleagues.

Particularly interesting is the possibility that the chameleon-like style of the high self-monitor helps rather than hurts leadership emergence. High self-monitors are likely to segregate their audiences from each other, acting out different and even incompatible roles across social settings (Snyder & Gangestad, 1982; Snyder, Gangestad, & Simpson, 1983). Although critics might characterize such role flexibility as detracting from leadership, the alternative possibility, suggested by our results, is that the high self-monitoring, purposively sociable orientation (Ickes & Barnes, 1977) toward quite different social settings can help high self-monitors play a vital role in brokering across social divides. Indeed, high self-monitors (compared to low self-monitors) show leadership in resolving social dilemmas by contributing to the general welfare of others (De Cremer, Snyder, & Dewitte, 2001).

Contribution to Theory and Research

Whereas prior work has speculated that high self-monitors may be perceived by others to lack leadership integrity because of the variability in their behaviors (Simons, 2002), our work has emphasized that high self-monitoring flexibility may enhance perceptions of leadership by facilitating coordination across social divides. Critics have tended to perceive the high self-monitoring style of leadership as lacking authenticity (Ilies, Morgeson, & Nahrgang, 2005) but research has failed to support this proposition (Tate, 2008). Our results show that high self-monitors tend to provide advice to more people than do low self-monitors, and that high self-monitors appear to be particularly well suited to playing the role of broker between parties that do not trust each other. The flexibility of high self-monitors, therefore, expresses itself in terms of centrality in advice networks and the ability to effectively broker trust relations to win attributions of leadership.

The current study contributes to brokerage theory and research (e.g., Burt, 2005) an emphasis on the ways in which different kinds of people can take differential advantage of brokerage positions. Being trusted by people who do not trust each other has been theorized in prior work to provide both the opportunity and the motivation for brokerage (Burt, 1992, pp. 34–35). However, we show that, with respect to being recognized by their peers as leaders, high self-monitors, relative to low self-monitors, are more likely to benefit from the occupation of a structurally advantageous network position. The occupation of a structurally advantageous position, therefore, may well be more advantageous for some (i.e., high self-monitors) relative to others (i.e., low self-monitors). The incorporation of theoretically relevant personality differences can enhance the predictive and explanatory power of network theory.

The paper addresses the controversy in the self-monitoring literature concerning the kind of leadership that high self-monitors are likely to bring to real organizations. From our research, we show that high self-monitors, relative to low self-monitors, are more central in the provision of advice to colleagues. As prior work has suggested (Ickes, Holloway, Stinson, & Hoodenpyle, 2006), high self-monitors work hard to ensure that social interactions are successful. In the present research this hard work involves being active in helping others with work-related matters. Leadership emergence, therefore, is not just a matter of impression management, as some critics of the self-monitoring and leadership relationship have suggested.

Future Research

It seems clear that high self-monitors emerge as informal leaders in organizations (Day et al., 2002). But we still do not fully understand the differences between high and low self-monitoring styles of leadership. If we assume that both low and high self-monitors can develop over time as leaders in the eyes of others (as research shows—Tate, 2008), then the interesting question becomes what leadership behaviors differentiate the two self-monitoring orientations. Brokerage across social divides may appeal to the interests and abilities of high self-monitors whereas strengthening connections among members of a team may appeal to the interests and abilities of low self-monitors (Oh & Kilduff, 2008). Some people may be recognized as leaders because of their institutional loyalty, their retention of the services of trusted subordinates over long periods of time, and their "straight talking." These would seem to be leadership characteristics associated with low self-monitoring. Other people may be recognized as leaders because of their flexibility in moving from one situation to another, their appeal to different types of people, and their reputation for saying the right thing at the right time. These would seem to be leadership characteristics associated with high self-monitoring. Thus, future research can move beyond the expectation that one type of personality will emerge successful in leadership tournaments. Different trajectories and behaviors may be associated with different personality types.

Indeed, high self-monitors' pursuit of informal leadership may be related to costs as well as benefits. Thus, evidence shows that high self-monitors (relative to low self-monitors) are more susceptible to role conflict in the workplace (Mehra & Schenkel, 2008) and are more likely to accept a range of responsibilities that negatively affect their workplace performance (Mehra et al., 2001). To the extent that the high self-monitors' attitudes and behaviors are driven by external cues (an orientation that may be conducive to getting ahead in organizational contexts), the high self-monitors (relative to the low self-monitors) may be susceptible to influences in the environment such as prompts to eat too much food leading to obesity (Younger & Pliner, 1976). It is necessary to avoid thinking that one self-monitoring orientation is inevitably superior to the other.

The current research is consistent with other research showing self-monitoring to be associated with leader emergence, but questions remain concerning how individuals different in self-monitoring orientation build bases of trust among colleagues and precisely what kinds of advice high and low self-monitors provide. Previous research has suggested that high and low self-monitors approach relationship building with different orientations. High self-monitors are concerned to project positive images of themselves and to suppress information that might trigger negative inferences (Gangestad & Snyder, 2000). High self-monitors are also motivated to produce social interactions that are successful (Ickes et al., 2006) and that promote social status (Flynn et al., 2006). By contrast, low self-monitors generate expressive behavior from inner affective states and attitudes (Snyder, 1979) and pay less attention to impression management (Turnley & Bolino, 2001). Low self-monitors may be strongly motivated to produce social interactions that reflect their genuine underlying values (Ickes et al., 2006). Thus, future research could investigate whether high self-monitors tend to build trusting relationships on the basis of diplomatic impression management, whereas low self-monitors tend to build such relationships on the basis of a match between strongly held values. Further, future research could investigate whether the advice provided by high self-monitors tends to reflect a status-seeking orientation whereas the advice provided by low self-monitors tends to reflect a sticking-up-for-principles orientation.

Limitations The research is limited in that it draws from cross-sectional data within a single organization. Confidence in the results is enhanced to the extent that they contribute to a consistent pattern that includes laboratory experiments and field studies showing self-monitoring effects on leader emergence (see the review by Day et al., 2002). Given that the culture of the focal organization explicitly valued cooperation, this could limit generalizability of the findings with respect to trust brokerage. Common method bias is always a concern in survey research. We have endeavored to reduce such concern by measuring leadership emergence and advice centrality as counts of nominations by others whereas self-monitoring orientation was based on a well-established self-report instrument. A further limitation of the research is that we were not able to explore in depth differences among high and low self-monitors concerning the reasons for the differential pattern of results concerning trust brokerage. An issue for future research is to investigate whether high self-monitors are better able to exploit brokerage positions in the trust network because they perceive their network positions more accurately (Flynn et al., 2006) or whether network brokers who happen to be high self-monitors have different motivations than their low self-monitoring colleagues.

Conclusion

Self-monitoring theory shows itself to be valuable in understanding the patterns of leadership emergence in an actual organization in which colleagues provide each other advice and establish patterns of trust and lack of trust. The current research may help to explain why it is that high self-monitors tend to get ahead in the race for promotion and advancement in organizations (Kilduff & Day, 1994). As individuals pursue their careers, they establish reputations in the eyes of others in terms of leadership behaviors. If self-monitoring theory as employed in this study has an overall message, it is that to understand the structures of social behavior that emerge in organizations we must first understand the psychology of the interacting individuals.

References

Aiken, L. S., & West, S. G. (1991). *Multiple regression: Testing and interpreting interactions*. Thousand Oaks: Sage.
Arvey, R. D., & Murphy, K. R. (1998). Performance evaluation in work settings. *Annual Review of Psychology, 49*, 141–168. doi:10.1146/annurev.psych.49.1.141
Bavelas, A. (1950). Communication patterns in task-oriented groups. *Journal of the Acoustical Society of America, 22*, 725–730. doi:10.1121/1.1906679
Bedeian, A. G., & Day, D. V. (2004). Can chameleons lead? *Leadership Quarterly, 15*, 687–718. doi:10.1016/j.leaqua.2004.07.005
Berscheid, E., Graziano, W., Monson, T C., & Dermer, M. (1976). Outcome dependency: Attention, attribution, and attraction. *Journal of Personality and Social Psychology, 34*, 978–989. doi:10.1037//0022-3514.34.5.978
Bono, J. E., & Anderson, M. H. (2005). The advice and influence networks of transformational leaders. *Journal of Applied Psychology, 90*, 1306–1314. doi:10.1037/0021-9010.90.6.1306
Borgatti, S. P., Everett, M. G., & Freeman, L. C. (2002). *UCINET 6 for Windows: Software for social network analysis*. Harvard: Analytic Technologies.
Borgatti, S. P., Jones, C., & Everett, M. G. (1998). Network measures of social capital. *Connections, 21*(2), 27–36.
Bretz, R. D. Jr., Milkovich, G. T., & Read, W. (1992). The current state of performance appraisal research and practice: Concerns, directions, and implications. *Journal of Management, 18*, 321–352. doi:10.1177/014920639201800206

Burt, R. S. (1992). *Structural holes: The social structure of competition.* Cambridge, MA: Harvard University Press.
Burt, R. S. (1997). The contingent value of social capital. *Administrative Science Quarterly, 42,* 339–365. doi:10.2307/2393923
Burt, R. S. (2005). *Brokerage and closure: An introduction to social capital.* Oxford: University Press.
Burt, R. S. (2007). Secondhand brokerage: Evidence on the importance of local structure for managers, bankers, and analysts. *Academy of Management Journal, 50,* 119–148. doi:10.5465/AMJ.2007.24162082
Burt, R. S., & Ronchi, D. (1990). Contested control in a large manufacturing plant. In J. Weesie & H. Flap (Eds.), *Social networks through time* (pp. 121–157). Utrecht: ISOR.
Carter, L., Haythorn, W., Shriver, B., & Lanzetta, J. (1951). The behavior of leaders and other group members. *Journal of Abnormal and Social Psychology, 46,* 589–595. doi:10.1037/h0059490
Cooper, C. D., Scandura, T. A., & Schriesheim, C. A. (2005). Looking forward but learning from our past: Potential challenges to developing authentic leadership theory and authentic leaders. *Leadership Quarterly, 16,* 475–493. doi:10.1016/j.leaqua.2005.03.008
Dabbs, J. M., Evans, M. S., Hopper, C. H., & Purvis, J. A. (1980). Self-monitors in conversation: What do they monitor? *Journal of Personality and Social Psychology, 39,* 278–284. doi:10.1037/0022-3514.39.2.278
Day, D. V., & Schleicher, D J. (2006). Self-monitoring at work: A motive-based perspective. *Journal of Personality, 74,* 685–713. doi:10.1111/j.1467-6494.2006.00389.x
Day, D. V., Schleicher, D. J., Unckless, A. L., & Hiller, N. J. (2002). Self-monitoring personality at work: A meta-analytic investigation of construct validity. *Journal of Applied Psychology, 87,* 390–401. doi:10.1037//0021-9010.87.2.390
De Cremer, D., Snyder, M., & Dewitte, S. (2001). The less I trust, the less I contribute (or not)?: The effects of trust, accountability and self-monitoring in social dilemmas. *European Journal of Social Psychology, 31,* 93–107. doi:10.1002/ejsp.34
Dirks, K. T., & Ferrin, D. L. (2002). Trust in leadership: Meta-analytic findings and implications for research and practice. *Journal of Applied Psychology, 87,* 611–628. doi:10.1037/0021-9010.87.4.611
Flynn, F. J., Chatman, J. A., & Spataro, S. E. (2001). Getting to know you: The influence of personality on impressions and performance of demographically different people in organizations. *Administrative Science Quarterly, 46,* 414–442. doi:10.2307/3094870
Flynn, F. J., Reagans, R. E., Amanatullah, E. T., & Ames, D. R. (2006). Helping one's way to the top: Self-monitors achieve status by helping others and knowing who helps whom. *Journal of Personality and Social Psychology, 91,* 1123–1137. doi:10.1037/0022-3514.91.6.1123
French, J. R. P. Jr., & Raven, B. (1959). The bases of social power. In D. P. Cartwright (Ed.), *Studies in social power* (pp. 150–167). Ann Arbor: University of Michigan.
Furnham, A., & Capon, M. (1983). Social skills and self-monitoring processes. *Personality and Individual Differences, 4,* 171–178. doi:10.1016/0191-8869(83)90017-X
Gangestad, S. W., & Snyder, M. (1985). "To carve nature at its joints": On the existence of discrete classes in personality. *Psychological Review, 92,* 317–349. doi:10.1037/0033-295X.92.3.317
Gangestad, S. W., & Snyder, M. (2000). Self-monitoring: Appraisal and reappraisal. *Psychological Bulletin, 126,* 530–555. doi:10.1037//0033-2909.126.4.530
Granovetter, M. S. (1973). The strength of weak ties. *American Journal of Sociology, 78,* 1360–1380. doi:10.1086/225469
Hilbe, J. M. (2008). *Negative binomial regression.* Cambridge, UK: University Press.
Hogan, R., Curphy, G. J., & Hogan, J. (1994). What we know about leadership: Effectiveness and personality. *The American Psychologist, 49,* 493–504. doi:10.1037/0003-066X.49.6.493
Homans, G. C. (1951). *The human group.* London: Routledge & Kegan Paul.

Hosch, H. M., Leippe, M. R., Marchioni, P. M., & Cooper, D. S. (1984). Victimization, self-monitoring, and eyewitness identification. *Journal of Applied Psychology, 69,* 280–288. doi:10.1037/0021-9010.69.2.280

Huelsenbeck, J. P., Rannala, B. (1997). Phylogenetic methods come of age: Testing hypotheses in an evolutionary context. *Science, 276,* 227–232. doi:10.1126/science.276.5310.227

Ibarra, H. (1992). Homophily and differential returns: Sex differences in network structure and access in an advertising firm. *Administrative Science Quarterly, 37,* 422–447. doi:10.2307/2393451

Ickes, W., & Barnes, R. D. (1977). The role of sex and self-monitoring in unstructured dyadic interactions. *Journal of Personality and Social Psychology, 35,* 315–330. doi:10.1111/j.1467-6494.2006.00388.x

Ickes, W., Holloway, R., Stinson, L. L., & Hoodenpyle, T. G. (2006). Self-monitoring in social interaction: The centrality of self-affect. *Journal of Personality, 74,* 659–684. doi:10:1111/j.1467-6494.2006.00388.x

Ilies, R., Morgeson, F. P., & Nahrgang, J. D. (2005). Authentic leadership and eudaemonic well-being: Understanding leader-follower outcomes. *Leadership Quarterly, 16,* 373–394.

Jenkins, J. M. (1993). Self-monitoring and turnover: The impact of personality on intent to leave. *Journal of Organizational Behavior, 14,* 83–91. doi:10.1002/job.4030140108

Jones, E. E., & Baumeister, R. (1976). The self-monitor looks at the ingratiatory. *Journal of Personality and Social Psychology, 44,* 654–674. doi:10.1111/j.1467-6494.1976.tb00144.x

Kilduff, M., & Day, D. V. (1994). Do chameleons get ahead?: The effects of self-monitoring on managerial careers. *Academy of Management Journal, 37,* 1047–1060. doi:10.2307/256612

Kulik, J. A., & Taylor, S E. (1981). Self-monitoring and the use of consensus information. *Journal of Personality, 49,* 75–84. doi:10.1111/j.1467-6494.1981.tb00847.x

Krackhardt, D. (1995). Entrepreneurial opportunities in an entrepreneurial firm: A structural approach. *Entrepreneurship Theory and Practice, 19,* 53–69.

Lippa, R. (1978). Expressive control, expressive consistency, and the correspondence between expressive behavior and personality. *Journal of Personality, 46,* 438–461. doi:10.1111/j.1467-6494.1978.tb01011.x

Lord, R. G., De Vader, C. L., & Alliger, G. M. (1986). A meta-analysis of the relation between personality traits and leadership perceptions: An application of validity generalization procedures. *Journal of Applied Psychology, 71,* 402–410. doi:10.1037/0021-9010.71.3.402

Lord, R. G., & Maher, K. J. (1993). *Leadership and information processing: Linking perceptions and performance.* London: Routledge. (Original work published 1991)

Markovsky, B., Willer, D., & Patton, T. (1988). Power relations in exchange networks. *American Sociological Review, 53,* 220–236. doi:10.2307/2095689

Mehra, A., Kilduff, M., & Brass, D. J. (2001). The social networks of high and low self-monitors: Implications for workplace performance. *Administrative Science Quarterly, 46,* 121–146. doi:10.2307/2667127

Mehra, A., & Schenkel, M. T. (2008). The price chameleons pay: Self-monitoring, boundary spanning and role conflict in the workplace. *British Journal of Management, 19,* 138–144. doi:10.1111/j.1467-8551.2007.00535.x

Merton, R. K. (1968). *Social theory and social structure.* New York: Free Press.

Neubert, M. J., & Taggar, S. (2004). Pathways to informal leadership: The moderating role of gender on the relationship of individual differences and team member network centrality to informal leadership emergence. *The Leadership Quarterly, 15,* 175–194. doi:10.1016/j.leaqua.2004.02.006

Oh, H., & Kilduff, M. (2008). The ripple effect of personality on social structure? Self-monitoring origins of network brokerage. *Journal of Applied Psychology, 93,* 1155–1164. doi:10.1037/0021-9010.93.5.1155

Podolny, J. M., & Baron, J. N. (1997). Resources and relationships: Social networks and mobility in the workplace. *American Sociological Review, 62,* 673–693. doi:10.2307/2657354

Rousseau, D. M., Sitkin, S. B., Burt, R. S., & Camerer, C. (1998). Not so different after all: A cross-discipline view of trust. *Academy of Management Review, 23*, 393–404. doi:10.5465/AMR.1998.926617

Santee, R. T., & Maslach, C. (1982). To agree or not to agree: Personal dissent amid social pressure to conform. *Journal of Personality and Social Psychology, 42*, 690–700. doi:10.1037/0022-3514.42.4.690

Seibert, S. E., Kraimer, M. L., & Liden, R. C. (2001). A social capital theory of career success. *The Academy of Management Journal, 44*, 219–237. doi:10.2307/3069452

Shaw, M. E. (1964). Communication networks. In L. Nerkowitz (Ed.), *Advances in experimental social psychology* (pp. 111–147), Vol. 1. New York: Academic Press.

Simmel, G. (1955). *Conflict and the web of group-affiliations*. New York: Free Press.

Simons, T. (2002). Behavioral integrity: The perceived alignment between managers' words and deeds as a research focus. *Organization Science, 13*, 18–35. doi:10.1287/orsc.13.1.18.543

Snyder, M. (1979). Self-monitoring processes. In L. Berkowitz (Ed.), *Advances in experimental social psychology* (pp. 85–128), Vol. 12. New York: Academic Press.

Snyder, M. (1987). *Public appearances, private realities: The psychology of self-monitoring*. New York: Freeman.

Snyder, M., & Gangestad, S. (1982). Choosing social situations: Two investigations of self-monitoring processes. *Journal of Personality and Social Psychology, 43*, 123–135. doi:10.1037/0022-3514.43.1.123

Snyder, M., & Gangestad, S. (1986). On the nature of self-monitoring: Matters of assessment, matters of validity. *Journal of Personality and Social Psychology, 51*, 125–139. doi:10.1037/0022-3514.51.1.125

Snyder, M., Gangestad, S., & Simpson, J. A. (1983). Choosing friends as activity partners: The role of self-monitoring. *Journal of Personality and Social Psychology, 45*, 1061–1072. doi:10.1037/0022-3514.45.5.1061

Snyder, M., & Monson, T. C. (1975). Persons, situations, and the control of social behavior. *Journal of Personality and Social Psychology, 32*, 637–644. doi:10.1037/0022-3514.32.4.637

Sorrentino, R. M., & Field, N. (1986). Emergent leadership over time: The functional value of positive motivation. *Journal of Personality and Social Psychology, 50*, 1091–1099. doi:10.1037/0022-3514.50.6.1091

Sparrowe, R. T., & Liden, R. C. (2005). Two routes to influence: Integrating leader-member exchange and social network perspectives. *Administrative Science Quarterly, 50*, 505–535. doi:10.2189/asqu.50.4.505

Tate, B. (2008). A longitudinal study of the relationships among self-monitoring, authentic leadership, and perceptions of leadership. *Journal of Leadership and Organizational Studies, 15*(1), 16–29. doi:10.1177/1548051808318002

Tetlock, P. E. (1992). The impact of accountability on judgment and choice: Toward a social contingency model. In M. P. Zanna (Ed.), *Advances in experimental social psychology* (pp. 331–376), Vol. 25. San Diego: Academic Press. doi:10.1016/S0065-2601(08)60287-7

Toegel, G., Anand, N., & Kilduff, M. (2007). Emotion helpers: The role of high positive affectivity and high self-monitoring managers. *Personnel Psychology, 60*, 337–365. doi:10.1111/j.1744-6570.2007.00076.x

Turner, R. G. (1980). Self-monitoring and humor production. *Journal of Personality, 48*, 163–167. doi:10.1111/j.1467-6494.1980.tb00825.x

Turnley, W. H., & Bolino, M. C. (2001). Achieving desired images while avoiding undesired images: Exploring the role of self-monitoring in impression management. *Journal of Applied Psychology, 86*, 351–360. doi:10.1037/0021-9010.86.2.351

Wherry, R. J. Sr., & Bartlett, C. J. (1982). The control of bias in ratings: A theory of rating. *Personnel Psychology, 35*, 521–551. doi:10.1111/j.1744-6570.1982.tb02208.x

Younger, J. C., & Pliner, P. (1976). Obese-normal differences in the self-monitoring of expressive behavior. *Journal of Research in Personality, 10*, 112–115. doi:10.1016/0092-6566(76)90089-1

Zaccaro, S. J., Foti, R. J., & Kenny, D. A. (1991). Self-monitoring and trait-based variance in leadership: An investigation of leader flexibility across multiple group situations. *Journal of Applied Psychology, 76,* 308–315. doi:10.1037/0021-9010.76.2.308

Zanna, M. P., Olson, J. M., & Fazio, R. H. (1980). Attitude–behavior consistency: An individual difference perspective. *Journal of Personality and Social Psychology, 38,* 432–440. doi:10.1037/0022-3514.38.3.432

Open Access This chapter is distributed under the terms of the Creative Commons Attribution 4.0 International License (http://creativecommons.org/licenses/by/4.0/), which permits use, duplication, adaptation, distribution and reproduction in any medium or format, as long as you give appropriate credit to the original author(s) and the source, provide a link to the Creative Commons license and indicate if changes were made.

The images or other third party material in this chapter are included in the work's Creative Commons license, unless indicated otherwise in the credit line; if such material is not included in the work's Creative Commons license and the respective action is not permitted by statutory regulation, users will need to obtain permission from the license holder to duplicate, adapt or reproduce the material.

Part III
Network Geographies of Learning

Chapter 12
How Atypical Combinations of Scientific Ideas Are Related to Impact: The General Case and the Case of the Field of Geography

Satyam Mukherjee, Brian Uzzi, Benjamin F. Jones, and Michael Stringer

Scientific enterprises are increasingly concerned that research within narrow boundaries is unlikely to be the source of the most fruitful ideas (National Academy of Sciences, National Academy of Engineering, & Institute of Medicine of the National Academies, 2004). Models of creativity emphasize that innovation is spurred by original combinations that spark new insights (Becker, 1982; Guimera, Uzzi, Spiro, & L.A. Amaral, 2005; Jones, 2009; Jones, Wuchty, & Uzzi, 2008; Schilling, 2005; Schumpeter, 1939; Usher, 1929/1998; Uzzi & Spiro, 2005; Weitzman, 1998). Current interest in team science and how scientists search for ideas is premised in part on the idea that teams can span scientific specialties, effectively combining knowledge that prompts scientific breakthroughs (Evans & Foster, 2011; Falk-Krzesinski et al., 2010; Fiore, 2008; Stokols, Hall, Taylor, & Moser, 2008; Wuchty, Jones, & Uzzi, 2007).

The production and consumption of boundary-spanning ideas can also raise well-known challenges (Azoulay, Zivin, & Manso, 2011; Collins, 1998; Einstein, 1949; Fleming, 2001; Henderson & Clark, 1990; Schilling & Green, 2011). If, as

S. Mukherjee
Indian Institute of Management, Udaipur, Rajasthan, India
e-mail: satyam.mukherjee@gmail.com

B. Uzzi (✉)
Kellogg School of Management, Northwestern University,
2001 Sheridan Road, 60208 Evanston, IL, USA
e-mail: uzzi@northwestern.edu

B.F. Jones
Department of Management and Strategy, Kellogg School of Management, Northwestern University, 2001 Sheridan Road, Jacobs Center 371, 60208-2001 Evanston/Chicago, IL, USA
e-mail: bjones@kellogg.northwestern.edu

M. Stringer
Northwestern Institute on Complex Systems, Northwestern University,
600 Foster, 60208 Evanston, IL, USA
e-mail: mike.stringer@datascopeanalytics.com

Einstein (1949) believed, individual scientists inevitably become narrower in their expertise as the body of scientific knowledge expands, then reaching effectively across boundaries may be increasingly challenging (Jones, 2009), especially given the difficulty of searching unfamiliar domains (Fleming, 2001; Schilling & Green, 2011). Moreover, novel ideas can be difficult to absorb (Henderson & Clark, 1990) and communicate, leading scientists to intentionally display conventionality. In his *Principia*, Newton presented his laws of gravitation using accepted geometry rather than his newly developed calculus, despite the latter's importance in developing his insights (Whiteside, 1970). Similarly, Darwin devoted the first part of *On the Origin of Species* to conventional, well-accepted knowledge of the selective breeding of dogs, cattle, and birds. Given these tendencies, the balance between extending science with atypical combinations of knowledge while maintaining advantages of conventional domain-level thinking is critical to the link between innovativeness and impact. However, little is known about the composition of this balance or how scientists can achieve it. In this paper, our analysis of 17.9 million papers spanning all scientific fields suggests that science follows a nearly universal pattern: The highest-impact science is primarily grounded in exceptionally conventional combinations of prior work yet simultaneously features an intrusion of unusual combinations. Papers of this type were twice as likely to be highly cited works. Notably, novel combinations of prior work are rare, yet teams are 37.7% more likely than solo authors to insert novel combinations into familiar knowledge domains.

Data and Methods

Data

We examined 17.9 million scientific publications across 15,613 journals, constituting all research articles indexed in the Thomson Reuters Web of Science (WOS) database that was published between 1950 and 2000. According to each journal's subject area, the Institute for Scientific Research (ISI, a.k.a. Web of Science) currently defines three fields and constituent subfields: science and engineering (171 subfields), social sciences (54 subfields), and arts and humanities (27 subfields) with coverage for research publications in science and engineering since 1945, social sciences since 1956, and arts and humanities since 1975. For each paper, the WOS records the citations, number of authors, and citation links to other papers in the database.

Methods

We measured the relative conventionality and novelty of the prior work that a paper combines by examining the papers referenced in a paper's bibliography (Small, 1973; Stringer, Sales-Pardo, & Amaral, 2010). This section first provides an overview of our methodology, followed by an illustrative example and further details.

Overview

Our basic measurement question is to assess how common or novel any pairwise combination of prior work is. To determine this, we want to know both the (i) observed frequency of any given pairing of references in the WOS and (ii) the frequency of that pairing that would have occurred by chance. Comparing the observed frequency to the frequency expected by chance creates a normalized z-score measure for whether any given pairing appears novel or conventional.

To measure the *observed frequency* of any given pairing in the WOS, we took the following five steps:

(1) Took the references listed in a given paper's bibliography.
(2) Considered all pairwise combinations of the papers referenced in the bibliography of the paper.
(3) For each pairwise combination, recorded the two journals that were paired.
(4) Repeated steps (1–3) for every paper in the WOS.
(5) Counted the aggregate, population-wide frequency of each journal pairing for all referenced pairs from a given publication year.

Figure 12.1 presents a stylized example for steps (1–3), showing for a given paper how pairs of references are counted from that paper's reference list. The algorithm repeats this counting process for every article in the WOS and aggregates the counts for each given publication year.

Our method counts specific journal pairings, using different journals as a proxy for different areas of knowledge. Journal-level analysis is well positioned to distinguish domains of knowledge while having precedence in the literature for being relatively transparent, interpretable, and computationally feasible (Bollen et al., 2006; Itzkovitz et al., 2003; Small, 1973; Stringer et al., 2010).[1]

Having determined the observed frequency of each journal pairing, we considered the frequency distribution for each journal pairing that would have occurred by chance. The null model randomly reassigns the citation links between papers. As further detailed below, the method uses a variation of the Markov Chain Monte Carlo (MCMC) algorithm to randomly switch co-citations between all 17.9 million papers into a synthetic network with 302 million citations (edges), the same number of papers and citations as the observed network. Note that this method preserved the detailed paper-level structure of the global citation network. The number of citations to and from each paper was preserved backward and forward in time.

Using this approach, we created 10 synthetic instances of the entire WOS, each with its own set of randomized citation links. For each instance of the WOS, we then repeated steps (1–5) above, calculating the frequency of each co-referenced journal pair. Looking at all 10 randomized cases of the WOS, we generated a distri-

---

[1] Other operationalizations might consider lower resolution pairings using the ISI's 252 subfield categories, text-based combinations, or conceptualizations for measuring novelty beyond combinatorial pairs (Rosenkopf & McGrath, 2011).

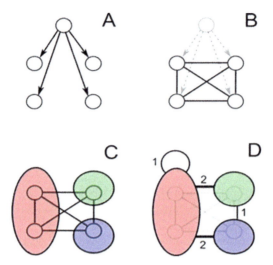

Fig. 12.1 Paper pairs and journal pairs. This figure presents a stylized example of how paper pairs and journal pairs are drawn from the network structure of citations. In *panel A*, the *circular nodes* represent papers; the directed links exist when the top paper cites the bottom four papers. In *panel B*, the *circular nodes* represent papers, and the undirected co-citation links between papers are shown in *black*. A co-citation exists between each pair of papers that occurs in the reference list of the focal paper. Here, there are 4 references and therefore 6 (i.e., 4 choose 2) co-citation links. In *panel C*, paper nodes are grouped by journal; the shaded ovals represent the three journals in which each of the cited papers is published. Finally, in *panel D*, the co-citation links between papers are mapped to the journal level, and the black links represent journal co-citations. Note that the total number of paper-to-paper co-citation links (6) is preserved at the journal co-citation level (From Uzzi et al. (2013b, p. 10). Copyright 2013 by *Science*. Adapted with permission from the authors and *Science*)

bution of frequencies for each journal pair. We could then evaluate the z-score for each observed journal pair relative to what was expected by chance:

$$z = (obs - \exp) / \sigma$$

Where *obs* is the observed frequency of the journal pair in the actual WOS while *exp* is the mean and σ is the standard deviation of the number of journal pairs obtained from the 10 randomized simulations of the paper-to-paper citation network.

Finally, returning to categorizing a paper's prior work regarding novelty and conventionality, we could then assign a z-score to each of the journal pairs in that paper's reference list. Each paper thus had a distribution of journal pairings, where any given pairing could be more or less common compared to chance. To summarize the information in this distribution, we took two primary summary statistics:

(i) The median z-score for that paper.
(ii) The 10th percentile z-score for that paper.

The first measure is a summary statistic for the central tendency of the combinations of journals that a paper cites. The larger the median z-score for a paper, the more common the main mass of journal combinations in that paper compared to chance. The second measure is a summary statistic for the left tail of combinations of journals that a paper cites—journal pairings that are relatively unusual, compared to chance, among the set of journal pairings in that paper's reference list.

Illustrative Example of Methodology and Further Detail

To illustrate these procedures, consider the following example, based on a single paper in the field of geography.

1. Step 1. Take the references in a bibliography in a given paper. Consider the paper, "The Tropical Cyclone Hazard Over the South China Sea 1970–1989: Annual Spatial and Temporal Characteristics," which was published in *Applied Geography* in 1995. This paper has 22 references, of which 10 are known references (Fig. 12.2).
2. Step 2. Consider all pairwise combinations of the papers referenced in the bibliography of that paper. As can be seen in Fig. 12.2, pairwise paper combinations include, for example, (i) Deser et al. 1992 with Black 1990, (ii) Deser et al. 1992 with Thompson 1987, and (iii) Thompson 1987 with Black 1990. With 10 known references, we have 45 (i.e., 11 choose 2) pairwise paper combinations.
3. Step 3. Map the observed paper pairs into observed journal pairs. The 45 paper pairs are mapped into 45 journal pairs, where some journal pairs in this list appear multiple times. For example, *Nature* and *Monthly Weather Review* are paired twice.
4. Step 4. Repeat steps (1–3) for every paper in the WOS. The above steps, shown in a single article, are now repeated for every paper in the WOS. References to materials outside the WOS (for example, books) are not included.
5. Step 5. Count the frequency of each observed journal pairing for a given publication year, using the referenced works of every paper published that year in the WOS. Information from the sample paper above would be counted as part of the year 1995. Hence, we allow journal pair frequencies varying over time.

Having completed steps (1–5) for the observed papers in the WOS, we repeated them for each synthetic instance of the WOS, as created by the null model. Comparing the observed frequency of journal pairs under the real WOS with the frequency distribution that appears across instances of the null model, we computed a z-score for each journal pair. Continuing our illustrative example, the observed frequency, expected frequency, and z-score for several journal pairings that appear in the paper, "The Tropical Cyclone Hazard Over the South China Sea 1970–1989: Annual Spatial and Temporal Characteristics," are presented in Table 12.1. As Table 12.1 demonstrates (for a subsample of journal pairs), each published paper has a distribution of journal pairs, some of which are highly conventional (such as

> Title: Long Term Variations in Western Tropical Pacific Cyclogenesis Associated With the Southern Oscillation
> Author(s): Harding, J.M.
> Source: *Nature, 262,* pp. 41–43, published 1976.
>
> Title: Network Autocorrelation in Transport Network and Flow Systems
> Author(s): Black, W. R.
> Source: *Geographical Analysis, 24,* pp. 207–222, published 1992.
>
> Title: Tropical Cyclone Activity in the Northwest Pacific in Relation to El Niño/Southern Oscillation Phenomenon
> Author(s): Chan, J. C. L.
> *Monthly Weather Review, 113,* pp. 599–606, published 1985.
>
> Title: Large Scale Atmospheric Circulation Features of Warm and Cold Episodes in the Tropical Pacific
> Author(s): Deser, C., & Wallace, J. M.
> Source: *Journal of Clamate, 3,* pp. 1254–1281, published 1990.
>
> Title: Rainfall at Tuvalu, Tokelau, and the Northern Cook Islands and Its Relationship to the Southern Oscillation
> Author(s): Thompson, C. S.
> Source: *New Zealand Journal of Geology and Geophysics, 30,* pp. 195–198, published 1987
>
> Title: Predictability of Interannual Variation of Australian Seasonal Tropical Cyclone Activity
> Author(s): Nicholas, N. N.
> Source: *Monthly Weather Review, 113,* pp. 1144–1149, published 1985.
>
> Title: El Niño and Tropical Cyclone Frequency in the Australian Region and Northwest Pacific
> Author(s): Dong, K.
> Source: *Australian Meteorological Magazine, 36,* pp. 219–225, published 1988.
>
> Title: El Niño/Southern Oscillation Modification to the Structure of the Monsoon and Tropical Cyclone Activity in the Australasian Region
> Author(s): Evans, J. L., & Allan, R. J.
> Source: *International Journal of Climatology, 12,* pp. 611–623, published 1992.
>
> Title: Temporal and Spatial Characteristics of Coastal Rainfall Anomalies in Papua New Guinea and Their Relationship to the Southern Oscillation
> Author(s): McGregor, G. R.
> Source: *International Journal of Climatology, 12,* pp. 449–468, published 1992.
>
> Title: El Niño: The Ocean–Atmospheric Connection
> Author(s): Rasmusson, E. M.
> Source: *Oceanus, 27,* pp. 5–12, published 1984.

Fig. 12.2 Reference list for example paper. The paper, "The Tropical Cyclone Hazard Over the South China Sea 1970–1989: Annual Spatial and Temporal Characteristics," cites 10 different known references. From Uzzi et al. (2013b, p. 11). Copyright 2013 by *Science*. Adapted with permission from the authors and *Science*

Monthly Weather Review–Monthly Weather Review) while others are unusual compared to chance (such as *Nature–Monthly Weather Review*). Fig. 12.4a presents the distribution of z-scores for this illustrative paper and indicates the median z-score and the 10th percentile z-score in that paper's distribution.

Table 12.1 Examples of journal pair frequencies for illustrative paper

Journal pairs	Observed	Expected	Z-score	
Mon. Weather Rev.– Mon. Weather Rev.	28,685	68.999	3252.658	
Int. Journ. of Climatology– Int. Journ. of Climatology	402	0.1	1339.667	More Conventional Combinations
Nature–Journ. of Climate	2720	1392.016	47.344	
Geogr. Anal.–Journ. of Clim.	3	2.199	0.743	
A z-score of zero means the actual journal pair frequency is the same as expected by chance pairings				
N.Z. Journ. Geol. & Geophys.– Journ. of Climate	4	4.0	0	More Novel Combinations
Nature–Aust. Meteorol. Mag.	89	95.494	−0.915	
Geogr. Anal.–Mon. Weather Rev.	2	6.192	−1.436	
Nature–Geogr. Anal.	30	138.889	−8.78	
Nature–Mon. Weather Rev.	2226	3779.287	−24.554	

Note. Mon. Weather Rev. Monthly Weather Review, *Int. Journ. of Climatology* International Journal of Climatology, *Geogr. Anal.* Geographical Analysis, *N.Z. Journ. Geol. & Geophys.* New Zealand Journal of Geology and Geophysics, *Aust. Meteorol. Mag.* Austrian Meteorology Magazine. From Uzzi et al. (2013b, p. 21). Copyright 2013 by *Science*. Adapted with permission from the authors and *Science*

Table 12.1 further shows the importance of normalizing the observed frequencies. For example, compare the pairings (1) *Nature* and *Journal of Climate* and (2) *Nature* and *Monthly Weather Review*. Both have similarly observed co-citation frequencies in the WOS: 2720 and 2226, respectively. However, compared to chance, the first pairing appears to have high conventionality while the second pairing seems to have high novelty.

Null Model Detail

The null model creates random synthetic instances of the WOS while incorporating realistic aspects of the data and its network structure. In particular, the null model incorporates two basic empirical facts about citation patterns:

- Citation distributions are skewed. Some papers and journals are cited far more often than other papers and journals and consequently are referenced more frequently in bibliographies.
- Citation counts are dynamic processes that vary by the journal (Stringer, Sales-Pardo, & Amaral, 2008), so that the rate at which papers accumulate citations is journal dependent.

Keeping these facts in mind, the null model preserves for each paper in the WOS the same number of references to past work, the same number of citations from

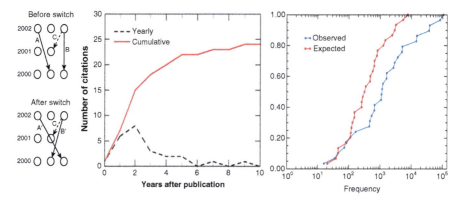

Fig. 12.3 Link switching in the null model and example distributions of observed and expected frequency of journal pairs. Citation links between papers are switched randomly but constrained to have the same origin year and target year. Thus in the *left panel*, switching links A and B are allowed, while switching links A and C are not allowed. The switching algorithm thus preserves for each paper its (i) number of references, (ii) citation count, (iii) citation accumulation dynamics, and (iv) the age distribution of referenced work. Performing QE switches converges to a random graph from the configuration model (Itzkovitz et al., 2003) where the number of and dynamics of citations are preserved, but the origin of the citations is randomized. Since each node is equally likely to be the originating node of any citation, given the constraints, we know a priori that no disciplines exist in this randomized citation network. The *middle panel* above demonstrates the citation history of a paper. The citation history of every paper is exactly preserved under our null model, ensuring that we control for both the variation in magnitude and dynamics of citation accumulation to papers. The *right panel* above further shows, for the example paper highlighted in Table 12.1, the frequency distribution for the observed journal pairings (*blue line*) and the frequency distribution for these journal pairings when averaged across instances of the null model (*red line*). From Uzzi et al. (2013b, p. 12). Copyright 2013 by *Science*. Reprinted with permission from the authors and *Science*

subsequent papers, and the same distribution of these citations over time (Fig. 12.3, left panel and middle panel). The right panel of Fig. 12.3 showed the distributions of observed frequency and expected frequency of journal papers for the example paper above.

Specifically, we used a variation of the Markov Chain Monte Carlo (MCMC) algorithm to construct randomized citation networks for all papers in the WOS database. The switching of endpoints of citation links was constrained to randomly chosen endpoints within the same class (Fig. 12.3), where the link classes are defined as having the same origin year and target year (Itzkovitz et al., 2003). One can think of each link class as a sub-graph of the global citation network, which can then be randomized in the usual way by performing Q*E switches, where E is the number of links in the subgraph. There is no proof for when the Markov Chain converges; however, it is suggested (Itzkovitz et al., 2003) to set Q at a safe value of 100. Since the citation network has 302 million edges, the scale of the computation is large, and we used a slightly less conservative value of $Q=2\log(E)$ to reduce computational burden. As can be noted in the original paper on the MCMC switching algorithm (Itzkovitz et al., 2003), this value of Q is well within the region where correlations with the original network cannot be detected.

Results

In this study, we examined 17.9 million research articles in the Web of Science (WOS) to see how prior work is combined. We present facts that inform (i) the extent to which scientific papers reference novel versus conventional combinations of prior work, (ii) the relative impact of papers based on the combinations they draw upon, and (iii) how (i) and (ii) are associated with collaboration.

We considered pairwise combinations of references in the bibliography of each paper (Small, 1973; Stringer et al., 2010). We counted the frequency of each co-citation pair across all papers published that year in the WOS and compared these observed frequencies to those expected by chance, using randomized citation networks. In the randomized citation networks, all citation links between all papers in the WOS were switched using a Monte Carlo algorithm. The switching algorithm preserves the total citation counts to and from each paper, and the distribution of these citations counts forward and backward in time to ensure that a paper (or journal) with n citations in the observed network will have n citations in the randomized network. For both the observed and the randomized paper-to-paper citation networks, we aggregated counts of paper pairs into their respective journal pairs to focus on domain-level combinations (Itzkovitz et al., 2003; Stringer et al., 2008, 2010). In the data, there were over 122 million potential journal pairs created by the 15,613 journals indexed in the WOS.

Comparing the observed frequency with the frequency distribution created with the randomized citation networks, we generated a z-score for each journal pair. This normalized measure describes whether any given pair appeared novel or conventional. Z-scores above zero indicate pairs that appeared more often in the observed data than expected by chance, indicating relatively common or "conventional" pairings. Z-scores below zero indicate pairs that appear less often in the observed WOS than expected by chance, indicating relatively atypical or "novel" pairings. For example, in the year 1995, the pairing *Nature* and *Journal of Climate* had a high z-score (47.344) indicating a conventional pairing, while *Nature* paired with *Monthly Weather Review* had a negative z-score (−24.554) indicating a pairing more unusual than chance.

The above method assigns each paper a distribution of journal pair z-scores based on the paper's reference list (Fig. 12.4a). To characterize a paper's tendency to draw together conventional and novel combinations of prior work, we took two summary statistics. First, to characterize the central tendency of a paper's combinations, we considered the paper's median z-score. The median allowed us to characterize conventionality in the paper's main mass of combinations. Second, we considered the paper's 10th percentile z-score. The left tail allows us to characterize the paper's more unusual journal combinations where novelty may reside.

We found that papers typically relied on very high degrees of conventionality. Figure 12.4b presents the distribution of papers' median z-scores for the WOS in the indicated decades. Considering that a z-score below zero represents a journal pair that occurs less often than expected by chance, the analysis of median z-scores sug-

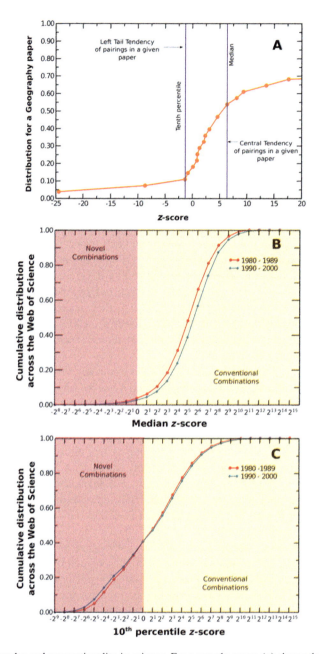

Fig. 12.4 Novelty and conventionality in science. For a sample paper, (**a**) shows the distribution of z-scores for that paper's journal pairings. The z-score shows how common a journal pairing is compared to chance. For each paper we take two summary measures: its median z-score, capturing the paper's central tendency in combining prior work, and the 10th percentile z-score, capturing the paper's journal pairings that are relatively unusual. For the population of papers, we then consider these values across all papers in the WOS published in the 1980s or 1990s. (**b**) considers the

gests very high degrees of conventionality. Half the papers had median z-scores exceeding 69.0 in the 1980s and 99.5 in the 1990s. Moreover, papers with a median z-score below zero were rare. In the 1980s only 3.54% of papers had this feature, while in the 1990s the percentage fell to 2.67%, indicating a persistent and prominent tendency for high conventionality.

Focusing on each paper's left tail combinations, we found that even among the paper's relatively unusual journal combinations, the majority of papers did not feature atypical journal pairs. Figure 12.4c shows that 40.8% of the papers in the 1980s and 40.7% in the 1990s had a 10th percentile z-score below zero. Overall, by these measures, science typically relies on highly conventional combinations and rarely incorporates journal pairs that are uncommon compared to chance.

Our next finding indicates a powerful relationship between combinations of prior work and ensuing impact. Figure 12.5 presents the probability of a "hit" paper conditional on the combination of its referenced journal pairs. Hit papers are operationalized as those in the upper 5th percentile of citations received across the whole dataset, as measured by total citations through 8 years after publication. The vertical axis shows the probability of a hit paper conditional on a 2×2 categorization indicating the paper's (i) "median conventionality" (an indicator of whether the paper's median z-score is in the upper or lower half of all median z-scores) and (ii) "tail novelty" (an indicator of whether the paper's 10th percentile z-score is above or below zero).

Papers with "high median conventionality" and "high tail novelty" display a hit rate of 9.11 out of 100 papers, or nearly twice the background rate of 5 out of 100 papers. All other categories show significantly lower hit rates. Papers featuring high median conventionality but low tail novelty displayed hit rates of 5.82 out of 100 papers, while those featuring low median conventionality but high tail novelty display hit rates of 5.33 out of 100 papers. Finally, papers low on both dimensions have hit rates of just 2.05 out of 100.

Further analyses suggest universality of these relationships for scientific work across time and fields. In Fig. 12.6, we show that the results hold (a) over five decades of data recorded in the WOS from 1950 to 2000 and (b) using the upper 1st or 10th percentiles of citation impact. In Fig. 12.7, we define the cutoff for high and low tail novelty at different percentiles of a paper's z-score: The 1st, 5th, 20th, 30th, and 40th. Figure 12.7 shows that using the 1st, 5th, 10th, or 20th percentile captures significant positive associations between impact and tail novelty in the 1990s. Beyond the 30th percentile, the significant association between impact and tail nov-

Fig. 12.4 (continued) median z-scores and shows that the vast majority of papers display a high propensity for conventionality; in the 1980s and 1990s fewer than 4% of papers have median z-scores below 0 and more than 50% of papers have median z-scores above 64. (**c**) considers the 10th percentile z-scores, which further suggest a propensity for conventionality; only 41% of papers in the 1980s and 1990s have a 10th percentile z-score below 0. Overall, by these measures, science rarely draws on atypical pairings of prior work. From Uzzi et al. (2013a, p. 469). Copyright 2013 by *Science*. Adapted with permission from the authors and *Science*

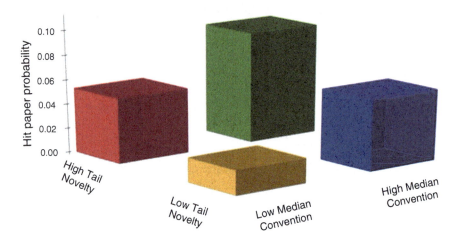

Fig. 12.5 The probability of a "hit" paper conditional on novelty and conventionality. Figure 12.5 presents the probability of a paper being in the top 5 % of the citation distribution, conditional on two dimensions: whether a paper exhibits (1) high or low median conventionality and (2) high or low tail novelty, as defined in the text. Papers that combine high median conventionality and high tail novelty are hits in 9.11 out of 100 papers, a rate nearly double the background rate of 5 %. Papers that are high on one dimension only—high median conventionality or high tail novelty but not both—have hit rates about half as large. Papers with low median conventionality and low tail novelty have hit rates of only 2.05 out of 100 papers. The sample includes all papers published in the WOS from 1990 to 2000. Figure 12.6 shows similar findings when considering (i) all other decades from 1950 to 2000; (ii) "hit" papers defined as the top 1 % or 10 % by citations, hinting at a universality of these relationships for scientific work. The difference in the hit probabilities for each category is statistically significant ($p<0.00001$). The percentage of WOS papers in each category are; Green Bar (6.7 %), Gold Bar (23 %), Red Bar (26 %), and Blue Bar (44 %). From Uzzi et al. (2013a, p. 470). Copyright 2013 by *Science*. Reprinted with permission from the authors and *Science*

elty disappears. These patterns suggest that the concept of tail novelty is not sensitive to a single value and that beyond a precise focus on the 10th percentile the construct is related to impact so long as one continues to consider the left tail of the distribution.

Results by Subfields

The following analysis shows that the results presented in the main text for the whole of the WOS continued to appear quite broadly when examining patterns within individual subfields. By subfield, we presented (1) the tendency for tail novelty and median conventionality, and (2) the relationship between novelty, conventionality, and hit papers. We examined all 243 subfields that appeared in the WOS over the 1990s.

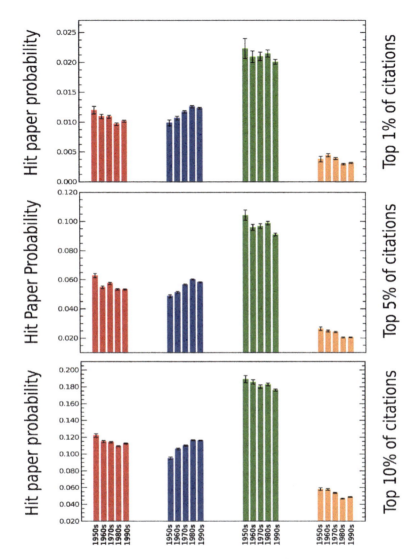

Fig. 12.6 Citation impact results generalize by decade and by definition of "hit" paper. This figure shows broadly consistent patterns both over time and by the definition of "hit" paper, suggesting a remarkably robust and strong empirical regularity between scientific impact and how prior work is combined. Specifically, the figure shows that high tail novelty combined with high median conventionality (*Green bars*) outperforms other categories in all decades from 1950 to 2000, regardless of whether a "hit" paper is defined as a top 1 %, 5 %, or 10 % by citations received, and broadly shows hit rates that are approximately twice the background rate. By contrast, papers that feature neither high tail novelty nor high median conventionality (*Orange bars*) see hit rates at only half or less the background rate. From Uzzi et al. (2013b, p. 13). Copyright 2013 by *Science*. Reprinted with permission from the authors and *Science*

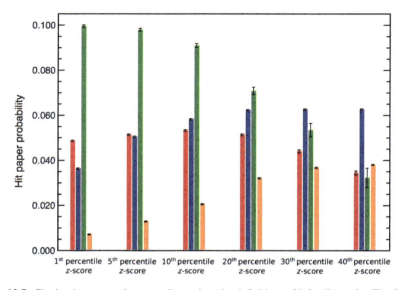

Fig. 12.7 Citation impact results generalize to broader definitions of left tail novelty. The figure presents the relationship between tail novelty and impact using alternative definitions of tail novelty. In each case, tail novelty is defined as an indicator for whether the eth percentile of a paper's z-score distribution is less than zero. The x-axis indicates the value of e. It is seen that for $e \leq 20$, high tail novelty combined with a high median conventionality (*Green bars*) outperforms other categories. The results in the main text, which use the 10th percentile, thus extend broadly to other definitions of tail novelty so long as the measure emphasizes the paper's left tail of combinations. From Uzzi et al. (2013b, p. 14). Copyright 2013 by *Science*. Reprinted with permission from the authors and *Science*

To examine any field-specific relationships between novelty, conventionality, and hit papers, we calculated the subfield-specific probabilities of a "hit" by the four categories used in Fig. 12.2 and defined in the text. We then ranked these four categories in each subfield, where 1 indicates the highest probability of a hit, 2 indicates the second highest probability of a hit and so on. Consistent with the main results, Table 12.2 shows that in 64.4% of fields, a paper's likelihood of being a hit paper was greatest when combining prior work characterized by high tail novelty and high median conventionality. This category (Row 3 in Table 12.2) is ranked first or second in 86.3% of subfields. Notably, to the extent that this category is not dominant within a subfield, the category featuring a more general shift toward novelty (Row 1 in Table 12.2) appears prominently, suggesting that tail novelty is an especially generic feature of the highest-impact papers. Conversely, the category featuring low tail novelty and low median conventionality (Row 4 in Table 12.2) ranks lowest in 70.4% of subfields. Thus, novelty and conventionality are not opposing factors in the production of science; rather, papers with an injection of novelty into an otherwise exceptionally familiar mass of prior work are unusually likely to have high impact. Next, we focus on the effect of teams on novelty.

Role of Teams in Production of Knowledge

Collaboration is often claimed to produce more novel combinations of ideas (Falk-Krzesinski et al., 2010; Fiore, 2008; Stokols et al., 2008; Uzzi & Spiro, 2005; Wuchty et al., 2007), but the extent to which teams incorporate novel combinations across the universe of fields is unknown. Team-authored papers were more likely to show atypical combinations than single or pair-authored papers. Figure 12.8a shows that the distribution of 10th percentile z-scores shifted significantly leftward as the number of authors increased (*Kolmogorov-Smirnov* [KS] tests indicate solo vs. pair $p = 0.016$, pair vs. team $p = 0.001$, team vs. solo $p < 0.001$). Papers written by one, two, three, or more authors showed high tail novelty in 36.1%, 39.8%, and 49.7% of cases, respectively, indicating that papers with three or more authors showed an increased frequency of high tail novelty over the solo-author rate by 37.7%.

Teams were neither more nor less likely than single authors or pairs of authors to display high median conventionality. Figure 12.8b indicates no significant statistical difference in the median z-score distributions (KS tests indicate solo vs. pair $p = 0.768$, pair vs. team $p = 0.417$, team vs. solo $p = 0.164$). Teams thus achieve high tail novelty more often than solo authors, yet teams were not simply "more novel" but rather displayed a propensity to incorporate high tail novelty without giving up a central tendency for high conventionality.

Regression Methods

In our final analysis, we examined the interplay between citation, combination, and collaboration using regression methods (Fig. 12.9). Papers were binned into eleven equally sized categories of median conventionality. We used logistic regression to

Table 12.2 Novelty, conventionality, and citation impact by field

	Rank			
	1st	2nd	3rd	4th
High tail novelty and low median conventionality	20.3%	44.5%	28.7%	6.5%
Low tail novelty and high median conventionality	9.7%	26.7%	50.6%	13.0%
High tail novelty and high median conventionality	64.4%	21.9%	3.6%	10.1%
Low tail novelty and low median conventionality	5.7%	6.9%	17.0%	70.4%

Note. For each of 243 subfields indexed by the WOS in the 1990s, we ranked the categories of papers according to their probability of producing hit papers. Hit papers are defined as those in the upper 5% of citations received in that subfield. We focused on all papers published across all subfields in the 1990s. This analysis revealed that high tail novelty and high median conventionality were the highest impact papers in 64.4% of subfields and either first or second in 86.3% of fields. By contrast, low tail novelty and low median conventionality rank lowest or second lowest in 87.4% of fields. From Uzzi et al. (2013a, p. 22). Copyright 2013 by *Science*. Reprinted with permission by the authors and *Science* predict the probability of hit papers in the 1990s and ran these regressions in a flexible manner that avoided imposing functional forms on the data. In particular, we first divided papers into subsamples based on their median conventionality (11 categories, from least to greatest median conventionality, as defined in the main text) and the number of authors (3 categories, for solo authors, two-author pairs, and three or more authors). This created 33 distinct subsamples. We then ran a separate regression for each subsample.

For a given subsample, a regression takes the form

$$\Pr(y_i) = f(\beta Tail\_Novelty_i + \sum_f \gamma_f Field_{fi})$$

where $y_{ij} \in \{0,1\}$ is an indicator variable for a "hit" paper, and $Tail\_Novelty_i \in \{0,1\}$ is an indicator variable for whether a paper's 10th percentile z-score is below zero. The regression includes a full set of fixed effects for each of 243 subfields indexed by the WOS in the 1990s, where the indicator variables $Field_{fi} \in \{0,1\}$ are equal to 1 if the paper i is in field f. The inclusion of these fixed effects accounts for any mean differences in hit probabilities and tail novelty across subfields. We further restricted the sample to papers with at least ten known references, which ensured that each paper in the sample had many pairwise combinations of prior work.

Figure 12.9 establishes a large positive relationship between tail novelty and hit papers, which appears independently in each of the 33 subsamples. The regressions further establish that the probability of hit papers increases with median conventionality, peaking at approximately the 85th percentile of median conventionality. These strong empirical regularities extend to alternative analyses. Figure 12.10 reconsiders these regressions defining hit papers to be in the top 1% of citations received. The results for this higher threshold for a "hit" paper look extremely similar.

Novelty and Conventionality in Geography

In Fig. 12.11 we show the novel and conventional combinations in papers written in the field of geography. We do not observe any high degrees of conventionality when compared with fields like physics and economics. Figure 12.11a presents the distribution of papers' median z-scores for papers published in geography in the indicated decades. Half the papers have median z-scores exceeding 16 in the 1980s in the 1990s. Papers with a median z-score below zero are rare; only 4% of papers displayed this feature in the 1980s and 1990s. Focusing on each paper's left tail combinations, we found that 25% of papers in the 1980s and 1990s have a 10th percentile z-score below 0 (Fig. 12.11b). Overall, by these measures, we observed that geography papers rarely draw atypical knowledge from prior works.

We investigated the role of team authors in geography in production of knowledge. Our findings support the previous observations in Fig. 12.8: Each team size

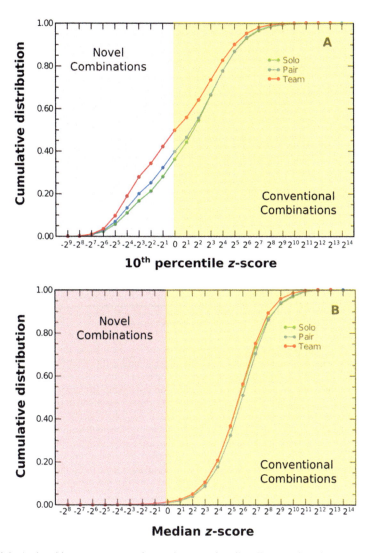

Fig. 12.8 Authorship structure, novelty, and conventionality. Team-authored papers are more likely to incorporate tail novelty but without sacrificing a central tendency for high conventionality. Papers introduce tail novelty (a 10th percentile z-score less than 0) in 36.2 %, 39.9 %, and 49.7 % of cases for solo authors, dual authors, and three or more authors, respectively (**a**). Kolmogorov-Smirnov tests confirm the distributions of tail novelty are distinct (solo vs. pair $p=0.016$, pair vs. team $p=0.001$, team vs. solo $p<0.001$). By contrast, each team size shows similar distributions for median conventionality (**b** KS tests indicate no statistically significant differences). These findings suggest that a distinguishing feature of teamwork, and teams' exceptional impact, reflects a tendency to incorporate novelty. From Uzzi et al. (2013a, p. 470). Copyright 2013 by *Science*. Reprinted with permission from the authors and *Science*

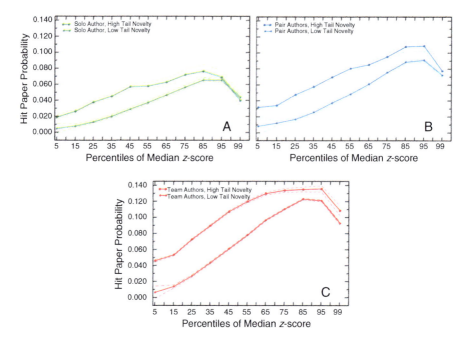

Fig. 12.9 Novel and conventional combinations in the production of science. The interplay between tail novelty, median conventionality, and hit paper probabilities show remarkable empirical regularities (**a–c**). First, high tail novelty papers have higher impact than low tail novelty papers at (i) any level of conventionality and (ii) regardless of authorship structure. Second, increasing median conventionality is associated with higher impact up to the 85–95th percentile of median conventionality after which the relationship reverses. Third, larger teams obtain higher impact given the right mix of tail novelty and median conventionality. Nonetheless, at low levels of median convention and tail novelty, even teams have low impact, further emphasizing the fundamental relationship between novelty, conventionality, and impact in science. From Uzzi et al. (2013a, p. 471). Copyright 2013 by *Science*. Reprinted with permission from the authors and *Science*

shows similar distributions for median conventionality (Fig. 12.11c) and papers with team authors show greater novelty than solo-authored or pair-authored papers (Fig. 12.11d).

We plot the average hit citations by considering the top 5 % of highly cited papers written in the fields of geography, economics, and physics over time (Fig. 12.12). The average of hit citations for geography is significantly lower than that of economics and physics. For papers published between 1980 and 2000, half the papers in geography have median z-scores above 36. Thus papers in geography combine less conventionality when compared to physics or economics, where half the papers have median z-scores above 145. Moreover, for geography, conventionality doesn't increase with time when compared with physics and economics (Fig. 12.13). This indicates that for geography, mixing novel and conventional combinations does not result in high impact work.

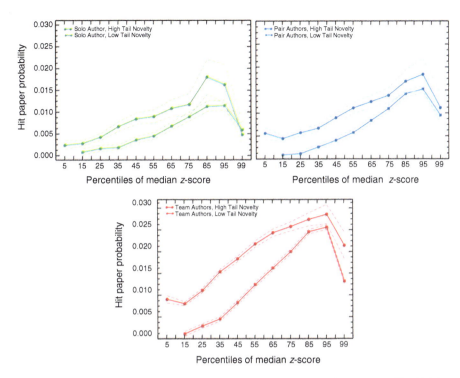

Fig. 12.10 Novelty, authorship and impact for top 1 % of papers. This figure repeats Fig. 12.9 but defines hit papers as those that receive citations within 8 years of publication that are in the upper 1 % of all papers published that year. From Uzzi et al. (2013b, p. 16). Copyright 2013 by *Science*. Adapted with permission from the authors and *Science*

Discussion and Conclusion

There were three primary findings. First, high tail novelty papers had higher impact than low tail novelty papers, an impact advantage that occurred at any level of conventionality and regardless of authorship structure. Second, peak impact occurs in the 85–95th percentile of median conventionality, an exceptionally high level. This peak and its position appeared irrespective of tail novelty/no tail novelty or authorship structure. These generic features suggest fundamental underlying rules relating combinations of prior work to the highest impact science.

Finally, Fig. 12.4 indicates that for virtually all possible mixes of tail novelty and median conventionality, larger teams were associated with higher impact. Thus, while teams incorporated the highest impact mixes more frequently (Fig. 12.3), teams also tended to obtain higher impact for any particular mix (Fig. 12.4). Nonetheless, despite this advantage in citations across virtually all fields of science (Wuchty et al., 2007), even teams had low impact at low levels of median conventionality and tail novelty.

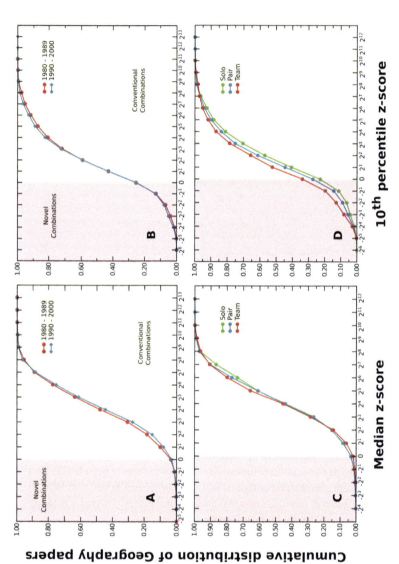

Fig. 12.11 Novel and conventional combinations in geography. The median z-scores shows that the vast majority of geography papers display a high propensity for conventionality; in the 1980s and 1990s fewer than 4 % of papers have median z-scores below 0 and more than 50 % of papers have median z-scores above 16 (**a**). The plot for 10th percentile z-scores, which further suggest a propensity for conventionality; ~ 25 % of papers in the 1980s and 1990s have a 10th percentile z-score below 0 (**b**). From these two figures, we observe that geography papers rarely draw atypical knowledge from prior works. For geography papers published in the 1990s, each team size shows similar distributions for median conventionality (**c**). Papers published in the 1990s introduce tail novelty (a 10th percentile z-score<0) in ~ 20 %, 25 %, and 35 % of cases for solo authors, dual authors, and three or more authors, respectively (**d**) (Design by authors)

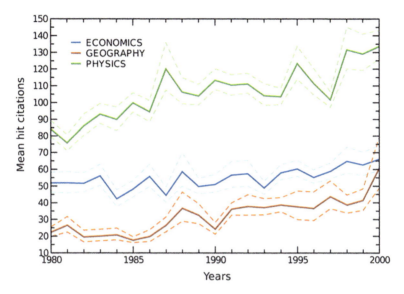

Fig. 12.12 Mean of hit citations with time for three fields. For each of the fields—geography, economics, and physics—we consider the "hit" papers. Hit papers are defined as those in the top 5% of citations. The plot shows the evolution of mean hit citations in time. For geography, the value of mean hit citations is much lower when compared to hit papers in physics and economics (Design by authors)

Our analysis of 17.9 million papers across all scientific fields suggests that the highest-impact science draws on primarily highly conventional combinations of prior work with an intrusion of combinations unlikely to have been joined before. These patterns suggest that novelty and conventionality are not factors in opposition; rather, papers that mix high tail novelty with high median conventionality have nearly twice the propensity to be unusually highly cited.

These findings have implications for theories about creativity and scientific progress. Combinations of existing material are centerpieces in theories of creativity, whether in the arts, the sciences, or commercial innovation (Becker, 1982; Collins, 1998; Guimera et al., 2005; Jones, 2009; Schilling & Phelps, 2007; Schumpeter, 1939; Usher, 1929/1998; Uzzi & Spiro, 2005; Weitzman, 1998). Across the sciences, the propensity for high impact work is sharply elevated when combinations of prior work are anchored in substantial conventionality while mixing in a left tail of combinations that are rarely seen together. In part, this pattern may reflect advantages to being within the mainstream of a research trajectory, where scientists are currently focused while being distinctive in one's creativity. For example, as mentioned in the beginning of the chapter, Newton remained in the mainstream of traditional geometry and at the same time remained creative while communicating the laws of gravitation in *Principia*. Combinations of prior work also relate to "burden of knowledge" theory, which emphasizes the growing knowledge demands upon scientists (Einstein, 1949; Fleming, 2001; Jones, 2009). New articles indexed by the WOS now exceed 1.4 million per year across 251 fields, encouraging specialization

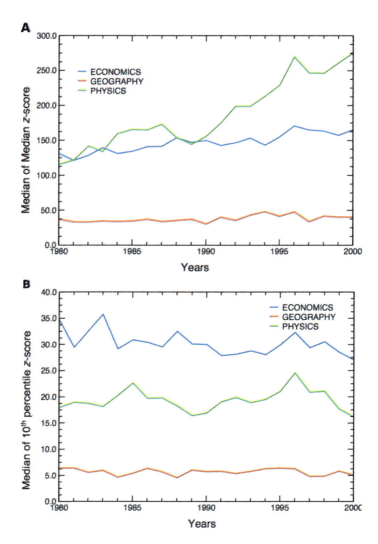

Fig. 12.13 Median of conventionality and novelty with time for three fields. (**a**) shows the median conventionality of papers published in geography exhibit no change with time. On the contrary, median conventionality of physics and economics papers increases with time, indicating a trend towards high conventionality for both these fields. Moreover, geography does not draw enough conventional knowledge as compared to physics or economics. In (**b**) we show the median novelty of geography, economics, and physics. While for physics and economics, novelty decreases with time, in the case of geography there is no such behavior—a trend we observed earlier in Fig. 12.11b (Design by authors)

and challenging scientists' capacity to comprehend new thinking across domains. The finding that teams preserve high conventionality yet introduce tail novelty suggests that teams help meet the challenge of the burden of knowledge by balancing domain-level depth with a capacity for atypical combinations.

Our methodology considered paper and journal pairings but can be applied at the level of disciplines, papers, or topics within papers, allowing the examination of combinations of prior work at different resolutions in future studies of creativity and scientific impact. Beyond science, links between novelty and conventionality in successful innovation also appear. E-books retain page-flipping graphics to remind the reader of physical books, and blue jeans were designed with a familiar watch pocket to look like conventional trousers. From this viewpoint, the balance between extending technology with atypical combinations of prior ideas while embedding them in conventional knowledge frames may be critical to human progress in many domains. Future research questions also arise from our findings. Science is dynamic, with research areas shifting and new fields arising. While we find that the regularities relating novelty, conventionality, and impact persist across time and fields, understanding how research trajectories shift and how new fields are born are questions that measures of novelty and convention may valuably inform. At root, our work suggests that creativity in science appears to be a nearly universal phenomenon of two extremes. At one extreme is conventionality, and at the other is novelty. Curiously, notable advances in science appear most closely linked not with efforts along one boundary or the other but with efforts that reach toward both frontiers.

Acknowledgements Sponsored by the Northwestern University Institute on Complex Systems (NICO), by the Army Research Laboratory under Cooperative Agreement Number W911NF-09-2-0053 and DARPA BAA-11-64, Social Media in Strategic Communication. The views and conclusions contained in this document are those of the authors and should not be interpreted as representing the official policies, either expressed or implied, of the Army Research Laboratory or the U.S. Government. 11B.

References

Azoulay, P., Zivin, J. G., & Manso, G. (2011). Incentives and creativity: evidence from the Academic Life Science. Howard Hughes Medical Investigator Program. *The RAND Journal of Economics, 42,* 527–554. doi:10.1111/j.1756-2171.2011.00140.x

Becker, H. S. (1982). *Art Worlds*. Berkeley: University of California Press.

Bollen, J., Rodriguez, M. A., & van de Sompel, H. (2006). Journal status. *Scientometrics, 69,* 669–687. doi:10.1007/s11192-006-0176-z

Collins, R. (1998). The sociology of philosophies: A global theory of intellectual change. Cambridge, MA: Harvard University Press.

Einstein, A. (1949). *The world as I see it*. Secaucus: Citadel Press.

Evans, J., & Foster, J. (2011). Metaknowledge. *Science, 331,* 721–725. doi:10.1126/science.1201765

Falk-Krzesinski, H. J., Börner, K., Contractor, N., Fiore, S. M., Hall, K. L., Keyton, J., & Uzzi, B. (2010). Advancing the science of team science. *CTS: Clinical and Translational Science Journal, 3*, 263–266. doi:10.1111/j.1752-8062.2010.00223.x

Fiore, S. M. (2008). Interdisciplinarity as teamwork: How the science of teams can inform team science. *Small Group Research, 39*, 251–277. doi:10.1177/1046496408317797

Fleming, L. (2001). Recombinant uncertainty in technological search management. *Management Science, 47*, 117–132. doi:10.1287/mnsc.47.1.117.10671

Guimera, R., Uzzi, B., Spiro, J., & Nunes Amaral, L. A. (2005). Team assembly mechanisms determine collaboration network structure and team performance. *Science, 308*, 697–702. doi:10.1126/science.1106340

Henderson, R. M., & Clark, K. B. (1990). Architectural innovation: The reconfiguration of existing technologies and the failure of established firms. *Administrative Science Quarterly, 35*, 9–30. doi:10.2307/2393549

Itzkovitz, S., Milo, R., Kashtan, N., Newman, M. E. J., & Alon, U. (2003). Subgraphs in random networks. *Physical Review E, 68*. doi:10.1103/PhysRevE.68.026127

Jones, B. (2009). The burden of knowledge and the death of the renaissance man: Is innovation getting harder? *The Review of Economic Studies, 76*, 283–317. doi:10.1111/j.1467-937X.2008.00531.x

Jones, B., Wuchty, S., & Uzzi, B. (2008). Multi-university research teams: Shifting impact, geography, and stratification in science. *Science, 322*, 1259–1262. doi:10.1126/science.1158357

National Academy of Sciences, National Academy of Engineering, & Institute of Medicine of the National Academies (2004). *Facilitating interdisciplinary research*. Washington, DC: National Academies Press.

Rosenkopf, L., & McGrath, P. (2011). Advancing the conceptualization and operationalization of novelty in organizational research. *Organization Science, 22*, 1297–1311. doi:10.1287/orsc.1100.0637

Schilling, M. A., & Phelps, C. C. (2007). Interfirm collaboration networks: The impact of small world connectivity on firm innovation. *Management Science, 53*, 1113–1126.

Schilling, M., & Green, E. (2011). Recombinant search and breakthrough idea generation: An analysis of high impact papers in the social sciences. *Research Policy, 40*, 1321–1331. doi:10.1016/j.respol.2011.06.009

Schumpeter, J. (1939). *Business Cycles*. New York, McGraw-Hill.

Small, H. (1973). Co-citation in scientific literature: A new measure of the relationship between two documents. *Journal of the American Society for information Science, 24*, 265–269. doi:10.1002/asi.4630240406

Stokols, D., Hall, K. L., Taylor, B. K., & Moser, R. P. (2008). The science of team science: Overview of the field and introduction to the supplement. *American Journal of Preventive Medicine, 35*, 77–89. doi:10.1016/j.amepre.2008.05.002

Stringer, M. J., Sales-Pardo, M. & Amaral, L. A. (2008). Effectiveness of journal ranking schemes as a tool for locating information. *PLOS ONE, 3*. doi:10.1371/journal.pone.00016

Stringer, M. J., Sales-Pardo, M., & Amaral, L. A. (2010). Statistical validation of a global model for the distribution of the ultimate number of citations accrued by papers published in a scientific journal. *Journal of the American Society for Information Science and Technology, 61*, 1377–1385. doi:10.1002/asi.21335

Usher, A. P. (1998). *A History of mechanical invention*. Cambridge, MA: Harvard University Press. (Original work published 1929)

Uzzi, B., Mukherjee, S., Stringer, M., & Jones, B. (2013a). Atypical combinations and scientific impact. *Science, 342*, 468–472. doi:10.1126/science.1240474

Uzzi, B., Mukherjee, S., Stringer, M., & Jones, B. (2013b). Supplementary materials for atypical combinations and scientific impact. *Science, 342*. Retrieved from www.sciencemag.org/content/342/6157/468/suppl/DC1

Uzzi, B., & Spiro, J. (2005). Collaboration and creativity: The small world problem. *American Journal of Sociology, 111*, 447–504. doi:10.1086/432782

Weitzman, M. L. (1998). Recombinant growth. *The Quarterly Journal of Economics. 113*, 331–360. doi:10.1162/003355398555595

Whiteside, D. T. (1970). The mathematical principles underlying Newton's principia mathematica. *Journal for the History of Astronomy, 1*, 116–138. doi:10.1177/002182867000100203

Wuchty, S., Jones, B., & Uzzi, B. (2007). The increasing dominance of teams in the production of knowledge. *Science, 316*, 1036–1039. doi:10.1126/science.1136099

Open Access This chapter is distributed under the terms of the Creative Commons Attribution 4.0 International License (http://creativecommons.org/licenses/by/4.0/), which permits use, duplication, adaptation, distribution and reproduction in any medium or format, as long as you give appropriate credit to the original author(s) and the source, provide a link to the Creative Commons license and indicate if changes were made.

The images or other third party material in this chapter are included in the work's Creative Commons license, unless indicated otherwise in the credit line; if such material is not included in the work's Creative Commons license and the respective action is not permitted by statutory regulation, users will need to obtain permission from the license holder to duplicate, adapt or reproduce the material.

Chapter 13
Connectivity in Contiguity: Conventions and Taboos of Imitation in Colocated Networks

Johannes Glückler and Ingmar Hammer

People and organizations learn from others. Cultures, traditions, opinions, behaviors, and technologies spread through imitation. Tarde (1903) was among the first to appreciate imitation as a key learning mechanism for inventions in social life to be diffused among society (Kinnunen, 1996; Rogers, 1995). Imitation, however, is not confined to the mere replication of existing knowledge. The process of imitation always implies potential deviation into invention (Barry & Thrift, 2007; Djellal & Gallouj, 2014) because the absorption of new knowledge requires learning and, hence, conscious recombination of knowledge, an activity that may lead to new ideas and new knowledge. Imitation is thus a crucial learning mechanism and a valuable source of innovation.

If imitation is such an economic advantage, then what are the conditions that favor learning by imitation? Essentially, two powerful perspectives—social networks and geography—have been proposed and used to unpack mechanisms of learning. Social networks focus on the quality of social relations and the effect of connectivity on knowledge outcomes. Geography focuses on the spatial dimension of social relations and facilitates theory development on the role that physical contiguity has in knowledge creation and innovation. Both these bodies of literature have contributed greatly to the understanding of the interorganizational production of knowledge, but few studies have integrated these viewpoints to capture the interdependencies of networks and space (Glückler, 2013a).

In this chapter we combine the network and geographical perspectives to theorize on the interactive effect of connectivity and spatial proximity on mechanisms of learning. We specifically examine social tensions generated by imitation among firms that are simultaneously in processes of colocation and organizational integration. This tension arises from the potential conduciveness of different spatial and

---

J. Glückler (✉) • I. Hammer
Department of Geography, Heidelberg University,
Berliner Straße 48, 69120 Heidelberg, Germany
e-mail: glueckler@uni-heidelberg.de; hammer@uni-heidelberg.de

organizational configurations to different forms of learning. Organizational integration, for example, typically supports the institutionalization of conventions of collaboration and two-way learning, whereas spatial proximity increases the visibility and observability among actors and thus leverages the undeniable incentive of competitive, one-way learning. If colocated competitors have agreed to collaborate, the key question arises as to how firms manage the tensions of cooperation and competition that accompany collective learning.

We begin by discussing imitation and invention in terms of the opportunities and relative advantages each can offer to learning and innovation. Specifically, we adopt a perspective of social conventions to distinguish two practices of imitation: the convention of collaborative learning through friendly imitation and the taboo of unfriendly imitation in a context of rivalry. We then analyze the conditions governing different forms of spatial organization for interfirm collaboration and imitation processes before we present the research strategy of the mixed-method network case study COMRA.DE, an organized interfirm network of 25 new media technology companies in eastern Germany. We follow up with an analysis of the empirical findings on the various mechanisms of interorganizational learning and the imitation practices between convention and taboo. The chapter closes with a discussion of the consequences for network governance.

Innovation by Imitation

Inventions are often the result of planned research and development. Although the directed search process may not always lead to the expected outcomes, as is the case with serendipitous and "false negative" inventions (Chesbrough, 2003, p. 3), research and development activities frequently entail high costs, risks, and long development phases. Innovation studies suggest that high levels of research and development intensity, that is, the allocation of major resources to inventive activity, are strongly correlated with a firm's economic performance (Ahuja, 2000; Mansfield, Rapoport, Romeo, Wagner, & Beardsley, 1977). Small and medium-sized enterprises (SMEs) often try to compensate for their diseconomies of scale by building alliances. In network organizations or, more precisely, organized interfirm networks (Glückler, Dehning, Janneck, & Armbrüster, 2012), firms are able to jointly develop resources that they would not be able to develop alone. So-called network goods are one way to achieve common goals that would be unattainable without partners. Essentially, network goods are collective outcomes from collaborative effort and have the additional advantage of being available to all members of a given social group regardless of their individual contributions to the creation of those goods (Glückler & Hammer, 2015). Because innovation refers to the process of introducing and disseminating new solutions on a market (Akrich, Callon, Latour, & Monaghan, 2002), it does not depend on invention alone. Instead, the process of imitation by observation offers an additional opportunity to learn from other organizations and to adopt and create new knowledge.

Jacobs (1969) draws on car-maker Henry Ford to illustrate that imitation or, as she calls it, "economic borrowing" (p. 64), can be a promising, often successful path to innovation. Instead of building cars himself, Ford focused on assembling premanufactured components. His innovation was not to create a new car but rather to offer to supply each individual component as a replacement part. In a continuing imitation process, he went on to build more and more parts himself until his company finally produced the majority of parts for his famous Model T. Japanese industry also applied imitation strategies to adopt external technologies, gradually developing its own competitive technological advantage (Bolton, 1993). The success of the Swiss watch-making industry is also the result of an intense period of imitation and reverse engineering of French and English watches in the seventeenth century (Maillat, Lecoq, Nemeti, & Pfister, 1995). Moreover, imitation is not only helpful for followers to catch up within an industry, it is an effective mechanism enabling cross-industry innovation (Enkel & Gassmann, 2010). When firms have sufficient absorptive capacity, they may detect and transfer to their own industry good practices and solutions from related and even unrelated industries. It is this unforeseeable potential for learning by imitation that makes the diversity of a city so crucial for long-term innovativeness (Jacobs, 1969).

The imitation process comprises three key mechanisms (Malmberg & Maskell, 2002): variation, observation, and imitation. It starts with variation stemming from parallel experimentation and the distributed search for innovations: "the tendency to variation is a chief cause of progress" (Marshall, 1890, p. 355). A firm's ability to compete derives from the heterogeneous nature of the solutions that firms create based on different competencies, experiences, strategies, and resources. To attain this competitiveness, firms need to create new solutions and new combinations of existing solutions:

> "Little progress would be made in a world of clones" (Lundvall & Maskell, 2000, p. 364). "The blind-variation-and-selective-retention model unequivocally implies that, ceteris paribus, the greater the heterogeneity and volume of trials the greater the chance of a productive innovation" (Campbell, 1960, p. 395).

If there is great variety in the available practices, organizations have the opportunity to identify suitable solutions by using a process of attentive searches and observations, and in the final stage they can transfer this knowledge to their own company by imitating them.

Unlike the generation of knowledge in partnerships, imitation refers to the unilateral transfer of existing solutions from one company to another. Imitation offers savings when established practices are transferred. Imitation cuts the costs of typical trial-and-error used in the research process (Jacobs, 1969). We distinguish between two fundamental situations for imitation (Glückler, 2013a). With friendly imitation, there is a cooperative transfer of solutions, with the owners of the solutions voluntarily agreeing to transfer them or even actively transferring them outright. With unfriendly imitation, the owners of the solutions try to prevent their imitation or disapprove of any secret imitation. In this section we investigate the circumstances under which imitation processes in a network are viewed as either legitimate and accepted (sometimes even planned) or as contested or sanctioned. Both forms of imitation, friendly and unfriendly, reflect the diametric opposition of competition and cooperation in a network.

Conventions of Friendly Imitation

In a cooperative context we assume that organizations and their members establish conventions to regulate the process of friendly imitation. Observing the good practice of others, and actively seeking and requesting aid when transferring existing solutions is accepted as legitimate or even as the actual reason for the cooperation if the current owner permits a solution to be imitated. According to (Weber, 1922/1978) conventions fall on a continuum extending from formal law to traditional customs and habits: "an order will be called convention so far as its validity is externally guaranteed by the probability that deviation from it within a given social group will result in a relatively general and practically significant reaction of disapproval" (p. 34).

A convention ranges between social custom and law: Unlike deviation from customs, deviation from convention is sanctioned; unlike law, a convention lacks an authority that enforces compliance to it. A convention thus constitutes an institutional order for exchange between parties to a transaction, creating a mutually sound basis for expectations. This order cannot penalize violations of the convention through the force of law. Instead, it uses social disrespect. Practices of friendly imitation always occur when one firm takes information or solutions from another firm with the latter's approval. These resources may even be actively provided, often without any direct compensation. That kind of transfer to a partner corresponds to the economic principle of a gift (Ferrary, 2003), a type of generalized exchange in which a transfer is not compensated directly but rather reciprocated over the long term, possibly also by other partners (Yamagishi & Cook, 1993). Examples of friendly imitation practices—processes that could lead to imitation—include recommendations, the exchange of experience or knowledge between employees within and between companies, and specialist discussions at trade fairs.

A key factor in maintaining long-term friendly imitation is the convention of reciprocity (Gouldner, 1960). Unlike goods traded on the market, gifts provided in networks can seldom be assigned a cash value, and that value often cannot be clearly allocated after the exchange. As a rule, reciprocal treatment (Stegbauer, 2011) is of fundamental importance in the convention of friendly imitation. Imitating without authorization or without providing anything yourself violates the convention. Conventions of friendly imitation are the foundations for learning and the rapid adoption, recombination, and dissemination of ideas and solutions within networks. Ultimately, each organization benefits from the solutions from all the other partners in a network, an outcome that offers cost advantages over the long-term innovation process. Imitation without immediate interaction may even forge the creation of collective identity, as Staber (2010) has demonstrated for colocated firms in southern Germany.

Imitation practices can always develop if firms and their employees cooperate with each other or if meetings offer opportunities for mutual observation. For example, projects are key drivers in imitation processes when companies jointly develop new knowledge and learn from each other, pooling their expertise to arrive at joint solutions. With concrete project results constantly accumulating in the company (Ibert, 2004), it should be easy for the project partners to integrate knowledge from other organizations in the firm's own knowledge base. Additional key ways in which imitation occurs are employee fluctuation and assignment of employees to multicompany project teams. When employees change their place of work, they contribute their own expertise and solutions to the new company (Malmberg & Power, 2005). As part of the European TSER project, Storper (1999) identified employee mobility as the most important mechanism for the regional exchange of knowledge between companies. In addition, the opportunities for imitating existing solutions are highly varied and are facilitated, for example,

> through skilled labour mobility within local labour markets, customer-supplier technical and organizational interchange, imitation processes and reverse engineering, exhibition of successful "climatisation" and application to local needs of general purpose technologies, informal "cafeteria" effects, complementary information and specialized services provision. (Camagni, 1991, p. 130)

The Taboo of Unfriendly Imitation

The conventions of friendly imitation are based on agreement and long-term reciprocity between the partners. There are mutually shared behavioral expectations with which network members comply in order to be accepted in the network permanently. If a network member transgresses these conventions, the network members will at least disapprove of this behavior and may even sanction it by excluding the member from communication within the network (Weber, 1922/1978). However, the processes for imitating time-tested solutions are certainly not linked to cooperation: "[N]o trust is required as a prerequisite for learning. The sequence of variation, monitoring, comparison, selection and imitation can take place without any close contact or even an arm's-length interaction between the firms" (Maskell, 2001, p. 930).

In these situations specific observation methods such as reverse engineering or other noninteractive spillover effects (Glückler, 2013a) certainly enable firms to imitate and employ tried-and-trusted solutions and innovations from other firms without their agreement and knowledge (Minagawa, Trott, & Hoecht, 2007). This unapproved acquisition of knowledge is what we call unfriendly imitation. Unfriendly imitation violates the convention of eliciting the owner's agreement when adopting solutions from someone else. Although unfriendly imitation is considered illegitimate by the originator of the idea or practice, it is still legal as long as it does not violate any intellectual property rights. In these situations firms cannot influence imitation and the use of their own knowledge by other organizations. In open competition and rivalry, unfriendly imitations do not violate any convention pertaining to cooperation, loyalty, or reciprocity, and firms simply have to accept that fact as a general environmental condition.

By contrast, unfriendly imitation is socially forbidden in cooperative relationships. However, the existence of cooperative or trusting relationships between members of a network reinforces the risk of unfriendly imitation. If actors trust in the cooperation and the joint work in which they are engaging, they are inclined to disclose much more about themselves than they would to competing firms with which they have no cooperative relationship. As more information is discovered, the risk of unfriendly imitation thus becomes greater in cooperative relationships than in open competition. This argument has its roots in the observation that the greatest damage from abuse can only arise under conditions of trust (Granovetter, 1985). Within cooperative relationships the gravity of this potential harm has institutionalized unfriendly imitation as a taboo that should not be broken given the prevailing conventions.

The Geography of Interfirm Relationships

The importance of the processes described above for cooperative and rival learning varies according to the underlying conditions for cooperation. The geographic context, for instance, figures prominently in rival learning in particular, affecting the capacity to exploit opportunities for imitation. The following section distinguishes between three geographic situations—clusters, organized networks, and the special form of colocated network organizations—bearing on interfirm relations that play a key role in discussing cooperative and rival learning (Fig. 13.1).

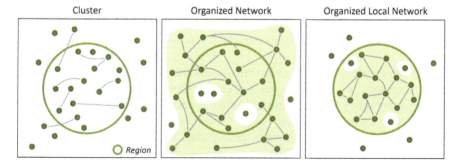

Fig. 13.1 Geographic organization of cooperation: Clusters, organized networks, and colocated network organizations (From Glückler et al. (2012, p. 168). Reprinted with permission of Springer)

Cluster

The cluster concept is associated with two elementary components in the definition: a geographical concentration of firms and a functional interrelation between them. Porter (1998) defines geographic clusters as regional concentrations of interlinked companies that perform similar activities in a common field. These two defining elements need to be assessed separately. Local concentration gives firms traditional localization advantages deriving from the joint use of infrastructure, labor markets and specialized services. The greater the number of a location's firms that require specialist employees, the cheaper and more probable it is that a corresponding segment of the labor market will form. These traditional localization advantages result, in particular, from external economies of scale. Local externalities evoke the theory of the club good (Buchanan, 1965), a reminder of why geographic concentrations are often referred to as regional club goods (Capello, 1999). The localization advantages work irrespective of any interorganizational action and require only that several firms with the same activities be colocated (Malmberg & Maskell, 2002).

The second part of the definition distinguishes between the narrow and the wide senses of the term *cluster*. The former predicates not only a geographic concentration but also functional links between the firms in a cluster. Concepts for industrial districts (Belussi & Pilotti, 2002; Sforzi, 1989) or the creative milieu (Maillat, 1998), for example, note the importance of cooperation relationships that benefit from their proximity and that are often based on trust (Bathelt, 1998). One can use transaction-cost theory (Scott, 1988) and the embeddedness approach (Uzzi, 1996) to argue that geographic proximity reduces communication costs and that face-to-face communication promotes the development of binding, trusting, and reciprocal relationships (Sabel, 1994). In this regard learning processes are due, in particular, to cooperation between local companies along the value chain. Despite the plausibility of the argument, the tendency for a firm to cooperate is often just as strongly geared to partners outside its cluster as to those within it. Empirical studies such as the software cluster in Darmstadt, southern Germany, show that lead firms and technology SMEs in the region attach substantially greater importance to strategic alliances with partners outside the region than to local opportunities for cooperation (Angelov, 2006). It is clear that functional links in a cluster are not as strong or important as supposed in traditional concepts.

Firms in a cluster are consequently a concentration of related activities based on a social division of labor between different stages of the value chain and in competition within the same stage. Malmberg and Maskell's (2002) knowledge-based theory of clusters thus incorporates the concept of rival learning. The two researchers explicitly explore the relative advantage of having a multiform cluster rather than a single integrated firm in one place. In the case of full internalization, a single firm could exploit internal economies of scale through the reduced unit costs of large production capacity, minimize external transaction costs through an authority-based governance mode, and smoothly organize the transfer of knowledge under a regime of hierarchical control. By contrast, multiple and colocated firms engaging in parallel and rival experimentation are more likely to generate variations of techniques and solutions that would be impossible within a single firm because of the common vision and corporate coherence it needs. This variety increases the opportunities for each firm to identify and imitate successful practices by attentively observing their competitors (Malmberg & Maskell, 2002; Malmberg & Power, 2005).

There are various mechanisms to promote observation and imitation. One is learning-by-hiring (Song, Almeida, & Wu, 2003), another is the adoption of new information and ideas from the "local buzz" within a communication ecology (Bathelt, Malmberg, & Maskell, 2004). Cluster structures favor competition and rivalry in these ways because competitors operate under the same environmental conditions, meaning that none can credibly claim any advantages—or excuse laggardness—deriving from external factors (Porter, 1998). Consequently, competition for innovation focuses purely on a firm's ability to develop new solutions and launch them on the market. Geographic proximity grants many competitors increased visibility and thus a greater opportunity to imitate new solutions more quickly than is likely for a spatially isolated firm. There was once a time when urban variety and density were considered the drivers of imitation and the recombination of existing knowledge in other sectors or functional areas and when the city was seen as the driver of economic innovation (on both counts see Jacobs, 1969). More recently, however, proponents of cluster approaches (Malmberg & Maskell, 2002; Porter, 1998) note that rivalry, observation, and imitation under the same local underlying conditions can also be the source of innovation for local production systems outside cities and urban regions. Unlike the concept of the industrial district, which highlights interactional collaboration, the concept underlying cluster approaches bases learning on noninteractional rivalry. In addition, rival learning can explain why firms in clusters enter into so few formal cooperations (Malmberg & Maskell, 2002; Angelov, 2006).

Organized Network

Unlike regional clusters, which are often only loosely linked, the organized network focuses on actively coordinated interfirm cooperation. We define an organized network as a voluntary and purposive association of members that aligns the multilateral collaboration between a finite number of independent organizations with a collectively shared utility (Glückler, 2012). Organized networks serve to generate cooperation gains and external savings. They are an organizational instrument for constantly reinforcing the competitiveness of the individual members (Araujo & Brito, 1997). This networking makes it possible to recombine various kinds of knowledge, something that no individual member would achieve in its entirety (von Hayek, 1945; Inkpen & Tsang, 2005). The tendency to cooperate enables corporate networks to offer a backdrop for cooperative learning; they jointly generate knowledge with friendly imitation.

To use the advantages of this cooperation jointly, rules and organs through which to implement them are developed by the members as part of their network governance. Members undertake to meet the expectations in the network, which are based on formal, contractual rules and standards and on established and collectively shared conventions. Particular importance is attached to the conventions. A member cannot just opportunistically use the knowledge of other members against their will and for his or her own purposes without violating the convention and having to fear sanctions. Violating a relationship of trust in networks implies far greater consequences than simply the disapproval of the damaged partner. If joint associated third parties find out about A's opportunistic behavior with B, then B as well as all of the other partners lose their trust in A (Glückler, 2001). Even though conventions have no legal character, their violation entails the risk of being shunned by the community or even excluded from it (Weber, 1922/1978). Hence, interfirm networks offer a suitable backdrop for cooperative learning in which practices of unfriendly imitation are not only illegitimate but effectively sanctionable.

Colocated Network Organization

The third context of geographic organization is the locally organized network. It includes features of both learning processes, that is, friendly and unfriendly opportunities for imitation. Outside the strategic alliances established in the network, the physical proximity of local companies makes for unplanned personal contact (Rallet & Torre, 1999) and many other forms of mutual observation, often dubbed local buzz (Bathelt et al., 2004). The simultaneity of geographic proximity and cooperative relationships allows both friendly and unfriendly imitation, albeit in the context of a network based on conventions and rules, which sanctions unfriendly imitation more strongly than in a geographic cluster. Misbehavior can thus be identified and sanctioned with relative ease. Locally organized networks constitute a special type of organized network. They link the advantages of physical proximity with the advantages of organized cooperation in developing and disseminating innovations. The following empirical case study on a network addresses the central issue of colocated network organizations: the perception and regulation of the diametric opposition that results in locally organized networks when the opportunities for unfriendly imitation benefit from physical proximity and when opportunities for friendly imitation benefit from cooperation.

The COMRA.DE Network Case Study

COMRA.DE: *Ideal Type of Local Interfirm Network*

COMRA.DE is an organized network of 25 technology SMEs that offer solutions and services for e-commerce and the new media market. The network was established in response to the crisis at SELLSOFT.[1] Sellsoft had held a leading market position in

---

[1] SELLSOFT is a pseudonym for a large technology company on the new media market.

the German e-commerce business until the New Economy's bubble burst in 2003. The upheaval led to mass dismissals of employees, many of whom eventually found new jobs through a transfer company. The head of the human resources department at that time wanted to offer the former employees new perspectives and encourage them to form their own companies. The easy access to infrastructure (e.g., office rentals and state-of-the-art communication technology) and continual professional exchanges were particularly important in this regard. From the outset, these activities took place in a highly concentrated geographic area, a common office building that also houses SELLSOFT. In 2005 the firms then officially adopted the legal form of a cooperative, and the network was formed as an organization. By 2010, COMRA.DE had grown from the initial 26 employees to 351 employees. Over the same period, SELLSOFT shrank from more than 1200 to 275 employees, making COMRA.DE larger than its former parent.

COMRA.DE was created without public subsidies, purely on the private initiative of the shareholders. As a type of network organization, the cooperative offers the advantages of binding its members more strongly than an association, but it is not as hierarchically structured as a GmbH (German public limited company). The network is formally governed by the executive and supervisory boards. A member company takes on the role of network spokesperson, and membership is due to the purchase of units in the cooperative. Each member has one vote, which means they have equal voting rights. This formal governance structure guarantees the members sufficient flexibility and independence. In addition to the cooperative rental of the office property, the individual companies reap collective benefits from bundling specialist expertise to solve complex tasks and from pooling capacity to process larger orders. As a result, the cooperative can work on the market as an end-to-end provider with the greatest possible bandwidth and, for example, pursue joint marketing activities and receive improved purchasing conditions.

Within the cooperative the member firms specialize in different areas of competence, such as developing software for online shops, mail-order solutions, mobile applications, online marketing, and Web design. These competencies are offered to SMEs and large enterprises alike. In addition, the network operates as an e-business service provider for other cooperatives. In 2007, COMRA.DE recorded revenues of €17.5 million, up 80 % from the previous year. This figure was the largest percentage increase in revenues the network had yet achieved. In the following year, revenues totaled €18.1 million; in 2009, €19.2 million (Beck, 2011).

Method

COMRA.DE agreed to participate in a network case study from May 2010 to September 2011. In preliminary discussions the spokesperson reported a series of problems and challenges for work in the network, which finally led him to agree to a scientific investigation of organized networks as part of the research consortium krea.nets (Glückler et al., 2012). The method for the study was based on the procedure for situational organizational network analysis, SONA (Glückler & Hammer, 2012), which integrates qualitative and quantitative research methods in six consecutive phases. The case study was based on expert interviews[2] with four company owners and the network spokesperson, who with his own company is also a member of the network. A customized network questionnaire was prepared from the interviews and offered to all of the network members for a standardized network survey. Of the 25 members invited, 20 participated in the study, a return rate of 80 %. The data collected in the survey was then evaluated with methods of social network analysis (Borgatti et al., 2002). The results of the network analysis and the interviews with the individual network members were presented and discussed at one of the monthly shareholder meetings to ensure communicative validation of our findings. The empirical research and data collection is based on joint contributions by Beck (2011) and Hammer, Beck, and Glückler (2012).

Results

Breaking Taboos

Friendly imitation is based at least on goodwill, and often also on active support in transferring existing solutions to another network member. If companies violate this convention through secret, unagreed-on imitation, then conflicts in the network are inevitable. But what does breaking taboos look like when it comes to unfriendly imitation? The case of COMRA.DE illustrates the breaking of a taboo. The members of the COMRA.DE network share information on the current trends in the e-commerce sector. In late 2010 social network technology was a major issue, so members discussed how COMRA.DE could further hone its profile in this area and generate additional benefits for the network. The discussions led to the idea of developing software that would link online shops with the most frequently used social networks in the Internet, without this connection having to be initiated. Three of the member firms decided to collaborate on a project and jointly implement this idea with a finished product. A fourth member firm observed their activities and broke the taboo. At a trade fair it published a press release stating that it, together with a major competitor outside the COMRA.DE network, would be the first provider to launch a standard shop for social networks on the market. However, this member had never worked together with the original developers or supported the joint development:

> The fourth member did that alone, was not involved in the design and development, and didn't say a word to anyone—"pssst"—and did this secretly with SELLSOFT, and then published the press release on this subject without saying anything to us beforehand. (Member of the original development group, November 2010)

---

[2] All of the interviews were recorded, transcribed, and coded with MAXQDA.

It was not the first time that this member had used rival learning against other members of the network. The chief executive had already attracted attention on several occasions in the network with his noncompliant activities. The members had repeatedly informed the entrepreneur that his behavior violated the conventions of cooperation they had agreed on at one of the cooperative's monthly meetings. In personal discussions, other members attributed the "persistence" of this unfriendly imitation to a lack of sanctions on such behavior and the ineffectiveness of the disapproval of actually engaging in opportunism. Nevertheless, no attempts were made to exclude this member from COMRA.DE:

> This is the legendary black sheep who will always be a black sheep. The fact that this company has a very similar level of knowledge makes this process [of imitation] much easier. I am concerned, once again, about this action. At some point or other he will have to learn — and yet apparently we haven't made a major impression — because he has never been thrown out. OK, he's a tenant here, he has a whole floor. If we throw him out, then we have a problem. He won't cease to exist in a city like this, either. He'll still be there. Until now, we thought that we would [keep] that crazy guy under control, give him a bit of guidance and influence him. (Network spokesperson, November 2010)[3]

The analysis of the interviews suggests two findings. First, although the deviant firm imitated a potential economic product from its network colleagues, a formal exclusion was not possible. According to the network policy that had been formalized and circulated among all members, competition between network members must not be hampered under any circumstances. Technically, the instance of unfriendly imitation was not a violation of codified rules, for the perpetrating firm produced its solution with own resources and partners for their own, separate customer. Second, the consequences of excluding the deviant firm from membership would have been more serious for the rest of the network than for the black sheep. Thus, the other members decided to maintain membership but to withdraw from the conventions of cooperation, that is, of exchange knowledge and friendly imitation. If they stopped knowledge exchange with the black sheep, they would still benefit from observing its activities as long as that member continued to have its offices in the same building as they did. The members thereby sanctioned the taboo-breaker not by formal exclusion but by articulated disapproval and soft exclusion from internal forms of cooperation: They no longer invited that member to joint activities and excluded it from open knowledge exchange and collaborative projects. Moreover, that member was suspended from the "cafeteria atmosphere" at lunch time and from unofficial management meetings. As one member firm reported, "[The black sheep] will be isolated, and nobody will talk to them any more" (Interview, November

---

[3] The term "black sheep" was used in this specific case of unfriendly imitation. Actually, both the rule-breaking member and the network have been very successful in business. Whereas the network relies on friendly imitation, the deviant member firm relies on a supply network consisting of business firms outside COMRA.DE. At the time of our investigation in 2010 and 2011, this firm reported 23 employees but had expanded to more than 100 people by the time of this chapter's publication in 2016. For lack of space in the joint office building, the member chose to resign from the network to pursue its own business and growth strategies, upon which it had embarked in the previous years.

2010). It is apparent from discussions with members of the network that violating the taboo of unfriendly imitation results in perceptible sanctions against illegitimate behavior, in particular through exclusion from the local communication ecology in the network. But what are the consequences for the excluded firm? Does the black sheep really experience disadvantages from soft exclusion?

Forms of Cooperation and the Consequences of Breaking the Taboo

In the first meeting and in personal interviews, network members highlighted the gains from collective learning among members. Employees often asked for assistance, and they exchanged program parts, codes, and other technical or organizational solutions with employees from other member firms just across the corridor. The physical proximity in the same building, together with the related activities of the firms in the same field of technology, was found to be a powerful source of collaborative learning. The information revealed in the interviews was used to develop a specific network questionnaire, which was then used for a network survey to capture all bilateral relationships across four distinct forms of cooperation among all members of COMRA.DE (see Fig. 13.2).

The first form of cooperation in this multilevel network was the imitation-of-solutions network. Firms in the network survey were asked to provide information on the use and transfer of solutions from other members.

> Over the past four years, have you introduced in your company new features or concepts that were developed by other members of COMRA.DE? Please consider novelties such as products, plug-ins, applications, code parts, marketing concepts, and organizational concepts. If this was the case, which companies developed these new features?

The responses were used to construct a network in which each link denoted an instance of one member imitating another member's solution. This type of imitation was of no legal relevance with regard to copyright violations. The companies freely disclosed their knowledge, and the imitation constituted reuse of artifacts in software or the company's organization, which are very difficult to protect under law.

The second form of cooperation was the knowledge-exchange network. In the interviews, members argued that network activities increased their opportunities for imitation and information transfer. The companies reported that knowledge was regularly exchanged both between employees and at a management level. Employees and managers either held informal discussions in the corridors or specifically looked for each other to obtain help and advice to solve concrete problems. On the basis of these interview descriptions, the members in the network survey were asked to indicate all partners who had helped them solve work-related problems, a proven survey item that conveyed valid representations of the knowledge network in previous studies (Glückler, 2008, 2013b, 2014; Glückler & Panitz, 2014).

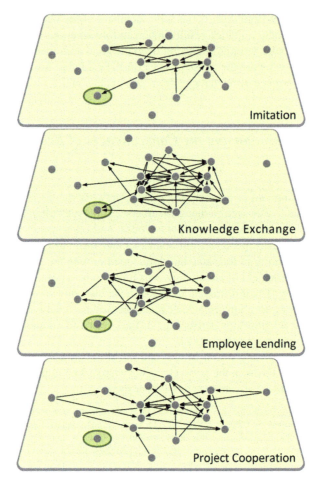

Fig. 13.2 Four forms of cooperation in the COMRA.DE corporate network. From Glückler et al. (2012, p. 177). The shaded circle highlights the position of the "black sheep" in the different forms of cooperation. Reprinted with permission of Springer

A third form of cooperation practiced within the network was employee-lending, that is, the temporary sharing of employees between the partner firms. Employees were used in the partner companies as consultants. When required, they also helped with the design of concepts for Internet purchasing systems. The amount of time spent as a temporary worker varied greatly. Some consultants were lent only for a specific project; others had been cooperating with the partner companies for several years. Lending employees was a widespread practice in the COMRA.DE network. The firms were then asked to state those members to which they had already deployed employees over the last years.

Finally, the fourth form of cooperation was the project-cooperation network. Network members were asked to state those partner firms with whom they had

Table 13.1 Four forms of cooperation in COMRA.DE

Variables	Number of network components	Network density[a]	Number of relationships	Relationships per member (mean)
Imitation	9	0.04	17	0.85
Knowledge exchange	7	0.10	38	1.90
Employee-lending	8	0.07	25	1.25
Project collaboration	4	0.09	35	1.75

[a]Network density is calculated by dividing the number of observed relations by the number of possible relationships. Adapted from Glückler et al. (2012, p. 177). Reprinted with permission of Springer

repeatedly collaborated in concrete projects in the past.[4] In professional software engineering, particularly in the IT industry, it is standard practice to modularize common project outcomes and reuse them in other projects. In the software industry joint projects can become a key process for knowledge imitation because developed project solutions such as programs, code, or parts of programs and code—so-called code snippets—can easily be reused in other projects.

The imitation network was the most highly fragmented of all the activities. Slightly more than half of the members had already used concepts, plug-ins, or code sections from other network members for their own operating purposes. This imitation allowed the companies to save development time and to make solutions to problems available in the company. Not only was friendly imitation as a network activity at a moderate level in the network, it was also the activity with the fewest relationships, the lowest density, and a comparatively low number of average relationships per network member (Table 13.1). The size and similarity of the member companies were statistically unrelated to engagement in imitation among network participants. In particular, the exchange of knowledge and the cooperation on joint projects were the strongest network activities in COMRA.DE. They included the largest number of members, the greatest density, and the largest number of relationships.

What was the position of the deviant firm that had repeatedly broken the conventions of the network? If the firm had really been sanctioned with disapproval and exclusion from the communication and cooperation relationships, that status would be reflected by a relatively peripheral or even isolated position in the network. Indeed, according to its own response and the responses of the other members to the items in the survey, the deviant firm was largely isolated from any activity. It did not lend any employees to other members, receive any solutions from other companies,

---

[4]To rule out other explanatory factors, we included many additional variables, such as the entrepreneurs' joint history, capital participations between member companies, and company prestige. Later analysis showed all these variables to be insignificant, however, so we do not address them in depth in this chapter.

participate in any exchange of knowledge, or cooperate in projects. The company was isolated especially from project work and was avoided by all three of the other companies. However, the other members of COMRA.DE reported that the company was a source of knowledge and imitable concepts and was a target for their own employee-lending. Yet on the whole, the noncompliant firm occupied only a peripheral position in the network (Fig. 13.2).

What was the benefit of a peripheral location in an organized network? The answer is quite simple: The physical proximity resulting from collective location in one building meant that imitation could never be stopped even if communication and collective projects and other work was very slow between the rule-breaker and all others. Therefore, the black sheep's continued membership let the other members benefit from the increased visibility and monitoring of new technical and industry-specific developments.

> If there are regular exchanges between 26 or 27 companies, then you are much more on the ball than if you were to be in the inner city with a team of 15 employees or in a commercial zone. You would never get the same value there. And I certainly don't mean that negatively, but the value of fast exchanges, including at an employee level, that's something we have only here in the network. (Interview with a member of the COMRA.DE corporate network, July 2010)

Despite the deviant firm's opportunism, the other members exploited the advantages of physical proximity and organizational membership. The fact that the taboo-breaker still belonged to the network meant that they believed it legitimate for them, too, to observe the company and to imitate its successful practices and solutions without approval. On the whole, the network analysis confirms the sanctions of disapproval detailed in the interviews, which were expressed by soft exclusion from the various forms of internal cooperation rather than by exclusion from membership altogether. The firm was thus forced into structural periphery of its relational activities. Despite the short-term advantage of unfriendly imitation, the violation of network conventions must ultimately be viewed as negative on the whole. Breaches of taboos place the culture of cooperation at risk, undermining the cooperative core of a corporate network. In the following section we analyze the mechanisms of friendly imitation, that is, the economic opportunities arising from the combination of connectivity and contiguity.

Practices of Friendly Imitation

Conventions of friendly imitation are based on either approval or even active support of one firm's reproduction of another firm's solution. Discussions with network members left no doubt that the different forms of exchange and cooperation were geared to providing other parties with solutions in eventual or immediate exchange for help and advice. The imitation network in Fig. 13.2 documents the results that relationships have for friendly imitation, but it provides no information on the enabling conditions. Network-related statistical methods can be used to investigate

Table 13.2 MRQAP: Effects of forms of cooperation on the dyadic imitation of solutions

Variable	Model 1	Model 2	Model 3	Model 4
Knowledge exchange	0.394**			0.370**
	(0.042)[a]			0.036)
Employee-lending			0.045	–0.170*
			(0.047)	(0.042)
Project collaboration		0.327**		0.292**
		(0.038)		(0.039)
adj. R^2	0.153	0.105	–0.001	0.228
p	0.000	0.000	0.319	0.000

[a]Standard deviations are in parentheses. *$p<0.05$. **$p<0.001$. $N=20$ members, 380 observations, 5000 permutations. Dependent variable: imitation network. Adapted from Glückler et al. (2012, p. 179). Reprinted with permission of Springer

whether the various forms of cooperation support imitation, with the imitation network being the dependent variable. The results of a series of multiple network regression models (MRQAP, see Krackhardt, 1988) have shown that bilateral project cooperation and exchange of knowledge significantly increase the propensity of two partners to learn from each other through successful imitation. Model 1 illustrates the significant positive association between knowledge exchange and successful imitation (Table 13.2), a finding also reflected by an interview in which a network member told of the effect that collaboration had had on imitation.

> There is an online shop called Magento…, and all of these member firms that I just mentioned use Magento. There's a lot of transfer here because the employees ask people, "Tell me, have you already written a plug-in for Magento? It can do such and such." And they say, "Yes, we've done that." (Interview, July 2010)

As with knowledge exchange, cooperation in projects also promoted imitation between companies (model 2). In projects, knowledge from different companies was merged and further developed to create new solutions. Companies reported that the newly developed solutions were stored not in a joint program library, as is often the case in the software industry or development syndicates, but rather in the companies participating in the projects. This practice may be due to two facts: (a) the use of standardized shop systems in the e-commerce industry, and (b) the use of many different software systems. In the COMRA.DE network, for example, more than six different shop systems were in use, with business firms mastering more than ten different development environments if one includes programming language as well. Therefore, the joint projects allowed the simplified development of specialist applications such as the use of new security systems on different standardized systems that were equally used by a large number of companies. The new media industry was characterized by standardization, modularization, and the accumulation of knowledge. However, this knowledge was stored in and used by the individual companies, not jointly (Grabher, 2004). Clearly, projects promoted the transfer of codified knowledge for the companies involved.

The fact that firms were engaged in employee-lending seems unrelated to the probability of their learning from each other (model 3, Table 13.2). The multivariate model 4 encompasses all three levels of cooperation and confirms the combined effects of knowledge exchange and project cooperation on imitation relationships. In summary, we see that various levels of cooperation and prevailing conventions of friendly imitation supported the transfer of solutions between members. This cooperative learning promoted the innovative abilities of the individual members and was fostered in particular by the mutual exchange of knowledge between the companies and their joint project work.

Conclusion

Although spatial contiguity and network connectivity have for the most part been investigated separately for their role in knowledge creation, we have combined the two perspectives to explore the opportunities and tensions that emerge from situations in which organized connectivity and spatial colocation come together. We have argued that connectivity among firms facilitates purposive collaboration and forms of friendly imitation, whereas spatial proximity also enhances the mutual visibility among even disconnected firms and thus increases the incentives for unfriendly forms of rival learning and unilateral imitation. The case of COMRA.DE has illustrated how an organized business network's members who are colocated in an office building have experienced both friendly and unfriendly imitation. Our analysis has shown the imitation of successful solutions from other members. Variation leads to a superior position, and imitation gives the company a head start when looking for new solutions. Even if the network promotes these collective gains from learning, not all of the companies are equally committed to cooperation. In particular, members learn from the partners with whom they have worked on earlier projects and with whom they have repeatedly exchanged knowledge that can be used in the company to solve work-related problems.

What are the consequences for the management of organized networks? Variation and imitation in organized networks are an opportunity to reduce the individual's costs of continuous learning. This process can be actively supported if the firms manage to share their knowledge and to work together on projects. As Dyer and Hatch (2006) ascertained for the automotive industry, a mutual opening of the firm is to the advantage of all of the partners. However, a convention of friendly imitation is also an opportunity to develop excellent practices for developing common learning processes and, at a later stage, to establish network goods (Glückler & Hammer, 2015). Network goods in COMRA.DE could be joint program databases or organizational concepts for cooperation based on the division of labor. We argue that awareness of the convention of friendly imitation is a fundamental requirement for successful cooperative learning.

However, variation and imitation in physical proximity also allow spillover effects from friendly imitation. One of these results was reconstructed in detail in the interviews with members. Unfriendly imitation is regarded as a breach of existing conventions, and its effects quickly circulate among members (Coleman, 1988). In the case of COMRA.DE, the sanctions have been expressed in collective disapproval (Weber, 1922/1978) of the member who has broken a taboo. Although the network management board or its shareholders at first refrained from tangible sanctions such as formal cancellation of membership, the members practiced various forms of soft exclusion leading to the deviant member's isolation from most forms of cooperation. That member ended up on the perimeter of the network for cooperative learning and finally resigned from the network. The new prevailing semiconvention in the relationship with this member was legitimacy for both parties to pursue rival learning practices. This case illustrates that interfirm collaboration involves a tension between cooperation and competition, especially in situations of spatial colocation where the actions of others are relatively observable and rather easy to imitate even against their consent. The legitimacy of imitation is therefore highly institutionalized in terms of conventions and taboos.

References

Ahuja, G. (2000). Collaboration networks, structural holes, and innovation: A longitudinal study. *Administrative Science Quarterly, 45,* 425–455. doi:10.2307/2667105

Akrich, M., Callon, M., Latour, B., & Monaghan, A. (2002). The key to success in innovation Part I: The art of interessement. *International Journal of Innovation Management, 6,* 187–206. doi:10.1142/S1363919602000550

Angelov, D. (2006). *Wege der Kooperation von Darmstädter IKT-Betrieben. Eine Netzwerkanalyse* [Cooperation between IT firms in Darmstadt: A network analysis]. Frankfurt am Main: Institute of Human Geography.

Araujo, L., & Brito, C. (1997). Agency and constitutional ordering in networks: A case study of the Port wine industry. *International Studies of Management and Organization, 27,* 22–46. doi:10.1080/00208825.1997.11656717

Barry, A., & Thrift, N. (2007). Gabriel Tarde: Imitation, invention and economy. *Economy and Society, 36,* 509–525. doi:10.1080/03085140701589497

Bathelt, H. (1998). Regionales Wachstum in vernetzten Strukturen: Konzeptioneller Überblick und kritische Bewertung des Phänomens "Drittes Italien" [Regional growth through networking: A critical reassessment of the "Third Italy" phenomenon]. *Die Erde, 129,* 247–271. Retrieved from http://www.digizeitschriften.de/dms/resolveppn/?PID=GDZPPN003001822

Bathelt, H., Malmberg, A., & Maskell, P. (2004). Clusters and knowledge: Local buzz, global pipelines and the process of knowledge creation. *Progress in Human Geography, 28,* 31–56. doi:10.1191/0309132504ph469oa

Beck, S. (2011). *Kooperation und Imitation in räumlich agglomerierten Unternehmensnetzwerken* [Cooperation and imitation in spatially clustered interfirm networks]. Unpublished master's thesis (*Diplom*), Department of Economic Geography, Heidelberg University.

Belussi, F., & Pilotti, L. (2002). Knowledge creation, learning and innovation in Italian industrial districts. *Geografiska Annaler B, Human Geography, 84,* 125–139. doi:10.1111/j.0435-3684.2002.00118.x

Bolton, M. K. (1993). Imitation versus innovation: Lessons to be learned from the Japanese. *Organizational Dynamics, 21*(3), 30–45. doi:10.1016/0090-2616(93)90069-D

Borgatti, S. P., Everett, M., & Freeman, L. (2002). *Ucinet 6 for windows.* Harvard: Analytic Technologies.

Buchanan, J. M. (1965). An economic theory of clubs. *Economica, New Series, 32,* 1–14. doi:10.2307/2552442

Camagni, R. (1991). Local "milieu," uncertainty and innovation networks: Towards a new dynamic theory of economic space. In R. Camagni (Ed.), *Innovation networks: Spatial perspectives* (pp. 121–144). London: Belhaven Press.

Campbell, D. (1960). Blind variation and selective retentions in creative thought as in other knowledge processes. *Psychological Review, 67,* 380–400. doi:10.1037/h0040373

Capello, R. (1999). Spatial transfer of knowledge in high technology milieux: Learning versus collective learning processes. *Regional Studies, 33,* 353–365. doi:10.1080/00343409950081211

Chesbrough, H. (2003). Managing your false negatives. *Harvard Management Update, 8*(8), 3–4. Reference no. U0805A Retrieved from https://hbr.org/product/harvard-management-update-august-2003-volume-8-number-8/U03080-PDF-ENG

Coleman, J. S. (1988). Social capital in the creation of human capital [Supplement]. *American Journal of Sociology, 94,* 95–120. Retrieved from http://www.jstor.org/stable/2780243

Djellal, F., & Gallouj, F. (2014). *The laws of imitation and invention: Gabriel Tarde and the evolutionary economics of innovation.* Retrieved from https://halshs.archives-ouvertes.fr/halshs-00960607/document

Dyer, J., & Hatch, N. (2006). Relation-specific capabilities and barriers to knowledge transfers: Creating advantage through network relationships. *Strategic Management Journal, 27,* 701–719. doi:10.1002/smj.543

Enkel, E., & Gassmann, O. (2010). Creative imitation: Exploring the case of cross-industry innovation [Special issue]. *R&D Management, 40,* 256–270. doi:10.1111/j.1467-9310.2010.00591.x

Ferrary, M. (2003). The gift exchange in the social networks of Silicon Valley. *California Management Review, 45*(4), 120–138. doi:10.2307/41166191

Glückler, J. (2001). Zur Bedeutung von Embeddedness in der Wirtschaftsgeographie [The importance of embeddedness in economic geography]. *Geographische Zeitschrift, 89,* 211–226. Retrieved from: http://www.jstor.org/stable/27818919

Glückler, J (2008). Die Chancen der Standortspaltung: Wissensnetze im globalen Unternehmen [The opportunities afforded by dispersed locations: Knowledge networks in the global enterprise]. *Geographische Zeitschrift, 96,* 125–139. doi:10.2307/27819147

Glückler, J. (2012). Organisierte Unternehmensnetzwerke: Eine Einführung [Introduction to organized business networks]. In J. Glückler, W. Dehning, M. Janneck, & T. Armbrüster (Eds.), *Unternehmensnetzwerke: Architekturen, Strukturen und Strategien* (pp. 1–18). Heidelberg: Springer Gabler.

Glückler, J. (2013a). Knowledge, networks and space: Connectivity and the problem of non-interactive learning. *Regional Studies, 47,* 880–894. doi:10.1080/00343404.2013.779659

Glückler, J. (2013b). The problem of mobilizing expertise at a distance. In P. Meusburger, J. Glückler, & M. El Meskioui (Eds.), *Knowledge and the Economy* (pp. 95–109). Knowledge and Space: Vol. 5. Berlin: Springer. doi:10.1007/978-94-007-6131-5_6

Glückler, J. (2014). How controversial innovation succeeds in the periphery? A network perspective of BASF Argentina. *Journal of Economic Geography, 14,* 903–927. doi:10.1093/jeg/lbu016

Glückler, J., Dehning, W., Janneck, M., & Armbrüster, T. (Eds.). (2012). *Unternehmensnetzwerke. Architekturen, Strukturen und Strategien* [Network organizations: Architectures, structures, and strategies]. Heidelberg: Springer Gabler.

Glückler, J., & Hammer, I. (2012). Situative Organisatorische Netzwerkanalyse [Situational organizational network analysis]. In J. Glückler, W. Dehning, M. Janneck, & T. Armbrüster (Eds.), *Unternehmensnetzwerke. Architekturen, Strukturen und Strategien* (pp. 73–93). Heidelberg: Springer Gabler.

Glückler, J., & Hammer, I. (2015). Cooperation gains and network goods. In S. Jung, P. Krebs, & G. Teubner (Eds.), *Business Networks Reloaded* (pp. 22–41). Surrey: Ashgate.

Glückler, J., & Panitz, R. (2014). Command or conviction? Informal networks and the diffusion of controversial innovations. In A. Berthoin Antal, P. Meusburger, & L. Suarsana (Eds.), *Learning Organizations: Extending the Field* (pp. 49–67). Knowledge and Space: Vol. 6. Dordrecht: Springer.

Gouldner, A. W. (1960). The norm of reciprocity: A preliminary statement. *American Sociological Review, 25,* 161–178. doi:10.2307/2092623

Grabher, G. (2004). Learning in projects, remembering in networks? Communality, sociality, and connectivity in project ecologies. *European Urban and Regional Studies, 11,* 103–123. doi:10.1177/0969776404041417

Granovetter, M. (1985). Economic action and social structure: The problem of embeddedness. *American Journal of Sociology, 91,* 481–510. doi:10.1086/228311

Hammer, I., Beck, S., & Glückler, J. (2012). Lernen im lokalen Unternehmensnetzwerk: Imitation zwischen Konvention und Tabu [Learning in local business networks: Imitation between convention and taboo]. In J. Glückler, W. Dehning, M. Janneck, & T. Armbrüster (Eds.), *Unternehmensnetzwerke. Architekturen, Strukturen und Strategien* (pp. 163–182). Heidelberg: Springer Gabler.

Hayek, F. A. v. (1945). The use of knowledge in society. *American Economic Review, 35,* 519–530. Retrieved from http://www.jstor.org/stable/1809376

Ibert, O. (2004). Projects and firms as discordant complements: Organisational learning in the Munich software ecology. *Research Policy, 33,* 1529–1546. doi:10.1016/j.respol.2004.08.010

Inkpen, A. C., & Tsang, E. W. K. (2005). Social capital, networks, and knowledge transfer. *Academy of Management Review, 30,* 146–165. doi:10.5465/AMR.2005.15281445

Jacobs, J. (1969). *The economy of cities.* New York: Random House.

Kinnunen, J. (1996). Gabriel Tarde as a founding father of innovation diffusion research. *Acta Sociologica, 39,* 431–442. doi:10.1177/000169939603900404

Krackhardt, D. (1988). Predicting with networks: A multiple regression approach to analyzing dyadic data. *Social Networks, 10,* 359–381. doi:10.1016/0378-8733(88)90004-4

Lundvall, B.-Å., & Maskell, P. (2000). Nation states and economic development: From national systems of production to national systems of knowledge creation and learning. In G. L. Clark, M. P. Feldman, & M. S. Gertler (Eds.), *The Oxford handbook of economic geography* (pp. 353–372). Oxford: University Press.

Maillat, D. (1998). Vom "Industrial District" zum innovativen Milieu: Ein Beitrag zur Analyse der lokalen Produktionssysteme [From "industrial districts" to "innovative milieus": A contribution to the analysis of local production systems]. *Geographische Zeitschrift, 86,* 1–15. Retrieved from http://www.jstor.org/stable/27818794

Maillat, D., Lecoq, B., Nemeti, F., & Pfister, M. (1995). Technology district and innovation: The case of the Swiss Jura. *Regional Studies, 29,* 251–263. doi:10.1080/00343409512331348943

Malmberg, A., & Maskell, P. (2002). The elusive concept of localization economies: Towards a knowledge-based theory of spatial clustering. *Environment and Planning A, 34,* 429–449. doi:10.1068/a3457

Malmberg, A., & Power, D. (2005). (How) do (firms in) clusters create knowledge? *Industry and Innovation, 12,* 409–431. doi:10.1080/13662710500381583

Mansfield, E., Rapoport, J., Romeo, A., Wagner, S., & Beardsley, G. (1977). Social and Private Rates of Return from Industrial Innovations. *The Quarterly Journal of Economics, 91,* 221–240. doi:10.2307/1885415

Marshall, A. (1890). *Principles of economics.* London: Macmillan.

Maskell, P. (2001). Towards a knowledge-based theory of the geographical cluster. *Industrial and Corporate Change, 10,* 921–943. doi:10.1093/icc/10.4.921

Minagawa, T., Trott, P., & Hoecht, A. (2007). Counterfeit, imitation, reverse engineering and learning: Reflections from Chinese manufacturing firms. *R&D Management, 37,* 455–467. doi:10.1111/j.1467-9310.2007.00488.x

Porter, M. E. (1998). Clusters and the new economics of competition. *Harvard Business Review, 76*(6), 77–90. Retrieved from https://hbr.org/1998/11/clusters-and-the-new-economics-of-competition

Rallet, A., & Torre, A. (1999). Is geographical proximity necessary in the innovation networks in the era of global economy? *GeoJournal, 49,* 373–380. doi:10.1023/A:1007140329027

Rogers, E. M. (1995). *Diffusion of innovations* (4th ed.). New York: Free Press.

Sabel, C. F. (1994). Flexible specialisation and re-emergence of regional economics. In A. Amin (Ed.), *Post-Fordism* (pp. 101–501). Oxford: Blackwell.

Scott, A. J. (1988). *New industrial spaces: Flexible production organization and regional development in North America and Western Europe.* London: Pion.

Sforzi, F. (1989). The geography of industrial districts in Italy. In E. Goodman, J. Bamford, & P. Saynor (Eds.), *Small firms and industrial districts in Italy* (pp. 153–173). London: Routledge.

Song, J., Almeida, P., & Wu, G. (2003). Learning-by-hiring: When is mobility more likely to facilitate interfirm knowledge transfer? *Management Science, 49,* 351–365. doi:10.1287/mnsc.49.4.351.14429

Staber, U. (2010). Imitation without interaction: How firms identify with clusters. *Organization Studies, 31,* 153–174. doi:10.1177/0170840609357369

Stegbauer, C. (2011). *Reziprozität: Einführung in soziale Formen der Gegenseitigkeit* [Reciprocity: Introduction into social forms of mutality] (2nd ed.). Wiesbaden: VS Verlag.

Storper, M. (1999). *TSER project "Networks, collective learning and RTD in regionally-clustered high-technology industries" evaluation.* Brussels. (Unpublished manuscript)

Tarde, G., (1903). *The laws of imitation.* New York: Henry Holt.

Uzzi, B. (1996). The sources and consequences of embeddedness for the economic performance of organizations: The network effect. *American Sociological Review, 61,* 674–698. Retrieved from http://www.jstor.org/stable/2096399

von Hayek, F. A. (1945). The use of knowledge in society. *American Economic Review, 35,* 519–530. Retrieved from http://www.jstor.org/stable/1809376

Weber, M. (1978). *Economy and society.* Vol. 1. (G. Roth & C. Wittich, Eds.; E. Fischoff, H. Gerth, A. M. Henderson, F. Kolegar, C. Wright Mills, T. Parsons, M. Rheinstein, G. Roth, E. Shils, & C. Wittich, Trans.). Berkeley: University of California Press. (Original work published 1922)

Yamagishi, T., & Cook, K. S. (1993). Generalized exchange and social dilemmas. *Social Psychology Quarterly, 56,* 235–248. Retrieved from http://www.jstor.org/stable/2786661

Open Access This chapter is distributed under the terms of the Creative Commons Attribution 4.0 International License (http://creativecommons.org/licenses/by/4.0/), which permits use, duplication, adaptation, distribution and reproduction in any medium or format, as long as you give appropriate credit to the original author(s) and the source, provide a link to the Creative Commons license and indicate if changes were made.

The images or other third party material in this chapter are included in the work's Creative Commons license, unless indicated otherwise in the credit line; if such material is not included in the work's Creative Commons license and the respective action is not permitted by statutory regulation, users will need to obtain permission from the license holder to duplicate, adapt or reproduce the material.

Chapter 14
Are Gatekeepers Important for the Renewal of the Local Knowledge Base? Evidence from U. S. Cities

Stefano Breschi and Camilla Lenzi

The Role of Gatekeepers for Knowledge Renewal: Review of the Literature and Research Questions

Recent research on the role of social networks for the creation and the spatial diffusion of scientific and technological knowledge has increasingly emphasized the importance of connecting and combining spatially dispersed sources of knowledge (Boschma & Frenken, 2010). Openness to global sources of knowledge provides some shelter from the risk of over-embeddedness, of lock-in to obsolete sets of technologies, of decrease in the variety of technological approaches and solutions, and of redundancy of localized knowledge exchanges by favoring a continuous expansion, rejuvenation, and update of the existing knowledge base (Bathelt, Malmberg, & Maskell, 2004; Uzzi, 1996).

In this regard, recent research has concentrated on the role played by specific actors in local networks, the so-called gatekeepers, by investigating their characteristics, attributes, and performances. The literature on industrial clusters has been particularly successful in emphasizing the crucial interfacing functions gatekeepers perform between the local and the external knowledge systems, such as screening external sources, accessing them, and conveying new knowledge to local actors (Giuliani & Bell, 2005; Graf, 2011).

S. Breschi (✉)
Department of Management and Technology, Università L. Bocconi,
Via Sarfatti 25, 20136 Milan, Italy
e-mail: stefano.breschi@unibocconi.it

C. Lenzi
Building Environment Science & Technology, Politecnico di Milano,
Via Bonardi 3, 20133 Milan, Italy
e-mail: Camilla.lenzi@polimi.it

Following the original definition put forward by Gould and Fernandez (1989), gatekeeping is a specific form of brokerage that corresponds to structural position in transaction networks, in which "an actor can selectively grant outsiders access to members of his or her own group" (p. 92). By extension, in regional studies gatekeepers are generally understood to be individuals (and sometimes organizations) that enable knowledge transfer among different spatial units, e.g., industrial clusters, cities, or regions (Giuliani & Bell, 2005; Graf & Krüger, 2011; Morrison, 2008; Morrison, Rabellotti, & Zirulia, 2013). The uniqueness of this function rests on two specific features: (a) Gatekeepers establish exclusive linkages with outside actors and/or knowledge sources and (b) they guarantee knowledge transfer and absorption within their proximate working and social environments. In short, gatekeepers not only can search for and collect relevant information outside the professional and social contexts in which they are embedded, but they are also able to transcode this information and diffuse it within their organizations and geographical areas.

Several distinctive attributes enable gatekeepers to perform this fundamental activity: high productivity and performance (Burt, 1992); creativity; novel points of view that allow new solutions (Burt, 2004; Fleming, Mingo, & Chen, 2007; Hargadon & Sutton, 1997; Obstfeld, 2005); and maintaining influential positions in their respective social structures (Fernandez & Gould, 1994; Padgett & Ansell, 1993). These characteristics can give gatekeepers comparative advantages with respect to other network members, leading to higher (private) economic and innovative outcomes, as well as to greater control power over (and relative accruable rents from) the bridging ties and knowledge exchanges they enable between internal and external actors (Burt, 2008; Gould & Fernandez, 1989).

This bright side, however, may also entail a dark side. In particular, a gatekeeper can strategically choose whether to grant access or block information flows from outside. Albeit an individual gatekeeper's impact may be slight, this possibility can have different and sizeable effects at the aggregate level of analysis, such as the regional one. In support of this line of argumentation, recent research has documented that gatekeepers can purposefully restrict the diffusion and circulation of valuable knowledge, as in the case of certain leading firms in industrial clusters (Giuliani & Bell, 2005; Hervas-Oliver & Albors-Garrigos, 2014; Morrison, 2008; Morrison et al., 2013).

In addition, gatekeepers can experience coordination costs and difficulties in managing and matching multiple external and internal connections, with a negative impact on the amount and efficiency of information flows (Whittington, Owen-Smith, & Powell, 2009). The increasing complexity of processing, coding, interpreting, and absorbing large amount of information from multiple sources (Dahlander & Frederiksen, 2012) can also hamper the efficiency of knowledge exchanges. In general, social structures in which gatekeepers dominate external linkages (and the related knowledge flows) are more exposed to disruptions of such links than social structures whose external ties are mostly direct, and possibly redundant. Finally, and more generally, direct linkages avoid leakages and noise in knowledge transmission, whereas longer chains of intermediaries imply slower knowledge transfer and a higher risk of distortion of the message content (Tushman & Scanlan, 1981).

The extant literature therefore suggests that openness and external ties are crucial for the renewal and expansion of the local knowledge base and, more generally, for innovation and creativity. However, it also suggests that, despite the importance often assigned to gatekeepers regarding the access and transfer of external knowledge (Graf, 2011; Munari, Sobrero, & Malipiero, 2012), their role is not unequivocally and unambiguously positive. Some research questions are thus still open. For example, is the open-mindedness, creativity, and innovativeness of gatekeepers sufficient to make the relations they mediate a more effective channel for knowledge transmission than direct external links? Are the disadvantages of the slower and noisier access to knowledge associated with gatekeepers compensated by the advantages of translation and transcoding of external information necessary for the successful transfer and application of externally sourced knowledge at the local level? In short, are all external relations alike with respect to expanding and renewing the existing local knowledge base?

We aim to offer an exploratory investigation of these issues and a preliminary assessment of the importance of gatekeepers for the renewal and expansion of the local knowledge base. We distinguish conceptually between direct external ties and external linkages mediated by gatekeepers and test their relative effectiveness as knowledge transfer channels. For this purpose, we propose a methodological approach to identifying and measuring the different types of external relations. In so doing, we also supply a methodological contribution to the modeling of the structure of external relations and the channels through which external knowledge flows into a city.

The empirical analysis was conducted on a large dataset of patents and their inventors in 196 U.S. Metropolitan Statistical Areas (MSAs) in the period 1990–2004. Urban settings particularly suit the study of the relationship between knowledge network properties and innovation, because invention in the United States has always been a predominantly metropolitan phenomenon (Carlino, Chatterjee, & Hunt, 2007).

In the next section, we discuss the construction of appropriate indicators to capture the intensity of a city's external linkages, the identification of gatekeepers, and of their importance in mediating external knowledge flows. We then describe our data sources and the econometric framework. The results of the empirical analysis are presented in section results, followed by our conclusions.

Measuring the Contribution of Gatekeepers to External Linkages

In this chapter, we use patents as relational data and apply the tools of social network analysis in analyzing the impact of social networks on innovation, as recent literature suggests (Breschi & Lissoni, 2009; Ter Wal & Boschma, 2009). In particular, inventors are regarded as nodes of a network, with co-invention (namely, the designation of multiple inventors on the same patent) representing the link between nodes.

Specifically, in this chapter we use all patent applications made by U.S. organizations at the European Patent Office (EPO) from 1990 to 2004 recorded in the CRIOS-PATSTAT database. Names and addresses of inventors have been thoroughly cleaned and standardized, because the accurate identification of individual inventors is key to a correct application of social network analysis tools. Inventors' addresses have been linked to one of the 370 U.S. Metropolitan Statistical Areas (MSAs), using the delineation files available on the U.S. Census Bureau website (specifically, the June 2003 delineations issued by U.S. Office of Management and Budget).

As customary in the literature, the co-invention network is constructed on the basis of a 5-year moving window, because the effectiveness of knowledge transmission through a network's ties decay with its age.

The intensity of connection of metropolitan inventors with inventors external to the city is measured through the average distance-weighted external reach (*ADWR*) between inventors located in a given city and all other inventors located in all other cities. In particular, for an individual inventor i, it is defined as the sum of the reciprocal distances to all other inventors he/she can reach in the co-invention network.[1] Accordingly, the average distance-weighted external reach of city c ($ADWR_c$) is the distance-weighted external reach averaged across all inventors located in the city. Formally, this index is defined as follows:

$$ADWR_c = \frac{\sum_{i=1}^{n_c} \sum_{j=1}^{n_h} \frac{1}{d_{ij}}}{n_c} \qquad (14.1)$$

where n_c is the number of inventors located in city c and n_h is the number of inventors located in other cities (i.e., not located in city c), and d_{ij} is the geodesic distance (i.e., shortest path) in the U.S. co-invention network between inventor i (located in city c) and inventor j (not located in city c).[2]

The index ranges from zero (i.e., all inventors in city c do not collaborate with any external inventor) to n_h (i.e., when every inventor directly collaborates with every other inventor in every other city).[3] As the literature suggests, we expect that a higher $ADWR_c$ has a positive impact on the rate of expansion and renewal of a city's knowledge base.

However, this aggregate indicator encompasses different types of external relations. In this paper, we make an effort to separate out different types of relationships between local and external inventors. In particular, we can classify external linkages

---

[1] In this paper, co-invention ties between two inventors located within the same city are considered as *internal* to that city, whereas a co-invention tie between two inventors located in different cities is considered as *external* to them, *regardless of the organizational affiliation of the two inventors*.
[2] For disconnected (i.e., unreachable) pairs of inventors $d_{ij} = \infty$ and therefore $1/d_{ij}$ is equal to $1/\infty$, in other words, zero.
[3] For a fuller discussion of the advantages of this index with respect to other measures used in the literature to capture the intensity of external relations, see Breschi and Lenzi (2015).

as *direct*, whenever a local inventor is directly connected to an external inventor, and *indirect*, whenever a local inventor needs the intermediation of another co-localized inventor to reach external inventors.

As far the indirect linkages are concerned, these are defined as those shortest paths between inventors such that the geodesic distance d_{ij} between inventor i (located in focal city c) and inventor j (not located in city c) goes through some other inventor also located in city c. Accordingly, the latter inventor can be defined as a gatekeeper, in the sense this inventor performs a bridging function between inventors located in a given city and other inventors located in other cities. This definition of gatekeeper is consistent with the original one proposed by Gould and Fernandez (1989), Allen (1977), and Tushman and Katz (1980). If we take all indirect linkages defined in this way and we aggregate them up to the city level, we can formally define the overall indirect reach of city c as:

$$INDREACH_c = \sum_{i=1}^{n_c}\sum_{j=1}^{n_h} \frac{1}{d_{ij}^{ind}} \qquad (14.2)$$

where d_{ij}^{ind} is the distance in the co-invention network between inventor i (in city c) and inventor j (not in city c) and the apex "ind" indicates that the shortest paths linking i and j involve the intermediation of at least one inventor (i.e., a gatekeeper) located in city c.[4]

As far as direct linkages are concerned, these are symmetrically defined as those paths between inventors such that the distance d_{ij}) between inventor i (located in focal city c) and inventor j (not located in city c) does not pass through any other inventor located in city c. In other words, direct linkages, in the sense used in this paper, are those that do not involve the intermediation of other inventors located in the same city. In this respect, any type of actors, including gatekeepers, can undertake direct linkages. As before, if all direct linkages defined in this way are aggregated up to the city level, the overall direct reach of city c can be formally defined as:

$$DIRREACH_c = \sum_{\substack{i=1\\i \in GK}}^{n_c}\sum_{j=1}^{n_h} \frac{1}{d_{ij}} + \sum_{\substack{i=1\\i \notin GK}}^{n_c}\sum_{j=1}^{n_h} \frac{1}{d_{ij}} \qquad (14.3)$$

where d_{ij} is the distance in the co-invention network between inventor i (in city c) and inventor j (not in city c) ; the first term of the summation refers to the subset of inventors in city c who perform the function of gatekeepers for some other co-located inventor, while the second term of the summation refers to the subset of inventors in city c who do not perform the function of gatekeepers for any other co-located inventor.

---

[4] Note that by definition $d_{ij}^{ind} \geq 2$ and thus $1/d_{ij}^{ind} \leq 1/2$. Paths of length 1, in fact, cannot involve any gatekeeper, in other words, they are direct linkages.

Importantly, the definitions above imply that the sum of (14.2) and (14.3) is equal to the numerator of (14.1), in other words, to the overall distance-weighted external reach of city c.

Armed with these definitions, we constructed several variables in order to test for the importance of gatekeepers. First, we computed (for each city c and each 5-year time window) the number of inventors who perform the function of gatekeepers. This variable tests whether the mere quantity of gatekeepers can be of relevance for a city's capacity to recombine and expand its knowledge domains.

Second, we computed the share of the overall external reach, which is either directly or indirectly mediated by gatekeepers. Formally:

$$SHREACH\_GK_c = \frac{\sum_{i=1}^{n_c}\sum_{j=1}^{n_h}\frac{1}{d_{ij}^{ind}} + \sum_{\substack{i=1 \\ i \in GK}}^{n_c}\sum_{j=1}^{n_h}\frac{1}{d_{ij}}}{\sum_{i=1}^{n_c}\sum_{j=1}^{n_h}\frac{1}{d_{ij}}} \qquad (14.4)$$

This variable captures to what extent a city's overall external reach would decrease when all gatekeepers are removed from the city (Borgatti, 2006; Valente & Fujimoto, 2010), in other words, how robust its external relations are to the removal of the links established by gatekeepers or, conversely, how much gatekeepers control the flows of knowledge across cities. Hence, it is suitable for testing whether gatekeepers are fundamental mediators of knowledge exchanges leading to higher technological recombination or whether direct relations (also not mediated by gatekeepers) are more effective. Higher values of the index correspond to cities in which external linkages mostly rely upon gatekeepers. On the other hand, lower values of the index imply that most of the linkages with externally located inventors are direct and do not need any intermediation (i.e., removing the gatekeepers would not diminish substantially the external reach).[5]

Third, we decomposed the overall distance weighted external reach mediated by gatekeepers (i.e., the numerator of (14.4)) into its two major components, i.e., the direct and the indirect and we computed the following shares:

$$SHDIR\_GK_c = \frac{\sum_{\substack{i=1 \\ i \in GK}}^{n_c}\sum_{j=1}^{n_h}\frac{1}{d_{ij}}}{\sum_{i=1}^{n_c}\sum_{j=1}^{n_h}\frac{1}{d_{ij}}} \qquad (14.5)$$

---

[5] For a fuller discussion of this index, see Breschi and Lenzi (2015).

$$SHINDIR\_GK_c = \frac{\sum_{i=1}^{n_c}\sum_{j=1}^{n_h}\frac{1}{d_{ij}^{ind}}}{\sum_{i=1}^{n_c}\sum_{j=1}^{n_h}\frac{1}{d_{ij}}} \qquad (14.6)$$

Expression (14.5) is the share of the overall external reach that is due to direct external linkages made by gatekeepers, whereas expression (14.6) is the share of the overall external reach that is due to indirect external linkages mediated by gatekeepers. Such a distinction allows addressing two questions:

(a) Whether indirect links mediated by gatekeepers are actually relevant for technological recombination in cities as claimed in the literature;
(b) whether direct relations held by gatekeepers are superior to direct relations held by other actors because of the higher inventiveness, creativity, and power characterizing gatekeepers as proposed in the literature.

Fourth, we measured to what extent the indirect external reach mediated by gatekeepers (i.e., expression (14.2) above) is concentrated in the hands of few individuals. To this purpose, we proceeded as follows. For each individual gatekeeper we computed how much the indirect external reach of the city would decrease by removing this gatekeeper. Then, we took the top 10% of gatekeepers in terms of impact and computed how much the indirect external reach would decrease by removing these individuals (*GKREMOV*). It is worth noting that this exercise is somehow related to the notion of network redundancy. To the extent that there are multiple shortest paths and thus gatekeepers between inventor i (in city c) and inventor c, removing a specific gatekeeper does not have any effect on the overall external reach of the city. On the other hand, if there is only one shortest path and thus only one gatekeeper between them, then there is no redundancy, namely the gatekeeper has full control over any information flow between i and j. In terms of the measure discussed above, the greater the impact of the top 10% of gatekeepers on the overall external reach, the lower the redundancy in information paths and the more the access to external sources of knowledge is concentrated in the few key individuals. A priori, the impact of this variable is uncertain. On the one hand, dispersion of the gatekeeping function among many inventors, with a certain amount of redundancy resulting, could improve the reliability and continuity of access to external knowledge sources and mitigate the control power individual gatekeepers exercise on these sources of knowledge. On the other hand, as long as performing an effective gatekeeping function requires the possession of distinctive skills and attributes that are unlikely to be evenly distributed, concentrating that function among key individuals might result in a better outcome.

Finally, the role played by gatekeepers could also vary according to their concentration or dispersion across firms within a city. To this purpose, we computed the share of the *indirect* external reach mediated by gatekeepers (i.e., expression (14.2) above), which is accounted for by the top four patenting firms (*CONCGK*). Once again, the effect of this variable is a priori uncertain. On the one hand, if one believes that performing effectively as a gatekeeper requires special attributes that are not widely distributed in the population, then a higher concentration of that function in few (possibly large) firms might lead to a superior outcome. On the other hand, as long as access to external knowledge is concentrated in few local firms, any benefit that might derive from the activity of gatekeepers does not spread (or spreads more slowly) across all firms in the local economy.

A Hypothetical Example

Figure 14.1 below illustrates the measures derived above by using a highly simplified, hypothetical example of a city with seven inventors (from a to g), who are connected either directly or indirectly to six inventors located outside the boundaries of the city (from H to M).

By applying the expression (14.1) above, it is straightforward to check that

$$\sum_{i=1}^{n_c}\sum_{j=1}^{n_h}\frac{1}{d_{ij}} = \left(\frac{1}{d_{aH}}+\frac{1}{d_{aI}}+\frac{1}{d_{aJ}}\right)+\left(\frac{1}{d_{bH}}+\frac{1}{d_{bI}}+\frac{1}{d_{bJ}}\right)+\left(\frac{1}{d_{cH}}+\frac{1}{d_{cI}}+\frac{1}{d_{cJ}}\right)$$

$$+\left(\frac{1}{d_{dK}}+\frac{1}{d_{dL}}\right)+\left(\frac{1}{d_{eK}}+\frac{1}{d_{eL}}\right)+\left(\frac{1}{d_{fK}}+\frac{1}{d_{fL}}\right)+\frac{1}{d_{gM}}$$

$$=\left(1+\frac{1}{2}+\frac{1}{2}\right)+\left(\frac{1}{2}+\frac{1}{3}+\frac{1}{3}\right)+\left(\frac{1}{3}+\frac{1}{4}+\frac{1}{4}\right)+\left(1+\frac{1}{2}\right)$$

$$+(1+1)+\left(\frac{1}{2}+1\right)+1=10$$

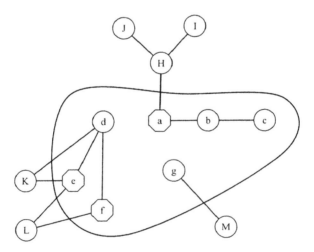

Fig. 14.1 Hypothetical example of external relations and gatekeepers (Source: Design by authors)

From this, it follows that the average (distance-weighted) external reach of the city is $ADWR_c = \frac{10}{7} = 1.43$. Of the seven inventors in the city, three perform the function of gatekeepers and are indicated by the octagon shape, in other words, *a*, *e* and *f*.

As far as the overall indirect external reach mediated by gatekeepers is concerned (expression (14.2) above), this is equal to:

$$\left(\frac{1}{d_{bH}}+\frac{1}{d_{bI}}+\frac{1}{d_{bJ}}\right)+\left(\frac{1}{d_{cH}}+\frac{1}{d_{cI}}+\frac{1}{d_{cJ}}\right)+\left(\frac{1}{d_{dL}}\right)+\left(\frac{1}{d_{fK}}\right)=\left(\frac{1}{2}+\frac{1}{3}+\frac{1}{3}\right)$$
$$+\left(\frac{1}{3}+\frac{1}{4}+\frac{1}{4}\right)+\left(\frac{1}{2}\right)+\left(\frac{1}{2}\right)=3$$

The overall direct external reach (expression (14.3) above) is instead equal to:

$$\underbrace{\left(\frac{1}{d_{aH}}+\frac{1}{d_{aI}}+\frac{1}{d_{aJ}}\right)+\left(\frac{1}{d_{eK}}+\frac{1}{d_{eL}}\right)+\left(\frac{1}{d_{fL}}\right)}_{\sum_{i=1}^{n_c}\sum_{j=1}^{n_h}\frac{1}{d_{ij}},\ i\in GK}+\underbrace{\left(\frac{1}{d_{dK}}\right)+\left(\frac{1}{d_{gM}}\right)}_{+\sum_{i=1}^{n_c}\sum_{j=1}^{n_h}\frac{1}{d_{ij}},\ i\notin GK}=5+2=7$$

The share of the overall external reach, which is either directly or indirectly mediated by gatekeepers (expression (14.4) above), is thus given by:

$$\frac{3+5}{10}=0.8$$

Similarly, the share of the overall external reach, which is due to direct external linkages made by gatekeepers (expression (14.5) above), is given by:

$$\frac{5}{10}=0.5$$

The share of the overall external reach, which is due to indirect external linkages mediated by gatekeepers (expression (14.6) above), is given by:

$$\frac{3}{10}=0.33$$

As far as network redundancy is concerned, we observed that removing either gatekeeper *e* or gatekeeper *f* has no impact on the overall indirect reach of the city. This is because there are two shortest paths (of length 2) linking inventor *d* to inventor *L*. On the other hand, removing gatekeeper *a* reduces the amount of indirect external reach by 2 (or 80%). In this over-simplified context, we can say that the overall indirect reach of the city is concentrated among few (in this case, one) individuals.

Data and Estimation Framework

We used information on the technological content of patent documents to measure the ability of cities to renew and expand their knowledge base. Patents can be described as a bundle of different technologies, whereby each is identified by the technology codes classification used at the U.S. Patent and Trademark Office (Strumsky, Lobo, & van der Leeuw, 2012). The technology fields and their combinations found in locally produced patents can therefore provide a good description of a city's knowledge base (Boschma, Balland, & Kogler, 2015; Kogler, Rigby, & Tucker, 2013). Importantly, this approach allows emphasis to be placed on the intrinsic recombinatorial nature of technical change and inventive processes (Fleming, 2001; Katila & Ahuja, 2002).

We defined our dependent variable as the number of new pairs of technology codes (i.e., combinations) introduced in a city at time t, in which both technology codes are new to the city, in other words, no local patent had been classified in those fields before time t. Differently from other studies (e.g., Fleming et al., 2007), new combinations of technology codes previously used in a city's patents have been excluded, because they simply recombine existing knowledge, with no renewal or expansion of a city's knowledge base resulting. Still, our estimates are robust to alternative (less restrictive) measuring of the dependent variable (not shown for the sake of brevity).

In order to compute the number of new combinations in each city, three filters have been applied. First, only cities showing persistent inventive activity (i.e., with a positive number of patents for each year in the period 1990–2004; i.e., 196 out of 370 cities) have been considered, so as to mitigate erratic patterns that may arise on a short time basis because of annual fluctuations and lumpiness in patent records.

Second, new combinations have been identified at the technology group level, as it corresponds to the lowest hierarchical level in the International Patent Classification (IPC, 2014) adopted at the EPO.[6] Importantly, the number of technology groups per patent class exhibits an extremely skewed distribution: 20 % of patents are classified in only one IPC technology group and, therefore, cannot lead to any new recombination (i.e., they do not enter in the computation of the dependent variable); 95 % of all patents in the sample are classified in eight or less technology groups, and 99 % in fifteen or less groups, with the remaining 1 % of all patents being outliers classified in a number of technology groups ranging from 15 to 63. It is quite obvious that the higher the number of technology groups the greater the number of new combinations. In order to mitigate the bias in the computation of the dependent variable due to the presence of such extreme observations, its construction is based on patents classified in up to eight groups.[7]

---

[6] Groups are next divided in subgroups; however, subgroups are nested into groups (i.e., their hierarchical level varies across groups) and therefore cannot be exploited in this study. Further details are available online, see IPC (2014).

[7] The number of total patents in the sample is 504400.

Third, the construction of the dependent variable is based on patents in which only inventors located in the focal MSA are reported in the document. The exclusion of new combinations that are the outcome of cross-city collaborative patents provides a more restrictive measure of a city's autonomous recombinatorial and inventive capabilities and should mitigate possible endogeneity concerns with reference to the main independent variables.

In addition to the variables described in the previous section, the empirical model includes other factors that may potentially affect the renewal and expansion of a city's knowledge base.[8] In order to account for the importance of agglomeration economies (see Duranton and Puga [2004] for a review), it includes two variables. First, the number of internal patents (*INTPAT*) in the city at time t (i.e., by excluding patents with inventors external to the city) captures both the scale effect associated with the agglomeration of inventive activities at the city level, as suggested by Bettencourt et al. (2007) and Lobo and Strumsky (2008), and the potential for technological recombination. Second, the degree of concentration of inventive activities among firms, computed as the Herfindahl index at the level of patent assignees (*HFIRMS*), accounts for (possible) effects of local market structure and competition (Beaudry & Schiffauerova, 2009).

A further set of variables controls for the nature of the local knowledge base. First, an index of absolute specialization, namely the Herfindahl index of the share of patents made in IPC four-digit (i.e., subclass) technology fields (*HPATENTS*), captures to what extent a city is specialized in a narrow set of fields, thereby controlling for the presence of externalities arising from technological specialization (Feldman & Audretsch, 1999).[9] Second, the average number of citations of the non-patent literature made by a city's internal patents (*NPLCIT*) measures the scientific orientation and generality of the local knowledge base. It is not a simple matter to anticipate the sign of this variable. More science-oriented knowledge can have more difficulties in finding its immediate technological application, leading to a negative effect of this variable on the recombinatorial capabilities of a city. On the other hand, more universal notions are more likely to find multiple applications at the junction of different technological domains (Fleming & Sorenson, 2004), meaning that a more general and science-based knowledge base could open greater possibilities of technological recombination. Third, because the Herfindahl index captures the absolute technological specialization of a city, the model also includes an index of relative technological specialization measuring the dissimilarity between the technological profile of city c and that of all the other cities with which inventors of city c have collaborative linkages, namely the so-called Krugman index (*KI*), at the level of technology groups in which a city's patents are classified. For each city c a time t, *KI* is defined as follows:

---

[8] The general logic of the empirical model is based on and expands Breschi and Lenzi (2015).

[9] This variable is computed at the technology subclass (i.e., 4-digit IPC) level and not at the technology group (i.e., the lowest technological aggregation level) level, because the use of groups would disproportionately and artificially inflate its value.

$$KI_c = \sum_{i=1}^{n}\left|\frac{P_{ci}}{P_c} - \frac{P_i}{P}\right| \quad (14.7)$$

where P_{ci} is the number of patents of city c in technology field i; P_c is the total number of patents of city c; and P_i is the total number of patents obtained in all U.S. cities (excluding city c) in technology field i. This index has been adjusted in order to make cities with which inventors of city c have more collaborative links (and thus knowledge exchange) have more weight in the computation of the Krugman index of city c. Similarly, only cities with which inventors of city c have external linkages enter into the computation of the index. In particular, P_i has been weighted by the frequency of co-inventing links between inventors of city c and inventors of city d, and P is the total number of patents obtained in all U.S. cities (except city c), weighted by the frequency of co-inventing links between inventors of city c and inventors of city d.[10]

The Krugman index ranges from 0 to 2, taking value 0 for cities whose technological profile is totally identical to the average technological profile of the cities with which it has external linkages, and taking value 2 for cities that are specialized in completely different fields. Dissimilarity from the average knowledge base of all other cities with which a city has linkages can make more fruitful (and necessary) communication, knowledge exchanges, and learning and, in turn, can stimulate the recombination of internal and external knowledge.

The last group of variables considered includes two further controls for other structural properties of the co-invention network within a city (i.e., based only on ties among inventors located in the same city). First, the largest connected component (*LARGE*) is the ratio between the number of inventors that are in the largest component of the network and the total number of metropolitan inventors. It ranges from zero (all inventors are isolates) to one (all inventors are directly or indirectly connected) and aims to capture the size and degree of internal connectivity in the co-invention network (Lobo & Strumsky, 2008). Second, the clustering coefficient (*CLUST*) captures the extent to which the partners of an inventor, within the city, are also partners with each other. This index ranges from zero to one, with higher values indicating that the internal city network is composed of dense cliques of collaboration.[11] Because cliquishness can cause isolation and localism; reduce exposure to alternative ideas; and limit the access, absorption, and recombination of externally

---

[10] More formally, P_i is defined as:

$$P_i = \sum_{d \neq c} w_{dc} P_{di}$$

where P_{di} is the number of patents that city d has obtained in technological field i, and w_{dc} is the weight of city d on all external collaborative links between inventors of city c and inventors in all other cities.

[11] The computation of this index excluded those triads of inventors connected through of a joint patent and only counted the number of triads that are the outcome of independent interactions between pairs of inventors as recommended by Opsahl (2013).

14 Are Gatekeepers Important for the Renewal of the Local Knowledge Base?... 303

Table 14.1 Definition of dependent and independent variables

Variables	Definition
	Number of new technological combinations in a city at time t (dependent variable)
INTPAT	Number of internal patents made in a city at time t (in logs)
HFIRMS	Concentration (Herfindahl) at the level of patent assignees in a city
HPATENTS	Concentration (Herfindahl) at the level of IPC 4-digits in a city
NPLCIT	Average number of citations to NPL of a city
KI	Krugman index (at the level of IPC groups) of a city
LARGE	Percentage of inventors in the largest component of the co-invention network within a city
CLUST	Clustering coefficient of the co-invention network within a city
ADWR	Average distance-weighted external reach of a city
NUMGK	Number of gatekeepers in a city
SHREACH_GK	Share of external reach mediated by gatekeepers in a city
SHINDIR_GK	Share of external reach indirectly mediated by gatekeepers in a city
SHDIR_GK	Share of external reach directly mediated by gatekeepers in a city
GKREMOV	Share of the external reach mediated by gatekeepers accounted for by the top 10% gatekeepers in a city
CONCGK	Share of the external reach mediated by gatekeepers accounted for by the top 4 firms in a city

Note. All independent variables are computed in the period ($t-1, t-5$), with the exception of *INTPAT* which is measured at time t. Source: Elaboration by authors

sourced knowledge; it has to be expected to have a negative effect on the recombinatorial capacity of a city (Uzzi & Spiro, 2005).

All the explanatory variables (except the number of internal patents) are 1-year lagged over a 5-year moving window (i.e., computed over the period $[t-1, t-5]$) with respect to the dependent variable to mitigate endogeneity concerns. The definition of variables is summarized in Table 14.1. Table 14.2 reports summary statistics, while Table 14.3 reports the correlation matrix.[12]

The empirical model estimated is based on a conditional negative binomial framework with fixed-effects by controlling for annual effects, which allows accounting for the integer and over-dispersed nature of the dependent variable, as was done in similar studies (Fleming, King, & Juda, 2007; Fleming et al., 2007 Schilling & Phelps, 2007).

---

[12] The correlation matrix reported some relatively high correlation coefficients. To test for risks of multicollinearity, we did run the collin Stata command on all variables included in the regression (with the exclusion of *SHDIR_GK* and *SHINDIR$_{GK}$*, because the sum of the two was simply equal to *SHREACH_GK*). The variance inflation ratio (VIF) tended to exclude serious risks of multicollinearity because it was below 2.5 for most of the variables with the exception of the (log) of internal patents (6.95), the number of gatekeepers (5.96), and the Krugman index (3.73). However, even for these variables, the VIF was well below 10, which is the rule of thumb value usually considered in order to detect serious problems of multicollinearity. The average VIF was slightly above 2.5 (2.59).

Table 14.2 Summary statistics of dependent and independent variables

Variable	Mean	SD	Min	Max
Number of new combinations	30.29	26.64	0	217
INTPAT	136.24	309.37	1	2916
HFIRMS	0.13	0.15	0	0.91
HPATENTS	0.07	0.06	0.01	0.49
NPLCIT	1.28	1.07	0	6.26
KI	1.40	0.35	0.37	1.99
LARGE	12.22	10.35	1	67.26
CLUST	0.25	0.23	0	1
ADWR	7.30	10.10	0.07	162.99
NUMGK	91.27	259.60	0	2876
SHREACH_GK	0.38	0.25	0	1
SHINDIR_GK	0.24	0.20	0	0.86
SHDIR_GK	0.14	0.09	0	0.67
GKREMOV	0.45	0.24	0	1
CONCGK	0.78	0.28	0	1

Note. 2940 observations (196 cities × 15 years). Source: Elaboration by authors

Results

Table 14.4 reports the results of regression estimates. The first columns present the model with only the control variables. The following columns progressively include the variables accounting for external linkages and gatekeepers. All models report estimated coefficients transformed to incidence rate ratios (IRR), defined as $\exp(b)$.

Concerning the control variables, the coefficient of the number of internal patents shows, as expected, that the scale of inventive inputs and experimentation matters. More specifically, estimates indicate that, all else being equal, a unit increase in the (log) number of internal patents is associated with a doubling in the number of new combinations of technology groups introduced in a city.

Concentration of inventive activities among relatively few firms is negatively associated with technological recombination, suggesting that competitive market structures are more conducive to a renewal of the local knowledge base. As far as the specialization variables are concerned, absolute technological specialization in a narrow set of technology fields has a negative impact on the ability to expand the knowledge base, whereas relative technological specialization (i.e., a dissimilarity of the technological profile to that of the other cities with which it exchanges knowledge) is positively related to the number of new combinations introduced in a city. A plausible interpretation of this result is that a lower cognitive overlap enhances complementarities and opportunities for learning.

Table 14.3 Correlation matrix of dependent and independent variables

		1	2	3	4	5	6	7	8	9	10	11	12	13	14
1	Number of new combinations	1													
2	INTPAT	0.458*	1												
3	HFIRMS	−0.235*	−0.156*	1											
4	HPATENTS	−0.336*	−0.201*	0.523*	1										
5	NPLCIT	0.0923*	0.119*	−0.249*	−0.0390*	1									
6	KI	−0.527*	−0.595*	0.351*	0.336*	−0.460*	1								
7	LARGE	−0.189*	−0.0670*	0.540*	0.367*	−0.150*	0.233*	1							
8	CLUST	0.293*	0.317*	−0.125*	−0.167*	0.0983*	−0.385*	−0.0244	1						
9	ADWR	−0.00479	0.0788*	0.145*	0.0839*	0.0647*	−0.283*	0.306*	0.108*	1					
10	NUMGK	0.317*	0.895*	−0.136*	−0.144*	0.147*	−0.563*	−0.0357	0.304*	0.202*	1				
11	SHREACH_GK	0.295*	0.416*	0.227*	0.103*	0.0795*	−0.451*	0.365*	0.317*	0.377*	0.404*	1			
12	SHINDIR_GK	0.313*	0.464*	0.263*	0.110*	0.0447*	−0.439*	0.462*	0.317*	0.401*	0.446*	0.953*	1		
13	SHDIR_GK	0.140*	0.146*	0.0566*	0.0473*	0.128*	−0.303*	0.00328	0.193*	0.176*	0.154*	0.721*	0.478*	1	
14	GKREMOV	−0.0619*	−0.109*	−0.0935*	−0.0632*	0.0698*	0.0732*	−0.177*	−0.0705*	−0.0922*	−0.104*	−0.120*	−0.164*	0.0260	1
15	CONCGK	−0.184*	−0.298*	0.289*	0.156*	−0.173*	0.277*	0.221*	−0.0938*	0.0315	−0.267*	0.120*	0.0796*	0.165*	0.471*

Source: Elaboration by authors
Note. *$p<0.05$

Table 14.4 Technological recombination and the role of gatekeepers

Dependent variable	Number of new combinations						
	1	2	3	4	5	6	7
INTPAT	1.904***	1.917***	1.959***	1.985***	1.991***	1.990***	1.989***
	(0.04)	(0.04)	(0.04)	(0.05)	(0.05)	(0.05)	(0.05)
HFIRMS	0.721*	0.668**	0.672**	0.726*	0.723*	0.727*	0.706*
	(0.13)	(0.12)	(0.12)	(0.13)	(0.13)	(0.13)	(0.13)
HPATENTS	0.132***	0.138***	0.152***	0.177***	0.180***	0.182***	0.183***
	(0.06)	(0.07)	(0.07)	(0.09)	(0.09)	(0.09)	(0.09)
NPLCIT	1.028	1.023	1.032	1.035	1.034	1.034	1.036
	(0.03)	(0.03)	(0.03)	(0.03)	(0.03)	(0.03)	(0.03)
KI	1.798***	1.931***	1.941***	1.864***	1.860***	1.856***	1.833***
	(0.19)	(0.21)	(0.21)	(0.20)	(0.20)	(0.20)	(0.20)
LARGE	0.995***	0.992***	0.993***	0.995**	0.995**	0.995**	0.995**
	(0.00)	(0.00)	(0.00)	(0.00)	(0.00)	(0.00)	(0.00)
CLUST	0.920	0.912	0.951	0.963	0.962	0.962	0.962
	(0.06)	(0.05)	(0.06)	(0.06)	(0.06)	(0.06)	(0.06)
ADWR		1.007***	1.008***	1.008***	1.008***	1.008***	1.008***
		(0.00)	(0.00)	(0.00)	(0.00)	(0.00)	(0.00)
NUMGK			0.9997***	0.9997***	0.9997***	0.9997***	0.9997***
			(0.00)	(0.00)	(0.00)	(0.00)	(0.00)
SHREACH_GK				0.796***		0.786***	0.771***
				(0.07)		(0.07)	(0.07)

14 Are Gatekeepers Important for the Renewal of the Local Knowledge Base?...

	(1)	(2)	(3)	(4)	(5)	(6)	(7)
SHREACH_GK				0.747**			
				(0.09)			
SHDIR_GK				0.897			
				(0.16)			
GKREMOV					1.108*		
					(0.07)		
CONCGK							1.115*
							(0.07)
Constant	0.178***	0.160***	0.142***	0.148***	0.146***	0.141***	0.139***
	(0.04)	(0.04)	(0.03)	(0.03)	(0.03)	(0.03)	(0.03)
N	2940	2940	2940	2940	2940	2940	2940
Log-likelihood	−10423.1	−10416.9	−10405.4	−10401.8	−10401.5	−10400.3	−10400.0
Chi-square	1438.1	1449.6	1489.0	1489.6	1486.8	1491.0	1488.4

Source: Elaboration by authors

Note: $*p<0.10$. $**p<0.05$. $***p<0.01$. Year dummies (not shown) included. The table reports the estimated coefficients transformed to incidence rate ratios (IRR) defined as $\exp(b)$. Robust standard errors in parentheses

Regarding the variables capturing the structure of the within-city co-invention network, the coefficients of the fraction of inventors in the largest component together with that of the clustering coefficient (albeit not significant) seem to suggest that in cities characterized by dense cliques of collaborators, knowledge may flow relatively quickly within cliques, but it may also be highly redundant, which hampers recombination.

Coming to the main variables of interest, external links prove to be an important mechanism to support the expansion and renewal of a city knowledge base (model 2). The IRR of *ADWR* is larger than 1 and statistically significant, even though the magnitude of the effect is not extremely large: Keeping all other variables constant, a standard deviation increase in the average external reach brings around $7.2\% \left(= \left[\exp(0.0068883 \times 10.10) - 1 \right] \times 100 \right)$ more new combinations in a city.

By decomposing the impact of external reach, it turns out that the sheer number of gatekeepers (*NUMGK*) is detrimental to recombination (model 3), even though the corresponding IRR is very close to 1. Nevertheless, this result is somewhat counterintuitive at a first glance, because gatekeepers are generally thought to be creative and imaginative actors. A possible interpretation, already anticipated in the previous sections of the paper, is that the control power these actors exert on the bridging ties and knowledge exchanges they govern can weaken indigenous capacity of recombination because they are in the position to grant, restrict, or even block the access to external knowledge flows. A further possible interpretation is that performing the gatekeeping function effectively requires skills and abilities that are not widely distributed in the population.

Both interpretations find further support in model (14.4). The share of the overall external reach mediated by gatekeepers (*SHREACH_GK*) shows a negative and statistically significant effect. All else equal, a standard deviation increase in this share is associated to a reduction of around 6 % in the number of new combinations introduced in a city.

To probe further into the impact of gatekeepers, model (14.5) splits the overall external reach mediated by gatekeepers into its direct and indirect components. Results show that the negative effect associated with gatekeepers is due precisely to the indirect external reach mediated by gatekeepers (i.e., *SHINDIR_GK*), rather than to the gatekeepers' direct external ties (i.e., *SHDIR_GK*). Overall, these results suggest that, all else equal, direct links to external sources of knowledge outperform indirect ones, namely those mediated by gatekeepers, in sustaining expansion and renewal of a city's knowledge base. In other words, the key message stemming from these results is that direct links, regardless whether developed by gatekeepers or other actors in the network, are far more reliable and fruitful in spurring technological recombination in cities.

Model (14.6) introduces into the regression the variable that captures the fraction of the indirect external reach accounted for by the top 10 % of gatekeepers (i.e., *GKREMOV*). The rather surprising result is that the IRR of this variable is larger than 1 and statistically significant, thereby indicating that a greater concentration of the gatekeeping function among few individuals is positively associated with technological recombination and may at least partially compensate for the generally negative effect of gatekeepers. Here, we can only offer a speculative interpretation of this finding. As already mentioned above and as pointed out in the organizational literature, effective gatekeepers are a relatively "rare breed and few networks have many of them" (Cross & Prusak, 2002, p. 109). Indeed, only few individuals are likely to have the intellectual expertise, social skills, and personality traits necessary to perform that role. Thus, one can advance the conjecture that the more diluted among many individuals the function of interfacing with the external environment is, the less effective, all else equal, the performance will be.

Model (14.7) further tests this conjecture by including in the regression the share of the indirect external reach accounted for by the top four firms in the city. The IRR of this variable is greater than 1 and statistically significant, thus suggesting that a greater concentration of the gatekeeping function in few firms is beneficial to exploration and technological recombination. Once again, advancing a definitive interpretation for this result is somewhat hazardous. At the same time, this result is consistent (or at least not in contrast) with several studies showing that leading large and technologically sophisticated firms are those more likely to act as gatekeepers and possibly generate externalities for other colocated entities (Agrawal & Cockburn, 2003). Still, we believe that this point represents an issue for further research.

Conclusions

We have offered an explorative perspective on the role of gatekeepers in the expansion and renewal of a city's knowledge base. Quite interestingly, the results indicate that external relations and their structure play a pivotal role in renewing, expanding, and regenerating a city's knowledge base, although only direct relations were particularly effective in this regard. Importantly, albeit considered imaginative, inspired, and open to new approaches and radical innovation, gatekeepers per se, and the indirect relations they mediate, do not necessarily contribute to enriching the knowledge base of the cities where they are located.

These results indeed challenge conventional wisdom that often invokes gatekeepers as the most important means of accessing and exploiting external knowledge as well as—more importantly—strategy and policy recommendations based on this assumption aimed at increasing the number and importance of gatekeepers in mediating knowledge flows across both organizational and geographical boundaries.

We contend that this conventional wisdom about the role and importance of gatekeepers is based on two misconceptions. First, external relations crucial to expanding and regenerating a city's knowledge base encompass several types of relations, but direct relations perform this function most effectively, by allowing faster, more trusted, and less noisy knowledge exchanges. Second, at an aggregate level of analysis such as the urban level, the control power that gatekeepers can exert on the knowledge flows they govern can more than offset the benefits accruing from their superior inventive performance. An excessive reliance upon indirect flows mediated by gatekeepers can signal a situation of knowledge dependence that is at higher risk of linkage disruption. Moreover, the intellectual expertise and skills necessary to act as effective gatekeepers are likely to be rather rare and possibly only present in large and technologically sophisticated organizations.

Should one conclude from what our analysis that gatekeepers are not necessary—or even detrimental to the renewal of a city's knowledge base? We believe that this conclusion is not warranted. In a companion article (Breschi & Lenzi, 2015), we show indeed that the role played by gatekeepers may indeed be important, but only in some specific circumstances. In particular, by confirming the longstanding intuition of Tushman and Katz (1980) and Tushman and Scanlan (1981), we show there that gatekeepers only play an important role when the knowledge base of a city is sufficiently different and specialized with respect to other cities to require the absorption of knowledge and the transcoding function of those actors.

In conclusion, the chapter is intended to provide a contribution to the literature on both conceptual and methodological grounds. First, we clarify and qualify the role and function of gatekeepers. Second, we propose an operational method to quantify the importance of gatekeepers in brokering knowledge flows across cities and a set of new indicators that allow measurement of the meso-level effects (i.e., at the city level) of individual behavior and interactions (i.e., of inventors, gatekeepers, and co-invention networks). We hope that they will be useful and deployed in future research.

References

Agrawal, A., & Cockburn, I. (2003). The anchor tenant hypothesis: Exploring the role of large, local, R&D-intensive firms in regional innovation systems. *International Journal of Industrial Organization, 21,* 1227–1253. doi:10.1016/S0167-7187(03)00081-X

Allen, T. J. (1977). *Managing the Flow of Technology.* Cambridge, MA: MIT Press.

Bathelt, H., Malmberg, A., & Maskell, P. (2004). Clusters and knowledge: Local buzz, global pipelines and the process of knowledge creation. *Progress in Human Geography, 28,* 31–56. doi:10.1191/0309132504ph469oa

Beaudry, C., & Schiffauerova, A. (2009). Who's right, Marshall or Jacobs? The localization versus urbanization debate. *Research Policy, 38,* 318–337. doi:10.1016/j.respol.2008.11.010

Bettencourt, L. M. A., Lobo, J., & Strumsky, D. (2007). Invention in the city: Increasing returns to patenting as a scaling function of metropolitan size. *Research Policy, 36,* 107–120. doi:10.1016/j.respol.2006.09.026

Borgatti, S. P. (2006). Identifying sets of key players in a social network. *Computational and Mathematical Organization Theory, 12,* 21–34. doi:10.1007/s10588-006-7084-x

Boschma, R., Balland, P.-A., & Kogler, D. F. (2015). Relatedness and technological change in cities: The rise and fall of technological knowledge in U.S. metropolitan areas from 1981 to 2010. *Industrial and Corporate Change, 24*, 223–250. doi:10.1093/icc/dtu012

Boschma, R., & Frenken, K. (2010). The spatial evolution of innovation networks: A proximity perspective. In R. Boschma & R. Martin (Eds.), *The Handbook of Evolutionary Economic Geography* (pp. 120–138). Cheltenham: Edward Elgar.

Breschi, S., & Lenzi, C. (2015). The role of external linkages and gatekeepers for the renewal and expansion of U.S. cities' knowledge base, 1990–2004. *Regional Studies, 49*, 782–797. doi:10.1080/00343404.2014.954534.

Breschi, S., & Lissoni, F. (2009). Mobility of skilled workers and co-invention networks: An anatomy of localized knowledge flows. *Journal of Economic Geography, 9*, 439–468. doi:10.1093/jeg/lbp008

Burt, R. S. (1992). *Structural holes: The social structure of competition*. Cambridge, MA: Harvard University Press.

Burt, R. S. (2004). Structural holes and good ideas. *American Journal of Sociology, 110*, 349–399. doi:10.1086/421787

Burt, R. S. (2008). Information and structural holes: Comment on Reagans and Zuckerman. *Industrial and Corporate Change, 17*, 953–969. doi:10.1093/icc/dtn033

Carlino, G. A., Chatterjee, S., & Hunt, R. M. (2007). Urban density and the rate of invention. *Journal of Urban Economics, 61*, 389–419. doi:10.1016/j.jue.2006.08.003

Cross, R., & Prusak, L. (2002). The people who make organizations go–or stop. *Harvard Business Review, 80*, 104–112. Retrieved from https://hbr.org/2002/06/the-people-who-make-organizations-go-or-stop

Dahlander, L., & Frederiksen, L. (2012). The core and cosmopolitans: A relational view of innovation in user communities. *Organization Science, 23*, 988–1007. doi:10.1287/orsc.1110.0673

Duranton, G., & Puga, D. (2004). Chapter 48 Micro-foundations of urban agglomeration economies. In J. V. Henderson & J.-F. Thisse (Eds.), *Cities and Geography* (pp. 2063–2117). Handbook of Regional and Urban Economics: Vol. 4. Amsterdam: Elsevier.

Feldman, M. P., & Audretsch, D. B. (1999). Innovation in cities: Science-based diversity, specialization and localized competition. *European Economic Review, 43*, 409–429. doi:10.1016/S0014-2921(98)00047-6

Fernandez, R. M., & Gould, R. V. (1994). A dilemma of state power: Brokerage and influence in the national health policy domain. *The American Journal of Sociology, 99*, 1455–1491. doi:10.1086/230451

Fleming, L. (2001). Recombinant uncertainty in technological search. *Management Science, 47*, 117–132. doi:10.1287/mnsc.47.1.117.10671

Fleming, L., King, C., & Juda, A. I. (2007). Small worlds and regional innovation. *Organization Science, 18*, 938–954. doi:10.1287/orsc.1070.0289

Fleming, L., Mingo, S., & Chen, D. (2007). Collaborative brokerage, generative creativity, and creative success. *Administrative Science Quarterly, 52*, 443–475. doi:10.2189/asqu.52.3.443

Fleming, L., & Sorenson, O. (2004). Science as a map in technological search. *Strategic Management Journal, 25*, 909–928. doi:10.1002/smj.384

Giuliani, E., & Bell, M. (2005). The micro-determinants of meso-level learning and innovation: Evidence from a Chilean wine cluster. *Research Policy, 34*, 47–68. doi:10.1016/j.respol.2004.10.008

Gould, R. V., & Fernandez, R. M. (1989). Structures of mediation: A formal approach to brokerage in transaction networks. *Sociological Methodology, 19*, 89–126. doi:10.2307/270949

Graf, H. (2011). Gatekeepers in regional networks of innovators. *Cambridge Journal of Economics, 35*, 173–198. doi:10.1093/cje/beq001

Graf, H., & Krüger, J. J. (2011). The performance of gatekeepers in innovator networks. *Industry & Innovation, 18*, 69–88. doi:10.1080/13662716.2010.528932

Hargadon, A., & Sutton, R. I. (1997). Technology brokering and innovation in a product development firm. *Administrative Science Quarterly, 42,* 716–749. doi:10.2307/2393655

Hervas-Oliver, J.-L., & Albors-Garrigos, J. (2014). Are technology gatekeepers renewing clusters? Understanding gatekeepers and their dynamics across cluster life cycles. *Entrepreneurship & Regional Development, 26,* 431–452. doi:10.1080/08985626.2014.933489

International Patent Classification (IPC) (2014). Guide. Retrieved from http://www.wipo.int/export/sites/www/classifications/ipc/en/guide/guide_ipc.pdf

Katila, R., & Ahuja, G. (2002). Something old, something new: A longitudinal study of search behavior and new product introduction. *Academy of Management Journal, 45,* 1183–1194. doi:10.2307/3069433

Kogler, D. F., Rigby, D L., & Tucker, I. (2013). Mapping knowledge space and technological relatedness in US cities. *European Planning Studies, 21,* 1374–1391. doi:10.1080/09654313.2012.755832

Lobo, J., & Strumsky, D. (2008). Metropolitan patenting, inventor agglomeration and social networks: A tale of two effects. *Journal of Urban Economics, 63,* 871–884. doi:10.1016/j.jue.2007.07.005

Morrison, A. (2008). Gatekeepers of knowledge within industrial districts: Who they are, how they interact. *Regional Studies, 42,* 817–835. doi:10.1080/00343400701654178

Morrison, A., Rabellotti, R., & Zirulia, L. (2013). When do global pipelines enhance the diffusion of knowledge in clusters? *Economic Geography, 89,* 77–96. doi:10.1111/j.1944-8287.2012.01167.x

Munari, F., Sobrero, M., & Malipiero, A. (2012). Absorptive capacity and localized spillovers: Focal firms as technological gatekeepers in industrial districts. *Industrial and Corporate Change, 21,* 429–462. doi:10.1093/icc/dtr053

Obstfeld, D. (2005). Social networks, the Tertius Iungens orientation, and involvement in innovation. *Administrative Science Quarterly, 50,* 100–130. doi:10.2189/asqu.2005.50.1.100

Opsahl, T. (2013). Triadic closure in two-mode networks: Redefining the global and local clustering coefficients. *Social Networks, 35,* 159–167. doi:10.1016/j.socnet.2011.07.001

Padgett, J. F., & Ansell, C. K. (1993). Robust action and the rise of the Medici, 1400–1434. *American Journal of Sociology, 98,* 1259–1319. doi:10.1086/230190

Schilling, M. A., & Phelps, C. C. (2007). Interfirm collaboration networks: The impact of large-scale network structure on firm innovation. *Management Science, 53,* 1113–1126. doi:10.1287/mnsc.1060.0624

Strumsky, D., Lobo, J., & van der Leeuw, S. (2012). Using patent technology codes to study technological change. *Economics of Innovation and New Technology, 21,* 267–286. doi:10.1080/10438599.2011.578709

Ter Wal, A., & Boschma, R. A. (2009). Applying social network analysis in economic geography: Framing some key analytic issues. *Annals of Regional Science, 43,* 739–756. doi:10.1007/s00168-008-0258-3

Tushman, M. L., & Katz, R. (1980). External communication and project performance: An investigation into the role of gatekeepers. *Management Science, 26,* 1071–1085. doi:10.1287/mnsc.26.11.1071

Tushman, M. L., & Scanlan, T. J. (1981). Boundary spanning individuals: Their role in information transfer and their antecedents. *The Academy of Management Journal, 24,* 289–305. doi:10.2307/255842

Uzzi, B. (1996). The sources and consequences of embeddedness for the economic performance of organizations: The Network Effect. *American Sociological Review, 61,* 674–698. Retrieved from http://www.jstor.org/stable/2096399

Uzzi, B., & Spiro, J. (2005). Collaboration and creativity: The small world problem. *American Journal of Sociology, 111,* 447–504. doi:10.1086/432782

Valente, T. W., & Fujimoto, K. (2010). Bridging: Locating critical connectors in a network. *Social Networks, 32,* 212–220. doi:10.1016/j.socnet.2010.03.003

Whittington, K. B., Owen-Smith, J., & Powell, W. W. (2009). Networks, propinquity, and innovation in knowledge-intensive industries. *Administrative Science Quarterly, 54,* 90–122. doi:10.2189/asqu.2009.54.1.90

Open Access This chapter is distributed under the terms of the Creative Commons Attribution 4.0 International License (http://creativecommons.org/licenses/by/4.0/), which permits use, duplication, adaptation, distribution and reproduction in any medium or format, as long as you give appropriate credit to the original author(s) and the source, provide a link to the Creative Commons license and indicate if changes were made.

The images or other third party material in this chapter are included in the work's Creative Commons license, unless indicated otherwise in the credit line; if such material is not included in the work's Creative Commons license and the respective action is not permitted by statutory regulation, users will need to obtain permission from the license holder to duplicate, adapt or reproduce the material.

Chapter 15
Learning Networks Among Swedish Municipalities: Is Sweden a Small World?

Christopher Ansell, Martin Lundin, and Per Ola Öberg

Distributed, networked learning processes are widely touted as a basis for superior performance. Public and private organizations, cities and regions, and even nations are exhorted to network, to innovate collaboratively, to benchmark, and above all to learn from one another (Agranoff, 2006; Betsill & Bulkeley, 2004; Cooke & Morgan, 1993; Goldsmith & Eggers, 2004; Kraatz, 1998; Lee & van de Meene, 2012; Powell, Koput, & Smith-Doerr, 1996; Slaughter, 2009). From case study research, we know a good deal about local strategies of networking, innovation, and collaboration (e.g., Saxenian, 1996). And from diffusion studies, we also know that the structure of networks shapes the diffusion of information, ideas, innovations, policies, and best practices (Cao, 2010; Davis, 1991; Granovetter, 1973; Gray, 1973; Hedström, Sandell, & Stern, 2000; Lee & Strang, 2006; Mintrom & Vergari, 1998; Stone, 2004). However, we know relatively little about how the local learning choices of individuals, firms, cities, or nations aggregate into global network patterns that may subsequently affect diffusion. In this chapter, we explore this question by examining how the learning strategies of Swedish municipalities aggregate to produce a national intermunicipal learning network.

Interdependence between the policy choices of local governments has attracted growing interest recently (Lee & van de Meene, 2012; Marsden, Frick, May, & Deakin, 2011). It has been argued that subnational governments can act like *demo-*

C. Ansell (✉)
Charles and Louise Travers Department of Political Science, University of California, Berkeley, CA, USA
e-mail: cansell@berkeley.edu

M. Lundin
Institute for Evaluation of Labour Market and Education Policy (IFAU), Uppsala, Sweden
e-mail: martin.lundin@ifau.uu.se

P.O. Öberg
Department of Government, Uppsala University, Uppsala, Sweden
e-mail: PerOla.Oberg@statsvet.uu.se

© The Author(s) 2017
J. Glückler et al. (eds.), *Knowledge and Networks*, Knowledge and Space 11,
DOI 10.1007/978-3-319-45023-0_15

cratic laboratories (Shipan & Volden, 2012; Volden, 2006) and that they can learn important lessons from each other. Literature on *urban policy mobilities* (Jacobs, 2012; McCann, 2011) and *policy diffusion* (Krause, 2011; Lee & van de Meene, 2012) has begun to explore the mechanisms of policy transfer and diffusion between cities. Our research shares this interest in policy mobility and diffusion but approaches the issue from a different angle. Rather than asking why a policy moves from city A to city B, our research is interested in uncovering the relational principles that constitute interurban networks in the first place. We approach the issue from this angle, in part, because of the character of our data, which does not enable us to track the mobility or diffusion of specific policies, but does give us an unusually detailed look at the relationships of learning between Swedish municipalities. Our contribution is therefore not to explain mobility or diffusion per se, but rather to utilize social network analysis to uncover the structuring principles of national learning networks.

Over the last decade or so, economic geographers and economic sociologists have been engaged in a similar exploration of the relational principles that guide learning in interfirm networks. Their research has shown that interfirm learning is often structured by geographical proximity, but that nonlocal networks may be critical pipelines that move knowledge between local clusters of firms (e.g., Amin & Cohendet, 1999; Bathelt, Malmberg, & Maskell, 2004; Bell & Zaheer, 2007; Glückler, 2013; Owen-Smith & Powell, 2004). Although geographical proximity is understood to enhance interactional learning, nonlocal networks are increasingly understood to be important for preventing local learning networks from becoming too parochial (Boschma, 2005; Maskell, 2014). Although research is beginning to reveal variations on this theme, this literature valuably highlights the composite character of learning ecologies, which are produced through the interplay of geography and networks. Our research builds on this literature, but extends this discussion from firms to municipalities. Our research therefore offers a bridge between this literature on interfirm learning and the literature on policy mobility and diffusion. To our knowledge, there has been little cross-fertilization between these two important bodies of literature.

Our exploration of intermunicipal learning networks is based on a unique survey of municipal civil servants conducted in 2010 as part of a wider study of municipal knowledge use in Sweden. In this survey, the senior civil servants in all Swedish municipalities were asked to name other Swedish municipalities from whom they had drawn lessons in a given period. When these choices are aggregated across all Swedish municipalities, the result is a unique glimpse into what an intermunicipal learning network looks like on a national scale. Swedish municipalities provide an interesting context in which to examine learning networks. Much of the fabled Swedish welfare state is actually administered by Sweden's 290 municipalities varying in size from roughly 3000 inhabitants to 750,000 inhabitants.[1] These municipalities have responsibility for a wide range of policy areas, including social ser-

---

[1] Prior research notes significant variation in welfare services across municipalities, leading some scholars to describe Sweden as a multitude of "welfare municipalities" (Trydegård & Thorslund, 2010).

vices, education, daycare, environmental protection, and planning, and municipal employees compose approximately 25% of the Swedish workforce (Sveriges Kommuner och Landting, 2014). Although they are organized into 21 counties, the county-municipality relationship is not a hierarchical one and while Swedish municipalities operate within a framework of national law, they have considerable latitude about how to organize and deliver government services and regulation.[2] Thus, their extensive and parallel responsibilities create powerful incentives to learn from one another, but their political autonomy means that they are relatively free to decide whom to learn from. We know that the Swedish Association of Local Authorities and Regions (SALAR) actively encourages the municipalities to learn from each other, but we do not know how their choice of whom to learn from aggregates to produce a national learning network.

The chapter is organized as follows: The first section describes our data. In the second section, we provide some basic information about the extent of learning among municipalities and about how municipalities try to learn from each other. In section three, we use social network analysis to explore how municipal clusters of learning are structured. Then, in section four, we examine whether the Swedish municipalities can be described as a small world through which ideas and information may easily diffuse. Section five focuses on what characterizes the municipalities whose nonlocal networks bridge between otherwise disconnected municipalities in the learning network. Section six concludes.

Data

Our data come from a survey of Swedish municipalities conducted in 2010. The survey asked a range of questions about knowledge use in each municipality and was answered by the top civil servant. This manager is in charge of the office responsible for preparing policy proposals for the municipal executive board, which is the most important and powerful local government institution in Sweden (Bäck, 2005). Composed of local politicians appointed in proportion to their party mandate in the municipal assembly, these boards have responsibility for managing and coordinating local administration and also have financial responsibility for the municipality.

The key variable of this study is *learning* or *lesson-drawing* (Freeman, 2008, p. 376; see also, Lundin, Öberg, & Josefsson, 2015). Learning is a voluntary activity involving a search for knowledge in order to solve problems. That is, in a learning process actors try to improve the understanding of the relationship between cause and effect by taking advantage of others' experiences (Lee & Strang, 2006;

---

[2] In a comparative perspective, Swedish local governments are considered to have a lot of power (Sellers & Lidström, 2007). Municipalities have taxing power and a constitutionally protected right of self-government. Swedish public agencies are also known to actively support innovation. The 2010 European Innobarometer Survey found that innovation in the Swedish public sector is much more bottom-up (initiated internally) rather than driven by policy mandate (Arundel & Hollanders, 2011).

Lee & van de Meene, 2012; Meseguer, 2005). The survey question used to elicit the municipal learning network was: "What other municipalities have you drawn important lessons from within your field during the last election period (since January 2007)?" In response, municipal managers could mention as many other municipalities as they liked.

A web survey was distributed as a first step, with three follow-up reminders. We then distributed a somewhat shorter version as a postal survey in a second step. This led to a response rate of 78 %. The remaining nonrespondents were telephoned, producing a 100 % response rate on the learning question.[3]

The information that can be spread among municipal head managers is of a diverse character because a wide range of policy decisions are handled in the municipal executive boards. Overarching issues like budgets, policies, programs, guidelines, and various action plans (e.g., wind power plans and school plans) are within the managers' purview. Somewhat more limited decisions are also frequently made, such as whether to shut down a certain school or where to locate a recycling station. Moreover, the committees handle minor issues such as what documents should be archived and for how long. We do not know exactly what issues respondents had in mind when answering our question, but they all have equivalent positions within the municipalities and were asked about lessons learned within their field, which includes all issues handled by the municipal executive boards. Furthermore, they were explicitly told to ignore issues that do not reach the political level and "routine matters" concerning individual citizens.

In addition to the key question, we use some other questions from the survey in order to describe learning processes in Swedish municipalities in more detail. Moreover, a series of interviews with municipal officials was conducted in order to develop a more qualitative understanding of how municipalities use knowledge to make policy decisions. Semistructured, open-ended interviews were conducted with 40 politicians and civil servants in six municipalities. These municipalities were strategically selected to maximize variation (two large, two medium-sized, and two small municipalities). For each pair, one municipality had a stable social democratic majority and the other had shifting majorities. The interviews lasted from 45 to 90 min and were recorded. Although we do not report systematically on these interviews in this chapter, they do provide some background information for our interpretation of learning networks.

Local Learning Through Informal Personal Connections

A first step in the analysis is to explore how important information from other municipalities is in municipal decision-making. We also want to know what channels are used to collect information. Table 15.1 provides some basic statistics on

---

[3] Note that the other survey questions presented in this chapter are based on a somewhat smaller sample (i.e., about 78 % of the population).

Table 15.1 Learning among Swedish local governments: Various survey responses

Q1. How many other municipalities have been learned from? ("Outdegree")		Q2. How often is information from (a) other municipalities (b) SALAR used when issues are prepared before political decision?		
Number of municipalities mentioned	%	Response alternative	Other municipalities (%)	SALAR (%)
0	8	Never or almost never	12	2
1	5	Less than half of the issues	54	39
2–5	39	About half of the issues	21	30
6–9	22	More than half of the issues	12	20
10–15	19	Always or almost always	1	9
16–26	7			
Average: 6.86				

Q3. Channels used "often" or "very often" in order to get information about activities in other municipalities?

Channel	%	Channel	%
1. Informal personal connections	81	5. Conferences, seminars etc.	28
2. Internet homepages	72	6. Written reports produced by other municipalities	21
3. Regular meetings with certain municipalities	67	7. Information in media	20
4. Written reports produced by SALAR	65	8. Official visits	19

learning among municipalities in Sweden according to the survey responses. Of the 290 municipalities surveyed, only 8% reported they had not learned something important from another municipality during the previous 4 years (since the last election period), whereas 61% reported learning from between two and nine other municipalities, and the maximum number reported was 26 other municipalities. On average, the municipal managers report that their municipality draws important lessons from about seven other municipalities.

The survey also included a question on how often information from other municipalities is used when issues are prepared before political decision. Table 15.1 reveals that although information from other municipalities is not used in a majority of issues, only 12% reported that they "never or almost never" use such input in the policy process. Furthermore, we asked how often information produced by the Swedish Association of Local Authorities and Regions (SALAR) is employed in the policy process. Around two percent claim that they "never or almost never" use information from SALAR, whereas 59% use information from SALAR in at least half of the issues. Thus, SALAR seems to function as an important bridge between local governments. This finding was reinforced in the in-depth interviews.

Table 15.1 verifies another conclusion drawn from the in-depth interviews: informal personal connections are the most important channel used to get information about activities in other municipalities. Other important channels include the internet homepages of other municipalities, regular meetings and written reports where SALAR describes various activities at the local level.

Learning Clusters Are Based on County Structure

In an analysis of dyads of municipalities by Lundin et al. (2015) using the same data analyzed in this chapter, it is demonstrated that Swedish municipalities primarily learn from their local neighbors.[4] The analysis reveals that geographic proximity greatly increases the probability that a municipality will learn from another municipality. For instance, if two municipalities are located in the same county, the predicted probability that a learning link will be established is .054, all else being equal. If the municipalities are not located in the same county, the probability is only .003. Our interviews point in the same direction. As one local civil servant told us:

> Above all, it is if you find somebody that is successful in a certain area, somebody that has given thought to something. Primarily it is often among neighbors that we look because they are quite similar and work under roughly the same conditions. (2011 interview with civil servant)

The importance of geographical proximity suggests that municipal learning networks in Sweden might be very parochial. If so, it is reasonable to expect that new knowledge, ideas, and best practices would be quite slow to diffuse to local governments in Sweden. But the dyadic analysis presented above does not account for the possibility of learning indirectly through less proximate networks. To explore this possibility, we employ ideas from social network analysis. The aim is to deepen our understanding of the clustering properties of a potential learning network: How are clusters structured? To find out more about this, we started by using the Girvan-Newman method of detecting *community structure* (Girvan & Newman, 2002). This method finds clusters by iteratively removing edges with high edge betweenness scores until it reaches some specified minimum number of clusters. A betweenness score summarizes the number of times an actor is a bridge between two other actors in the network (Freeman, 1977).

The analysis is presented in Table 15.2 and it reinforces findings in Lundin et al. (2015): county is a very strong predictor of cluster membership. There are 21 counties in Sweden and when directed to detect 21 clusters, the community structure

---

[4]The main research question in Lundin et al. (2015) is whether local governments tend to learn from governments that are more successful than others; the empirical findings support this hypothesis. However, the importance of proximity, similarity, and power is also examined in the study.

Table 15.2 Girvan-newman clusters by county

Cluster number	Counties (number of municipalities per county)	E-I index
1	Stockholm (26); Södermanland (1); Skåne (1)	−0.411
2	Södermanland (7); Uppsala (2)	0.000
3	Gävleborg (10); Västernorrland (4); Uppsala (1)	−0.310
4	Västmanland (7); Uppsala (4); Södermanland (1); Gotland (1); Örebro (1)	0.162
5	Östergötland (12); Halland (1)	−0.197
6	Västra Götaland (22); Östergötland (1); Jönköping (1)	−0.338
7	Jönköping (12); Halland (4); Blekinge (1)	−0.116
8	Kronoberg (8)	−0.195
9	Kalmar (12)	−0.417
10	Blekinge (4)	0.130
11	Skåne (16)	−0.452
12	Skåne (12)	−0.282
13	Jämtland (8); Skåne (1); Västernorrland (1)	−0.020
14	Skåne (1)	0.000
15	Västra Götaland (11); Halland (1)	−0.416
16	Västra Götaland (14)	0.262
17	Västerbotten (15); Västmanland (1); Västra Götaland (1); Västernorrland (1); Norbotten (1)	−0.371
18	Värmland (16)	−0.247
19	Örebro (11)	−0.426
20	Dalarna (14); Västmanland (2)	−0.229
21	Norrbotten (13); Västernorrland (1)	−0.277

identified by the Girvan-Newman method is very close to the structure of counties. Although some clusters contain municipalities from more than one county, the county structure is clear. Twenty of the clusters are dominated by municipalities from a single county (cluster 14 is an exception with only one municipality). Municipalities from some counties are divided between clusters (Västra Götaland, Skåne), but a single county still dominates each cluster. Only a few counties have the municipalities distributed across clusters without clearly dominating at least one cluster (Uppsala, Västernorrland). The county structure of clusters remains robust even if the algorithm is told to produce a different number of clusters.[5]

We can also look at what is called the E-I index for each of these clusters. The E-I index is a measure that varies between −1 and +1. At +1, all ties are external to

---

[5] With 10 clusters, the method identifies a regional organization that resembles the three old Swedish provinces (Norrland, Svealand, and Götaland). However, municipalities still tend to cluster with other municipalities from their own county. The northern region includes Norrbotten, Västerbotten, and Västernorrland. The center region includes Stockholm, Uppsala, Södermanland, Gävleborg, Dalarna, Västmanland, Gotland, and Jämtland. Then there are seven small regions in the south: (1) Västra Götaland, Halland, and Jönköping; (2) Örebro; (3) Östergötland; (4) Kronoberg and Blekinge; (5) Värmland; (6) Kalmar; and (7) Skåne.

a group (in this case the cluster); at −1, all ties are internal to the group.[6] We can see in Table 15.2 that a large majority of the E-I indexes for the clusters are negative. These findings suggest that learning within clusters is much stronger than more global learning.

Because the pattern of emergence of the global network works via a principle of local proximity, we might expect local clusters to cluster together on a geographical basis. In other words, we should expect the clusters identified above to cluster into larger regions. To examine this, we wanted a clustering technique that did not require us to assign the number of clusters. We selected Markov clustering, which uses a different strategy of community detection (van Dongen, 2008). The Girvan-Newman community detection procedure used above identifies community structure by removing edges with high betweenness centrality until nonoverlapping groups appear. Markov clustering identifies community clusters by "walking around"; it identifies clusters as places where the algorithm spends a lot of time walking. This strategy intuitively captures the way information might circulate geographically.

The Markov clustering identified 22 clusters, which at first glance might seem to approximate the county structure of Sweden. However, two of these clusters are very large and many others are quite small. Our interpretation is that the Markov clustering algorithm identifies the regional as opposed to the local clustering structure of the network. These larger regional clusters attracted our attention because they suggest that one of the ways the national learning network might be integrated is through larger learning regions. These regional clusters could be significant in the circulation of knowledge among Swedish municipalities. A study of regional innovation and networks by Fleming, King, and Juda (2007), for example, found that such large components are positively correlated with innovation in patent co-authorship networks.

The two large clusters are indeed regions in a spatial sense. One of them (Fig. 15.1) represents the northern coast plus the Stockholm region (minus Stockholm itself). The second region (Fig. 15.2) runs spatially east to west in the southern part of Sweden and contains the Göteborg region. We also observe that a distinctive subregion can be detected in the Southern region (Fig. 15.2). This subregion is an extremely tight cluster of municipalities around the city of Göteborg. A possible explanation for this tight clustering is the formal creation of a metropolitan region. The formal association is called the Göteborg Region Association of Local Authorities, and the member municipalities are Ale, Alingsås, Göteborg, Härryda, Kungsbacka, Kungälv, Lerum, Lilla Edet, Mölndal, Partille, Stenungsund, Tjörn, and Öckerö. All these belong to the distinctive subregion visually detected in Fig. 15.2.

The West Sweden region (Västra Götalandsregionen) that includes the Göteborg Region Association of Local Authorities has been studied in prior research. Gren (2002) notes that this is one of the best organized regions in Sweden, partly through

---

[6]The E-I index for all the municipalities using this clustering was −.271 (the expected E-I index was .893, significant at <.05).

15 Learning Networks Among Swedish Municipalities: Is Sweden a Small World?

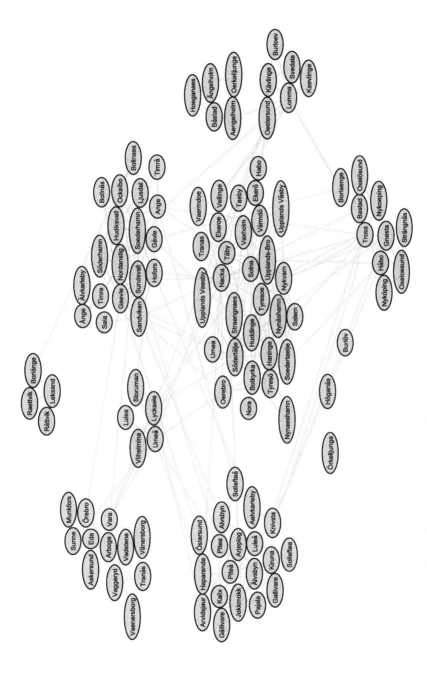

Fig. 15.1 Northern Coast-Stockholm region (Design by authors)

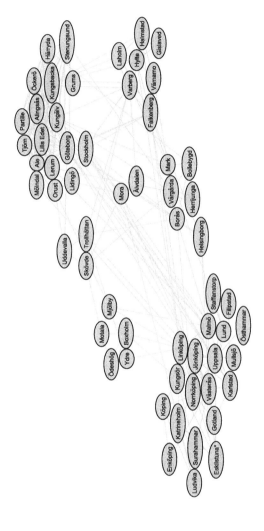

Fig. 15.2 Southern East–west region (Design by authors)

support from the European Union. Lidström (2011) found that citizens in the municipal regions of Göteborg (13 municipalities) and Umeå (6 municipalities) adopted more of a city-regionalist attitude (emphasizing the importance of intermunicipal coordination on a regional basis), as opposed to a localist attitude (strong municipal autonomy). The findings of Gren (2002) and Lidström (2011) suggest explanations for the existence of this subregion in the learning network.

A Small World?

The previous analysis has shown that learning networks in Sweden are to a large extent structured by county. However, we want to know more about whether the municipalities are efficiently integrated on a national scale. The literature on small-world networks suggests that networks might be well connected despite highly localizing tendencies (Watts, 1999; Uzzi, Amaral, & Reed-Tsochas, 2007). Small-world networks are more cosmopolitan than expected because of the connections that occur among local clusters. If Swedish municipalities compose a small world, knowledge, ideas, and best practices might be diffused widely and rapidly despite the localism of learning networks.

A small-world network is defined as a graph with high clustering but low path length.[7] A random graph typically has low clustering but also short average path lengths. A highly clustered network, by contrast, generally has high path lengths. A small-world network is a network with higher clustering than a random graph but with similar path lengths. A key feature of a small-world network is that despite the high clustering, which is expected to impede communication across the network, links between clusters can greatly shorten the path lengths and hence facilitate more rapid and cosmopolitan communication. In small worlds, path lengths are often reduced through the influence of highly connected hubs that link different clusters together. Well-connected hubs are not a necessary feature of small worlds, but it is reasonable to expect them to be important in networks with high local clustering. A number of scholars have pointed to the potential for small-world networks to diffuse knowledge and enhance innovation. Cowan and Jonard (2004), for example, simulated knowledge diffusion in innovation networks and found that diffusion in small-world networks produces higher knowledge levels (in the network as a whole) than either a more local network or a random network.

Two measures have been used to identify whether a network exhibits small-world properties: a clustering coefficient (as defined by Watts, 1999; labeled *cc* for

---

[7] *Clustering* refers to the density of interconnections in each social network actor's local *neighborhood*—the set of other actors with whom the focal actor is directly connected. The overall clustering of a network is the mean clustering across all the actors in the network. *Path length* is the mean number of steps it takes each actor in the network to reach every other actor in the network when taking the shortest path.

Table 15.3 Clustering and average path length in municipal learning networks in Sweden

	Sweden	Random
Clustering (cc)	0.293	0.025
Length (L)	5.080	3.215

clustering coefficient) and a measure of average path length (labeled L).[8] These measures are then compared to a random graph of the same size and density (an Erdos-Renyi random graph). Table 15.3 shows the basic measures in the Swedish case.

In comparing the results in Table 15.3, we see that the Swedish local learning network is much more clustered than the random graph, but the path lengths are also longer. We can take this a step farther by estimating the small-world quotient (Q), which is given by Eq. [15.1]:

$$Q = \frac{cc_{Sweden}}{cc_{Random}} / \frac{L_{Sweden}}{L_{random}} \quad (15.1)$$

A small world is usually defined as having a quotient greater than 1. In this case, the result is: $11.72 / 1.58 = 7.44$. So by this standard, the learning network of Swedish municipalities is indeed a small world, though the path lengths are a little high. The higher path lengths might indicate there are fewer hubs in the Swedish network than in an ideal small world.

Learning Hubs

As noted above, hubs are important in small-world networks because their more cosmopolitan ties allow information to widely and rapidly diffuse. Amin and Cohendet (1999) claim that nonlocal networks are particularly crucial for path-breaking innovation, whereas local networking results in more incremental innovation. Thus, hubs are expected to fulfill a crucial role in the diffusion of innovations

---

[8] The clustering coefficient (cc) is measured using the clustering coefficient algorithm in UCINET VI (there are various versions of cc; UCINET uses Watts's version; see, Watts, 1999). The algorithm produces both a weighted and an unweighted coefficient. The unweighted coefficient was used here. (There is a discussion in the literature about the tradeoffs between the two. But it does not make too much difference in this case because the results are similar. The weighted cc is slightly lower than the unweighted cc for the Swedish network; for the random network, weighted and unweighted cc's are the same). Path length is measured using the geodesic distance algorithm in UCINET VI, which produces a matrix of shortest path lengths between nodes. UCINET VI's univariate statistics algorithm then calculates mean path length. To produce the Erdos-Renyi random graph, the random graph algorithm in UCINET VI (subcommand Erdos-Renyi) is used, specifying that the graph should be same size and density as the Swedish network—290-x290; .0237 density).

Table 15.4 Correlation between Hub measures

	Hub A	Hub B	Hub C
Hub A	1.00		
Hub B	.56	1.00	
Hub C	.78	.43	1.00

among the clusters. Accordingly, identifying the hubs and finding out what characterizes these municipalities is important.

We devised three ways to measure the extent to which each municipality can be characterized as a learning hub. Based on our view that hubs are transit points for learning, hubs should not only be learned from, but they must also learn from others. They should stand out from other municipalities in this respect. Our first measure is based on degree centrality, which captures the local connectedness of a municipality. By multiplying together how many other municipalities reported learning from a municipality (*indegree*) by how many others that municipality learned from (*outdegree*), we get a simple variable capturing the extent to which a municipality takes on the role as a transit point in the Swedish municipal learning network (Hub A).

One problem with this measure is that it does not take indirect ties into account. Potentially, a municipality can have high indegree and high outdegree without being that well connected to distant (in network terms) municipalities. Another approach is therefore to use the concept of *closeness centrality* developed by Valente and Foreman (1998). Valente and Foreman distinguish two measures, integration and radiality. Integration is a measure of how closely other actors in the network are connected to you via a chain of contacts; a municipality is more integrated if other municipalities must take fewer steps (path lengths) to reach you. Radiality is a measure of how well you are connected outwards to others—that is, how easily you can reach others through direct or indirect networks. These measures go beyond a local measure of degree centrality by incorporating the indirect links to the entire network.[9] By multiplying integration and radiality we get a second hub measure (Hub B).

A third possible measure (Hub C) is *betweenness centrality* (Freeman, 1977), that is, the number of times a municipality sits on the shortest possible path between all other municipalities in the network. Actors with high betweenness scores may perform brokering roles by connecting otherwise disconnected actors and clusters.

Table 15.4 shows positive correlation coefficients between the three hub measures. The correlations are not exceptionally strong, which suggests that they capture somewhat different dimensions of what it means to be a hub. Beyond suggestive interpretations, theoretical arguments for why one of these hub measures might be

---

[9] The Valente-Foreman measures use the reverse of the average distances between nodes. The reversed distance is the diameter minus the geodesic distance. The diameter is the longest path between any two points, whereas the geodesic distance is the shortest path. Basically, they reverse the distance measure, turning it into a closeness measure.

better than the others are not well articulated in the small-world literature. We therefore approach hub identification ecumenically by looking for municipalities that score well on all three measures.

To get a sense of how well hubs are spread out geographically, Fig. 15.3 depicts the percentage of municipalities over the 75th percentile on each hub measure within each county. The pattern is quite robust to the selection of measure, although there is some obvious variation. Västra Götland and Halland, two neighboring counties in western Sweden, have a substantially larger share of cosmopolitan municipalities than other counties. At the other extreme, we find Gotland and Kronoberg. In most other counties, around 10–30 % of the municipalities have a clear transit point character. Overall, the impression is that the hubs are fairly evenly distributed geographically, but that some counties depart from this general pattern.

Above, in Fig. 15.2, we discovered a tight network in western Sweden consisting of the members of the Göteborg Region Association of Local Authorities. Many of the municipalities belonging to this association also score high on the three hub measures. If we once again use the 75th percentile to separate out more cosmopolitan cities, 54 % of the Associations' members are hubs if we focus on the most basic hub measure (Hub A). Using the other two hub measures yields 85 % (Hub B) and 31 % (Hub C), respectively.[10] At first glance, at least, this region has done an impressive job of promoting regional cooperation and diffusion of information. However, it is of course also possible that the association was formed around municipalities already having a lot of cooperation. If this is true, the causality runs in the opposite direction.

In order to find out more about what characterizes hubs as transit points, we explore the correlation between the three hub measures introduced above and various municipal characteristics. A first idea is that county seats and larger or more urban municipalities could be important. Such cities might function as regional centers where large companies, authorities, universities, and other organizations are located and where infrastructure is more developed. These features might increase the probability that knowledge diffuses through such municipalities. A second idea is that healthy fiscal conditions or a favorable economic climate might characterize the transit points. Cities like this are perhaps more innovative and outward-looking. Lastly, features of the local population could be important—perhaps transit points have a younger and more educated population?

Table 15.5 provides descriptive statistics of the variables of interest. Log population, inhabitants/km^2 and whether the municipality is a county seat or not are the variables designed to capture the importance of being a large and urban area. Economic climate and fiscal conditions are measured by the unemployment rate and the tax base (in Swedish crowns per inhabitant). Mean age in years and the percentage of the population having a college degree are assumed to capture potentially important citizen characteristics. Table 15.5 displays large variation in all variables. To find out which factors are correlated with high scores on the

---

[10] If hubs were randomly distributed, we would have expected 25 % of the hubs in the Göteborg Region Association of Local Authorities to be hubs.

15 Learning Networks Among Swedish Municipalities: Is Sweden a Small World?

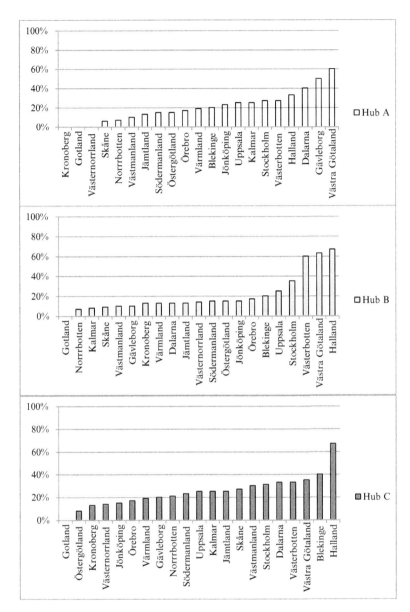

Fig. 15.3 Share of municipalities scoring high (>75th percentile) on hub measures, by county (Design by authors)

three hub measures, OLS regression is employed. Table 15.6 summarizes the results of this explorative exercise.

A robust and statistically significant finding (at the .05 level) is that county seats (the municipality where the county government resides) are more often learning hubs. This finding applies regardless of which hub measure is employed. County seats score, on average, 0.15–0.22 of a standard deviation higher on the hub indices

Table 15.5 Descriptive statistics: Swedish municipalities

	Mean	Min	Max
Hub A (indegree × outdegree)	45.3	0.0	280.0
Hub B (integration × radiality)	49.9	0.0	70.4
Hub C (betweenness centrality)	907.5	0.0	11133.4
Log population (number of inhabitants)	2.9	0.9	6.7
Inhabitants/km^2	135.0	0.2	4410.4
County seat (1 = Yes; 0 = No)	0.1	0	1
Unemployment rate (percent)	6.3	1.8	13.8
Tax base (SEK/citizen)	155,642.1	125,829.0	300,491.0
Population characteristics			
Mean age (in years)	42.8	36.3	48.5
College degree (percent of population)	13.0	6.6	43.8

than other municipalities. Moreover, there is some indication that population size and a young population are positively correlated with being a learning hub. However, these findings are sensitive to the choice of hub measure. For instance, population size is not related to *closeness centrality* (Hub B) and average age of the municipal citizen is basically not related to *betweenness centrality* (Hub C). The other background variables included in the analysis do not correlate with the hub measures.

The main conclusion from Table 15.6 is that county seats are important. One way to further investigate this is to examine the E-I index for county seats (using the Girvan-Newman clusters as partitions). Table 15.7 shows the results. The mean E-I index for all municipalities is −.345, indicating that the ties of most municipalities are local (e.g., within county). By contrast, the average E-I index for county seats is .130. This means that in contrast with the localism of most municipalities, county seats have on balance more external than internal ties. However, there is also variation among the county seats. For example, the municipalities of Nyköping and Falun are quite insular, whereas Malmö, Visby, and Örebro are quite cosmopolitan.

Taken together, the evidence clearly suggests that county seats are acting as hubs in the learning network of Swedish municipalities. This conclusion is reinforced by looking at the network connecting county seats (Fig. 15.4; note that the figure roughly organizes the county seats geographically). Nyköping and Falun are isolates, but the rest of the county seats are linked together.

Conclusion

The purpose of this analysis was to better understand how a global learning network emerges from the local learning choices of autonomous Swedish municipalities. We found that the county is a basic structuring property of the global network. Municipalities learn from their near neighbors, especially from neighbors in the

Table 15.6 What characterizes cosmopolitan municipalities?

	Hub A		Hub B		Hub C	
	Unstandardized coefficients	Standardized coefficients	Unstandardized coefficients	Standardized coefficients	Unstandardized coefficients	Standardized coefficients
Log population	10.2889**	0.21**	−0.4154	−0.02	452.9517**	0.29**
	(4.4301)		(1.6692)		(197.7984)	
Inhabitants/km^2	−0.0025	−0.03	0.0012	0.03	−0.0048	−0.01
	(0.0066)		(0.0015)		(0.2537)	
County seat	28.5011**	0.16**	9.3094***	0.15***	1252.4590**	0.22**
	(12.4988)		(3.2782)		(577.8630)	
Unemployment rate	−1.1010	−0.05	−0.2249	−0.03	11.3899	0.02
	(1.9823)		(0.8029)		(47.0081)	
Tax base	−0.0002	−0.10	−0.0000	−0.09	−0.0012	−0.02
	(0.0003)		(0.0001)		(0.0067)	
Mean age	−2.8083*	−0.16*	−1.6788***	−0.26***	−47.7297	−0.08
	(1.5429)		(0.6379)		(0.0067)	
College degree	0.5640	0.07	0.1766	0.06	1.5119	0.01
	(0.9812)		(0.6379)		(28.5191)	
Constant	157.7529**		124.2963***		952.6489	
	(78.5295)		(31.9230)		(2267.613)	
N	290		290		290	
Adj. R^2	0.23		0.24		0.27	

Note: The table reports unstandardized regression coefficients and robust standard errors (in parentheses), as well as standardized regression coefficients, using OLS regression analysis. Three different outcome measures are used: Hub A, Hub B and Hub C. All models include county fixed effects. * <.10; ** <.05; *** <.01

Table 15.7 Internal vs. External learning in county seats

County Seat	County	E-I index
Stockholm	Stockholm	.273
Uppsala	Uppsala	.294
Nyköping	Södermanland	−1.00
Linköping	Östergötland	.217
Jonköping	Jönköping	.429
Växjö	Kronoberg	−.077
Kalmar	Kalmar	−.222
Visby	Gotland	.555
Karlskrona	Blekinge	.400
Malmö	Skåne	.579
Halmstad	Halland	.333
Göteborg	Västra Götaland	−.043
Karlstad	Värmland	.176
Örebro	Örebro	.500
Västerås	Västmanland	.355
Falun	Dalarna	−.833
Gävle	Gävleborg	.048
Härnösand	Västernorrland	.167
Östersund	Jämtland	.333
Umeå	Västerbotten	.259
Luleå	Norrbotten	.000
Averages		
All municipalities		−.345
County seats		.130

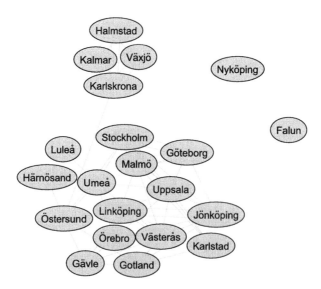

Fig. 15.4 The network of county seats (Design by authors)

same county. Informal personal connections seem to be the main channel through which municipalities learn from one another.

The high degree of clustering in the municipal learning networks prompted us to examine whether the global network met the criteria for a small-world network, and we have shown that it does. This is important because it suggests that ideas, knowledge, and best practices may diffuse through the network of Swedish municipalities despite the relatively parochial learning patterns of many municipalities. One possible mechanism of integration might be regional agglomeration of networks. Using Markov clustering, we found two very large regions in the global network—a northern coast-Stockholm region and a southern east–west region. These regions extend the pattern of local clustering to the regional level and may be an important basis for nonparochial learning.

Another important mechanism for national integration of municipal learning networks is the role of important network hubs—key transit points in the flow of knowledge. We found that the county seats play this transit-point role for knowledge diffusion. County seats are comparatively well networked outside the county and most of the county seats are linked to one another on a national basis. Hence, although the high clustering of a small-world network is explained by geographic proximity and county, the global integration of this small world works through county seats to a substantial extent. Using county seats as transit points in order to spread best practices more rapidly might therefore be a promising avenue to improve policies.

Interviews suggested that municipalities were quite aware that they learned from geographically proximate neighbors, especially from municipalities within their own county. There may be several reasons why learning is structured this way. Spatially proximate governments often share certain policy-relevant problems, conditions and experiences (Karch, 2007). It is also probably easier to develop a closer relationship with neighboring municipalities; the costs of searching for information from these governments might be lower than looking for information elsewhere (Lundin et al., 2015). Anecdotal evidence from our interviews indicates that municipal bureaucrats tend to circulate between positions in municipalities within counties. This could make it easier to establish the necessary personal connections that, according to our findings, are so important for intermunicipal learning.

There are also other potential explanations for the distinct county pattern that emerges in our analysis. A first possibility is that the role of counties reflects a deep historical legacy. The counties are very close to the old Swedish provinces, whose history reaches back to the seventeenth century. These provinces had a fair degree of political and cultural autonomy and this historical legacy may have structured long-term patterns of intermunicipal interaction. Moreover, in each county, there is a national government authority (Länstyrelsen) acting as a representative of national government to help align local and national policy. Länstyrelsen are also charged with promoting cooperation and working in the interest of the municipalities within the county. This role presumably requires them to work closely with the municipalities in the county. The tendency of municipalities to learn from other municipalities in the same county might be a reflection of the Länstyrelsen's coordinating role.

Our findings suggest that learning networks are likely to aggregate according to a set of factors that systematically shape learning choices. In the Swedish case, these factors include geographical proximity, personal social relations, urban and regional economic and demographic structure, and political-administrative institutions. Although the important role of geographical proximity and county government are not entirely surprising, we have shown that such factors produce clear global patterns of learning—the small world of Swedish municipalities. This global learning pattern is likely to have important consequences for how knowledge, ideas, and best practices spread to and among Swedish municipalities.

References

Agranoff, R. (2006). Inside collaborative networks: Ten lessons for public managers. *Public Administration Review, 66,* 56–65. doi:10.1111/j.1540-6210.2006.00666.x

Amin, A., & Cohendet, P. (1999). Learning and adaptation in decentralized business networks. *Society and Space, 17,* 87–104. doi:10.1068/d170087

Arundel, A., & Hollanders, H. (2011). *A taxonomy of innovation: How do public sector agencies innovate?* INNO Metrics 2011–2012 report, Brussels, Belgium: European Commission, DG Enterprise. Retrieved June 28, 2015, from http://ec.europa.eu/enterprise/policies/innovation/files/psi-studies/taxonomy-of-innovation-how_en.pdf

Bäck, H. (2005). Borgmästarens makt [The power of mayors]. *Kommunal ekonomi och politik, 9,* 7–36. Retrieved May 15, 2015, from http://hdl.handle.net/2077/20675

Bathelt, H., Malmberg, A., & Maskell, P. (2004). Clusters and knowledge: Local buzz, global pipelines and the process of knowledge creation. *Progress in Human Geography, 28,* 31–56. doi:10.1191/0309132504ph469oa

Bell, G. G., & Zaheer, A. (2007). Geography, networks, and knowledge flow. *Organization Science, 18,* 955–972. doi:10.1287/orsc.1070.0308

Betsill, M. M., & Bulkeley, H. (2004). Transnational networks and global environmental governance: The cities for climate protection program. *International Studies Quarterly, 48,* 471–493. doi:10.1111/j.0020-8833.2004.00310.x

Boschma, R. (2005). Proximity and innovation: A critical assessment. *Regional studies, 39,* 61–74. doi:10.1080/0034340052000320887

Cao, X. (2010). Networks as channels of policy diffusion: Explaining worldwide changes in capital taxation, 1998–2006. *International Studies Quarterly, 54,* 823–854. doi:10.1111/j.1468-2478.2010.00611.x

Cooke, P., & Morgan, K. (1993). The network paradigm: New departures in corporate and regional development. *Environment and Planning D, 11,* 543–564. doi:10.1068/d110543

Cowan, R., & Jonard, N. (2004). Network structure and the diffusion of knowledge. *Journal of Economic Dynamics and Control, 28,* 1557–1575. doi:10.1016/j.jedc.2003.04.002

Davis, G. F. (1991). Agents without principles? The spread of the poison pill through the intercorporate network. *Administrative Science Quarterly, 36,* 583–613. doi:10.2307/2393275

Fleming, L., King, C., & Juda, A. I. (2007). Small worlds and regional innovation. *Organization Science, 18,* 938–954. doi:10.1287/orsc.1070.0289

Freeman, L. C. (1977). A set of measures of centrality based on betweenness. *Sociometry, 40,* 35–41. doi:10.2307/3033543

Freeman, R. (2008). Learning in public policy. In R. E. Goodin, M. Moran, & M. Rein (Eds.), *The Oxford Handbook of Public Policy* (pp. 367–388). Oxford: University Press. doi:10.1093/oxfordhb/9780199548453.003.0017

Girvan, M., & Newman, M. E. J. (2002). Community structure in social and biological networks. *Proceedings of the National Academy of Sciences, 99*, 7821–7826. doi:10.1073/pnas.122653799

Glückler, J. (2013). Knowledge, networks and space: Connectivity and the problem of non-interactive learning. *Regional Studies, 47*, 880–894. doi:10.1080/00343404.2013.779659

Goldsmith, S., & Eggers, W. D. (2004). *Governing by network: The new shape of the public sector.* Washington: Brookings Institution Press.

Granovetter, M. S. (1973). The strength of weak ties. *American Journal of Sociology, 78*, 1360–1380.

Gray, V. (1973). Innovation in the states: A diffusion study. *The American Political Science Review, 67*, 1174–1185. doi:10.2307/1956539

Gren, J. (2002). New regionalism and West Sweden: The factors of change in the regionalism paradigm. *Regional & Federal Studies, 12*, 79–101. doi:10.1080/714004766

Hedström, P., Sandell, R., & Stern, C. (2000). Mesolevel networks and the diffusion of social movements: The case of the Swedish social democratic party. *American Journal of Sociology, 106*, 145–172.

Jacobs, J. M. (2012). Urban geographies I: Still thinking cities relationally. *Progress in Human Geography, 36*, 412–422. doi:10.1177/0309132511421715

Karch, A. (2007). Emerging issues and future directions in state policy diffusion research. *State Politics and Policy Quarterly, 7*, 54–80. doi:10.1177/153244000700700104

Kraatz, M. S. (1998). Learning by association? Interorganizational networks and adaptation to environmental change. *Academy of Management Journal, 41*, 621–643. doi:10.2307/256961

Krause, R. M. (2011). Policy innovation, intergovernmental relations, and the adoption of climate protection initiatives by US cities. *Journal of Urban Affairs, 33*, 45–60. doi:10.1111/j.1467-9906.2010.00510.x

Lee, C. K., & Strang, D. (2006). The international diffusion of public-sector downsizing: Network emulation and theory-driven learning. *International Organization, 60*, 883–909. doi:10.1017/S0020818306060292

Lee, T., & Van De Meene, S. (2012). Who teaches and who learns? Policy learning through the C40 cities climate network. *Policy Sciences, 45*, 199–220. doi:10.1007/s11077-112-9159-5

Lidström, A. (2011, November). The limits of rational choice: Localism and city-regionalism in two Swedish city-regions. Paper prepared for XX Nordiska kommunforskarkonferensen, Göteborg. Retrieved May 27, 2015, from http://www.pol.gu.se/digitalAssets/1350/1350051_the-limits-of-rational-choice-anders-lidstr--m.pdf

Lundin, M., Öberg, P., & Josefsson, C. (2015). Learning from Success: When Can Local Government Serve as a Role Model to Others? *Public Administration*, 93 (3), 733–752.

Marsden, G., Frick, K. T., May, A. D., & Deakin, E. (2011). How do cities approach policy innovation and policy learning? A study of 30 policies in Northern Europe and North America. *Transport Policy, 18*, 501–512. doi:10.1016/j.tranpol.2010.10.006

Maskell, P. (2014). Accessing remote knowledge—the roles of trade fairs, pipelines, crowdsourcing and listening posts. *Journal of Economic Geography, 14*, 883–902. doi:10.1093/jeg/lbu002

McCann, E. (2011). Urban policy mobilities and global circuits of knowledge: Toward a research agenda. *Annals of the Association of American Geographers, 101*, 107–130. doi:10.1080/00045608.2010.520219

Meseguer, C. (2005). Policy learning, policy diffusion, and the making of a new order. *Annals of the American Academy of Political and Social Science, 598*, 67–82. doi:10.1177/0002716204272372

Mintrom, M., & Vergari, S. (1998). Policy networks and innovation diffusion: The case of state education reforms. *The Journal of Politics, 60*, 126–148. doi:10.2307/2648004

Owen-Smith, J., & Powell, W. W. (2004). Knowledge networks as channels and conduits: The effects of spillovers in the Boston biotechnology community. *Organization Science, 15*, 5–21. doi:10.1287/orsc.1030.0054

Powell, W. W., Koput, K. W., & Smith-Doerr, L. (1996). Interorganizational collaboration and the locus of innovation: Networks of learning in biotechnology. *Administrative Science Quarterly, 41*, 116–145. doi:10.2307/2393988

Saxenian, A. (1996). *Regional advantage: Culture and competition in Silicon Valley and Route 128*. Cambridge, MA: Harvard University Press.

Sellers, J. M., & Lidström. A. (2007). Decentralization, local government, and the welfare state. *Governance, 20,* 609–632. doi:10.1111/j.1468-0491.2007.00374.x

Shipan, C. R., & Volden, C. (2012). Policy diffusion: Seven lessons for scholars and practitioners. *Public Administration Review, 72,* 788–796. doi:10.1111/j.1540-6210.2012.02610.x

Slaughter, A. M. (2009). *A new world order* (2nd ed.). Princeton: University Press. (Original work published 2004)

Stone, D. (2004). Transfer agents and global networks in the "transnationalization" of policy. *Journal of European Public Policy, 11,* 545–566. doi:10.1080/13501760410001694291

Sveriges Kommuner och Landting (2014, March 28). Swedish Association of Local Authorities and Regions. Retrieved March 28, 2014, from http://english.skl.se/municipalities_county_councils_and_regions

Trydegård, G.-B., & Thorslund, M. (2010). One uniform welfare state or a multitude of welfare municipalities? The evolution of local variation in Swedish elder care. *Social Policy & Administration, 44,* 495–511. doi:10.1111/j.1467-9515.2010.00725.x

Uzzi, B., Amaral, L. A., & Reed-Tsochas, F. (2007). Small-world networks and management science research: A review. *European Management Review, 4,* 77–91. doi:10.1057/palgrave.emr.1500078

Valente, T. W., & Foreman, R. K. (1998). Integration and radiality: Measuring the extent of an individual's connectedness and reachability in a network. *Social Networks, 20,* 89–105. doi:10.1016/S0378-8733(97)00007-5

van Dongen, S. (2008). Graph clustering via a discrete uncoupling process. *SIAM Journal on Matrix Analysis and Applications, 30,* 121–141. doi:10.1137/040608635

Volden, C. (2006). States as policy laboratories: Emulating success in the children's health insurance program. *American Journal of Political Science, 50,* 294–312. doi:10.1111/j.1540-5907.2006.00185.x

Watts, D. J. (1999). *Small worlds: The dynamics of networks between order and randomness*. Princeton: University Press.

Open Access This chapter is distributed under the terms of the Creative Commons Attribution 4.0 International License (http://creativecommons.org/licenses/by/4.0/), which permits use, duplication, adaptation, distribution and reproduction in any medium or format, as long as you give appropriate credit to the original author(s) and the source, provide a link to the Creative Commons license and indicate if changes were made.

The images or other third party material in this chapter are included in the work's Creative Commons license, unless indicated otherwise in the credit line; if such material is not included in the work's Creative Commons license and the respective action is not permitted by statutory regulation, users will need to obtain permission from the license holder to duplicate, adapt or reproduce the material.

Chapter 16
The Coevolution of Innovative Ties, Proximity, and Competencies: Toward a Dynamic Approach to Innovation Cooperation

Uwe Cantner, Susanne Hinzmann, and Tina Wolf

The growing complexity and shortening of cycles inherent in the innovation process have changed the industrial and technological environment in which firms operate. The associated increase in uncertainty and costs accompanying R&D projects has shaped a landscape that favors collaboration (Hagedoorn, 2002). Especially in high-tech industries, where knowledge creation and accumulation is a crucial input factor and competition has become a learning race, joint research has steadily grown since the 1980s (Mowery, Oxley, & Silverman, 1996; Powell, 1998).

A basic feature of joint research is the exchange and sharing of knowledge among the cooperation partners. Actors choose research cooperation in the expectation that it will maximize their potential gain in knowledge. In this context several scholars have stressed the importance that similarity between cooperation partners has for knowledge transfer and successful collaboration. Similarity determines with whom one connects, for it creates trust, facilitates knowledge flows, and increases the mutual attractiveness of potential collaboration partners (Boschma, 2005; McPherson, Smith-Lovin, & Cook, 2001). Similarity or proximity in three dimensions—cognitive, social, and competence-related—seems to play a cardinal role in knowledge exchange in collaborations intended to generate innovation.

These three dimensions are not simply exogenously given and static; they develop in the course of the partners' collaboration. Continued collaboration eventually leads trust, experience, and common understanding to increase and knowledge differences to decrease. These dynamics are expected to determine whether the

---

U. Cantner • S. Hinzmann • T. Wolf (✉)
Department of Economics, Friedrich Schiller University Jena, Carl-Zeiss-Straße 3, 07743 Jena, Germany
e-mail: uwe.cantner@uni-jena.de; susanne.hinzmann@uni-jena.de; tina.wolf@uni-jena.de

same partners always cooperate or whether they switch partners over time. Increasing trust, experience, and common understanding tend to contribute to the continuation of the partnership because they increase the efficiency of knowledge exchange and sharing. Conversely, the declining difference between knowledge stocks of continuously cooperating partners—that is, an increase in their cognitive proximity (the degree of similarity of their knowledge bases)—indicates that opportunities to exchange and share knowledge have been exploited by them and should therefore lead to partner-switching.

Hence, the relation between certain proximity dimensions and continuation of collaboration is by no means unidirectional (Ter Wal & Boschma, 2011). In fact, individual characteristics (e.g., technological capabilities), and thus the proximity to others, coevolve with continuous collaboration (Balland, Boschma, & Frenken, 2015; Ter Wal & Boschma, 2011). These dynamics have undergone little empirical analysis (Balland et al., 2015). Although the coevolution of factors driving collaboration choice and the evolution of ties can be explored only with a dynamic approach, most of the studies on the relation between proximity and cooperation have been rather static (e.g., Cantner & Meder, 2007; Paier & Scherngell, 2011; Wuyts et al., 2005).

In this chapter we want to contribute to the field of dynamic approaches and analyze the interplay between cognitive proximity, knowledge exchange, and collaboration. We focus our analysis on ties within innovator networks defined as an ensemble of direct and indirect connections, with the direct ones being research collaborations intended to produce innovations (Cantner & Graf, 2006). Tracking the individual actors and their collaborations over time, we pursue the following core research question: To what extent do knowledge dynamics between two cooperating actors determine the continuation of their innovative ties? Accordingly, we concentrate mainly on the dynamics of partners' cognitive proximity. In addition, we analyze the other two dimensions, trust and competencies, as further important covariates.

Our descriptive analysis suggests that firms are generally prone to switching their cooperation partner rather than to repeating the collaboration with that partner. We thus find that the knowledge transfer and cooperation that partners have experienced with each other have no significant effect on the likelihood that they will repeat their cooperation. Our empirical analysis also shows that cooperation is promoted by several factors: an overlap between the firms' knowledge bases, an uneven distribution of the reciprocal potential for knowledge exchange, general collaboration experience of the partners, and similarity in the degree of popularity of the collaboration partners. We also find that firms prefer to cooperate with partners that are different in organizational nature and age.

We begin by providing a general overview of basic concepts and principle arguments that describe the relation between similarity in knowledge, experience, and their effect on tie formation. After characterizing how these relations dynamically coevolve with ongoing collaboration, we present our hypotheses. In the second section we explain our methodological approach, including descriptions of the data and variables. The third section presents the final results and our discussion of them. We conclude with suggestions for further research.

Knowledge Dynamics and the Evolution of Innovation Linkages

The Role of Cognitive Proximity, Social Proximity, and Similarity in Competencies in the Formation of Innovative Ties

The increased orientation to collaboration, especially in research and development (R&D), has led to an upsurge of studies analyzing the advantages and incentives that are encouraging the trend toward the formation of alliances (e.g., Ahuja, 2000; Gilsing, Nooteboom, Vanhaverbeke, Duysters, & van den Oord, 2008; Gulati, 1999; Hagedoorn, 2002; Hamel, 1991; Khanna, Gulati, & Nohria, 1998; Mowery et al., 1996; Powell, 1998). Essentially, most alliances are prompted by concerns about access to external resources that are too costly to be acquired internally (Kogut, Shan, & Walker, 1992). In innovation-oriented alliances the access to a partner's technology and knowledge-related resources—be they a particular technical infrastructure or, more important, technological capabilities and complementary skills—is the primary motive for joint research, besides the sharing of risks and R&D costs (Hagedoorn, 2002). Firms, especially those in high-tech industries, are unable to generate internally all the resources they need in order to survive the rapid pace of technological change (Powell & Grodal, 2006). According to the knowledge-based view of the firm (which draws on the resource-based view of the firm originally proposed by Penrose, 1959), a firm's knowledge base, understood as a unique resource difficult to imitate, is a key competitive advantage (Grant & Baden-Fuller, 1995). In this regard firms can be seen as bundles of competencies (Hamel, 1991, p. 83) that they have accumulated throughout their lifespan. Because environments and solutions to problems differ between firms, knowledge gathered by firms is an idiosyncratic property and quite heterogeneous among them (Cantner & Graf, 2011). Even firms operating in the same industry or market differ in what they know and what they are able to accomplish with their competencies. Although this proprietary knowledge resource affords a basis for opportunities, its exploitation within the firm's boundaries is limited and leads mostly to incremental, not necessarily optimal, improvements (Ahuja, 2000; March, 1991; Yang, Phelps, & Steensma, 2010). To broaden the knowledge base and explore new possibilities for recombination and radical innovations, firms depend on external sources of knowledge (March, 1991; Yang et al., 2010). In looking for solutions to complex problems, successful innovators extend their search to the environment beyond their own boundaries (Freeman, 1991). The generation of knowledge and innovation thus results progressively from a collective learning process among various actors interacting formally or informally (Asheim & Gertler, 2005).

In innovation-oriented alliances rational actors choose their potential interaction partners according to the highest expected outcome in terms of successful knowledge exchange and potential innovations. The efficacy of knowledge exchange between two or more actors is governed by the degree of heterogeneity between them. The proximity approach, proposed originally by Boschma (2005), emphasizes that similarity (conceptually the inverse of heterogeneity)—or, as he calls it, proximity—affects the ease of knowledge transfer between actors. He thereby differentiates between various dimensions of proximity whose prominence can differ from one type of alliance to another. In R&D alliances explicitly conceived to generate novel ideas and innovations, cognitive proximity might predominate over other forms of proximity as the basis for potential knowledge flows, and social proximity (also called the strength of social ties between collaborators) might take precedence as the control mechanism for knowledge flows.

Understood as the similarity of knowledge bases, cognitive proximity can determine the degree of knowledge exchange between actors through two central characteristics representing a trade-off in collective learning: mutual understanding and learning potential. Mutual understanding is the degree to which different actors comprehend each other, and it increases with cognitive proximity. Potential partners therefore need to exhibit some minimum degree of cognitive proximity to warrant mutual understanding.[1] Learning potential has to do with the amount of what can be mutually learned, and it decreases with cognitive proximity. The heterogeneity of firms in knowledge space is a source of learning effects because relatively great dissimilarity can increase learning potential and the exchange of knowledge (Nooteboom, 2005).

The idea of combining the two dimensions of cognitive proximity—that of being a condition for mutual understanding and that of being a source of knowledge exchange—suggests the existence of an intermediate degree of proximity at which beneficial exchange of knowledge is maximized (Boschma, 2005; Gilsing et al., 2008; Nooteboom, 1999). A deviation from this level will lead either to increased potential for exchanging knowledge combined with lowered common understanding or to increased common understanding combined with lowered potential for novelty. Consequently, an actor conducting a strategic and rational search for a research partner should, at least theoretically, try to connect with a candidate who is similar in knowledge stocks and who partly complements his or her own so as to acquire the potential for creating novelty.

Besides the relevance of an optimal degree of cognitive proximity for understanding and learning, the second condition for effective collaboration to take place is the controllability of the knowledge-exchange-and-sharing relation. It is here that social proximity comes in. Social proximity accounts for familiarity and trust between cooperation partners, two facets that facilitate the transfer of tacit knowledge and reduce the occurrence of opportunistic behavior. Trust affects the efficiency of knowledge transfer, for familiar and trusting partners have internalized

---

[1] The concept of cognitive proximity is closely related to that of absorptive capacity (the ability to assimilate external knowledge). Absorptive capacity is largely a function of the extent to which the knowledge bases of collaboration partners are related (Boschma, 2005; Cantner & Meder, 2007; Cohen & Levinthal, 1990). A lack of absorptive capacities tends to result in a sharing of knowledge rather than in its exchange, for the partners are not able to integrate the external knowledge into their own knowledge stock.

norms of communication and can therefore improve their control of undesired behavior such as free riding (Granovetter, 2005). Hence, the cooperation with trusted partners warrants increased reciprocity for their efforts. Frequently proposed mechanisms for developing social proximity include mobile inventors, who often maintain social relations with their former workplace; the existence of positive experience gained in previous collaboration; familiarity with each other before cooperation; and acquaintance through a common partner (Ter Wal & Boschma, 2009). A strategic and rational actor should therefore prefer to link up with actors who are already in his or her circle of acquaintances. In addition to cognitive and social proximity as means to develop social proximity, Boschma (2005) suggested geographic, organizational, and institutional proximity between partners to support learning and innovation. For successful R&D collaboration and the generation of innovations, we assume that social and cognitive proximity outweigh other dimensions of proximity because the creation of new ideas and the generation of innovation is a costly and uncertain process primarily determined by the knowledge involved (Mowery, Oxley, & Silverman, 1998). In focusing on the examination of learning dynamics in R&D collaborations, we concentrate our argumentation on these two relevant dimensions of proximity. The likelihood of collaboration increases with the social proximity and shows an inverted-U relationship with respect to the cognitive proximity of the potential partners.

Recent empirical findings underpin these arguments. Despite the differences in measuring the proximity dimensions, the positive effect of social proximity on the probability of collaboration has become stylized fact in most of the studies on bilateral collaboration and the factors explaining its establishment and the exchange of knowledge (Ahuja, 2000; Broekel & Boschma, 2012; Cantner & Meder, 2007; Criscuolo, Salter, & Ter Wal, 2010; Gulati, 1995, 1999; Gulati & Gargiulo, 1999; Mowery et al., 1998; Paier & Scherngell, 2011; Powell, 1998; Singh, 2005).

The results concerning *cognitive* proximity's effect on the probability of collaboration are less consistent, chiefly because it is difficult to find appropriate proxies and the divergence of applied measures. Paier and Scherngell (2011), Cantner and Meder (2007), and Singh (2005) found that knowledge proximity had a purely positive effect on tie formation, whereas Criscuolo et al. (2010), Mowery et al. (1998), and Wuyts, Colombo, Dutta, and Nooteboom (2005) gave evidence of the inverted-U relationship between cognitive proximity and the proclivity to cooperate or to share knowledge as originally proposed by Nooteboom (1999). Consistently, Gilsing et al. (2008) and Wuyts et al. (2005) observed an inverted U-shaped curve also for the relation between cognitive proximity and the innovative performance of R&D projects. By contrast, Broekel und Boschma (2012) observed what is called the proximity paradox in their analysis of link formation and link performance in the aviation industry: Although proximity seemed to guide the formation of new R&D alliances, cognitive proximity especially hindered the innovative performance of the observed links.

Scholars have likewise identified factors that go beyond the link-specific proximity as inducers of opportunities for actors to collaborate. Among them are economic factors (e.g., accumulated capabilities and resources) and the general embeddedness of a firm in its relevant environment (e.g., the industry, the region). Signaling competence to other actors in the network (Ahuja, 2000; Stuart, 2000), both aspects enhance the perceived attractiveness of actors as a potential collaboration partner. In general, firms relatively well endowed with resources, such as innovative capabilities (past innovation activity) or technical capital (technology stock), can exploit more opportunities to form links than less well-endowed firms can, for potential partners perceive them as more competent than other firms and as better able to offer more knowledge and relevant information (Ahuja, 2000). In turn, the number of connections that the firm already possesses—its embeddedness—favors new collaborations. In network studies the popularity of actors (or centrality as defined by their number of linkages with other partners) is highly contingent on the degree of their popularity in prior periods. This continually recurring phenomenon, often referred to as *preferential attachment* (Barabási & Albert, 1999, p. 510),[2] is attributable to two effects. First, highly connected actors have broader access to information about potential partners than less connected actors do (Gilsing et al., 2008). The more connections an actor has, the more information that actor automatically also has about the partners of his or her partners, and the more visible potential partners are. Second, potential partners perceive the central firm or actor as more attractive than other candidates because the information about the central actor diffuses more widely and quickly among a high number of potential partners than is the case with noncentral firms. Moreover, a high number of connections signals to potential partners a high level of competence and experience in managing and organizing alliances, a large repertoire of technical capabilities, and access to a broad and diverse knowledge pool (Ahuja, 2000; Gulati, 1999). Giuliani (2007), for instance, found that the most central actors in the knowledge network possess the most comprehensive knowledge base. The causal direction of this link is not clear, however.

Firms or actors do not have infinite capacity to establish new links. The returns on the creation of new links decrease with the total number of linkages because the costs of managing all the linkages increase as the information benefits decrease (Ahuja, 2000; Hagedoorn & Frankort, 2008). Besides, overembeddedness poses the risk of becoming locked in, of forfeiting access to novel and nonredundant information, and of thereby losing innovative potential (Gilsing et al., 2008; Uzzi, 1997). Corroborating this curvilinear relationship for the composition of linkages as well, Wuyts et al. (2005) found that the diversity of the collaboration portfolio positively influences innovativeness up to a certain optimal threshold. Actors whose popularity and opportunities are growing have to be increasingly selective in their partner choice (Ahuja, 2000).

In the context of mutual agreements on collaboration and the search for the optimal linkages out of a pool of potential partners, reciprocity becomes paramount. Firms or actors want a return on the effort and resources they invest in the collaboration. Reciprocity creates trust among the potential partners and makes collaboration

---

[2] *Preferential attachment* essentially refers to the tendency of a network's new entrants to be partial to connecting to central actors (Barabási & Albert, 1999).

more likely and sustainable (Cantner, Meder, & Wolf, 2011). Furthermore, the balance between partners' invested effort and reciprocated learning determines how well the alliance functions and how long it endures. Unilateral learning or an imbalance of resources might result in asymmetric bargaining power and dependency (Hamel, 1991; Khanna et al., 1998). Firms (actors) find that their attractiveness in terms of resources and efforts is reciprocated in collaborations with others similarly endowed. In sociological studies on the relations of individuals, the attractiveness of similarity has been termed *homophily* (McPherson et al., 2001; Rogers & Bhowmik, 1970). In the context of R&D collaborations, homophily might be driven by the search for reciprocity. If so, then actors similar in experience and competence will exhibit higher reciprocal potential than will dissimilar actors and will thus have mutual incentive to associate with each other (Cantner & Meder, 2007).

The Dynamics of Tie Formation

Although much work has been done to identify factors that lead to the formation of innovative alliances, little is known about the factors that determine the continuation[3] of these alliances (Dahlander & McFarland, 2013). Because comprehensive longitudinal data on collaboration is difficult to find, most studies on innovation networks have relied on static analyses. Conceptual frameworks, too, such as Boschma's proximity approach, are basically static in nature (Balland et al., 2015). In addition, the relation between the competence, proximity, and collaboration of a firm is characterized by strong interconnectedness. The embeddedness of firms also feeds back into the proximity to other actors, influencing their attractiveness as potential partners and future collaboration opportunities (Balland et al., 2015). The proximity of the partners changes throughout their bilateral collaboration as well, a shift that has consequences for its continuation. Both the underexplored coevolution of these factors and the evidence of the paradoxical effects of proximity and embeddedness make it unclear whether collaboration alliances are finite (develop toward a specific date of expiration) and whether one can use an alliance's continuation or termination to indicate an R&D alliance's success. These coevolutionary processes can be captured only by dynamic approaches.

Advances in this direction have been recently made mainly in the research on networks by scholars such as Balland, de Vaan, & Boschma (2013), Broekel (2015), and Ter Wal (2014). They have developed frameworks for empirically analyzing the parallel development of proximity, structural embeddedness, and the overall linkage distribution. One of this literature's foremost contributions has been the inclusion of endogenous network forces (the feedback effects of structural position in the network) as an explanation for the probability of link formation other than relational

---

[3] In this chapter the continuation of a linkage is synonymous with its persistence, recurrence, or repetition. It is defined technically as the reappearance of a link over multiple years in our time frame of observations.

effects (proximity) (Gilsing et al., 2008). Initial findings consistently have shown that the relevance of different proximity dimensions for the network configuration changes over time. Ter Wal (2014) elaborated the role of geographic proximity and triadic closure (which is close to social proximity; see Boschma & Frenken, 2010) in the network dynamics of the German biotech industry.[4] He found that the effect of geographic proximity disappears over time, whereas the effect of social aspects increases in importance over time. Conversely, analysis of a creative industry, such as that of video games, showed that the effects of geographical and social proximity were pronounced throughout all stages of the industry, whereas cognitive aspects were relevant only in later stages (Balland et al., 2013). The interrelations between the various proximity dimensions have also come under study. Cognitive, social, institutional, and geographical proximity were found to coevolve over time, but the association between cognitive and institutional proximity did not decrease over time (Broekel, 2015). At the regional level, Cantner and Graf (2006) examined the network of innovators in Jena over two periods and found that the configuration of technological proximity among the actors changed over time in conjunction with the instability of collaboration. From this observation they concluded that the very process of knowledge exchange depletes the cooperation potential between two partners and eventually renders cooperation obsolete.

However, neither the various mechanisms that cause a change of proximities nor the association with actions at the microlevel has been sufficiently considered yet (Balland et al., 2013). Given this gap in the literature, we adopt a dynamic perspective to take a step toward describing the coevolution of collaboration decisions, proximity, and competencies. By analyzing the endurance of innovative ties and relating them to the change in the underlying cognitive and social proximity and to the competencies of actors, we go beyond the mere explanation of the formation of these linkages.

Two opposite dynamics have been identified in the ongoing debate about the effects that social aspects and cognitive aspects have on the continuation and discontinuation of collaborative ties, respectively. First, familiarity breeds trust and facilitates communication among partners (Gulati, 1995), so building up link-specific social capital and the social proximity it entails contributes to the continuation and stability of linkages (Cantner, Conti, & Meder, 2010; Gulati, 1995; Gulati & Gargiulo, 1999). Second, an increase in cognitive proximity between collaborating partners fosters their mutual understanding but depletes the potential for novelty and reduces incentive to continue the collaboration (Wuyts et al., 2005). As for the development of innovation potential over time, we expect the positive returns of increased social proximity and mutual understanding between partners to be outweighed by the negative returns of excessively similar knowledge bases. The argument against long-term relations derives from the need for a diversity of knowledge for successful innovation (Nooteboom, 1998; Gilsing et al., 2008). In summary,

---

[4] According to the concept of triadic closure, actors indirectly linked to one another by a third actor in period $t - 1$ are more likely to establish a direct link in period t than are actors with no indirect linkages (Ter Wal, 2014).

repeated ties accelerate the diffusion of information, whereas infrequent ties serve as a source of novel and nonredundant knowledge (Granovetter, 2005).

Cognitive Proximity

Adding to what has already been done, we unravel the multifaceted concept of cognitive proximity into *overlap*, *reciprocal potential*, and *knowledge transfer* and track their dynamics within the evolution of collaboration. Basically, the decision to form or maintain a link is continuously evaluated according to the potential gains in knowledge and in innovation (Hamel, 1991; Wuyts et al., 2005). The knowledge endowment of partners can be considered a pool of potential knowledge flows. For these flows to be take place, two conditions must be met. First, a certain minimum similarity of knowledge bases, the overlap, is necessary to provide a basis for mutual understanding. The ability to absorb external knowledge is largely a function of the relatedness of the knowledge bases of collaboration partners (Boschma, 2005; Cantner & Meder, 2007; Cohen & Levinthal, 1990). Second, the exchange of knowledge requires potential knowledge that can be acquired because it is novel for the partner and not similar to the knowledge that the partner already possesses. The implication is that the dissimilarity of knowledge bases is also fruitful for potential knowledge flows. Collaboration will be established or continued only if the expected knowledge gains are positive.

From a dynamic perspective partners move along this proposed scale of cognitive proximity by increasing their overlap when collaborations evolve. After collaboration has been initiated, partners who are able to learn will experience an assimilation of knowledge bases that results in both an increase in overlap and a decrease in novelty potential (Balland et al., 2015; Nooteboom, 1998; Wuyts et al., 2005). The positive effects that overlap has on mutual understanding will eventually be offset by the negative effects on novelty creation (Balland et al., 2015). These dynamic reverse effects have been found in empirical studies on the persistence of collaboration between researchers (Dahlander & McFarland, 2013) and on the performance of continuing cooperation between organizations (Beaudry & Schiffauerova, 2011; Wuyts et al., 2005). At Stanford University, too much intellectual similarity (overlap) of the literature cited in publications by collaborating researchers has hampered the perpetuation of their collaborative ties (Dahlander & McFarland, 2013). Lack of diversity decreases innovative performance in repeated collaborations as patent rates and the quality of patents diminish in long-term collaborations (Beaudry & Schiffauerova, 2011), and the less variation a collaboration portfolio has, the less likely it is to result in technical novelty (Wuyts et al., 2005). We therefore assume that strategic actors who seek to maximize the benefits of collaboration for innovation will terminate their teamwork after it has exceeded the optimal level of overlap.

Hypothesis 1a The relation between the cognitive overlap of two actors and the likelihood of their continued collaboration follows an inverse-U curve.

Considering only the sheer overlap of knowledge does not necessarily imply the full exploitation of learning potential, for the remaining novel and complementary knowledge in the partner's knowledge base is not taken into account (Mowery et al., 1998). The need to broaden that perspective becomes especially relevant in a dynamic examination of collaborations. If the knowledge bases of partners increase disproportionally to the overlap, the novelty potential does not necessarily decrease with overlap over time. Remaining potential for novelty is a key incentive to continue collaboration. Furthermore, collaborations as mutual agreements are established or continued only if both partners have incentives to engage in them. In general these incentives encompass a certain level of reciprocity: Actors want their invested efforts and competencies to be reciprocated. Seeking potential knowledge flows, actors search for collaboration that they can expect to reciprocate the amount of new knowledge they "offer" the partner (Cantner et al., 2011). The greater this reciprocal potential is, the more attractive they rate the collaborative opportunity to be (Cantner & Meder, 2007). In other words, the likelihood of collaboration increases as the knowledge gains of the respective partners approach equality (referred to as the increase in reciprocal potential). We assume that the search for reciprocity in knowledge gains is also relevant for the continuation of collaboration.

Hypothesis 1b The reciprocal potential between two actors is positively correlated with the likelihood of their continued collaboration.

Apart from overlap and reciprocal potential, the very process of learning by the partners has consequences for the continuation or termination of collaboration (Hamel, 1991; Khanna et al., 1998). We define learning as the outcome of successful knowledge transfer, that is, as the successful integration of external knowledge into the given partner's own knowledge stock. This definition includes the possibility that the newly integrated knowledge is applicable outside the cooperative activity as well (Khanna et al., 1998). When learning potential has been exhausted and the associated knowledge has been transferred, the collaboration becomes obsolete to the partner who benefits from learning (Hamel, 1991). Learning also influences the power distribution among the partners. An asymmetry in learning might lead to an imbalance in bargaining power and dependency structures. Competitive collaboration can be understood as a learning race in which the "first learner" gains a higher bargaining power than the lagging partner, who thereby becomes less attractive (Hamel, 1991; Khanna et al., 1998). Hence, learning might cause the termination of collaboration by shifting the power balance and by decreasing innovative potential. In this regard the continuity of an alliance can be interpreted as learning failure rather than as success (Hamel, 1991). We hypothesize that the degree of learning determines the continuation of collaboration. In line with the cognitive and power-related arguments, our assumption is that effective knowledge exchange will decrease the incentives to maintain the collaboration. If, on the contrary, knowledge is only shared but not transferred, actors will retain sufficient diversity in knowledge to benefit from the continuation of the collaboration. We thus expect that knowledge exchange between partners will lead to the termination of their collaboration, whereas mere knowledge-sharing will result in continued collaboration.

Hypothesis 1c Knowledge transfer between two actors is negatively correlated with the likelihood of their continued collaboration.

Social Proximity

In the case of the collaboration among researchers at Stanford University, a shared history likewise has increased the probability of continuing the relationship (Dahlander & McFarland, 2013). Established link-specific social capital seems to reinforce collaboration (Gulati, 1995). A reason for this conjecture lies in the effect that social proximity has on the degree of comfort that accompanies communication. Social proximity is associated with trust, the establishment of mutually agreed social norms, and the control over undesired, noncooperative behavior such as opportunism (Boschma, 2005; Granovetter, 2005; Walker et al., 2003). Because social proximity is rooted in experience gained through successful cooperation, its supportive effects on knowledge exchange become increasingly evident with repetition of the cooperation. In this sense, increasing trust could explain the persistence of cooperation observed for alliances of firms (e.g., Gulati, 1995; Mowery et al., 1998). However, the relevance of social aspects might be contingent on the context of the collaboration. Cantner et al. (2010), for instance, found that social capital as measured by the frequency of the contact plays a role only for innovative outcomes of cooperation with research institutes. In a dynamic context we expect that social proximity as indicated by the experience that partners have shared through cooperation on innovation will promote future collaboration, all other factors remaining the same.

Hypothesis 2 The likelihood of continued collaboration between two actors increases with their prior common experience.

Competence

Other factors that coevolve with collaboration and that are subject to temporal changes are the actor's capabilities, overall experiences, and embeddedness in the overall network. Innovative capabilities and experience in managing collaborative agreements have been found to increase an actor's attractiveness as a collaboration partner (Ahuja, 2000; Gulati, 1999; Stuart, 2000). As the number of innovative collaborations increases, the experience in running an alliance, managing skills, and developing innovative capabilities mounts, attracting further potential partners. Assuming that the condition of reciprocity needs to be fulfilled if collaboration is to be maintained, we expect the likelihood of continued cooperation to be positively correlated with the combined innovative and collaborative experience of both partners.

Hypothesis 3a The greater the general inventive or innovative experience of both partners is, the higher the likelihood of their continued collaboration.

Hypothesis 3b The greater the general collaboration experience of both partners is, the more likely it is that their collaboration will continue.

The embeddedness of an actor as defined by the number of collaborative ties that the actor has established also determines the number of opportunities for additional collaborations. The mechanism by which the rich eventually get richer explains a certain path dependency in the evolution of networks: Central actors tend to become more central over time (Barabási & Albert, 1999). This phenomenon is known as preferential attachment, or cumulative advantage (Barabási & Albert, 1999; Dahlander & McFarland, 2013). This process might be explained by the broad access that central actors have to information about potential partners and by the high visibility that central actors have for other potential partners (Ahuja 2000). However, the reciprocity criterion applies as well. When seeking to maximize the benefits of the collaboration, central actors are more likely to find that their invested efforts are reciprocated by actors who exhibit the same degree of popularity. Moreover, the bargaining power of central firms is greater than that of the less connected actor (Gilsing et al., 2008). If collaboration is to continue, then that power needs to be equally distributed among the partners so as to avoid unilateral dependence (Hamel, 1991). Partners are therefore more likely to connect with each other and to maintain this connection if they possess a similar number of collaborative ties (Dahlander & McFarland, 2013).

Hypothesis 3c The more similar the degree of popularity of two actors is, the more likely it is that their collaboration will continue.

Methodology

In our theoretical considerations we identified three main factors that might explain the repetition of innovative linkages in our longitudinal study: (a) cognitive proximity between the cooperation partners, (b) social proximity between the cooperation partners, and (c) similarity in competencies that the partners bring to the collaboration. This section presents the database we used, the variables we created, and the methodology we applied.

Data

To construct potential and realized linkages, we used relational information found in patent applications. Successful collaboration leaves a trail in public patent data because patented inventions can be considered the output of a preceding intensive cooperative research process (Singh, 2005). By definition, cooperative patents comprise inventive success in this context. Although patent data come with certain limitations (see Griliches, 1990; Ter Wal & Boschma, 2009), they offer a rich and comprehensive database on inventive activities. While working with patents, one must carefully define the scope of analysis in order to avoid the bias stemming from unobserved heterogeneity in patenting behavior (across industries and nations, for example). To reduce this bias arising from intercountry and interindustry differences, we narrowed our analysis to patents that were filed by German applicants in the field of biotechnology between 1978 and 2010. The biotech industry is characterized by a high propensity to patent and a high frequency of joint research (Griliches, 1990; Powell & Grodal, 2006; Ter Wal, 2014). We gathered the data from the OECD REGPAT database[5] (January 2012 ed.), which covers patent applications to the European Patent Office (EPO) and the United States Patent and Trademark Office (USPTO). To match the collaborative actors to their respective other patents, we used the OECD Harmonised Applicants' Names (HAN) database, "which provides a dictionary of applicants' names which have been elaborated with business register data, so that it can easily be matched by all users" (retrieved July 15, 2015, from http://www.oecd.org/sti/inno/oecdpatentdatabases.htm).

The use of patent data in our analysis requires some qualifications. First, our pool of potential collaborators encompassed all applicants with at least one patent application between 1978 and 2010. The influx of entries meant that this pool was not fixed over time; it grew from year to year, so we had to deal with an unbalanced panel. Second, a link between actors occurred when actors appeared together as applicants on one patent document (coapplication). The probability of false positives in detecting collaborations was assumed to be very small because a coapplication reduces the applicants' claim to the patent. Third, it was debatable whether continuous cooperation was evident in patent data. If two applicants were persistently copatenting, we assumed that they were still conducting joint research. In this sense, we were able to identify long-lasting relationships but may have underestimated the number of ongoing partnerships that did not result in patents. Fourth, patents have been established as a measure of technological capabilities (Mowery et al., 1996). The suitability of patent data as a proxy for firms' knowledge stock derives from the disaggregate information they convey. The International Patent Classification (IPC) offers a standardized and detailed technological classification system that enables one to assign the protected invention to a certain field of technology and to characterize the firms' research activities by constructing firm-specific technology portfolios (Griliches, 1990; Jaffe, 1986; Benner & Waldfogel, 2008).

---

[5] "The OECD REGPAT database presents patent data that have been linked to regions according to the addresses of the applicants and inventors. The data have been 'regionalised' at a very detailed level so that more than 2 000 regions are covered across OECD countries. REGPAT allows patent data to be used in connection with other regional data such as GDP or labour force statistics, and other patent-based information such as citations, technical fields and patent holders' characteristics (industry, university, etc.), thus providing researchers with the means to develop a rich set of new indicators and undertake a broad range of analyses to address issues relating to the regional dimension of innovation." (Maraut, Dernis, Webb, Spiezia, & Guellec, 2008, p. 3).

Jaffe (1986) was one of the first researchers to use patent data as a proxy for technological competencies of firms. He constructed the knowledge portfolios as a vector of patent classes in which firms patented, and he computed the distances between technology vectors of firms to obtain a measure of proximity among them. Researchers subsequently adopted Jaffe's approach in using patent classes to show a firm's technology portfolio, technological distances among firms, or potential pools of knowledge spillover in the firm's environment (Benner & Waldfogel, 2008; Boschma & Frenken, 2010; Cantner & Graf, 2006; Cantner & Meder, 2007). We, too, made use of this rich information by constructing the knowledge portfolios of the actors and tracing their changes over time. Because it is unfeasible to approximate knowledge portfolios of the individual inventor by means of patent information, we focused our analysis on the organizational level.

Sample

The basic characteristics of the sample are presented in Table 16.1. The sample consisted of 197 firms that applied for patents with partners between 1983 and 2010, the period for which we sought to explain links between partners. Because our objective was to explain a link between actors by examining their prior patenting activities, we consulted patent information on the 5 years before the actors' first link as of 1983. Our calculation of the variables is therefore based on all patents the two actors applied for between 1978 and 2010. To analyze the dynamics of cooperation choice, we considered only the 91 firms that had cooperated at least twice between 1983 and 2010, and we observed their collaborative behavior over the years that followed the firms' first appearance in the dataset. When a firm was cooperating in 1 year, we paired it with each of the potential cooperation partners that were active in the pool at the same time. The pool of a firm's potential cooperation partners consisted of all patenting actors who were active in the focal year or had entered the sample before that point (Cantner & Meder, 2007). For all possible combinations, we assigned a 1 for each realized cooperation and a zero otherwise. Double pairs were excluded. The size of the pool of potential partners was nondecreasing from year to year. It amounted to a maximum of 2369 potential partners.

By definition, the collaborations we looked at included the subject firm and, from the pool, one potential partner that could be of any type (e.g., firm, university), implying that the observations were not symmetric. All told, the 27-year span covered by our analysis encompassed 321,683 possibilities to form dyads, of which 293 were ultimately realized.

When we grouped actors according to their overall collaboration activity over the whole period or over their all-time partner portfolio (Wuyts et al., 2005), we identified 106 firms that had collaborated only once (one-shot), 27 that had collaborated at least twice but with different partners (hop-on, hop-off), 24 that had collaborated persistently with the same partner (persistent), and 40 that had pursued a mixed strategy (mixed-type). For the purpose of our analysis, we focused on the

Table 16.1 Description of firms in the sample analyzed for the dynamics of cooperation, 1983–2010

Actors	
Characteristics	No.
Size of the pool of potential partners	2369
Cooperating firms	197
One-shot	106
Repeaters	91
Hop-on-Hop-off	27
Mixed-type	40
Persistent	24
Partner diversity (collaboration partners of focal firms)	
Minimum	1
Maximum	17
Median	2
Links	
Possible links	321,683
Realized links	293
Repeated links	60
Nonrecurring link	138
Continuity of links (distribution of linkages across times of repetition, without duplicates)	
0	138
1	41
2	11
3	3
4	3
5	1
6	1

firms that had collaborated at least twice (i.e., excluding the one-shot collaborators). As for the continuity of linkages, we found that 60 of the 293 linkages were persistent and that 138 did not recur. Most of the 293 linkages had been repeated once, and the maximum number of times that a link was subsequently observed to have recurred was 6.

Variables

We aim to explain the reappearance of linkages that were established between 1983 and 2010. Assume, for example, that we observed a certain firm to have cooperated with a partner in 1997 and that this link recurred in 1998. This activity is what we call repeated cooperation. Assume also that recurrence of this link ceased from 1999 on. With our analysis we seek to explain why the variable for cooperation (the dependent variable) became zero after 1998. To do so, we constructed variables based on the cooperation partners' characteristics that had accumulated in the years before the cooperative relationship in 1998. All explanatory variables have been lagged by 1 year. Assuming that collaboration was the outcome of a mutual agreement, we derived the explanatory variables (except for Knowledge Transfer, that is, *TransKnowledge*) by matching the attributes of a given firm with those of the partner it selected or was assigned to. In our analysis we have evaluated the mutual attractiveness of the collaboration opportunity according to social, technological, and experiential aspects of reciprocity. Table 16.2 gives a comprehensive description of the variables used.

Dependent Variable

The dependent variable, *Coop*, represents the cooperation between two actors in the current year and is binary. It has the value of 1 if there is cooperation between the actors as a pair; zero, if there is no cooperation. With our interest in explaining continuous collaboration and the dissolution of cooperation, previously existing nonrecurring links (expressed technically by the change of the dependent variable from 1 to zero) are detected by the variable for common experience (see Social proximity between the cooperation partners, below).

Independent Variables

Cognitive Proximity Between the Cooperation Partners

Overlap

A widely accepted procedure to operationalize the construct of cognitive proximity is to categorize the innovative pursuits of the actors in some way. For this purpose, the IPC offers a practical, detailed system for documenting their technological activities. In empirical studies it is claimed that the IPC is useful for measuring technological proximity as an aspect of cognitive proximity (Gilsing et al., 2008, pp. 1719–1720, 1723). In keeping with previous studies (e.g., Cantner & Graf, 2006; Cantner & Meder, 2007; Gilsing et al., 2008; Jaffe, 1986), we, too, adopted this resource to classify patent documents and used technological proximity as a proxy for the multifaceted concept of cognitive proximity.

To test hypothesis 1a, we included a simple measure used in previous studies (e.g., Singh, 2005; Cantner & Graf, 2006). To observe whether a minimum level of mutual understanding of both partners was guaranteed, we calculated the two partners' overlapping areas of knowledge (technically, just the count of the IPC classes that partners or potential partners share). To correct for the fact that a potential overlap is more likely between firms with relatively large portfolios than between for firms with smaller ones, we divided the overlap by the sum of the IPC classes in

Table 16.2 Description of variables explaining the reappearance of linkages between partners in the sample, 1978–2010

Use	Name of variable	Description	Number of observations	Mean	SD	Min	Max
Dependent variable	*Coop*	Binary variable indicating whether the pair actors cooperated in a certain year	321,683	0.0009	0.0302	0	1
Hypothesis 1a	*RelOverlap*	Continuous variable indicating the overlap of the partners' knowledge relative to the overall knowledge both partners possess. Measured as the ratio of common IPC classes to the sum of all IPC classes both partners cover.	319,323	0.05197	0.0662	0	0.5
	RelOverlap²	The squared values of knowledge overlap	319,323	0.0071	0.0158	0	0.25
Hypothesis 1b	*ReciPot*	Continuous variable ranging from zero to one and measuring the ratio between the minimum and maximum of nonoverlapping knowledge classes of both partners. The higher the value, the closer the partners are to having an equal number of potential new classes.	319,256	0.2307	0.2730	0	1

(continued)

Table 16.2 (continued)

Use	Name of variable	Description	Number of observations	Mean	SD	Min	Max
Hypothesis 1c	*TransKnowledge*	Binary variable indicating whether a knowledge exchange occurred in the previous period	321,683	0.0006	0.0254	0	1
Hypothesis 2	*CoopExp*	Count variable to measure social proximity. It indicates how often the partners cooperated before the cooperation in question.	321,683	0.0016	0.0655	0	7
Hypothesis 3a	*DyadSinglePAT5*	Logarithm of the sum of single patents held by each of the partners in the previous 5 years	311,728	4.4010	2.7340	0	10.75658
Hypothesis 3b	*DyadCoopPAT5*	Logarithm of the sum of the number of copatents held by each partner in previous 5 years	311,728	3.4156	1.6567	0	8.9363
Hypothesis 3c	*DCentrality*	Absolute difference in the degree centrality of the two partners	321,683	1.4467	0.9919	0	11
Controls	*DPatAge*	Difference in age (year of first patenting activity) of the two partners	321,683	7.7953	6.3583	0	30

	DStatus	Binary variable indicating whether the partners are of the same type: 1 means not of the same type, zero means both partners are firms.	321,683	0.5480	0.4977	0	1
Interactions	TransKnowledge × CoopExp	Interaction of knowledge TransKnowledge with CoopExp	321,683	0.0010	0.0560	0	7
	TransKnowledge × RelOverlap	Interaction of TransKnowledge with RelOverlap	319,323	0.0001	0.0035	0	0.3478

the portfolios of both partners, using the relative overlap as one measure of cognitive proximity (*RelOverlap*). We also included this measure as a quadratic term to capture the trade-off between minimum levels of knowledge overlap (as a warrant for mutual understanding) and maximum levels of overlap (as a hurdle that knowledge redundancy poses to innovation) (*RelOverlap^2*).

Reciprocal Potential

Following Cantner and Meder (2007), we tested hypothesis 1b by operationalizing the potential knowledge benefits from a potential collaboration as the relation between partner A's and partner B's new knowledge that is brought to the collaboration. However, we extended the approach of that earlier study by differentiating the individual classes that were new to the partner rather than solely considering the absolute number of patents. We counted the number of nonoverlapping IPC classes for each actor and took the ratio between the minimum number and the maximum number of new knowledge classes. This measure is named *ReciPot*. It is a continuous variable that ranges between 0 and 1, taking a 1 when the amount of new knowledge that the one partner offers is equal to that of the other (perfect reciprocity). The greater the divergence between the amount of partner A's and partner B's nonoverlapping knowledge (i.e., the less reciprocal the gain is between the partners), the more the measure of potential benefit approaches zero.

Knowledge Transfer

To test hypothesis 1c, we needed to measure the knowledge transfer between collaborators. Citations of previous documents (patents and publications) pertaining to the patent have become a favored instrument with which scientific authors detect knowledge spillovers (e.g., Griliches, 1990; Hall, Jaffe, & Trajtenberg, 2001; Jaffe, Trajtenberg, & Henderson, 1993; Mowery et al., 1996; Nelson, 2009; Nomaler & Verspagen, 2008; Schmoch, 1993; Singh, 2005). A frequent criticism, however, has been that patent citations may not imply real knowledge flows, for many citations are added by the patent examiner rather than the inventor or applicant.

We took a different avenue and measured knowledge transfer between partners. To do so, we defined the vector of a firm's patented technological classes as its cumulated knowledge stock and compared pre- and postcollaboration knowledge stocks. We defined knowledge transfer as the appearance of a new patent class in the firm's patent portfolio after the collaboration had taken place (i.e., after the copatent had been filed).[6] To attribute the portfolio changes to the cooperation, the newly added class had to have been part of the partner's precollaboration knowledge base. This measure enabled us to differentiate pure knowledge-sharing (as the pure access to knowledge) from knowledge exchange (the integration of new knowledge into the firm's own knowledge base). We assumed that if a class was subsequently

---

[6] *New* in this context meant that the patent class did not appear in the firm's precooperation portfolio before the application for the copatent.

assigned to single patents, then the knowledge had been successfully integrated and was applicable afterward without further collaboration. Used in conjunction with this procedure, the binary variable *TransKnowledge* indicates whether knowledge has been exchanged in prior collaborations. This variable takes the value 1 if either partner has gained new knowledge; otherwise it takes the value zero. That is, the variable captures both symmetric and asymmetric learning.

Our three measures of cognitive proximity—*RelOverlap*, *ReciPot*, and *TransKnowledge*—do not develop independently of each other. Their changes over time go hand in hand. Figure 16.1 illustrates the dynamics of these three variables. Two actors, I and II, hold specific knowledge portfolios before cooperating with each other (precollaboration). Actor I's portfolio comprises ABCDEF; actor II's, ABGH. The knowledge overlap in t-1 is given by AB and amounts to .2, relative to the overall knowledge. The reciprocal potential equals .5 because actor II possesses two knowledge units that actor I can gain as opposed to four knowledge units that actor II might be able to acquire from actor I. In other words, actor I can gain at most only half the amount of knowledge that actor II, the partner, stands to gain. Formulated differently, actor II can earn twice the amount of new knowledge that is being offered to actor I. In this example, the potential gains are unequal. Assume that collaboration then leads to symmetric learning in that C and G are exchanged. Actor I's postcollaboration portfolio is thereby enlarged to ABCDEFG; actor II's, to ABCGH. As a result, the overlap has increased to ABCEG and amounts now to .3 in relation to the overall knowledge possessed by the two firms. In turn, the ratio between the potential knowledge gains has decreased to .3 because actor II now offers only one new knowledge unit to actor I, whereas actor I now offers three knowledge units to actor II. The potential for knowledge flows has thus decreased and become more uneven. The attractiveness of this fictive alliance and the likelihood that it will continue have therefore declined. This example illustrates the case of knowledge having been efficiently exchanged. When actors collaborate but are unable to integrate new knowledge into their stock, then knowledge has only been shared and the collaboration is more likely to continue than if they are able to integrate the new knowledge. In this sense, a continuation of collaboration can be interpreted as a failure to learn (Hamel, 1991).

Social Proximity Between the Cooperation Partners

To test whether the probability for the creation or re-creation of a link increases with the social proximity between the partners (hypothesis 2), we included a variable for common experience, *CoopExp*, as a proxy for social proximity. *CoopExp* measures how often the pair was cooperating prior to the cooperation in question. The number of prior research projects with the partner is commonly used as a measure of the strength of the tie and is assumed to capture the trust and ease of communication between the partners (Cantner & Meder, 2007).

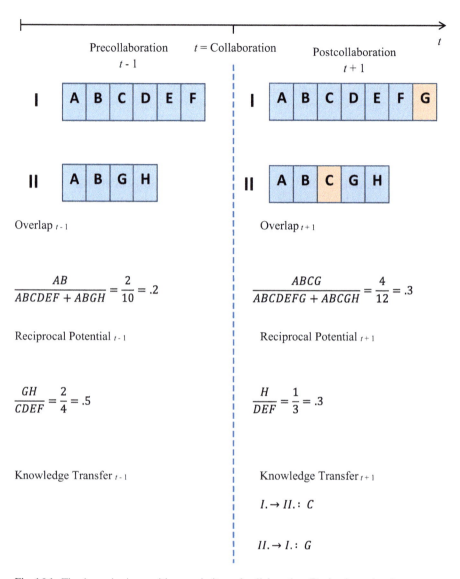

Fig. 16.1 The dynamics in cognitive proximity and collaboration (Design by authors)

Similarity in Competencies

Innovative Capabilities

Patents are an approved proxy for innovative activities, for the number of patents an actor holds is highly correlated with that actor's R&D activities (Mowery et al., 1996). To elaborate on the relation between accumulated technological capital and the continuation of linkages (hypothesis 3a), we therefore added up the single patents (not copatents) that both partners owned in the 5 years prior to their collaboration. We regarded that sum as a proxy for their accumulated innovative capabilities (*DyadSinglePAT5*). To delimit the domain of the variable, we took the logarithm of these values. We limited the observation period to the 5 years preceding the collaboration of the two firms, assuming the knowledge to be almost obsolete thereafter and accounting for the depreciation of innovative capabilities. Studies on the depreciations of R&D activities (Czarnitzki, Hall, & Oriani, 2006; Edworthy & Wallis, 2009; Hall, 2007) have indicated that R&D investment is completely depreciated after 3–5 years.

General Collaboration Experience Analogously, to capture the attractiveness of the collaboration opportunity in terms of management ease, we took the sum of the shared patents (copatents) that both actors held in the 5 years prior to the collaboration as a proxy for their accumulated collaboration experience (*DyadCoopPAT5*). Because we wanted to detect the general collaboration experience, we used this measure to add up all collaborations except the one in question. The greater the collaborative experience is, the higher the likelihood of further collaborations. We also assumed average capability depreciation after 5 years and applied the logarithmic transformation to delimit the range of the variable.

Popularity Taking reciprocal incentives into account, Giuliani (2007) has argued that central actors who are popular (as measured by their number of other linkages) tend to connect to similarly embedded actors. We believe that the potential for knowledge spillovers might be greater when partners are equally popular and possess a similar pool of potential knowledge sources (links). To test this relation (hypothesis 3c), we followed Dahlander and McFarland (2013) in using the absolute difference between the two partners' degree of centrality (the number of links) in the year before actual or potential collaboration. We called this variable *DCentrality*. Theoretically, this measure is closely related to the general collaboration experience. In our analysis, however, it captures the reciprocity of popularity in collaboration activity rather than the pure amount of previous collaboration activity.

Control Variables

Apart from technological, social, and competence aspects, we also wanted to control for additional effects stemming from organizational and age similarity. Both variables might increase the likelihood of collaboration due to ease of communication when the cooperating partners are exposed to the same institutional factors and environments (organizational similarity) or when they have had the same amount of time to operate in these environments and to accumulate experience and resources (age similarity). Organizational dissimilarity—*DStatus*—is a binary variable taking the value 1 when the two actors differ in organizational nature and zero when they are of the same organizational type (interfirm collaboration). *DPatAge* is the absolute difference between the ages of the actors (measured as the length of time since their first patent application). Our age variable was also assumed to capture the effect of firm size because the age and the size of the firm are usually highly correlated.

Estimation Strategy

The choice of a pair of partners to cooperate was modeled as the probability of observing the realization of a link ($coop_{i,j,t}$ taking the value 1) contingent on the explanatory variables we have discussed in this section. The decision to collaborate in the form of a copatent is a binary one (see Fig. 16.2). We therefore estimate the following logistic model (see Kennedy, 2009).

We included all realized and potential i,j combinations over the period from 1983 to 2010. To prevent potential biases from confining our sample to collaborative actors only, we included all possible combinations between the focal firms and all actors who had patented at least once. However, inclusion of combinations with all potential actors in the sample (even those that have never collaborated) introduces a source of bias due to unobserved heterogeneity. That is, control-group dyads that were never realized might differ systematically in unobserved factors from dyads that were realized at least once. These differences in unobserved characteristics might account for systematic differences in the general propensity of actors to collaborate. Furthermore, other specific factors that are not observable and that therefore cannot be included in our model might have caused the formation of each dyad (Gulati & Gargiulo, 1999; Heckman, 1981). To account for pair-specific heterogeneity, we applied a random-effects panel model by including a random intercept for each pair. We thereby assumed that the unobserved differences in the dyads were the results of a random process. However, this method also comes with the strong assumption that the unobserved factors are not correlated with any of the explanatory variables. This assumption is hard to test empirically. Conversely, the fixed-effects estimator would remove these time-invariant factors but would dramatically shrink the size of the sample. This change would come at a cost: The number of observations would drop from more than 300,000 to 501. Moreover, random-effects estimation allows the model to include additional time-invariant variables, such as *DStatus*. Given these considerations, we preferred the random-effects over the fixed-effects model.

Another issue that arises in the analysis of network data is the dependence of observations. The observations are not completely independent; individual actors might be part of multiple dyads. Consequently, the estimates are consistent, but the standard errors might be underestimated (Kennedy, 2009). Because we could not make any distributional assumption, we obtained robust standard errors by resorting to bootstrapping methods for panel data. We calculated the standard errors from the empirical distribution that was drawn by resampling the original dataset in 1000 iterations. Another form of bootstrapping commonly used to analyze dyadic data is

$$\log\left[\frac{P(\text{Coop}_{i,j,t} = 1)}{1 - P(\text{Coop}_{i,j,t} = 1)}\right] = \beta_0 + \beta_1 \text{RelOverlap}_{i,j,t-1} + \beta_2 \text{RelOverlap}^2_{i,j,t-1} + \beta_3 \text{ReciPot}_{i,j,t-1}$$

$$+ \beta_4 \text{TransKnowledge}_{i,j,t-n} + \beta_5 \text{CoopExp}_{i,j,t-n} + \beta_6 \text{DyadSinglePAT5}_{i,j,t-1}$$

$$+ \beta_7 \text{DyadCoopPAT5}_{i,j,t-1} + \beta_8 \text{DCentrality}_{i,j,t-1} + \beta_9 \text{TransKnowledge}_{i,j,t-n} \times \text{CoopExp}_{i,j,t-n}$$

$$+ \beta_{10} \text{TransKnowledge}_{i,j,t-n} \times \text{RelOverlap}_{i,j,t-1} + \beta_{11} \text{DPatAge}_{i,j,t} + \beta_{12} \text{DStatus}_{i,j,t} + \varepsilon_{i,j,t}$$

Fig. 16.2 The model of the cooperation decision that is estimated to explain cooperation by the presented explanatory variables

that of gathering the empirical distribution by repeated random permutation of the complete adjacency matrix—an approach known as multiple regression quadratic assignment procedures (MRQAP). Although this method has proven to be appropriate for linear models with a continuous dependent variable, it is still unclear how it performs when employed to analyze binary models (Broekel, Balland, Burger, & van Oort, 2014; Dekker, Krackhardt, & Snijders, 2007). Besides, MRQAP has not been tested much in panel settings.

Results

Descriptives

Diversity in Partner Portfolio

For an initial overview of the diversity of the firms' partner portfolios, we considered the number of different partners firms cooperated with in the years from 1978 to 2010. Table 16.1 contains summary statistics about the number of partners and the continuity of links. As shown by the distribution of actors across the different partners (see Fig. 16.3), most firms cooperated with two different partners, the median being 2. Only a few firms cooperated with a larger variety of actors. The maximum number of different partners in one portfolio was 17. In other words, one firm cooperated with 17 different actors during the period under study. For the firms in our sample, the implication was that repeated collaboration with only one partner was not a dominant behavior.

Dynamics of Link Formation

Concerning the recurrence of links, we found that 138 of the 293 realized links came about just once (nonrecurring), whereas 60 links were repeated at least once (the sum of repetitive links was 155). Without double-counting the repeated links,

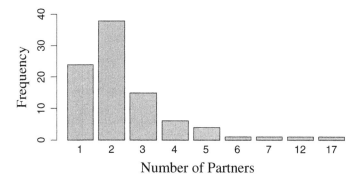

Fig. 16.3 Diversity of the partner portfolio among firms in the sample (Design by authors)

we found 198 realized combinations, of which most (138, or 70%) were nonrecurring. Most (41) of the sustainable links were repeated only once, and the maximum number of link repetitions was 6. Unlike the findings reported by Gulati (1995) and Gulati and Gargiulo (1999), who found stability in link formation, our first findings suggest that firms are inclined to change partners regularly rather than repeat collaboration with the same partner. Our findings complement the results by Wuyts et al. (2005) and Cantner and Graf (2006), which support the contention that the search for diversity of knowledge sources tends to lead firms to switch their R&D partners.

Estimation Results

Table 16.3 shows the bilateral correlations between the variables included in the estimations. With regard to correlations between the explanatory variables, we do not seem to have a severe problem of colinearity. With respect to the correlation between the explanatory variables and the dependent variable (*Coop*), we find that *RelOverlap, TransKnowledge, CoopExp, DyadSingle-PAT5, DyadCoopPAT5,* and *DStatus* have a weak positive correlation with cooperation, whereas *ReciPOT, DCentrality,* and *DPatAge* are negatively correlated.

To deepen our understanding of the forces that determine the partner choice, we ran a random-effects logistic regression on our panel data. Table 16.4 shows the outcome of our estimations for seven model variations. The results for the base model, which comprises the two control variables, *DStatus* and *DPatAge*, are shown in the last column. We found that *DStatus* was highly significant and positively correlated to the probability to cooperate (*Coop*), indicating that firms prefer to cooperate with partners that are of a different organizational form.

Concerning the dynamics of cognitive proximity, we analyzed three dimensions: overlap (*RelOverlap*), reciprocal potential, and knowledge transfer. First, we found

Table 16.3 Correlation between explanatory variables and dependent variable (Coop)

Variables	Coop	RelOverlap	RelOverlap²	ReciPot	TransKnowledge	CoopExp	DCentrality	Dyad SinglePAT5	Dyad CoopPAT5	DStatus	DPatAge
Coop	1										
RelOverlap	0.0471*	1									
RelOverlap²	0.0673*	0.9098*	1								
ReciPot	−0.0079*	0.2081*	0.1861*	1							
TransKnowledge	0.2332*	0.0250*	0.0219*	−0.0019	1						
CoopExp	0.2479*	0.0265*	0.0253*	−0.0058*	0.6577*	1					
DCentrality	−0.0182*	−0.0381*	−0.0255*	0.0252*	0.0059*	−0.0004	1				
DyadSinglePAT5	0.0105*	−0.1366*	−0.1083*	−0.4396*	0.0241*	0.0172*	0.0222*	1			
DyadCoopPAT5	0.0215*	−0.1455*	−0.1079*	−0.3693*	0.0351*	0.0298*	0.0770*	0.6526*	1		
DStatus	0.0123*	−0.0120*	−0.0001	−0.0652*	0.0071*	0.0058*	0.0005	−0.1169*	−0.0053*	1	
DPatAge	−0.0021	−0.2131*	−0.1684*	−0.1866*	−0.0029	−0.0046*	0.0937*	0.1638*	0.2781*	−0.0054	1

*$p <= .01$

that the squared term of the relative overlap ($RelOverlap^2$) between the knowledge bases of the two partners had a highly significant positive correlation to the probability of collaboration. However, we found no evidence of a moderate overlap and, hence, no support for hypothesis 1a. When controlling for combined effects of experience and overlap (see the column labeled "Interactions"), we found only a pure positive correlation between overlap and the likelihood of collaboration. Thus, the degree of mutual understanding seems to increase the likelihood that linkages will be recreated.

Second, our impression of the search for diversity as illustrated in Fig. 16.2 was confirmed by the results of our estimation. We found that firms were more likely to reconnect with actors who differed from them in the amount of potentially new knowledge than with actors who were the same or similar in that respect. The negative relation between reciprocal potential (*ReciPot*) and the likelihood of collaboration indicates that reciprocity in knowledge gains is not a necessary precondition for the continuity of collaborations. Our result was opposite to the assumed relation stated in hypothesis 1b.

Third, concerning hypothesis 1c, we did not find a significantly positive correlation between collaboration and previous knowledge transfer (*TransKnowledge*). Our results seem to contradict our hypotheses on the relevance of knowledge diversity in the evolution of cooperation. Concerning cognitive proximity, the need for mutual understanding seems to predominate over need for reciprocity in potential knowledge gains.

Regarding social proximity, we found no empirical connection between the chances for cooperation and prior common experience (*CoopExp*), a result that does not support our suggestion in hypothesis 2 that the propensity of collaboration increases with prior common experience.

Even though common experience did not play a significant role in partner choice among the firms in our sample, the combined overall cooperation experience (*DyadCoopPAT5*) was positively and significantly correlated with the re-creation of linkages. That is, choices to collaborate were preferred when at least one actor exhibited great capability in managing cooperation. This finding is consistent with the results reported by Gulati (1999), who observed the same supportive effect that an actor's general experience with collaboration has on that actor's chances of forming linkages. The importance of cumulative advantages is also reflected in the negative relation between collaboration propensity and the difference in the degree of popularity (*DCentrality*). Firms tended to seek reciprocal incentives when it came to accumulating experience and building their cooperation capability but not when they were interested in gaining knowledge benefits. Our results indicate that firms prefer to link up with actors who offer an equal amount of accumulated resources. Dahlander and McFarland (2013) found the same negative correlation between the difference between the "cumulative advantage" (p. 72) of both partners and the persistence of collaboration between researchers at Stanford University. Conversely, the common cumulative innovative potential as measured by the total number of single patents held by both actors (*DyadSinglePAT5*) seems rather irrelevant when it comes to partner choice. Therefore, we find support for our hypotheses 3b and 3c but not for hypothesis 3a.

16 Coevolution of Innovative Ties, Proximity, and Competencies

Table 16.4 Estimation results of the random-effects logistic regression (Method)—Dependent variable Coop

Explanatory variables	Hypothesis 1a	Hypothesis 1b	Hypothesis 1c	Hypothesis 2	Hypotheses 3 a–c	Interactions	Controls
RelOverlap	5.5655					27.0777***	
	(1.58)					(7.79)	
RelOverlap^2	49.7110***						
	(5.59)						
ReciPot		−2.2486***					
		(−3.88)					
TransKnowledge			0.9032			1.6796	
			(1.19)			(1.53)	
CoopExp				0.0077		−0.1455	
				(0.03)		(−0.33)	
DyadSinglePAT5					−0.0431		
					(−1.00)		
DyadCoopPAT5					0.6109***		
					9.53		
DCentrality					−1.1718**		
					−1.97		
TransKnowledge × CoopExp						−0.9984	
						(−1.51)	
TransKnowledge × RelOverlap						−4.3422	
DStatus	1.2470***	1.1283***	0.9980***	1.0228***	1.1042***	1.4245***	1.0215***
	(4.18)	(4.39)	(4.40)	(4.29)	(4.42)	(4.06)	(4.15)
DPatAge	0.0743***	−0.0003	−0.0041	−0.0039	−0.0393**	0.1149***	−0.0039
	(−3.43)	(−0.01)	(−0.23)	(−0.23)	(−2.19)	(4.69)	(−0.23)

(continued)

Table 16.4 (continued)

Explanatory variables	Hypothesis 1a	Hypothesis 1b	Hypothesis 1c	Hypothesis 2	Hypotheses 3 a–c	Interactions	Controls
Constant	−20.9707***	−17.1154***	−14.1513***	−14.3361***	−14.8631***	−24.0424***	−14.3457***
	(−15.62)	(−13.09)	(−8.44)	(−8.17)	(−7.66)	(−8.81)	(−9.34)
No. of observations	319323	319256	321683	321683	311728	319323	321683
No. of Groups	142417	142384	142984	142984	139318	142417	142984
LR chi^2	−1610.31	1019.03	479.56	613.07	542.03	−1604.7	−1808.19
Prob>chi^2	0.0000	0.0000	0.0000	0.0000	0.0000	0.0000	0.0000
Wald chi^2(3)		33.08	19.68	19.89			
Wald chi^2(5)					178.66		
Wald chi^2(7)						146.14	
Wald chi^2(2)	164.27						17.62
Wald chi^2(4)							
/lnsig2u	3.4286	3.2234	2.7003	2.7382	2.7401	3.6029	2.7404
Sigma_u	5.5528	5.0114	3.8579	3.9318	3.9355	6.05834	3.9362
Rho	0.9036	0.8842	0.8190	0.8245	0.8248	0.9177	0.8249

**means significant at 5 %
***means significant at 1 %

Our findings lend support to the hypothesis that similarity in knowledge and accumulated capabilities enhance the attractiveness of collaboration options and link maintenance. Nevertheless, firms also seek some degree of heterogeneity in the controls *DStatus* and *DPatAge*, for the probability of repeated collaboration increases when the partner is not a firm or when the partner is significantly different in patenting experience. However, these findings can be partially attributed to the specificities of research in biotechnology. One reason is that relationships between industry and the university are prevalent in German biotechnology. Because the innovation process is rather linear, with discoveries being introduced by public research institutes, collaboration between industry and the university is an important mechanism of technology transfer and thus increases its likelihood. Furthermore, the influence of the difference between the patenting ages of the partners might reflect another widespread form of collaborative combination in biotechnology: young, small companies as the creative engine of joint research and large pharmaceutical companies as a source of financial resources (McKelvey, 1997; Powell, Koput, & Smith-Doerr, 1996; Ter Wal, 2014).

In summary, our findings generally suggest that both similarity and diversity of actors afford incentives to form alliances. Similarity plays a specific role in partner choice with regard to general collaboration experience (*DyadCoopPAT5*) and the accumulation of resources (*DCentrality*). Actors seek to connect to actors who can reciprocate their general collaboration expertise and provide a certain basis for mutual understanding. The reciprocity in knowledge gains and the amount of innovative capability seem to play a comparatively subordinate role. As far as organizational similarity and patenting age are concerned, actors are inclined to choose diverse partners.

Conclusion and Further Research

The aim of this study was to elaborate on the coevolution of several attributes of cognitive proximity, social proximity, and similarity in competencies as collaboration between two actors progresses. We have contributed to the debate on whether networks are rather stable (i.e., with actors always cooperating with the same partners) or volatile (i.e., with actors changing partners regularly). Our findings suggest that firms are prone more to switching their cooperation partner than to repeating the collaboration with a given partner. We found no significant effect of knowledge transfer and prior common experience on repeated link formation. Instead, we found that firms prefer to cooperate with a partner whose knowledge bases and accumulated collaboration experience are rather similar to their own and whose organizational nature and patenting age are rather dissimilar to their own. We did not find evidence to support the hypothesis that potential for innovation and collaboration decreases as the overlap of the knowledge bases increases (Gilsing et al., 2008; Nooteboom, 1998; Wuyts et al., 2005).

Our methodology has limitations and drawbacks that one must consider when interpreting the final results. First, the degree to which the number of linkages observable in our data matches that in the real world heavily depends on the patenting practices among actors (e.g., cross-patenting or cases in which a central institution may administrate the patenting process and is therefore the only applicant). Including only those collaborations that are defined by coapplication might underestimate the number of actual linkages. Yet if we were also to take account of the connections realized through shared inventors, we might overestimate the number of linkages (Ter Wal & Boschma, 2009). In addition, we expect the number of disregarded cases to be rather small because inventor mobility is rare in Europe (Ter Wal & Boschma, 2009). Crescenzi, Gagliardi, and Percoco (2013) estimated that barely 5% of inventors change their employer. A closely related drawback to our methodology is the underrepresentation of informal ties, for we considered only formal collaboration agreements. Prior studies have emphasized the importance that informal ties have for innovative outcomes (e.g., Powell & Grodal, 2006), but it has been found that formal ties, especially in the life sciences, are generally preceded by informal ties (Powell et al., 1996). On this basis we argue that preceding informal ties are manifest in formal ties and are therefore captured in the study of the latter.

Second, by focusing on the research of the dynamics in bilateral R&D collaboration, we set aside the study of the effects of the micromechanism on the overall network structure. We thereby also opted to forgo explicit consideration of the feedback effects that an actor's position in the overall network has on partner choices at the microlevel. We tried to control for this limitation by incorporating information on whether an actor was highly connected (central) or rather peripheral and by adapting the standard errors accordingly. However, recent research on networks has made advances regarding the explicit modeling of endogenous structural mechanisms such as triadic closure and preferential attachment (Broekel et al., 2014). Our analysis could be extended by elaborating the overall network evolution as a result of partner choice at the microlevel, a selection that is itself determined by similarity and diversity aspects. Stochastic actor-oriented models, for instance, allow for examination of the relationship between the individual partner choice and overall network dynamics (Balland et al., 2013). In this context, however, it is debatable to what extent firms can directly influence and are aware of the network beyond their ego network (direct connections) (Gilsing et al., 2008).

The third concern about studies that focus on analyzing a certain pattern in a specific industry is the generalizability of their results. Application of our results is limited, for example, by the appearance of patterns that might be caused by industry specificities. However, some of the factors that our analysis identifies (e.g., positive effects of overlap, the reciprocal cumulative advantage, and reciprocal general collaboration experience) have also been observed in other environments and at other levels of observations (Cantner & Meder, 2007; Dahlander & McFarland, 2013; Gulati, 1999).

In view of our results and the type of analysis suggested with this study, we have taken a further step in the effort to disentangle the coevolution of the proximity of collaboration partners and the formation and repetition of cooperative ties. In doing so, we have already taken into consideration factors that go beyond dyadic relationships, factors such as network characteristics. Extending this dimension in future research will help improve the understanding of the dynamics of cooperation networks at the core of clusters and of local and regional innovation systems.

References

Ahuja, G. (2000). Collaboration networks, structural holes, and innovation: A longitudinal study. *Administrative Science Quarterly, 45,* 425–455. doi:10.2307/2667105

Asheim, B. T., & Gertler, M. S. (2005). The geography of innovation: Regional innovation systems. In J. Fagerberg, D. Mowery, & R. Nelson (Eds.), *The Oxford handbook of innovation* (pp. 291–317). Oxford: University Press. doi:10.1093/oxfordhb/9780199286805.003.0011

Balland, P.-A., Boschma, R. A., & Frenken, K. (2015). Proximity and innovation: From statics to dynamics. *Regional Studies, 49,* 907–920. doi:10.1080/00343404.2014.883598

Balland, P.-A., de Vaan, M., & Boschma, R. A. (2013). The dynamics of interfirm networks along the industry life cycle: The case of the global video games industry, 1987–2007. *Journal of Economic Geography, 13,* 741–765. doi:10.1093/jeg/lbs023

Barabási, A.-L., & Albert, R. (1999). Emergence of scaling in real networks. *Science, 286,* 509–512. doi:10.1126/science.286.5439.509 [ISSN No. 1095–9203]

Beaudry, C., & Schiffauerova, A. (2011). Impacts of collaboration and network indicators on patent quality: The case of Canadian nanotechnology innovation. *European Management Journal, 29,* 362–376. doi:10.1016/j.emj.2011.03.001

Benner, M., & Waldfogel, J. (2008). Close to you? Bias and precision in patent-based measures of technological proximity. *Research Policy, 37,* 1556–1567. doi:10.3386/w13322

Boschma, R. A. (2005). Proximity and innovation: A critical assessment. *Regional Studies, 39,* 61–74. doi:10.1080/0034340052000320887

Boschma, R. A., & Frenken, K. (2010). The spatial evolution of innovation networks: A proximity perspective. In R. A. Boschma & R. Martin (Eds.), *The handbook of evolutionary economic geography* (pp. 120–136). Cheltenham: Edward Elgar. doi:10.4337/9781849806497.00012

Broekel, T. (2015). The co-evolution of proximities—A network level study. *Regional Studies, 49,* 921–935. doi:10.1080/00343404.2014.1001732

Broekel, T., Balland, P.-A., Burger, M., & van Oort, F. (2014). Modeling knowledge networks in economic geography: A discussion of four empirical strategies. *The Annals of Regional Science, 53,* 423–452. doi:10.1007/s00168-014-0616-2

Broekel, T., & Boschma, R. A. (2012). Knowledge networks in the Dutch aviation industry: The proximity paradox. *Journal of Economic Geography, 12,* 409–433. doi:10.1093/jeg/lbr010

Cantner, U., Conti, E., & Meder, A. (2010). Networks and innovation: The role of social assets in explaining firms' innovative capacity. *European Planning Studies, 18,* 1937–1956. doi:10.1080/09654313.2010.515795

Cantner, U., & Graf, H. (2006). The network of innovators in Jena: An application of social network analysis. *Research Policy, 35,* 463–480. doi:10.1016/j.respol.2006.01.002

Cantner, U., & Graf, H. (2011). Innovation networks: Formation, performance and dynamics. In C. Antonelli (Ed.), *Handbook on the economic complexity of technological change* (pp. 366–394). Cheltenham: Edward Elgar.

Cantner, U., & Meder, A. (2007). Technological proximity and the choice of cooperation partners. *Journal of Economic Interaction and Coordination, 2,* 45–65. doi:10.1007/s11403-007-0018-y

Cantner U., Meder, A., & Wolf, T. (2011). Success and failure of firms' innovation co-operations: The role of intermediaries and reciprocity. *Papers in Regional Science, 90,* 313–329. doi:10.1111/j.1435-5957.2011.00366.x

Cohen, W. M., & Levinthal, D. A. (1990). Absorptive capacity: A new perspective on learning and innovation. *Administrative Science Quarterly, 35,* 128–152. doi:10.2307/2393553

Crescenzi, R., Gagliardi, L., & Percoco, M. (2013). Social capital and the innovative performance of Italian provinces. *Environment and Planning A, 45,* 908–929. doi:10.1068/a45221

Criscuolo, P., Salter, A., & Ter Wal, A. (2010). *Summer Conference 2010 on "Opening Up Innovation: Strategy, Organization and Technology": The role of proximity in shaping knowledge sharing in professional services firms.* London: Imperial College London Business School.

Czarnitzki, D., Hall, B. H., & Oriani, R. (2006). Market valuation of US and European intellectual property. In D. Bosworth & E. Webster (Eds.), *The management of intellectual property* (pp. 111–131). Cheltenham: Edward Elgar.

Dahlander, L., & McFarland, D. A. (2013). Ties that last: Tie formation and persistence in research collaborations over time. *Administrative Science Quarterly, 58,* 69–110. doi:10.1177/0001839212474272

Dekker, D., Krackhardt, D., & Snijders, T. A. B. (2007). Sensitivity of MRQAP tests to collinearity and autocorrelation conditions. *Psychometrika, 72,* 563–581. doi:10.1007/s11336-007-9016-1

Edworthy, E., & Wallis, G. (2009). Research and development as a value creating asset. In OECD and the swiss federal office of statistics (FSO), *Productivity Measurement and Analysis* (pp. 303–335). Paris: OECD. doi:http://dx.doi.org/10.1787/9789264044616-16-en

Freeman, C. (1991). Networks of innovators: A synthesis of research issues. *Research Policy, 20,* 499–514. doi:10.1016/0048-7333(91)90072-X

Gilsing, V., Nooteboom, B., Vanhaverbeke, W., Duysters, G., & van den Oord, A. (2008). Network embeddedness and the exploration of novel technologies: Technological distance, betweenness centrality and density. *Research Policy, 37,* 1717–1731. doi:10.1016/j.respol.2008.08.010

Giuliani, E. (2007). The selective nature of knowledge networks in clusters: Evidence from the wine industry. *Journal of Economic Geography, 7,* 139–168. doi:10.1093/jeg/lbl014

Granovetter, M. (2005). The impact of social structure on economic outcomes. *Journal of Economic Perspectives, 19,* 33–50. doi:10.1257/0895330053147958

Grant, R. M., & Baden-Fuller, C. (1995, August). A knowledge-based theory of inter-firm collaboration. In D. P. Moore (Ed.), *Academy of Management Best Papers Proceedings 1995* (pp. 17–21). Fifth Annual Meeting of the Academy of Management, Vancouver. doi:10.5465/AMBPP.1995.17536229

Griliches, Z. (1990). Patent statistics as economic indicators: A survey. *Journal of Economic Literature, 28,* 1661–1707. doi:10.3386/w3301

Gulati, R. (1995). Does familiarity breed trust? The implications of repeated ties for contractual choice in alliances. *Academy of Management Journal, 38,* 85–112. doi:10.2307/256729

Gulati, R. (1999). Network location and learning: The influence of network resources and firm capabilities on alliance formation. *Strategic Management Journal, 20,* 397–420. doi:10.1002/(SICI)1097-0266(199905)20:5<397::AID-SMJ35>3.0.CO;2-K

Gulati, R., & Gargiulo, M. (1999). Where do interorganizational networks come from? *American Journal of Sociology, 104,* 1439–1493. doi:10.1086/210179

Hagedoorn, J. (2002). Inter-firm R&D partnerships: An overview of major trends and patterns since 1960. *Research Policy, 31,* 477–492. doi:10.1016/S0048-7333(01)00120-2

Hagedoorn, J., & Frankort, H. T. W. (2008). The gloomy side of embeddedness: The effects of overembeddedness on inter-firm partnership formation. In J. A. C. Baum & T. J. Rowley (Eds.), *Network strategy* (pp. 503–530). Advances in Strategic Management: Vol. 25. Binglay: Emerald Group Publishing limited. doi:10.1016/S0742-3322(08)25014-X

Hall, B. H. (2007). *Measuring the returns to R&D: The depreciation problem* (NBER Working Paper No. 13473). Cambridge, MA: National Bureau of Economic Research. doi:10.3386/w13473

Hall, B. H., Jaffe, A. B., & Trajtenberg, M. (2001). *The NBER Patent Citations Data File: Lessons, Insights and Methodological Tools* (NBER Working Paper No. 8498). Cambridge: National Bureau of Economic Research. doi:10.3386/w8498

Hamel, G. (1991). Competition for competence and interpartner learning within international strategic alliances. *Strategic Management Journal, 12(S1),* 83–103. doi:10.1002/smj.4250120908

Heckman, J. J. (1981). Heterogeneity and State Dependence, NBER Chapters. In S. Rosen (Ed.), *Studies in labor markets* (pp. 91–140). Chicago: University of Chicago Press.

Jaffe, A. (1986). Technological opportunity and spillovers of R&D: Evidence from firms' patents, profits and market value. *American Economic Review, 76,* 984–999. doi:10.3386/w1815

Jaffe, A. B., Trajtenberg, M., & Henderson, R. (1993). Geographic localization of knowledge spillovers as evidenced by patent citations. *Quarterly Journal of Economics, 108,* 577–598. doi:10.2307/2118401

Kennedy, P. (2009). *A guide to econometrics* (6th ed.). Cambridge: Wiley-Blackwell.

Khanna, T., Gulati, R., & Nohria, N. (1998). The dynamics of learning alliances: Competition, cooperation, and relative scope. *Strategic Management Journal, 19,* 193–210. doi:10.1002/(SICI)1097-0266(199803)19:3<193::AID-SMJ949>3.0.CO;2-C

Kogut, B., Shan, W., & Walker, G. (1992). The make or cooperate decision in the context of an industry network. In N. Nohria & R. Eccles (Eds.), *Networks and organizations: Structure, form, and action* (pp. 348–365). Boston: Harvard Business School Press.

Maraut, S., Dernis, H., Webb, C., Spiezia, V., & Guellec, D. (2008, June 3). *The OECD REGPAT database: A presentation* (OECD Science, Technology and Industry Working Papers No. 2008/02). doi:10.1787/241437144144

March, J. G. (1991). Exploration and exploitation in organizational learning. *Organization Science, 2,* 71–87. doi:10.1287/orsc.2.1.71

McKelvey, M. (1997). Coevolution in commercial genetic engineering. *Industrial and Corporate Change, 6,* 503–532. doi:10.1093/icc/6.3.503

McPherson, M., Smith-Lovin, L., & Cook, J. M. (2001). Birds of a feather: Homophily in social networks. *Annual Review of Sociology, 27,* 415–444. doi:10.1146/annurev.soc.27.1.415

Mowery, D. C., Oxley, J. E., & Silverman, B. S. (1996). Strategic alliances and inter-firm knowledge transfer. *Strategic Management Journal, 17,* 77–91. doi:10.1002/smj.4250171108

Mowery, D. C., Oxley, J. E., & Silverman, B. S. (1998). Technological overlap and interfirm cooperation: Implications for the resource-based view of the firm. *Research Policy, 27,* 507–523. doi:10.1016/S0048-7333(98)00066-3

Nelson, A. J. (2009). Measuring knowledge spillovers: What patents, licenses and publications reveal about innovation diffusion. *Research Policy, 38,* 994–1005. doi:10.1016/j.respol.2009.01.023

Nomaler, Ö., & Verspagen, B. (2008). Knowledge flows, patent citations and the impact of science on technology. *Economic Systems Research, 20,* 339–366. doi:10.1080/09535310802551315

Nooteboom, B., (1998). Cost, quality and learning based governance of buyer-supplier relations. In M. G. Colombo (Ed.), *The changing boundaries of the firm* (pp. 187–208). London: Routledge. doi:10.4324/9780203443408.pt3

Nooteboom, B. (1999). Innovation and inter-firm linkages: New implications for policy. *Research Policy, 28,* 793–805. doi:10.1016/S0048-7333(99)00022-0

Nooteboom, B. (2005). *Learning and governance in inter-firm relations* (Center for Economic Research Discussion Paper No. 2005-38). Tilburg, The Netherlands: Tilburg University. Retrieved from https://pure.uvt.nl/portal/files/773588/38.pdf

Paier, M. F., & Scherngell, T. (2011). Determinants of collaboration in European R&D networks: Empirical evidence from a discrete choice model. *Industry and Innovation, 18,* 89–104. doi:10.1080/13662716.2010.528935

Penrose, E. G. (1959). *The theory of the growth of the firm.* New York: Oxford University Press.

Powell, W. W. (1998). Learning from collaboration: Knowledge and networks in the biotechnology and pharmaceutical industries. *California Management Review, 40,* 228–240. doi:10.1002/9780470755679.ch14

Powell, W. W., & Grodal, S. (2006). Networks of innovators. In J. Fagerberg, D. C. Mowery, & R. L. Nelson (Eds.), *The Oxford handbook of innovation* (pp. 56–85). Oxford: University Press. doi:10.1093/oxfordhb/9780199286805.003.0003

Powell, W. W., Koput, K. W., & Smith-Doerr, L. (1996). Interorganizational collaboration and the locus of innovation: Networks of learning in biotechnology. *Administrative Science Quarterly, 41,* 116–145. doi:10.2307/2393988

Rogers, E. M., & Bhowmik, D. K. (1970). Homophily–heterophily: Relational concepts for communication research. *Public Opinion Quarterly, 34,* 523–538. doi:10.1086/267838

Schmoch, U. (1993). Tracing the knowledge transfer from science to technology as reflected in patent indicators. *Scientometrics, 26,* 193–211. doi:10.1007/BF02016800

Singh, J. (2005). Collaborative networks as determinants of knowledge diffusion patterns. *Management Science, 51,* 756–770. doi:10.1287/mnsc.1040.0349

Stuart, T. E. (2000). Interorganizational alliances and the performance of firms: A study of growth and innovation rates in a high-technology industry. *Strategic Management Journal, 21,* 791–811. doi:10.1002/1097-0266(200008)21:8<791::AID-SMJ121>3.0.CO;2-K

Ter Wal, A. L. J. (2014). The dynamics of the inventor network in German biotechnology: Geographic proximity versus triadic closure. *Journal of Economic Geography, 14,* 589–620. doi:10.1093/jeg/lbs063

Ter Wal, A. L. J., & Boschma, R. A. (2009). Applying social network analysis in economic geography: Framing some key analytical issues. *The Annals of Regional Science, 43,* 739–756. doi:10.1007/s00168-008-0258-3

Ter Wal, A. L. J., & Boschma, R. A. (2011). Co-evolution of firms, industries and networks in space. *Regional Studies, 45,* 919–933. doi:10.1080/00343400802662658

Uzzi, B. (1997). Social structure and competition in interfirm networks: The paradox of embeddedness. *Administrative Science Quarterly, 42,* 35–67. doi:10.2307/2393808

Walker, W. E., Harremoes, P., Rotmans, J., Van der Sluijs, J. P., Asselt, M. B. A., Janssen, P., & Krayer von Krauss, M. P. (2003). Defining uncertainty: A conceptual basis for uncertainty management in model-based decision support. *Integrated Assessment, 4,* 5–17. doi:10.1076/iaij.4.1.5.16466

Wuyts, S., Colombo, M. G., Dutta, S., & Nooteboom, B. (2005). Empirical tests of optimal cognitive distance. *Journal of Economic Behavior & Organization, 58,* 277–302. doi:10.1016/j.jebo.2004.03.019

Yang, H., Phelps, C. C., Steensma, K. (2010). Learning from what others have learned from you: The effects of knowledge spillovers on originating firms. *Academy of Management Journal, 53,* 371–389. doi:10.5465/AMJ.2010.49389018

Open Access This chapter is distributed under the terms of the Creative Commons Attribution 4.0 International License (http://creativecommons.org/licenses/by/4.0/), which permits use, duplication, adaptation, distribution and reproduction in any medium or format, as long as you give appropriate credit to the original author(s) and the source, provide a link to the Creative Commons license and indicate if changes were made.

The images or other third party material in this chapter are included in the work's Creative Commons license, unless indicated otherwise in the credit line; if such material is not included in the work's Creative Commons license and the respective action is not permitted by statutory regulation, users will need to obtain permission from the license holder to duplicate, adapt or reproduce the material.

The Klaus Tschira Stiftung

Fig. A.1 Klaus Tschira at his welcoming address at the 11th symposium, "Topographies and topologies of knowledge," in the series on knowledge and space, the Villa Bosch studio, Heidelberg, Germany. © Johannes Glückler, Heidelberg

In 1995 physicist Dr. h.c. Dr.-Ing. E. h. Klaus Tschira (1940–2015) created the German foundation known as the Klaus Tschira Stiftung. This organization is one of Europe's largest privately funded non-profit foundations. It promotes the advancement of natural sciences, mathematics, and computer science and strives to enhance the understanding of these fields. The focal points of the foundation are "Natural Science—Right from the Beginning," "Research," and "Science Communication." The involvement of the Klaus Tschira Stiftung begins in kindergartens and continues in primary and secondary schools, universities, and research facilities. The foundation champions new methods in the transfer of scientific knowledge, and supports both the development and intelligible presentation of research findings. The Klaus Tschira Stiftung pursues its objectives by conducting projects of its own but also awards subsidies after approval of applications. To foster and sustain work on selected topics, the Stiftung has also founded its own affiliates. Klaus Tschira's commitment to this objective was honored in 1999 with the "Deutscher Stifterpreis," the award conferred by the National Association of German Foundations.

The Klaus Tschira Stiftung is located in Heidelberg and has its head office in the Villa Bosch (Fig. 16.1), once the residence of Carl Bosch, a Nobel laureate in chemistry.

www.klaus-tschira-stiftung.de

Fig. A.2 Villa Bosch, the head office of the Klaus Tschira Stiftung, Heidelberg, Germany. © Peter Meusburger

Fig. A.3 Participants of the symposium "Topographies and topologies of knowledge" at the Villa Bosch studio in Heidelberg, Germany. © Johannes Glückler, Heidelberg

Index

A
Academic engagement, 103
Actions and thoughts, 106
Advice
    centrality, 228, 230, 232, 235
    network, 5, 14, 124–130, 133, 223, 226, 228, 233
    seeking, 5, 124–128, 136
Agency, 4, 6, 10, 12, 14, 15, 131–138, 194, 195, 202, 204, 206, 207, 210, 212, 213
Agglomeration economies, 301
Alliances, 7, 8, 16, 270, 275, 277, 339–343, 347, 367
Artist's success, 150
Attitudes, 107, 221–224, 235
Atypical
    combinations, 15, 243
    journal pairs, 15, 253
Automotive
    cluster, 198, 201
    system, 208, 209

B
Behavior, 4, 54–57, 59, 62, 63, 69, 90–92, 94, 97, 99, 107, 109, 120, 122, 126, 131, 134, 171, 174, 186, 221–224, 226, 233–236, 264, 269, 273, 277, 280, 281, 310, 340, 341, 347, 349, 350, 361
Beliefs, 107, 109
Berlin agency for electromobility, 202, 207
Bilateral relations, 98, 281
Biotech industry, 344, 349

Block
    information, 292
    model, modeling, 89, 153, 173, 179–181, 183, 186
    prespecified -model, 14, 179
Bonding, 37, 39
Bop cool era, 161–162
Bourdieu, P., 27, 56, 103, 105–107, 113, 146, 147
Breaking taboos, 279–281
Bridging cores, 180, 182, 183, 187
Broker
    opportunities, 233
    research, 233
    theory, 233
    trust, 233
Brokerage, 157, 160, 163, 164, 180, 222, 224, 225, 227, 229, 230, 234, 236, 292
Business
    community, 70, 73, 74, 80, 124
    law, 125
    practices, 104, 124

C
Capabilities, 14, 170, 204, 301, 338, 339, 341, 342, 347, 349, 358, 359, 367
Capital, 4, 27, 29, 37, 57, 69, 70, 105, 106, 113, 121, 169, 170, 192, 198, 358
Career
    pathways, 105, 111
    track, 146
Case study, 123, 136, 171, 174–176, 198, 201, 270, 277–279, 315

Cassirer's philosophy of science, 55
Catch-up dynamics, 131–136
Centrality
  betweenness, 150–152, 158, 159, 162–164, 322, 327, 330
  closeness, 327, 330
  degree, 159, 160, 162, 359
Centrifugal forces, 144, 145
Centripetal tendency, 145
Changes, 16, 30, 36, 53, 88, 105, 106, 108, 120, 121, 132, 134, 137, 138, 143–145, 148, 150, 161, 165, 170, 174, 175, 184, 186, 187, 194, 202, 343, 344, 347, 350, 356, 357
Citation pattern, 9, 249, 356
City's knowledge base, 16, 294, 300, 301, 308–310
Civil servants, 316, 318
Client service, 108, 109
Closeness tendency of strong ties, 71
Cluster
  analysis, 150, 151
  concept, 169, 275
  model, 169
Clustering
  approach, 94
  coefficient, 88, 302, 303, 308, 325–326
Coapplication, 349, 368
Co-citation, 245, 246, 249, 251, 356
Coevolutionary
  approach, 164
  processes, 343
Cohesive
  cores, 180, 183
  field, 162
  group, 97, 154, 156, 162, 163, 176, 186
Co-invention network, 294, 295, 302, 303, 308, 310
Collaboration
  activity, 350, 359
  experience, 338, 348, 359, 367, 368
Collaborators, 308, 340, 349, 351, 356
Collective
  action, 4, 10, 122, 123, 127, 134–137
  agency, 131
  learning, 4–6, 9–11, 14, 15, 123–131, 134, 136, 137, 170, 270, 281, 339, 340
Collinearity, 107
Combination, 15, 29, 34, 75, 77, 78, 109, 145, 160, 199, 200, 243, 271, 284, 300, 301, 303, 304, 308, 350, 360, 362, 367
Commercial court, 124, 129

Community, 3, 26, 41, 43, 71, 73–78, 96–97, 152, 172–173, 277, 322
Community structure, 320, 322
Competencies, 29, 31, 63, 104, 106, 109, 110, 113, 201, 203, 208, 210, 212, 213, 271, 278, 338, 339, 344, 346, 348, 350, 358, 367
Competitive
  fields, 143–147, 160, 164, 165
  structure, 14, 165
Competitiveness, 35, 170, 174, 200, 203, 271, 276
Component, 26, 29, 44, 56, 60, 62, 74, 92, 95, 97, 99, 105, 107, 109, 126, 127, 198, 271, 275, 283, 296, 302, 303, 308, 322
Concept of family, 59, 73
CONCOR, 92, 153–155
Conflict, 4, 5, 57, 89, 90, 92, 99, 100, 120, 124–125, 127, 128, 130, 135, 203, 235, 279
Connectedness, connectivity, 1, 2, 4, 8–11, 15, 32, 88, 104, 269–287, 302, 327
Connected periphery, 160, 162
Context, 1, 3, 4, 6, 8–10, 14, 26–30, 34, 35, 39, 41, 42, 44, 53, 56, 60, 61, 63, 68, 70, 73, 106, 111, 119–138, 174, 187, 194, 196, 198, 199, 208, 222, 235, 270, 272, 274, 277, 299, 316, 337, 342, 343, 347, 349, 368
Controllable stress, 61
Controversial
  innovations, 173
Conventionality, 13, 15, 33, 39, 44, 196, 244, 246, 249, 251–261, 263, 265, 309
Conventions, 15, 67, 109, 269–287
Conventions of cooperation, 280
Cooperation, 4, 6, 13, 16, 57, 70, 90, 96–100, 235, 270, 272–277, 280–287, 328, 333, 337–372
Cooperation choice, 350
Cooperative patents, 349
Coordination
  cost, 292
  mechanisms, 170
Core
  actors, 145, 150, 172
  members, 150, 151
  periphery, 5, 14, 79, 131, 143–146, 163, 164, 171–173, 180–183, 186, 187
Corporate
  culture, 104, 109
  research center, 170, 174

County seats, 16, 328–330, 332, 333
Creative industries, 198
Creativity, 38, 57, 150, 165, 210, 243, 263, 265, 292, 293, 297
Crowdsourcing, 26, 30, 31, 33, 42, 44
Cultural
   capital, 56, 105
   distance, 53
   embodied capital, 105
   shock, 53
Cultures of practice, 110, 114
Cultures, firm-specific, 110
Cyclical process, 5, 125, 129

D
Decision-making, 57, 90, 94, 98, 318
Devastation, 43
Difference, 12, 25, 26, 33, 34, 38–40, 63, 73, 79, 127, 169, 200, 206, 210, 225, 234, 236, 254, 257–259, 337, 338, 341, 349, 359, 360, 364, 367
Direct
   linkages, 292, 295
   reach, 295
Discourse, discursive, 109, 110, 192, 210
Displaced musicians, 147
Distance-weighted external reach, 294, 296, 303
District, 14, 34, 37, 103, 107, 109–113, 169–190, 275, 276
Distrusted, 230
Diversification, diversity, 31, 39, 57, 106, 161, 172, 191, 194, 210, 211, 213, 271, 342, 344–346, 351, 361, 362, 364, 367, 368
Dominate interactions, 161
Drawbacks, 91, 368
Dynamic
   approaches, 16, 55, 337–372
   models, 120
   process, 55, 126, 249

E
Early-career
   elites, 107, 109–111, 113, 114
   financial elites, 104, 107, 108, 110–113
E-commerce, 277, 279, 285
Economic
   background, 12
   borrowing, 271
   capital, 56
   credentials, 13
   development, 2, 3, 41, 68–70, 73, 74, 78, 90, 94, 95, 192, 193, 197, 204, 213
   education, educational, 13
   elites, 103–114
   experience, 105, 107
   geography, 7, 25, 35, 38, 68, 79, 103, 114, 143, 193, 194, 213
   landscape, 169
   undergraduate, 13
Educators and managers, 107
E-I index, 321, 322, 330, 332
Electromobility, 14, 191–214
Electromobility pilot regions, 201, 205
Elite
   action, 107
   city, 107
   class, 107
   education, 106, 111
   financial labor markets, 104, 106, 107, 111–113
   formation, 103, 104
   practice, 107
   universities, 105
Embeddedness, 35, 173, 176, 275, 341–343, 347, 348
E-mobility, 14
Emotional problems, 223
Empirical
   analysis, 6, 293, 338
   model, 301, 303
   research, 7, 11, 107, 279
Employee mobility, 273
Endogenous evolution, 127
Entrepreneur, 70, 73, 74, 76–78, 80, 161, 280
Epistemic status, 124–130
Equilibrium, 55, 126–128, 162
Establish links, 57, 342
Estimation, 172, 300–303, 360, 362–367
European commission, 94–97
Evolutionary
   economics, 7, 196
   perspective, 171, 174
   trajectory, 171, 181, 183, 186
Evolution of ties, 156, 338
Exchange, 1, 3, 4, 7, 10, 16, 26, 33, 35, 36, 57, 89, 122–124, 129, 133, 134, 137, 173, 203, 208, 224, 272, 278, 280, 281, 283–286, 291, 302, 304, 308, 310, 337–340, 344, 346–347, 356
Excluded communities, 43
Exclusion, 25, 26, 34, 43, 44, 120, 135, 136, 280, 281, 283, 284, 287, 301
Expatriates, 53, 58–62
Expertise pooling, 273

Exploitation, 134, 135, 173, 192, 213, 339, 346
Exploratory investigation, 293
External
  links, 292–299, 308
  reach, 294, 296, 297, 299, 303, 308, 309
  sources, 29, 30, 291, 297, 308, 339
  ties, 292, 293, 308

F
Family
  bridge, 73–75, 78, 80
  ties, 68–80
Field
  articulation, 160
  configuring events, 144, 164
  dynamics, 143, 144
  of geography, 1, 11, 243
  research, 26, 42, 43, 121
  structure, 145
  theory, 54–57, 63
Financial
  centers, 112, 114
  crisis, 13, 69, 103, 114, 192, 201, 211
  elite labor markets, 105, 111
  elites, 104–113
  intermediation, 106
  services, 103, 104, 106, 108, 110, 111
Flow studies, 87, 88
Foreign
  assignment, 12, 53–66
  sojourn, 53, 60, 62
Formal
  authority, 221
  knowledge transfer, 172
  power, 221
Fragmentation, 163, 222
Friend, friendly, 15, 79, 80, 226, 271, 272
Friendship, 5, 10, 13, 68, 71, 72, 74, 76–79, 126

G
Gatekeepers
  characteristics, 292
  disadvantages of, 293
  impact of, 308
  importance of, 15
Generalized
  exchange, 272
  trust, 13, 77, 79, 80
Gentlemanly capitalism, 105, 106, 108, 109, 114

Geographic, geographical
  localism, 164
  network analysis, 86
  proximity, 3, 7, 8, 75, 85, 172, 173, 316, 320, 334, 344
Geopolitical
  geography, 86
  perspective, 100
  research, 100
Gestalt psychology, 55
Gift, 272
Girvan-Newman method, 320, 321
Global
  economy, 25, 28–32
  investment banking labor markets, 110
  learning network, 330
  network patterns, 315
Globalization, 12, 53–66, 85, 87, 88, 98, 99, 169
Globalization of markets, 53
Goodwill, 279
Governance shift, 85
Graph
  bipartite, 94–97
  multibipartite, 92
  random, 250
Group
  dynamics, 55, 98
  processes, 57
Growth, 13, 31, 69, 70, 74, 80, 106, 114, 161, 169, 213

H
Habitus, 105, 113
Herfindahl index, 301
Heterogeneity, 174, 184, 271, 339, 340, 349, 360, 367
High median conventionality, 255, 263
High tail novelty, 253–257, 260, 261, 263
High-tech
  company, 67, 70, 75, 337, 339
  district, 14, 170
Historical legacy, 333
Hit papers, 253, 254, 256–258, 261, 263
Homophily, 129, 343
Hub measures, 327–330
Human
  capital, 104, 114, 122
  resource managers, 107
Hybrid system, 32

I
Ideological considerations, 95
Illustrative paper, 248, 249

Imitation
    friendly, 270, 272, 273, 284
    of solutions, 285
    strategies, 271
    unfriendly, 15, 273, 274, 277, 280, 281, 286
Impact, 7, 14, 16, 60, 122, 144, 147, 148, 150, 172, 174, 181, 210, 211, 243, 292–294, 297, 299, 304, 308
Inclusivity, 33
Inconsistencies, 174, 179–186
Indicators, 15, 62, 85, 171, 293, 310
Indirect
    external reach, 297, 299
    linkages, 295, 299
    reach, 295, 299
Industrial
    clusters, 68, 70, 73, 74, 79, 291, 292
    community, 73, 74, 79, 80
Informal
    connections, 318–320
    know-how, 109
    leader, 15, 221–223, 228, 234, 235
Information spread, 318
Innovation
    capabilities, 29, 342, 347, 358
    externalizing, 29
    open, 28–32
    process, 206, 272, 337, 367
    studies, 270
    systems, 169, 170, 174, 203, 206, 369
Institutional
    capital, 105
    infrastructure, 209, 211
Instrumentality of the social, 12, 25, 26, 33
Intercultural adjustment, 54
Interdisciplinary, 6, 16, 37, 85, 138
Interfirm relations, 29, 274–277
International
    business schools, 107
    financial centers, 104
    patent classification, 300, 349
Interorganizational, 6, 8, 10, 28, 57, 131–134, 137, 138, 174, 201, 203–206, 208, 210, 212, 213, 269, 270, 275
Interorganizational platform, 203
Interpersonal
    exchange, 58
    trust relations, 226
Interviews, semi structured, 198
Inventions, 30, 31, 269, 270, 348
Inventive activities, 301, 304, 349
Inventors, 9, 31, 42, 293–299, 301–303, 308, 310, 341, 368
Investment
    advice, 108, 111
    bankers, banking, 103–113
Ivory tower, 151, 153, 156, 158, 160, 162
Ivy League, 151, 153, 156, 158–160, 163

J
Jazz
    field structure, 152, 165
    renaissance, 162–163
Job performance, 62, 63, 228, 230, 232
Joint session recordings, 147, 148
Joint venture, 206

K
Key players, 164
Knowledge
    assimilation of, 345
    based view, 339
    bases, 16, 110, 170–175, 183, 184, 187, 198, 201, 208, 212, 338, 340, 344–346, 364, 367
    burden of, 263
    creation, 1–4, 6, 9–11, 15, 67–69, 76, 77, 80, 192, 193, 213, 269, 286, 337
    diffusion, 4, 74, 76, 325, 328, 333
    dispersed, 25, 30, 31
    economy, 13, 67, 70, 71, 76, 79, 80, 171, 213
    exchange network, 137
    exchange of, 72, 272, 273, 283–286, 340, 341, 345
    flows, 15, 75, 79, 80, 292, 293, 309, 310, 337, 340, 345, 346, 356, 357
    generation, 12, 26, 35, 36, 39, 71
    nonoverlapping, 356
    overlap, 356, 357
    path, 192, 194, 199, 209–213
    portfolios, 350, 357
    relational, 2, 11
    stocks, 338, 340, 346, 349, 356
    topology of, 14, 213
    transfer, 16, 36, 172, 206, 292, 293, 337, 338, 340, 345, 346, 352, 356, 362, 364, 367
    transmission, 292–294
    types of, 10, 25, 26, 32, 33, 35
    use, 316, 317
Krugman index, 301–303

L

Labor market, markets, 13, 28, 30, 41, 42, 69, 103–106, 110–114, 119, 120, 275
Leaders, 5, 15, 43, 127, 130, 175, 221–223, 225, 227, 228, 230, 233, 234
Leadership
  emergence, 221–236
  perceptions, 222, 226, 227
Leading-edge cluster competition, 201, 206
Learning
  among municipalities, 317–319
  ecologies, 316
  hubs, 326–330
  by imitation, 269, 271
  indirectly, 320
  intercultural, 13, 53–66
  intraorganizational, 123, 126, 129, 130
  networks, 16, 68, 123, 315–336
  processes, 1, 13, 16, 53–69, 76, 79, 80, 106, 125, 126, 171, 208, 275, 277, 286, 315, 317, 318, 339
Lesson-drawing, 317
Limitations, 131, 192, 213, 235, 349, 368
Link formation, 341, 343, 361, 367
Living wage, 33, 42, 44
Localization advantages, 275
Local, locally
  buzz, 172, 276, 277
  clustering, 16, 173, 174, 316, 322, 325, 333
  cohesion, 222
  governments, 174, 315, 317, 320
  knowledge base, 15, 291–313
  organized network, 135, 184
Lock-in, 36, 170, 172, 193, 194, 196, 198, 199, 291
London, 3, 88, 103–113, 158, 159
Longitudinal analyses, 125
Low tail novelty, 253, 254, 256, 257, 260, 261

M

Managerial goals, 221
Managing relationships, 225
Markov
  chain, 146, 245, 250
  clustering, 322, 333
Mathematics, 2, 112
Mechanisms
  of cooperation, 97
  of learning, 15, 269
Mediated crowdsourced project work, 33
Mediators, 31, 32, 42–44, 296
Mentoring programs, 54
Meso- and macrolevels, 138

Migration, 85, 88, 121
Misinformation, 34
Mobile, mobility, 77, 79, 103–114, 119–138, 169, 171, 208, 273, 316, 368
Modeling skills, 108
Modes of communication, 39, 42
Monopoly, 159, 161
Monte Carlo Markov Chain, 245, 250
Multidimensionality, 26, 42
Multilateral collaboration, 276
Multilevel, 6, 9, 10, 12, 14, 88, 98, 131–138
Multiple network regression models, 285
Multistakeholder platform, 203

N

National
  educational systems, 104, 111
  electromobility development plan, 201, 202
  innovation system, 203, 206
  strategy conference, 200
Neoliberal practices, 27
Neostructural approach, 122, 135
Network
  analysis, 2–4, 9, 38, 86, 88, 89, 99, 100, 123, 135, 154, 170, 284
  case study, 277–279
  collaboration, 14
  constraint, 227
  elite, 105
  ego-centered, 57
  ephemerality, 40
  of expatriates, 59
  family, 13, 67–69
  financial, 114
  friendship, 13, 68, 71, 72, 76, 77
  goods, 270, 286
  inclusive knowledge, 26
  interpersonal, 53–66
  metaphor, 6
  multilevel, 6, 132, 133, 281
  municipal learning, 318, 320, 326, 327, 333
  networking strategies, 28
  organization, 173
  organized, 2, 15, 270, 274, 276–278, 284, 286
  redundancy, 297, 299
  as relational flows, 87
  social, 1, 3–6, 11–13, 54, 56, 59, 60, 63, 64, 68, 71, 73, 74, 76–79, 105, 152, 196, 227, 269, 279, 291
  spatial, 2, 88
  star, 150

Index　　　　　　　　　　　　　　　　　　　　　　　　　　　　　　　　383

strategies, 25, 26, 28, 41, 315
synthetic, 245
as technical infrastructures, 85
topological, 110, 113
trust, 222, 224–227, 230, 236
two-mode network, 175
Niche, 5, 9, 32, 122, 137
Normalizing, 249
Normative field, 143–146, 164
Norms of communication, 341
Novel, novelty
　combinations, 15, 244, 251, 257
　ideas, 244, 340
Null model, 245, 247, 249, 250

O
Occupational segregation, 34
Opportunism, 4, 5, 15, 16, 36, 42, 43, 76, 86, 109, 132–135, 147, 150, 192, 223, 224, 227, 270, 273–277, 280, 281, 284, 286, 304, 338, 339, 341–343, 347, 348
Opportunity, 4, 5, 15, 16, 36, 42, 43, 76, 86, 109, 132–135, 147, 150, 192, 223, 224, 227, 270, 273–277, 280, 281, 284, 286, 304, 338, 339, 341–343, 347, 348
　hoarding, 134
　structure, 120–123, 132–135
Organizational
　change, 55, 97
　development, 55
　dissimilarity, 359
　fields, 144
　network analysis, 279
　path dependence, 193, 194
　rule, 131
　structure, 125, 134, 210, 226
Organized mobility and relational turnover (OMRT), 14, 119–138
Oscillation, 128, 130

P
Partner choice, 342, 362, 364, 367, 368
Partner-switching, 16, 338
Patent
　applications, 11, 294, 348, 349, 360
　data, 348–350
Path
　breaking, 14, 15, 191–214, 326
　dependence, dependent, 14, 40, 171, 173, 191–199, 211–213, 348
　length, 325–327

Patterns
　of collaborations, 171, 186
　of cooperation, 13
　of interaction, 88, 99
　of relationships, 153, 160
Peak impact, 261
Pecking order, 5, 126–128, 130, 131
Perpetual cyclical pattern, 129
Personal
　initiative, 54, 62, 63
　relations, 37, 40, 120
Phonographic field, 159, 162
Physics, 112, 258, 260, 263, 264
Platform
　ing strategy, 211
　organizers, 204, 208
　policies, 192, 196, 212, 213
Poisson-based regression, 229
Political regionalization, 13, 85–102
Popularity, 16, 123, 129, 159, 338, 342, 348, 359, 364
Position, 4, 5, 7, 9, 11, 13, 15, 40, 74, 76, 89, 90, 94, 97, 99, 121, 122, 128, 132, 135, 136, 144, 146, 147, 150, 151, 154, 164, 165, 171, 178, 222, 225–227, 230, 233, 234, 236, 261, 277, 282–284, 286, 292, 308, 318, 333, 343, 368
Positional advantages, 103, 112, 114, 172
Positions of autonomy, 225
Postgraduate landscape, 104
Power relations, 38
Preferential attachment, 173, 342, 348, 368
Pre-swing era, 158, 159
Probability of collaboration, 341, 364
Project(s)
　cooperation network, 282
　lighthouse, 205
　R&D, 175, 176, 180, 205, 206, 210, 337, 341
　work, 26, 33, 37, 39–44, 284, 286
Promoters, 161
Property rights, 32, 172, 274
Proximity
　cognitive, 16, 172, 173, 338–345, 348, 352, 356–358, 362, 364, 367
　dimensions, 338, 341, 344
　paradox, 341
　social, 339, 344, 347, 348, 352, 357, 364, 367
　spatial, 15, 37, 100, 269, 270, 286
　technological, 344, 352

Q
Qualitative study, 58

R
Random-effects panel model, 360
Randomized citation networks, 250, 251
Rank, 88, 228, 230, 232, 256, 257
Reappearance of linkages, 351, 353–355
Reciprocal potential, 16, 338, 343, 345, 346, 356, 357, 362, 364
Reciprocity, 129, 272–274, 341–343, 346–348, 352, 356, 359, 364, 367
Reconfiguration, 26, 40, 41, 164, 201
Reference list, 245–248, 251
Regional
   club goods, 275
   clustering, 16, 191, 193, 195, 276, 322
   clusters, 16, 191, 193, 195, 276, 322
   configuration, 98
   development, 12, 14, 192, 193, 196, 202–204, 208, 212, 213
   economies, 13, 67, 70, 79, 80, 209
   groups, 13, 91, 95–99
   innovation network, 13, 169, 202, 322
   institutions, 198, 204, 206, 212
   knowledge base, 197, 204
   path dependence, 194, 196
   resource configurations, 191, 196
Regions
   developed, 67–69
   developing, 67–80
Reindustrialization process, 204
Related variety, 14, 191, 194–197, 209–211, 213
Relational
   capital, 37, 136
   data, 14, 147, 148, 178, 293
   principles, 316
   turnover, 11, 14, 119–138
Relations, relationship, 2, 4–12, 14–16, 25, 27–29, 36–39, 54–56, 58–64, 68, 70–74, 77, 85–91, 94, 97–100, 105–107, 111, 113, 120–123, 126, 128, 130, 132, 134, 135, 138, 147, 148, 153, 154, 158, 160–164, 170, 172, 173, 178, 180, 182, 183, 191, 193, 196, 199, 210, 211, 213, 222–226, 230, 232–235, 253, 254, 256, 258, 260, 269, 274, 275, 277, 283, 284, 286, 287, 293, 294, 296–298, 309, 316, 317, 333, 334, 338, 340–345, 347, 349, 352, 356–359, 364, 367–369
Reproducing, 107–109, 170, 195
Reputation, 61, 71, 127, 128, 146, 224, 225, 234, 236

Resolution
   based selection, 92
   proposal, 91
Resource, 2, 10, 14, 30, 34, 37, 40, 42, 54, 56, 57, 59–61, 67, 69, 70, 73, 79, 80, 123, 125, 126, 132–134, 144, 145, 150, 161, 165, 169, 191, 192, 196, 197, 200, 208–211, 225, 228, 270–272, 278, 280, 339, 341–343, 352, 359, 364, 367
Reverse engineering, 271, 273
Rival learning, 15, 274–276, 280, 286, 287
Rock music, 161

S
Sanction, 15, 273, 277, 280, 281, 284, 287
Scientific
   fields, 15, 244, 263
   progress, 263
   work, 253, 254
Search for diversity, 362, 364
Secondary market for innovation, 32
Securitization, 103, 106, 108
Segregation, 25, 26, 34, 42
Self
   efficacy, 54
   monitoring, monitors, 15, 221–236
   segregation, 40
Sequence process, 199
Shared history, 347
Sharing of knowledge, 40, 337
Shooting stars, 151–153, 156, 159, 161–163
Shortest paths, 2, 294, 295, 297, 299
Showcases, 198, 205, 207
Simple cores, 180, 181, 183
Small and medium-sized companies, 58, 60, 206, 270
Small-world networks, 325, 326, 333
Social
   capital, 4, 27, 30, 56, 77, 121, 136, 165, 344, 347
   class, 134
   cleavages, 135
   conventions, 270
   costs, 121, 123
   dilemmas, 233
   discipline, 123, 135
   divides, 15, 222, 233, 234
   division of labor, 137, 275
   ecology, 60
   enterprises, 41
   goals, 25–27
   instrumentality of, 12, 25–51
   interactions, 2, 34, 54, 63, 71, 222, 225, 234, 235

knowledge, 12, 26, 33–35, 39, 44
learning, 40, 67–69, 77, 79, 80
network analysis, 6, 85, 87–89, 170, 173, 175, 180, 279, 293, 294, 316, 317, 320
organization, 69, 80, 122, 126, 196
phenomena, 4, 120, 132
process, 3–5, 9, 14, 87, 99, 120–123, 131, 134, 136, 137
status, 5, 122, 123, 137, 235
support, 54, 57–63
system, 10, 121, 143, 146, 147
Socialization, 4, 34, 109, 110, 120
Socioeconomic
activity, 107, 109
life, 106
polarization, 25, 28, 41, 44
practice, 104–110, 112–114
Solvers, 31–33, 40, 41, 43–44
Spatiality of networks changes, 36
Speeches, 13, 90, 94–102
Speech patterns, 90
Spillover effects, 273, 286
Spinning-top model, 14, 123–130
Split plot, 230
Stable position, 318
Status
competition, 123, 128, 131
game, 130
hierarchy, 126
Strategies, 7, 12–14, 25, 27–31, 38, 39, 41, 43, 44, 78, 112, 123, 128, 129, 132–133, 150–158, 171, 175, 187, 191, 192, 199, 202–204, 208, 210–212, 270, 271, 309, 315, 322, 350
Strong ties, 71, 73, 75, 78, 80
Structural
change, 160, 187
emergence, 137
equivalence, 164, 178–180
evolution, 178
hole, 5, 30, 176, 181, 224
linked design, 132
periphery, 284
position, 171, 292, 343
transformation, 182
variation, 171, 180, 181, 183–186
Stylistic
crisis, 163
rules, 146
Subfields, 244, 254, 258
Subsamples, 247, 258
Support
from locals, 61
model, 41

Supranational structures, 85, 98
Swedish municipalities, 16, 315–336
Swing era, 159–161
Switching algorithm, 250, 251
Systems of places, 119, 121, 136–142

T
Tacit knowledge transfer, 36, 340
Team-authored papers, 257, 259
Team science, 243
Technical know-how, 74, 80, 108–110, 113
Technical nature, 108, 111
Technological
capabilities, 14
districts, 174–177, 179, 182, 184, 185
environments, 201, 337
performance, 202
recombination, 16, 296, 297, 301, 304, 306–309
Technologies, technology groups, 300, 301, 304
Technosocial framework, 37
Temporal
bracketing, 199
dimension, 173
Temporary clusters, 196
Tenure, 124, 226, 228, 230, 232
Territorially, 110–113
Threshold, 92, 258, 342
Topographical
dimensions, 104, 114
requirements, 113
space, 104
specificity, 104
Topological
changes, 143
financial networks, 104
hypothesis, 179
mobility, 104
nature, 114
networks, 110, 113
Training experiences, 107
Trajectory, 29, 39, 143–165, 170, 171, 173, 181–183, 263
Trajectory types, 14
Transit points, 327, 328, 333
Transnational community, 70, 80
Triadic closure, 344, 368
Trust
based relationships, 113
brokerage, 225, 227, 230, 232, 235, 236
Turnover, 11, 119–138
Type of groups, 95

U

United Nations General Assembly (UNGA), 13, 89–97, 99, 100
UN organization, 90
Up-Starters, 85–102, 152, 153, 156, 163
Urban policy mobilities, 316

V

Vacancy chains, 119
Value chain, 173, 201, 204, 206, 275
Variables, 88, 129, 150–152, 227–230, 232, 258, 283, 285, 296, 297, 300–305, 308, 309, 317, 327, 328, 330, 338, 348, 350–357, 359–363, 365–366
Variation, 13, 36, 92, 130, 171, 174, 181, 183, 187, 245, 250, 271, 273, 276, 286, 316, 318, 328, 330, 345, 362

Voting
  behavior, 90–92, 94, 99
  results, 91

W

Wanna-be, 146, 151–153, 156
Weak ties, 68, 71, 74, 76
Web
  of science, 244, 251
  survey, 318
Windows of opportunities, 212
Working
  groups, 203, 205
  practices, 103, 104, 107
Workplace problems, 224
World
  decisions, 97
  governance, 89, 100
  regionalization, 94

Printed by Printforce, the Netherlands